DO NOT BE
DECEIVED

A **CHRISTIAN** WORLDVIEW RESPONSE TO **GAY** THEOLOGY

ERIK F. WAIT

Aventine Press

Published by Aventine Press
55 East Emerson St.
Chula Vista CA 91911
www.aventinepress.com

ISBN: 978-1-59330-835-3

Library of Congress Control Number: 2013916793
Library of Congress Cataloging-in-Publication Data
Do Not Be Deceived/ Erik F. Wait

Printed in the United States of America

Acknowledgements

I would like to thank Pastors Dr. Philip Kayser and Peter Allison for their willingness to read the rough draft of the manuscript and offer valuable feedback. I would especially like to offer my sincere gratitude to David Gill who proof-read the manuscript and provided numerous suggestions for improvements. But most of all, I am most grateful for the grace and mercy of my Lord Jesus Christ without whom nothing is possible.

Table of Contents

- A revisit of the story of the destruction of Sodom and Gomorrah and how the term "Sodomite" was coined. Defining the terms "Sodomite" "Gay" and "homosexual" and how they have been used in various English translations of the Bible.

- Define and explain the basic construct of a worldview and how the Gay Theological movement is not a mere variance within the Christian faith, but a very subtle and deceptive cultic heresy akin that undermines not only Biblical sexual ethics but every essential doctrine of the historic Christian faith.

Biblical Worldview of Epistemology
vs.
The Gay Theological Worldview

In this chapter the Biblical doctrines of the inerrancy, infallibility and authority of Scripture are defined and defended against the majority view of Gay Theological "scholarship."

In this chapter I address the Queer Theory and Liberal Gay Theology lens of trajectory hermeneutics and Liberation theology which determines how they interpret marriage, polygamy, the roles of men and women, Christian liberty and the passages that prohibit same sex acts.

In this chapter I address the hermeneutical lens of Dispensational Gay Theology which seeks to promote Gay Theology as an acceptable view within the Bible-believing evangelical church. Specifically I address its theoretical antinomianism, its inherent self-contradictions and cult-like twisting of the relevant Biblical passages.

In this chapter I address how the growing trend of neo-liberal hermeneutics interprets the Bible through the lens of extra-biblical literature, rather than reading the text within its own literary and historical context. This is one of the key errors being taught in even so-called conservative seminaries and it is the lens through which Gay Theology reinterprets the stories of Ruth and Naomi, David and Jonathan and Jesus and the Beloved Disciple as being gay lovers.

Biblical Worldview of Ethics vs. The Gay Theological Worldview

In this chapter I address how the unfolding of redemptive history and revealing of God's law incrementally "fences in" sin and restores God's intended original order, eventually finding its *telos* in Christ who corrects the errors of the Pharisees while upholding the moral law revealed to Moses.

In this chapter I continue the same theme of chapter 12 as it is developed in Apostle Paul's Epistle to the Romans.

In this chapter I continue the same theme in chapter 13 and 14 as it is developed in Apostle Paul's First and Second Epistles to the Corinthians.

In this chapter I discuss Leviticus 20:13 and the various means and degrees to which God Himself has carried out His penal sanctions from Genesis to Revelation.

- In this chapter I refute the Gay Theological assertion the nebulous notion that "love" as opposed to law is a moral standard (rather than the motive) for Christian ethics.

In this chapter I refute the Gay Theological assertion that Ruth and Naomi were lesbians, David and Jonathan were gay lovers, that Jesus and the Beloved were gay lovers, that the Roman Centurion and his servant were gay lovers or that being a "eunuch" was an ancient equivalent to a "gay" man.

- In this chapter I discuss the prescriptive nature of the ordinance of marriage, the fallacy of the neoplatonic Complementarian theory, the ontological equality and economic subordination of the husband and wife, the jurisdiction of the family, church and state and finally the issue of homosexuality and loneliness.

Biblical Worldview of Metaphysics
vs.
The Gay Theological Worldview

In this chapter I discuss Queer Theology's rejection of the created order of the binary gender of male and female, transgender theology, transgenderism, transexuality and intersexuality (hermaphroditism) and the revival of pagan and Gnostic theology.

The Fruit of the GLBT Theological Movement

In this chapter I discuss the cultic nature of the Metropolitan Community Church and other Gay affirming congregations. In doing so I reveal how they distort every essential doctrine of the historic Christian faith, the sacraments and overtly promote pagan sexuality.

Introduction

Over the past half century, Western Civilization has witnessed a significant shift in the thinking of its citizens. Critical observers of post-Enlightenment thought will note the broad intellectual waltz of the past few centuries – from an abstract rationalism to a skeptical empiricism to a wandering existentialism – to which the historian of ideas is treated. But of special note at the outset of the present manuscript is the eagerness with which our Late Modern neighbors are turning from these "Western options" to ancient, pagan spiritualties for knowledge and wisdom. Places in which devoutly Biblical thinking was once a dominant mental habit are evolving into variations on a post-Christian theme, in which both the volume and the apparent integrity of the Christian Church's prophetic voice are diminishing. In several quarters, seminaries that were established to train generations of men for the ministry have come to mimic the prevailing philosophies of the day. Pastors by the handful, purportedly called to shepherd God's people, too commonly are found guilty of fleecing the flock for their own material gain and "cult of personality." And the compromising of Christian leadership doesn't stop there. To hear of adulterous affairs or other sexual mis-adventures within the pastorate is, today, all too common; indeed, we have ample documentation to the effect that scores of preachers and priests of recent vintage have preyed upon and polluted young children in order to feed their own fleshly lusts. This decline from a more robust Christian devotion and conviction has, for many onlookers (both inside and outside of its walls), undermined the Christian Church's credibility. As a further consequence, many contemporary critics are seeking to disqualify Christians in particular from proclaiming their Lord's message publicly. The Church and the Bible it has too often used as an instrument of prideful dismissals has no answers, one might think, for it seems to have too often forsaken its divinely procured theological and moral moorings. Readily citing such facts as excuses, then, people are looking elsewhere for answers to life's questions.

These are the times in which we live. Meanwhile, the Sexual Revolution has issued new behavioral standards. Foes formerly known as fornication, adultery, multiple sex partners, pornography, "swinging", serial divorce, and homosexuality have been added to our "friends" list. Along the way, forms of Eastern mysticism and ancient paganism have made themselves comfortable within the confines of the popular mindset. One feels the impact of these developments pervasively. Just flip on the television, watch a film, or log on to the internet. By consent of an increasingly law-less consumer, our entertainment brokers have replaced Christian self-control with self-*worship* and a libidinous appetite. But the disturbing changes are not restricted to entertainment industries and universities. Theological seminaries, those arterial bloodlines leading to the broader Church, are commonly found following rather than challenging prevailing cultural trends. In particular, a collection of doctrines and practices under the guise of a "new" Christian spirituality has oozed its way onto the contemporary ecclesial landscape. One sub-cluster within this collection is known as Gay Theology. The latter, it ought to be recognized, figures as no mere "ethereal" speculation or set of theological propositions. Rather, the sustained effort to construct and articulate a "gay" theology constitutes a personal strike at the very core of how Christians have historically understood humanity, creation, and God. Rooted in one's understanding of these are the norms by which sexual practices and identities are evaluated and established. Yet, the leaders within Christian churches do not, on the whole, appear equipped to take the side of sound Biblical theology and respond to the promoters of Gay Theology in a sophisticated, irenic fashion. As a result, laymen and lay-women find *themselves* conforming to prevailing cultural opinions rather than *the Lord* transforming them and those to whom they would minister through the renewing of their minds. Indeed, sadly, the Church's response to the cultural pressures mentioned above has frequently consisted of a mixed-up montage of unkind reactions, obtuse denunciations, political grand-standing, and unlearned psychobabble.

If you are a Christian (or have something of a Christian background) that you haven't fully abandoned and are wrestling with same sex attractions (SSA) perhaps even secretly, and are struggling with your faith, then this book was written specifically for you. I want you to know that you are not alone and that this book is primarily designed to help you hold on to your Christian faith rather than be persuaded by the errors of Gay Theology or, in a downward spiral of skepticism, repudiate that faith. In what follows, I will give you a detailed means of understanding the Bible and defending your faith against the lies of the Gay Theological movement. The present text, however, has a limited scope. It focuses a spotlight on the Biblical and theological issues raised by Gay Theology advocates. However important the matter may be, I do not have space in this volume to discuss, analyze and critique all the prevailing theories of the etiology of SSA or the counseling or therapeutic methods that are offered and then provide a more Biblical alternative of my own. Those chapters will have to wait for another book. My heart's desire for this work is to arm my readers against the deceit of Gay Theology as well as offer hope to those in the grip of SSA, paving the way for a life of joy and integrity rather than one of despair and compromise.

This book has as its second intended audience Christian leaders, teachers, and counselors interfacing with those who already self-iden-tify as gay or with those who, feeling a tug toward same-sex attraction, seek the ethical insight of God's Word and a greater understanding of their psycho-sexual condition. Many well-meaning pastors today are being confronted with the reality of congregants who express a desire to follow Christ while also identifying themselves as "gay." Even when the former have grasped some of the Bible's ethical teachings on these matters, however, they have too often come up short in addressing the complex and emotional issues surrounding SSA. The persistence of such shortcomings only works to the detriment of individual Christians and the corporate body. Moreover, the clamor for an embrace of Gay Theology's doctrinal and moral distinctives continues to escalate at the expense of a sound, Biblical understanding of marriage and homosex-uality. Well-meaning Christian communicants are being socially mar-ginalized and told that they hold antiquated views of sexuality. I seek to turn them from this trajectory.

Toward that end, this study will not content itself with a simplistic or narrow treatment of a hand-full of well-worn Scripture texts (though the well-worn ones are certainly not to be cast aside or forgotten, to be sure). Far more than is typically found in other works on this subject, I look to present a full-orbed picture of the attributes of Scripture, the history of redemption, the law of God, and the Biblical covenants, thereby establishing a fairly detailed context for the passages of Scripture that I judge to be germane to our subject. In doing so, I hope to introduce readers to a more consistent and defensible understanding of the Biblical, Christian Worldview.

Finally, I aim to present clearly the claims and implications of the Christian Scriptures, especially reflecting on historical context as well as on some key literary features. Success in doing so will act to silence the mouths of those who would wolfishly plague the Christian church with the false gospel of Gay Theology. Alongside these efforts, I sincerely pray that God will have mercy on the Church's enemies and release them from the bondage of both self- and other-deception, as He has for so many other former deviants from "straight" Christian faith and practice.

The Structure of This Book

As shall be shown in the chapters that follow, a worldview (something all humans have) consists of a network of beliefs that themselves have not been verified by the procedures of natural science, beliefs about knowledge and its requirements (epistemology), behavioral standards (ethics), and the nature of reality (metaphysics). The structure of this book follows these three areas. In addressing epistemological matters, I will contend for the ultimate authority of Scripture as a necessary presupposition of one's reasoning, for its inerrancy, for its infallibility, and for its role as our chief hermeneutical (interpretative) standard. Once these issues are addressed, I will articulate a foundational perspective in terms of which the relevant Scripture texts as well as the ethical and metaphysical claims of Gay Theology may be examined. In the process of doing so, I will critically discuss three sub-categories of Gay Theology: Liberal Gay theology, Dispensational Gay Theology, and Queer Theology.

Chapter 1
Defining Our Terms

As do many who address the Bible's ethical attitudes toward homo-sexual acts and proclivities, I wish to define terms such as "homosexual" "gay" and "Sodomite." This way, readers are more likely to grasp the sense of my claims and follow the flow of my arguments. Let's begin our discussion by taking a look at one of the most infamous stories in the Bible, often pejoratively referred to by Gay Theology advocates as a *clobber passage* and *text of terror*, from which the antiquated term "Sodomite" was coined.

Two common arguments are thought by some to remove the story of the destruction of Sodom and Gomorrah from the question of whether consenting, Christian adults are morally permitted to engage in homo-sexual sex acts in a monogamous committed relationship. The first concludes that the destruction-worthy sin of Sodom's inhabitants was not sexual in nature. Rather, Sodom suffered divine judgment due to a wanton neglect of the common cultural Middle Eastern custom of practicing hospitality towards strangers. The great sin of the Sodomites, according to this reading, was their violent reaction to the strangers who wanted to "get acquainted with them." The late Yale historian, John Boswell, for example, took up this understanding of the Genesis passage:

> When the men of Sodom gathered around to demand that
> the stranger be brought to them, 'that they might know
> them,' they meant no more than to 'know' who they were,
> and the city was consequently destroyed not for sexual
> immorality, but for the sin of inhospitality to strangers. [1]

Often, those presenting this argument stress that there are numerous passages throughout Scripture referring to the sin of Sodom but none specifically mentioning homo-sexual sex acts. Rather, the scriptural

---

[1] John Boswell, *Christianity, Social Tolerance, and Homosexuality* (University Of Chicago Press; 8th Edition, 2005), 94.

concern appears to center on inhospitable acts of greed and an oppression of the poor, as seen in this passage from the prophet Ezekiel:
"Behold, this was the guilt of your sister Sodom: she and her daughters
had arrogance, abundant food and careless ease, but she did not help the
poor and needy" (Ezekiel 16:49).

What this passage makes clear is that if the member-citizens of
Sodom and Gomorrah were condemned for sexual sins, then certainly
that was not their only noteworthy fault. Clearly, they earned a reputation (at least among some of God's Old Covenant prophets) for enjoying
material privilege to the neglect of those not so privileged. The prophet
Jeremiah, however, while not explicitly mentioning same-sex acts, does
mention that one of the sins of Sodom and Gomorrah was the act of
adultery:

> Also among the prophets of Jerusalem I have seen a hor-
> rible thing: The committing of adultery [Hebrew: *na'aph*]
> and walking in falsehood; and they strengthen the hands of
> evildoers so that no one has turned back from his wicked-
> ness. All of them have become to Me like Sodom, and her
> inhabitants like Gomorrah (Jeremiah 23:14).

Likewise, it is often argued that Jesus' own mention of Sodom and
Gomorrah alludes to an inhospitality toward his disciples and that He
does not mention homo-sexual sex:

> Whoever does not receive you, nor heed your words, as
> you go out of that house or that city, shake the dust off your
> feet. Truly I say to you, it will be more tolerable for the
> land of Sodom and Gomorrah in the day of judgment than
> for that city (Matthew 10:14-15).

Notice, however, that Jesus is not asserting that the sin of Sodom
and Gomorrah was inhospitality, but rather that people will be judged
for rejecting the gospel proclaimed by His disciples. Certainly, the sin
of Sodom and Gomorrah involved more than inhospitality and indeed
included at least a significant sexual component.

This judgment finds confirmation when one studies the word-choice
of the Genesis narrator. Richard Davidson, for instance, contends that

the Hebrew word '*yada*' found in Genesis 9 and rendered as "know" in English translations clearly functions for the composer of the passage as a euphemism for sexual intimacy:

> [T]he Achilles heel of the argument of Baily, Boswell, and others who see only issues of inhospitality in this narrative is the use of "to know" in the immediate context. In v.8 the verb *yada* is used in connection with Lot's daughters and unmistakably refers to sexual intercourse. The close proximity of its usage in v. 5 to this clear sexual meaning of *yada* in v. 8 makes it very difficult to conclude that it has a different, nonsexual meaning in the former.[2]

Lot is not offering his daughters to the crowd for the purpose of making friends; rather he is using the term *yada'* to indicate that they are virgins. To paraphrase, Lot is saying, "Don't have sex with (*yada'*) these men which is a wicked thing, but rather have sex with (*yada'*) my daughters who, because they are virgins, are eligible as wives."

Also consider that in the New Testament Epistle of Jude the writer describes the sin of Sodom, Gomorrah, and the surrounding cities as being of a sexual variety. He writes that they "indulged in gross immorality and went after strange flesh" and "are exhibited as an example in undergoing the punishment of eternal fire" (Jude 7). Regarding this passage, DeYoung notes: "Jude specifies neither inhospitality nor pride as the sin of Sodom, nor does John in the final reference to Sodom in Revelation 11:8, where Jerusalem in figuratively called Sodom and Egypt."[3]

The reality that the sin of Sodom included a form of same sex acts is acknowledged by many Gay Theology advocates. Among them is R.D. Weekly, who writes:

> [C]ontrary to what some would have us believe – the townsmen intended nothing less than to engage in sexual

---

2   Richard Davidson, *Flame of Yahweh: Sexuality in the Old Testament* (Peabody, MA: Hendriksen Publishing, 2007), 146-147.

3   James B. De Young, *Homosexuality: Contemporary Claims Examined in the Light of the Bible and Other Ancient Literature and Law* (Grand Rapids, MI: Kregel, 2000), 47.

relations with the visitors… It's impossible to be faithful to
the text and consider the intentions of the townspeople as
anything other than sexual intercourse.[4]

Weekly's astute observation, however, underscores the illogic of
concluding that *all* of the men present wanted to commit same-sex acts
or that doing so was their primary intention. "[A] lot more was going
on in Sodom than simply homosexual lust, considering that if this was
the only problem of sexual arousal, they could have easily satiated their
desires with one another."[5] If all they were after was to commit same-
sex acts, after all, they could have had sex with each other

Therefore, the most we can justifiably conclude regarding the intentions of the men of Sodom towards the angels is that they wanted to
commit a violent act of same-sex rape. John Frame states:

> The Hebrew word 'know' (*yada*') often refers to sexual
> intercourse, as in Genesis 4:1, where it is said that Adam
> "knew" his wife. Lot's response, that these men were act-
> ing 'so wickedly' (v. 7), indicates that their desire was for
> homosexual rape. Lot even offers his daughters to them, as
> if that were a lesser evil (v. 8). This is the event that leads to
> the total destruction of Sodom and Gomorrah. [6]

If we are going to be honest and do justice to the text we must
acknowledge with Richard Davidson that, "Most modern interpreters
now acknowledge that homosexual activity along with inhospitality is
described in Gen 19 but insist that the sexual issue is that of rape or violence and that thus this passage gives no evidence for the condemnation
of homosexual practice in general."[7]

It has long been taught that God destroyed Sodom and Gomorrah
because their residents engaged in homo-sexual sex and many commentators and preachers go on to tie the sexual prohibitions of Leviticus to

---

4   R.D. Weekly, *Homosexianity (Judah First Ministries, 2009), 5.*

5   R.D. Weekly, *Homosexianity (Judah First Ministries, 2009), 6.*

6   John Frame, *Doctrine of the Christian Life (Phillipsburg, NJ, P & R Publishing, 2008), 757.*

7   Richard Davidson, *Flame of Yahweh: Sexuality in the Old Testament* (Peabody, MA: Hendriksen Publishing, 2007), 147.

this text.[8] Nevertheless, it is evident that we cannot justifiably use the term "Sodomite" to refer exclusively to those who participate in same-sex acts. Contrary to this traditional interpretation and many English translations, they were destroyed for homosexual rape and a multitude of others sins and crimes. The sins of Sodom and Gomorrah involved arrogantly neglecting and oppressing the poor and needy (Ezekiel 16:49), walking in falsehood, strengthening the hands of evildoers, failing to repent from wickedness, committing adultery (Jeremiah 23:14) and seeking to rape angels (Genesis 19:7).

Because Gay Theology advocates are not defending violent (a.k.a., non-consensual) acts of homosexual sex, such behaviors more often being associated with desires to dominate, shame and disgrace victims rather than with desires for sexual pleasure, the destruction of Sodom and Gomorrah is not directly applicable to people who identify themselves as being gay or homosexuals. Therefore, we must acknowledge that "the story does not deal directly with consensual homosexual relationships, it is not an 'ideal' text to guide contemporary Christian ethics."[9]

Are there wealthy people today who oppress the poor? Are there fundamentalist pastors on television who have committed adultery? Are there Christians who are proud and arrogant and neglect the widow and orphan? If so, then they can be justifiably called Sodomites just as much as we could use the term to refer to people who commit violent same-sex acts.

If the term "Sodomite" more accurately describes a person who commits homosexual violence, then surely those homosexuals that desecrated Communion hosts at St. Patrick's Cathedral and attacked pastors and their families for standing up for what the Church has rightly taught for nearly 2,000 years fit the definition. In fact, Queer Theologians such as Robert E. Goss endorse the violent, militant actions of organizations such as ACT UP, Queer Nation, and Outrage who vandalize churches in San Francisco, New York and Los Angeles.[10] Having lived in the

8 Gary DeMar for example writes, "This wicked city was destroyed for breaking God's law: in particular, the sin of homosexuality (Genesis 19:4-5; Leviticus 18:22; 20:13)." *The Debate Over Reconstruction* (Powder Springs, GA: American Vision Press, 1988), 149.
9 Robert A. J. Gagnon, *The Bible And Homosexual Practice* (Nashville, TN: Abingdon Press, 2001), 71.
10 Robert E. Goss, *Queering Christ: Beyond Jesus Acted Up* (Eugene, OR: The Pilgrim Press, 2007), 250.

San Francisco Bay Area most of my life, it is my experience that gay activists, such as those involved in ACT UP, who behave in a violent manner, have earned the label "Sodomite." Consider the following first-hand account which accords with my own experiences while serving as an elder at the First Orthodox Presbyterian Church of San Francisco:

> As a minister and his wife working in this city since 1973, the Lord has given us many opportunities to speak of righteousness and biblical morality. For such threatening speech – according to the gay community – we have experienced repeated attacks against us, our children, and our congregation by militant gays. We have been subject to two lawsuits brought by a homosexual church organist and later two lesbians. By God's mercy, we won both lawsuits, but it cost tens of thousands of dollars. Our home has been subjected to firebombing, vandalization and graffiti numerous times; we have received multitudes of obscene phone calls and death threats; and for the sake of the children, we've been forced to flee the city in fear for our lives on several occasions.[11]

Some may be tempted to think that this account was an isolated incident that took place in the gay-mecca of the world. But as other Christian churches take their stand against the culture's increasing tolerance and avocation of "alternative lifestyles" we are sure to see these types of events repeated. To vocally take a stand for Biblical sexual ethics and Godly marriages will increasingly become a penalized form of "hate speech." This is not a paranoid prognostication of the future of the Church, it has already happened in other countries around the world.

The Term "Homosexual" in the Bible

Before we get any deeper on this subject, we need to understand some terms and discuss how various English Bible translations may be muddling the issue in the Church rather than bringing greater clarity. Some translations, in fact, may even be causing undue harm to those

11 Charles & Donna McIlhenny, *When the Wicked Seize A City* (New York, NY: Authors Choice Press, 2000), 19.

Christians who, after reading their Bible, may wonder if God has rejected them merely for having same-sex attractions.

For example, 1 Corinthians 6:9-10 in the New American Standard Bible says, "Or, do you not know that the unrighteous will not inherit the kingdom of God? Do not be deceived; neither fornicators... nor homosexuals... will inherit the kingdom of God." Many same-sex attracted Christians respond in fear when Scripture speaks negatively in this way about "homosexuals" and "Sodomites." Looking up the word 'homosexual' in a dictionary, they might find that their own condition is aptly characterized as "a tendency to direct sexual desire toward individuals of one's own sex."[12] Discovering that the definition of the term "homosexual" includes those who have desires for their own sex, even if those desires have never acted upon, and then reading such a definition into passages such as Romans 1, 1 Corinthians 6:9, or 1 Timothy 1:10, these Christians may begin to wonder, "Am I truly a Christian? Have I been fooling myself, thinking that I'm a Christian when in fact I have been 'given over' to my desires by God?" Tragically, some, having lost hope in the face of an overwhelming fear that they might act on their desires, have chosen to commit suicide.[13]

Do passages such as these refer to everyone who has same-sex attractions? Does same-sex attraction constitute an essential aspect of who and what we are? Should we think of ourselves and identify ourselves as being homosexual or gay? How do we identify ourselves in relation to our emotional desires and sexual attractions? These are very important questions and the terminology that we use to refer to ourselves and other people who have same-sex attractions and those who act on these desires is a very controversial matter. However, in order to answer these questions we must first rightly understand the key texts. We must additionally understand *what* we are as male or female created in the image of God and understand *who* we are as Christians -- that is, our perception of "self" and our identity, in Christ.

Throughout history there has often been an underlying problem with the use of language in theological, philosophical, and ethical disputes. Terms such as "homosexual," "Sodomite," or "Gay" are no different. In addition to debates about textual exegesis and doctrinal formulations,

12 http://dictionary.reference.com/browse/homosexual
13 Jallen Rix, *Ex-gay No Way: Survival And Recovery From Religious Abuse* (Findhorn Press, 2010), 7.

disputes have sometimes ensued because parties differ over certain key terms. When this happens, disputants may only succeed in arguing past each other. The failure to resolve such terminological differences can lead to absurdities such as this: "I know you believe you understand what you think I said, but I'm not sure you realize that what you heard is not what I meant."

Sometimes there is a necessity to use words that are more common in one field of study (philosophy, psychology, theology, the physical sciences etc.) than in another. Furthermore, a particular field of study will have its own technical jargon to which outsiders are unaccustomed. Sometimes these technical terms may not translate well from one field of study to another or from one culture to another. Consequently, there is a sense in which people working in these narrow fields of study can to some degree have a sub-culture of their own in how they think and speak.

Various types of cultures (ethnic, religious, demographic, academic etc.) tend to have their own language and terminology that may not translate completely word-for-word from one to another. When translation does occur there are often various idioms, figures of speech, metaphors, and historical allusions that are derived from the original language and not the translated language. In other words, behind the translation there still remains a cultural understanding of the terms from the original language.

In the post-apostolic era, for example, the Church consisted primarily of Greek (Gentile) believers, some of whom, in their eagerness to explore the nature of God and the identity of Christ, did not always sufficiently cling to the concrete language and exemplars of the Bible. This fact helps to account for why the Athanasian Creed contains some heavy philosophical jargon. "And the Catholic Faith is this: That we worship one God in Trinity, and Trinity in Unity, neither confounding the Persons, nor dividing the Substance." Some of the terms found here only turn up in the Bible in root form (such as "substance" cf. Hebrews 11:1). They do not take the nuanced roles in which Athanasius casts them. The word "Trinity," for example, was engineered to convey the idea that God is a single "substance" (ontologically unified) who yet exists in three "persona" (individual identities), all of whom are distinct from each other. Thus, a Trinitarian would do well to answer to the question "*what* is God?" with "He is one." Whereas, the same Trinitarian would do well to answer the question "*who* is God?" with "He is three."

All of these ideas are abstract philosophical ideas used in an attempt to convey what the Bible teaches concerning the nature of God and the relationship of the Father, Son, and Holy Spirit. The early Church Fathers were not trying to Hellenize the Christian faith. Rather, they were seeking to explain what the Bible teaches in what might be considered philosophical technical language.

Now, let us jump forward to our own day and try to discuss the inner workings of the human mind - the mental, emotional, and sociological development of people's thinking – using only terms from the Bible. Is this possible? My goal is to begin with the Bible to understand the nature of sin and how it affects the human mind and soul. Put in another way, I want to develop a psychology using the worldview of the Bible.

But does the Bible provide a technical terminology (should this become necessary) that would allow us to explain the formation and evolution of particular human mental and emotional states or conditions? Or do new technical terms need to be introduced in order to explain what I believe the Bible teaches and what we observe in human mental, emotional, and sociological development? If I use technical terminology to develop a Biblical understanding of psychology, do I start from scratch or do I use terms that are already in use in this science even if such terms are being used differently by non-Christians?[14] If I decide to use technical terms to discuss psychology ("study of the soul") that are also used by non-Christians, then I will need to do so in the terms of a distinctly Christian worldview. As such, my explanations will differ significantly from the forms that explanations take in the thought of Sigmund Freud, Carl Jung, and J.B. Watson, to name a few secular "mental doctors" of the past century. These men built upon fundamental premises that are antithetical to historic Christianity. Against such approaches, I will build an anthropology (a study of man) based upon Biblical specifics. In doing so, I will accommodate common terms, but I will also work to see these terms placed within the unique, governing context of God's self-revelation.

---

14 Koine Greek is not "Bible language" but was rather the common language of the day. The New Testament authors were using a language and terminology already in existence but with an eye towards idioms and concepts inherited from the Old Testament.

There is a danger in doing this, of course. As already mentioned, many of the early Church Fathers (such as Origen) did not merely use Greek philosophical terminology. They often incorporated Greek philosophical ideas that were antithetical to the Bible. When they "baptized" the terminology their penchant for Neo-platonic thought forms often polluted the Christian water. Neoplatonism also permeated the theological architecture of the thirteenth-century Dominican, Thomas Aquinas, whose "baptism" of Aristotle's philosophy played out in his doctrines of natural law, sin, grace, and the sacraments. Something similar can happen when Christian psychologists, whose indoctrination at the knees of secular guides may only be equaled by their lack of theological training, approach various moral, mental, and emotional questions pertaining to the human condition. Sadly, it is not difficult to find Christians adopting substantial portions, for instance, of Freudian jargon, leaving them and others, at best, with a less than fully Biblical understanding of man and sin. Even worse, these same people frequently adopt the faulty diagnoses and prescriptions of Freudian psychology.[15]

One ancient example of a theological dispute pervaded by terminological differences comes from the fourth century. At the Council of Nicaea in A.D. 325, conflict arose between Eastern (predominantly Greek) and Western (predominantly Latin) churchmen over the meaning of the term *homoousios*. That's right, another "homo" word! This Eastern-Western division persisted for centuries and succeeded in frustrating Eastern theology and confusing Western churchmen about the East's position. The terminological dispute, to be sure, was not the only point of contention at Nicaea but it was a significant one.[16] At the council of Alexandria, "it was formally recognized that what mattered was not the language used but the meaning underlying it."[17]

Similarly, discourse pertaining to same-sex relations and relationships in the Church has sometimes courted confusion due to lack of care with respect to terms such as "homosexual," "gay" and "orientation." It is therefore very important to understand how these terms have been used with different connotations. If a person believes that their desires

---

15 See Richard Ganz, *Psychobabble* (Wheaton, IL: Crossway Books, 1993).

16 See Williston Walker, *A History of the Christian Church* (New York, NY: Scribner; 4th edition, 1985), 131-137.

17 J.N.D. Kelly, *Early Christian Doctrines* (San Francisco, CA: Harper Collins, 1978), 253

and preferences to have sex with a person of their own gender (male or female) are innate, something with which they are born and are a gift from God, then he may accept for himself the labels "homosexual" or "gay" as identity markers and even perhaps as ontologically definitive (i.e., constitutive of her fundamental "being").

But if a person believes that desires to have intercourse with a member of their own sex is an acquired and developed proclivity and that the term "homosexual" only refers to one's objective actions and not subjective feelings, then the term will have a different connotation. The consequence of hearing and understanding the term "homosexual" differently is severe; if two people go on to have a debate about the morality of same-sex relationships without defining their terms or settling the issue of whether such desires are innate or acquired then they will be equivocating on some crucial terms. They will talk past each other and neither side will truly understand where the other is coming from on the issue.

There are two problems with using the term "homosexual" in English translations of the Bible. The first is how the English term "homosexual" has changed over the past century. The second is the question of whether the word accurately reflects the words and intents of the New Testament writers.

The Bible contains terms that are unique to its time and culture that do not exactly correlate to anything in our own time or culture. Consequently, we often lack a single term that corresponds to the concept that is being conveyed. In such translation situations one either leaves the reader to research terms, explains his own usage in a footnote, invents a word for the reader's language, or transliterates the term into his own language. This is, in fact, what early English translators did with the word "baptism," which hails from the Greek *baptizo*. In the Septuagint, the term *baptizo* is used to speak in places of sprinkling, pouring, and dipping; it carries the general idea of "washing" rather than any particular mode of applying water. However, when used in a religious context, particularly in the New Testament, it takes on additional connotations and so is transliterated as "baptism" rather than as "wash."

Unfortunately, many exegetes of Scripture have not been properly exhorted to consider these issues when they read, translate, interpret and apply the text of Scripture. The result is that many unlearned and poorly taught people take a simplistic "cut and paste" approach to

using various language tools, thinking that a simple dictionary definition will provide the correct understanding of a word which is used in
Scripture. To make matters worse, many contributors to popular Greek
language dictionaries, such as Kittel's *Theological Dictionary of the
New Testament*, reckon the Bible to be less than the fully breathed-out
Word of God. For this reason, they often superimpose meanings native
to classical Greek onto New Testament texts without sufficiently considering the distinctive nuances the latter may feature due to commonly
Hebraic historical experiences and concepts. The New Testament was
written by Jews with a Jewish history and culture, whose language and
understanding of God and morals stemmed from the Hebrew Scriptures.
Scholarly neglect of this fact threatens to blind us to ways in which the
Biblical writers may have endowed common linguistic symbols with a
novel sense or reference-function.

This brings us to the word "homosexual," how it has been used in
theological, ethical, and political conversations, and how it has been
used in English translations for the past century. Many Gay Theology
apologists argue that, along with constituting a "moral good," the desire to have sex with a member of one's own gender is an innate and
immutable (because it is divinely granted) inclination. "[T]o claim that
Jesus can change one's sexual orientation," Michael Piazza writes, "is
as ludicrous as suggesting that He can change one's race. Perhaps He
can, but He won't. That is how God made you and who God intended
you to be."[18]

Promoters of this proposition do not look to Scripture for justification
but rather to a selection of psychological studies, faulty interpretations of
animal behavior, and personal experiences. Too frequently, the former
are driven to embrace such studies by (sometimes legitimate) complaints
they have about the ways in which persons with same-sex desires have
been treated in our society. They argue that to deny people the freedom
to express a supposedly God-given desire is a form of oppression. In
this connection, when they come across "homosexual" in their English
Bibles they find themselves asserting that this is a mistranslation of the
Greek word *arsenokoitai* (1 Corinthians 6:9; 1 Timothy 1:10). The term
is so ambiguous, they will contend, that we cannot know what it truly

---

18 Michael S. Piazza, *Gay By God* (Dallas, TX: Source of Hope Publishing, 1998),
15.

means or that it can only be understood within the narrow confines of either an exploitative pederastic (man-boy) sexual relationship or ritualistic cultic pagan practice. Therefore, according to them, the modern use of the term "homosexual" should not be used to translate the word *arsenokoitai* and all anti-homosexual sentiments in the Church, at least in part, result from a poor translation of the Bible.[19]

Here is where the use of the term "homosexual" can become rather complicated. The term was coined in C.G. Chaddock's translation of Krafft-Ebing's *Psychopathia Sexualis* (originally written in 1886), and it is from a combination of the Greek word *homo* which means "same" and the Latin word *sexus* which means "a state of being either male or female, gender." The noun was first recorded 1912 in English and in 1907 in French. Technically used, it can refer to either a male or female; in non-technical usage its almost always refers to a male. According to Webster's Dictionary, the term "homosexual," when used as an adjective, refers to a person who is sexually attracted to members of his or her own sex. When it is used as a noun it means someone "who practices homosexuality" or "having a sexual attraction to persons of the same sex." Likewise, it says that the term "gay" can either mean "having or showing a merry, lively mood" or it is used as a synonym for a homosexual.[20]

Word meanings can shift and alternate over time. In 1892, the term "gay" meant a happy person. Today it is a slang term that refers to a person who is sexually attracted to members of their own sex. In common parlance, it distinguishes male homo-sexuals from "lesbians," women who are sexually attracted to other women. *Originally,* the term "lesbians" referred to the residents of an island in the east Aegean, off the North West coast of Turkey. Likewise the term "homosexual" has changed since 1892 and commentators on different sides of the Gay Theology debate use it in different ways. Some use it to refer to anyone who is attracted to members of the same sex and still others use it to refer to only people who engage in homogenital acts. For those who believe that their same-sex desires are an innate gift of God, the term "homosexual" is not merely a descriptive word of their actions. It forms an essential part of their personal identity, the core of many "deep"

19 Jefferey Miner, *The Children Are Free* (Digital Imagery, 2001); Daniel Helminiak, *What The Bible Really says About Homosexuality* (Alamo Square Press, 2000). 19.
20 http://dictionary.reference.com/browse/homosexual

thoughts and feelings. This is why when they hear that homosexuality is a sin to them it is akin to saying, "Being a dark-colored skinned person is a sin."

The person who believes that men having sex with other men in any context is a sin usually does not usually use the term "homosexual" to refer to an innate identity of a person but rather a descriptive term that defines a person according to their actions, not merely their sexual attractions. In this sense the term is used in the same way "fireman" might be used to define a man whose occupation is to put out fires. However, many Christian theologians who have argued against Gay Theology have not been consistent with their use of the term. Sometimes they will refer to a person as a "homosexual" even after the person has become a Christian and ceased from all sexual activity with other men. [21] The problem with this should be clear. If Christian theologians are going to be consistent in their use of their terms, to continue to refer to such a person as a homosexual is to assert that the condemnation of homosexuals in the Bible, as they interpret it, would still be applicable even though they ceased to have sex with other men.

The word "homosexual," like any other English word, is a term that some translators borrowed from the English language but did not exist until about a century ago. They believed that this term was a close equivalence to what the Greek term *arsenokoitai* conveys. The problem is that the word "homosexual" is borrowed from the field of psychology and it includes the inward mental processes of a person and not just his actions. Hence, according to most English dictionaries if you are sexually attracted to another person of your own gender you are identified as a homosexual whether or not you have ever engaged in same-sex copulation. The problem of miscommunicating arises when using the term to translate *arsenokoitai* in 1 Corinthians 6:9 and 1 Timothy 1:10 as "homosexual." In these passages Paul is not referring to a mental-emotional process but to an *action*, which is prohibited in Leviticus 18:22 just as the person mentioned in 1 Corinthians 5:1 is violating Leviticus 18:8.

21 For example, Greg Bahnsen states that the church should reject unrepentant homosexuals and then states, "When converted by God's grace, the homosexual must be wholeheartedly received by the church as a person for whom Christ died...", in *Homosexuality: A Biblical View* (Grand Rapids, MI: Baker Book House, 1978), 98. If the person has repented why are they still being identified as a homosexual? Bahnsen should have said, "When converted by God's grace, the ex-homosexual must be wholeheartedly received by the church as a person for whom Christ died..."

There are some English translations that seek to bring clarity to this passage by adding an additional qualifying terms such as "homosexual offenders" or "homosexual acts" (NIV) or "men who practice homosexuality" (ESV). But the NIV's use of term "homosexual offenders" can sound as if the sin is to offend a homosexual and the ESV's can leaves one to wonder, "What does it mean to 'practice' homosexuality?" Because of such potential confusion, as I have later argued in this book, the word *arsenokotai* in 1 Corinthians 6:9 and 1 Timothy 1:10 might be better translated not as "homosexuals" or "sodomites" (a misnomer) but rather more precisely as "men who have sex with other men" to rightly reflect the apostle Paul's allusion to the Septuagint translation of Leviticus 18:22 and 20:13. This translation rightly renders the objective nature of the sin and makes it clear that it does not apply to anyone who is merely tempted to engage in such activity. Instead the reader will clearly know that if he is not having sex with a member of the same gender the text does not condemn him. Consequently, people who experience same sex attractions should not identify themself as a "homosexual" or any of its synonyms without qualification. Wesley Hill makes such a qualifying statement in his book *Washed and Waiting*:

> In this book I have chosen not to discriminate between various terms for homosexuality. So, for instance, I use 'same-sex attraction,' 'homosexual desires,' 'homosexuality,' and related terms interchangeably. Likewise, I've used a variety of designations for gay or lesbian people. Instead of sticking to one term, such as 'homosexual Christian,' I also refer to myself as a 'gay Christian' or 'a Christian who experiences homosexual desires.' These phrases are all synonymous for me, and though they are open to misunderstanding, in my judgment the gains in using them outweigh the potential hazards. None of them should be taken necessarily to imply homosexual practice; in each case I am often placing the emphasis on the subject's sexual orientation and not the corresponding behavior.[22]

---

22 Wesley Hill, *Washed and Waiting: Reflection on Christian Faithfulness and Homosexuality* (Grand Rapids, MI: Zondervan, 2010), 21.

What should additionally be kept in mind is that Paul mentions a number of other sins in 1 Corinthians 6:9, including fornicators. Does this mean that any heterosexual man that does not actually fornicate but is tempted to do so in his heart shall not inherit the kingdom of God? It is true that Jesus made it clear that if a man lusts after a woman who is not his wife he has committed adultery in his heart (Matthew 5:27-28). But nowhere in either the Old or New Testament is there any penal sanction for what only goes on in the mind or heart. While this does mean that lust is unjustifiable and morally inexcusable, it does *not* mean that a person tempted to commit acts of a certain type should have his identity invariably defined by or associated with such acts. Passages such as Romans 1:18-32 and 1 Corinthians 6:9 also mention various other sins such as being greedy. But only the person who lives as an *unrepentant* sinner stands under God's condemnation.

Understandably, some Christians may object to a person who has same-sex attractions referring to themselves as a "Gay Christian," if in fact the person is not involved in same-sex acts and do not subscribe to Gay Theology. This is the stated objection within the Ex-Gay movement. This objection, however, is sometimes built on false premises of Pentecostal and Charismatic theology as taught by advocates of the Word of Faith movement.

In this heretical movement faith is viewed as a force and words are a container of the force such that if you speak health, wealth and prosperity into your life declaring "I'm healthy," then you can create your own reality. But, if you say, "I am sick" you are speaking a negative confession into your life and by the power of your words you are actually making yourself ill. The solution then is to deny the symptoms of the illness and refrain from using medicine, which would be a form of negative confession. The solution then, according to this theology, is to repeatedly assert, "I am healed in the name of Jesus! By His stripes I am healed!" even if your body is telling you differently.[23] When this same line of thinking is carried over into the "Ex-Gay" movement the result is people declaring, "I am healed in the name of Jesus! I'm no longer gay!" when in fact the person still experiences same-sex attractions. Inevitably, the person eventually grows weary of living a lie. Instead of

---

23 For a critique of this theology I recommend reading: *Hank Hanegraaff, Christianity In Crisis: The 21st Century* (Thomas Nelson, 2009); Gordon D. Fee, *The Disease of the Health and Wealth Gospels* (Regent College Publishing, 1985)

denying the truth of the presence of their attractions, they stop fighting the emotional and sexual desires and give into them which can end either in some form of sexual scandal or an embrace of Gay Theology which necessitates a departure from Biblical Christianity. This all too common scenario has given rise to the self-named "Ex-Ex Gay Movement."

Because of this, some Christians who continue to experience same-sex attractions and yet are convinced that acting on them is not a viable ethical option choose to dissociate with the "Ex-Gay" movement. Many such disaffected individuals believe they show greater honesty and transparency by openly declaring themselves to be a "celibate" or "Side B" Gay Christian. Less of an identity, it is an open and honest admission of an ongoing temptation.

That a man finds himself tempted or wages an ongoing battle with homosexual desires does not imply that he is among those who God has "given...over" to their lusts. The mark of a true Christian is continual repentance and the very fact that this war against the desires of the flesh rages within him indicates that the law of God has indeed been written on his heart (Jeremiah 31:33; Romans 2:14-15). Therefore, a Christian who is tempted to commit adultery but does not actually carry out the lusts of his heart should not be labeled an adulterer. Neither should a person who has desires to have sex with a member of his own gender but does not act on those lusts be labeled "homosexual." The marked difference between one who is a Christian tempted to do such acts and a person who has been given over to the lusts of their heart by God is "although they know the ordinance of God, that those who practice such things are worthy of death, they not only do the same, but also give hearty approval to those who practice them" (Romans 1:32).

We are not judged on the basis of our temptations. Jesus was tempted in all ways like us and yet without sin (Hebrews 4:15). Instead, how we respond to those sinful desires with our actions is what determines how we are judged. The dictionary defines this term "homosexual" in a psychological manner whereas Paul is using the word *arsenokoitai* to convey the idea of "a man who lays with another man," euphemistically meaning "a man who has sex with another man." Therefore, as I have argued, the word *arsenokoitai* should not be translated as "homosexual" but rather spelled out as "a man who has sex with another man."

But in a discussion or debate on the ethics of same-sex acts non-Christians do not use the term "homosexual" in this way. One side in the debate uses the term ontologically, whether or not they ever act on their emotional desires. The other side uses it to talk about someone who acts on those desires. When a Christian then says on the issue of homosexuality that we are to "love the sinner, hate the sin," this assumes a distinction that many individuals who act (sexually) out of a "gay" sense of self will not countenance as legitimate. In their minds, the "sin" (a sexual way of life) is so interwoven with the homo-sexual's personal identity that one cannot hate the sin without also hating the sinner. "Gayness" comes to expression not merely in the bedroom or bath-house but at life's every turn.

Christians are coming to the issue on the basis of the Bible which classifies sinners according to particular actions and not their temptations. Others have a broader use of the term in which "homosexual" or "gay" defines a person whether or not the person ever acts on the feelings. Ultimately, this is an extremely important distinction to make. We are seeking to understand what God requires from the believer in addition to faith in Jesus Christ. I think Michael Saia is correct when he states, "God does not demand that a person be healed, heterosexually oriented, or happy - God demands *holiness*."[24]

Having the distinction between how the Bible uses the term *arseno-koitai* and how the English dictionaries use the term "homosexual" we now need to consider whether the trait of having same sex attractions constitutes something akin to being right-handed or whether it is a developed and acquired characteristic, much like preferring chocolate over vanilla ice cream. Returning to the story of Sodom and Gomorrah, which we examined in the beginning of this chapter, we read of two angels disguised as men who have come to visit Abraham's nephew Lot in the wicked city of Sodom. Lot then invites them into his home to spend the night, fearing the dangers of the city. But then things take a turn for the worse:

> Before they lay down, the men of the city, the men of
> Sodom, surrounded the house, both young and old, all
> the people from every quarter; and they called to Lot and
> said to him, 'Where are the men who came to you tonight?
> Bring them out to us that we may know (Hebrew: *yada'*)

24 Michael Saia, *Counseling The Homosexual* (Minneapolis, MN; Bethany House Publishers, 1988), 97.

them.' But Lot went out to them at the doorway, and shut
the door behind him, and said, 'Please, my brothers, do not
act wickedly. Now behold, I have two daughters who have
not known (*yada'*) a man; please let me bring them out to
you, and do to them whatever you like; only do nothing to
these men, inasmuch as they have come under the shelter
of my roof.' But they said, 'Stand aside.' Furthermore, they
said, 'This one came in as an alien, and already he is acting
like a judge; now we will treat you worse than them.' So
they pressed hard against Lot and came near to break the
door. But the men reached out their hands and brought Lot
into the house with them, and shut the door. They struck
the men who were at the doorway of the house with blind-
ness, both small and great, so that they wearied themselves
trying to find the doorway (Genesis 19:1-11).

Historically, this text has been interpreted to be an account of God's
display of wrath on a city for the sin of committing same-sex acts.
Subsequently, same-sex acts took on the name "sodomy" in various
English translations of the Bible which translated *arsenokoitai* in 1
Corinthians 6:9 as "sodomites" as in the RSV. I am convinced that such
a reading of the text is unjustifiable and to refer to all homosexuals
as Sodomites is a misnomer at best and tends to mislead the Church
at worst. The sexually ravenous behavior of the men in Sodom or the
greedy murderous God-hating idolaters described in Romans 1 by the
apostle Paul does not describe the average self-identified gay person.

The consequence of this misunderstanding of the sin of Sodom is
that many fundamentalist Christians, who have never actually met or
interacted with gay people (that they know of), will have a caricature of
them in their mind as fitting the description of the Sodomites in Genesis
19 or homosexuals in Romans 1 as being consumed with sexual violence. Some will even argue with a wrong reading of Romans 1 that God
turns people into homosexuals as a judgment for their suppressing the
knowledge of the truth concerning God. I often heard arguments growing up in the Church and as a young adult in the various Calvary Chapel
congregations I attended, things such as "If God doesn't soon judge

San Francisco He will have to apologize to Sodom and Gomorrah."[25] The rhetoric I have heard in Reformed and Presbyterian churches has been worse as I heard from fellow seminary students, "The government should kill all the queers!" I have also heard men, who often lead worship in church, singing as we stood in line in during the potluck, "Burn the faggots! Burn the faggots!" Even more tragic, theologians whom I admire and respect who train future pastors have said in their lectures, "If just a few of them were executed the rest would go back into the closet."

Hearing preachers talk this this, many Christians in the Church who then find themselves having unchosen and unwanted same-sex attractions live in fear of acknowledging that they struggle with such desires, concluding that God has judged them and turned them into a homosexual. They, sooner or later, sink into depression, thinking that God does not love them and that there is no hope of salvation regardless of the depth of their faith or the quality of their love for Jesus Christ. Or, as so often is the case, once they discover that the average gay person does not meet the descriptions of Genesis 19 or Romans 1, they come to the conclusion that the Bible and the Church are misinformed about the average self-identified gay person who, other than the fact that they engage in a sexual sin, behave no better or worse than the average Christian.

On the flip side, when the average civil gay person who works a normal job, pays his taxes, spends his spare time raising funds for breast cancer research, and helps his elderly neighbor take out her garbage hears nothing but words of contempt for him, he will be quick to dismiss Church's condemnation of same-sex acts as being the result of a primitive backwards religion as he hears preachers conveying misinformation concerning modern homosexuals. Add to this the innumerable public sex scandals of gay-hating Christian leaders in the Church, and his first reaction to preaching on Genesis 19 becomes a reason to dismiss the Bible and the gospel itself.

Many people who have grown up in the Church and have same sex attractions, after listening to such rhetoric, then develop great sympathy for Gay rights advocacy groups. They then learn how Nazi Germany used anti-gay, religion-based propaganda to justify imprisoning, torturing and putting to death many homosexuals. As a consequence, they

25 In fact, Calvary Chapel of Sahurita has this statement on their web site, attributing it to the wife of Billy Graham: http://www.ccos.org/notes/61-2Peter-02-03-jk.html

become fearful of Bible-believing Christians and even develop what might be termed "Christo-phobia." Motivated by their fear of experiencing the horrors of Nazi-Germany they see political activism not merely as a means to be able to act on their sexual inclinations in private but as a necessary means to overcome the perceived homophobia in a society which seeks to deny them fair employment, a right to have place to live, and equal representation in the political system. The fear-mongering of the Church provides fuel for the fire of Gay activists. A collection of quotes from fundamentalist preachers added to the history of mistreatment of homosexual in Nazis German feeds the formation in many of a persecution complex, whether or not this is warranted by the evidence. They then see themselves as an oppressed minority group that has suffered injustice in the way African slaves did in America, much of which was also supported and defended by conservative fundamentalist churches.

At this point it may seem to some that I am playing "right into the hands of Gay activists." However, I am convinced that if the Christians are going to address the issue of homosexuality in the Church with integrity, they need to be willing to change their views when confronted with a correct understanding of the text of Scripture, even if it means contradicting some of our previously held interpretations and traditions. To do otherwise is to continue foolishness and failure to obey the Biblical mandate to rightly interpret and apply it to our culture as Paul exhorted Timothy, "Be diligent to present yourself approved to God as a workman who does not need to be ashamed, accurately handling the word of truth" (2 Timothy 2:15). Furthermore, if Christians are going to be credible and viewed as honest in the public realm of debate on this issue, they need to confess and repent of how the Church has wrongly used the Scriptures in the past. For example, many churches sought to use the Bible to justify slavery and the brutal treatment of black people in the United States. This was done on the mistaken premise that they were sub-human or the cursed race of people descended from Ham based on a faulty interpretation of Genesis 9:20-27. For example, Southern Presbyterians such as R. L. Dabney began to say things such as:

> But while we believe that 'God made of one blood all
> nations of men to dwell under the whole heavens,' we

know that the African has become, according to a well-known law of history, by the manifold influence of the ages, a different, fixed species of the race, separated from the white man by traits, bodily, mental and moral almost as rigid and permanent as those of genus.[26]

This assertion was based on an incorrect but popular interpretation of the curse of God regarding the sin of Ham. In the Middle Ages, it was a popular idea to view Africans as the "sons of Ham" who were cursed and "blackened" by their sins. Though early arguments to this effect were sporadic, they became increasingly common during the slave trade of the 18th and 19th centuries.[27] The justification of slavery itself through the sins of Ham was well-suited to the economic interests of the slave trade which sought to justify the exploitation of a ready supply of African labor and the subsequent mistreatment of blacks as being sub-human, even within the confines of the Church.

Finally, the leaders of the Church must repent of their own sin, get the plank out of their own eye before they judge others (Matthew 7:1-4). If they are going to be deemed credible, they need to obey the ninth commandment since Christians cannot justifiably misrepresent their neighbors by bearing false witness against them (Exodus 20:16). This includes repenting of real homophobia which fails to be gracious and merciful towards self-identified gays and lesbians, seeing that no one is beyond the saving power of the gospel. In this vein, Charles McIlhenny writes:

Unfortunately,…there are individuals who are fearful and even hate homosexuals. Some Christians have the idea that homosexuals are so sinful that they're beyond God's redeeming grace. We had a minister acquaintance tell us that if he found out that a homosexual was merely sitting

---

26 Ernest Trice Thompson, *Presbyterians in the South*, Vol. 2, 1861-1890 (Richmond: John Knox Press, 1973), 200.

27 Benjamin Braude, "The Sons of Noah and the Construction of Ethnic and Geographical Identities in the Medieval and Early Modern Periods" in "William and Mary Quarterly LIV" (January 1997): 103–142. See also William McKee Evans, "From the Land of Canaan to the Land of Guinea: The Strange Odyssey of the Sons of Ham," in "American Historical Review 85" (February 1980), 15–43.

in his service, he'd have the ushers throw him out. This kind of attitude is totally unscriptural and just provides the gays with ammunition to condemn the whole church for being hateful and homophobic. Homosexual behavior is no worse than any other sexual sin. The adulterer and homosexual both need the same sovereign grace of God in Christ to bring them to repentance. Both can avail themselves of God's mercy and forgiveness.[28]

---

28 Charles & Donna McIlhenny, *When the Wicked Seize A City* (New York, NY: Authors Choice Press, 2000), 20.

Chapter 2
Worldviews in Conflict

The challenge of the rise of Gay Theology in the Church is nothing less than a battle for the Bible, its meaning, and application in the modern era. As we will see, the issues at hand concern not merely abstract or tangential doctrines but the very foundation of the historic Christian faith and the heart of the gospel – namely the person and work of Jesus Christ. This movement, which has been steadily growing since the so-called "sexual revolution" of the 1960's, is not merely a different interpretation of a handful of passages in the Bible. Rather it is an entirely different worldview, a pseudo-Christian cultic movement that is a revival of the syncretism of paganism and Christianity and a theoretical antinomian doctrine of libertine Gnosticism which confronted the early church. Many Gay Theology advocates may identify themselves as evangelical such as Rick Brentlinger and Virginia Mollenkot and Gay affirming churches may claim to uphold the historic creeds of the Church. Yet Gay Theology's philosophical, epistemological and hermeneutical framework is completely antithetical to the historic Christian faith. This movement, as I will demonstrate, promotes a different Jesus than the one revealed in the gospels and preached by the apostles as do many other modern cults.[29]

When we address the issue of same sex acts and the Bible it is crucial to understand that what is at hand is a conflict in worldviews. It is a spiritual and theological battle between a consistently Biblical understanding of same sex acts and an opposing worldview whose foundation is antithetical to Biblical Christianity. Gay Theology is heretical and the organizations that promote it, such as the Metropolitan Community Church and the Gay Christian Network, are a radical departure from Biblical Christianity. This does not mean that there are no well-meaning and sincere Christians within their midst. Rather, many ill-equipped and uninformed Christians who subscribe to the Gay Theological movement have been duped by their leaders who are themselves self-deceived.

29 For further reading, I highly recommend "Scaling the Language Barrier" in Walter Martin's classic text *The Kingdom of the Cults* (Minneapolis, MN: Bethany House Publishers, 1985), 18-24.

These false teachers consequently twist Scripture in order to present a false gospel and justify going beyond Biblical ethical boundaries for expressing love towards someone of the same gender.

It is extremely important to understand that the growing popularity and acceptance of Gay Theology is a revival of an ancient heretical paradigm which seeks to replace a historic understanding of sexual ethics and the Bible. As it does so it subtly introduces a different gospel than the one preached by the apostles with a revised version of a Gnostic hermeneutical system. In order discern the errors of Gay Theology, it is crucial that we understand the presuppositions of this movement which create the lens through which its promoters interpret the Bible, for no one comes to the issue of same sex acts and the text of Scripture in a neutral fashion without any philosophical bias as Ronald H. Nash explains:

> Whether we know it or not – whether we like it or not – each of us has a worldview. These worldviews function as interpretive conceptual schemes to explain why we 'see' the world as we do, why we often think and act as we do.[30]

Therefore, when addressing this issue it is important to first examine the presuppositions that support the worldview of Gay Theology before we address the various passages in the Scriptures that are relevant to this topic. No one comes to the historical and doctrinal texts of the Bible in a neutral fashion without a set of presupposed parameters for interpreting the facts life. This becomes especially clear when it comes to the relevant texts on same sex acts as James B. De Young points out:

> Every person comes to the matter of homosexuality with an established opinion, which has been shaped by a worldview. By *worldview* I mean a person's concept of self, the world, and everything else. Every worldview encompasses what one views as real, the nature of truth, how we come to know what is true, and how we define what is

---

30 Ronald H. Nash, *Worldviews In Conflict* (Grand Rapids, MI: Zondervan, 1992), 33.

'good' in an ethical sense. One's worldview determines whether homosexuality is perceived as right or wrong.[31]

It is common for believers to regard the Christian faith as merely a collection of independent doctrines rather than as a total conceptual system providing a lens through which they are to interpret history, culture and the meaning of life. However, Christianity is a total world and life-view and biblical theism is a total system of belief that includes sexual ethics as Ronald H. Nash aptly states, "Instead of thinking of Christianity as a collection of theological bits and pieces to be believed or debated, we should approach our faith as a conceptual system, as a total world-and-life view." [32] A worldview entails the sum total of propositions a person believes which results in what R.C Sproul refers to as a "unifying system of thought" [33] or as James Sire states, "A worldview is a set of presuppositions (assumptions which may be true, partially true or entirely false) which we hold (consciously or subconsciously, consistently or inconsistently) about the basic make-up of our world."[34]

A worldview then encompasses the "big picture" concerning the nature of reality in an effort to grasp it all together as a whole in a web of beliefs. This web of beliefs forms a hermeneutical lens through which we interpret all facts of life, things in the exterior world outside of ourselves (the Bible and the created order) but also our feelings, experiences and desires -- what we might think of as our interior world. Consequently, a worldview functions as a means of interpreting facts within God's created order (General Revelation) as well as His written Word (Special Revelation). Our worldview then determines how we answer questions concerning epistemology, the nature of reality and how we should live:

> In its simplest terms, a worldview is a set of beliefs about
> the most important issues in life... A Worldview, then, is

---

31 James B. De Young, *Homosexuality: Contemporary Claims Examined in the Light of the Bible and Other Ancient Literature and Law* (Grand Rapids, MI: Kregel, 2000), 13.

32 Ronald H. Nash, *Worldviews In Conflict* (Grand Rapids, MI: Zondervan, 1992), 19.

33 R.C. Sproul, *Lifeviews: Make a Christian Impact on Culture and Society* (Grand Rapids, MI: Fleming H. Revell, Publishing, 1986), 29

34 James W. Sire, *The Universe Next Door: A Basic Worldview Catalogue*, expanded ed. (Downers Grove, IL: InterVarsity, 1988), 17.

a conceptual scheme by which we consciously or uncon-
sciously place or fit everything we believe and by which
we interpret and judge reality.[35]

Some doctrines within this web of beliefs are more central to the
worldview while others are more peripheral and subject to change while
still maintaining the worldview's central and foundational presuppositions. The entirety of a worldview then is viewed from the standpoint
of some particular philosophy or theology that is defined by its core
presuppositions. Consequently the more peripheral convictions of the
web of belief may be considered non-essential or variables within the
defining characteristics of the worldview.

As an example, two people may be orthodox Bible-believing
Christians and consider each other to be brothers in Christ with essentially the same worldview because they hold to the same core doctrines
concerning Scripture, the nature of God and Jesus Christ. Yet they may
differ on certain peripheral theological issues such as an eschatological
perspective (amillennial, premillennial, postmillennial) or how they
understand the proper form of ecclesiastical government (Episcopalian,
Congregational, Presbyterian). This does not mean that these more peripheral theological issues are unimportant. Rather they are not the essential defining characteristics of what constitutes Biblical Christianity.

At this point many Gay Theology advocates may insist that they
uphold the central core doctrines of the Christian faith but, as we shall
see, error begets error and when the trajectory of the Gay Theological
movement is taken to its logically consistent end it is a very clear departure from historical Christianity. What must be clearly understood
is that Gay Theology is not merely a variant on a peripheral doctrinal
issue that can Christians can in good faith "agree to disagree agreeably."
The issue of sexual conduct is not a matter of debate, such as modes of
baptism, in which we can differ and yet continue to consider each other
to be in good standing within the Body of Christ. Scripture requires that
the obstinate, those who persist in sin, be removed in order to curtail its
leavening affect on the Christian community. While Christian Jews and
Christian Gentiles may break bread together in celebrating the Lord's
Supper, those who are unrepentant of sexually immorality are to be
excluded (1 Corinthians 5:7-13).

35 Ronald H. Nash, *Worldviews In Conflict* (Grand Rapids, MI: Zondervan, 1992), 16.

Every worldview, philosophy of life, seeks to answer three basic questions, "How can I know?" "What is the nature of reality?" and "How should I live?" These three questions are then answered within the three fundamental studies within philosophy -- epistemology, metaphysics, and ethics. Whether it is well thought out in philosophical categories or not, a worldview is formed by one's theory of *knowledge* (epistemology) which determines how facts are known and interpreted, which then determines a method of understanding the nature of *reality* (metaphysics), as well as establishing how one discerns how one *ought to live*; in distinguishing between right from wrong (ethics).

Ultimately what governs one's worldview is a presupposed *authority* whether it is the Scriptures, an earthly ecclesiastical ruler, or oneself. Consequently central to one's worldview are beliefs that are presupposed without support from other beliefs, arguments, or evidence. These presuppositions are taken upon by faith whether a person realizes it or not. A person may think to themselves, "This is the way reality truly is" not realizing that they have certain assumptions which they may have inherited from the culture around them or their educational upbringing.

Not only does every person have presuppositions of a worldview, such assumptions are necessary in order to function in this world. For example, scientists in order to do research make certain important epistemological assumptions (knowledge is possible, there is a real correspondence between physical phenomena and the human mind), metaphysical assumptions (nature is uniform, the law of physics are universal) and ethical assumptions (medical research to alleviate human suffering is good) in order to do research. The issue, as we shall see, is whether a given worldview can provide the necessary foundation and authority for such assumptions.

Authority and Epistemological Certainty

We now want to consider the importance of epistemology in relation to developing a justifiable worldview. By "justifiable" I am referring to how we demonstrate that a particular worldview is warranted. While many people go through life without consciously asking specific philosophical questions, the way in which they conduct their lives and the goals they pursue in life demonstrate that they do have some sort of an opinion as to how the basic questions of life ought to be answered. That which determines how these questions are answered will be one's ultimate faith commitment and authority in life. It will be the starting point for answering not only these questions but answering all opposing arguments to this faith commitment. Hence, how one answers these questions will not only depend on one's worldview but also one's religious belief whether or not one consciously believes in a god or ever attends a church, synagogue, shrine, or temple. Consequently even atheists are "religious" in that they have a worldview that has an ultimate authority, even if that authority is their proclaimed autonomous self-ruling mind as Ronald H. Nash wrote:

> ...there really is no such thing as an atheist. Someone named Jones may deny that the God of the Bible exists. He may even be foolish enough to believe that there is no god at all. But perceptive people will readily observe that there is something in life that functions as an object of ultimate concern for Jones... that something may be nothing more than the betterment of self. But whatever the object of ultimate concern is for us, that will be our god.[36]

The relationship between the three fields of study in philosophy (epistemology, metaphysics, and ethics) is co-determinative – that is, one's method of determining a system of epistemology will also, if consistent, determine one's understanding of metaphysics and system of ethics as Greg Bahnsen states, "Each worldview has its presuppositions about reality, knowledge, and ethics; these mutually influence and support each other."[37] Consequently there is circularity between these fields of philosophy. Likewise, just as there are three basic fields of study within philosophy, so too there are three categories or aspects of these three fields such that the issues of life can be approached from a rational, empirical, or existential perspective.[38]

36 Ronald H. Nash, *Worldviews In Conflict* (Grand Rapids, MI: Zondervan, 1992), 27.
37 Greg Bahnsen, *Presuppositional Apologetics: Stated and Defended* (The American Vision, 2009), 15.
38 John Frame uses the terms "Normative" "Situational" and "Existential" in *The Doctrine of the Knowledge of God*, (Phillipsburg: P&R., 1987). Greg Bahnsen uses the terms "deontological," "existential," and "teleological" in *By This Standard* (Tyler, TX: Institute for Christian Economics, 1985), 78-79.

One of the key issues of any worldview is not only the previously stated questions but also how epistemology relates to each question, "How I can I know what I know?", "How can I know the nature of reality?" and "How can I know how I should live?" Consequently, epistemology takes an economic priority as the starting point for creating a system of belief that seeks to answer these three basic questions although ethics may often be the motive for seeking to answer such questions.

As previously stated, there are within epistemology, three aspects or perspectives of our knowing all of which must be present to truly and fully know anything. Hence, we know things by reason (rational), through the empirical senses, (sight, smell, sound, taste, touch) and from subjective experience (existential). Within the history of philosophy, there have been attempts to make one of the three perspectives of epistemology the ultimate starting point for a worldview. While there are many other philosophical schools of thought, if you examine their ultimate starting point, though they may be more sophisticated and nuanced they nonetheless are reducible to being essentially one of these three.

Empiricism holds that all justifiable claims to knowledge come from the senses (hearing, seeing, touching, and smelling). The empiricist's motto is "seeing is believing" for he asserts that unless something can be proved by the "scientific method" then such stated facts cannot be substantiated. The modern "scientific method" when used as a means to formulate an epistemology is, in fact, a form of philosophical empiricism. It has in its presuppositions the nonexistence of God since it claims His existence cannot be tested by empirical observation. In fact, Gay Theology apologist Patrick M. Chapman bases on his own worldview and self-determined definition of science on this premise asserts that science cannot include the possibility of the existence of God since it by its very natures excludes the supernatural.[39]

The errors of empiricism and all systems of thought that insist on beginning with the senses are fairly simple to test. Relying only on the physical senses (hearing, seeing, touching, smelling) cannot account for the existence of the non-empirical such as the laws of logic or provide a justifiable ethical system. Neither can it make universal statements based on its own criteria because one cannot observe all things at all

39 Patrick M. Chapman, *"Thou Shalt Not Love": What Evangelicals Really Say to Gays* (New York, NY: Haiduk Press, 2008), 55.

times. Consequently when empiricists make any universal claim such as "all squares have four sides" they do so contrary to their professed epistemology. In fact, empiricism cannot account for itself because empiricism cannot be known empirically. How can you test the "scientific method" by the scientific method? Empiricists believe in the so-called scientific method as an axiom of faith. And, although empiricists can assert that they are able to make valid observations concerning the universe, thus giving them something that "works," further examination of the conclusions they reach reveals that they are, in fact, operating on assumed premises. Their worldview cannot account for these premises in and of itself. In essence, empiricism can be categorized as a religious faith commitment and presupposed worldview that must operate on borrowed epistemological capital in order to function.

As a Christian, I believe in conducting true science, which is, by definition, a quest for knowledge as the word is derived from the Latin *scientia* which means "knowledge." Science, therefore, is keenly concerned with issues of epistemology which the average scientist ignores thinking that such concerns are in the unrelated field of study known as philosophy. As a Christian (not merely a theist) my worldview can account for such things that the non-Christian scientist takes for granted. His worldview cannot account for such things as the uniformity of nature, the reliability of the senses, or provide a universal ethical standard.

Rationalism, in contrast to empiricism, holds that all justifiable claims to knowledge come from reason and not the empirical senses. As Rene Descartes concluded, the senses can be deceptive and therefore one must start self-reasoning, *"Cogito ergo sum"* or "I think therefore I know I am." Descartes reasoned that since he is thinking, there must be a thinker and therefore he must exist. However, in coming to this conclusion, Rene Descartes was not primarily declaring his existence but rather that he *knew* he existed. Consequently he was not primarily making a metaphysical statement. Rather he was declaring a method for how one may know one exists. His famous declaration therefore is an assertion that reason is the ultimate standard and the starting point for acquiring knowledge. The problem with rationalism and all systems of thought that insists on beginning with the autonomy seeking mind is rather obvious. It cannot account for anything outside of one's own mind because it eliminates sense experience as a valid form of knowledge. What we need to ask is, "How can the rationalist connect what is going on in his mind with what is going on around him? How can he know that what is going on in his mind is the same thing which is going on in your mind? When two people look at the sky and both say that it is "blue" how can the rationalist know that what is being observed by his eyes is the same thing as that which is being observed by your eyes?" In fact, according to the rationalist's criteria, he could not know anything is going outside of his own mind. While Descartes may declare that he exists he couldn't declare anything or anyone else existed.

The third attempt to make absolute one of the three aspects of epistemology is existentialism. Essentially existentialism is an expression of what one has subjectively experienced. Its focus is not on the empirical senses or what may be rationally deduced in order to obtain knowledge but rather it asserts that by "being," one comes to know truth. Consequently, existentialism holds that it is not objective truth that one needs to be concerned with for it is what one experiences that is important. The problem with existentialism and all systems of thought that insist on beginning with oneself is that if truth is not objective then we are not obligated to believe in existentialism since, on its own claim, it is not objectively true. If an existentialist were to tell me, "You can know the truth by experience" then, by his own standards, I should merely assert, "That is your experience which may or may not be true because I have not experienced it." Existentialism consistently followed is pure subjectivism. Since existentialism is not objectively true and merely the expression of the existentialist, then it is not incumbent on me to believe it. Consequently existentialism cannot account for existentialism itself, let alone anything else.

The reader should notice that in each of these scenarios the necessity to justify one's claim is crucial. This is why "knowledge" is rightly defined as "true, justifiable, belief."[40] One cannot justifiably say, "I know a round square exists" because such a statement is a contradiction. A square by definition has four sides and is not round. Likewise one cannot justifiably assert that "I know who the next President of the United States will be after the next election" apart from being able to justify

---

40 The term "justify" has several meanings. It can mean "to make right" such when we "justify" a word processing document, to "prove" or "vindicate," as I am using the term here and finally Paul uses the term in a forensic, or declarative sense (cf. Romans 5:1).

such a statement, such as proving that the election is rigged. A person may think that he knows who the next President of the United States will be, he may even believe it to be true, and he may even be correct in his assertion who the next president will be, but apart from being able to justify such an assertion it is a mere guess. Guessing correctly does not constitute knowledge. Finally, one cannot say that one knows something that he does not believe. For example, an atheist cannot justifiably say, "I know God exists" and remain an atheist. If he consciously knew God exists he would believe it and hence not be an atheist. So something could be true and justifiable but if it is not believed it is not genuinely known. From these three basic fields of epistemology other attempts have been made to combine various aspects of each but all the while failing to form a cohesive system of thought; to establish a system for true, justifiable, belief.[41]

Some have attempted to appeal to two equal epistemological starting points but such a method establishes a dialectical tension. The empiricist who tries to add rationalism to his system has no basis or foundation for his epistemology. Does he start with the empirical data for his mind's perception of the data? Which is more reliable, the data or the mind? Which establishes ultimate certitude? How does the one account for the other? How can he connect that which he perceives with his senses (the external world) with that which occurs in his mind? To which does he give precedence, his reason or his perceptions? What is his normative, guiding rule for making rational judgments?

The cause of such a failure is due to the system's ruling authority. At the root of each system that does not begin with the fear of the Lord for the beginning of knowledge and wisdom, is the autonomous mind. In contrast, the ultimate authority for determining truth for the faithful Christians is the fear of God as He has revealed Himself in Scripture for, "The fear of the LORD is the beginning of knowledge; But fools despise wisdom and instruction" (Proverbs 1:7). The faithful Christian begins his worldview in submission to the will of God as revealed in the Word of God. The Christian therefore begins with a *revealed* knowledge from God.

The fatal flaw of all the philosophical schools (and their derivatives) that are opposed to this Christian worldview is the inability to form

41 Such other schools of thought include idealism, realism, anti-realism, objectivism, pragmatism, positivism, Kantian transcendentalism, postmodernism and so on.

a cohesive relationship between the rational, empirical, and existential perspectives. What is needed to form such a cohesive relationship is an ultimate objective authority which not only establishes a right relationship between the rational, empirical, and existential aspects of knowledge but the prerequisites of knowledge itself – *transcendental norms*.

> Transcendental reasoning seeks to discover what general conditions must be fulfilled for any particular instance of knowledge to be possible. It asks what view of man, mind, truth, language, and the world is necessarily presupposed by our conception of knowledge and our methods for pursuing it.[42]

A transcendental norm then is that standard which provides the necessary preconditions for intelligibility. In other words they are necessary before one can make empirical observations, rational deductions and make sense of one's own experiences. Included are universal norms such as the laws of logic, ethics, and the uniformity of nature -- all of which are necessary prerequisites for life to make sense. For example, without the laws of logic, communication becomes impossible for without the law of non-contradiction to say, "The light is on" could just as well mean, "The light is off." Without a universal ethical norm "just" and "unjust" are merely personal preferences and consequently there is no absolute right or wrong. All that remains to determine how citizens are to conduct themselves is the will of the majority or the tyrannical assertions of those in power.

However, not only are transcendental norms needed but a singular personal ultimate ruling transcendental norm is necessary to provide and account for such transcendental norms. That Transcendental Norm must be a personal being Who can and does reveal His will as an absolute ethical normative standard, sustains the laws of nature and is Logic. It is the claim of the Biblical Christian worldview that it alone can provide such a cohesiveness of knowledge and the necessary preconditions for intelligibility for the Triune God of the Bible is that singular personal

---

42 Greg L. Bahnsen, *Pushing the Antithesis* (Powder Springs: American Vision, 2007), 280.

transcendental norm. [43] All other systems borrow from the Biblical Christian worldview when they make any universal statements concerning metaphysics, the uniformity of nature and ethics. Therefore, the Christian worldview is known to be true because of the impossibility of the contrary; without the true Christian worldview all thinking leads to futility and foolishness as Paul states concerning those who reject the God of the Bible, "…they became futile in their speculations, and their foolish heart was darkened. Professing to be wise, they became fools" (Romans 1:21-22).

It must be noted here that what I am arguing for is a consistently *Biblical* Christian worldview which is opposed to many systems of thought that claim to be Christian when in fact they are at their very core antithetical to Biblical Christianity. Such worldviews would include ancient forms of Gnosticism and their modern counterparts as well as Arianism and its modern form taught by the Watchtower Bible and Tract Society (the Jehovah's Witnesses). This would also include authoritarian cults such as Mormonism, denominations which deny the inerrant and infallible Scriptures as the sole ultimate infallible and inerrant authority. It also includes "churches" that contradict and are opposed to the Gospel and the Word of God as the standard for Christian ethics. As we shall see, this would also include the Metropolitan Community Church, liberal mainline denominations and other organizations that promote Gay Theology.

One might ask, "But can't another 'revealed religion' (Judaism, Islam etc.) also provide the necessary preconditions for intelligibility? What makes the Biblical Christian worldview uniquely necessary to account for transcendentals?" This is a worthy question which, for the purpose of this book I cannot answer at length and in detail. But, should any other revealed religion which makes claim to provide the necessary preconditions for intelligibility, the task of proving the solitary right of the claim of Christianity is conducted by doing an internal critique of each opposing revealed religion. The claims of opposing revealed religions are self-refuting, such as Judaism's and Islam's inability to uphold the Law of Moses, as well as the Koran's internal

---

43 Cornelius Van Til goes even further, "…it is the Reformed Faith, not some denominator 'core' of Christianity, that must be defended. By the 'Christian philosophy of life' I mean the truths of Scripture as set forth by the classical Reformed theologians…" *The Defense of the Faith* (Phillipsburg: P&R, 1967), 21.

contradictions and historical inaccuracies as they conflict with the Bible which Islam claims as authoritative. Islam undermines its own claim for the trustworthiness of the Koran for it asserts that God did not preserve the Old and New Testament from corruption and therefore He had to issue a third book. It must be asked then, "If the god of Islam did not preserve his first Testaments, why should the believer have a confidence that he has preserved the third testament?" Likewise, the fatal flaw of all non-monotheistic systems is that not only do they not have the ability to form a cohesive relationship between the rational, empirical, nor the existential aspects of knowledge but they also cannot provide the necessary preconditions for intelligibility – a singular ultimate authority. Instead they advocate the worship of a multitude of competing gods, none of whom are sovereign, with conflicting wills.

It is at this point that I would argue that not only can the Biblical Christian worldview alone provide such a cohesiveness of knowledge and the necessary preconditions for intelligibility, but the Protestant Christian worldview in particular. As stated previously, what is needed to form a cohesive worldview is not only an ultimate objective authority, but a singular ultimate objective authority.[44] If any authority attempts to supplant the authority of Scripture, or claim co-authority with Scripture, it will, in the end, rule over the Scriptures as *the* ultimate authority, whether or not its adherents are willing to admit it.

The challenge then of answering Gay Theology apologists is not merely to offer our interpretation of various texts, but rather to defend the very foundation of the Christian worldview itself. An internal critique of the flawed hermeneutical system of those who wish to claim that Gay Theology can be reconciled with Biblical Christianity would need to be included in that defense. If we approach the text, offer our interpretation of the relevant texts and expect the detractors to come to the same conclusion while still maintaining their presuppositions then we are

---

44 Notice that I am not saying that the Church has no authority and that creeds, confessions, catechisms etc. aren't necessary and helpful to summarize, codify, and organize what the Scriptures as a whole teach concerning God and what He requires of us. Thus I am not arguing for *Solo Scriptura*. What I am saying is that there can only be one infallible, binding, and ultimate authority. All civil, familial and ecclesiastical authorities as well as creeds and confessions are subordinate to the Scriptures and subject to potential, if not actual, revision based on further study of the Scriptures. Hence we ought to believe in the ecumenical creeds not because "the Church says so" but because they are Biblically justifiable.

sadly mistaken. Instead of encouraging consistency in the application of their worldview, biblical Christianity should call Gay theologians to repentance while demonstrating to them the futility of their thinking. Their ultimate faith commitments must be challenged and refuted as folly lest they think they are wise in their own eyes (Proverbs 26:4-5). The Apostle Paul tells us that the mind of those who are unrepentant in same sex acts, whether male or female, have been given over…

> …in the lusts of their hearts to impurity, so that their bodies would be dishonored among them… to degrading passions; for their women exchanged the natural function for that which is unnatural, and in the same way also the men abandoned the natural function of the woman and burned in their desire toward one another, men with men committing indecent acts and receiving in their own persons the due penalty of their error. And just as they did not see fit to acknowledge God any longer, God gave them over to a depraved mind, to do those things which are not proper (Romans 1:24-28).

While Christians may be tempted toward and fight against all the vices mentioned by Paul such as greed, envy, murder, strife, deceit, malice, and gossip (Romans 1:30-31), it is those who are darkened in their understanding that persist in their sin and are unrepentant. The apostle warns the Christian not to be deceived, presumably by those who were teaching contrary to the commandments of God, "…neither fornicators, nor idolaters, nor adulterers, nor passive participants in same sex acts [*malakoi*], nor men who have sex with other men [*arsenokoitai*], nor thieves, nor the covetous, nor drunkards, nor revilers, nor swindlers, will inherit the kingdom of God" (1 Corinthians 6:10). But Paul immediately gives comfort to believers who wrestle against such sin, "Such *were* some of you; but you were washed, but you were sanctified, but you were justified in the name of the Lord Jesus Christ and in the Spirit of our God" (1 Corinthians 6:11; cf. Galatians 5:17).

Merely professing to believe in Christ is not sufficient to be justified; one must prove the genuineness of that claim to faith by seeking to obey the commandments of God as the Apostle John wrote, "The one who says, 'I have come to know Him,' and does not keep His commandments, is a liar, and the truth is not in him" (1 John 2:4). Those who would call themselves Christians but who proudly and without repentance persist in their sin are self-deceived due to their suppressing the truth in unrighteousness (Romans 1:18). Consequently on Judgment Day they will stand before Christ and boast of doing many good deeds in His name and yet they will be rejected by Christ:

> Beware of the false prophets, who come to you in sheep's clothing, but inwardly are ravenous wolves. You will know them by their fruits. Grapes are not gathered from thorn bushes nor figs from thistles, are they? So every good tree bears good fruit, but the bad tree bears bad fruit. A good tree cannot produce bad fruit, nor can a bad tree produce good fruit. Every tree that does not bear good fruit is cut down and thrown into the fire. So then, you will know them by their fruits. Not everyone who says to Me, 'Lord, Lord,' will enter the kingdom of heaven, but he who does the will of My Father who is in heaven will enter. Many will say to Me on that day, `Lord, Lord, did we not prophesy in Your name, and in Your name cast out demons, and in Your name perform many miracles?' And then I will declare to them, `I never knew you; depart from me, you who practice lawlessness' (Matthew 7:15-23).

It is true that Gay and Queer affirming churches feed the poor just as many Bible-believing Christian churches do. But so do atheists, Mormons, and a host of other cultists. As we shall see, what distinguishes true Christians from mere professors is whether they seek to obey and honor God's commandments by faith, in love and from the heart.

The Worldview of Biblical Christianity

The ultimate presupposition of Biblical Christianity is that God exists (Hebrews 11:6) and that He has revealed Himself in various ways and means but ultimately through His Son Jesus Christ, the Word made flesh as recorded in the Scriptures (John 1:1; Hebrews 1:1-2). These Scriptures themselves are fully God-breathed (2 Timothy 3:16) and

God, through the apostles and prophets, has promised in both the Old and New Testaments to preserve His Word for all time for "the Word of the Lord endures forever" (Isaiah 40:8 1 Peter 1:25). Jesus Himself promised, "Heaven and earth will pass away, but My words will not pass away" (Matthew 24:35). These providentially preserved God-breathed Scriptures include the entire Old Testament, the Gospels which contain the teaching and ministry of Jesus Christ, the General Epistles and the writings of the Apostle Paul as he stated that what He taught and wrote was the very Word of God:

> For this reason we also constantly thank God that when you received the word of God which you heard from us, you accepted it not as the word of men, but for what it really is, the word of God, which also performs its work in you who believe (1 Thessalonians 2:13).

The truth that Paul's epistles are the very Word of God was also confirmed by the Apostle Peter who stated that Paul's wisdom was given to him and that it is the unlearned and untaught who twist them as they do rest of the Scriptures (2 Peter 3:15-16). The Scriptures of the Old and New Testaments were given by the Holy Spirit who moved men to write them, "...for no prophecy was ever made by an act of human will, but men moved by the Holy Spirit spoke from God" (2 Peter 1:21). Likewise the authority of the apostles was given to them by the Lord as Paul states, "For you know what commandments we gave you by the authority of the Lord Jesus" (1 Thessalonians 2:4; cf. 2 Corinthians 10:8; 13:10; 1 Thessalonians 13:6). Therefore, the Old and New Testaments are not the mere words of men but were given by the Holy Spirit and are the authoritative Word of God. In addition, since He has promised to preserve them, they must be without error and true on everything they teach including matters of faith, history, and morality. It follows then that if all Scripture is given by God and He has promised to preserve it that it is to be believed, rightly interpreted and obeyed.

In His Word the Lord has principally taught us what we are to believe concerning Him and what duties He requires of us.[45] The Bible

---

45 As the Westminster Shorter Catechism states, "The Scriptures principally teach, what man is to believe concerning God and what duty God requires of man." (WSC #2)

then is His revealed will for all mankind, especially to His covenant people. Since He is the author of the Scriptures, He alone has the authority to tell us what must still be obeyed in the New Covenant and what from the Old Covenant is obsolete and no longer binding. Therefore, the commandments of the Old Testament (also referred to as the Old Covenant or the *Tanakh*) are still required to be obeyed unless God has directly revoked or abrogated such laws, has replaced them with new corresponding laws, or by good and necessary consequence such commandments are no longer binding because the implications of the New Covenant reveals completion of their redemptive-historical task making them obsolete in keeping with their designed purpose.

The Antithesis of Worldviews In Biblical History

One of the root causes of God's people failing to remain faithful to their covenant with Him is not maintaining the antithesis between worldviews. This antithesis begins with how we are to interpret and obey His commandments verses what the world and the god of this age declares to be believed and obeyed as he, "…has blinded the minds of the unbelieving so that they might not see the light of the gospel of the glory of Christ, who is the image of God" (2 Corinthians 4:4).

We first see the importance of maintaining the antithesis in the Garden of Eden when the LORD (YHWH) told Adam regarding the fruit from the tree of the knowledge of good and evil, "From any tree of the garden you may eat freely; but from the tree of the knowledge of good and evil you shall not eat, for in the day that you eat from it you will surely die" (Genesis 2:16-17). Then the Lord gave to Adam his wife Eve from his side who was then confronted by the devil in the form of a serpent who challenged God's interpretation of the tree and His commandments, "Indeed, has God said, 'You shall not eat from any tree of the garden'?" To which the woman replied, "From the fruit of the trees of the garden we may eat; but from the fruit of the tree which is in the middle of the garden, God has said, 'You shall not eat from it or touch it, or you will die.'" Then the serpent twisted, or what some Gay Theologians refer to as "queered," the Word of God and said to the woman that rebelling results in becoming divine, "You surely will not die! For God knows that in the day you eat from it your eyes will be opened, and you will be like God, knowing good and evil" (Genesis 3:4-5). The woman then took it upon herself to think autonomously apart from God's revealed will and then determined for herself that she ought to eat from the tree, "When the woman saw that the tree was good for food, and that it was a delight to the eyes, and that the tree was desirable to make one wise, she took from its fruit and ate; and she gave also to her husband with her, and he ate" (Genesis 3:6).

The Bible presents Adam and Eve as having a choice to believe what God said about the tree and obey Him or to take it upon themselves to question God, interpret the tree for themselves and consequently have faith in the lie of the serpent. In failing to take dominion over the serpent and subdue him in the garden as God had commanded (Genesis 1:26, 28), Adam allowed his wife to be deceived by the serpent; Adam, in turn, sinned by eating the forbidden fruit as well (Genesis 3:6). The entire human race fell into sin and the text reports that Adam and Eve were subsequently "driven out" of the garden (Genesis 3:24). Throughout the Scriptures the idea of "driven out" from the land is also referred to as being "cut off," (Genesis 17:14; Leviticus 18:29) "vomited out" (Leviticus 18:28; Revelation 3:16) or what we might refer to today as "excommunicated."

This pattern of being cut off, vomited out or excommunicated from the land due to breaking covenant with God is seen repeated throughout redemptive history. The fall into sin is the result of failing to maintain the antithesis between the lies of the serpent and the truth of God's Word. The root of the fall is the failure to begin one's epistemology with the fear of the Lord and instead make oneself an autonomous judge to interpret God's creation and consequently put God's law to the test (Matthew 4:7).

But the antithesis between God's Word and the lie of the serpent did not end there for after the fall there would begin two spiritual lineages of humans, one which would follow the Lord and another that would opposed to His commandments as the Lord pronounced judgment upon the serpent:

> And I will put enmity between you and the woman, and
> between your seed [zera] and her seed [zera]; He shall
> bruise you on the head, and you shall bruise him on the
> heel (Genesis 3:15).

The enmity and antithesis that is between the woman and her seed and the serpent and his seed is not biological but rather spiritual. Often the seed of the serpent are false teachers who dwell amongst God's people. Jesus explicitly states that the Pharisees are as the descendants of the devil:

> You are of your father the devil, and you want to do the desires of your father. He was a murderer from the beginning, and does not stand in the truth because there is no truth in him. Whenever he speaks a lie, he speaks from his own nature, for he is a liar and the father of lies (John 8:44).

Here Christ clearly states that the Pharisees are the descendants of the one who was the liar in the garden, who speaks according to his nature just as the Pharisees are speaking and acting according to their nature. Therefore the fatherly relationship between the serpent, or devil, is obviously not biological but rather spiritual. Likewise, the head that was crushed was not the physical head of a serpent but rather the spiritual lineage as the power of the serpent, Satan, was defeated at the cross when the seed of the woman, Jesus Christ, was bruised - put to death - by the spiritual descendants of the serpent who were the Pharisees and the Roman Empire.

In this pronouncement of the judgment in Genesis 3:15 we see that there is an antithesis between those who are followers of the serpent and those who are of the holy lineage. The descendants or "seed" of the woman are not every human being on the planet but rather those who are by faith holy in the Lord, the holy covenant community. Throughout history there has been hostility between those who are of the line of the woman according to their spiritual nature and those who are of the line of the serpent according to their spiritual nature. Often times these two exist within the same family and even within the same covenant community, even the Church.

We see the antithesis and enmity of the two "seeds" again when Cain kills his brother Abel (Genesis 4:8) and when Ishmael persecutes Isaac the son of the promise (Genesis 21:9; Galatians 4:29). We also see it in Israel's rebellion after God delivered His people from slavery in Egypt and established a covenant with them and gave them His Word through Moses.

The Bible tells us that in His law God made a clear antithesis be-tween worshipping the LORD (YHWH) as Israel's king and obeying His commandments verses worshipping the foreign gods and following the commandments of foreign kings who also sought to be worshipped as god. The Lord delivered His people and called them to be a holy (sep-arate, consecrated) nation from the rest of the world (Leviticus 11:44). They were to think, dress, eat and worship differently from the Gentile nations. The tendency to fail to maintain the antithesis of worldviews and consequently integrate idolatrous worship with the true worship of YHWH was one of the chief errors of Israel when they came out of Egypt. Having lived amongst idolaters for 400 years they quickly began to worship like them and the inhabitants of the land of Canaan who worshipped Baal in the form of a golden calf through sacralized sex (Exodus 32). What was even worse was that Aaron capitulated to the idolatrous desires of the people and formed with his own hands from their jewelry an image of the Canaanite god (a bull calf) and yet called it YHWH (Exodus 32:4). This is the exact sin which was later repeated by Jeroboam (1 Kings 12:28) and on numerous occasions the nation had to be rebuked for following foreign gods and obeying foreign command-ments. The law of God was not the product of the culture of the day but was, in fact, antithetical to the culture of the surrounding nations, particularly in its theology of worship and sexual ethics. Israel's chief sin was a failure to maintain this antithesis and as we shall see in the fruit of the Gay Theology movement, that the Metropolitan Community Churches repeat this exact same sin in their sexual idolatry.

The history of YHWH's people in the Old Testament is one in which we read of their repeated failure to believe His promises, heed His warnings and maintain the antithesis between the Word of God and the word of the serpent. Throughout the Old Testament, since man's fall from grace, the majority of God's people have been disobedient but He reserved for Himself a remnant of faithful prophets, priests and kings (Genesis 45:7; 2 Kings 19:31; Ezra 9:8, 15; Nehemiah 1:3; Isaiah 10:20, 22; Jeremiah 6:9; Ezekiel 6:8; Micah 2:12; 4:7; 5:7-8.). The underling sin of Israel is the failure to maintain the antithesis of worldviews that resulted in their idolatry, sexual immorality and the civil and religious leader's injustice in oppressing the poor.

But YHWH, the faithful persistent husband who is long-suffering and slow to wrath pursued Israel His bride and repeatedly called her to repentance and covenant faithfulness through His faithful prophets. We see in the history of God's people, a repeated cycle of disobedience, judgments, repentance and then deliverance such as during the time of the Judges. Following the period of the Judges YHWH gave Israel the prophet Samuel to speak to them on God's behalf. But Israel rejected YHWH as her king and demanded to have an earthly king like the surrounding nations (1 Samuel 8:7). Once Saul the earthly king was established YHWH soon rejected him as he proudly offered up a forbidden sacrifice (1 Samuel 13:9-14). Another king, one who was a man after God's own heart, was chosen but he set in motion a pattern of sin within his family such that the heart of his son Solomon would be turned from the Lord by pagan wives to establish the worship of pagan gods, who are depicted as foreign husbands, in the land (1 Kings 11:1-5). Though Solomon in his last days exhorted His son Rehoboam to follow the Lord (Ecclesiastes 12), he too followed in the footsteps of his father and consequently Israel was judged by YHWH and eventually became a divided nation like Egypt.

Hundreds of years later the Messiah came and reconciled man to God through the cross (Ephesians 2:15-18). The consequence was that Jews and Gentiles were reconciled to each other by faith in the death, burial and resurrection of Jesus Christ resulting in a single worldview which is antithetical to that of the Pharisees and the Greek philosophers (Galatians 3:28; 1 Corinthians 1:19-22). It was at this time that two problems arose within the early Church. There were Christian Jewish Pharisees that were trying to bring Gentiles under the Mosaic Covenant asserting that they needed to be circumcised and live like Jews (keeping the feasts, obeying the Sabbaths, observing the kosher laws) in order to be saved (Acts 15:1, 5). Paul's Epistles to the Romans and Galatians address this error of the doctrine of the Christian Pharisees. In the Epistle to the Romans the apostle Paul is defending the inclusion of the Gentiles into the covenant promises of Abraham by faith. In the Epistle to the Galatians he is addressing the "foolish" Gentiles (Galatians 3:1) who are succumbing to the Pharisee's doctrines which were even persuading Peter and Barnabas to compel Gentiles to live like Jews (Galatians 2:11-14). Paul also warns the Philippian believers, "beware of the false circumcision" and states that Jews and Gentiles in Christ are "the true circumcision, who worship in the Spirit of God and glory in Christ Jesus and put no confidence in the flesh" (Philippians 3:2-3). He likewise warns

Titus, "...there are many rebellious men, empty talkers and deceivers, especially those of the circumcision" (Titus 1:10). He also addresses this error in his Epistle to the Colossians in regards to their insistence that Gentiles follow the Old Covenant Feast Days, "Therefore no one is to act as your judge in regard to food or drink or in respect to a festival or a new moon or a Sabbath day" (Colossians 2:16). These Pharisees are also said to be "wanting to be teachers of the law" (1 Timothy 1:7) and purveyors of the traditions of men which Paul refers to as "Jewish myths" (Titus 1:14).

Paul also had to exhort the Gentile converts to put off the former way of life and walk in the light (Ephesians 4:17-5:20) and not integrate the so-called wisdom of the world of Greek philosophy with the Christian worldview for their faith is not based on the "wisdom of men" (1 Corinthians 2:5). Rather, they need to see that they are the new Israel (Galatians 6:16), who need to "clean out the old leaven" as they keep the new Passover which is Christ (1 Corinthians 5:7) rather than follow in the footsteps of their forefathers (the Jews of the Old Testament) who rebelled against God (1 Corinthians 10:1-6).

In his exhortations to the Gentile Christians, Paul cited the Law of Moses as the ethical standard for maintaining the antithesis between the worldview of the apostate Jews who rejected Jesus as the Messiah and the pagan Gentiles. In fact, Paul and the other authors of the New Testament repeatedly cite Leviticus which is the clearest Old Testament book that prohibits, among other sexual vices, men having sex with men (Leviticus 18:22; 20:13). For example, Paul uses Leviticus 19:19 to illustrate the need for separation of Christians (2 Corinthians 6:14ff) and upholds Leviticus 18:8 when he rebukes the congregation for tolerating a man who is having sex with his father's wife (1 Corinthians 5:1). He even upholds the penal sanction of cutting the violator off from the people of God by removing him from their midst (1 Corinthians 5:13; Leviticus 18:29; Deuteronomy 13:5). Likewise, Peter cites Leviticus 19:2 as the standard of holiness, calling Christians away from "former lusts" (1 Peter 1:14-16; cf. Leviticus 11:44-45; 20:7). The Apostles Paul and James both quote the law of love (Leviticus 19:18; Romans 13:8-10; Galatians 3:12; James 2:8) and Jesus Christ Himself cited Leviticus 19:12 against making vain vows (Matthew 5:33).[46] Clearly, the sexual

---

46 James B. De Young, *Homosexuality: Contemporary Claims Examined in the Light of the Bible and Other Ancient Literature and Law* (Grand Rapids, MI: Kregel, 2000), 54.

prohibitions in Leviticus have not been completely abrogated by the New Covenant.

In contrast, the Gay Theology worldview adopts a theoretical anti-nomian hermeneutical framework. Much like Ancient Gnosticism, they despise the law of God and deny that it has *any* binding authority for Christians.[47] James B. De Young in his analysis of the Gay theological paradigm rightly equates this with the ancient heresy of Marcionism:

> Revisionist interpreters [Gay theology advocates] have such a disparaging attitude toward the Old Testament that their work is tantamount to a new Marcionism – a rejection of most of the Old Testament as irrelevant. But the use Old Testament quotes in the New Testament in the area alone compels one to acknowledge that early Christians did view the Old Testament as relevant in ethics.[48]

What we must keep in mind is that the Apostle Paul had to remind the Gentile Christians that the saints of the Old Testament were their forefathers, who ate of the same spiritual food, consumed the same spiritual drink from the rock that was Christ (1 Corinthians 10:1-4). Yet God was not pleased with them and the punishment that Israel received serves as an example to them:

> Now these things happened as examples for us, so that we would not crave evil things as they also craved. Do not be idolaters, as some of them were; as it is written, 'The people sat down to eat and rink and stood up to play.' Nor let us act immorally, as some of them did, and twenty-three thousand fell in one day (1 Corinthians 10:6-8).

---

47 As R. D. Weekly asserts, "We needn't turn to the pages of the Mosaic Law in determining God's moral code. Let's simply accept and celebrate what Christ accomplished on Calvary, remaining faithful to our new husband by allowing the Mosaic Law to keep its rightful place – history, not establishing or informing Christian moral conduct." *Homosexianity* (Judah First Ministries, 2009), 60.

48 James B. De Young, *Homosexuality: Contemporary Claims Examined in the Light of the Bible and Other Ancient Literature and Law* (Grand Rapids, MI: Kregel, 2000), 59.

While the two peoples were to be integrated into one, neither was to bring with them into the New Covenant the old way of life – the types and shadows of the Old Covenant that were fulfilled in Christ or the Greek Pagan philosophy and its immorality. As we shall see, the conflict we are facing is between Biblical Christianity and the Gay Theological worldview, that is slithering its way into the Church and our culture, is another example of the lie of the apostate seed of the serpent that was confronted by Paul and the other apostles:

> ...our present culture is locked in a struggle between two antithetical views on ultimate meaning and value – what Paul calls the great struggle between the Truth and the Lie. Each side seeks control of the sacred canopy, under which society lives. Sacred canopies are chosen by general consent, and presupposed as true. Replacing them usually involves conflict... The need for antithetical worldview thinking has never been more needed. If Christian, in the name of love, harmony and human flourishing, fail to recognize the clamor of the religious war, they will not be armed to defend the Truth of the Christian gospel.[49]

The Antithesis of Worldviews In Church History

Since the dawn of the New Covenant era and the ushering in of the Gentiles the sin of failing to maintain the antithesis of worldviews has been a persistent problem. Christians have constantly been tempted to integrate into the Christian Worldview such things as Platonism (as did the early Church apologists), Aristotelianism (as did the Medieval scholastics), Rationalism and Empiricism (as the men of the enlightenment) out of which came Darwinian evolution, Marxist sociology, and Freudian psychology.

During the first five centuries of the Church Christians were prone to integrating the philosophy of Plato with the doctrine and practice of the Church. They did this because many of them thought that the Greek philosophers were a preparation for the gospel for the Gentiles as Moses

---

49 Peter Jones, *One or Two: Seeing A World of Difference* (Escondido, CA; Main Entry Editions, 2010), 65.

was a preparation for the Jews. For example, Clement of Alexandria (Titus Flavius Clemens) taught that the Gospel was not a departure from Greek philosophy but rather a meeting point for the convergence of two worldviews, Hellenism and Judaism. To him all history is one, because all truth is one and therefore Philosophy and Christianity are the product of "one river of truth."[50] This, as we shall later discover, is a monistic view of reality. Then during the middle ages Christian theologians and philosophers shifted from Plato to Aristotle. This is particularly true of Thomas Aquinas. Consequently, the history of philosophy in the Church has been a mixed bag of worldly and Christian thought.

The Roman Catholic Church and the Eastern Orthodox Church are particularly prone to integrating worldly philosophies with Christian doctrine and practice. Wherever Roman Catholic missionaries have ventured they have assimilated the local culture by baptizing pagan gods and renaming them as saints or blended pagan philosophies, such as Confucianism, with the Christian faith with an attempt to show that the two worldviews are compatible rather than antithetical to each other.[51] In doing so they have adopted their local customs and rather than seeing this as scandalous they defend this practice as a virtue:

> Whatever is good - even in paganism - can and should be incorporated into Christian life and practice so as to enrich our faith and to make converts realize that so much of their former way of life was a true preparation for the Gospel message.[52]

In contrast, the Protestant Reformation began as a quest to purify Christian doctrine and worship. But more often than not Protestants have also have failed to maintain the antithesis of worldviews as they have assimilated Enlightenment Rationalism, Marxist Liberation Theology and Madison Avenue tactics for evangelism. The result is that these congregations are so closely identified with pagan culture that they can hardly be called a true Church. There are also many so-called

---

50 *Strom.* 1.5.29.
51 Geoffrey Barraclough, ed. *The Christian World: A Social and Cultural History* (New York: Harry N. Abrams Publishers, 1981), 29.
52 Peter M. J. Stravinskas, *The Catholic Response* (Our Sunday Visitor Publishing Division, 2001), 47.

evangelical Christian churches and seminaries that, although they have professed to maintain a high view of Scripture, they have in practice abandoned it in many ways. Some have capitulated to the culture in their form of worship and exchanged the preaching of the Word for seeker-sensitive entertainment. While the Bible teaches that it is sufficient for all that pertains to doctrine and life (1 Timothy 3:15-17; 2 Peter 1:3) many churches in practice deny this truth. While claiming to maintain the orthodox doctrine of inerrancy and infallibility they adopt Freudianism and use pop-psychology to provide answers to man's deepest problems. This has been most clearly seen in many elements of the ex-Gay movement who have preached the false-gospel of Reparative Therapy.

Others have given lip service to the inerrancy, infallibility and authority of Scripture but then go on to deny its sufficiency. They grant ultimate authority for interpreting the Bible to sources outside of Scripture which forms the lens through which they interpret the Scriptures. Once they do this they then construct a natural theology from which is developed an unbiblical view of man derived from Darwinian philosophy, a Marxist understanding of liberation, a humanistic view of ethics and they integrate a Freudian view psychology in the place of Biblical truth.

The Worldview of Gay Theology

The worldview of Gay Theology is not monolithic, but rather multifaceted. While it consistently rejects the Biblical prohibitions and condemnation of same sex acts (Leviticus 18:22; 20:13; Romans 1:18-25; 1 Corinthians 6:9; 1 Timothy 1:10) and seeks to assert that some relationships within the Bible are closeted stories of homosexual interest (Ruth and Naomi, David and Jonathan, Jesus and the Beloved Disciple, the Roman Centurion and his servant) there are essentially three different segments to the Gay Theological Worldview. Yet these segments often overlap and borrow from each other.

The first segment is a liberal higher-critical view that rejects the inerrancy and infallibility of Scripture and asserts that the Church has misinterpreted the "clobber passages" incorrectly for almost 2,000 years. It subsequently reinterprets the Bible as being "Gay friendly" (John Boswell, John McNeil and many others).

The second segment is a supposedly evangelical wing (R.D. Weekly, Rick Brentlinger) that promotes itself as genuinely holding to a Biblical doctrine of Scripture and the Gospel. It then follows the assertions of liberals and borrows their exegesis of the so-called clobber passages and the supposed "closet gay" stories of the Bible. This segment is much more subtle and consequently more deceptive for its proponents attempt to present the exact same doctrines as the liberal Gay Theologians but in a manner that will be accepted by an evangelical audience. The primary error of this seemingly Bible-believing evangelical Gay Theology is a flawed set of sub-presuppositions conveyed as a set of hermeneutical axioms that have their root in the theoretical antinomianism of classic Dispensationalism. The consequence of this antinomianism is, "They profess to know God, but they deny him by their works" (Titus 1:16). We shall examine these proponents of Gay Theology further when we consider the hermeneutical lens of Gay Theology.

The third segment of Gay Theology is more radical. Yet it is also a more consistent with the Gay Theological Worldview, which is the Marxist/Feminist wing of Queer theologians. These Queer Theorists (Robert Goss, Gary Comstock, Patrick S. Cheng) do not read the Bible as "gay friendly." Instead they see it has hostile to their homosexuality and then in order to subvert its authority they seek to deconstruct the text (or as they call it "queer" the text) to make it suit their purpose. This segment of Gay Theology also includes a Transgender Theology (Virginia Mollenkot, Justin Tanis) which takes Queer Theology a step further. What is crucial to recognize is that this is a more consistent form of Gay Theology and it is the logical end to the trajectory of the presuppositions of this worldview. Yet, this is not a new interpretation of the Bible. Rather, it is an ancient monism that was advocated by ancient libertine Gnostics who sought to break down any and all biblical distinctions such as Creator/creature, male/female, good/evil, and life/death in the name of an eroticized "radical love" as Queer Theologian Patrick S. Cheng describes:

> So what exactly is queer theology? If theology is "talk about God," then, in light of the above three definitions of "queer," there are at least three possible definitions for "queer theology." First, queer theology is LGBT people

"talking about God." Second, queer theology is "talking about God" in a self consciously transgressive manner, especially in terms of challenging societal norms about sexuality and gender. Third, queer theology is "talk about God" that challenges and deconstructs the natural binary categories of sexual and gender identity... in light of the definition of "queer" as transgression, queer theology can be understood as a theological method that is self-consciously transgressive, especially by challenging societal norms about sexuality and gender... in light of the definition of "queer" as erasing boundaries, queer theology can be understood as a way of doing theology that is rooted in queer theory and that critiques the binary categories of sexuality (that is, homosexual vs. heterosexual) and gender identity (that is, female vs. male) as socially constructed. In other words, queer theology argues that the discourse of classical Christian theology ultimately requires the erasing of the boundaries of essentialist categories of not only sexuality and gender identity, but also more fundamental boundaries such as life vs. death, and divine vs. human.[53]

The goal of the Queer component of the Gay Theological Worldview is to end not only the so-called "binary social construct" of heterosexuality but also put an end to the antithesis between Christianity and other worldviews and spiritual practices. The goal then is that while there would remain different forms of religion they would all be worshipping the same god, goddess or "Spiritual Source."[54] The abolishing of binary sexuality and gender is the natural outcome of this spirituality which, although it finds a revival in the 20th century is rooted in ancient forms of eastern mysticism and Gnosticism. There are two primary evidences for this - the first is their repeated references to Gnostic Texts (Gospel of Thomas, Secret Gospel of Mark) for their support of the understanding

53 Patrick S. Cheng, *Radical Love: An Introduction to Queer Theology* (Seabury Books; 1 edition, 2011), 9,10.
54 Virginia Ramey Mollenkott, *Omnigender: A Trans-religious Approach* (Cleveland, OH: The Pilgrim Progress, 2007), 17-18; Patrick S. Cheng, *Radical Love: An Introduction to Queer Theology* (Seabury Books; 1 edition, 2011), 26.

of the New Testament.[55] The second is their frequent appeal to pagan religions for alternative views of sexuality including the Hindu *hijdras* and Native American "two-spirit" folk.[56] In essence, the end of the binary gender worldview of historic Christianity is a rise of what Peter Jones refers to as spiritual monism or "One-ism."[57]

The Biblical Christian Worldview teaches that there are ontological and anatomical distinctions without advocating a simplistic dualist view of reality. Biblical distinctions include such categories as the Creator/creature ("God is not a man..." Numbers 23:13), male/female (Genesis 1:27), spirit/matter ("God is spirit..." John 4:24), and humans/angels (man is flesh, angels are "ministering spirits" Hebrews 1:14). It also teaches that there are moral distinctions such as the intentions of good/evil (Genesis 50:20), lawful/lawless deeds (Titus 2:14), desires (works, fruit) of the spirit/desires (works, fruit) of the flesh (Galatians 5:16-26), as well as metaphorical moral categories such as light/darkness (1 John 1:5). Likewise it also teaches that there are role or functional economic distinctions such as the Father/Son/Holy Spirit (Matthew 28:19), Husband/Wife/Child (Ephesians 5:22-6:4), and the prophet/priest/king of the Old Testament.

A platonic worldview introduces unbiblical dualisms which confuse ontological distinctions with moral distinctions such as asserting that *spirit* (an ontological category) is good while *matter* is evil (a moral category). When this dualism manifested itself in Gnosticism it tended either to advocate asceticism as a means of combating moral evil or abandonment of all sexual boundaries into licentiousness. It also creates a number of false dualities in creation such as a realm of forms/ideas, or in Kantian terms the noumenal/phenomenal realms. Due to the influ-

---

55 Theodore W. Jennings, Jr., *The Man Jesus Loved: Homoerotic Narratives From the New Testament* (Cleveland, OH: Pilgrim Press, 2003), 114; Susannah Cornwall, *Sex and Uncertainty in the Body of Christ: Intersex Conditions and Christian Theology (Gender, Theology and Spirituality)* (Sheffield, England: Equinox Publishing, 2010), 71; Virginia Ramey Mollenkott, *Omnigender: A Trans-religious Approach* (Cleveland, OH: The Pilgrim Progress, 2007), 118-121.

56 Susannah Cornwall, *Sex and Uncertainty in the Body of Christ: Intersex Conditions and Christian Theology (Gender, Theology and Spirituality)* (Sheffield, England: Equinox Publishing, 2010), 24; Virginia Ramey Mollenkott, *Omnigender: A Trans-religious Approach* (Cleveland, OH: The Pilgrim Progress, 2007), 173-177;

57 Peter Jones, *One or Two: Seeing A World of Difference* (Escondido, CA; Main Entry Editions, 2010), 13.

ence of Greek philosophy in the early Church neo-platonic dualisms and unbiblical forms of asceticism were practiced by many Christians and grotesque masochistic forms of mistreatment of the body were common in the Middle Ages. Yet the Apostle Paul made it clear that mistreatment of the body was not a means of sanctification (Colossians 2:23). When derived from various forms of Eastern Mysticism such dualisms often are formulated in a monistic fashion such that the two opposites are merely different sides of the same coin such as ying/yang, or as in the movie Star Wars trilogy the light/dark side of the force.[58] In this monism two polar or seemingly contrary forces are interconnected and interdependent in the natural world such that they are actually two sides of the same thing.

Monism is the fundamental worldview advocated by Queer Theologians. The chief evidence of this is that while they label their opponents Platonic dualists, they prove themselves to be monists when they advocate androgyny and sexual fluidity. In doing so they seek to put an end to the Biblical categories that make distinctions between male and female as mere social constructs:

> Queer theory rejects the traditional view that categories of sexuality (that is, homosexual vs. heterosexual) and gender identity (that is, female vs. male) are "natural," essentialist, or fixed. Instead, as articulated in the work of theorists such as Judith Butler and Michel Foucault, queer theory argues that the meanings of such categories are socially constructed. This is not to deny that there are in fact physiological differences between people in terms of sexual attraction and bodies. These differences do exist. Furthermore, this is not to deny that sexuality and gender identity can effectively be immutable characteristics for many people and thus are deserving of legal protections akin to race. However, the significance of such differences in terms of sexuality and gender identity is not simply a matter of "nature," but rather is socially constructed.[59]

---

58 For more reading on this see: Peter Jones, *Spirit Wars: Pagan Revival in Christian America* (Wine Press Pub; First edition, 1997) and *The Gnostic Empire Strikes back: An Old Heresy for the New Age* (P & R Publishing, 1992).

59 Patrick S. Cheng, *Radical Love: An Introduction to Queer Theology* (Seabury Books; 1 edition, 2011), 17.

Equating the erotic with "radical love," Queer theologians reject Biblical distinctions and in their place argue for an erotic gender fluidity that dissolves boundaries not only between male/female, but also between homosexual/heterosexual, adult/child, good/evil, and lawful/lawless deeds and the Creator/creature distinction:

> ...queer theology can be understood as a way of doing theology that is rooted in queer theory and that critiques the binary categories of sexuality (that is, homosexual vs. heterosexual) and gender identity (that is, female vs. male) as socially constructed. In other words, queer theology argues that the discourse of classical Christian theology ultimately requires the erasing of the boundaries of essentialist categories of not only sexuality and gender identity, but also more fundamental boundaries such as life vs. death, and divine vs. human.[60]

What must be understood then when we examine the Gay Theological movement is that we're looking not merely at individuals with independent thoughts. But rather an entire worldview which has variations within it and if followed through to its a logical trajectory, leads to what is known as Queer Theology. Yet the seemingly "evangelical" wing and its leaders cannot distinguish or separate themselves from what may be considered the more "radical" elements of Gay Theology, since they would be accused of being "divisive" "oppressive" and "discriminatory." All forms of Gay Theology require that its adherents practice a "radical inclusion" that rejects any form of genuine Church discipline.

As we shall see throughout the course of this book, the presuppositions of the Gay Theology worldview opposes the Scriptures as the ultimate, inerrant, infallible and final authority for man's epistemology and ethics. Whereas the Bible teaches that the fear of the Lord is the beginning of knowledge, Gay Theologians pretend to be Christians but as fools they despise wisdom and instruction (Proverbs 1:7).

Furthermore, Gay Theology opposes what the Scriptures teach on metaphysics. They dismiss Scripture's teaching concerning mankind being fallen in sin. Instead they look to the folly of modern culture to interpret the ontological state of man as well as their own autonomous

60 Ibid, 10.

reasoning for interpreting their experiences. Consequently the ultimate presupposition of Gay Theology is that modern culture is ultimately authoritative for one's understanding of faith, history, and morality. Gay Theology then is antithetical in every way to the Christian Worldview in matters of epistemology, metaphysics and ethics.

Whereas the Christian Worldview teaches that mankind and all of creation is fallen in sin, subject to futility because of the act of the first man (Romans 8:19-20), many Gay Theology apologists, such as Michael Carden, Patrick M. Chapman and Daniel A. Helminiak, treat the historical event recorded in Genesis 1-3 as mythical rather than as a historical account of the creation of man and the origin of the fall.[61] In doing so they repeat the sin of Adam in denying commandments of God, instead thinking and acting like Eve, believing and obeying the lie of the serpent.

In contrast, the Biblical Christian Worldview founded on the Scriptures teaches that God Himself referred to Adam as a historical person who broke covenant with Him (Hosea 6:7) and the New Testament records Jesus as being a historical descendent of Adam (Luke 3:38). Likewise, the Apostle Paul refers to Adam as a historical person through whom he says came the entire human race (Acts 17:26) as well as the fall of mankind into sin and death. Paul also states that Jesus Christ is the second Adam who likewise represented the human race as a covenantal head in His act of obedience order in order to give them eternal life (Romans 5:12-19; 1 Corinthians 15:22, 45). If there was no historical Adam and no historical fall into sin the logical conclusion is that there is no need for the historical saving work of the second Adam.

Another important point of contrast between the Christian Worldview and the worldview of Gay Theology is in regards to Moses and the law. In the New Testament Jesus, the Apostle John and the Apostle Paul tell us that the historical figure Moses gave us the law of God (Matthew 8:4; 19:8; Luke 5:14; John 1:17; 7:19; Romans 10:5; Hebrews 9:19). In contrast, Gay Theologians, borrowing from Julius Wellhausen, insist that according to the Documentary Hypothesis theory, that the first five books of the Bible, are the product of a primitive misogynistic culture

---

61 Michael Carden, "Genesis/Bereshit" in *The Queer Bible Commentary;* Deryn Guest (Author, Editor), Robert E. Goss (Editor), Mona West (Editor), *Thomas Bohache* (Editor) (SCM Press, 2006), 23; Patrick M. Chapman, *"Thou Shalt Not Love": What Evangelicals Really Say to Gays* (New York, NY: Haiduk Press, 2008), 60.

with multiple authors.[62] Hence, according to Gay Theologians, it does not reflect the mind of God but rather the ignorant oppressive culture dominated by men who dictated laws to suit their self-interests.[63]

Gay Theological Worldview Apologetics

The Gay or Queer theologian has a worldview with which they seek to take dominion over every sphere of society – the Church, the state and the family – using a particular apologetical methodology. In short, it takes a three-pronged approach. First, in a negative fashion it seeks to deny that any of the so-called "clobber passages" or "terror texts" (Genesis 19; Leviticus 18:22; 20:13; Romans 1:26-27; 1 Corinthians 6:9, 1 Timothy 1:10) may be applied to modern day same sex relationships. In doing so they may deny the authority of the Scriptures and that the law of God is applicable to Christians today. They then assert that the context of the so-called "terror texts" only refer to abusive same sex acts, pederasty, prostitution or part of a cultic form of worship. In the case of Queer theologians, they assert the relevant passages merely reflect a primitive "binary gender construct" that was ignorant of the reality that gender and sexuality is a fluid continuum in nature.

Second, many Gay Theology apologists seek to argue for a positive reading of the Bible for same sex acts. In doing so they assert that many heroes of the Bible were in fact closeted homosexuals who need to be "outed" through what is referred to as a Queer hermeneutic. These include, but are not limited to, King David and Jonathan, Ruth and Naomi, the Roman Centurion and his servant as well as Jesus and the Beloved Disciple.

Third, they seek to identify their political-spiritual-sexual cause with the down-trodden and oppressed people (the poor, the outcasts, the widow and orphan) of the Bible. These three apologetical tasks are referred to as "deflecting textual violence," "outing the text" and "befriending the text."[64] Queer Theologian Robert E. Goss explains the strategy as follows:

---

62 Patrick M. Chapman, *"Thou Shalt Not Love": What Evangelicals Really Say to Gays* (New York, NY: Haiduk Press, 2008), 99-102.
63 Gary David Comstock, *Gay Theology Without Apology* (Cleveland, OH: Pilgrim Press, 1993), 13.
64 Robert E. Goss, *Queering Christ: Beyond Jesus Acted Up* (Eugene, OR: The Pilgrim Press, 2007), 205.

The first interpretive strategy consists of a 'negative' apologetics, aiming to critique the heterosexist interpretations of texts applied to homosexuality and deflect the resulting social violence... The second and third reading strategies consist of forms of positive apologetics, promoting queer reading strategies over the heterosexual erasures of homoeroticism from the text. Whereas the negative apologetics engage in defensive strategies, positive apologetics remain offensive in promoting their truth-claims.[65]

The second stage of Gay Theological apologetics asserts that various persons in the Bible were in fact closet homosexuals whose true sexuality is hidden by the authors. The Queer theologian reads into the text their own experiences which then supposedly gives them the ability to discover a new queer-truth by "outing" the supposed closeted homosexual in the passage:

'Outing' is a transgressive strategy that publicly reveals a person's sexual orientation. It breaks the conspiracy of silence, forcing queers out of the closet by speaking the unspeakable and disrupting the codes of silence... [this methodology] counters pervasive biblical heterosexism by outing 'eunuchs' and 'barren women,' Ruth and Naomi, Jonathan and David, the gay centurion, Lydia in Acts, and Jesus as bisexual... The next stage in negative apologetics would be to engage these groups in their method of argumentation and epistemological criteria of knowledge. This may provide even greater challenge for queer scholars, demanding that they abandon historical, literary, and cultural criticism for such an engagement and try novel attempts to engage evangelical Christians on their own terrain. The battle has just begun over biblical texts.[66]

---

65 Ibid, 206, 211.
66 Ibid, 208-209.

Biblical Christian Worldview Apologetics

Religious and philosophical critical attacks against the Biblical Christian Worldview cannot be rightly responded to by merely arguing over an exegesis of a handful of relevant passages, Natural Law, the brute facts of history, medical science or an appeal to a common sense playing field of interpreting facts on a "neutral ground."[67] In the long run the Biblical Christian must respond to opposing worldviews, such as that of the Gay Theologian, by confronting its very foundation. The faithful Christian must challenge their presuppositions, their claims to epistemological certainty, particularly in regards to the Scriptures and their hermeneutical methodology. The faithful Christian who seeks to uphold a Scriptural view of the person and work of Jesus Christ and Biblical ethics cannot forever be defensively constructing atomistic answers to the endless variety of unbelieving criticisms; he must take the offensive and show the Queer Theologian that he has no intelligible place to stand, no grounds for a justifiable epistemology, that his worldview is inherently self-contradictory, his hermeneutical axioms cannot be supported by Scripture and his conclusions regarding relevant texts cannot be vindicated. The pseudo-wisdom of his worldview must be reduced to foolishness - in which case none of his criticisms have any force – for as Paul states the one who has suppressed the knowledge of the truth and subsequently in his foolishness has been given over to his homosexual lusts is *anapologetous*, "without a defense" or more literally "without an apologetic" (Romans 1:20).

The Gay Theology advocate has forsaken the source of true wisdom of God revealed in His Law-Word in order to rely on his own (allegedly), self-sufficient, intellectual powers. He utters self-confidence and imagines himself to be intellectually autonomous and consequently reveals himself to be a fool (Proverbs 28:26). The Gay Theologian judges matters according to his own pre-established standards of truth

---

67 For more reading on how to develop a consistent Christian Worldview approach to apologetics I recommend reading: Greg L. Bahnsen, *Presuppositional Apologetics: Stated and Defended* Joel McDurmon (ed.). (The American Vision, 2009); *Van Til's Apologetic: Readings and Analysis* (Presbyterian & Reformed Pub Co, 1998); Always Ready: Directions for Defending the Faith. *Robert R. Booth (ed.). (Covenant Media Press, 1996); John M. Frame,* Apologetics to the Glory of God. *(Phillipsburg: Presbyterian & Reformed, 1994)*

and justice as he judges the one true God of the Biblical Worldview to be oppressive.

If the Church is going to rightly respond to the Gay Theology Worldview we must begin our thinking by presupposing the Word of God as the ultimate authority over all matters of faith and life. We must begin by sanctifying Christ as Lord of our hearts so that we may then give a reason for the hope that is within us, yet with gentleness and respect (1 Peter 3:15). Being respectful means that the Christian cannot justifiably seek to uphold Biblical ethics and love his neighbor while referring to those who engage in homosexual acts as "faggots" or "Sodomites." Yet, rather than heeding the lies of the serpent and his interpretation of God's Word and of the created order, we must begin with Scripture in the same way that the Gay Theologian begins with his autonomy-seeking mind and call him to repentance.

This consistent presuppositional apologetical method of the Christian who argues against the claims and assertions of opposing worldviews, such as the Gay Theology proponent, is two-fold: Presupposing the Scriptures as the ultimate authority for all matters concerning faith, life and doctrine we will, rather than "dialoguing" with the Queer Scripture twister in a supposed neutral fashion, recognize that the Bible is God's Word which He has given to His bride. It is not given to the reprobate who seeks to subvert and "queer" it as the serpent did in the Garden or Satan in the desert (Matthew 4:6). In doing so faithful Christians will not "…answer a fool according to his folly" otherwise we "will also be like him" (Proverbs 26:4).In doing so the faithful Christian in responding to the Gay Theological arguments must place himself upon the position of the Gay Theologian. For the sake of argument we will assume the correctness of his method in order to show him that his worldview and subsequent denial of the applicability of the relevant passages of Scripture that condemn him is unjustifiable in the form of a *reductio ad absurdum*. As we shall see, the interpretations of the Gay Theology apologist cannot be consistently held within the Christian worldview and the Queer Theologian contradicts himself and his fellow Gay Theology advocates.

Then we will rightly, "Answer a fool as his folly deserves, that he not be wise in his own eyes" (Proverbs 26:5). In doing so we will answer Gay Theologians according to their self-proclaimed presuppositions (i.e. according to his folly). In doing so we will show them the outcome of their assumptions and the incoherency of the sub-presuppositions of their hermeneutical system. It will be demonstrated that their interpretation of Scripture creates conflicts with other portions of Scripture, it cannot be justified within the passage's own context and it even contradicts other Gay Theological arguments.

The Apostle Paul provides for us a useful and instructive summary of the presuppositional approach to apologetics when he wrote:

> But refuse foolish and ignorant speculations, knowing that they produce quarrels. And the Lord's bond-servant must not be quarrelsome, but be kind to all, able to teach, patient when wronged, with gentleness correcting those who are in opposition, if perhaps God may grant them repentance leading to the knowledge of the truth (2 Timothy 2:23-25).

First, this passage makes it very clear that the faithful Christian simply cannot have an arrogant attitude in dealing with the self-identified homosexuals or "Gay Christian." He must be loving, gentile, patient, courteous, and not quarrelsome. Confidence in the Scriptures and in the correctness of the Biblical Christian Worldview and assertiveness in our position should not be confused with arrogance or prideful quarreling. Our zeal for the truth should not lead us to be unloving or rude and failing to truly hear what they have to say. Our attitude is to be peaceable and gentle which demonstrates that our wisdom is from above (James 3:13-17).

Second, this passage teaches that those who are challenged to defend the Biblical Christian Worldview must not consent to answer in terms of foolish interpretations of the Bible. We are not to submit to the autonomous outlook that suppresses the truth of God; we are not to comply with the demand for neutrality in our discussions. A response to their assertions is to be given, but not one that conforms to the presuppositions behind the their faulty conclusions much in the way that Jesus responded to foolish assertion that He cast demons by the power of Beelzelbul (Luke 11:16-26). The goal is not to win an argument but to reach a deceived sinner who is seeking to respond to the desires of his flesh and a legitimate desire to be loved in an unbiblical manner.

Third, it will be demonstrated that the Gay Theology advocate hates God's law and in doing so he "opposes himself." By his foolish presuppositions he actually works against himself. He suppresses the clear truth about God's commandments that is foundational to a true understanding of creation, morality and salvation. He then affirms a position that is contrary to genuine knowledge. As we shall see, in the manner in which they mishandle the New Testament, the Gay theology advocate is intellectually schizophrenic. This is demonstrated by the fact that he asserts that none of the Holiness Code is applicable to the New Covenant Christian even though Jesus Christ and the apostles repeatedly cite the law including commandments from Leviticus 18-20. As we shall see, this confused double-mindedness is also demonstrated when they assert that the apostle Paul was a self-hating misogynistic homophobe and yet they then argue that Paul advocated an eschatological egalitarianism that does away with gender and sexual distinctions.

Fourth, Paul indicates that what the one who thinks in opposition to the Word of God needs is not simply additional information. Instead he needs to repent and have his thinking completely turned around; he must undergo a conversion, a paradigm shift, unto genuine knowledge of the truth. Until this repentance takes place they will only have a knowledge of God which condemns him (cf. Romans 1:18ff). A genuine or sincere knowledge of the truth - a saving knowledge - can only come with conversion. The so-called "Gay Christian" who engages in homogenital acts must be taught to renounce his supposed autonomy and submit to God's clear Word of authority and what it declares concerning homosexual behavior.

Finally, the passage quoted above leaves no doubt that the source of apologetic success must be God's sovereign will. A person will be converted only if it is granted to him from God since it is He who determines the destinies of all men (cf. Ephesians 1:1-11). Therefore it is the Holy Spirit alone who also determines whether our apologetic will be fruitful or not.

The ultimate ground of the Christian's certainty and the authority backing up his argumentation must be the Word of God. In doing so we will be able to rightly interpret facts in accordance with the foundational axioms of Biblical epistemology. We need to recognize that the debate between Biblical Christianity and Gay Theology is fundamentally a dispute between two completely different worldviews - between ultimate commitments and assumptions that are antithetical to each other. The Gay Theologian is not simply wrong concerning a hand full of passages of the Bible. His antagonism is rooted in an overall worldview which is according to the world's tradition (Colossians 2:8). Like all adherents to unbelieving worldviews, he is an enemy of God in his mind (Colossians 1:21; James 4:4) and he uses his mind to nullify, twist and queer God's law (Mark 7:8-13). He cannot receive or know the things of the Spirit (1 Corinthians 2:14), because he suppresses the truth (Romans 1:18) and exalts his reasoning against the knowledge of God (2 Corinthians 10:5). Consequently even though he may attend a church and do many otherwise respectable charitable deeds, the unrepentant homosexual has received a spirit of self-deception, "For this reason God will send upon them a deluding influence so that they will believe what is false, in order that they all may be judged who did not believe the truth, but took pleasure in wickedness" (2 Thessalonians 2:11-12).

All theological and exegetical debate will ultimately come down to the question of ultimate authority. In principle the two options will be understood as antithetical to each other. Fundamentally, the conflict within the Church on the matters of same sex acts are two philosophies or systems of thought that collide: one submits to the authority of God's Word as a matter of presuppositional commitment and the other does not. Appeals to fact such as matters of biology, psychology and interpretation of Scripture will be arbitrated in terms of the conflicting presuppositions held by the two worldviews. The debate between two perspectives will thus eventually work down to the level of one's ultimate authority and hermeneutical methodology. Far from ending in stalemate in which each person arbitrarily chooses the course which is "right for them," this situation shows the great need for a Biblical presuppositional method of defending the faith.

In terms of a Biblically-guided method, the core of proper apologetics is not mere experienced facts but God's revelation in its self-attesting truthfulness. As Christ-honoring defenders of the faith, we are obligated to "test the spirits, whether they are from God" (1 John 4:1); that discernment and defense is required at the level of starting point and presupposition, just as at every higher level. The final standard by which all theological claims are to be tried is the apostolic teaching (1 John 4:2-3). There is no higher authority than God's self-evidencing word. Nor do any earthly authorities whether ecclesiastical, scientific, or political have an equal say on the matter for there is one Lord who is sovereign over all earthly kingdoms and magistrates.

Therefore, when the apologetic debate centers on the issue of conflicting presuppositions, the faithful Christian must defend God's Word as the ultimate starting point, the unquestionable authority, the self-attesting foundation of all thought and commitment and do so with a consistent methodology for interpreting it. Otherwise we ourselves will twist it to our own destruction (2 Peter 3:16). At the level where there are conflicting truth-claims the choice is between either complete submission to Lordship of Christ for obtaining knowledge and wisdom (Colossians 2:3) or utter intellectual vanity striving after the wind (Ecclesiastes 1:13-17). The fundamental truth of the Biblical Christian Worldview and what it teaches concerning sexual ethics cannot be given a more ultimate or rigorous defense than this. Simple evidences from nature, biology, psychology or history cannot suffice when the debate reaches the presuppositional level: they cannot cast down every high reasoning which exalts itself against the knowledge of God and demand that every thought be made captive to the obedience of Christ (2 Corinthians 10:4-5).[68]

---

68 Much of the preceding on presuppositional apologetics was adapted from the lectures and writings of Greg Bahnsen.

Chapter 3
The Antithesis of Biblical Christianity and Gay Theology

In the preceding chapters we defined our terms that refer to people who experience same sex attractions and a fundamental understanding of how a worldview is formed in terms of epistemology, ethics and metaphysics. The following chapters will further examine the foundational *epistemological* issues related to the attributes and the authority of Scripture. Then having laid this foundation we will consider secondary epistemological issues, namely the hermeneutical process which forms the lens through which we read God's Word, understand our experiences and interpret the world around us. Once that groundwork has been laid we will be in a better place to examine the redemptive-historical nature of the law of God revealed in the Old Testament and the apostolic interpretation of it in the New Testament as the basis for Christian *ethics*. Once that has been accomplished we shall consider the *metaphysical* issues related to human ontology, particularly in relation to our gender identity and sexual attractions.

The rise and growing popularity of Gay Theology is rooted in two fundamental errors – a denial of the ultimate and final authority of Scripture and a distorted understanding of how Scripture ought to be interpreted and applied today. If the Christian is going to make a faithful decision to obey Christ and be able to defend his faith from the numerous attacks on the Bible, it is necessary to have at least a rudimentary understanding of Bibliology and hermeneutics. Bibliology is the study of the Scriptures that deals with issues such as the doctrines of Biblical inspiration, inerrancy, infallibility and canonicity. Hermeneutics, which we shall consider further in subsequent chapters, entails the science of Biblical interpretation and application to all of life.

Since the dawn of time whether or not you believe and obey God's Word has been the deciding factor in any ethical issue as the enemy always seeks to call into question the authority and meaning of God's Word as he challenges God's people, "Did God say...?" (Genesis 3:1) The controversy over same sex relationships in the Church today is no different. What you believe concerning the Bible and how it ought to be interpreted and applied will determine your convictions concerning what Christians ought to believe and how they ought to seek to live, especially in their sexual behavior.[69] This is why Gay or Queer Theologians will attack the veracity of Scripture and then intentionally subvert, or as they say "queer," the relevant passages that address the subject of same sex activity. They do so because they recognize that if they should acknowledge the Bible as being the very Word of God then it would be clear that the Almighty does not condone their behavior:

> If the Bible is the literal and inspired 'word of God' in the sense that God communicated each word to the writers, then any biblical condemnation of homosexuality represents God's opinion and is not a reflection of societal values at the time of writing, or of the authors' personal biases. [70]

Scripture presents itself as God's self-disclosure in which He has finally and sufficiently revealed Himself, His character and His will for

---

69 Daniel R. Heimbach demonstrates that the only mainline denomination to faithfully defend Biblical morality has been able to do so because they took a stand on the inerrancy and infallibility of Scripture. Consequently, while mainline denominations such as Anglicans (ECUSA), Methodists (UMC), Lutherans (ELCA) and Presbyterians (PCUSA) continue to battle with egalitarians and Gay Theology advocates within their midst, which is the fruit of their failure to uphold Scripture, the Southern Baptist Convention (SBC) was able to successfully change their seminaries and the defend the church because they stood on the solid ground of the authority of God's Word as he states, "Because the SBC has taken a clear stand reaffirming biblical authority, which includes continuing to uphold biblical standards on sexual morality, sexual revisionists have ceased to be a source of agitation. Instead they have been leaving to find accommodation elsewhere." *True Sexual Morality: Recovering Biblical Standards for a Culture in Crisis* (Crossway Books, 2004), 107.
70 Patrick M. Chapman, *"Thou Shalt Not Love": What Evangelicals Really Say to Gays* (New York, NY: Haidukpress, 2008), 21-22.

mankind, "…seeing that His divine power has granted to us everything pertaining to life and godliness, through the true knowledge of Him who called us by His own glory and excellence" (2 Peter 1:3). The Scriptures state that they are God-breathed as the Holy Spirit moved men to write the very words of the text so that it is "…profitable for teaching, for reproof, for correction, for training in righteousness; that the man of God may be adequate, equipped for every good work" (2 Timothy 3:16-17; 2 Peter 1:19-21). Because the Scripture's origin is from God, not the imaginings or mere observations of men, the Bible is supremely authoritative in all matters of doctrine and ethics which is why Jesus Himself quoted it when He was tempted to sin by the devil, "It is written…" (Matthew 4:4, 7, 10).

Furthermore, God has preserved His Word as He promised throughout the centuries so that while the grass whithers and the flowers fade the Word of the Lord abides forever (Isaiah 40:6; 1 Peter 1:24). If He did not preserve His Word for all generations then the Bible is a lie for not only would it be insufficient for matters of faith and life but also having become corrupt it would no longer teach the truth. In fact, Jesus, who throughout His earthly ministry repeatedly cites the Scriptures authoritatively, would be a deceiver for He said that His Word would never pass away (Matthew 24:35). Therefore, if we are going to believe what the Scriptures testify concerning God and His Word then we must believe that not only did the Holy Spirit move men to write the Scriptures but He also superintended it throughout time in His providence.

According to the Bible, not only were copies of the original writings (commonly referred to as the *autographa*) treated authoritatively but also portions of translations (such as the Greek Septuagint) were also cited as being the very Word of God by both Jesus and the apostles. The Scriptures do not merely bear witness to the acts of God in history; rather they are in themselves a revelation from God. In fact, the Scriptures represent the supreme revelation of God, for apart from them the other forms of revelation would be misinterpreted by man. While Jesus is the final unveiling of God as the Word of God made flesh we only know of Him through the written Word (John 1:14, 18: Hebrews 1:1-3). It is important, therefore, that we hold to the Bible as the supreme revelation of God for He has communicated this revelation by actual words, and not merely through His actions in history.[71]

The faithful Christian will begin with the Word of God as his standard for all that is to be believed concerning God and His revealed will. In doing so, the Scriptures will be presupposed as the lens of his worldview; it will determine how he interprets facts, for the fear of the Lord is the beginning of knowledge and wisdom while fools despise Godly instruction (Proverbs 1:7, 29; 9:10). In doing so he will develop an epistemology that is consistent with the Biblical Christian Worldview from which he will develop a biblical view of reality (metaphysics and ontology) as well as ethics and aesthetics.[72]

Gay Theology and The Bible

The orthodox view of Scripture as the inerrant, infallible and authoritative Word of God is more often than not denied by Gay Theology advocates. Subsequently they deny the reliability of Scriptures in what it teaches on matters of creation, cosmology, history, morals and theology. They then go on to argue that in certain contexts it is ethical and morally justifiable for men to have sex with other men (and women with

71 For further reading on this subject I recommend: James Boice, *Foundations of the Christian Faith* (Downers Grove, IL: InterVarsity Press; 1986); F. F. Bruce, *The Canon of Scripture* (Downers Grove, IL: InterVarsity Press, 1960); L. Glaussen, *The Divine Inspiration of the Bible* (Grand Rapids, MI: Kregel, 1971); Bruce Metzger, *Chapters in the History of New Testament Textual Criticism* (Grand Rapids Michigan: Eerdmans, 1963); Bruce Metzger, *The Text of New Testament: Its Transmission, Corruption, and Restoration* (Oxford University Press, 1992); James Orr, *Revelation and Inspiration* (Grand Rapids MI: Eerdmans, 1952); James I. Packer, *God Has Spoken* (Grand Rapids MI: Baker Book House, 1979); Bernard Ramm, *Special Revelation and the Word of God* (Grand Rapids, MI: Wm. B. Eerdmans Publishing Company, 1961); Robert B. Strimple, *The Modern Search For The Real Jesus: An Introductory Survey of the Historical Roots of Gospels Criticism* (P & R Publishing, New Jersey, 1995.); Cornelius Van Til, *In Defense of the Faith* Vol I. "The Doctrine of Scripture" (den Dulk Christian Foundation, 1967.); Benjamin B. Warfield, *Revelation and Inspiration* (Oxford University Press, 1927.); Edward Young, *Thy Word is Truth* (Grand Rapids, MI: Wm. B. Eerdmans Publishing Company, 1957.)

72 For more reading on developing a thoroughly Biblical Christian epistemology and defense of the Christian faith I highly recommend reading: Greg L. Bahnsen, *Presuppositional Apologetics - Stated and Defended* (Nacogdoches, Texas: Covenant Media Press, 2008); Greg L. Bahnsen, *Van Til's Apologetic* (Phillipsburg, NJ: P&R Publishing, 1998).

women) because they deny that God has actually communicated to men in words on this issue to the modern man. For example, Gay Theology apologist L. William Countryman, author of *Dirt, Greed & Sex: Sexual Ethics in the New Testament and Their Implications for Today,* writes in another book, *Biblical Authority or Biblical Tyranny?*:

> The universe, as conceived by most of the Old Testament writers, was very different from what we now know it to be. They envisioned the earth as a relatively flat expanse, over which God had placed the crystalline vault of the firma-ment, rather like a giant cheese dome. There were waters above this dome (which might fall down through widows in the firmament in the form of rain and precipitation), and there were waters below it, which welled up in the form of springs… In other words, the whole view of the universe (cosmology) accepted by the Old Testament writers was quite different from ours; and it is quite reasonable for us to say that it was also quite wrong.[73]

This leads his readers to question the Bible in what it says about the creation of man:

> The same is true with regard to the scientific hypothesis of biological evolution, first clearly and persuasively set forth by Charles Darwin… But why should we expect the author of Genesis 1 to be accurate in matters of biology when he was wrong about even the most basic matters of astronomical observation?[74]

He then subsequently and quite logically, given his preceding prem-ise, concludes that the Bible is also in error on matters of history:

> If the Bible contains errors of a scientific nature, it is no surprise that it also makes mistakes in that most slippery of area, human history… The events of the past, simply

73 L. William Countryman, *Biblical Authority or Biblical Tyranny?* (Harrisburg, PA: Trinity Press, 1994), 2-3.
74 Ibid, 4.

because they are the past, are subject to forgetfulness, misunderstanding, misinterpretation, and outright distortion. In this respect, the Bible is not different from other historical works. [75]

Following this trajectory Countryman then takes the next logical step to deny the Bible's inerrancy on the matters of morals and ethics:

> Yet there are problems of another kind, too. The Bible is not only fallible in matters of science and history but also capable of contradicting itself in matters of faith and morality.[76]

Once this line of reasoning is adopted, whether or not the so-called "clobber passages" prohibit same sex acts of any kind becomes irrelevant for the entire Bible can be dismissed as a collection of scientific, historical, theological and ethical myths. The conclusion that Gay Theology apologists, such as L. William Countryman, come to is that while the Scriptures may record the "mighty acts" of God in history they refuse to accept that any words, including those of the Bible, are really the words of God. According to their view, derived from so-called Neo-Orthodoxy, God acted and then the Spirit opened the eyes of certain observers to perceive something about God's character and will in these acts. Then that which rings true in the experience of the believer as he reads the text *becomes* the Word of God as Jack Rogers asserts:

> Neo-orthodoxy's defining insight, taken from the Danish philosopher Soren Kierkegaard, was that people and God are known by personal encounter, not by rational analysis. The revelation of God comes *not* in an inspired book, but in the person of Jesus Christ, who is God incarnate… the Bible *becomes* the word of God to people of faith.[77]

Gay Theology advocates go on to assert that the men who wrote the Bible were oppressive to women and other sectors of society. Therefore

75 Ibid, 4-5.
76 Ibid, 9.
77 Jack Rogers, *Jesus, The Bible, and Homosexuality* (Louisville, Kentucky; Westminster John Knox Press, 2006), 38.

the Bible is to be criticized as a product of "male gender dominance" - a bigoted work of a society where men dominated women rather than the Spirit-breathed Word of God.[78] Subsequently, the Bible is to be read with "suspicion" rather than in faith and obedience as J. Michael Clark states, "...my hermeneutic of suspicion, including my suspicions of objectivity, further lead me to ask whether the scriptures really have much positive value to say to gay and lesbian experience."[79]

This line of thinking comes from Friedrich Nietzsche (1844 - 1900) and Michel Foucault (1926 - 1984) which was further developed within Marxist Liberation theology and became the basis for Feminist Theology which then gave rise to Queer Theology.[80] Without exception every book by a Gay Theology apologist that I have read operates either subtlety or overtly from a premise of liberation theology. Taken to its logical conclusion, this methodology leads Gay Theologians to assert that Ruth and Naomi, Saul and David, Jonathan and David as well as Jesus and the Beloved Disciple were same sex partners. But this can only be accomplished by reading these stories from a presupposed Gay Theological Worldview:

> Now this case can only be made by rereading the biblical materials. The issue is not just a matter of the five isolated verses that presumably disqualify persons who engage in same-sex erotic behavior. It is a question of rereading the biblical witness much more broadly and appropriating the Bible for a gay-positive perspective. This kind of rereading of the Bible is related to the sort of rereading that has gone on in a variety of liberationist contexts.[81]

---

78 Jack Rogers states, "Both the Hebrew and Greek cultures were patriarchal. Men were and were intended to remain, dominant over women. Paul assumes the conventions of these cultures that he is addressing." *Jesus, The Bible and Homosexuality* (Louisville, KY: Knox Press, 2006), 78

79 J. Michael Clark, *Defying the Darkness* (Cleveland, OH: The Pilgrim Progress, 1997), 11

80 The "hermeneutic of suspicion" is a method of interpretation which assumes that the literal or surface-level meaning of a text is an effort to conceal the political interests which are served by the text. The purpose of interpretation is to strip off the concealment, unmasking those interests.

81 Theodore W. Jennings Jr., *The Man Jesus Loved* (Cleveland, OH: The Pilgrim Press, 2003), 3.

This method of interpreting the Bible includes reading the text from a presupposed "pro-gay" perspective which entails "…reading the texts from the perspective of contemporary gay or queer sensibility. Here the aim is to discover how the texts appears when it is read from a standpoint affirmative of gay or queer reality – that is, what the text means now, when viewed from this perspective."[82] The goal then is to "queer" the warning passages concerning same sex behavior in order to make them "gay friendly" at which time they *become* the Word of God:

> When queer people think about their relationship with the Bible, the phrase 'Word of God' is probably the last thing that comes to mind… When we approach the Bible as a [queer] friendly text, as a text that 'does no harm,' the terror of the Scriptures is transformed into the life-giving Word of God.[83]

Liberation theology in its various forms (African, South American, Feminist and Queer) begins with the premise that all theology is biased in favor of the wealthy and powerful. They then argue that the books of the Bible reflect the theology of the economic and social classes of those who developed them. Accordingly, they hold that the Bible perpetuates the interests of patriarchal heterosexual males while oppressing women and other sectors of society, including homosexuals, as Gary David Comstock states, "As a patriarchal document that places great value on men heading families and women bearing children, the Bible's homophobia should not surprise me." [84] He then goes on to assert:

> The Bible is, after all, a patriarchal document. The social structure of biblical times was patriarchal – a man ruled a nation as a man ruled a tribe as a man ruled his family. That the theological document to emerge from these times would be an expression by those men about their God is illustrated in the so-called 'household codes' of the New

---

82 Ibid, 7.
83 Robert E. Goss, Mona West (ed.) *Taking Back The Word: A Queer reading of the Bible* (Cleveland, Ohio, Pilgrim Press, 2000), 1, 5.
84 Gary David Comstock, *Gay Theology Without Apology* (Cleveland, OH: Pilgrim Press, 1993), 13.

Testament. In these codes wives were told to 'be subject to your husbands, as fitting in the Lord... for the husband is the head of the wife as Christ is the head of the church.' The Bible reflects the religious concerns and sociopolitical position of men; it was largely written by and addressed to them. The Bible is a product of those who controlled and managed the social order of that time... To maintain the role of provider is to maintain power over others.[85]

The justification for such assertions is determined by the liberation theological lens through which he reads the Bible. He then makes the following conclusions concerning the Scripture's treatment of women:

Throughout the Bible, four themes reinforce the centrality and superiority of men in procreative sexual ethics. These themes are: (1) male lineage and genealogy, (2) the tragedy of 'barren' women and the value of women as childbearers, (3) the use of 'harlotry' as a metaphor for Israel's corporate sin, and (4) the wickedness of lesbians and gay men.[86]

Ironically, we could, utilizing the very same methodology, read the Bible as a feminist document which is anti-male leadership in four themes: (1) Adam, not Eve, is held responsible for the fall from grace and expulsion from the Garden of Eden even though it was Eve, not Adam, who was the first to eat the forbidden fruit. Consequently it is Adam who broke covenant (Hosea 6:7) and it was his one act of transgression that plunged the human race and all of creation into death and corruption (Romans 5:15; 1 Corinthians 15:22, 45). (2) It is male kings and priests who are held responsible for leading Israel into exile and not women. (3) Men, not women, were commanded to go to war and potentially die for their country. (4) Men, not women, in the Old Covenant had to undergo having part of their genitals removed as a sign of the covenant whereas women were included without undergoing circumcision. The truth is, if you presuppose a "hermeneutic of suspicion" you can twist the text against anything or anyone depending on your presupposed political, social, theological and sexual agenda.

85 Ibid, 34-35, 36.
86 Ibid, 37.

Queer theologian Gary Comstock then concludes that the Bible cannot be read as "Gay friendly" (contrary to other Gay Theologians) but must be manipulated to make it so:

> But in the interest of convincing ourselves and the church that the Bible does not condemn us, we have brought our own bias to our reading of it. We have tended to overlook the danger and hostility that lurk in the very passages with which we have tried to become friends. We have not been sufficiently skeptical of the patriarchal framework within which these passages occur. I would suggest that our approach to the Bible become less apologetic and more critical – that we approach it not as an authority from which we want approval, but as a document whose shortcomings must be cited.[87]

The conclusion then is not to submit to the authority of Scripture and what it teaches concerning the roles of men and women and the family. Rather the goal is to criticize the Bible in light of a presupposed liberation theology:

> Quite obviously the Bible is stacked in favor of heterosexual males ruling the household, tribe and nation; and a central factor in maintaining position is their control of sexual behavior. With such a patriarchal framework, therefore, lesbians and gay men should not be surprised to find passages that malign us. Our tendency, however, has been to apologize for those biblical passages that appear to condemn homosexuality and attack lesbians and gay men.[88]

According to Gay Liberation Theology or Queer Theology, the Bible is to be read with suspicion as the product of a heterosexual male dominated society rather than the self-disclosure of a Holy God. Following Karl Marx, liberation theology asserts that all of man's problems are the direct result of this class exploitation. It then sees men who have sex with other men (or women with other women), as a social class of peo-

87 Ibid, 39.
88 Ibid, 38.

ple who have been politically oppressed rather than as those who have a strong, even overwhelming, indwelling sinful sexual desire. The result is that the historical understanding of same sex relations by the Church is not viewed as Biblical but rather, as they call it, the consequence of oppressive and unenlightened heterosexual "man on top" dominancy. Likewise, the Biblical roles for husbands, wives and children are also viewed as a form of oppression rather than part of God's created order that reflect the ontological equality and economic subordination of the Father, Son and Holy Spirit. This view is also advocated by some Dispensational Gay Theology advocates as well.[89]

The majority of these Gay Theology advocates put on par with Scriptural authority a selection of opinions of modern psychologists and "scientists" as well as their own experiences:

> I take the Bible to be the highest authority for Christians in theological and ethical matters, although I recognize also the legitimacy of tradition, reason, and experience. Authority does not mean perfection or inerrancy or complete consistency. The authoritative norm is the one that you finally listen to in a situation of competing norms... The experiential or existential view says that the Bible is authoritative only in those parts that are existentially engaging and compelling - that give grounding and meaning to existence.[90]

Ultimately, then, because the Bible does not have the final "say so" the final word on any given ethical issue rests on the wisdom of man:

> ...as a Roman Catholic - and more importantly, a thinking person - I do not presume the bible provides the last word on sexual ethics. In my mind, the matter is more complicated than that. Historical, cultural, philosophical,

---

89 R.D. Weekly, *The Rebuttal: A Biblical Response Exposing Deceptive Logic of Anti-Gay Theology* (Judah First Ministries, 2011), 51.
90 Dan O. Via, *Homosexuality and the Bible* (Minneapolis, MN: Fortress Press, 2003), 2.

psychological, sociological, medical, spiritual and personal factors all come to bear on the matter.[91]

While Gay Theology apologist Jeff Miner says, "We hold the Scriptures in highest esteem..." he does not believe that the Scriptures are infallible, inerrant or ultimately authoritative for Christian ethics because, as he asserts, it has errors and contradictions. Simply put, the god of Gay Theology has not inspired the Scriptures nor preserved it for all generations. Rather, this god has allowed men of an oppressive and culturally naive culture to write the books of the Bible so that where it contradicts the opinions of some modern social scientists and the testimony of gay people's experiences it must be dismissed:

> This canon (normative list) provides a rich and diverse - sometimes contradictory - context in which to try to understand individual texts... we will also want to consider our own cultural context. How does the unambiguous condemnation of homosexual acts in certain biblical texts accord with what recent social science has taught us and with the contemporary experience of gay and lesbian Christians?[92]

The conclusion is that each individual must become his own standard for what is to be deemed right or wrong as he feels led by the "spirit," even if he must live in contradiction to the clear principles of the law of God in Scripture. This is not merely something that a self-identified homosexual may do, but according to the Gay Theology apologist Jeff Miner declares he has a moral *obligation* to do so:

> We have a moral obligation to think, to reason, and to be guided by the Holy Spirit, even if that leads us to occasionally to conclude that a certain rule in the Bible is inapplicable to us as followers of Jesus.[93]

---

91 Daniel Helminiak, *What the Bible Really Says About Homosexuality* (Estancia, NM: Alamo Square Press, 2000), 19.
92 Dan O. Via, *Homosexuality and the Bible* (Minneapolis, MN: Fortress Press, 2003), 3.
93 Jeff Miner; John Connoley, *The Children Are Free* (Indianapolis, IN: Jesus Metropolitan Church, 2002), 70.

What is the Christian who has same sex attractions to do when he finds the New Testament, such as in the Epistle of James, upholding the moral standards found in the Old Testament law of God? Gay Theology apologists assert that we are to judge James as a legalist and therefore excuse ourselves from heeding his wisdom:

> The book of Acts makes James' legalistic tendencies clear, but we also have the New Testament book of James, which was attributed to this Apostle and was likely written by one of his followers (if not by him). That New Testament book, written in a style similar to Proverbs, shows a respect for the Hebrew Scriptures, with an emphasis on living a holy life by the law of Moses.[94]

The result of this theology is that the requirement to obey the law of God as advocated in the Epistle of James is to be dismissed. Because these Gay Theology apologists deny the inerrancy and infallibility of Scripture they assert that they are free to pick and choose which texts are applicable and which are not. When they find moral requirements that contradict their homosexual experience they insist that they are free to dismiss what the Bible says in regards to sexual ethics in the name of giving other commandments a higher priority, "When there is theological or ethical conflict within the canon, conscientious Christians simply have to decide to which side they give priority."[95]

The truth is the contradiction is not in the Word of God, rather it is between Gay Theology and the Bible. Taken to its logical conclusion, authority is not found in the Scriptures, but in the theological and political agenda of the Gay Theology apologist:

> ...it is not the scripture that holds authority, it is the standpoint of oppression and the concomitant demand of justice that are authoritative... the scriptures are neither authoritative nor particularly informative for gay/lesbian being, relationships, or liberation...[96]

---

94 Ibid, 87.
95 Dan O. Via, *Homosexuality and the Bible* (Minneapolis: Fortress Press, 2003), 10.
96 J. Michael Clark, *Defying the Darkness* (Cleveland, OH: The Pilgrim Progress, 1977), 11-12.

Whatever does not affirm Gay Theology and same sex acts is deemed "oppressive" and therefore it can be "dismissed" as "irrelevant, out of date or vague."[97] In doing so the Queer Theology apologist abandons Scripture as coming from the authority of God the Father and instead lowers it to that of the words of an equal with whom he is free to disagree, criticize and disregard:

> Instead of making the Bible into a parental authority, I have begun to engage it as I would a friend - as one to whom I have made a commitment and in whom I have invested dearly, but with whom I insist on a mutual exchange of critique, encouragement, support and challenge.[98]

Therefore, with a liberation theology's interpretation of Exodus and the ministry of Jesus the Queer Theology apologist is free to judge the Scriptures, "I criticize and call it to account for its homophobia."[99] For the Queer Theology apologist, Christians are not to seek to conform their thinking and their lives to the Scriptures nor seek the approval of God from it. Instead, they merely glean from it here and there as to what might be useful for one's own social-political-sexual agenda:

> Christian Scripture and tradition are not authorities from which I seek approval; rather they are resources from which I seek guidance and learn lessons as well as institutions that I seek to interpret, shape, and change. I am not afraid to look for, face, and criticize those parts of Scripture and tradition that condemn us or treat us badly.[100]

Not only are the Scriptures viewed as being corrupted by these Gay Theology apologists, but any preaching or teaching in the Church is corrupted which assumes the Bible to exercise any supreme authority in Christian ethics is likewise in error, "...preaching is unhelpful if it becomes corrupted by notions of biblical authority" because "...we

---

97 Gary David Comstock, *Gay Theology Without Apology* (Cleveland, OH: Pilgrim Press, 1993), 11
98 Ibid, 11.
99 Ibid, 12.
100   Ibid, 4.

cannot demonstrate that it is God's word through these human words..."[101] Having exposed the typical understanding of Scripture of the Liberal and Queer Gay Theology apologists, later chapters will address the hermeneutical systems and fallacy of the theological presuppositions that they use to interpret the Bible.

The Doctrine of Biblical Infallibility, Inerrancy and Authority Defended

Entire books have been written on the various doctrines within the field of Bibliology and to attempt to exhaustively cover the subjects of Biblical inerrancy, infallibility and subsequently the authority of Scripture is beyond the scope of this book. However, before we move on to further discuss Gay Theology let us take a closer look at these Biblical doctrines. If the Bible is not the fully inspired Word of God from which we can know Him and His will for our lives then we are left to a worldly philosophy, whether from ourselves or another, to understand ourselves and how to live in the world around us. If the Apostle Paul is not to be believed or obeyed in what he states concerning sexual ethics, particularly in his epistles to the Romans and Corinthians, there is no basis for believing his testimony of being an eyewitness to the resurrected body of Jesus Christ or that we ought to believe in the Gospel which is founded on testimony of the Scriptures as Paul wrote:

> Now I make known to you, brethren, the gospel which I preached to you, which also you received, in which also you stand, by which also you are saved, if you hold fast the word which I preached to you, unless you believed in vain. For I delivered to you as of first importance what I also received, that Christ died for our sins *according to the Scriptures*, and that He was buried, and that He was raised on the third day *according to the Scriptures*... (1 Corinthians 15:1-4).

While Paul goes on to state that there were more than 500 eyewitnesses to Christ's post-resurrection appearances, the basis for believing

101   Murray A. Rae and Graham Redding, *More Than a Single Issue* (Hindmarsh, SA; Australian Theological Forum, 2000), 19-20.

in the historical bodily resurrection of Jesus Christ is "according to the Scriptures." The Scriptures Paul is referring to are the Old Testament passages that Gay Theology despises as the product of a backwards unenlightened misogynistic culture (Psalm 16:9-11 cf. Isaiah 53:10-11).

To believe what the Scriptures teach concerning the resurrection but deny the same author's teaching concerning sexual ethics is arbitrary. It leaves the believer without a foundation for any certainty on which to base his hope for his own forgiveness of sin and his own resurrection from the dead and turns the gospel into a vain proclamation (1 Corinthians 15:13-19).

The only foundation on which there can be any epistemological certainty and true knowledge is by building one's system of knowledge on the Scriptures that are breathed-out by God through the Holy Spirit in which we also find the very words of Christ:

> Therefore everyone who hears these words of Mine and acts on them, may be compared to a wise man who built his house on the rock. And the rain fell, and the floods came, and the winds blew and slammed against that house; and yet it did not fall, for it had been founded on the rock. Everyone who hears these words of Mine and does not act on them, will be like a foolish man who built his house on the sand (Matthew 7:24-26).

The doctrine of the infallibility of the Bible is a necessary and proper deduction from the doctrines of revelation and inspiration. The Church has generally presumed this doctrine for well over 1,800 years, until the rise of higher Biblical criticism and skepticism that has been so prevalent in the last two hundred years or so.

One of the most common views of infallibility comes from a new form of liberalism (neo-liberalism) that is being taught and advocated in even otherwise conservative seminaries and denominations. The neo-liberal view of infallibility states that the purpose of Scripture is to lead men to salvation (2 Timothy 3:15), and that any other subject that it might touch on (like botany or cosmology) is unimportant to that purpose, so that what it says about those things may not be correct. They stress that the authors did not intentionally deceive us with these false statements. The historical, scientific or moral errors are in the

Bible because the authors of Sacrid Writ did not know better or they simply accommodated themselves to the popular views of the times so that they could get their main point across, which had to do with salvation. Consequently, once it is seen that writers of the Bible, such as the apostle Paul, were ignorant of the "homosexual orientation" as we know it today their statements concerning same sex acts can be dismissed as the product of a primitive unenlightened worldview.[102] Therefore, we can proudly reject anything that Moses or the Apostle Paul has to say about sexual ethics:

> Some people think the Bible and its writers were homophobic, especially Paul. To coin a word, I think they were homo-ignorant. Attempting to reconcile first and second century understanding of sexuality into a modern framework is virtually impossible. What the apostle Paul, his Christian contemporaries, and the society around him believed about sexuality would be rejected as ridiculous myth by even the most conservative, prudish Christian today. Though homosexuality existed, it was not scientifically understood.[103]

In fact, Gay Theology proponents will even go on to argue that given the more inclusive trajectory of the New Testament, if Paul knew what we know today, he too would be condone consensual non-exploitive same sex relationships.[104] The New Testament as well as the rest of the

102   Daniel Helminak states, "Taken on its own terms and in its own time, the Bible nowhere condemns homosexuality as we know it today." *What the Bible Really Says About Homosexuality* (Estancia, NM: Alamo Square Press, 2000), 13.

103   Samuel Kader, *Openly Gay, Openly Christian: How the Bible Really Is Gay Friendly* (San Francisco, CA: Leyland Publications, 1999), 69. Kader then refers to the Epistle of Barnabas 10:6-8, a non-canonical book, which allegorizes some of the Old Testament food laws as being references to sexual prohibitions and in doing so makes some absurd statements concerning sexuality and biology. Kader then argues that this non-inspired book, an epistle not given to the church by an apostle or the Holy Spirit, is representative of the apostle's understanding of sexuality. It is absurd that to assert that such a book tells us anything about the understanding of the apostles or that the Holy Spirit was incapable of communicating through the apostles God's will regarding heterosexual or homosexual conduct.

104   Jack Rogers states, "The trajectory of Christian history is in the direction of ever-greater openness and inclusiveness." *Jesus, The Bible, and Homosexuality* (Louisville, Kentucky; Westminster John Knox Press, 2006), 111.

Bible then becomes the tool of the Gay Theology proponent in which he sets himself up as judge over Scripture. He then chooses, according to his own agenda, which Scriptures are profitable for teaching and reproof and which are to be dismissed as the result of the misconceived notions of the primitive unenlightened worldview of its author.

The consequence of this is a view of limited infallibility which extends only to certain portions of Scripture, with human reason determining the actual extent, is in the end the ultimate authority is in the autonomous reasoning of the Gay Theology advocate. One person may say that it extends to doctrine only, another says doctrine and ethics, while another says doctrine, geography, and history. With this view of Scripture the Gay Theology advocate declares himself to be free to pick and choose which texts he deems to be the Word of God and which are the mere ideas of ancient culturally primitive patriarchal oppressive men. In the hands of such theologians the Scripture becomes a waxed nose with which the Gay Theology apologist can bend and twist to justify his sexual desires and actions. The consequence is that the canon ("rule") of Scripture ceases to be the source for knowing the will of God and man is left up to his own to "do what is right in his own eyes" (Judges 17:6; Proverbs 12:15).

In contrast to the assertions of Gay Theology apologists, Biblical Christianity maintains that the Scriptures are infallible in that they are incapable of error and not liable to mislead, deceive, or disappoint and incapable of error in defining doctrines touching on history, faith and morals. To say that the Bible is infallible is to assert that it is not only without error but also incapable of error because of its origin. For example, I may say, "2+2 = 4" and the statement is without error. But because I am not infallible the statement, though inerrant, is in the realm of possibilities fallible because I am the one who said it.

When the Church teaches that the Bible is infallible this means that, according to Scripture itself, it is not nor can it ever be "broken." Infallibility refers to the divine character of Scripture that necessitates its truthfulness (John 10:35). The doctrine of infallibility teaches that the Scriptures have full trustworthiness as a guide for they do not deceive having come from the One who is Truth and whose word is truth.[105] The true Christian Church accepts and preserves the infallible word as the

105   J.I. Packer, *New Dictionary of Theology* (Downers Grove, IL: InterVarsity Press, 1988), 337.

true standard of its apostolicity; for Scriptures owes their infallibility, not to any intrinsic or independent quality, but to the divine Subject and Author to whom the term infallibility may properly be applied.[106]

It should be apparent at this point that one's view of inspiration is directly related to, and ultimately determines, one's view of infallibility. Revelation is the communication of divine truth, God's self-disclosure, to human beings. Inspiration is the means of the transfer of that revelation from God to human beings in the form of human language in written form. Infallibility deals with the infallible transfer of the truth which results in the fact that the written record does not have the ability or capability of teaching any kind of deception. Therefore, if the revelation is complete, and if the inspiration is both verbal (extending to every single word) and plenary (extending equally to every part), then we conclude that the entire Bible is a complete and infallible revelation in everything that it says, and about everything is speaks about. If the Church is to remain faithful to the Word of God and resist the lies of the serpent we must confess the following:

> We affirm that Scripture, having been given by divine inspiration, so that, far from misleading us, it is true and reliable in all matters it addresses. We deny that it is possible for the Bible to be at the same time infallible and errant in its assertions. Infallibility and inerrancy may be distinguished, but not separated.[107]

Having established the Biblical doctrines of both the inspiration and infallibility of the Scripture, we must now ask an additional important question. Is the Bible merely infallible (in its truth content) or is it also inerrant (the absence of any error in anything it says)? Higher-critical, or "liberal" seminaries, denominations and churches, out of which Gay Theology arises, have generally accepted the position that the Bible surely contains errors which are evident in light of modern scientific discoveries, historical documentation, modern psychology, the social

---

106   W.C. G. Proctor, *Baker's Dictionary of Theology* Everett Harrison, ed., (Grand Rapids, MI: Baker Book House, 1987), 284.
107   "The Chicago Statement on Biblical Inerrancy" 1978. Signed by such theologians as R.C. Sproul, James Boice, John Gerstner, Carl Henry, John Warwick Montgomery, Francis Schaeffer, J.I. Packer and approximately 300 others.

sciences and so-called "common sense."[108] In order to justify their claims Gay Theology proponents must denigrate the Bible as the ultimate authority over our epistemology, metaphysics and ethics for, as Patrick Chapman recognizes, "If the Bible is the literal and inspired 'word of God' in the sense that God communicated each word to the writer, then any biblical condemnation of homosexuality represents God's opinion and is not a reflection of societal values at the time of the writing, of the authors' personal biases."[109]

However, the infallibility and inerrancy of Scripture hangs together. If you one pull a single thread from either, the integrity of Scripture unravels:

> The Scripture, therefore, is a rule sufficient in itself, and was by men divinely inspired at once delivered to the world. If there be any mistakes in the Bible, there may well be a thousand. If there be any falsehood in that book, it did not come from the God of truth.[110]

The Church has maintained the inerrant integrity of Scripture for almost 2,000 years. In fact, in spite of Church disagreements throughout the centuries on matters of doctrine, church polity, and Christian practice, there was virtual unanimous agreement regarding the inerrancy and authority of Scripture. Our goal then as faithful Christians ought to be to refute the modern denial of the inerrancy of Scripture upon which Gay Theology is built. Only then can we have solid ground to develop the reasons for the orthodox position on sexuality. Christians need to be better equipped to defend the absolute inerrancy of Holy Scripture so that, despite whatever temptations and feelings we might have, we will be able to maintain our moral integrity according to the Scriptures by the power of the Holy Spirit.

There is a close relationship between inerrancy and infallibility, with the general definitions of each somewhat overlapping. However,

108   Patrick M. Chapman states, "It seems untenable to insist that the Bible is the literal, inerrant 'word of God,' when there are obvious mistakes and contradictions." *"Thou Shalt Not Love": What Evangelicals Really Say to Gays* (New York, NY: Haiduk Press, 2008), 18.

109   Ibid, 21-22.

110   James Boice, *Foundations of the Christian Faith* (Downers Grove, IL: InterVarsity Press; 2 Sub edition, 1986), 69.

the following definition seeks to specifically clarify the exact meaning of inerrancy:

> Being wholly and verbally God-given, Scripture is without error or fault in all its teaching, no less in what it states about God's acts in creation, about the events of world history, and about its own literary origins under God, than in its witness to God's saving grace in individual lives.[111]

The word *inerrant* from the Latin infinitive *errare* means "to wander," and the "in" indicates a negation of the action of erring, departing or going astray from the truth. Hence the word simply denotes the quality of freedom from error, and it is in this sense that the word is applied to the Holy Scriptures. The doctrine of the inerrancy of the Scriptures teaches that every assertion of the Bible is true, whether the Bible speaks of what to believe (doctrine), or how to live (ethics), or whether it recounts historical events. On whatever the subject the Scripture speaks, it speaks truth, and one may believe its utterances. This does not mean that every word in the Bible is to be understood in a wooden sense for it also conveys inerrant truth in various forms of speech metaphor, hyperbole, and non-literal genres such as poetry or parables. Nevertheless, what Scripture teaches in these forms of speech is without error.

There have been many objections raised to discredit the idea of an inerrant Bible. Some object to the doctrine of inerrancy and state, "The books of the Bible are basically human documents." "To err is human" is the battle cry of these critics and they state that the claim that the writers did not abandon their natural human capacities surely makes the writings fallible and thus subject to error.

Another complaint is that there are variations in the text. This is the age-old idea of the manuscript and translation variations. The assertion that the parallel accounts of the same events all differ, the literary polish of material differs, and that the actual manuscripts themselves all differ, only serves to prove that the Bible is only a human book. As such, it is subject to human limitation and error just as would be the case with any other book.

One assertion which is common in liberal universities is that modern scientific and historical research have supposedly demonstrated the

111   "The Chicago Statement on Biblical Inerrancy" 1978

fallibility and errancy of the Bible. This is the assertion that no thinking person would still give "blind" acceptance to an infallible and inerrant Bible. This is surely an interesting position, in light of the fact that much of our scientific knowledge contradicts that of previous years. In other words, if our "scientific" views are constantly undergoing revision and modification, why does science seem to have the final word on what Scripture records as fact?

Another factor which is often brought up by Liberals and Gay Theologians is the unavailability of the original autographs. Inerrancy is claimed only for the original documents (*autographa*) penned by the authors of the Scriptures. Because we do not have the autographs and no one has seen them critics claim that inerrancy cannot be verified. It is argued that since it cannot be proven to be true, but it can be demonstrated to be suspect, inerrancy must be rejected as being a valid position for a thinking person to subscribe to. Thus the appeal to autographs which we cannot produce is deemed meaningless by liberal Gay Theologians such as Patrick M. Chapman who states:

> Unfortunately, we do not have the original texts so no one can authoritatively say what they actually state. This begs the question as to how evangelicals can trust anything in the Bible.[112]

In response to this argument, we must keep in mind that Jesus Christ and the apostles authoritatively cited not only copies of the Torah, the Psalms and the Prophets but they also quoted the Septuagint, a Greek translation of the Old Testament. In fact, of the approximately 300 Old Testament quotes in the New Testament, approximately two-thirds of them come from the Septuagint. To argue therefore that one can only have assurance that the Scriptures have been preserved and can only cite the Word of God by quoting directly from the original *autographa* contradicts the teaching and practice of Jesus Christ and the apostles. In addition, the necessity of having the *autographa* would only be true if the number of variants in the various manuscripts remained constant as we traced the history of manuscripts back to the original writings. But because inerrancy is determined by the plethora of manuscripts avail-

---

112   Patrick M. Chapman, *"Thou Shalt Not Love": What Evangelicals Really Say to Gays* (New York, NY: Haiduk Press, 2008), 97.

able we can determine the nature of the original text and the content of the autographs.[113]

A proper understanding of the true nature of Biblical inerrancy will be sufficient to refute most of the previous objections and misconceptions. In addition, it will prevent those who hold to inerrancy from making a shipwreck of their faith, and eventually follow deceptive heresies of the Gay Theology movement or abandon the faith altogether. In understanding Biblical inerrancy and infallibility and the authority of Scripture the following needs to be considered.

First, inerrancy does not negate the variety of human expression. Or, to put it the other way around, human expression does not in any way nullify inerrancy. God can say the same thing, through a variety of human authors, in many different ways. For example, the confession of Peter at Caesarea Philippi:

> "Thou art the Christ, the Son of the living God" (Matthew 16:16).
> "Thou art the Christ" (Mark 8:29).
> "The Christ of God" (Luke 9:20).

At this point some might argue that there is a contradiction between these three quotes because some include more data than others. It is argued if they are authentic quotes, how can they be different? If one reads the critiques of higher-critics (errantists) they have a "Damned if you do, damned if you don't methodology." In other words, where the gospel writers have the exact same quote, word for word, they accuse the authors of plagiarizing from another text and thus of not being an actual eye witness to the event. On the other hand, errantists will accuse the text of error when they do not have the exact same quote word for word. Consequently whether or not the quotes are exactly the same they reject the authenticity of the eyewitness account. Needless to say, it is their presupposition that the Bible is not the Word of God rather than an honest scholarly approach to the text that drives their conclusions.

Second, the guarantee that we have from the Bible is that the authors are accurate eyewitnesses to the events being depicted and that the texts

---

113   For more reading on the issue of Biblical inerrancy, textual criticism and the preservation of the New Testament I highly recommend reading: Philip G. Kayser and Wilbur N. Pickering, "Has God Indeed Said?" and Philip G. Kayser, "How To Deal With Objections to Innerrancy" available at: http://www.biblicalblueprints.org/shop-displayproducts.asp?id=9&cat=Apologetics

are God-breathed. It is not a guarantee that the phrases being quoted are word for word. In other words, the quotation marks are from the English translation and not the original text. For example, compare the following:

(a) Bob said, "You are to go to the grocery store."
(b) Bob said you are to go to the grocery store.

Both of the above clearly and accurately indicate the message conveyed by Bob. But was the command exactly word for word "You are to go to the grocery store" or is the phrase, you are to go to the grocery store, a summary of what was said? In the original Hebrew and Greek texts there were no punctuation or quotation marks so we do not know whether the author was giving an exact quote or merely a summary of what was said. In either case the message is the same and the intent of the sentence is clear. In addition, in the case of the Bible as an inspired text the message desired to be conveyed by the Holy Spirit, such as Peter's confession, is not any less authoritative whether or not the quote is exact or is merely a summary of what was said.

Third, inerrancy does not negate the use of individuality and personality. Those who hold to inerrancy readily admit to the human authorship of the Bible. The doctrine of inerrancy recognizes that God used a variety of people, employed their full personalities, worked through unique circumstances and used their literary styles. For example, Luke manifests an interest in medical phenomenon, James is intensely practical like Wisdom literature (Proverbs), and Paul is highly polemical at times (Galatians 5:12). The differences of personality are expressed in their writing, but these differences do not demand fallibility or error.

Fourth, inerrancy does not exclude the use of pictures and symbols. It must be remembered that the symbols used were peculiar to that particular audience and setting such as cultural metaphors, idioms and euphemisms. The wise interpreter of Scripture will study the various figures of speech in order to acquaint himself with the communication technique of each individual author. For example, Jesus frequently used parables to illustrate His point, Paul frequently uses Old Testament idioms, and there are several books written primarily in a poetic style. The context will generally assist the interpreter to determine what is symbolic and what is to be understood "to the letter." To not read a passage "literally" does not mean that the text conveys a non-historical fact, but that the text is using something other than a strict narrative genre to report events. For example, while Henry Wadsworth Longfellow's "Paul Revere's Ride" is written in a poetic genre, like the creation narrative in Genesis Chapter 1 and the prayer in Jonah chapter 2, we should not necessarily conclude that he did not intend to convey an actual historical event.

Fifth, inerrancy does not necessarily imply the use of technical language or scientific vocabulary. The Biblical writers wrote to their generations in the human language of the time. Many critics seem to think that the Bible should have been written in the modern scientific language of our present time. When the Bible speaks of the "sun setting" (Exodus 17:12; Judges 19:14) the critics cry out "error" for science has proven that the sun does not actually set as in geocentric theory, but rather the earth revolves around the sun and is itself rotating on its axis (Heliocentricity). What these critics fail to recognize is that it is not unusual to hear the modern weather forecaster on the evening news speaking of the "sun rising." This is phenomenological language in which one speaks according to appearances, from the human perspective, not technical scientific language. Likewise, while it is true that Genesis 1-2 isn't a scientific text book, as some Gay Theologians insist, this does not mean that it conveys historical error or was not intended to convey not only *what* was created but *how* it was created. Even if we do not take the 7 days to be literal 24 hour days this does not mean we can justifiably dismiss Adam and Eve as mythical persons or deny the fall as an actual historical event.[114]

Sixth, inerrancy does not negate the use of noninspired documents. The Bible is not errant simply because an author employs a non-Biblical source or uninspired writing. Many conservative scholars state that Moses may have used genealogical records available to him, Luke's gospel was based upon his research of the written documents of his day, Joshua used the Book of Jasher for his famous quotation about the sun standing still (Joshua 10:13), the Apostle Paul quoted a heathen poet without any hesitation (Acts 17:28), and Jude cited a non-canonical source about the prophecy of Enoch (v. 14). These free use of sources in no way reduces Biblical inspiration, and therefore does not negate

114   Virginia Ramey Mollenkott, *Omnigender: A Trans-religious Approach* (Cleveland, OH: The Pilgrim Progress, 2007), 96.

infallibility or inerrancy. As a point of illustration, we might imagine that if the Apostle Jude was to write an epistle today he might quote the *Encyclopedia Britannica*. Does a modern encyclopedia contain accurate historical information? Yes, but it is obviously not inspired and may contain some historical and factual inaccuracies. It is conceivable that Jude could be moved by the Holy Spirit to use an accurate portion of the encyclopedia of his day without validating the entire document. Likewise, an inspired document quoting an accurate portion of a non-inspired book neither negates the validity of the inspired document nor does it make the source quoted an inspired document or even entirely historically reliable. Therefore, just because Jude quotes the Book of Enoch does not indicate that it should be added to the canon of Scripture and neither does it mean we should remove Jude's epistle from the New Testament.

Seventh, inerrancy does not imply omniscience on the part of Biblical authors. In other words, the Biblical authors were not acquainted with all facets of the subjects created. The Bible does not claim to be a textbook on science, or an exhaustive historical record. It is was not the intent of the authors to reveal everything that they did know. The gospels, for example, were not intended to be exhaustive accounts of all that they had observed about the life and ministry of Jesus. Inerrancy simply claims that what any given author did record is actually true and accurate, for they were kept from error through the superintendence of God.

Eighth, inerrancy does not imply that everything the Bible recorded is true or normative for Christian practice. For example the Bible records the lies of Satan and various people as it records falsehoods in an accurate manner, and without any error whatsoever. Likewise, the Bible does not endorse everything it records such as Solomon's accumulation of wives, David's infidelity or Peter's denial of Christ.

Ninth, inerrancy does not extend beyond the original autographs. Inerrancy does not extend to the copies of the autographs or the translations from the copies. In other words, we are not making claim to completely inerrant copies or completely inerrant translations. The authority of copies and translations is only in so far as they accurately represent the original autograph. In addition, inerrancy extends only to the original text itself, and never to the interpretations of the text.

Finally, inerrancy does extend to the entire Bible and the entire message of the Bible. Biblical Christianity does not support any kind of "limited inerrancy" notion. The doctrine of inerrancy teaches that the Bible is inerrant in what it teaches about all matters, even down to the tenses of the verbs and the very last letters of words. In addition, the doctrine of inerrancy teaches that the entire Bible message is inerrant, and not merely those sections that have to do with "faith and practice."

The Christological Analogy of Inerrancy

Throughout Church history, particularly the first three centuries, there have been various theological heresies concerning the dual nature of Christ. Usually the errors have been due to an over emphasis on one nature (human or divine) to the neglect, confusion, or even denial of the other.[115]

The Biblical orthodox view of Christ was codified in 451 A.D. at the Council of Chalcedon which established the official position of the historic Christian faith. This creed states that Jesus Christ is one person with two natures - the human and the divine. He is truly God and truly man, composed of body and rational soul. He is consubstantial with the Father in his deity and consubstantial with man in his humanity, except for sin. In His deity He was begotten of the Father before time, and in His humanity born of the Virgin Mary. The distinction between His two natures is not diminished by their union, but the specific character of each nature is preserved and they are united in one person. Jesus Christ is not split or divided into two persons; He is one person, the Son of God.

The Christological errors come from an over emphasis on either Jesus Christ's humanity and thus err in understanding His divine nature, or over emphasize His divinity and negate His human attributes. The difficulty in understanding this Biblical truth lies in our inability to be able to fully comprehend two things concerning the person of Jesus

---

115   These heresies include various forms of Gnosticism such as Cerinthianism and Docetism, Arianism (which denied the deity of Christ), Monophysitism (which denied the two distinct natures of Christ), Nestorianism (which denied the real union of the two natures of Christ into one person and implied a twofold personality), and Sabbellianism (also known as modalism or dynamic monarchianism) was an early heresy that held to a unity of essence but not a distinction in the persons in the Godhead.

Christ. First, how God can become flesh so that the finite contains the infinite. Second, how Christ could be truly tempted in all ways as we (Hebrews 4:15), yet not only not sin but not be able to sin (*posse non peccare*) and still truly be human born under the law suffering all the human frailties of life such as sleep, pain, and hunger.

In a similar fashion, the errors which have arisen concerning the inerrancy of Scripture in relation to its human and divine origin are due to an over emphasis on either human or divine aspects. Again, the difficulty in understanding this truth arises from our inability to be able to fully comprehend how God can inspire an inerrant human document and how humans can be involved in an inerrant divine document. But what must be affirmed is that the Scriptures, like Christ, are fully human and fully divine in their origin. Their origin is not half human and half divine, or only divine or only human. They are both completely human and completely divine just as Christ is both human and divine without a mixture or confusion of the two aspects, yet without error or sin. To say that Christ and the Scriptures are both completely human and divine is not a contradiction, a paradox, or an antinomy but rather a mystery. There is an aspect to both which has either not been revealed to us or cannot be revealed to us because of our finitude and inability to fully comprehend (Isaiah 55:7-8; Romans 11:33-36).

Having established the dual nature of Scripture we now need to understand the importance of having a correct understanding of the authority of Scripture. The root of all sin is the quest for autonomy (self-law) rather than submitting to the authority of God's Word, whether it is the direct verbal command given in the garden or God's written Word in Scripture. Yet this is exactly what Gay Theology proponents are advocating when they write such things as:

> I skirt established Christian Scripture and tradition to gain autonomy, to locate myself within my own life, to escape an external authority and find an internal authority, to respond to my own need for the company of others... I have begun to assemble and name as my Scripture a small body of literature in which I find myself accepted for who I am.[116]

---

116   Gary David Comstock, *Gay Theology Without Apology* (Cleveland, OH: Pilgrim Press, 1993), 108.

However, the problem of submitting to the authority is not merely an issue with non-Christians but within the Church as well as James Boice wrote, "…a primary cause of the confusion within the Christian church today is its lack of a valid authority."[117] The issue of the authority of Scripture is ultimately an issue of the authority of God Himself, for Scripture is God's self-revelation. Our view and acceptance of the authority of that revelation will be no greater than our view of the authority of the Revelator. Therefore a high view of the majesty of God, linked together with a high view of inspiration of Scripture, alone will produce an adequate view of an authoritative Bible. Our study of Biblical authority must begin with God Himself, and we affirm the following statement about God as our starting point:

> All ultimate authority rests in God. As Creator and Sustainer of the universe He has absolute right over all created beings and an all-embracing authority in heaven as on earth. This final and supreme authority gives Him the unlimited prerogative to command and enforce obedience, to unconditionally possess and absolutely govern all things at all times in all places of the universe.[118]

Alleged Discrepancies of the Bible

We come now to that important section of our defense of the Bible against the claims of liberalism and Gay Theology that pertains to the alleged discrepancies of Scripture. There is a general consensus of Gay Theologians that the Bible is full of errors, mistakes, and contradictions as one of them asserts:

> The Bible is not a coherent rule book with a consistent, reliable, and currently applicable list of sins, but it does provide some guidelines for naming and changing what is wrong.[119]

117   James Boice, *Foundations of the Christian Faith* (Downers Grove, IL: Inter-Varsity Press; 1986), 47.
118   Norval Geldenhuys, "Revelation and the Bible" *Authority and the Bible*, Carl F. Henry (ed.) (Grand Rapids, MI: Baker Book House, 1958), 371.
119   Gary David Comstock, *Gay Theology Without Apology* (Cleveland, OH: Pilgrim Press, 1993), 39.

As Bible-believing Christians we must be both willing to admit that there are some Bible difficulties, and be prepared to answer those who challenge us (Jude 3; 1 Peter 3:15; Proverbs 26:5). However, in doing so, we should approach the entire issue with the following presuppositions:

> The burden of proof rests on the critics... Like an American citizen, the Bible should be presumed innocent until proven guilty. Like a reliable friend, it should be given the benefit of the doubt. A scientist always assumes that there is an explanation when faced with some unexpected anomaly. In the same way, a Bible student assumes that there is a harmony in the Bible in light what appear to be contradictions.[120]

This is the premise upon which we will proceed as we examine the various types of apparent contradictions, the manner of resolving them, the examples of many that have been resolved. However, as stated before, the argument of "burden of proof" or "innocent until proven guilty" is a difficult one because the burden of proof is almost always equal. The USA has such a policy in its courts because the British in the 1700's had the view of "guilty until proven innocent." Not only this, but the argument is almost always stated in such a manner: "You can't prove me wrong." This supposes that the burden of proof is on the other's side, when in fact, the assertion itself must be proven before it is even worth disproving. However, in cases that an assertion is against a widely held belief, it will have to be reinforced with more than the usual circumstantial evidence; thus, a greater burden of proof. However, the fallacy is usually instigated when the opponent wants to "assert without proving," and claims that his assertions are innocent until proven guilty. Also note that in some cases there is a burden of proof when a change in policy is advocated. Nevertheless, since the Bible for 2000 years has dominantly been viewed as the authoritative Word of God, for critics in the Church (such as liberal Gay theologians) to assert otherwise the burden of proof is placed upon them. But for critics outside the Church the case for burden of proof may be more difficult.

---

120   Norman L. Geisler, Ronald Brooks, *When Skeptics Ask* (Wheaton: Victor Books, 1990), 163-164.

There are a variety of principles that must always be observed as we deal with the alleged discrepancies of the Bible. First, always be sure you know what the text actually *says*. This means that we must try to ascertain, as much as we can within the realm of possibility, exactly what the original text actually said. There may be variants in the manuscript copies that are also reflected in our modern translations. These are textual problems with which we are still in doubt, but we must know where they are in our Bibles, and we should know something of the reasons for the apparent problem. In addition, an apparent problem may be due to the translation of the text from Greek or Hebrew to English. Whenever any text (whether it be the Bible or secular literature) of one language is translated into another there is often some degree difficulty in completely conveying the same meaning in a word for word translation. Consequently sometimes a discrepancy might be solved when returning to the original language. If you do not know Hebrew or Greek, good commentaries will usually address known translation problems.

Second, always be sure you know what the text actually *means*. The Bible frequently uses phrases and terminology that don't mean exactly what they might appear to mean because of idioms and metaphors tied to the culture at the time it was written. Clearly there are times in which a statement must be understood as hyperbole for it could hardly be argued that Jesus actually advocated self-mutilation as a means to avoiding sin (Matthew 5:30). The text must be understood and studied in relation to the author's purpose for writing. Also, some words change their meaning according to their different context even within the Bible and even within texts written by the same human author. In English for example, a "trunk" might belong to an elephant, a car, a salesmen, or a tree. A word's meaning then is determined by the context, rather than being arbitrarily imposed by the author.

Third, never confuse error with imprecision, rounded or approximate use of numbers, or paraphrases of Scriptures. Precision with measurements is critical in our modern age of science. However, the ancient world and Biblical writers were less concerned with such precision. They often used round numbers in order to give the general size of an object or an army or a quantity of years. For example, Acts 7:6 states that Israel was in bondage in Egypt for 400 years whereas Exodus 12:40 states they were in bondage for 430 years. But this is not so unusual for even in modern times if someone were to ask your age you would not reply in exact years, months, days, hours, and seconds but would give a round number. Another example would be New Testament author's freedom in quoting previously written Scriptures. New Testament authors frequently do not quote the Old Testament text verbatim, but what they do quote is faithful to the meaning of the author. In fact, the quotation marks are not from the Greek text but are inserted by the English translators and perhaps wrongfully so. Given the above factors we should not use a modern criteria to judge a methodology freely used in an ancient culture.

Fourth, never confuse falsity with perspective. Any given witness to an automobile accident will testify concerning that which he actually saw, and only from his unique perspective. Just because a testimony is in part does not mean that it is false. The same is true with a Biblical writer, particularly the Gospel writers, who records an event from what he actually saw, but does not communicate all the details, including some of those included by other authors.

Next, always remember that language about the world, as it is expressed in the Bible, for the most part is in everyday language. While there are at times various genres which may use unusual language, the Bible by and large uses language we speak and is generally written from the writer's perspective. For example, we speak of space travel from the perspective of the earth but that does not imply that we think earth is the center of the universe. In other words, we use "earth language" universally. We see an example of this in science fiction television shows and movies in which aliens often say to earthlings, "It would take X amount of your earth years to travel to such and such a place..." The script writers of the show are taking into account that the fictional alien characters would want to convey a meaningful message to a people who are oriented to earth's frame of reference. Likewise, the writers of the Bible describe heaven as being above the earth as if one might fly there in a space ship at warp speed for X amount of years and eventually get there. But this does not mean that we should think of heaven as being somewhere out past Pluto anymore than we should think of hell as being in the center of the earth because it is described as being "below" (cf. Job 11:8; Psalm 55:15).

Finally, always remember that the Bible records things that it does not approve. Much of the Bible is historical narrative and is not intended to be normative for Christian behavior. Thus it records many historical events that it does not necessarily endorse such as the sins of King David (2 Samuel 11), Solomon's polygamy (1 Kings 11:1-8), and the serpent's lie to Eve (Genesis 3:4-5). Contrary to the assertion of many Gay Theology advocates, the fact that there may not be any immediate condemnation of these sins in the context in which they are recorded does not imply that God is either unaware of them or is approving of them. They are simply historical facts condemned elsewhere in the Bible.

In addition, there are also other seeming discrepancies in the Bible, many of which are asserted in L. William Countryman's book *Biblical Authority or Biblical Tyranny?,* that are generally classified around the following subject headings:

(1) Genealogical problems: Usually in Genesis 5 and in Christ's genealogies in Matthew 1 and Luke 3.

(2) Quotation problems: Usually associated with Old Testament quotes in the New Testament and the quoting of extra-Biblical sources.

(3) Scientific problems: Usually associated with the origin of the universe; the creation of life; the creation of new life forms; Joshua's extended day; etc.

(4) Doctrinal problems: Usually associated with the person of God and or with one of the individuals within the Trinity.

(5) Ethical problems: Usually associated with issues such as the slaughter of apparently innocent people; God's use of Satan and evil to accomplish His purposes.

(6) Historical problems: Usually associated with the dating of events; the apparent numerical discrepancies contained in the Bible; the lack of harmonization in the historical narratives such as those found in the gospels etc.

Having listed the various general classifications, we now want to examine in more detail a specific example from several of the categories. Of course we do not have space here to cover every subject heading nor every example in the few categories. However, we shall discuss a few examples of what I think demonstrate the basic nature of alleged discrepancies.

Another type of discrepancy is quotation problems. An example of this is found in a comparison between Numbers 25:9 which states that 24,000 Jews fell in one day, and 1 Corinthians 10:8 which says that 23,000 fell on that particular day. Some argue vehemently that this proves that the Bible contains errors in its recording of facts and figures, although it is generally conceded that it is inerrant in its intent and purpose. Some suggest that there is a scribal error and thus the *autographa* (the original text written by Paul) agreed with Numbers 25:9 while others suggest that Moses was speaking in round numbers with the exact number being somewhere between 23 and 24 thousand. Thus Moses was rounding up whereas Paul was rounding down. On the other hand it may be that that Paul is not taking into account those who were slain by the judges themselves, whereas Moses is simply giving the total number. The point is, this is an alleged discrepancy based on the Bible's use of round numbers.

In addition, there are texts that appear to be in conflict with science. Rather than citing a specific scientific problem the real issue behind this category is that "the greatest conflict between people who consider themselves scientifically minded and people of faith is the question of miracles."[121] Supernatural miracles have always been a great stumbling block to the natural man and anti-supernaturalism is the driving presupposition of higher criticism liberal theologians.[122]

How then should we approach alleged discrepancies in this category? First, always recognize that the real problem is a philosophical problem that is behind any scientific approach. Those who discount the Bible because of its recorded miracles do so on a presupposed naturalism rather than on any true empirical evidence. In other words, it is impossible to empirically prove a universal absolute for to do so would require that one be present everywhere at all times in order to prove that such a universal statement is valid. Their denial of miracles is not based on empirical observation but a preconceived bias. The historical validity of miracles is not determined by empirical proof but by the

---

121   J. Robertson Mc Quilkin, *Understanding and Applying the Bible* (Moody Publishers; Rev Sub edition, 1992), 209.

122   Some of the most influential include: Ernst Troeltch, Hermann Samuel Reimarus, H. E. G. Paulus, C.H. Weisse, Albert Ritschel, George Wilhelm Friedrich Hegel, David Friedrich Strauss, Ferdinand Christian Baur, Adolf von Harnack, William Wrede, Martin Kahler and Rudolph Bultmann.

authority of God. We must remember that miracles were signs and were always related to the revelation of God's person and/or His purposes. Consequently they are not normative for human history. Most alleged scientific problems of the Bible may be adequately answered in the spite of the fact that the naturalist will continue to disbelieve the evidence.

Another type of apparent conflict in Scripture is doctrinal problems. Most apparent doctrinal problems are due to seemingly contradictory passages that seem to be asserting completely opposite theological ideas. However, doctrinal problems are easily resolved through developing a coherence of truth by the studying the Word of God and developing a proper hermeneutical method, not from one's presuppositions, but from the text of Scripture itself. Then we can create a consistent systematic theology in which we develop harmonized understanding of the proper meaning of a text and the author's intentions.

For example, we allow the New Testament to teach us how to interpret the Old Testament as we see how Christ and the Apostles interpreted the Old Testament. On the other hand there may be at times an element of mystery, an inability to understand due to our lack of knowledge, a text that presents an apparent problem. Such doctrinal problems may be due to our finitude and creatureliness (Isaiah 55:8). Or the doctrinal problems may be something we can apprehend but not fully comprehend, such as the doctrine of the Trinity and the incarnation of Christ. There may be times in which we must be content with a gap in our comprehension though ever pursuing to understand the text of Scripture. Therefore, doctrinal problems are only apparent which may be resolved with further study and the confidence that the Lord does not contradict Himself.

Another issue that is often raised, particularly by modernists, and Gay Theologians are so-called ethical problems. One of the most frequently asserted ethical problems is found in 1 Samuel 15:2-3. In this passage God is giving instructions to Israel to utterly destroy the entire Amalekite nation, commanding them to slaughter every man, woman, child, infant, ox, sheep, camel, and donkey and that God uses Israel as His means of carrying out this judgment. How should we respond? Is it morally right for God to use one race to destroy another? Is it morally right for God to destroy "innocent" people?

First, we ask the opponent to God's Word on what basis they call anything right or wrong? Are we to judge something based on how we feel? If so, then the one who says he feels the actions of God in this passage are wrong could just as well be refuted by saying, "Well, I feel God's actions are right." The consequence would be that there is no absolute standard for making an absolute judgment about anything being right or wrong. This is called a *reductio ad absurdum* response in which one assumes the opponent's methodology and demonstrates how it is absurd by taking it to its logical conclusion.

Second, if someone states that the actions of God in this passage are wrong because of other passages in Scripture, such as the command "Thou Shalt Not Kill" (Exodus 20:13), then the person is making an appeal to an authority that He himself does not accept or submit to. If he is then willing to submit to the authority of Scripture as an absolute standard by which we can make judgments then other passages may be appealed to such as when the Psalmist declares, "But our God is in the heavens: He hath done whatsoever He hath pleased" (Psalm 115:3).

Ultimately it is God who is judge and sovereign Lord and we do not have the right to question His actions. In addition, God's use of Israel was not because they were morally superior to the Amalekite nation but because they were the elect unto salvation. Like the Pharaoh and his army, the Amalekite nation were those who were "vessels of wrath prepared for destruction" for their abominable practices that included cultic sexual priests and human sacrifices (Romans 9:21-22). Israel was merely the tool for God's judgment at that particular occasion just as at other occasions God uses His elect angels to judge.

In addition, God reserves judgment and vengeance for Himself (Leviticus 19:18; Deuteronomy 32:35, 41, 43; Matthew 7). The command "Thou Shalt Not Kill" is applicable to personal vengeance and not civil justice, let alone God, who uses even non-Christian rulers as His agents of wrath (Romans 13:4). Finally, no one, not even a newborn child is ultimately "innocent" for we are all born sinners with the Adam's guilt imputed to us (Romans 5:12; Psalm 51:5). Therefore the apparent moral problem is more of a subjective sentiment and is based on a sinful appraisal rather than God's declarative indictment which will always be consistent with what and who He has revealed Himself to be.

Another issue which is often brought up are apparent historical problems from both within the Biblical text itself and as it relates to secular historical information. The following would be a representative example of the latter type:

> Many archeologists and scholars date Israel's Exodus from Egypt about 1290 B.C. This is based primarily on the reference in Exodus 1:11 to the city of Ramses as the site where the Israelite slaves worked. The assumption is that, if the city were named after Ramses the Great, then the Exodus must have taken place after 1300. However, 1 Kings 6:1 says that it was 480 years from the date of the Exodus to the commencement of Solomon's temple in 966 B.C., dating the Exodus around 1446 B.C. - 150 years earlier than supposed. Who is right? The Bible or these scholars?[123]

The late date for the Exodus as proposed by these archaeologists is used for liberal scholars who teach a Documentary Hypothesis for the origin of the five books of Moses (the Pentateuch / Torah). The Documentary Hypothesis, first articulated by Julius Wellhausen in the nineteenth century, theorizes that the Torah is actually the work of four authors edited into one collection of four books. These four authors or parties are identified primarily by the name that is used for God and by their writing style. This theory is used by many Gay Theology apologists to dismiss the authority and reliability of the Torah. [124]

When we are faced with this kind of alleged discrepancy we must follow two paths of exploration. The first is to determine the weight of Biblical evidence in favor of what it declares. In other words, does the Bible confirm in other places what it has stated in one place? In this case, the Bible does in Judges 11:26 and Acts 13:19-20. The second is to allow further historical and archeological evidences to either confirm or refute their former discoveries and claims. This is also true in the case we are looking at, for the evidence is mounting against the later dating of the Exodus. For example, literary analysis demonstrates that the Pentateuch could not have been written during the exile as the documentary hypothesis proposes. The covenant between God and

---

123   Norman Geisler & Ron Brooks, *When Skeptics Ask* (Wheaton: Victor Books, 1990), 171.

124   Patrick M. Chapman, *"Thou Shalt Not Love": What Evangelicals Really Say to Gays* (New York, NY: Haiduk Press, 2008), 99-102.

Israel follows, with appropriate modifications, the form of a suzerainty treaty, which defined the relationship between a Lord and a servant people. Suzerainty treaties of this type existed during the time that the Pentateuch purports to have been written. At the time that the documentarians theorize the Pentateuch's alleged constituent documents were written, this type of suzerainty treaty had not been used for centuries. It is unclear how the writers could have gained such accurate knowledge of an obsolete literary form or what their motivation could have been in using it. It is also unclear how the literary features of the suzerainty treaty could have survived a complex editing process by editors who were largely unaware of the form that they accidentally preserved. It is like supposing that a Shakespearean sonnet in Elizabethan English was the unwitting product when twentieth-century editors harmonized nineteenth-century documents from disparate sources. Therefore, it is more logical to assume that the Pentateuch was written more or less at the same time as latest events that it describes. It is a stretch of the imagination to theorize that a document, coalescing out of disparate accounts many centuries after the fact, could have accurately reproduced events and conditions several centuries in the past. However, it is quite reasonable to assume that Moses would have learned about suzerainty treaties during his royal education. There is nothing to prohibit the Holy Spirit from moving Moses to cast the covenant with God in that form just as the apostle Paul used the common epistle form of his day when he wrote to the New Covenant churches.[125]

In regard to archeological evidence, generally speaking given sufficient time it always refutes archeologist's former claims and endorses the Bible's claims. I believe then that any current discrepancy between archeologists and the Bible will sooner or later be resolved as support for the Bible continues to mount.[126]

---

125   For further reading see: Meredith Kline, *The Structure of Biblical Authority* (Grand Rapids, MI: Wm. B. Eerdmans Publishing Company, 1972.) Also, compare the literary form of "A Letter From Son to Father" written in the early third century A.D. with the writing form of Paul's epistles in C.K. Barret, *The New Testament Background: Selected Documents* (San Francisco, CA: Harper Collins Publishing, 1987), 41.

126   For more reading on this other archeological evidences that support the Bible historical reliability of the Bible see: Josh McDowell, *Evidence That Demands a Verdict* (Vol. 1) (Thomas Nelson; Revised edition, 1992), 65-78.

Liberalism, Textual Criticism and Gay Theology

The word "criticism" is from the Greek word *krinein* which means "to judge." There are various forms of textual criticism including Historical criticism, Form Criticism, Genre Criticism, Source Criticism, as well as Higher and Lower Textual Criticism.[127] On the one hand, all criticism which leads to better comprehension of the Bible is not to be rejected, and we have nothing to fear from genuine scientific research made in the attempt to discover truth. On the other hand, that form of Biblical criticism that seeks to elevate the autonomy of man from God and by seeking to destroy the integrity of the Bible as God's Word, and fails to recognize that the Bible is indeed a unique book is extremely dangerous and should be rejected as such. Criticism is not to be evaluated primarily by which type it is, but rather by the person who is conducting it. In other words, there is some valid contribution in each of the classifications of criticism. The other types must be evaluated in light of the person doing the work and the contribution they are making to conservative Biblical scholarship.

There have arisen many erroneous views of Scripture that have come out of "higher criticism" and these are commonly taught in liberal seminaries that deny the inerrancy, infallibility and consequently the ultimate authority of the Bible. One of the most common errors is the previously mentioned Documentary Hypothesis for the authorship of the Pentateuch. This erroneous view of the first five books of the Bible asserts that multiple sources were used by an editor who compiled the

---

127   Historical Criticism is the method of Scripture analysis that seeks to discover what actually happened in the Biblical narrative by studying the narrative, extra-biblical materials, and the possibility of miracles actually happening. An element of skepticism is inherent in this methodology. Form Criticism is the method of Scripture analysis that builds on source criticism in attempting to understand the collection and editing of the materials used to make up the books of the Bible. Genre criticism is the method of Scripture analysis that studies the style of communication of the text such as poetry, narrative, apocalyptic, and so forth in order to determine the rules of speech of the text. This type of criticism is concerned with not only what the text says, but what it also means and hence is tied to the science of hermeneutics. Source Criticism is an analytical attempt to discover the underlying sources used in writing the gospels. Higher Criticism is concerned with the matter of dating and authorship of Biblical books through studying the underlying sources used in the writing of Scripture. Lower Criticism is the method of Scripture analysis which is concerned with the text of Scripture through the study of the many variant readings of the many manuscripts.

Pentateuch and Mosaic authorship is absolutely denied. The motive for this view is that if we can deny that Moses received the law directly from God and subsequently wrote the first five books of the Bible we can then attribute political and oppressive patriarchal motives to the editors who picked and chose which texts, and portions of texts, they wished to keep and discard to serve their own self-serving agenda. The formula of sources that were supposedly used for the Pentateuch is as follows:

J = The hypothetical J document was characterized primarily by the use of 'Yahweh' [Jehovah] as God's name. This document also contains lively narratives of God's providence to Israel. This document is supposed to be the product of a scribe living in Solomon's time and was motivated by the desire to preserve the old traditions.

E = The hypothetical E document was characterized primarily by the use of 'Elohim' to designate God. This document contains lively stories about old heroes, and is supposed to be the product of the northern tribes, sort of the northern counterpart of J.

P = The hypothetical P document was the priestly code. It is a collection of laws and rituals and was supposed to have been drawn up by the priests during the Babylonian exile to preserve the priestly traditions that would have been lost during the captivity, when there was no Temple in which to carry them out.

D = The hypothetical D document, which is primarily Deuteronomy, was supposed to be the product of a religious reform movement during the reign of King Josiah.

The result is a "cut and paste" job that makes the authorship of the Pentateuch look something like this:

Genesis 1:1-2:4a belongs to P
Genesis 2:4b - 4:26 belongs to J
Genesis 5:1-28 belongs to P
Genesis 5:29 belongs to J

Genesis 5:30-32 belongs to P
Genesis 6:1-8 belongs to J
Genesis 6:9-22 belongs to P
Genesis 7:1-5, 7, 10, 12, 16b, 17b, 22a-23a; 8:2b-3a, 6-12, 13b, 20-22; 9:18-27 all belong to J

This pattern continues for each book of the Pentateuch. To think someone (without a computer) using manuscripts written on vellum (animal skins) could piece together such a monumental work as the Pentateuch in such a pattern is to stretch all credulity. It would be a miracle if someone could undertake such a monumental task and arrive at such a coherent document as the Pentateuch.

Sadly, there are theologians who argue against Gay Theology such as Robert A. J. Gagnon author of *The Bible And Homosexual Practice* who assert this same view of the Bible.[128] The problem with this is that he denies the Mosaic authorship of the Pentateuch, asserts a dual authorship of Isaiah and states that Paul didn't write all of the Pauline epistles. The logical question that must be asked is, "If the law didn't come through Moses then why should we believe what John says about Jesus?" (John 1:17) Clearly Jesus, the apostles and even the Pharisees believed that Moses (not the "Yahwist") wrote the first five books Bible as Jesus states, "…go, show yourself to the priest and present the offering that Moses commanded…" (Matthew 8:4) As much as I might appreciate many of the exegetical insights of Gagnon, his view of Scripture undermines rather than bolsters the historic Christian faith. Consequently, his book lacks the ability to strengthen the Church's assurance of the reliability and authority of the Word that prohibits any sexual act outside the relationship of a marriage between a man and a woman.

The epistemological root of this view of the Documentary Hypothesis (JEPD theory) is found in German rationalism that has infected our seminaries over the past century. This view of Scripture denies not only the Mosaic authorship of the Pentateuch but also asserts that there are dual authors for Isaiah. The very foundation of this line of thinking is flawed as it is based on an unjustifiable epistemology. The main criterion that these scholars use for detecting the contributing authors of the Torah is the various combinations of the name for God such as *elohim*

---

128   Robert A. J. Gagnon, *The Bible And Homosexual Practice* (Nashville, Abingdon Press, 2002), 43.

and YHWH. If we assume this methodology for the sake of argument and take it to its logical conclusion we find that it leads to absurdity. For example, in the New Testament we often find references to "Jesus," to "Christ," and to "Jesus Christ" and "Christ Jesus" in the same document, yet no one has offered up the theory that any of these documents were are the product of different sources being woven together by a redactor or editor. No scholar has offered the theory that there was a J tradition, in which Jesus was called 'Jesus,' and a C tradition, in which He was called 'Christ,' and that portions of documents that refer to 'Jesus Christ' are narratives that stem from both traditions that were editorially combined by a redactor. No one offers such a theory because it would be absurd. Yet they fail to see why it is not just as absurd to ascribe the J passages to one writer and the E passages to another. The terms "Christ" and "Elohim" are essentially titles and the names "Jesus" and "Yahweh" are personal names. Just as the Christians found out that the office of Messiah was uniquely and exclusively held by someone named "Jesus" so too Moses and the ancient Hebrews were informed in the Torah that the office of Elohim was uniquely and exclusively held by someone named "Yahweh." Dividing the Torah into source documents based on divine names is unjustified.

Chapter 4
The Hermeneutics of Liberal Gay and Queer Theology

As stated in the previous chapters, the contrast between Biblical Christianity and Gay Theology is an antithesis between two radically different worldviews built on two very different foundations and presuppositions for epistemology, metaphysics and ethics. Another way of thinking of a worldview is that of a *paradigm*. A paradigm is a set of assumptions, concepts, values, and practices that constitutes a way of viewing reality for an individual or a community (scientific, religious, ethnic, cultural or otherwise) that shares them. When a person or community experiences a dramatic change in its core assumptions and presuppositions this is referred to as a *paradigm shift*. We might also think of this as a form of *conversion*. However, there can also be minor adjustments within a paradigm in the peripheral beliefs of a worldview, such that the core or ultimate presuppositions remains the same while other more seemingly tangential beliefs are modified in order to be more consistent with the core belief and presupposed authority for the worldview.

Some of these peripheral beliefs are held to as sub-presuppositions; beliefs that act in conjunction with and in support of the ultimate presupposition. If a person's sub-presuppositions are found to be in conflict with their ultimate presupposition, the core and foundation of their worldview, a person may either adjust or modify the sub-presuppositions, the beliefs that are on the periphery of the web of belief, in order to make them more consistently in line with their core belief and faith commitment. However, a person may also decide to abandon their core belief or adjust it in order to align with their sub-presuppositions. In doing so, what was once thought of as being a peripheral belief has actually taken the place of being the core presupposition with the result being where they once had the dog wagging the tail, the tail is now wagging the dog.

An example of a peripheral belief becoming so dominant that it eventually replaces the original presupposition can be seen in how a theologian can hold on to a view of the autonomous freedom of the will of man that he is willing to adjust his view of Scripture, God and the gospel in order to do so. The result is a person can go from once upholding and defending the inerrancy and infallibility of Scripture as well as the freedom and omniscience of God to reducing his view of God and the Bible in order to maintain his view of the libertarian view of the freewill of man.[129] The chain of events in the paradigm shift goes like this - the theologian once contended for the historic Biblical view that God is omniscient and sovereign over all things and has given the Church a fully inspired, inerrant and infallible text. But, this person also wants to maintain a libertarian view of the freewill of man, such that man is not born in bondage to sin and at birth has the intellectual and moral freedom to choose or reject the gospel without any need for preceding grace or regeneration from the Holy Spirit. This view of freewill began as a peripheral belief in his worldview but then the theologian realized that if God is omniscient and already knows the choices of man then, even in the Arminian view of election and predestination, the will of man is not ultimately free (in a libertarian sense). In both the Arminian and Calvinist views the sinner is not free to choose Christ as his savior for God has already seen the choice he will make ahead of time and therefore his eternal destiny is predetermined before he is even born. Since the theologian wants to maintain his libertarian view of the freewill of man he then adjusts his view of God to assert that God only knows all things that may be possibly known, but that cannot include the free choices of man. Therefore, God acts in history are more like a superior chess player who, because of his vantage point, can continually adjust His strategies and actions in order accommodate the previously unknown choices of man. Man then, rather than God, becomes the determiner of history. God merely responds to the sovereign choices of man. The theologian then realizes that if man is totally free and that God does not interfere with the free choices of man (according to the libertarian view of the freewill) that it is not possible for God to provide

129   A libertarian view of the freewill of man contends that our choices are free from the determination or constraints of human nature and free from any predetermination by God. All "free will theists" hold that libertarian freedom is essential for moral responsibility, for if our choice is determined or caused by anything, including our own desires, they reason, it cannot properly be called a free choice. Libertarian freedom is, therefore, the freedom to act contrary to one's nature, predisposition and greatest desires.

man with an inerrant and infallible Bible. It is reasoned that "to err is human" and in order create such a book God would have to interfere with the libertarian freewill of man. In this scenario, what we have seen is the result of libertarian view of the freewill of man, the tail of a dog, becoming the functional ultimate presupposition of the worldview with the result that what was once claimed to be the core of the belief system (the Bible and the sovereignty of God) has been abandoned for the sake of what is essentially a man-centered theology. But this scenario is not a hypothetical scenario; this is in fact what has occurred in once-ortho-dox and evangelical apologists who now advocate a heretical doctrine known as "Open Theism."[130]

This same sort of event often occurs when people who profess faith in Jesus Christ and the Bible find themselves with a conflict between their same sex attractions and their faith. When they discover that their core belief in the Bible and the Christian faith are in conflict with their emotional longings and sexual desires, rather than submitting their sex-ual proclivities and inclinations to the revealed will of God, they adjust their view of Scripture and how it ought to be interpreted. They do so in order to accommodate their desire for relational and sexual intimacy with a member of their own biological gender. One of the primary pur-poses of this book is to provide a defense for the faith of those who may be tempted to do this very thing.

It is important then to understand that within the field of theological and Biblical exegesis the primary sub-presupposition of a paradigm is one's hermeneutical methodology. That is, a reader has a set of rules and hermeneutical axioms of how to translate, read, interpret and apply the text that is presupposed before coming to the text itself. Hermeneutics then acts as a particular prescription of a lens in a set of spectacles through which we read the Bible. The mindset of the faithful Christian then is to be willing to listen to the Scriptures and read them in such a way that one does not create conflict between one text and another. In doing so the reader has to be willing to adjust their understanding of the text so that there is greater harmony, clarity and consistency in understanding redemptive history and God's revealed will.

If, however, one does not believe that the Bible is the inspired inerrant and infallible Word of God the reader will presuppose and

---

130   For an excellent response to "Open Theism" see: John Frame, *No Other God: A Response to Open Theism* (P & R Publishing, 2001)

consequently see conflicts and errors within the text rather than conclude that perceived conflicts and contradictions are a result of misreading and misinterpreting the passage of Scripture. This is exactly what occurs when Gay Theology proponents twist the Scriptures in order to justify their theology and sexual behavior. As we shall see, Gay Theology pits the New Testament against the Old Testament, Jesus Christ against the Apostle Paul, and the attributes the work of the Holy Spirit to being the product of culturally primitive misogynistic men whose writings are to be condemned for their oppression of women and homosexuals.

In contrast to Gay Theology, if you hold to Biblical Christianity by faith you will believe that the Scriptures are the plenary inerrant, infallible inspired Word of God that have been providentially preserved throughout the ages. Consequently you will (if consistent) also believe that they are ultimately authoritative for all matters concerning doctrine and life. In doing so there will be an expectation of consistency within text in what it teaches about the nature of God, His saving work and what He requires of men concerning obedience to His revealed moral will. It will be recognized that there is a progression of revelation in which more light is given in each epoch in the succession of covenants throughout redemptive history from Genesis to Revelation. The faithful reader will also see that some ethical commands are only binding to particular individuals as determined from within the text, and that there may be a distinction between the specifics of a commandment and the moral principle of the commandment (the spirit of the law). The Bible as a whole will be understood as providing a consistent ethical system which has prescribed universal moral laws as well as a grand histor- ical narrative which culminates in the final revelation of Jesus Christ (Hebrews 1:1-2).

What you believe concerning the text affects the hermeneutical methodology that you use when reading the text. Your view of the Bible determines whether or not you have the expectation to find a consistent thread of doctrine and ethics through all of its various books as unfolded in redemptive history. If, however, the foundational Christian beliefs concerning the attributes of Scripture (inerrancy, infallibility, perspicui- ty and authority) are denied then the reader, not the Bible, is ultimately authoritative for how one is to live. Furthermore, from such a view of the Bible there arises an expectation in one's interpretation of the text to find inconsistency, contradictions and errors within the text of Scripture.

The consequence is that one's method for interpreting the Bible will be reduced to being no different than interpreting any other Ancient Near Eastern text, such as the Gilgamesh Epic. In fact, rather than seeing the Biblical text as that which depicts contemporary events of the author as antithetical to the various mythical religions you will interpret the Biblical stories as being derived from the same source as other religions of the Ancient Near East. The consequence of this is that the reader will then place himself, as a self-proclaimed enlightened modernist, to be the judge of Scripture as to how it ought to be understood and whether or not it ought to be applied to matters of faith and life in the modern era. This is in fact what Gay Theologians do in their conclusion that the sexual prohibitions of Leviticus 18 – 20 have nothing to do with same sex relationships and intercourse as we know them today.

Your view of the Bible then determines, in part, your hermeneutical methodology. In a circular fashion, your method of interpreting the Bible is both the result of your worldview and a key factor in forming and developing your worldview which determines your claims to knowledge (epistemology), your view of reality (metaphysics) and how you believe you ought to live (ethics). Since the days of Liberal Higher Criticism, it has become increasingly common, at least in academia, to read Scripture just like any other ancient writing. Consequently there is a lack of distinction between "general hermeneutics" in which a merely manmade document is read with an expectation to discover errors, inconsistencies and contradictions from "special hermeneutics" in which the reader and interpreter submits His understanding of God, doctrine and ethics to a consistent reading of the canon of Scripture.

In contrast, with a high view of Scripture and the development of an ever increasing consistent system of hermeneutics with subsequent doctrine and ethics from that system, there arises a more consistent Biblical Worldview with a distinctly Christian epistemology, metaphysic and ethics. In other words, if a Christian has a high view of Scripture the reader will be willing to constantly revise his understanding of God, ethics and various doctrines upon further and a more consistent humble reading of the text. Without a high view of Scripture and a willingness to submit all areas of one's doctrine and life to God's Word, then one's presupposed epistemological, metaphysical and ethical system (motivated by a particular political, philosophical, or sexual agenda that is opposed to Biblical Christianity) will determine the reading of the text rather than the text determining one's worldview.

The first task then in testing the arguments of a Gay Theology proponent is to examine his presupposed view of Scripture followed by an internal critique of his hermeneutical methodology. Having presented various examples of Gay Theologian's view of the Bible in the previous chapters, at this point we'll focus our attention on the various hermeneutical methodologies and schools of interpretation which stem from the presuppositions of the Gay Theological Worldview. Then we'll consider some basic principles in Biblical Hermeneutics that will be employed throughout this book.

Liberal Gay Theological Hermeneutics
and Queer Liberation Theology

As previously stated, there are three different theological spectrums under the umbrella of Gay Theology. The first is promoted by higher-critical Gay Theologians who deny the inerrancy and infallibility of Scripture. Another is led by Dispensational Gay Theology advocates that argue that monogamous same sex acts ought to be accepted within orthodox evangelical Christianity. Both of these groups hold to an essentialist understanding of same sex attractions, that it is a fixed and immutable trait. They also see the Bible as a gay-affirming text and insist that it has been misread, misinterpreted and misapplied by the Church for centuries.

Then there are Gay Theologians who advocate "Queer Theology" and assert that gender and sexual attractions are fluid and changeable who do not view the Bible as "gay friendly." They recognize that the text of Scripture cannot be interpreted in its own context to support any kind of homosexual behavior. Rather they insist that the Bible reflects its oppressive authors whose writing is the product of a culture that mistreated women and homosexuals. Therefore, in order to overcome the Bible's cultural influence in the church and society it must be "queered" (twisted, disrupted, deconstructed) in order to be used to support the Gay Theological worldview:

...queer theology draws upon scripture—that is, the Hebrew and Christian scriptures (also known as the First and Second Testaments)—in creative ways. Although scripture (and, in particular, the handful of "texts of terror" for LGBT people) traditionally has been used as a means of oppressing LGBT people, queer biblical scholars in recent years have not only countered these antiqueer readings with alternative readings, but they have also "taken back" or "reclaimed" the Bible by interpreting it positively and constructively from their own perspectives.[131]

This segment of the Gay Theological movement stems from Queer Theory proponents who argue that gender and sexuality are socially constructed. Their goal is not to assimilate into the society by arguing that homosexual behavior is acceptable in the culture as do the other Gay Theologies. Rather they aim to subvert it in order to become the dominate intellectual force that redefines all social norms of society in the state, family and the Church.[132] The philosophical roots of Queer Theology operates from the same foundation as postmodern Marxist and Feminist Liberation Theology that seeks to redefine the hermeneutical process, the nature of sin and salvation:

> Put briefly, liberation rests on three key premises: (1) theology must be culturally contextual; (2) sin is defined as structural oppression of others, not simply individual wrong doing; and (3) salvation is construed not as a reward in the afterlife but as the construction of a just society in this life.[133]

Queer Theology seeks to subvert the authority of the Bible and the Church by intentionally twisting ("queering") the text to produce a positive gay reading of any passage regardless of the author's original intent and meaning. It is a reader-centered approach to the Bible ("What

131   Patrick S. Cheng, *Radical Love: An Introduction to Queer Theology* (Seabury Books; 1 edition, 2011), 12.
132   For more reading on this subject, see Nikki Sullivan, *A Critical Introduction to Queer Theory* (New York, NY: New York University Press, 2003)
133   Michelle Wolkomir, *Be Not Deceived: The Sacred and Sexual Struggles of Gay and Ex-Gay Christian Men* (New Brunswick; Rutgers University Press, 2006), 22.

does the Bible mean to me?") and experience approach to reading the text ("How can I pour my experiences into the text?") with a specific political goal in mind:

> Queering is a method that I use theologically. As a verb 'to queer' means to spoil or interfere with. If the theological system is already spoiled [i.e. doesn't condone same-sex acts], spoiling the spoiled system to make it more inclusive of folks disenfranchised from Christianity is a good.[134]

In this hermeneutical process the Queer reader deconstructs the Bible (attacks and tears down the Bible as a perceived inherently wom-an-hating, misogynistic, heterosexist and homophobic text) and then reconstructs the text (making the text say and suit the queer reader's desired ends) so that the reader can use the text for his own political self-interests (feminism or "translesbiegaism"). In this methodology there is an intentional and admitted twisting ("queering") of the text, an attack on the Bible as the Word of God, in order to subvert the authority of the Scriptures and the authority of the Church that does not affirm same sex acts.

It should be noted that "queering" the Word of God to subvert the Church and lead people astray is not new. It was used by the serpent to deceive Eve (Genesis 3:1), when Satan tempted Jesus by twisting the Scriptures (Matthew 4) and Peter warned that in his day heretics did the same thing with the writings of the apostle Paul, "…which the untaught and unstable distort, as they do also the rest of the Scriptures, to their own destruction." Peter then exhorts the Church:

> You therefore, beloved, knowing this beforehand, be on your guard so that you are not carried away by the error of unprincipled men and fall from your own steadfastness, but grow in the grace and knowledge of our Lord and Savior Jesus Christ. To Him be the glory, both now and to the day of eternity. Amen (2 Peter 3:16-18).

---

134   *Robert E. Goss,* Queering Christ: Beyond Jesus Acted Up *(Eugene, OR: The Pilgrim Press, 2007), xiv.*

According to Queer Theologians, statements against same sex acts are to be construed as an act of violence against those who self-identify as gay, lesbian, transsexual and transgendered people. Queer hermeneutics begins by taking what is interpreted as a misogynistic and abusive patriarchal text and turning it against historical Christianity. It then associates the Queer political cause with a perceived marginalized class of people within the text. The next step is to reconstruct the Bible to not be about God redeeming lost people from their sin and its consequences (which includes forms social and political oppression) but rather as a means to use the identity of victim in order to obtain power for the Queer political-sexual-spiritual objective. Subsequently, these theologians not only dismiss the Bible as having any authority for sexual ethics today they will even go so far in their queering of the Bible as to assert that the Apostle John was Jesus' gay lover and that the Apostle Paul was a self-hating closet homosexual:

> Yes, I am convinced that Paul of Tarsus was a gay man, deeply repressed, self-loathing, rigid in denial, bound by the law that he hoped he could keep this thing, that he judged to be so unacceptable, totally under control, a control so profound that even Paul did not have to face this fact about himself.[135]

Yet, contrary to this view of the law the oppression of the weak, the poor, widows and the stranger is a reprehensible sin which is condemned in the Old Testament law (Exodus 22:21; 23:9). In fact it was one of the major complaints of the Lord against His people for which He sent them into exile (Amos 4:1). God also judged His people for tolerating sin such as idolatry (which is likened to sexual adultery) and for assimilating the immorality of the pagan nations. However, the ultimate "oppression" of God's people is not what they do to each other but what the devil and sin has done to them. Satan, sin and death are the ultimate slave masters as depicted in the New Testament and it is from this bondage that Christ has come to cleanse us and set us free (John 8:32-26; Romans 6:9, 14, 16-18; 1 Corinthians 6:11).

---

135   John Shelby Spong, *The Sins of Scripture* (San Francisco, CA: Harper Collins, 2005), 140.

Queer or Gay Liberation Theology operates from a misleading hermeneutical principle and it is a serious departure from the historic Christian faith. Rather than seeking to determine what the author's intent was in the text and what it meant to the original recipients and subsequently how it may be applied in other contexts, Gay Liberation Theology stemming from postmodernism takes a reader-centered approach as it seeks to use it as a means of accomplishing one's own end:

> With the rise of postmodernism we have seen a shift in biblical hermeneutics that considers the role of the reader in assigning meaning to the biblical text. Not only have we come to realize that readers make meaning of texts, but readers also bring a particular 'self' to the text which is shaped by a variety of factors such as race, ethnicity, gender, class, religious affiliations, socioeconomic standing, education, and we should add, sexual orientation.[136]

The conclusion from this line of reasoning is, if all reading of a text is an interpretation and we all bring to the text certain worldview assumptions and biases, then we cannot ever really know what the author intended in the text. All we are left then is a culture war of communities that fight to use the text as a weapon for their political-social ends. The problem with this line of thinking is that it presumes that no one and no community is willing to adjust their paradigm, their exegesis of a text or theological conclusions, upon further reading and harmonization of the Bible in what it teaches on any given subject. If this mentality is assumed, then the reader will never humbly submit to the text of Scripture and subsequently change his theological or ethical conclusions. Rather they will simply circle the wagon within their chosen theological community and attempt to change things politically by "acting up" (revolution) within the Church or society to force their views upon others. It is Queer Theology then that in acting out this worldview that does violence not only to the text of Scripture, but to the Church and the moral fabric of society. Gay or Queer Theology is not without its spiritual and political revolt against orthopraxy:

---

136   Robert E. Goss, *Queering Christ: Beyond Jesus Acted Up* (Eugene, OR: The Pilgrim Press, 2007), 204.

Initially gay/lesbian Jews and Christians formed interpretive communities to read the biblical texts to protect
themselves from religiously sanctioned violence, yet they
also brought their theological grid of affirming lesbian/gay
lives to take back the word in a cultural war over the Bible.
The Bible has become a hotly contested book in the culture
wars between the religious right and queers.[137]

This methodology then has absolutely no qualms with intentionally
reading into the text to suit one's own agenda:

My 'queerness' is a priori before my reading a biblical text,
and it is the horizon or social location from which I enter
into the text, queer it, and bring it into my own queer world
of meaning and empowered Christian practice... Queer
readers can become the subject of these narrative texts,
discovering within them their voices and agency. They
can reconfigure the texts or biblical figures imaginatively
within their lives because they already have come out and
found their sexuality as an original blessing from God.[138]

It then can read into any text and the life of any person in a Biblical
narrative as being a homosexual with some sort of fetish using a "gaydar" to read the Bible:

[Timothy] Koch speaks of using 'gay radar' or 'gaydar'
when approaching the text. I believe Koch's approach is
innovative and erotically titillating, but what is significant
is that he brings his life experiences as an out gay man
to engage the text by cruising and finding characters who
enrich his life in this erotic encounter. He read Elijah as a
'hairy leather-man' in 2 Kings 1:2-8 and reads other biblical texts in a similar fashion... He contextualizes Elijah
within the idea of the holy man attracted to men, wrapped
in goat skins..."[139]

137   Ibid.
138   Ibid, 215.
139   Ibid, 218.

Ecclesiastical authority subsequently comes not from God or the text of Scripture but from the Gay reading of the text:

> ...authoritative readings come not from the biblical text itself but from the assumptions that translesbigay (and other) readers bring to the text.[140]

While historical Liberation Theology rightly condemns a tradition that attempts to use God for its own ends, it wrongly denies God's definitive self-disclosure in biblical revelation. It then chooses "oppression" passages and ignores other portions of Scripture which teach the universal sinfulness of mankind and the need for repentance and forgiveness from a God who will judge sinners.

Gay Liberation Theology, following this methodology, selectively cites Scriptures while ignoring others as it chooses those passages that will fit into its presupposed sexual and political ideology. Its chief hermeneutic is to take the "oppression/freedom" motif of the Bible and remove from it the gospel that offers mankind freedom from the bondage to Satan, sin and death. Instead they turn the Bible into a Marxist notion of a social-economic story of the proletariat (the class of workers) fighting against the bourgeoisie (the upper class). For example, in this theology the Exodus is viewed purely in social-economic terms and Jesus becomes an exemplary martyr of the socially oppressed (like Ghandi and Martin Luther King Jr.) rather than the victor over Satan, sin and death.

Gay Liberation theologians believe that the orthodox doctrine of God tends to manipulate God in favor of the male patriarchal heterosexual social structure. Consequently they discount the human authors of the Scriptures as being part of the problem of the oppression conducted by patristic male heterosexuals. Instead they favor a feminist ideology over the authority of the Bible as John J. McNeill states, "Feminist Theology has thrown a sharp light on the fact that most traditional theologies were based exclusively on a patriarchal view of reality."[141] They then argue for a more "inclusive" translation/interpretation of the Bible which ceases to refer to God in the masculine or Christians as "sons" of God.

---

140   Ibid, 219.
141   John J. McNeill, *Taking A Chance On God* (Boston, MA: Bacon Press, 1996), xv.

Gay Liberation theologians then take the biblical notion of salvation from sin as being equated with the process of liberation from a perceived sense of oppression of sexual liberty and injustice towards homosexuals as an ontological and social class. Hence "sin" is re-defined in terms of man's inhumanity to man or the failure to condone non-exploitative and consensual same sex acts rather than a violation of God's law:

> Sin is the violation of mutuality and reciprocity, typically in the form of dominance and submission. Sin is the exercise of power over others that compromises their loving fully. We recognize sin as the institutionalized denial of equal opportunity, participation, and representation in the social order.[142]

Whether or not the Bible condones or condemns men having sex with other men is viewed as irrelevant for whatever the Scriptures teach on the subject is relegated to the human author's heterosexual and homophobic patriarchal worldview. Biblical redemptive history is then reduced to stories that illustrate this quest for a preconceived understanding of justice and human dignity defined apart from God's law. For example, Israel's liberation from Egypt in the Exodus and Jesus' life and death stand out as the prototypes for the contemporary human struggle for liberation. These biblical events signify the spiritual significance of the struggle for sexual liberation.

Gay Liberation theology equates loving your neighbor, as defined by Joseph Fletcher's *Situational Ethics*, with loving God in such a way that the two are not only inseparable but virtually indistinguishable including one's erotic behavior. In Gay Liberation Theology the Church and the world are no longer distinguished as they assert that the Church must allow itself to be inhabited and evangelized by the world. Joining in solidarity with the oppressed against the oppressors is an act of "conversion," and "evangelization" is redefined as announcing God's participation in the human struggle for justice and sexual liberty. Gay Liberation theologians consequently refer to fellow homosexuals as "brothers" whether or not they claim to be Christians simply because they self-identify as being gay.

---

142   Gary David Comstock, *Gay Theology Without Apology* (Cleveland, OH: Pilgrim Press, 1993), 130.

The meaning of Jesus' life in Gay liberation theology is reduced to an exemplary struggle for the poor, the outcast and the sexually oppressed. Consequently Jesus' incarnation is reinterpreted for, according to Gay Liberation Theology, He is not God in an ontological or metaphysical sense. Rather Jesus shows us the way to God as He reveals the way to become divine:

> Salvation comes from recognizing that the Sacred Presence within the human core of ourselves and all other creatures and learning to abandon the ego in favor of communion with that Presence. To the degree that we become fully human, we become divine; and to the degree that we realize our divinity, we become fully human. From my Christian perspective, as the first born of *many* sisters and brothers, Jesus led the way and made all this possible for the rest of us.[143]

The meaning of Jesus' incarnation is found in his total immersion in a historical situation of conflict and oppression. Gay Liberation Theology destroys the one true Gospel in that it asserts that the uniqueness of Jesus' cross lies not in the fact that God, at a particular point in space and time, experienced the suffering intrinsic to man's sinfulness in order to provide a way of redemption. Hence Jesus' death is not a vicarious offering on behalf of mankind who deserve God's wrath. Rather, according to their view, Jesus' death is unique because He historicizes in exemplary fashion the suffering experienced by God in all the crosses of the oppressed.

It is commendable that Gay Liberation Theology has compassion for the poor and it rightly teaches that Christians should not remain passive and indifferent to their plight, man's inhumanity to man is sin and deserves the judgment of God as well as Christian resistance. However, if the message preached is merely about a temporal social liberation then all that has taken place is a short term relief from the aliments of this world all the while the sinner is still bound for a Christ-less eternity in hell.

---

143   Virginia Ramey Mollenkott, *Omnigender: A Trans-religious Approach* (Cleveland, OH: The Pilgrim Progress, 2007), 95.

While Gay Liberation Theology rightly exposes the fact of oppression in society and that there are oppressors and the oppressed, the Bible teaches that sin causes alienation from God that confronts both the oppressor and the oppressed. Furthermore, Gay Liberation Theology threatens to politicize the gospel to the point that minority groups, the poor and various marginalized sectors of society are offered a solution that could be provided with or without Jesus Christ. While it rightly urges Christians to take seriously the social and political impact of Jesus' life and death it fails to ground His uniqueness in identity as the God-man. It claims He is different from us by degree, not by kind, and that His cross is the climax of his vicarious identification with suffering mankind rather than a substitutionary death offered on our behalf to turn away the wrath of God and triumph over sin, death, and the devil. A theology of the cross which isolates Jesus' death from its particular place in God's redemptive-history is powerless to bring us to God and offer a true hope for freedom from the bondage to sin.

Gay Liberation Theology and Egalitarianism

One of the consequences of the errors of Gay Liberation Theology is its quest for radical egalitarianism in society. This is due to a failure to distinguish between ontological equality and the economic differences in the roles that God has assigned for men and women. These distinctions are ordained by God to reflect the ontological equality and economic distinctions within the Godhead of the Father, Son and Holy Spirit. Ironically, in a movement that claims to be about equality and diversity they fail to see how God Himself has provided us with the perfect model for this endeavor. This is due to, by and large, an over reaction to brutish hyperpatriarcialism. The consequence is that they falsely assert that in order to be truly equal men and women must be able to have equal authority and responsibility in every segment of society. This is rooted in Feminist Liberation Theology which fails to recognize that even within the Trinitarian Godhead there is an ontological equality (John 10:30) between the Father, Son and Holy Spirit and yet Jesus is subordinate in His role in history and the Spirit is subordinate to the Father and the Son. Hence, the Father is the head of Jesus and Jesus is the head of the husband and the husband is the head of the wife (1 Corinthians 11:3). The subordination of roles does not mean a decrease in equality for both the husband and the wife are created in the image of God (Genesis 1:27). In the Bible women are not subordinate to men in general. Rather, a daughter is subordinate to her father and a wife is subordinate to her husband. Also, headship requires taking responsibility so that one cannot be the head without also being responsible for all that is under your sphere of responsibility. This is why the human race and all of creation are fallen in Adam and not in Eve (Romans 5:14-19; 1 Corinthians 15:22, 45). Adam failed in his responsibility to take dominion in the garden and protect his wife from the serpent. Then, rather than obeying God, he allowed her to be deceived and then followed her in the deception by eating from that which was forbidden by the Word of God. In his economic headship Adam had both the authority and the responsibility to care for his wife and all that was placed under him by God.

Feminist Liberation Theology rejects the God given roles for husbands and wives in an overreaction to an ungodly conduct of brutish men who want authority without responsibility. The Feminist Liberationist insists on an egalitarianism which confuses ontological equality with economic equality and rejects role-subordination. As a consequence they insist that women be able to act like men in leading the Church, the home and the state. Yet, God has assigned these roles and responsibilities to men (1 Timothy 2:11-14) and whenever women are in these roles it is because men are not accepting and acting rightly in their God given responsibilities (Judges 4:9). Hence feminism is the result of the sin of men. It is tolerated and promoted by lazy and brutish men who wish to abdicate their responsibilities under God.

Gay Theology follows in the footsteps of feminism and egalitarianism in that it seeks to undermine the distinctions of men and women. It is a confusion of the sexes in a fallen world of chaos and disorder. When Gay Theology apologists assume a Liberation Theology and Feminism's understanding of gender roles they tend to speak of homosexuals as a social class with an innate biological identity as if they were an ethnicity. They then affiliate the rejection of an ethical system that promotes men having sex with other men or women with women as a form of social-economic oppression. The result is the accusation against Christians who maintain that men having sex with other men is a sin as being hateful and oppressive. Anyone who takes a stance against

Gay Theology are then falsely accused of being hateful and oppressive because they view the arguments through the lens of a pro-Gay-Feminist-Liberation-Theology. They then respond to the arguments emotionally rather than intellectually without any solid Biblical, theological or philosophical grounds. Even worse, they will then assert that Christians that uphold Biblical gender roles as being no better than those who kidnapped Africans and brought them to the United States to be forced into slavery.

The truth is that the Biblical Christian will neither hate homosexuals, fornicators or adulterers. They will simply refuse to classify a life of habitual sin (however much it is in line with one's sexual preferences) with people who are born of a particular ethnic heritage. Furthermore, the mistreatment of people of African decent in America was not from a solid exegesis and application of Scripture. Rather it was due to a Darwinian view of man which asserts that dark skinned people, including the natives of South America, are of a different race than those of European descent and are on lower stage of evolution as Thomas Huxley wrote:

> No rational man, cognizant of the facts, believes that the average Negro is the equal, still less the superior, of the white man. And if this be true, it is simply incredible that, when all his disabilities are removed, and our prognathous relative has a fair field and no favor, as well as no oppressor, he will be able to compete successfully with his bigger-brained and smaller-jawed rival, in a contest which is to be carried on by thoughts and not by bites.[144]

This doctrine infiltrated and was tolerated in liberalizing seminaries and consequently was promoted in many denominations and churches in the south. Hence "racism" (a misnomer) is due to Darwinism infiltrating the church - not a Biblical view of ethnicities. A Biblical view of man that recognizes that all ethnicities are of the same race which all stem from one man and are appointed where they live by God (Acts 17:26). In Christ and in the Church there is no distinction between Jew or Gentle before God (Galatians 3:28). Therefore to treat darker skinned people as less than lighter skinned people is a theological heresy as well

144   *Lay Sermons, Addresses, and Reviews*, 1871.

as a moral sin. To equate the rejection of the morality of men having sex with other men with a Darwinian oppression of black people is a false analogy unless people are asserting that homosexuals are a lower stage of evolution than heterosexuals.

Having said this, the Church does need to see that homosexuals have been treated sinfully and this cannot be denied. I have on many occasions heard pastors from the pulpit, not just ignorant lay people, make jokes about homosexuals and those dying from A.I.D.S. It is a sin to beat or mistreat prostitutes, fornicators, adulterers and homosexuals or to look the other way when they are being mistreated. Jesus loved sinners of all kinds but He did not tolerate their sin but rather commanded them to "go and sin no more" (John 8:11).

Restorative Hermeneutics vs. Trajectory Hermeneutics

One of the main features of the hermeneutical lens through which Gay Theology proponents view the Bible is that of Trajectory Hermeneutics. This is a method of reading the Bible within postmodernism which asserts that the text can have different meanings as a culture unfolds, advances, and matures in a social Darwinian fashion. In other words, rather than viewing the Bible as an unfolding of God's redemptive plan in which the affects of the fall are incrementally overturned, the stories of the Bible reflect an ever increasing social evolutionary advancement such that supposed patriarchal attitudes, the oppressive social status of slavery, and the sexual taboos that were common amongst the patriarchs become passé during the time of Jesus and the apostles. The conclusion of the Gay Theology Worldview is that if the Church follows this per-ceived trajectory into our modern times, the homogenital acts that were once a taboo become acceptable due to cultural changes and advances in understanding of psychology, biology and the social sciences as R.D. Weekly asserts:

> Most modern Christians understand that Scripture must be interpreted in light of the culture surrounding the writers and the original readers. My goodness, if we didn't recog-nize this fact, the abolitionist movement never would have gotten off of the ground, for slavery had biblical support in

both Testaments! It isn't that God has changed throughout the generations. The culture has.[145]

In contrast to this Trajectory Hermeneutic, the Bible provides us with a Redemptive-Restorative view of history. In this view we see a progressive restoration of mankind and society in an incremental fashion in which God's law turns back the tide of the consequences of the fall. The law of God places greater restrictions on slavery, it limits the power of priests and kings within their jurisdiction, and restores God's intended design for marriage as well as hedges in the boundaries for sexual relationships towards that of the pre-fall condition. But, what the law could not do in the Old Testament, being weak and incomplete, the New Covenant accomplishes through the power of the gospel, for both Jews and Gentiles. The result of Redemptive-Restorative History is that the abuses of slavery is reduced giving greater liberty, the roles of husbands and wives are corrected to reflect the economic Trinity, and the boundaries of sexual expression is restored to that of the pre-fall condition to a one man and one woman marriage.

Biblical Christianity and Gay Theology have antithetical presuppositions concerning the nature and authority of Scripture and they have two radically opposing views of the progress of redemptive history in which we see the incremental unfolding of God's plan for salvation. This is due to the expectations that they have when they approach the text. When a Gay Liberation Theologian reads the law of God and what it states concerning the status of slaves and women and it does not meet his expectations he then judges the Bible as not being given by a just and holy God. Rather they conclude that it is the product of an oppressive patriarchal culture.

In contrast, the God-honoring Christian will approach the text with an attitude of humility rather than expect the law of God to meet his preconceived notions of what it ought to prohibit and require of God's people. In doing so he will not read the Old Testament with an expectation of God's covenant laws to meet his own criteria. He will recognize they were not a means to create a utopian society. Rather, the humble Christian will recognize that God as a gentle Father and Shepherd guided His people by slowly fencing them in from their fallen state in their family and culture. In doing so, the Lord leads His people towards a

145   R.D. Weekly, *Homosexianity* (Judah First Ministries, 2009), 83.

more ideal standard incrementally throughout redemptive history rather than radically uprooting them from their immature state of understanding of how they ought to live. In other words, as His children the Lord patiently dealt with them as a toddler who continues to defecate in his diapers rather than expecting them to act as mature Christian adults. Consequently God's law condescended to their primitive state and it frequently acquiesced to the hardness of their heart, their stiffed necks and their stubborn will and yet to some degree it hedged in their sinful traits and it reigned in their sinful and abusive behaviors.

The Old Testament law was an incremental step in its restorative nature that fell short of that found in the New Covenant. In doing so, it held in place many social effects of the fall in place (such as slavery) rather than immediately putting them to an end that would have caused more immediate harm than good. When an object has punctured and penetrated a person's eyeball you may intuitively want to pull it out. But to do so would cause more harm than good. Instead, what is needed is to hold the object in place to prevent further movement and injury to the eye until the injured person can receive proper medical treatment from a doctor. In a similar fashion, the Old Testament law kept many things in place until the arrival of the Great Physician who bore our injuries and heals us of our diseases through the Gospel (Isaiah 53:5). This healing is not only the judicial forgiveness of our sin, but it also by implication heals and restores the results of the fall in our personal lives, our family, the Church and society. This is the restorative trajectory of the Gospel and the Kingdom of God such that Paul can appeal to Philemon to receive his runaway slave Onesimus as a brother not by compulsion (a law) but by grace and of a free will (Philemon 14-16).

But many Gay Liberation Theology advocates reject the teachings of the Apostle Paul for, according to them, he advocated slavery when he (or the supposedly "Pauline party" who wrote in his name) instructed Christians to submit to their masters. But what if the Roman Empire or the Church had immediately outlawed slavery? Would that of done more harm than good, like immediately pulling out a foreign object in one's eye? Estimates for the prevalence of slavery in the Roman Empire vary but as much as one third of the population in the first century may have been slaves. The life of a slave under Roman law was without a doubt very harsh as they could be legally treated as subhuman by today's standards. In fact, boyslaves could lawfully be anally penetrated by their masters without any loss of social status of the slave master.[146] However, if slavery would have been suddenly ended then one third of the empire would have been unemployed, homeless, and destitute causing the economy to collapse with the result of crippling all of society. A more gracious approach then is to change the nature of the relationship of people through the preaching of the gospel. The result of the gospel is that masters and slaves begin to see one another as brothers as taught by the Old Testament law. This would require humane treatment and a mutually supportive relationship without leading the culture and society into chaos as Paul wrote:

> Slaves, be obedient to those who are your masters according to the flesh, with fear and trembling, in the sincerity of your heart, as to Christ; not by way of eye service, as men-pleasers, but as slaves of Christ, doing the will of God from the heart. With good will render service, as to the Lord, and not to men, knowing that whatever good thing each one does, this he will receive back from the Lord, whether slave or free. And masters, do the same things to them, and give up threatening, knowing that both their Master and yours is in heaven, and there is no partiality with Him (Ephesians 6:5-9).

The reason Paul gives this exhortation is not because slavery is good. In fact he uses slavery negatively as a metaphor for sin and being an idolater (Romans 6; Galatians 4:8). Rather, his greater concern is for the gospel and therefore he states, "All who are under the yoke as slaves are to regard their own masters as worthy of all honor so that the name of God and our doctrine will not be spoken against" (1 Timothy 6:1). Nevertheless, the Apostle Paul also urged slaves to gain their freedom if possible, "Were you called while a slave? Do not worry about it; but if you are able also to become free, rather do that... You were bought with a price; do not become slaves of men" (1 Corinthians 7:21, 23). In the mean time, as the Kingdom of God spread it would penetrate society as yeast permeates dough with the result that it would bring a

---

146   Craig A. Williams, *Roman Homosexuality* (Oxford University Press, USA; 2 edition, 2010), 16.

gradual, peaceful and incremental end to slavery if they followed and obey Paul's public exhortation to Philemon:

> I appeal to you for my child Onesimus, whom I have begotten in my imprisonment, who formerly was useless to you, but now is useful both to you and to me. I have sent him back to you in person, that is, sending my very heart, whom I wished to keep with me, so that on your behalf he might minister to me in my imprisonment for the gospel; but without your consent I did not want to do anything, so that your goodness would not be, in effect, by compulsion but of your own free will. For perhaps he was for this reason separated from you for a while, that you would have him back forever, no longer as a slave, but more than a slave, a beloved brother, especially to me, but how much more to you, both in the flesh and in the Lord. If then you regard me a partner, accept him as you would me. (Philemon 10-17)

A Biblical Christian Worldview approach to Scripture will see the history of redemption as God's story of restoration in which the Lord incrementally leads His people through a series of covenants in which there is greater liberty and restoration from the fall into sin. In doing so, the reader will recognize that the Old Covenant and its law does not present the ideal culture intended by God nor a plan for an immediate utopian society. Rather, in incremental baby steps it leads His people towards the full restoration found in the New Covenant, which finds its full culmination in the eschaton. Therefore, when interpreting the Old Testament Law the faithful Christian will recognize the weakness of the Old Covenant laws, which were better than the laws of the surrounding nations, provided greater liberty. Yet they still fell short of the greater liberty that we find in the New Covenant.

What is important to note is that the Scriptures in redemptive history do provide for us a trajectory of redemption away from the fall into sin towards the ideal in the New Covenant. But the working out of that ideal was not accomplished during the time of the apostles, for slavery was still in place. However, the implications of the gospel when lived out in the hearts of the believer would by its very nature eventually change society by changing the heart and minds of a culture.

The Status Of Women, Slaves and Marriage
in Redemptive History

One of the most important things to keep in mind when reading the historical accounts of the lives of the Old Testament saints is that they are being called out of the surrounding culture. They are commanded to live according to God's law which is to a great degree antithetical to that of the surrounding nations. However, when we do not see the Old Testament saints living up to the expectations of God's law (especially before it was written) we also see that the Lord is often patient with His people. He calls them "righteous" because of their faith even when they do things which are morally shocking to the modern reader.

Consequently at times we see the lives of many saints in the Old Testament reflects the more oppressive patriarchal nature of the surrounding culture. For example, due to a lack of faith and living in fear of Pharaoh we see Abraham convincing his wife to say that she is his sister which puts her moral virtue in great danger (Genesis 12:13). A modern reader might read such an account and judge the Bible as being the product of an oppressive patriarchal culture because we do not see God chastising him for doing so. However, to do so is to fail to see the patient character of God as He is progressing the faith of Abraham from the first time he is given covenant promises in Genesis 12 until he is finally matured in his faith in chapter 22. It is only then that he is willing to obey God in offering up his son Isaac as we read, "By faith Abraham, when he was tested, offered up Isaac, and he who had received the promises was offering up his only begotten son" (Hebrews 11:17). Just as a parent does not rebuke a child for every act of immaturity, so too the Lord doesn't rebuke Abram for his actions. In fact, He even goes so far as to bless Abram (later renamed Abraham) not only when he is faithful but also at times despite his unfaithfulness in order to show Abram His graciousness. This is clearly seen when Abram leaves Egypt with the wealth provided by Pharaoh even though the blessing is subsequent to his lying to Pharaoh concerning the identity of his wife Sarai (later renamed Sarah) (Genesis 12:16).

Likewise, we might be shocked when we read of Lot offering his daughters as a sexual substitute to the men of Sodom and then read that the Bible refers to him as "righteous Lot" (Genesis 19:8; 2 Peter 2:7). What must be kept in mind is that both Abraham and Lot are "righteous" not because everything they do is good or virtuous, but because of their faith. The Lord often is very patient towards His people in their sin as He does not chastise us every time we sin or do something foolishly, even when we blatantly violate the explicit commands of His law. In fact, sometimes the Lord allows us to violate the law and then suffer the subsequent repercussions of it such as when David and Solomon violate the prohibition of kings multiplying wives as the law commands, "He shall not multiply wives for himself, or else his heart will turn away; nor shall he greatly increase silver and gold for himself" (Deuteronomy 17:17).

Rather than rebuke David and Solomon for accumulating wives by sending him a prophet, such as when He sent the prophet Nathan to rebuke David, we see Solomon suffering the consequences explicitly stated in the law:

> He [Solomon] had seven hundred wives, princesses, and three hundred concubines, and his wives turned his heart away. For when Solomon was old, his wives turned his heart away after other gods; and his heart was not wholly devoted to the LORD his God, as the heart of David his father had been (1 Kings 11:3-4).

Yet, Gay Theology proponents would have us to believe that polygamy was an acceptable alternative form of marriage in the Old Testament.[147] Nothing could be further from the truth. Polygamy was a practice of the surrounding cultures, particularly of the kings, who used the multiplying of women as a demonstration of wealth and prowess.[148] While the Lord tolerated it to some extent and it was legal, as was divorce, it was neither the ideal nor according to God's original design. Both divorce and polygamy were tolerated and regulated because of the hardness of the people's heart (Matthew 19:8). But both in the Old

---

147   Rick Brentlinger, *Gay Christian 101 - Spiritual Self-Defense For Gay Christians* (2007), 19.; R.D. Weekly, *Homosexianity* (Judah First Ministries, 2009), 74-75.
148   Douglas Wilson, *Fidelity* (Moscow, ID: Canon Press, 1999), 93.

and New Testaments those in leadership, kings and elders, were called to lead by example by being a one-woman man (Deuteronomy 17:17; 1 Timothy 3:2).

Another important factor to keep in mind when we read what to our modern culture is a mistreatment of women by the Old Testament saints, is that the Bible isn't necessarily giving an approval of their actions just because it records it. The historical narratives tell us what happened but they are not an endorsement of everything that did happen whether it is the mistreatment of women, an act of adultery or when Abram takes his wife's handmade (at Sarah's urging) to bear a child. While we do not see the Lord rebuking Abram for his actions, like Solomon's sinful polygamy we see the negative outcome of his actions:

> After Abram had lived ten years in the land of Canaan, Abram's wife Sarai took Hagar the Egyptian, her maid, and gave her to her husband Abram as his wife. He went in to Hagar, and she conceived; and when she saw that she had conceived, her mistress was despised in her sight (Genesis 16:3-4).

Probably one of the most troubling factors in the Old Testament law was the legality of selling one's daughter into slavery (Exodus 21:7). What must be kept in mind is that there was a hierarchy of laws such that if one followed the "weightier matters of the law" of justice and mercy (Matthew 23:23) then they would not need to be concerned with the lawful boundaries of this law. A loving father would not treat his neighbor, let alone his daughter, in this fashion (Leviticus 19:18). But during times of famine and destitution, sometimes people sold their children into slavery in order to pay off debts (2 Kings 4:1).

As previously stated, not everything that was legal is necessarily good. These laws are equivalent to a modern law stating, "If you get drunk, don't drink and drive." Such a law is not an endorsement of drunkenness or selling one's children into slavery. They only set boundaries as to how far one could go and they attempt to keep the negative consequences of such an action to a minimum.

Such laws were also an accommodation to the economic and social conditions of the day. This is a weakness of the Old Testament Law in that they were not exhaustive in their redemptive and restorative nature.

The law fell short of providing a sufficient sacrifice for sin (Hebrews 10:4), and a lasting and permanent prophet, priest and king. Its redemptive and restorative nature fell short of the New Covenant in which we find Christ the perfect sacrifice as well as prophet (Hebrews 1:1-2), priest (Hebrews 11:7) and King of kings (Revelation 19:16) whose law of love exceeds the restorative nature of the Old Testament law. The law of Christ returns the conduct and status of believers to that of the pre-fallen condition as the ideal as it furthers the trajectory of God's order by freeing slaves, putting an end to polygamy and severely restricting divorce (Matthew 19:5).

Therefore, contrary to the assertions of Gay Theology proponents, the trajectory of the Bible and the New Covenant is not an open ended "liberty" without a specific *telos*, or goal, in mind. Rather, the pre-fallen created order is what the New Covenant has in mind as the ideal for God's people with a few notable exceptions which must await the coming of the New Heavens and New Earth. The New Covenant is restorative in granting greater freedom from sin, greater liberty to wives, greater responsibility to husbands and it restores marriage to its original order of a one man and one woman covenant. It also prohibits sex outside of the one-man and one-woman relationship including fornication, adultery and homogenital same sex acts (1 Corinthians 6:9).

Chapter 5
The Hermeneutics of Dispensational Gay Theology

One of the most deceptive forms of Gay Theology is that which comes under the guise of conservative Bible-believing evangelicalism. It begins by promoting itself as being a seemingly conservative Christian movement which makes it deceptively palatable to orthodox evangelical churches. It then borrows all the exegetical arguments of liberal higher-critical Gay Theology for the so-called "clobber" passages and then adds a wholesale rejection of the law of God. The justification for doing so is the hermeneutical system of Dispensationalism that has become popular in the American evangelical Christian church over the past century. Most evangelicals tend to think of Dispensationalism as an eschatological system with a particular view of Premillennialism. Consequently many do not strictly adhere to its tenets when they read much of the Bible. The fact is Dispensationalism is a hermeneutical system that has serious implications for understanding Redemptive-History in the Old and New Testaments, the structure of God's covenants with man, the identity of Israel and the Church and Christian ethics.[149] Thankfully, most evangelical Dispensationalists have not taken it to its logical conclusion as did its early founders that led to the Lordship Salvation controversy.[150]

Dispensationalism is a theoretical antinomian system and when Dispensationalists (such as John Mac Arthur) don't fall into its traps it is because they are distancing themselves from their historical and theological roots and are primarily maintaining their "dispensational" title for the sake of their Premillennial eschatology. When I say that Dispensationalism is antinomian, I do not mean that its founders were

---

149   For a refutation of the Dispensational hermeneutic I recommend reading: Keith A. Mathison, *Dispensationalism: Rightly Dividing the People of God?* (Phillipsburg, NJ: P & R Publishing, 1995); *John H. Gerstner and R.C. Sproul, Wrongly Dividing the Word of Truth: A Critique of Dispensationalism* 3rd Edition (Nicene Council, 2009).
150   For a helpful critique of this see Michael Horton, *Christ The Lord* (Grand Rapids, MI: Baker Book House, 1992).

advocates of going out sinning so that grace might abound as if they were advocate, "Why not do evil that good may come?" (Romans 3:8). In other words, Dispensationalists don't advocate extreme libertinism. In fact, a great many theoretical antinomians are known for their advocacy of holiness, and yet not one that is determined or measured by God's holy law. Rather, theoretical antinomians teach that Christians are not bound by any of the precepts of any of the laws given to Moses at Mount Sinai. For example, Dispensationalist Norman Geisler asserts the following:

> Jesus did away with the Old Testament laws. First of all, it is true that Jesus came to fulfill the righteous demands of the Old Testament law (Matt. 5:17-18; see also Rom. 10:2-3). He did not do away with it by destroying, but rather by fulfilling it... The law was in place only until Christ came. The 'law was put in charge to lead us to Christ that we might be justified by faith. But 'now that faith has come, we are no longer under the supervision of the law' (Gal. 3:24-25). Here too it is clear that Paul includes the moral law of Moses because he refers to it as what was given at Sinai some 430 years after the promise was confirmed to the patriarch (v. 17). And what was given at Sinai were the Ten Commandments which contain the very heart and basis of the moral law. So the whole law of Moses which was given to Israel was taken away by Christ.[151]

As we shall see, Dispensational Gay Theology advocates assert the very same "all or nothing" argument regarding the binding nature of the Holiness Code as does Norman Geisler:

> The law of Moses was a unit. There were civil aspects to the moral law and moral dimensions of the civil law. Indeed, there were moral aspects of the ceremonial law, as is evident from the fact that it was said to reflect God's holiness (Lev. 11:45). Surely God's holiness is not an amoral issue. Nowhere in the Old Testament is there a separation

---

151   Norman Geisler, *Christian Ethics* (Grand Rapids, MI: Baker Book House, 1989), 204, 206-207.

made between the moral and the civil or between the civil and the ceremonial aspects of Moses' law. And nowhere in the Old Testament does it declare that only the ceremonial aspects of the law of Moses have been abolished... The Ten Commandments have faded away. Paul told the Corinthians that what 'was engraved in letters on stone [the Ten Commandments]" has faded away since Christ (2 Cor. 3:7, 11).[152]

Yet elsewhere he states:

Jesus changed the dietary laws of the Old Testament (Mark 7:18; Acts 10:12), but the moral prohibitions against homosexuality are repeated in the New Testament (Rom. 1:26-27; 1 Cor. 6:9; 1 Tim. 1:10; Jude 7).[153]

Clearly there is some sort of cognitive dissonance taking place here. How can Jesus and Paul set aside the entirety of the Law of Moses "as a unit" including the Ten Commandments in an "all or nothing" fashion and then turn around and repeat the moral aspects of the law by citing the Old Testament in the New Testament? If the first assertion were true, any time Paul or one of the other apostles quoted the Decalogue as the standard for Christian conduct all the Christians would have to do is reply to Paul, "But you said there is no obligation to obey any of the Law of Moses!"

In contrast to theoretical antinomians, the Reformers saw three proper uses of the moral precepts of Moses' law. Some of which were still required to be obeyed as an act of faith in response to the grace given at Calvary and others that had become obsolete as of the Lutheran Formula of Concord (Article VI) states:

The Law has been given to men for three reasons: 1) to maintain external discipline against unruly and disobedient men, 2) to lead men to a knowledge of their sin, 3) after they are reborn, and although the flesh still inheres in them, to give them on that account a definite rule according to which they should pattern and regulate their entire life.

152   Ibid, 205, 206.
153   Ibid, 262.

In other words, the "third use of the law" makes the law's moral standards the normative standard for ethical conduct. In this sense, the moral principles of the law remain binding on Christians, even though we are "not under the law" as the apostle Paul states. Likewise, John Calvin understood the third use of the law is "the principle use" as he wrote:

> The third use of the Law (being also the principal use, and more closely connected with its proper end) has respect to believers in whose hearts the Spirit of God already flourishes and reigns. For although the Law is written and engraven on their hearts by the finger of God, that is, although they are so influenced and actuated by the Spirit, that they desire to obey God, there are two ways in which they still profit in the Law. For it is the best instrument for enabling them daily to learn with greater truth and certainty what that will of the Lord is which they aspire to follow, and to confirm them in this knowledge; just as a servant who desires with all his soul to approve himself to his master, must still observe, and be careful to ascertain his master's dispositions, that he may comport himself in accommodation to them. Let none of us deem ourselves exempt from this necessity, for none have as yet attained to such a degree of wisdom, as that they may not, by the daily instruction of the Law, advance to a purer knowledge of the Divine will. Then, because we need not doctrine merely, but exhortation also, the servant of God will derive this further advantage from the Law: by frequently meditating upon it, he will be excited to obedience, and confirmed in it, and so drawn away from the slippery paths of sin. In this way must the saints press onward...[154]

Dispensational theoretical antinomianism is, in essence, a denial of the historical Protestant third use of the law as taught by its leaders which was passed down to the Church through the historic Reformed confessions. Yet they falsely teach that such use of the law is contrary to the Protestant doctrine of justification and that they are the ones who

154   John Calvin, *Institutes of the Christian Religion* (2.7.12)

are their true heirs of the Reformation when they assert that the moral commandments provided in the law given at Sinai are not binding on Christians.[155] Dispensational Antinomianism is the teaching that the relevance of the law was confined entirely to the Mosaic dispensation, the era between Israel's exodus from Egypt and the resurrection of Jesus Christ (referred to by dispensationalist writers as the *dispensation of law*). The whole law, according to Dispensational antinomianism, has been abrogated in our so-called *dispensation of grace*. Some even go so far as to assert that even New Testament passages with a legal emphasis, such as the Sermon on the Mount, are assigned to other dispensations.

This type of antinomianism is found in differing degrees in the teachings of Lewis Sperry Chafer (founder of Dallas Theological Seminary), Charles Ryrie and Zane Hodges who were its chief proponents that sparked the Lordship Salvation controversy.[156] The consequence of this theology naturally lead to what is referred to as "No-lordship antinomianism" which asserts submission to the Lordship of Christ and sanctification is an optional choice of the Christian. It is asserted that a believer can have an assurance of his salvation if he has chosen Jesus as his savior even though he has not chosen to submit to His lordship. According to this theology, made popular by the Scofield Reference Bible, such a person who has not chosen to take the second step is classified as a "carnal Christian" who, while he may lose certain rewards in heaven, can nonetheless have a genuine assurance of pardon of his sin even though he continues to live as an unbeliever.[157] This version of antinomianism argues that if salvation is by grace through faith alone, then nothing can possibly be viewed as required of the Christian or essential to salvation if it involves the believer's obedience to the

---

155   Zane Hodges, *Absolutely Free!* (Grand Rapids, MI: Zondervan Publishing House, 1989), 20.
156   Lewis Sperry Chafer's book *Grace* and Zane Hodges' book *Absolutely Free!* are the classic works that assert this view.
157   In a footnote on 1 Corinthians 2:14 the Scofield Reference Bible states, "Paul divides men into three classes: *psuchikos,* 'of the senses' (Jas. iii:15; Jude 19), or 'natural,' i.e. the Adamic man, unrenewed through the new birth (John iii:3, 5); *pneumatikos,* 'spiritual,' i.e., the renewed man as Spirit-filled and walking in the Spirit in full communion with God (Eph. v:18-20); and *sarkikos,* 'carnal,' 'fleshly,' i.e. the renewed man, who walking 'after the flesh,' remains a babe in Christ (I Cor. iii:1-4)." (Scofield Reference Bible, Second Edition pp. 1213, 1214, Cf. Rom. 8:5-15). See also Charles Ryrie, *Balancing the Christian Life,* (Moody Press, 1969), 170.

law, even Christ's commandments, or submission to Christ's lordship. Faith, according to this theology, is nothing more than mere assent to the facts of the gospel. In this view, sanctification itself is seen as legal in character and is therefore regarded as an optional, additional step of the Christian life. The thesis of this theology is that the sole purpose of the law is to show us our need for salvation and then point us to Christ. Once it has accomplished this task, the law serves no further purpose for the Christian. This is the exact form of theoretical antinomianism advocated by so-called "evangelical" Gay Theology proponents. In fact, they cite Dispensational authors such as Charles Ryrie who argued that a person is saved even if he, like Judas, rejects Christ:

> Normally one who has believed can be described as a believer; that is, one who continues to believe. But… a believer may come to the place of not believing, and yet God will not disown him, since He cannot disown himself.[158]

Likewise, Zane Hodges (contradicting Paul in 1 Corinthians 6:9-10) states that a woman caught in adultery can continue in her sin and still be saved:

> If the mind of man recoils from so daring an expression of divine generosity, it recoils from the Gospel itself. If it should be thought necessary to add some intrinsic guarantee that the woman would not continue her illicit liaisons – and according to Jesus she was currently engaged in one (4:18!) – that guarantee would add to the words of our Lord himself. The result could only be a false Gospel.[159]

In contrast to theoretical antinomian Dispensationalism that does not require repentance and obedience to the law of God as part of the call of the Gospel, John Calvin rightly taught, "For when this topic is rightly understood it will better appear how man is justified by faith alone, and simple pardon; nevertheless actual holiness of life, so to speak, is not separated from the imputation of righteousness."[160] John Gerstner there-

---

158   Charles Ryrie, *So Great A Salvation* (Moody Publishers, 1997), 41.
159   Zane Hodges, *The Gospel Under Siege* (Redencion Viva; 1st edition, 1981), 48.
160   John Calvin, *Institutes of the Christian Religion*, Vol. III 3.1.

fore rightly presents the historical, Biblical and evangelical position in regards to the relationship between faith and works as follows:

> ... good works may be said to be a condition for obtaining salvation in that they inevitably accompany genuine faith. Good works, while a necessary complement of true faith, are never the meritorious grounds of justification, or acceptance before God. From the essential truth that no sinner in himself can merit salvation, the antinomian draws the erroneous conclusion that good works need not even accompany faith in the saint. The question is not whether good works are necessary to salvation, but in what way are they necessary. As the inevitable outworking of saving faith, they are necessary for salvation. As the meritorious ground of justification, they are not necessary or acceptable.[161]

This is why the faithful Christian must heed Paul's warnings to those who would seek to call themselves Christians yet dismiss God's law. He clearly warned that those who dismiss the moral law of the Holiness Code, such as a man having sex with his father's wife (Leviticus 18:8 cf. 1 Corinthians 5:1) or a man having sex with another man (Leviticus 18:22 cf. 1 Corinthians 6:9), "shall not inherit the Kingdom of God" (1 Corinthians 6:10).

While the majority of Gay Theology advocates are self-identified liberals and Liberation Theology proponents, the Dispensational Gay Theology advocates claim to be conservative in their view of the Bible. They then go on to dismiss all of the Old Testament as having any normative application for Christian ethics today because they misconstrue what Paul meant when he said that Christians are "not under law but under grace." They then go on to essentially lift all the Gay Theology arguments from Liberal Scripture-denying theologians. This includes the assertions that David and Jonathan were gay lovers, Ruth and Naomi were lesbians, that Jesus approved of men having sex with boys as young as fourteen years old, and Paul's statements regarding same sex acts only refer to exploitative pederasty, male prostitution or ritualistic cultic

---

161   John Gerstner, *Wrongly Dividing the Word of Truth: A Critique of Dispensationalism* (Brentwood, TN: Wolgemuth & Hyatt Publishers, Inc., 1991), 210.

sex acts. In fact, as we shall later see some advocates of Gay Theology, following their own hermeneutic consistently, even go so far as to assert that Jesus Himself engaged in same sex acts, the disciple John being his lover and that He had sex with a boy prostitute just before His arrest.

At the time of writing this book, there are two authors who attempt to present the exact same interpretation of the Bible as Liberal Gay Theologians and yet under the guise of Bible-believing evangelicalism. The first is Rich Brentlinger author of *Gay Christian 101 - Spiritual Self-Defense For Gay Christians* who claims:

> This book is a conversation about the Bible and homosexuality. It is an honest attempt by a born again, conservative, Bible-believing evangelical, gay Christian, to present historical and scriptural viewpoints which nongay Christians may not have considered.[162]

The second proponent of such a view is R.D. Weekly, author of *Homosexianity* for which Justin Lee, the founder of the Gay Christian Network, wrote the forward to his book. The problem with their arguments is in order to agree with their conclusions all of the New Testament quotations the Old Testament law, including the Holiness Code, which are applied to Gentile Christians and the warning to them not to repeat the error of their Old Testament forefathers or return to their former Gentile ways of living must be ignored.

What must be noted is that Rick Brentlinger and R.D. Weekly present themselves as being evangelicals whose interpretation ought to be accepted within the pail of orthodoxy, which makes them more deceptive than the liberals. While it may seem that Brentlinger and Weekly have the same ultimate faith commitment and presuppositions as this author, what we shall see is that the sub-presuppositions that form the lens through which they read the Scriptures are what leads them to view the Bible through a Gay Theological Worldview. Like the Jehovah's Witness or the Mormon who will likewise claim to uphold a conservative view of the Scriptures, it is their hermeneutical methodology that is heavily influenced by their personal experiences that leads them into error. The result is that while they may cite Scriptures to support their

162   Rick Brentlinger, *Gay Christian 101 - Spiritual Self-Defense For Gay Christians* (2007), 1.

arguments, if the reader actually takes the time to read the texts in their context they will find that these Gay Theologians either mistakenly or intentionally seek to mislead their readers. The irony is, these authors repeatedly exhort their readers to read the pertinent texts in their context yet they have failed to do so.

In addition to advocating the Dispensational hermeneutic, Rick Brentlinger also employs a set of axioms which cannot be supported by the apostolic methodology of interpreting and applying the Old Testament law. The first and often repeated one is "Scripture cannot mean now, what it did not mean then."[163] Brentlinger argues that "antigay" theologians are reading back into the text of Scripture from the modern era what was not believed or taught when the text of Scripture was originally written. Hence, according to Brentlinger and many other Gay Theology apologists, those who assert that same-sex unions are prohibited by Scripture are reading the Bible anachronistically.

What these Gay Theology apologists fail to observe in the apostolic method of interpreting the Bible is that though the specifics of a rule or commandment may be given in a particular redemptive-historical and cultural setting, the underlying ethical principle is applied universally by the New Testament authors. In other words, while a text of Scripture may have but one meaning it may have multiple applications. What must be discerned then is the intent of the law (sometimes referred to as the *principle* or *spirit* of the law) and then determine how we may apply a modern application of that same ethical principle even though some of the specifics of the situation have changed. This is accomplished by carefully following the apostolic example provided for us in the New Testament. Hence, the reader and interpreter need to learn not only how to *interpret* the text in its original historical context but also learn how to *apply* the principle of text in other social and cultural contexts.[164]

The apostle Paul does this when he upholds the Old Testament law in the New Covenant era, with the exception of those which were mere types and shadows or served to make a distinction between Jew and Gentile, and applies the principle of the law even though the specifics of

163   Rick Brentlinger, *Gay Christian 101 - Spiritual Self-Defense For Gay Christians* (2007), 11.
164   Although I don't agree with all his conclusions, for a helpful book on this approach to interpreting and applying the Scriptures in a cross-cultural context see William J. Webb, *Slave, Women & Homosexuals: Exploring the Hermeneutics of Cultural Analysis* (Downers Grove, IL: IVP Academic, 2001).

the situation have changed. One example is when he cites Deuteronomy 25:4 which was given to Jews in Palestine under the Old Covenant and applies the law to Gentile Christians, outside of Palestine in the New Covenant:

> Am I not free? Am I not an apostle? Have I not seen Jesus our Lord? Are you not my work in the Lord? If to others I am not an apostle, at least I am to you; for you are the seal of my apostleship in the Lord. My defense to those who examine me is this: Do we not have a right to eat and drink? Do we not have a right to take along a believing wife, even as the rest of the apostles and the brothers of the Lord and Cephas? Or do only Barnabas and I not have a right to refrain from working? Who at any time serves as a soldier at his own expense? Who plants a vineyard and does not eat the fruit of it? Or who tends a flock and does not use the milk of the flock? I am not speaking these things according to human judgment, am I? Or does not the Law also say these things? For it is written in the Law of Moses, 'You shall not muzzle the ox while he is threshing' God is not concerned about oxen, is He? Or is He speaking altogether for our sake? Yes, for our sake it was written, because the plowman ought to plow in hope, and the thresher to thresh in hope of sharing the crops. If we sowed spiritual things in you, is it too much if we reap material things from you? (1 Corinthians 9:1-11)

Contrary to the Dispensational hermeneutic and Brentlinger, the apostles applied the law given by Moses as a requirement to be followed and obeyed by Christians. This requirement to obey the law was not in order to merit their justification. Instead, just as the Old Testament saints were to obey in response to the good news of being delivered from slavery in Egypt by YHWH, so too the Christian's obedience was to be in response to the freedom from slavery to sin given them in Christ who is YHWH in the flesh (Exodus 20:2; Romans 6:17-18). Paul and the other apostles uphold the Old Testament laws in a New Testament context because while the immediate context has changed the ethical principle of the law remains. In fact, even though many of the Christians he addressed were ethnically Gentile, he asserts that the Jews in Israel in the Old Testament were their forefathers (1 Corinthians 10:1).

The Apostle Paul in the above cited text makes an argument from the lesser to the greater in that if the law required a mere animal to be able to benefit materially and be sustained from his labor in plowing a field then how much more so for a servant of God who is planting spiritual seed and harvest a spiritual crop in his progression of the Kingdom of God (1 Corinthians 9:9; 1 Timothy 5:18). If Brentlinger's supposition is correct then the Corinthian believers should have responded to Paul, "The law refers to oxen, not ministers of the Gospel. Scripture cannot mean now, what it did not mean then! Besides, we cannot be required to obey the law because we are not Jews and we do not live in the land in which it was applied. Besides all that, we are not under the law but under grace!"

The classic Dispensational view of the law and gospel is that the Mosaic Covenant was a system of a works based relationship with God and that the entire purpose of law was to demonstrate the impossibility of maintaining that relationship by doing good needs. Subsequently, under the New Covenant the believer is now under grace and the binding nature of those laws has come to an end. Therefore, according to this view, the Christian is not required to obey the laws of the Old Testament as these laws are now relegated to the realm of good advice and optional for the Christian. As one Dispensationalist put it: "He [Paul] is suggesting a wholesale shift in jurisdictions, from a period where the law had jurisdiction to a new period where the spirit reigns. The age of the church has rendered the law inoperative."[165]

But the error of this teaching lies in the fact that the salvation was never expected to be earned or merited, it was always by grace through faith and the atonement for sin was always accomplished by the sacrifice of the lamb as prescribed in God's law. Both God's moral standard and the gospel that atones for sin through the blood of another, by means of substitutionary atonement, are found in the law. One cannot pit the gospel against the law without pitting the law against itself. Israel's failure was not that they didn't maintain their relationship with YHWH their savior by meriting His favor, but rather that they lacked faith and

---

165   Wayne Strickland, "The Inauguration of the Law of Christ with The Gospel of Christ: A Dispensational View" *The Law, The Gospel, And the Modern Christian: Five Views* (Grand Rapids, MI: Zondervan Publishing House, 1993), 259.

consequently sought after the gods of the surrounding nations because they were a stiff necked people with hardened hearts. Obedience to God's commandments was always to be in response to their redemption already accomplished when He had redeemed them from slavery in the land of Egypt as well as their future hope and He had provided a typological means of atoning for sin in the sacrificial system. What the Lord then required of them was to be a faithful bride and not whore after other gods.

Therefore, the apostles can justly require that Christians be obedient to the law of God with the exception of those which were mere types and shadows or had the purpose of distinguishing Jews from Gentiles such as circumcision and food laws (Acts 10:10-15; Colossians 2:16-17). The typological commandments and the stipulations that made a distinction between Jew and Gentile was the pedagogical use of the law which Paul refers to when he states, "Therefore the Law has become our tutor to lead us to Christ, so that we may be justified by faith. But now that faith has come, we are no longer under a tutor" (Galatians 3:24-25).

In other words, as Wilhelmus á Brakel (1635–1711) so brilliantly argued, it was not what we usually call the "moral Law" which was a pedagogue but rather what is commonly referred to as the "ceremonial Law" which was the tutor.[166] The historical context of Paul's epistles to the Romans and the Galatians is a response to the Pharisees' heresy which insisted that in order to be saved the Gentiles must be circumcised and keep the Jewish distinctives of the law (Acts 15:1). This is why Paul had to confront Peter to his face for siding with the Pharisees and not eating with the Gentiles because:

> When I saw that they were not straightforward about the truth of the gospel, I said to Cephas in the presence of all, "If you, being a Jew, live like the Gentiles and not like the Jews, how is it that you compel the Gentiles to live like Jews?" (Galatians 2:14)

To "live as a Jew" is not a reference to the requiring Gentiles to obey the law's prohibitions of particular sexual behaviors (adultery,

---

166   Wilhelmus á Brakel, *The Christian's Reasonable Service* (Vol. 3) (Phillipsburg, NJ: Soli Deo Gloria Pub., 1984), 62-63.

fornication, incest, same-sex acts, bestiality). Rather, it is a reference to those elements of the law that made a distinction between Jew and Gentile, namely circumcision, the food laws and the old feast days. This is why Paul and the other apostles could cite commandments from both Leviticus and Deuteronomy as the standard for moral conduct and require that Gentiles be obedient to the non-Jewish distinctives of the law given at Sinai including Gentile believers at Corinth and Ephesus (Ephesians 6:2).

Contrary to theoretical antinomianism of Dispensationalism, the New Covenant has requirements for believers, especially for leaders of the Church as Paul states, "In this case, moreover, it is *required* of stewards that one be found trustworthy" (1 Corinthians 4:2). Likewise, the apostle James warns that few should seek to be teachers in the Church because they will be held accountable for their actions and undergo a stricter judgment (James 3:1).

Obedience to the moral requirements of the law and personal sacrifice is and has always been the believer's response of faith to the salvation provided through the redemptive acts of God (Exodus 20:2; Romans 12:1-2). In fact, the requirements for the Gentiles laid down by the apostles at the Jerusalem Council parallel the moral requirements of Leviticus 17-18. At this council it was decided that Gentile Christians did not need to be circumcised in order to be saved and yet they were given repeated laws from the Old Testament that were required to obeyed in order to maintain peace in the Church:

> For it has seemed good to the Holy Spirit and to us to lay on you no greater burden than these requirements: that you abstain from what has been sacrificed to idols, and from blood, and from what has been strangled, and from sexual immorality. If you keep yourselves from these, you will do well. Farewell (Acts 15:28-29, ESV).

In James' immediately preceding sermon (Acts 15:16-17) he cites several "prophets" in which he conflates Jeremiah 12:15 ("After this I will return"), Amos 9:11 ("and will rebuild the tabernacle of David, which has fallen down; I will rebuild its ruins, and I will set it up"), Zechariah 8:20-23/Amos 9:12 ("So that the rest of mankind may seek the LORD, even all the Gentiles who are called by My name, says the LORD who does all these things") with Zechariah 2:14-17 (Acts 15:16-17).[167] James is applying these prophecies to the inclusion of the Gentiles. The subsequent requirements given to them from the apostles in Acts 15:28-29 likewise include the requirements given to the Gentiles in the Old Testament in their inclusion into the covenant. These included the prohibition of meat sacrificed to idol sacrifices (Leviticus 17:7-9), blood laws (Leviticus 17:10-12), eating strangled animals (Leviticus 17:13-16), and *porneia* which is an all inclusive term that would refer to the sexual laws (Leviticus 18:1-19) such as not marrying within the prohibited degrees of consanguinity, not marrying within the prohibited degrees of affinity, not engaging in marital relations during the monthly period, and the sexual sins of adultery, same sex acts and bestiality in Acts 15:20-23.[168]

To argue then that the Christian faith is only about relationship and does not also require us to be obedient to His law is contrary to the Scriptures. The law of God is not a cruel task master to the one who lives and is justified by faith and this was true of the Old Testament:

> Then the LORD your God will prosper you abundantly in all the work of your hand, in the offspring of your body and in the offspring of your cattle and in the produce of your ground, for the LORD will again rejoice over you for good, just as He rejoiced over your fathers; if you obey the LORD your God to keep His commandments and His statutes which are written in this book of the law, if you turn to the LORD your God with all your heart and soul. **For this commandment which I command you today is not too difficult for you**, nor is it out of reach (Deuteronomy 30:9-11).

It is the same in the New Testament:

---

167   Phillip G. Kayser, "The Laws of Acts 15" (Unpublished Paper, ©Copyright by Phillip G. Kayser 2007)

168   Richard Davidson likewise states, "In Acts 15 the four categories of prohibitions imposed of Gentile Christians are precisely the same four, in the same order, as those listed in Lev 17-18 that are applicable to the stranger, with the final prohibition, *porneia*, summarizing the illicit activities described in Lev 18." *Flame of Yahweh: Sexuality in the Old Testament* (Peabody, MA: Hendriksen Publishing, 2007), 155.

> By this we know that we love the children of God when
> we love God and observe His commandments. For this is
> the love of God, that we keep His commandments; **and
> His commandments are not burdensome** (1 John 5:2-3).

The moral requirements of the law only seems like a burden when you ignore the fact that the law also provided a means for atoning for sin through the blood of the lamb which typified Christ or when you are trying to merit your salvation. Now that the Lamb of God has come, through Christ's onetime act of death and resurrection, the life of the believer is now one of walking by the power of the Holy Spirit who enables the believer to obey the commandments of God by faith and from the heart. The law is only a burden or a cruel task master when you seek to earn or merit your salvation and, in so doing, establish a righteousness for yourself through the Old Covenant sacrificial system of circumcision and feast days as did the Pharisees (Romans 10:3). What the Gentiles were freed from at the Council of Jerusalem was from having to undergo circumcision, which understandably would have been a burden – especially for adult males!

Brentlinger argues, however, that the Jerusalem Council freed Gentiles from having to keep the moral commands of the Old Testament law, despite the fact that the text itself laid down a list of moral commandments derived from the law:

> Although the first century church, in Acts 15, settled the
> issue of whether Christians must keep the Law of Moses
> to be right with God (they decided we are not required to
> keep the Law), since nongay Christians in the twenty-first
> century keep trying to put gay Christians back under the
> Law, the question of sexual orientation is one which the
> church still wrestles.[169]

This radical Dispensational discontinuity of the Old and New Covenants blinds Brentlinger from seeing what is clearly stated in Acts

---

169   Rick Brentlinger, *Gay Christian 101 - Spiritual Self-Defense For Gay Christians* (2007), 10-11.

15 and yet he claims to being doing so on the basis of the "Grammatical Historical Hermeneutic." In fact, he then says:

> We would not, for example, take promises about Palestine, given to Israel, during the Exodus, and claim them for Gentiles in the twenty-first century. The individual books of scripture were written in different historical contexts to address then current situations.[170]

Far from being a "Grammatical Historical Hermeneutic," it is purely a Dispensational hermeneutic which asserts that *none* the laws with their warnings or promises given to the saints of the Old Testament are to be applied to Christians in the New Covenant. Brentlinger then goes further to assert that to apply any of Leviticus 18-20, commonly referred to as the Holiness Code, to the New Covenant Christian, who is also an ethnic Gentile, is to bring them "under the law" as the Pharisees did in the first century:

> Modern Pharisees operate the same way ancient Pharisees operated in Jesus' day. They compel gay Christians to keep part of the Levitical Holiness Code to be right with God while refusing to keep the Levitical Holiness Code themselves.[171]

There are two things that need to be addressed here. First, Brentlinger presents a wrong view of the Pharisees when he states:

> Pharisees had rules about food, rules about gathering firewood and rules about clothing. Their lives were bound up in legalistic rules which are not found in scripture.[172]

Contrary to his assertion, the Old Testament Scriptures themselves had rules concerning food (Leviticus chapter 11; Deuteronomy chapter 14) gathering firewood on the Sabbath (Numbers 15:32) and clothing (Leviticus 19:19). Second, the error of the Pharisees was that they did

---

170   Ibid, 5.
171   Ibid, 29.
172   Rick Brentlinger, *Gay Christian 101 - Spiritual Self-Defense For Gay Christians* (2007), 20.

not seek to obey the law by faith. In fact, what we repeatedly find in all forms of Gay theology is a caricature of Jesus and his view of the law as well as that of the Pharisees.

Jesus, The Pharisees and the Law of God

Much of this chapter is focused on the law of God; what it is, how to interpret it, apply it and the continuities and discontinuities of the law of God as standard for ethical behavior for the believer in the New Covenant. We have also looked at the inherent antinomianism of both Liberal Gay Theology and Dispensational Gay Theology. In addition to understanding the law, we also need to rightly understand Jesus Christ's view of the law and the errors of the Pharisees. Whenever Christians cite the Old Testament commandments Gay Dispensationalists typically assert that the New Covenant has made the commandments of the Old Testament null and void, eliminating the need for Christians today to obey them. They then put forth of a caricature of Jesus as one who was all about grace, not about obeying the law and even assert that He disobeyed the law by violating the fourth commandment or that He overruled the penal sanction for adultery. They then put forth a carica-ture of Pharisees as legalists who were supposedly sticklers for the law and assert that anyone who seeks to uphold the law of God as a moral standard for Christian living are modern Pharisees:

> Modern Pharisees operate the same way ancient Pharisees operated in Jesus' day. They compel gay Christians to keep part of the Levitical Holiness Code to be right with God while refusing to keep the Levitical Holiness Code themselves.[173]

In the same way, R. D. Weekly refers to people who are believe that same-sex acts are sinful regardless of the circumstance as Pharisees.[174] In response to these characterizations we need to examine the life and teaching of the Pharisees, Jesus' condemnation of them and then see how Jesus upheld and taught the law's true meaning so that His follow-ers would know how to obey it.

---

173   Ibid, 20.
174   R.D. Weekly, *Homosexianity* (Judah First Ministries, 2009), 124-125.

The Life and Teaching of the Pharisees

Although the Pharisees believed in the Word of God they tended to err by granting equal authority to oral tradition (Matthew 9:14; 15:1-9; 23:5; 23:16, 23, Mark 7:1-23; Luke 11:42), which is forbidden by God's law (Deuteronomy 4:2). Some of these traditions were later codified in the Talmud. While some may think of the Pharisees as legalists the truth is that since they nullified God's Law with their traditions they were actually antinomian (or, against God's law). It is Jesus who truly upheld and defended God's law, not the Pharisees, which is why He said:

> Do not think that I came to abolish the Law or the Prophets; I did not come to abolish but to fulfill. For truly I say to you, until heaven and earth pass away, not the smallest letter or stroke shall pass from the Law until all is accomplished. Whoever then annuls one of the least of these commandments, and teaches others to do the same, shall be called least in the kingdom of heaven; but whoever keeps and teaches them, he shall be called great in the kingdom of heaven. For I say to you that unless your righteousness surpasses that of the scribes and Pharisees, you will not enter the kingdom of heaven (Matthew 5:17-20).

In this passage Jesus, from the meaning of the word "fulfill" and the structure of the text, is clearly contrasting His a correct understanding of the law with the tradition of the Pharisees. In doing so He upholds, or fulfills, the law which is contrasted with the Pharisees' nullifying the law with their traditions. This construction of this passage is similar to many of the Proverbs in which we see a synonymous parallelism in which a concept is emphasized by being repeated (Proverbs 1:5) and two principles are contrasted in an antithetical parallelism (Proverbs 3:1).[175] Twice Jesus states that He did not come to destroy the Law and the Prophets (synonymous parallelism) and then in antithesis to such an assertion He states He came to fulfill (uphold) the Law and the Prophets. However the structure of the text goes on to show that Jesus' use of antithesis and synthesis does not end with verse 17. Is it by His teaching

---

175   For example, Proverbs 3:1 states, "My Son, do not forget my teaching. But let your heart keep my commandments."

and demonstration of the Law and constitutes His fulfillment of the law. In fact, the point of the text is that someone cannot be a true teacher of the law without also being a doer of the law.

In continuing the antithetical structure of verse 17 Jesus goes on to state what the opposite of what He is declaring in verse 19a, "Whosoever therefore shall break one of these least commandments, and shall teach men so, he shall be called the least in the kingdom of heaven." The person who breaks (not merely endorses breaking) the law shall be least in the Kingdom. In antithesis He goes on to state in 19b, "but whosoever shall do and teach them, the same shall be called great in the kingdom of heaven." The person who does (not merely endorses) the Law shall be great in the kingdom.

When Jesus states, "…but whoever keeps and teaches them, he shall be called great in the kingdom of heaven" (Matthew 5:19b) He is referring to none other than Himself. He is the antithesis of the Pharisees who break and teach others to break the law. He then goes on to state, "For I say to you that unless your righteousness surpasses that of the scribes and Pharisees, you will not enter the kingdom of heaven" (Matthew 5:20). The one that has a righteousness that exceeds the righteousness of the scribes and Pharisees is He who does and teaches them. Ultimately this is none other than Christ Himself. The rest of Matthew chapter 5 is an exposition (application) of the Law to its fullest:

> You have heard that the ancients were told, "You shall not commit murder" and "Whoever commits murder shall be liable to the court." But I say to you that everyone who is angry with his brother shall be guilty before the court; and whoever says to his brother, "You good-for-nothing," shall be guilty before the supreme court; and whoever says, "You fool," shall be guilty enough to go into the fiery hell (Matthew 5:21-22).

Already from the context of the passage we see that Jesus has stated in a synonymous fashion it is "whosoever shall do and teach them" is what He is doing in the Sermon on the Mount and in His entire ministry. He is doing and teaching the moral principles of the law "as an example" to follow (1 Timothy 1:16).

In addition, the term "fulfilled" (Greek: *plerosai* an aorist active infinitive of *plero*) does not refer to a prophetic culmination of an Old Testament prophecy. Rather it means "to do to the fullest." Consider for example Paul's use of the same term elsewhere in a similar context regarding how one handles the Scriptures:

> Of this church I was made a minister according to the stewardship from God bestowed on me for your benefit, that I might *fully carry out* (*plerosai*) the preaching of the word of God (Colossians 1:25).

The structure of the passage and context of *plerosai* in Matthew 5:17 clearly demonstrates that Jesus is contrasting what He is doing in His teaching on the law with those who break the law and teach others to do so as well by following their traditions. Obeying God's law in sincerity rather than hypocrisy is "a righteousness that exceeds the righteousness of the scribes and Pharisees." He is contrasting what He is teaching and doing with what others are teaching and doing. He fulfills and teaches others to keep the law whereas the hypocritical scribes and Pharisees break the law and teach others to do so as well (cf. Matthew 23). Jesus' obeying and teaching on the law in Matthew 5 indicates that He is endorsing and upholding the moral elements of the Mosaic Law by teaching a correct understanding and application of them.

Notice that Jesus says nothing about His fulfilling the types and shadows of the sacrificial system of the Mosaic Covenant or any of the foretelling of the prophets. The context of his teaching is on the universal moral requirements of the law which includes the sexual prohibitions of the law. He is not speaking of what we usually refer to as the "ceremonial law" which includes the types and shadows of the law such as the sacrificial system, the old temple worship, the old priesthood nor those laws which served the purpose of making a distinction between Jews and Gentles such as circumcision, kosher laws and clothing laws.

In addition, we must not conclude that because Jesus is teaching others to keep the law to the fullest, by His teaching and example, that therefore once He has perfectly kept the law in His work of active obedience that in His doing so He abolishes the Law, as many have concluded. [176] If this were so Jesus would have been saying, "Do not

176   Ibid.

think I have come to abolish the law, I have come to fulfill the law and doing so abolish the law." Such as interpretation of the passage would be illogical. Therefore, the moral requirements of the Law of Christ are not a replacement of the moral requirements of the Law of Moses.

Jesus goes on to reinforce the abiding nature of the law as He gives us an eschatological promise that it will continue to be upheld until the end of the earth as He states, "For verily I say unto you, until heaven and earth pass, one jot or one tittle shall in no wise pass from the law, till all be accomplished." Unfortunately the KJV translates the last word in verse 18 (Greek: *genetai*) as "fulfilled" which makes it seem as if Jesus is using the same word translated "fulfilled" in verse 17. The word *genetai* is from the word *ginomai* which means "to happen, take place" or "until all is past." Here Christ is speaking eschatologically concerning the sustaining of the Law. The text says that the law will continue to abide, "…until heaven and earth pass away…" which have not passed away and so neither has God's moral law. Although Jesus died, rose again, ascended to His throne and has sent the Holy Spirit the Kingdom of God continues to be spread until He has placed all His enemies at His footstool (Psalm 110; Hebrews 1:13; 10:13). Jesus is still in the process of making His enemies His footstool and therefore not all has been accomplished as His kingdom still goes forward and along with the ethics of His Kingdom. Therefore the moral principles of God's law as taught and applied by Jesus and the apostles remains the standard for Christian living today.

Jesus' fulfilling the law in the context of this passage has nothing to do with His passive obedience on the cross, but it is His upholding the law of God, teaching others to keep it, demonstration of how to obey it, and refuting the Pharisee's distortion of it. Read the entire context of the Sermon on the Mount. It is all about the ethics of the Kingdom of God! Jesus says absolutely nothing about the shedding of blood, but He expounds and applies the moral requirements of the law and counteracts the tradition of the Pharisees which contradicted and nullified the moral requirements of the Law of God. Ironically, though these Gay Dispensationalists accuse their opponents of being Pharisaical it is *they* who are wantonly violating God's law and teaching others to do likewise just like the tradition of the Pharisees.

Some might be tempted to argue that "heaven and earth" in Matthew 5:17-18 refers to the destruction of the temple and Jerusalem in 70 A.D.

They would argue that the entire Old Testament law was done away with the destruction of Jerusalem and that consequently the "Law of Christ" in Galatians 6:2 is something other than what we find in the 10 Commandments. While "heaven and earth" can refer to the Mosaic Economy, which ended with the destruction of the temple and Jerusalem in 70 A.D., this term does not necessarily refer to the temple. There are 192 references in the Old Testament and New Testament where this or similar phrases are used. Sometimes "heaven and earth" refers to the abode where God and the angels dwell (the third heaven) and the universe (2 Corinthians 12:2), sometimes it means the sky and the planet earth (Exodus 31:17; 2 Samuel 18:2), and at other times it refers to the temple in Jerusalem which was a copy of what was in heaven. The picture has been done away with, but not the reality. But at the end of time heaven and earth shall become one when all is accomplished. In the mean time Jesus remains sitting at the right hand of the father until all His enemies have been made his footstool (Hebrews 10:13).

If "until all is accomplished" refers to Christ's work on the cross, then we have a conflict between Paul and Jesus for Paul cites the law as the ethical authority for the Church, to equip the saints for every good work (2 Timothy 3:15-17). If "until all is accomplished" refers to the destruction of the temple, then the Epistle to the Hebrews is pointless for the sacrifices would still be binding on the first Christians since the temple was not destroyed until 70 A.D.

Let us, for the sake of argument, grant that no commandment from the Old Testament is binding for the Christian today. Therefore, only what Christ Himself has given us, via the evangelists, in the gospels is now binding. For, after all, since we are going to split the law that Christ gave to Moses from that which He gave to anyone else, then we are restricted to the gospels as the definition of the "Law of Christ." In doing so we have to exclude any commandments given by Paul for, after all, just as we ought to be "Christonomists not Mosonomists" so too we should be "Christonomists not Paulonomists." Now the liberals have their day, men can have sex with other men, we can engage in bestiality, and a whole host of other things that were forbidden in the Law of Moses for Jesus says nothing concerning such sexual behaviors in the gospels. But perhaps the Gay Dispensationalist would wish to include the entire New Testament as part of his definition of the "Law of Christ" including Paul's epistles. If so, then we now have a conflict between Christ and Paul for he included the Mosaic Law as that which was able to fully equip us for every good work and lead us to Christ (2 Timothy 3:14-17). What Timothy had from his childhood was the entire Old Testament which Paul says leads Him to Christ and is profitable for teaching, for reproof, for correction, for training in righteousness; that the man of God may be adequate, equipped for every good work.

Furthermore, Jesus is the "I AM" (John 8:58) who gave the Law to Moses and then during His ministry corrected the errors of the Pharisee's traditions in His Sermon on the Mount. This cannot be denied unless of course the Gay Dispensationalist wants to concede that he is a Marcionite and further his dualism more explicitly by stating that we have a different God in the Old Testament than in the New Testament. Therefore, the "Law of Christ" we are to live by is the moral commandments which Christ gave at Sinai and upheld during His earthly ministry.

Christ explained and upheld the law in His Sermon on the Mount. He continued to teach on the law through His appointed apostles and writers of the New Testament through His Spirit who inspired their writings. I do not pit Jesus against Paul as do Liberal Gay Theologians because I do not pit Jesus against Moses. God has not changed His ethical requirements for they are a reflection of His immutable holy character. God and His moral standards have not changed. His laws that were but types and shadows or made a distinction between Jews and Gentiles had a designed obsolescence. These laws alone have expired in their observance in the Church for they found their designed in Christ (Hebrews 7:27).

The alternative to the Gay Dispensational Worldview states that only those laws that are repeated in the New Testament are binding. However, if this is so then we must also reject any reference to the Law in the New Testament. The New Testament writers do not merely repeat Old Testament Laws. They cite the Old Testament as their authority for New Covenant ethics. For example, in Paul's exhortation in Ephesians 6, to the children in the Church, he says that they are to obey their parents in the Lord. However, Paul does not merely say, "Obey your children in the Lord" and thus merely repeat what the Old Testament law states and thereby reinstate the fifth commandment. Rather he cites the Old Testament law as the authority for Christian ethics and the reason for obeying it, "which is the first commandment with a promise" (Ephesians

6:2). The laws from the Old Testament are not merely repeated in the New Testament, as if it were a new version of Deuteronomy. Rather the New Testament constantly cites the law and the prophets as the standard for Christian doctrine and life.

What Bible did the entire Church have and use as an objective standard for Christian ethics until 70 A.D. by which time the New Testament canon was most likely completed? What did they preach from until they received the New Testament epistles and gospels? They had Old Testament Law and the Prophets and what they did then was interpret texts such as the Psalms or Isaiah 53 in light of Christ (Acts 8:32-33).

The Gay Dispensationalist needs to heed the warning Jesus gave, "Whoever then annuls one of the least of these commandments, and teaches others to do the same, shall be called least in the kingdom of heaven; but whoever keeps and teaches them, he shall be called great in the kingdom of heaven" (Matthew 5:19). Instead of seeking to abolish God's law, they ought to say with King David:

> O how I love Your law! It is my meditation all the day.
> Your commandments make me wiser than my enemies, for
> they are ever mine. (Psalms 119:97-98)

The Pharisees in contrast to Jesus upheld some of God's laws while ignoring others, particularly the more important commandments, and acted as if they were righteous when in fact they were full of hypocrisy as they committed the very same sins for which they condemned others (Romans 2:1). Jesus explained the moral law in the Sermon on the Mount and applied it to the heart whereas the Pharisees seemed righteous on the outside but inwardly they were corrupt (Matthew 23:27). The Pharisees often seemed to be righteous as they appeared to be very concerned about keeping the minute areas of the law but if they had been truly concerned with the law of God they would not have neglected what Jesus referred to as the "weightier matters of the law" (Matthew 23:23). It was not that tithing their mint and cumin was wrong, the problem was they ignored more important laws as Jesus went on to say, "...justice and mercy and faithfulness; but these are the things you should have done without neglecting the others." The Pharisees *said* what should be done, but they often did not do it for they were mere hearers of the law and not doers of the law by faith (Matthew 23:3).

The Pharisees were not only hypocrites, when they did good deeds they did so to be seen by men such as when they gave alms to the poor, fasted and prayed in public (Matthew 6:1-6) and they loved religious titles (Matthew 23:6-9). This is why Jesus said, "But all their works they do for to be seen of men" (Matthew 23:5).

The doctrine of the Pharisees also taught that you merit your righteousness by your good deeds, rather than receiving it by faith. The apostle Paul made it clear that while we are to do good works, following our calling as Christians, those deeds are in response to the good news of the gospel and the working *out* of our salvation (not working *for* our salvation) (Philippians 2:12). We have been saved by grace through faith in Christ and are called to do good works which He has prepared for us in advance (Ephesians 2:8-10). This calling may include suffering for Christ:

> Therefore do not be ashamed of the testimony of our Lord or of me His prisoner, but join with me in suffering for the gospel according to the power of God, who has saved us and called us with a holy calling, **not according to our works**, but according to His own purpose and grace which was granted us in Christ Jesus from all eternity (2 Timothy 1:8-9).

The Pharisees after Pentecost also attempted to require Christians to keep and follow the types and shadows of the Mosaic Covenant and obsolete covenantal signs and Feast Days such as circumcision and Passover. The Old Covenant signs and Feast Days were about the repeated shedding of blood. Circumcision was a bloody rite (for boys) and Passover included the shedding of the blood of a lamb (Exodus 12:21). The signs and feast days have been replaced with New Covenant signs of baptism and the Lord's Supper, which does not shed blood because Christ's blood was sufficient as our Passover (1 Corinthians 5:7). Therefore, nobody is required to observe the rite of circumcision or keep the Old Covenant feasts and holidays that Paul says were "a mere shadow" (Colossians 2:16-17). The Christian Pharisees insisted that Gentiles needed to be circumcised and keep the Old Covenant feast days in order to be saved (Acts 15:1, 5). The Jerusalem council concluded that because the Gentiles had received the Holy Spirit by faith that they did not need to be circumcised. However, the apostles along with the Holy Spirit then gave them various commandments to follow which are from the Old Testament (Acts 15:29). Paul likewise argued in his epistles that Gentiles are children of Abraham by faith and that in their obedience of the law they demonstrate that their heart has been circumcised and that it is not the mere hearers of the law that are justified (which is a perfect description of the Pharisees). Rather, it is those who have a genuine faith and consequently are doers of the law that are justified, not on the basis of their works but because they have a genuine faith which is not alone but always produced the fruit of the Spirit (Romans 2:13-29). What is clear though, is that we are *not* justified by an alone faith and anyone who says that they love God but hates their brother or says that they have faith but have no works, is a liar and cannot be justified by that kind of faith (James 2:14; 1 John 2:4).

Chapter 6
The Hermeneutical Fallacies of Gay Theology

It is not easy to briefly provide a thorough understanding of proper Biblical Hermeneutics. Entire volumes can be and have been written on this subject.[177] Nor is it necessary for the purpose of this book to do so. Therefore, I will narrow my focus on hermeneutics on how it relates to the God's Covenant with His people and the law of God found in both the Old and New Testaments in which we find the relevant texts to the topics at hand such as marriage, sin, and sexual behavior. Finally, I will demonstrate how Gay Theology advocates wrongly use extra-Biblical literature as a lens to reinterpret Scripture.

A correct understanding of Biblical hermeneutics may be understood as the theological principles of exegesis; that is the Biblical method explaining the intended meaning of the text from within its own historical and literary context. This process of exegesis takes into consideration numerous issues from within the text in a series on contextual circles which include the original language of the text, the style of writings of the text (such as historical narrative, poetry, parables, apocalyptic genres) and any combination of these and how they are used within the given passage. It also takes into consideration the use of forms of speech such as metaphors, synonyms and cultural idioms and the text's place in redemptive history. Furthermore, proper Biblical hermeneutics takes into consideration the structure of the covenants as they unfold in redemptive history and find their culmination in the New Testament. Finally, when reading the New Testament an analysis is made as to how the writers of the Gospels and Epistles interpret and use the language and historical events of the Old Testament, particularly in reference to Christ and the identity of the Church. In doing so we will develop

---

177   For further reading on this subject I suggest: R. C. Sproul, *Knowing Scripture* (IVP Books, 1978); Gordon D. Fee, Douglas Stuart, *How To Read the Bible For All Its Worth* (Grand Rapids, MI: Zondervan; 3rd edition, 2003); William W. Klein, Craig L. Blomberg, and Robert L. Hubbard Jr. *Introduction to Biblical Interpretation* (Thomas Nelson; Revised & Updated, 2004); Grant R. Osborne, *The Hermeneutical Spiral: A Comprehensive Introduction to Biblical Interpretation* (Grand Rapids, MI: IVP Academic; Rev Exp edition (November 30, 2006).

an apostolic method for interpreting and applying the Old Testament, particularly the law, rather than imposing a presupposed foreign set of hermeneutical rules and axioms on the text.

For example, when exegeting the New Testament the interpreter needs to take into consideration the fact that the writers of the Gospels are living in post-exilic Israel, under the dominion of the Roman Empire, and that they are using the common Greek language of the day. While they are surrounded by the Greco-Roman culture, the primary literary, cultural and ethical influences on the New Testament writers is the Hebrew Scriptures. In particular, it is the language of the Septuagint which influences their historical-cultural mindset in how they use the Greek language to convey Old Testament Hebraic ideas. The New Testament consequently is laced with direct citations of the Septuagint as it uses the Greek language with a Hebrew mindset, not that of a Greek philosopher. Therefore, when reading the Apostle Paul we have to keep in mind that he is a Hebrew of Hebrews, not a Hellenist, and consequently his use of the Greek language will be different than that of Plato or Philo (Philippians 3:5). This will be especially important to keep in mind when we consider Paul's use of the phrase "contrary to nature" (*kata physin*) and the term *arsenokoitai* which I translate as "men who have sex with other men" (1 Corinthians 6:9; 1 Timothy 1:10).

Furthermore, we must remember that the only canon of Scripture and rule of faith to lead people to Christ and equip the man of God for the work of service that was universally available before the completion of the New Testament (as early as 70 A.D.) was the Old Testament (2 Timothy 3:15-17). Consequently, the early Church read the Psalms, the sacrificial laws and the prophecies from Moses to the Prophets as pointing us to the Messiah as we are told Jesus taught, "Then beginning with Moses and with all the prophets, He explained to them the things concerning Himself in all the Scriptures" (Luke 24:27).

We see then in their epistles that the apostles directly quote the Old Testament law as a standard for ethics (Ephesians 6:2-3; Deuteronomy 5:16; Exodus 20:12 cf. 1 Timothy 5:18; Deuteronomy 25:4), even to the Gentile Christians. They refer to the Old Testament saints as the forefathers of all Christians (both Jew and Gentile) and freely use Old Testament metaphors and allude to Old Covenant customs (such as sacrifices) as models for the Christian life (Romans 12:1-2; Philippians

4:18). The post-resurrection writers also freely interpret the events, po-etry, and prophecies as all being foreshadows of Jesus as did Philip for the Egyptian Eunuch (Isaiah 53:7; Acts 8:32-33).

In light of this, it is axiomatic that the canon of Scripture must be viewed as an organic whole from which the Christian is to develop a consistent worldview. This is antithetical to the Gay Theological Worldview that sees the Bible as an accumulation of disparate individual texts written and edited in the course of history by a group of redactors with differing and competing agendas known as "The Jahwist Party," "The Elohim Party" of the Old Testament or "The Pauline Party," "The Petrine Party" or the "James Party" of the New Testament as if the epistles are not uniform in their teaching on doctrine and ethics. Any interpretation of these epistles or the Gospels that contradicts any other part of Scripture or pits one portion of the Bible against another is not to be considered to be sound exegesis. This is why the hermeneutical prin-ciples of Gay Theology that are built on a non-cohesive understanding of Scripture are to be rejected at the outset.

In the interpretation of a text, Biblical hermeneutics seeks to dis-cover what the language of the authors says and implies. The process consists of several steps for best attaining the Scriptural author's in-tended meaning such as a Lexical-Syntactical, historical, cultural, and contextual analysis. This is often referred to as a Historical-Grammatical interpretation. In this method of interpretation the meaning of the liter-ary expression of the Bible is best learned by a thorough knowledge of the languages in which the original text of Scripture was written, and by acquaintance with the Scriptural way of speaking, including the various customs, laws, and habits which influenced the writers as they were moved by the Holy Spirit to compose their respective books.

However, there may be some challenges that need to be overcome when interpreting a text correctly that may be particularly difficult to some. These include speaking a different language, the chronological distance in time from which the text was written, and the fact that we bring different literary expectations to the text. This does not, of course, mean that the Christian who can only read the English text is somehow inferior to the "scholar" who can come to the correct meaning of the text. Rather, it ought to make the reader aware that a great deal of hu-mility, prayer and patience is required before coming to any dogmatic conclusions. This is especially important if an interpretation of the text is novel or not in accord with the historical teaching of the Church.

Finally, the exegesis of a text must be handled in what is referred to as a hermeneutic circle. In doing so, one seeks to understand the particular verse or pericope in light of the entirety of the text and all of the individual parts of the passage are understood in reference to every other individual part within the entire book, gospel or epistle. Neither the entire book, gospel, or epistle nor any individual part can be understood without reference to the others. Hence there is a series of concentric circles that correlate how the individual part is understood in light of the whole and the whole is understood in light of the individual parts. This circular character of interpretation stresses that the meaning of a text must be found within its cultural, historical, and literary context. In other words, a verse is understood within the context of a chapter of a book and the entire book is understood in relation to its various parts. The books of the Bible are then understood in their redemptive historical context and in light of any other books that are written by the same author such as Moses, the Apostle Paul, or the Apostle John.

The science of interpreting a text therefore follows a step-by-step process in which the reader, by the power of the Holy Spirit, method-ically seeks to understand the passage as it was written by the original author to the original audience. It then determines how the theological and ethical implications of the passage may be applied in the present day. When interpreting a passage of Scripture, first consider the larger context and structure of the text. If possible, read the entire book in one sitting in an attempt to get "the big picture." Before studying the minute details of a single leaf the reader needs to know, in general, what the forest looks like. When applicable, write an outline of the book noting major themes and transitional points. In epistles these are frequently marked by transitional statements such as "therefore." This reveals the general thought development of the book but be careful not to rely on the chapter divisions, verse numbers, or translator headings that are not part of the original text. Some books, such as the Psalms and Proverbs, are not written by a single author but are a collection of writings from multiple authors thus there may not be an overall structure or consistent theme throughout them. In the process of examining an entire book written by a single author, determine such factors as the genre and historical setting. Then determine the passage's place in redemptive history in which you establish the author's identity, the original audience and recipients and the purpose of the text whether it is to record historical events, correct a problem in the church or foretell what was to take place in the future.

Then consider the immediate context and structure of the text. In doing so, consider the immediate context within the few verses preceding and following the text being considered. Then conduct Grammatical-syntactical analysis of words. Consider the verse within the context of the major section then within the context of the entire book and then within the context of all of that author's writings (Moses, Paul, John, etc.). Finally, consider the verse in light of the entire New Testament and finally in light of the entire Bible.

The importance for understanding this interpretive methodology will be made clear as we further examine Gay Theology. As we shall see, their conclusions and assertions is the consequence of abandoning this fundamental hermeneutical process.

Cultural Context

One issue that is frequently raised by Gay Theologians is the matter of handling a text not only within its literary context but also taking into consideration the passage's cultural context. Most of the arguments concerning the interpretation of relevant Biblical passages that address sexual behavior are discussed not only in regards as to how to best translate the given Hebrew or Greek words, but also what those words specifically refer to in their cultural context and whether or not there are any parallels between their religious culture and our own.

For example, in the Gospel of John we read of Jesus washing the disciple's feet and then he says to them, "…I gave you an example that you also should do as I did to you" (John 13:15). Should modern Christians in the twenty-first century wash each other's feet? In consideration of the passage's cultural context we need to keep in mind that at that time they wore open-toed sandals, walked on dirt roads, and they had no indoor plumbing. The custom of the day was that a servant would wash the feet of the guests which was a very humble and dirty job. While it is conceivable that Christians might reenact this event and imitate

Jesus' example of humble service, our cultural context neither expects nor needs such a service. Today, we have the ability to bathe regularly, wear socks and shoes and walk on hard pavement. This keeps our feet, in comparison, relatively clean. However, there is an underlying principle behind Jesus' actions which can be applied to our modern context which is the willingness to perform humble acts of service for others in a Christ-like manner.

In a similar fashion, even if the author of the various passages regarding homogenital acts has some cultural differences than our modern day, we cannot rightly immediately dismiss them without first seeking to determine what parallels exist between ancient and modern cultural settings and behaviors. However, if we, like Gay Theologians, presume that the sexual ethics of the writers of Scripture were due to their particular cultural squeamishness, a primitive cultural backwardness that was bent on oppressing women and maintaining a "man on top" dominance, then regardless of what the text meant we will consider the passage totally irrelevant to our modern sensibilities and social sciences produced by sexual revolutionary ideals. This sort of modern chronological snobbery, "we're the enlightened ones," creates what we might think of as of a form of *cultural relativism*. This is *exactly* what Gay Theologians are asserting when they insist that they are interpreting the passage under consideration "in its cultural context" such as when Dan Via asserts:

> We will also want to consider our own cultural context. How does the unambiguous condemnation of homosexual acts in certain biblical texts accord with what recent social science has taught us and with the contemporary experience of gay and lesbian Christians?[178]

The result is it does not matter what the text prohibits for the presuppositions of the Gay Theology proponent leads him to dismiss the text as being inapplicable to those enlightened by the modern social sciences which has supposedly proven that same-sex attractions are an innate desire and are akin to being born left handed. The assumption then is that an innateness of a proclivity excuses one from moral culpability of

---

178   Dan O. Via, *Homosexuality and the Bible: Two Views* (Minneapolis, MN: Fortress Press, 2003), 3.

acting on those desires. It is then postured that if it can be demonstrated that there is any biological component to the origin (etiology) for a desire to conduct a particular act that is categorized as sin in the Bible, it can be dismissed by modern socially enlightened Christians.[179]

A second form of "cultural context" argument that is frequently made by Gay Theology apologists is that the prohibited sexual acts can only be understood as to condemn a very specific behavior tied to a very particular religious cultic ritual. It is asserted that if modern Christians are not behaving in that particular cultic act then the text does not prohibit their same-sex behavior which is taking place in a non-cultic context between mutually consenting persons in a non-exploitative manner. However, such an assertion is *eisegetical* as it reads into the text what is not clearly in the passage rather than *exegetical*, which seeks to read from the text. It assumes that the author did not know in his own day of any mutual same-sex acts and therefore he could not have had in mind their particular type of homosexual act when the prohibition was written. As we shall see, the modern equivalence to homosexual relationships, gay marriages, and even the opinion that it was an innate nature, was known in the day of the writers of the Old and New Testament.[180] In fact, in Paul's day the Roman emperor himself was involved in two gay marriages, and one with the ancient equivalency to a post-operational male to female transsexual.[181]

The Historical-Critical Method and Literal Interpretation

Because many Gay Theologians assume that the Bible is not inerrant and infallible, their mind is already set against the Word of God as the ultimate authority for all of life, including sexual ethics. Rather than reading the text with their heart in submission to the Spirit of God, they read it through the eyes of self-deception, suppressing the knowledge of the truth which results, as we shall see, in the twisting of the Scriptures. They then set up straw-man arguments and assert that anyone who does

---

179   However, Queer and Transgender Theology advocates reject these Gay essentialist notions.

180   Robert A. J. Gagnon, *The Bible And Homosexual Practice* (Nashville, TN: Abingdon Press, 2001), 385, 393.

181   Peter Jones, *One or Two: Seeing A World of Difference* (Escondido, CA; Main Entry Editions, 2010), 21.

not agree with their conclusions is a fundamentalist who fails to take the hermeneutical process seriously as Daniel Helminiak states:

> The literal reading claims to take the text simply for what
> it says. This is the approach of Biblical Fundamentalism.
> It claims not to be interpreting the text but merely to be
> reading it as it stands.[182]

Helminiak doesn't cite any opponents to Gay Theology who advocate such a method of reading the Bible. While there may be some simple-minded fundamentalist preachers who advocate such a simplistic method for reading the Bible, these can hardly be said to be representative of Bible-believing scholarship. Such an assertion is a straw-man representation of how people who insist that same-sex acts are contrary to the teaching of God's Word interpret the Bible. Gay Theologians, such as Helminiak, then go on to knock down this fictional hermeneutic that not one conservative Bible-believing scholar advocates. Subsequently, the designation "literalist" becomes a fictional character that supposedly represents anyone who disagrees with the assertions of Gay Theology apologists.

Helminiak illustrates this idea by asserting that anyone who believes that God actually created the universe in six chronological twenty-four hour time periods is using the simplistic "literalist approach" that ignores all the proper rules for hermeneutics as he states:

> The literal approach would take words to mean exactly
> what they say... reading in the first chapter of Genesis that
> God created the world in seven days, the literal approach
> would insists that the universe was formed in one week.
> For if creation did not happen that way, the Bible is mis-
> taken.[183]

I do not want to get on a tangent on the issue of whether or not the universe was created in six literal days. However, it is fallacious to assert that six-day creationists use such a superficial and simplistic approach

---

182   Daniel Helminiak, *What the Bible Really Says About Homosexuality* (Estancia, NM: Alamo Square Press, 2000), 33.
183   Ibid, 35.

to reading the Bible and thereby imply that anyone who believes that the Bible prohibits all same sex acts is likewise reading the Scriptures in such a manner.[184]

To interpret the Bible literally is not to do an injustice to the genre or literary structure of the text. Rather it is to understand the text in the manner in which the author intended in his use of historical narrative, poetry, parable, or metaphorical and abstract concepts. That which is concrete (such as a person or event) is that which is physical and extends into space and time or exists in history. If I were to say, "My car is a rust bucket" I am referring to something concrete in history but I am using the term "rust bucket" metaphorically to describe the condition of my automobile. When we say that we want to interpret a text literally that does not settle what the text actually refers to, whether the author intends to convey an abstract idea (such as a parable that uses concrete sounding fictional stories to convey moral and spiritual truths) or whether it intends to convey an actual historical person such as when the Gospels tell us that Jesus was crucified. In the case of Genesis 1-3, the question then is whether the text is intended to be *completely* metaphorical containing no historical concrete events or persons or a poetic story that conveys actual persons and actual events and yet some elements are not intended to convey a "to the letter" account. The Bible contains poetic accounts of historical events much like the way in which Henry Wadsworth Longfellow (1807-1882) speaks of a historical event in the form of a poem in "Paul Revere's Ride." The fact that both Jesus and the apostle Paul authoritatively cite Genesis 1:27 and Genesis 3 to substantiate the historical creation of marriage, its divine origin, and the relationship between the husband and wife as well as the origin of sin indicates that at least these elements are in fact actual historical, concrete persons and events. In fact, there are many non-six-day creationists who also conclude that the Scriptures clearly indicates the historicity of

---

184   There are many contextual indicators that the author of Genesis fully intended to convey that the earth was created mature within six days for it was in commemoration of this historical event that Moses then commanded the children of Israel to keep the Sabbath (Exodus 20:11). The six-day creationist view then is that, like the fine wine that Jesus Christ instantly created at the wedding at Cana which normally would require a great deal of time to create from grapes (John 2), so too the universe is of relatively recent origin (6,000-10,000 years ago) and yet it was created mature.

Adam and Eve and the event of the fall and that the Bible prohibits all homosexual conduct.[185]

Many liberals and so-called "evangelicals" who argue that the Bible is "gay friendly" assert that they are making their claim based upon the "historical-critical" method:

> ...the historical-critical method has a serious disadvantage. It is not easy. This method makes Bible interpretation a technical science. Archaeology, history, ancient languages, anthropology, minute analysis of words and texts are all required for proper interpretation.[186]

There are several things that must be noted about this supposed "historical-critical" method. First, it asserts that the Scriptures are insufficient in themselves to rightly understand them. Some other source (extra-biblical documents, an understanding of anthropology from a Darwinian worldview) is needed and can only be used in the hand of self-proclaimed "scholars" who deny such things as the inerrancy and infallibility of the text penned by the original writers, the Mosaic authorship of the Pentateuch, Pauline authorship of many of the epistles and that the Gospels represent eye-witness accounts of the life, teaching and resurrection of Jesus Christ. Second, this presupposed method of interpreting the Bible in which extra-Biblical documents are implemented are not used in a supplementary fashion to support a thesis, but in a primary fashion in which such sources outside the text are misused to reinterpret the text. Martti Nissinen illustrates this point when he says that:

> Greco-Roman and Jewish sources are a good basis for examining the arguments of Paul, who clearly shares with Josephus, Philo and others Jewish repugnance towards homoeroticism. Paul's language is deeply rooted in the Hellenistic Jewish tradition of his time, influenced by Stoic philosophy.[187]

---

185   C. John Collins, *Did Adam and Eve Really Exist?* (Crossway Books, 2011)
186   Daniel Helminiak, *What the Bible Really Says About Homosexuality* (Estancia, NM: Alamo Square Press, 2000), 38.
187   Martti Nissinen, *Homoeroticism in the Biblical World* (Augsburg Fortress Publishers, 1998), 104.

There are three problems with this view of Paul. First, it asserts that interpreting the text via extra-biblical resources are the basis for understanding Paul. Second it totally distorts the character of Paul as being of the Hellenistic Jewish tradition influenced by Greek Stoic Philosophy. We see from Scripture that Paul identifies himself as being a "Hebrew of Hebrews" which means he is a Jewish Jew, not a Hellenist, which was typical of the Pharisees who were not prone to compromise with the Hellenistic Jews (Philippians 3:5). Third, Paul clearly contrasts his way of thinking, writing and preaching with Greek philosophers (1 Corinthians 1:22). In fact he confronts them face to face concerning their errors, not by acquiescing to their worldview but by contradicting it and showing them the inconsistencies of their idolatry. While Paul was familiar with their philosophy, he was not one of them (Acts 17:18-31).

There has been for quite some time, even in seemingly Bible-believing seminaries and churches, a growing trend in which the inerrancy, infallibility and authority of Scripture is affirmed out of the one side of the professor's mouth but then out of the other the sufficiency of Scripture is denied. This denial may not be apparent outright and it may not even be explicitly stated. Yet, when observing how they interpret the Bible and how they limit its sufficiency to merely matters of theology and not history or ethics one cannot help but see how they are denying in *practice* what they claim to uphold with their *profession* of faith. This is done particularly in how Scripture is interpreted and how it is applied. This denial of the sufficiency of Scripture is a refusal to believe what Scripture tells us concerning itself and it grows out of a worldly view of esteemed "scholarship."

The Necessity, Authority and Sufficiency of Scripture

In order to rightly uphold and defend a Christian Worldview of Scripture a fundamental understanding of its attributes needs to be understood. We can remember the attributes of Scripture with the acronym "N.A.P.S." (Necessity, Authority, Perspicuity, Sufficiency). Scripture is *necessary* because while the invisible attributes of God have been made known through that which has been made since the foundation of the earth (Romans 1:19-20), the will of God and His plan of redemption is not found in that which has been made (Natural Revelation). Therefore Special Revelation, the Word of God, is necessary in written form in order to preserve it for all generations. Scripture is *authoritative* because ultimately it is not derived from man's observation of the work of God but rather it is breath-out (inspired) of God as it was written by men who were moved by the Holy Spirit the way in which the wind moves a sailing ship (1 Peter 1:21). Although some portions of Scripture may be difficult to understand (2 Peter 3:16) the Word of God is *perspicuous* (clear) in what it declares concerning the will of God, the attributes of God, the personhood of Jesus Christ and the Holy Spirit and what He requires of us in order for our sins to be forgiven.

Finally, Scripture is materially *sufficient* in that we do not anything outside of itself to know and understand the Word of God. We do not need the traditions of the Pharisees, the Midrash, the Talmud, the Gospel of Thomas, the so-called Secret Gospel of Mark, the Apocrypha, the latest archaeological find or other near-eastern documents in order to rightly interpret the Bible. We do not need pagan creation accounts to understand the first three chapters of Genesis. The Church does not need the suzerain treaties of pagan dynasties to understand the covenants of the Bible nor do we need extra-biblical flood stories to understand the Bible's account of Noah and the flood. Nor do we need Ancient Near East "hero myths" to interpret passages concerning the relationship between Jonathan and David. To insist that we cannot rightly understand the Scriptures apart from any of these things is to deny the sufficiency of Scripture and to assert that only a special class of people who have access to such resources can truly know God and understand His will. Furthermore, to insist that one must interpret the Bible in light of extra-Biblical documents asserts that God has not given His people everything that they need to know Him and understand His revealed will and that only the mystic with special knowledge or specialized "scholar" can truly understand the Bible.

One of the chief hermeneutical errors that all of the various forms of Gay Theology employ is that of reading the text of Scripture through the lens of extra-Biblical literature. This practice has become widely taught even in supposedly conservative seminaries in which the creation week is interpreted in light of pagan creation myths,[188] Noah's flood is interpreted in light of extra-Biblical flood accounts,[189] and foreign covenants are used to define Biblical covenants. After reading extra-biblical creation accounts, scholar Paul Sealy concludes:

> Certainly also it is not the purpose of Gen 1:7 to teach us the physical nature of the sky, but to reveal the creator of the sky. Consequently, the reference to the solid firmament 'lies outside the scope of the writer's teachings' and the verse is still infallibly true.[190]

Because Sealy narrows the intent of Genesis 1 to merely teaching monotheism, and that its purpose is to be a polemic against the surrounding pagan culture, he asserts that Moses is free to present a wrong view of the universe, according to Sealy's interpretation of the Hebrew word *raqiaà*, because his intention is theological and not scientific. He asserts that the text is inerrant concerning doctrine and morals, but not on its scientific presentation of the universe. Sealy then concludes in the second part of this article:

> The divine intent of this picture was not to communicate natural science, but to teach the fact that the God of Scripture is Creator and absolute Sovereign over the supposedly independent forces of the natural world. This is an important revelation which men still need today. Of

---

188   For example of reinterpreting of the creation week through extrabiblical evidence is found in Mark D. Futato, "Because it Had Rained: A Study of Genesis 2:5-7 With Implications for Genesis 2:4-25 and Genesis 1:1-2:3" *Westminster Theological Journal* 60 (1): 1–21. In this work Futato discounts the historical account of the creak week in Genesis 1-2 in favor of it being merely a polemic against Baal worshippers. In doing so he does little more than adapt the criticisms of liberals very similar to that found in the *Harper Bible Commentary* on Genesis 2. The problem is if Futato is correct the issue of Baal worship occurred from the time of Moses to Elijah hence Genesis chapters 1-3 can be completely dismissed in regards to tells us anything about the origin of the universe, the origin of man, marriage and sin.

189   For example of reinterpreting of the flood narrative through extrabiblical evidence is found in, Davis A. Young's book, *The Biblical Flood: A Case Study of the Church's Response to Extrabiblical Evidence.* (Carlisle: The Paternoster Press, 1995).

190   Paul H. Seely, "The Firmament and the Water Above Part I: The Meaning of raqiaà in Gen 1:6-8" *Westminster Theological Journal* - Vol. 53, No. 2 (Fall 1991).

course, the ancient science employed in giving this revelation cannot be completely harmonized with modern science. This gives us a clue, I think, as to why, as Davis Young has pointed out, neither concordism nor literalism has genuinely been able to harmonize modern science with Genesis. Nevertheless, the divine revelation endures. We need simply to see with Warfield [who allowed for theistic evolution] that divine inspiration does not bestow omniscience, and hence God has sometimes allowed his inspired penmen to advert to the scientific concepts of their own day. This fact in no way effaces the point and purpose of Genesis 1 to reveal the sovereign power and glory of the one true Creator. The divinely intended message of Genesis 1 does not err, but stands out in glorious contrast to the dark mythological polytheism of its own time, and by its divinely inspired excellence endures yet today as a bright revelation for all time.[191]

To summarize what the author is asserting, Moses' intent was not to give a scientific view of the universe. Therefore it was permissible for him to present a scientifically naïve and historically inaccurate view of the universe, so long as the correct theological message was given. This is the hermeneutical methodology and view of the creation account proposed by Gay Theology apologist L. William Countryman:

The universe, as conceived by most of the Old Testament writers, was very different from what we now know it to be. They envisioned the earth as a relatively flat expanse, over which God had placed the crystalline vault of the firmament, rather like a giant cheesedome. There were waters above this dome (which might fall down through widows in the firmament in the form of rain and precipitation), and there were waters below it, which welled up in the form of springs... In other words, the whole view of the universe

191   Paul H. Seely, "The Firmament and the Water Above Part II: The Meaning of 'The Water Above the Firmament' in Gen 1:6-8" *Westminster Theological Journal* - Vol. 54, No. 1 (Spring 1992).

(cosmology) accepted by the Old Testament writers was quite different from ours; and it is quite reasonable for us to say that it was also quite wrong.[192]

To say that Moses can present a wrong view of the universe without erring in theological doctrine, as Sealy wants to assert, is to deny the inerrancy and infallibility of Scripture. This is what is known as "limited inerrancy" in which one believes that the Bible may be in error concerning historical and scientific matters, but not on moral or theological because these are the truly important issues. To argue for limited inerrancy is detrimental to the faith. If we introduce the possibility of error even in the slightest degree, the foundation of our faith would be destroyed. Fallible human interpreters would then have the intolerable obligation of determining, according to their own autonomous judgment, which portions of Scripture are true and which are false. The modern exegete could relegate Scriptural teachings regarding women's ordination or the status of homosexual behavior to scientific and sociological ignorance and conclude that such teachings are not binding on the Church.[193] In sum, one could not affirm with the Westminster Confession that, "The supreme judge by which all controversies of religion are to be judged and in whose sentence we are to rest, can be no other but the Holy Spirit speaking in the Scripture" (WCF 1.10).

Using the same hermeneutical method of Sealy the reader could say the same thing concerning the Biblical account of Israel crossing the Red Sea by ascribing the splitting of the sea to the blast of Jehovah's nostrils merely to a providentially low tide. Or Christians could attribute Jesus' "virgin birth" to Mary's actual pregnancy coming from her being raped by a Roman Soldier or as Queer Theologians assert, to a parthenogenetic birth.[194] One could also contribute the historical bodily resurrection of Christ to mistaken identity, mass delusion or reinterpret it to refer to an existential experience of the reader of the gospels. To deny the actual historical accuracy of these events all the while claim

---

192   L. William Countryman, *Biblical Authority or Biblical Tyranny?* (Harrisburg, PA: Trinity Press, 1994), 2-3.
193   R.D. Weekly, *The Rebuttal: A Biblical Response Exposing Deceptive Logic of Anti-Gay Theology* (Judah First Ministries, 2011), 111.
194   Virginia Ramey Mollenkott, *Omnigender: A Trans-religious Approach* (Cleveland, OH: The Pilgrim Progress, 2007), 105-116

justification for such assertions because it wasn't the intent of the author to give a scientific view of these events, but to communicate a theological message is the potential result of such an misunderstandings of Scripture. There are no hermeneutical boundaries in this method to keep one from doing so.

With the same hermeneutical method we could make similar conclusions concerning the Bible teaching on same-sex acts insisting that the author's had a primitive understanding of the psychological orientation of gay men. In fact we could insist that they did not know of or even address the issue of orientation since they were only concerned with the biological survival of the race and heredity lines of passing down the family inheritance as well. It also might be asserted that the concerns of same-sex acts were theological and not ethical. Hence we might argue along with the Gay Theologians that the Bible is wrong sociologically and psychologically but since it is not a book on psychology it is still inerrant in its purpose "so long as a theological message is being conveyed." Therefore it is okay for the author to present such an accounts of creation due to the influence of his culture since Genesis 1 is actually a polemic against pagan theology and texts such as Leviticus 18-20 and Romans 1 are merely polemics against pagan idolatry, not condemnations of consenting "loving" committed same sex relationships. This is in fact the paradigm through which many Gay theology proponents read the Scriptures. As we shall see in later chapters, both Liberal and Dispensational Gay Theologians use this same methodology for interpreting the relationship between Jonathan and King David.

There are several problems with interpreting the Bible in light of extra-Biblical literature in this fashion. It is one thing to find additional support to an understanding of a passage from an outside source; it is another to have one's understanding of a text be completely dependent on something which God did not give to His Church to properly understand His revealed will. If an interpretation of a text can not be achieved apart from the use of extra-biblical materials then faithful Christians ought to seriously question the validity of the understanding of the passage. If the entire case for an interpretation of a text depends on the use of something outside of the Scripture, that conclusion ought to be rejected.

In liberal theological circles and in a growing number of supposedly conservative seminaries the Scriptures are being reinterpreted not according to a continuing study of Scripture, but according to an authority, influence and weight being given to extra biblical documents. The result of this methodology is that one must conclude that apart from these documents one could never come to a correct understanding as to the meaning of Scripture. Consequently, due to the lack of access to these documents for generations the Church has been in the dark concerning certain texts solely because they did not have access to the most recent archaeological find and extra-biblical documents.

Yet the Scriptures themselves tell us that they are materially sufficient to equip the saint for the work of service (2 Timothy 3:16-17) and "that His divine power has granted to us everything pertaining to life and godliness, through the true knowledge of Him who called us by His own glory and excellence" (2 Peter 1:3). The Church is lacking nothing that is required to know and prove that which is acceptable and pleasing to God (Romans 12:2). The Church needs neither Freudian psychology to understand the problems of man or the solution to his wrongful thinking nor an understanding of extra-Biblical literature to rightly interpret the Scriptures.

One of the primary justifications for using extra-biblical documents for interpreting the Bible is the assertion that the Canon of Scripture does not contain all that was taught by Jesus and the apostles. Reading the Bible with "suspicion," Liberation, and Queer Theology advocates, assume that a male dominant ecclesiastical leadership included in the canon only those texts which suited their patriarchal agenda. Then, supposedly, they edited those texts that were included while excluding others that should have been included, specifically the Gnostic gospels and epistles. Liberal "scholars" of the Jesus Seminar and Gay/Queer Theologians have sought to reintroduce various Gnostic texts, such as the Gospel of Thomas and the so-called Secret Gospel of Mark:

> The Secret Gospel of Mark represents an alternative tradition of make homodevotionalism to Jesus that has countered the dominant sexless constructions of Jesus. Today,

gay men have reclaimed the text for themselves and Jesus
as a paradigm for make same-sex relationships.[195]

Hermeneutics, Etymology and Gay Theology

Another common hermeneutical fallacy of Gay Theology proponents is to selectively cite passages and meanings of words which fit
into their paradigm while ignoring others that clearly contradict their
interpretation and shed more light on the meaning of the passage. In
doing so, when arguing for a meaning of a word they will look at the
semantic range from a lexicon and choose the definition which suits
their presupposed interpretation, not the one that fits the context of the
passage. It is the context in which words are found that determines their
meaning, not the frequency of their use, and we may determine the
meaning of words (such as the Hebrew word *ahab*) by comparing their
use in their immediate context and in other similar passages. As we shall
see, Gay Theology advocates tend to read a menu of possible lexical
meanings for a word and then select which definition will best suit their
presupposed understanding of the text and best suits their agenda. This
is far from anything worthy to be deemed "scholarship."

Experience Oriented Hermeneutics and Gay Theology

It is not uncommon for people when they read the Bible to read
into the text their own experiences or read the text as if it was addressing the theological or social concerns of their own day. Because many
well-meaning Christians want to read the Bible devotionally before they
determine what the text meant to its original recipients they ask, "What
does this text mean to *me*?" Or, they look at the issues and concerns of
the Church of their own day and before determining what the author
was addressing in his day they immediately read and apply the text to
the circumstances at hand.

An example of this type of reading into the text the issues of one's
own day can be found in commentaries written by the Protestant
Reformers in which they comment on Paul's epistles as if he was

195   Robert E. Goss, *Queering Christ: Beyond Jesus Acted Up* (Eugene, OR: The
Pilgrim Press, 2007), 122.

addressing Roman Catholicism and their doctrine of justification by faith plus meritorious works. Consequently they read Paul's term "works of the law" through the lens of the concerns of the 16th century rather than understanding it light of the concerns of the Jerusalem council, which is, "Do Gentiles need to be circumcised and lived like Jews in order to be saved?" (Acts 15:1; Galatians 2:14) They also read John's references to the coming of the antichrist and assumed that the apostle was to referring to the Pope of their day.[196]

The fallacy of reading into the text the issue of one's own day is especially common with cryptic eschatological passages which refer to things that were about to take place in the author's day ("…which must soon take place… for the time is near…" Revelation 1:1-3) and yet modern day "end times experts" read the passage as if it is referring to event that will take place in the modern era. They subsequently read passages such as Daniel Chapter 7, Matthew Chapter 24 and the Book of Revelation through the lens of a modern newspaper in an America-centered reading of the text. They simultaneously conclude that the text could not be understood by the original recipients of the text and it had nothing to say to previous generations of the Church or that one could not possibly understand them until the modern era.

The error of reading a text through the lens of our own experiences is most keenly seen in the way in which proponents of Gay Theology tend to read the Scriptures through the lens of their own homo-emotional longings, sexual arousals and experiences. Because they have sexualized their close male friendships they see any other close same sex friendship as being romantic rather than as a close familial relationship. Common examples include the relationship between Ruth and Naomi, King Saul and David, Jonathan and David, Jesus and the Beloved Disciple, and the Roman centurion and his servant.

In order to avoid committing these same exegetical fallacies it is necessary for us to first read Biblical passages which address the issue of same-sex acts within their immediate historical context. Once we have determined the meaning of these passages in their original context, an ethical and theological principle from the text can be derived and applied to the present day.

---

196   John Calvin, *Commentary On The First Epistle of John* (Calvin's Commentaries, Vol. 22) (Grand Rapids, MI: Baker, 1999), 190.

Gay Theology and Historical Revisionism

In order to convince people that the Bible does not condemn same sex acts Gay Theologians need to either assert that the Church has misread the Bible for almost 2,000 years or rewrite history in order to convince moderns that the Church's prohibition of same-sex acts is a relatively recent phenomenon. Historical revisionism becomes another tactic and hermeneutical grid of Gay Theology proponents who insist that the Bible actually affirms same sex relationships even amongst men who are already married to a woman. The most popular works on this front is by John Boswell author of *Christianity, Social Tolerance, and Homosexuality*. Boswell asserts that homosexuality was tolerated and accepted in the church until the 13th century when for a number of reasons he claims the Church suddenly changed its position on the Bible. The problem is that unlearned Christians who do not know their history or are unwilling to examine the facts herald this book because they want Boswell to be telling the truth and consequently they just accept it.

While Boswell does demonstrate that men having sex with other men has been a long running issue in the Church his argument that it took no official stance on the issue has been discredited by numerous historians (including those theologically sympathetic to him). It has also been demonstrated that he misquotes his sources and uses citations out of context.[197]

But Boswell is not alone is his historical revisionism. Robin Scroggs, author of *The New Testament and Homosexuality*, asserts that the only model of same sex relations that the apostle Paul could have been aware of was pederasty. Therefore, in his view, Romans 1 and 1 Corinthians 6:9 do not refer to men having sex with other men, but with boys. The historical record demonstrates that homosexuality among the Greeks is well attested by the fifth-century philosophers and it was deemed a normal and valuable relationship, chiefly associated with teachers and their students and mutual friendship. Commercial exploitation and pederasty

197   For more critiques of Boswell's works read: Robert B. Hays, "Relations Natural and Unnatural: A Response to John Boswell's' Exegesis of Romans 1" *Journal of Religious Ethics* pg. 14 [1986]; Richard John Neuhaus, "The Public Square: In the Case of John Boswell" First Things, 41 [November 1994]; Michael Sheehan, "Christianity and Homosexuality," *Journal of Ecclesiastical History* 33 [1982], 438-436; 441-446.; J. Robert Wright, "Boswell on Homosexuality: A Case Demonstrated," *Anglican Theological Review,* 66 [1984].

especially among older men and immature boys was disapproved. The Romans knew and had *clear disdain* for forms of same sex acts other than pederasty. In fact, Julius Caesar and King Nicodemus were two consenting adults who engaged in consensual same sex acts and at the time their behavior was considered scandalous. Also, as previously noted, in the Apostle Paul's day, Emperor Nero had a polygamous gay marriage with a man and a transsexual. [198]

198   For more documentation on the existence of consensual same sex relationships in ancient times see: James B. De Young, *Homosexuality: Contemporary Claims Examined in the Light of the Bible and Other Ancient Literature and Law* (Grand Rapids, MI: Kregel, 2000), 205ff.; Ronald M. Springett, *Homosexuality In History and The Scriptures* (Washington DC: Biblical Research Institute, 1988), 83-98.

Chapter 7
The Restorative Nature of the Law

In the previous chapters I addressed the *epistemological* issues regarding the Biblical Christian Worldview, namely the attributes and authority of Scripture and the basic principles of sound hermeneutics and the application of Scripture. At this point we now move on to the *ethical* component of a consistent Christian worldview, namely a proper understanding and application of God's law revealed in the Old and New Testaments.

Before we can delve into the specific issue of what the law of God says about same-sex acts we need to answer a few questions such as, "Does the New Covenant free the believer from obeying all of the Old Testament laws?" Or "Is the Christian only required to obey from the Old Testament that which is repeated in the New Testament?" Or, "May a person have faith (or at least clam to) in Jesus Christ and live in any manner that he wishes and still hope that his sins are forgiven?"

The Creation Covenant – The New World Order

In order to answer these questions we need to first understand the structure of Biblical covenants. Then we need to have a clear understanding of the purpose of God's law in its covenant context and consider how the New Testament uses the commandments of God in a New Covenant era as it calls Christians to obedience to Jesus as Lord.

The structure of a covenant relationship between God, who is both King and Redeemer, and His people, who metaphorically are His bride and children, always begins with what He has done for them. The grace and work of God *always* precedes the obligation to obey His commandments. This is made clear throughout the Scriptures from Genesis to Revelation in the five-fold structure of His covenants in which we see:

(1) An identification of the king/redeemer.
(2) An accounting of the historical events that led to the establishment of the covenant.

(3) Stipulations (terms) of the covenant of which include love, faith and fidelity.

(4) A warning of judgment and penal sanctions against anyone who is not faithful but a promise to those who maintain fidelity.

(5) A means of confirming the covenant (signs involving food, oaths, memorials).

This pattern is seen in Genesis, Deuteronomy, the Psalms, the Gospel of Matthew, Hebrews chapter 8, many of Paul's epistles, in the Ten Commandments and the book of Revelation.[199] For example, we read in Genesis the following in the Creation Covenant:

(1) An identification of the king in the identity of God (*elohim*) as the LORD (YHWH) (Genesis 2:4).

(2) An accounting of the historical events that led to the establishment of the covenant in the recounting of His creative acts through a series of Ten Commands ("And God said..." Genesis 1:3, 6, 9, 11, 14, 20, 24, 26, 28, 29) in which He brings chaos to order.[200]

(3) Stipulations of the covenant with Adam and representation his "seed" or descendants (Genesis 1-2), in which we see the requirement to name the animals (Genesis 2:19-20), to take dominion and subdue the earth (Genesis 1:28) and the prohibition against eating from the Tree of the Knowledge of Good and Evil.

(4) The warning of that the failure to obey would result in death (Genesis 2:16-17).

(5) The provision for confirming the covenant in the Tree of Life from which he could eat and live forever (Genesis 2:9; 3:22).

In the creation period we see a trajectory in which God brings into the universe life from non-life, order from chaos, establishes freedom

---

199   For similar understandings of the five-fold structure of the covenant see: Meredith Kline, *The Structure of Biblical Authority* (Grand Raids: Eerdmans, 1972); David Chilton, *The Days of Vengeance* (Tyler, TX, Dominion Press, 1987), xvii-xviii.; Ray R. Sutton, *That You May Prosper: Dominion By Covenant* (Tyler, Texas: Institute for Christian Economics, 1987); James B. Jordan, *Covenant Sequence in Leviticus and Deuteronomy* (Tyler, Texas: Institute for Christian Economics, 1989).

200   As Ray Sutton points out, "The creation account of Genesis 1 says ten times 'Then God said'... With 'ten words' God creates the world, just as He speaks the law (covenant) with ten words (Deut. 4:13)." *That You May Prosper: Dominion By Covenant* (Tyler, Texas: Institute for Christian Economics, 1987), 125.

within the covenant stipulations and creates man to have a relationship with one woman (Genesis 1:24). The relationship of a one-man and one-woman marriage was endorsed as God's original order by Jesus as well as the apostle Paul (Matthew 19:5; Ephesians 5:31).[201]

Darwinian evolution teaches that man ascended from non-living matter and his current state is the result of billions of years of improvement. Consequently death and suffering are part of the natural order through which life evolves from lower simple life forms to higher more complex life forms. Same sex acts then are just part of the variation of behaviors among animals of which mankind is simply in a higher stage of development. Therefore, if animals conduct same sex acts and man is merely a cousin to the ape, then same sex acts are to be accepted as merely a variation of the natural order:

> Scientists believe that humans are not biologically different from animals in any significant way. For instance, homosexuality is observed in a wide range of animal species, including apes, and is considered a natural variant of sexual expression and behavior.[202]

The Gay Theological Worldview teaches that the worldview of the Bible and its laws stemmed from a chauvinistic and misogynistic culture which promoted slavery, treated women as property and was genocidal in nature.[203] In contrast, the Biblical Christian Worldview teaches that it was the fall into sin that brought into this world a trajectory of death, social disorder, slavery, divorce, polygamy, and brokenness in our humanity. This fallenness is so radical that it affects the very core of our being in sexual brokenness which manifests itself in homosexuality, sexual promiscuity, frigidity and gender confusion. Man did not derive his existence from pre-existing animals. Rather, he was formed by God from the dust of the ground (Genesis 2:7), his wife from his side and they are both equally created in the image of God (Genesis 1:26-27).

201   While Gay Theology apologists maintain that the Bible endorses many types of marriage, we shall see that polygamy and divorce are a result of the fall which were restricted, not endorsed, by the law of God.

202   Patrick M. Chapman, *"Thou Shalt Not Love": What Evangelicals Really Say to Gays* (New York, NY: Haiduk Press, 2008), 59.

203   L. William Countryman, *Biblical Authority or Biblical Tyranny?* (Harrisburg, PA: Trinity Press, 1994), 12.

As a creature endued with a reasonable soul and the mental faculties for making moral decisions he is expected to live according to the revealed will of God. What must be kept in mind is that animals which do not bear God's image not only commit same sex acts; they also engage in cannibalism, eat their young and most have sex with whatever convenient partner suits their urges. To reason that "animals do it" justifies mankind doing so is contrary to the Biblical Christian Worldview.

Yet this is exactly what many Gay Theology advocates assert. Then based on this evolutionary view of man, that we are merely a higher form of animal, they go on to promote the syncretizing pagan religions, namely the worship of the Mother Goddess also known as Gaia, and its bondage and sadomasochistic practices (BDSM) with the Christian worldview:

> [T]he doctrine of creation is uniquely queer because God was not content to create just one kind of creation, but rather an incredibly diverse and multifaceted universe. This diversity of creation counters the fundamentalist and natural law argument that there should only be one kind of relationship because God created only "Adam and Eve, not Adam and Steve." In fact, by observing creation, we see that there are numerous animal species that engage in same-sex and gender variant acts. For example, Bruce Bagemihl, a biologist, has documented in his book *Biological Exuberance* hundreds of animal species that engage in homosexual, bisexual, and transgender behavior, including primates, marine mammals, hoofed mammals, carnivores, marsupials, rodents, bats, waterfowl, shore birds, perching birds, songbirds, flightless birds, reptiles, fishes, and insects… In the end, this ethic of "Gay and Gaia" encourages LGBT people to reexamine their patterns of consumption as well as their relationships with each other and with animals (for example, even with respect to the use of leather in the BDSM community).[204]

---

204   Patrick S. Cheng, *Radical Love: An Introduction to Queer Theology* (Seabury Books; 1 edition, 2011), 64.

Contrary to Gay Theology, the Bible speaks derogatively toward people who behave like or are treated as mere animals (Proverbs 26:11; 2 Peter 2:22; Job 18:3; Ecclesiastes 3:18; Daniel 5:21; Titus 1:12). Mankind as image bearers of God is called to reflect His holy character as revealed in His law and not think and behave like lower animals which *do not* bear His image. To behave like a mere beast is the very essence of what it means to suppress the knowledge of God.

In the midst of judging the serpent for his role in the deception that lead to the fall of man the Lord states that there would be an antithesis between the seed of the serpent and the seed of the woman. This would ultimately lead to the serpent crushing the heel of the seed of the woman and the seed of the woman crushing his head (Genesis 3:15). In this first form of the Gospel, the *protoevangelion*, we see the beginning of two lines of people throughout redemptive history in the Scriptures: the seed of the woman and the seed of the serpent.

In the pronouncement of judgment in Genesis 3:15 we see that there will be an antithesis between those who are followers of the serpent and those who are of the holy lineage. More often than not, the followers of the serpent disguise themselves as seed of the woman when in reality they are tares and not wheat, goats and not sheep and wolves rather than shepherds (Matthew 7:13; 10:16; 13; 25:32-33). The descendants or "seed" of the woman are not every human being on the planet. Instead this seed are those who are by faith holy in the Lord, the holy covenant community united to Christ. Throughout history there has been hostility between those who are of the line of the woman according to their spiritual nature and those who are of the line of the serpent according to their spiritual nature.

Eventually the line of the serpent becomes so great that the Lord enacts a judgment upon the earth in which He destroys every human and animal on the earth except those whom He would save in an ark. After the flood we see the first covenant after the fall that was made by the Lord with Noah and his seed in the ark:

> Behold, I, even I am bringing the flood of water upon the earth, to destroy all flesh in which is the breath of life, from under heaven; everything that is on the earth shall perish. But I will establish My covenant with you; and you shall enter

the ark - you and your sons and your wife, and your sons' wives with you. And of every living thing of all flesh, you shall bring two of every kind into the ark, to keep them alive with you; they shall be male and female (Genesis 6:17-19).

Not only do we see an antithesis and conflict between two lines we also see the Lord incrementally begin to turn the tide of the trajectory of the affects of the fall (death, slavery, polygamy, sexual sin) in a series of redemptive covenants with Noah, Abraham, Moses, and King David which all lead up to the New Covenant instituted by Jesus Christ. The Lord accomplishes this by establishing His holy line of people and incrementally in history He reveals Himself and His will to them through the means of the covenant. In these covenants His identity and saving acts are revealed by means of a promise followed by a series of commands to be obeyed with accompanying signs to seal the covenant. For example, in the Noahic Covenant we read:

> Now behold, I Myself do establish My covenant with you, and with your descendants [Hebrew: *zera* "seed"] after you; and with every living creature that is with you, the birds, the cattle, and every beast of the earth with you; of all that comes out of the ark, even every beast of the earth. And I will establish My covenant with you; and all flesh shall never again be cut off by the water of the flood, neither shall there again be a flood to destroy the earth." God said, "This is the sign of the covenant which I am making between Me and you and every living creature that is with you, for all successive generations; set My bow in the cloud, and it shall be for a sign of a covenant between Me and the earth it shall come about, when I bring a cloud over the earth, that the bow will be seen in the cloud, and I will remember My covenant, which is between Me and you and every living creature of all flesh; and never again shall the water become a flood to destroy all flesh. When the bow is in the cloud, then I will look upon it, to remember the everlasting covenant between God and every living creature of all flesh that is on the earth." And God said

to Noah, "This is the sign of the covenant which I have established between Me and all flesh that is on the earth" (Genesis 9:9-17).

Just as we saw in the Creation Covenant we see in this covenant the pattern of the declaration of identity and acts of God, a re-establishment of created order, the giving of a sign of the covenant, and the warning that those who are outside of the covenant are "cut off." This will also be said repeatedly of those who break covenant in the Abrahamic Covenant (Genesis 17:14), the Mosaic Covenant (Leviticus 18:29) and the New Covenant (Romans 11:22).

As we read in Genesis 3:15 the "seed" refers to not merely those who are somehow distantly genetically related to Eve (or Noah), but rather those who are in spiritual covenantal union with the holy line. The "descendants" refers to those of faith like Noah, not everyone who is genetically related to him. This use of "seed" or "descendants" is seen in Genesis 17 and Romans 4:16-18 as well. We see then that the covenant mentioned in Genesis 6 is ratified in Genesis 9 with the covenant sign (the rainbow) and therefore they are the one and the same covenant. We shall see this again in the Abrahamic Covenant that is established in Genesis 12, repeated in Genesis 15 and then ratified with the sign of circumcision in Genesis 17.

Though the "seed" ultimately refers to those who are of faith, the spiritual descendants of Eve and Noah, this does not mean that those who are in the covenant is a secret. The term "seed" is not without its literal aspect for the covenant speaks objectively concerning those who are in it. Noah's sons and daughters were in the ark, they had been baptized with Noah, and yet we see that some of his sons departed from the faith. They then became the father of a revived line of the seed of the serpent who became the Canaanites, Amorites and other pagan Gentile nations. We see then in the recipients of the blessings of the Noahic Covenant that not all "ark-people" are truly "ark-people" just as not all who are called "Israel" are truly "Israel." Rather it is those who are faith and obey the stipulations of the covenant from the heart are the true children of God (Romans 9:6). The Noahic covenant spoke objectively concerning those who were in it, but in time some descendants of Noah departed from the covenant.

In the Noahic Covenant, Noah had to believe God concerning what He said of the pending judgment and the means of salvation - the ark, a type of Jesus Christ. The only way to escape that judgment was to act in faith and build the ark as the writer to the Hebrews states:

> By faith Noah, being warned by God about things not yet seen, in reverence prepared an ark for the salvation of his household, by which he condemned the world, and became an heir of the righteousness which is according to faith (Hebrews 11:7).

If Noah had not built the ark he and his entire family would have perished with the rest of the unbelieving world. But because Noah had faith, he did works in accordance to that faith so that he and his family were saved. In saving Noah and his family the Lord re-establishes clear distinction between male and female for repopulating the earth (Genesis 7:3). The pre-flood world and the post-flood world began with a clear distinction between male and female. The Lord also provides a sign to remember the covenant made with Noah and his descendants – the sign of the rainbow.

The next major step in redemptive history is seen in the Lord's covenant with Abraham in which there is a series of repeated promises throughout Genesis 12-25. In these chapters there is a development of the covenant between God and Abraham (Abram) in which it is first initiated (chapter 12), then confirmed by God in an oath (chapter 15), and then years later it is ratified by the sign of circumcision (chapter 17). Throughout Abraham's life the Lord repeated several promises; that he would have countless descendants or "seed" (Genesis 12:1-2; 7; 13:15-16; 15:18; 17:7, 8, 10; 22:12-18) who will inherit a particular land (Genesis 12:1,7; 13:15, 17; 15:7, 18; 17:8) and that many nations and kings would come from him (Genesis 12:3; 17:4-6).

In Genesis we see the establishment order from chaos in a series of ten commands, "And God said..." God's Creation Covenant brings life from non-life (death), establishes freedom and order. Then in the Restorative Covenants (Noahic, Abrahamic, Mosaic, the New Covenant) where the fall brought sin, death and disorder God establishes a new trajectory in which He begins to reverse the tide of the fall. This is finally accomplished at the second coming of Christ when all of His enemies have been conquered and placed under His footstool (Hebrews 1:13; 10:13).

Approximately five hundred years after the death of Abraham the Lord resumes His Restorative Covenant at Mount Sinai. Like the Creation Covenant, the Mosaic Covenant revolves around Ten Commands or more literally ten "words" (Exodus 20: 2-17). In this covenant we see again the five-fold structure in the summary of the law, as well as in the five books of Moses, in which the name and the acts of the LORD are declared followed by the stipulations of the covenant and its accompanying signs:

(1) An identification of the king, "I am the LORD (YHWH) Thy God…" (Exodus 20:2)

(2) An accounting of the historical saving events that led to the establishment of the covenant, "…who brought you out of the land of Egypt, out of the house of slavery" (Exodus 20:2).

(3) Stipulations (terms) of the covenant (Exodus 20:3-17).

(4) A warning of judgment against anyone who was not faithful (Exodus 20:7, "…for the LORD will not leave him unpunished…") but a promise to those who maintain fidelity, "So you shall keep My statutes and My judgments, by which a man may live if he does them; I am YHWH." (Leviticus 18:5) Though false teachers like the Scribes and Pharisees would later violate God's law and burden YHWH's people with their traditions (Matthew 15:3, 6; Mark 7:9, 13), the law of God itself was not a burden, "For this commandment which I command you today is not too difficult for you, nor is it out of reach" (Deuteronomy 30:11; cf. 1 John 5:3).

(5) A means of confirming the covenant; circumcision in addition to the Passover meal (Exodus 12; 34).

While the Ten Commandments are a summary of the Mosaic Covenant, the rest of the law in Numbers, Deuteronomy and Leviticus further explain how these commandments were to be applied to daily living. What needs to be clearly understood is that the covenant which the Lord establishes with His people is not a business contract or a land-lease agreement between a landlord and a tenant. Rather, it is pictured throughout the Scriptures as a husband-bride relationship that reflects the original one-man and one-woman marriage (Genesis 2:24; Matthew 19:5; Ephesians 5:21).

The Mosaic initiation of the Law, as does all of God's command-ments, begins with the gospel of the Old Covenant – God's redemption of His bride from bondage (Isaiah 54:5-6; Jeremiah 2:2). This is the very same act that we later see Boaz do for his bride Ruth (Ruth Chapter 4). At Sinai the LORD was bringing to Himself His bride Israel who He had redeemed – YHWH is the near-kinsman redeemer! What follows in the commandments is a series of wedding vows that Israel was to keep as an act of love towards her husband, "You shall have no other gods before Me" (Exodus 20:3).

Throughout the Scriptures the Lord equates the seeking after oth-ers gods as a form of spiritual adultery (Jeremiah 2:20; Ezekiel 16:32, 36:16-18; Hosea 1:2). This was the chief sin for which Israel was sent into exile and it was the precursor to all of her others sins. Israel was commanded to have no other god beside her husband:

> You shall not make for yourself an idol, or any likeness of what is in heaven above or on the earth beneath or in the water under the earth. You shall not worship them or serve them; for I, the LORD your God, am a jealous God, visiting the iniquity of the fathers on the children, on the third and the fourth generations of those who hate Me, but showing loving-kindness to thousands, to those who love Me and keep My commandments (Exodus 20:4-6).

The husband-bride language could not get any stronger than in this commandment. When a spouse is unfaithful the other becomes jealous. For a wife, who was redeemed by a loving husband, the adulterous act is an act of hatred towards the husband. The law requires the bride to, "Love Me and keep My commandments." The requirement of the New Covenant is the same as Jesus said to His bride, the Church, "If you love Me, you will keep My commandments" (John 14:15). In fact, to love God and our neighbor is the summary of the Law and is at the very core of the Holiness Code of Leviticus 18-20. As Jesus said, "On these two commandments depend the whole Law and the Prophets" (Matthew

22: 37-38, 40). The rest of the marriage vows go on in the following manner:

> "You shall not take the name of the LORD your God in vain...
> Remember the Sabbath day, to keep it holy...
> Honor your father and your mother...
> You shall not murder.
> You shall not commit adultery.
> You shall not steal.
> You shall not bear false witness against your neighbor.
> You shall not covet..." (Exodus 20:7-17)

Some might object to viewing Israel's encounter with the LORD at Sinai as a wedding ceremony. But, how does a bride respond after the minister reads her the wedding vows? Does she not say, "I do"? This is exactly what we find Israel saying when she is betrothed and the wedding vows have been read, "All that the LORD has spoken we will do!" (Exodus 19:8; 24:3, 7).[205] Yet, after their rejection of Christ the nation was divorced and became the Great Whore of Babylon (Revelation 14:8; 17:5; 18:2, 10, 21).[206]

We see then that the spiritual enmity between seed of the woman and the serpent prophesied in Genesis 3 leads to the confrontation between those who claimed to be teachers of the law and Jesus:

> You are of your father the devil, and you want to do the desires of your father. He was a murderer from the beginning, and does not stand in the truth because there is no truth in him. Whenever he speaks a lie, he speaks from his own nature, for he is a liar and the father of lies (John 8:44).

In the New Covenant as well as the Old the Lord requires the faith that justified Abraham (Genesis 15:6). In response to this redemption He desires that His bride would love Him. In the New Covenant the Lord requires the exact same thing and Paul makes his entire argument

---

205   Roy Gane, *Leviticus, Numbers* (NIVAC 3) (Grand Rapids, MI: Zondervan, 2004), 321.
206   For further reading see: Gary De Mar, *Last Days Madness* (American Vision, 1999), 359.

for the inclusion of the Gentiles by faith on the Old Covenant (Romans Chapters 3-4). In fact, Paul makes it clear that the true Israelites were always those who were of faith (Romans 9:6) and that circumcision of the flesh in itself was nothing - it was *always* the circumcision of the heart that constituted the true Jew (Deuteronomy 10:16; 30:6; Jeremiah 4:4; Romans 2:29). The true children of Abraham have always been those who lived by faith and this was testified to "...by the Law and the Prophets" (Romans 3:21-30).

One of the clearest texts that the New Covenant is not any less demanding is Paul's "love chapter" (1 Corinthians 13). Paul reminds the Church of the covenant wedding vows of the Law of God and that their behavior towards each other and God is not in keeping with their promise to love their husband. Until the Church understands God's commandments as wedding vows Christians will never clearly understand either the gospel or the law. They will continue to pit these two against each other as if a person can somehow have Jesus as their Savior without also having Him as their Lord. In doing so the Church will see Him as the Redeemer without seeking to submit and obey Him as the Husband (Ephesians 5:22).

The New Covenant has the same five-fold structure as all the previous covenants. It identifies the King, recounts His saving work, stipulates the requirements of the covenant, warns against infidelity and it is confirmed by a sign and seal:

(1) An identification of the redeemer-king, "...and you shall call His name Jesus, for He will save His people from their sins" (Mathew 1:21).

(2) An accounting of the historical events that led to the establishment of the covenant, "...for this is My blood of the covenant, which is poured out for many for forgiveness of sins" (Matthew 26:28; 1 Corinthians 15:3-8).

(3) Stipulations of the covenant, "Repent, and each of you be baptized in the name of Jesus Christ for the forgiveness of your sins; and you will receive the gift of the Holy Spirit" (Acts 2:38).

(4) A warning of judgment against anyone who was not faithful, "I tell you, no, but unless you repent, you will all likewise perish" (Luke 13:3). But a promise to those who maintain fidelity, "If

you keep My commandments, you will abide in My love; just as I have kept My Father's commandments and abide in His love" (John 15:10).

(5) A means of confirming the covenant; Baptism (Ephesians 4:5) and the Lord's Supper, "This cup is the new covenant in My blood; do this, as often as you drink it, in remembrance of Me" (1 Corinthians 15:25).

Having examined the "big picture" of redemptive history we now need to determine how to apply God's law revealed in both testaments in our modern context. In doing so we will seek to determine the underlying principles of the law, observe the apostle's application of the law in their time and then seek to do likewise in our time and culture.

Chapter 8
The Meaning and Application of God's Law

Having discussed the framework of the Biblical covenants and the redemptive nature of the law we will look at the structure of the law and its various kinds, purposes, types and applications. It is common to hear preachers and theologians define "law" simply as "the Old Testament" or they say, "'Law' refers to any command, from Genesis to Revelation."[207] However, these definitions are overly simplistic and do not accurately represent the entirety of what Scriptures teach concerning the law. Just as there are various types of sin (commission, omission, original sin, premeditated sin) and many synonyms for sin (trespasses, iniquities, transgressions, uncleanness) so too the word "law" has various meanings which must be understood according to how the term is used in its context and in relation to its various synonyms. The words "law" (Hebrew: *tôrâ*; Greek: *nomos*) and "commandment" (Hebrew: *mitsvâh*; Greek: *entole*) are interchangeable terms in both testaments (Deuteronomy 4:45; 6:17) and other related words include "testimonies" (Hebrew: *'eduwth*), "judgments" (Hebrew: *mishpat*), "precepts" (Hebrew: *piqquwd*) or "statutes" (Hebrew: *chûqqâh*). For example, we read that God blessed Abraham because he "...obeyed my voice and kept my charge, my commandments (*mitsvâh*), my statutes (*chûqqâh*), and my laws (*tôrâh*)" (Genesis 26:5).

Just as in America the word "trunk" can refer to the storage compartment of an automobile, the base of a tree, or an appendage on the front end of an elephant so too the word "law" can also be used in different ways. It can refer to the first five books of the Bible, the "Law of Moses" (Luke 2:22, 24:44; John 7:23), and can also refer to the distinctive economy of the Mosaic Covenant during which the sacrificial system was a valid means of atoning for sin and circumcision was required for entrance into the covenant and participating in the Passover (Romans 6:14). The word "law" can also refer to the moral commandments given at Sinai (Romans 7:7). In antithesis to the law of God the word "law" can refer to a conflicting sinful ruling principle within us (Romans

---

207   Michael Horton, *The Law of Perfect Freedom* (Moody Publishers, 2004), 21.

7:21). "Law" can also be used as synonymous with "the Word of God" in general as Jesus refers to the Psalms as being in "the law" (John 10:34; Psalm 82:36) and the apostle Paul refers to the Book of Isaiah as "the law" (1 Corinthians 14:21).

It is extremely important then that when we use the term "law" and read Paul's phrase "not under the law" that we are clear on what he is addressing. As we shall see, contrary to Dispensationalism and Gay Theology, when Paul tells Christians that they are "not under law" he is *not* asserting that all of the Old Testament moral commandments are no longer required to be obeyed by faithful God-honoring Christians.

Categories of Law in The Old and New Covenant Contexts

There was a time when food and wine pairing was overly simplistic and it was commonly asserted, "Red wine goes with beef, white wine goes with chicken and fish." Due to the advancement of understanding the varieties of grapes and the complexities of food and wine flavors and styles this is no longer the case. The days of ignoring the vast differences in types of grapes and the great variety in which pairing can be made has ended the simplistic categorization of "red wine with beef" and "white wine with poultry."

In a similar fashion it has been common to assert in theological confessions and systematic theologies a simplistic categorization of the law of God as "moral law" "ceremonial law" and "civil law" or in terms of three uses - to convict the sinner, a standard for sanctification, and provide a standard for justice in the civil realm.[208] It is then it is commonly asserted that while the "ceremonial laws" of the Old Testament are no longer binding, having been fulfilled in Christ, the moral laws are still applicable and the "general equity" of the civil laws should still be upheld.[209] It has also been common to hear references to "two tables" of the law, one which relates to our relationship to God and the other that relates to our relationship to man.[210] While these classifica-

208   Greg Bahnsen, *By This Standard* (Tyler, TX: Institute For Christian Economics, 1985), 203ff.
209   As the Westminster Confession states, "To them also, as a body politick, he gave sundry judicial laws, which expired together with the state of that people, not obliging any other now, further than the general equity thereof may require." (19.4)
210   Michael Horton, *The Law of Perfect Freedom* (Chicago: Moody Press, 1993), 9

tions may be a convenient way of talking about the law, we cannot find these categories explicitly stated anywhere in Scripture nor can the fine lines of distinction between moral, ceremonial and civil be easily made. Consequently in response to such categorizations, there are those reject any sort of differentiation in the Old Testament law and insist that the entire body of Old Testament law is not applicable in the New Covenant era except those which are repeated in the New Testament. However in light of the fact that the first generation of Christians did not have the New Testament and only the Old Testament was available as an objective standard for Christian conduct, as well as the testimony of the apostle's frequent citation of the law for Christian ethics and morality, such a conclusion is not justifiable.

In order to have a right understanding of the apostolic use of God's law, there are several things that we must keep in mind. First and foremost, God alone is sovereign over His Word and He alone may tell us which laws are still binding and which are not in the New Covenant. Therefore, unless the New Testament either explicitly, or by good and necessary consequence, has abrogated or made obsolete an Old Testament law it is still applicable and its principle is to be observed in a New Covenant fashion. As we shall see, when we read the New Testament the apostles continue to cite the Old Testament laws as an objective standard for Christian conduct while also insisting that some of the laws are no longer applicable to believers. While they do not provide us with handy categories in which we may classify which laws are binding and which are not, we can determine their justification for maintaining some laws while abrogating others by observing how they apply the law.

Second, contrary to the two-table theory all of the laws relate to our relationship with God and man. Consequently when King David sinned against his neighbor by committing adultery with Bathsheba and murdering her husband he declared to God, "Against You and You only have I sinned" (Psalm 51:5). Likewise, when Achan sinned against God by taking the golden idols, his neighbors including his family and all of Israel suffered the consequences of His sin as well (Joshua 22:20). Our sin against God is also a sin against our neighbor and our sin against our neighbor is a sin against God.

Third, we also need to see that all of the Ten Commandments over lap each other and are interconnected. For example, the sin of coveting (10th Commandment) is a precursor to the sin of theft (8th Commandment) and adultery (7th Commandment). Likewise, adultery is a form of theft of another person's spouse and it constitutes a violation of bearing false witness in one's marriage vows (9th Commandment). Undoubtedly this is why James wrote, "For whoever keeps the whole law and yet stumbles in one point, he has become guilty of all" (James 2:10). However, his point was not that we should then cease to obey the Decalogue. Rather his point is that if we say we have faith we should not exploit or mistreat the poor person who is our neighbor, for the same law that says "Do not commit adultery" and "Do not murder" (Exodus 20:14, 13) also says in the very heart of the Holiness Code, "Love you neighbor as yourself" (Leviticus 19:18; James 2:8-11).

Fourth, we need to understand the various laws in terms of their covenantal jurisdiction (family, church, state), as well as those who are responsible for upholding the commandments (family elders, ecclesiastical elders, civil elders).[211] Then having done so, we need to look at the purpose of the laws and how they are used by the authors of Scripture redemptive-historically within the Old and New Testaments. This approach does justice to the text rather than simplistically categorizing the laws of the Old Testament in three different categories and then determine which category ought to be abrogated as obsolete.

Fifth, as we shall see, we need to understand that the law of the Old Testament was not intended to create a utopian society but rather in a redemptive fashion it was designed to turn the tide of the fall of mankind into sin and chaos. Incrementally God's covenant with man and His revealed will in the law restore society and creation to order in every aspect of life. God's law restrains the consequences of the fall while

---

211   As Gary North states, "I am suggesting the need for a restructuring of this traditional tripartite division in civil, ecclesiastical, and familial. In other words, the divisions should match the Bible's tripartite covenantal and institutional division. There are continuities (moral law) and discontinuities (redemptive-historical applications) in all three covenantal law-orders. It is the task of the interpreter to make these distinctions and interrelationships clear. The church has been avoiding this crucial task (exegetical and applicational) for over three centuries. The result has been the dominance of ethical dualism in Christian social theory: natural law theory coupled with pietism and/or mysticism." "Hermeneutics and Leviticus 19:19" *Theonomy: An Informed Response* (Tyler, Texas: Institute For Christian Economics, 1991), 260.

tolerating it within certain limits. We see a modern example of this form of fencing in the legalization of tobacco cigarettes within the U.S.A.. There is presently no law that forbids becoming addicted to tobacco products. This is not because the government or our culture thinks that becoming a slave to cigarettes is morally justifiable. Rather cigarettes are "legal" but they are confined, restricted and heavily discouraged and their harmful affects to your health made publicly known. Likewise, certain forms of pornography and prostitution are also legal in some parts of the country. Yet this does not indicate that the U.S. government and the majority of American citizens believe that pornography is morally good. Rather the U.S. government taxes, restricts the age accessibility and confines the areas in which strip joints may exist but such guarded "legal" activity does not mean that such license is to be deemed morally justifiable. What we need to understand is that within the law given to Moses, not everything that was legal in the civil laws is morally right and not everything that is immoral or unethical is civilly illegal for there was no penal sanction against coveting within one's heart.[212]

The government operates this way because it is not possible to micromanage individual lives or penalize every sinful action. This is why the first and most important form of government is self-government. Only when individuals in a society fail to live and act responsibly does the state have the moral necessity to increase laws and intervene into the lives of its citizens to maintain order and curb evil. Therefore, rather than trying to make every sin illegal a just society attempts to maintain some civility by restricting it and confining it within certain parameters.

The law of God in the Bible in the Mosaic Covenant is written in a similar way. After restricting and confining various sinful actions, it provides an overarching principle to love God and love one's neighbor. If this law is obeyed, the laws that restrained and regulated such things as slavery and divorce become unnecessary. In application, if the Israelites truly loved their neighbor they wouldn't need to be controlled by slavery laws that restricted and held them accountable for how they treated slaves.

---

212   For example, divorce in the law was legal, but it was not always morally right as Jay Adams states, "…Deuteronomy 24:1-4 refers (as does 1 Cor. 7:10, 11 – with which it has affinities, as we have seen) to a divorce given on unbiblical (or illegitimate) grounds. Such a divorce is legally proper, but sinful." *Marriage, Divorce, and Remarriage in the Bible* (Grand Rapids, MI: Zondervan, 1980), 64-65.

In the first century, the Pharisees that Jesus encountered often mistook "legality" for "morally justifiable." But Jesus made it clear that some things were legislated and allowable not because they are good or according to God's original design, but rather they were put in place because of the hardness of people's hearts (Matthew 19:8). Hence, not everything which is "legal" can be declared to be morally "good." By fencing certain actions and social circumstances the law of God in the Old Testament hedged in the affects of the sin as it incrementally turned the trajectory of the fall as the law protects life, restricts slavery, restricts divorce and prohibits men having sex with other men. And it penalizes those who break these laws. In the New Testament the implications of the Gospel and the coming of the Kingdom of God catapults this trajectory even further.

Finally, another popular misconception, especially within Lutheran circles and Dispensationalism, is that "law" refers to any command in the Bible whereas "Gospel" refers to any place in Scripture where there is a promise of salvation. Michael Horton illustrates such confusion when he says that:

> 'Law' refers to any command, from Genesis to revelation. 'Gospel' refers to any place in either testament where the promise of salvation by grace alone through faith alone is found. The law tells us what we *ought* to do, and this leads us to despair of meeting God's standard. Then the gospel tells us what God has done for us already in Christ, meeting the standard as our substitute and taking our punishment on Himself so that we could be regarded as righteous.[213]

This understanding of "Law" and "Gospel" is seriously flawed. The Gospel of the Old Testament which speaks of the redemptive acts of God says, "I am the Lord your God who brought you out of Egypt" foreshadows the redemptive work of Christ and it is found in the law of God (Exodus 20:2). All of the regulations concerning the blood atoning sacrifices that foreshadowed Christ were given in the law. Likewise the call of the Gospel of the New Testament declares that there is something which we are to do in response to the work of Christ, "Repent and be

---

213   Michael Horton, *The Law of Perfect Freedom* (Chicago: Moody Press, 1993), 21.

baptized for the remission of your sin in the name of Jesus Christ" (Acts 2:28; 22:16). You cannot simply define "law" as the "you ought to do this" passages or "Gospel" as "God has done this for you" passages. The texts that tell us of the work and promises of God are intertwined with the texts that require a response from the believer. The "law/Gospel" hermeneutic is not workable and cannot be found in the Scriptures. You cannot go through the Bible and say "that is a law text" simply because it tells us what we ought to do. Faith and obedience are not to be confused but neither are they to be separated from each other for all the acts of obedience of the saints are done by faith as we read:

> By faith Abel offered to God a better sacrifice than Cain... By faith Noah, being warned by God about things not yet seen, in reverence prepared an ark for the salvation of his household... By faith Abraham, when he was called, obeyed by going out to a place which he was to receive for an inheritance... By faith Abraham, when he was tested, offered up Isaac..." (Hebrews 11:4, 7, 8, 17)

The faith that justifies is an obedient faith for without works that claim to faith is dead (James 2:14-26). On Judgment Day the basis upon which one's claim to faith will be either accepted or dismissed will be one's obedience to the law by faith and from the heart (Matthew 25:31-46). What must be clearly understood is that the Gospel does indeed place on us moral demands, to deny oneself, pick up our cross and follow Jesus Christ which may include saying "no" to our sexual desires when they are in conflict with the revealed will of God:

> From the gospel's point of view, then, there is no absolute right or unconditional guarantee of sexual fulfillment for Christian believers... If *all* Christians must surrender their bodies to God in Christ whenever they enter the fellowship of Christ's body, then it should come as no great shock that God might actually make demands of those Christians and their bodies – demands proving that God, and God alone, has authority over us... this kind of long-suffering endurance is not a special assignment the gospel gives to gay and lesbian persons. Many believers of all stripes and

backgrounds struggle with desires of various sorts that
they must deny in order to remain faithful to the gospel's
demands…The sorrow and suffering we experience as
homosexual Christians is that of saying good-bye to any
sure hope of satisfying our sexual cravings. In choosing
fidelity to the gospel, we agree to bear up under the burden
for as long as it is necessary.[214]

The Letter And Principle Of The Law

One of the most important ideas which must be understood concerning God's law is that there is a distinction, though not a separation,
between the letter of the law and the spirit of the law. A person may
observe the spirit and intent of the law even if the details of the law are
not followed to the minutest detail. Likewise, a person may violate the
intent of the law even if the action is different than the specific requirements or prohibitions of the stated law. Also a law may be broken even
if the action only takes place within one's heart without actually fully
carrying it out in one's actions.

For example, the sixth commandment tells us that we are not to
commit murder (Exodus 20:13). However, we then read that you may
justifiably kill a person in order to defend yourself from a criminal who
is breaking into your home (Exodus 22:2). Therefore, there is within
the intent of the sixth commandment an allowance for justifiable ho-
micide. Furthermore, like all of the God's laws and precepts, the sixth
commandment is not merely concerned with the external observance of
the law as it is also to be applied to every thought, word, and deed as
Jesus states:

> You have heard that it was said to them of old time, 'You
> shall not commit murder; and whosoever shall commit
> murder shall be in danger of the judgment:' But I say unto
> you, that everyone who is angry with his brother shall be in
> danger of the judgment… (Matthew 5:21-22).

---

214   Wesley Hill, *Washed and Waiting: Reflection on Christian Faithfulness and
Homosexuality* (Grand Rapids: Zondervan Publishing House, 2010), 70, 71, 75.

The sixth commandment also forbids unjust anger and murderous thoughts as well, though it is inaccurate to say that the actual acting out of the sin is the same as merely doing it in your heart. The control of our temper is important because one sin leads to another as James writes:

> Let no one say when he is tempted, 'I am being tempted by God'; for God cannot be tempted by evil, and He Himself does not tempt anyone. But each one is tempted when he is carried away and enticed by his own lust. Then when lust is conceived, it gives birth to sin; and when sin is accomplished, it brings forth death (James 2:13-15).

Not only is the Decalogue applicable in the New Covenant era, but the Apostle Paul provides for us an example of the intent of the case laws found in the "Law of Moses" as still being applicable as well. In doing so, he applies the principle of the law regarding not muzzling a working ox in Deuteronomy 25:4 to the provision of a minister of the Gospel (1 Corinthians 9:1-11).

The principle of Deuteronomy 25:4 is that a worker has the right to benefit from his labor and to not allow him to do so would be a form of theft, a violation of the 8th commandment. The same method of applying Old Testament laws in different New Covenant contexts can be used for other laws. For example, the requirement of placing a parapet on a flat-topped roof to protect life can be applied to putting a fence around a backyard swimming pool to protect children from accidental drowning (Deuteronomy 22:8). As we shall see, there are other laws which, given in a particular ritualistic religious context, in the Old Testament can be applied in non-ritualistic contexts as well even in the New Testament such as the principle of the sacrificial libation offering being applied to financial support for the ministry (Exodus 29:18; Philippians 4:18). In a similar fashion, the laws that regulate sexual behavior can also be applied in a modern context even though the text does not specifically mention such things as pornography on the internet, non-married couples participating in consensual mutual masturbation, or same sex acts within a "committed relationship."

Types and Shadows In The Law

One of the most important things to understand about the Law of Moses are the elements which were typological in form. Some of these types refer to Christ and have found their intended purpose in Him while the moral and spiritual principle of others is still to be followed in a New Covenant era.

Some of these types and shadows in the Old Testament are found in the poetic, prophetic and apocalyptic genres in which we see that animals symbolically represent people. For example, the beasts in Daniel chapter 7 represent a succession of rulers and John refers to the persecutor of the Church, the Roman emperor Nero, as "the Beast" (Revelation 13:18).[215] The bulls and dogs in Psalm 22:12 and Psalm 22:16 represent the Jews and Romans who mocked and crucified Christ on the cross and Paul tells us the naturally opposing animals (wolf and lamb, leopard and goat, calf and lion) in Isaiah 11 that are made to be at peace with one another represent Jews and Gentiles who have been made one in Christ in the New Covenant (Romans 15:11). More importantly, we need to see that the sacrificial Passover lamb, as do many of the other atoning animal sacrifices, represented Christ (Exodus 12:27; John 1:29, 36; 1 Corinthians 5:7).

However, many of the other sacrifices of the Old Testament are also carried over into the New Testament in different forms. For example, the thanksgiving animal sacrifices in the Old Testament are represented by people in the New Testament who are to offer up themselves as living sacrifices of worship (Leviticus 7:12-15; 22:29; Romans 12:1-2). Likewise, the libation offering of the Old Testament that pictured Christ pouring Himself out as a sacrifice is continually observed by Paul pouring himself out in following Christ's example as well as the Philippian believers who contributed financially to Paul's missionary efforts (Exodus 29:18; Philippians 2:7, 17; 4:18).

Not only are animals in the poetic texts, prophetic passages and the sacrificial system typological of the people in the New Testament but so also the building of the temple and its form of worship was a shadow and a type of the New Covenant Church. Old Covenant worship was primarily symbolic (typological) because it was pre-incarnational. The

---

215   For more reading concerning the identity of the Beast see: Kenneth L. Gentry Jr., *The Beast of Revelation* (American Vision, 2002)

temple worship consisted of types and shadows of that which was yet to come in the New Covenant (Hebrews 8:5; 10:1). Jerusalem, the temple, the priests, the altars, the incense and the sacrifices were central to Old Covenant worship because through them God provided pictures of the coming Messiah. The types and shadows were temporary and necessarily inferior to the revelation of the Anti-type in the gospel (Hebrews 10:19-22). The shadows however were surpassed by the genuine, Jesus Christ, who having come is apprehended not by continuing types but by faith through the proclamation of the gospel from Scripture.

Jesus told Peter that He was going to build His Church upon a new foundation, which was to be him and the other the apostles (Matthew 18:13-19). The apostles John, Peter and Paul all used the imagery of the temple, which was then obsolete, as a picture of the New Temple, the Church, the New Jerusalem, which they built by the authority given to them by Jesus Christ (Revelation; 21:14; 1 Corinthians 3:16-17; 6:17-20; Ephesians 2:19-22; 1 Peter 2:4-8).

Seeing how Old Testament imagery and laws regulating worship are used in the New Testament in governing the Christian life, particularly sexual behavior, is extremely important. We need to keep these images and metaphors in mind when we later consider Paul's citation of the Holiness Code in the judgment of a man having sex with his father's wife (Leviticus 18:8; 1 Corinthians 5:1), his upholding of the penal sanction (Leviticus 18:29; 1 Corinthians 5:13, Deuteronomy 13:5) and his call upon Christians to not become "one flesh" with a prostitute for to do so is a desecration of God's temple (1 Corinthians 6:13-20).

The Law of God and Liberty

One of the most common tactics of liberals and proponents of Gay Theology is that anytime anyone cites an Old Testament passage against same sex acts is to then cite other passages that regulated slavery as if they were an endorsement of it.[216] It is then rhetorically asked, "Are you going to endorse slavery too?" This is a misrepresentation of what the Bible teaches on slavery and indentured servitude.

Throughout Scripture sin is equated with debt, particularly in being a debtor to God. One of the primary purposes of the law given at Sinai

216   Daniel Helminiak, *What the Bible Really Says About Homosexuality* (Estancia, NM: Alamo Square Press, 2000), 81.

was not to put the believer in bondage, but rather to establish liberty. In contrast to many of the surrounding pagan nations, the law in the Mosaic Covenant established parameters to protect slaves, restrict the abuse of slaves and to set a new trajectory towards liberty and freedom. While the kings used foreign slaves as labor (1 Kings 5:15; 2 Chronicles 2:17-18) the law also made a clear distinction between the benefits of being one of God's people for they had greater protections against long term slavery. For example, the manumission laws (commandments regarding the freeing of slaves) in Exodus, Leviticus and Deuteronomy stipulated the release of Hebrew debt-slaves who were released after a six-year (Exodus 21:2-6; Deuteronomy 15:12-18) or forty-nine year period of service (Leviticus 25:39-42).[217]

What must be kept in mind is that it was sin that put the believer in debt but it was the law of God that restricted the depth and length to which a person could go into debt and be without his God-given inheritance. It is a misrepresentation of Scripture to assert that the Mosaic Covenant promoted or endorsed slavery as God's desire for mankind. The condition of slavery was a given circumstance in the fallen and broken world. The treatment of slaves in the Pentateuch is discussed in many different legal stipulations which can be categorized according to the following topics:

1. Manumission (male slave) (Exodus 21:2-6; Leviticus 25:39-42, 47-55)
2. Marriage and Manumission (female slave) (Exodus 21:7-11; Deuteronomy 21:10-14)
3. Sex outside marriage (Leviticus 19:20-22)
4. Coveting (Exodus 20:17 = Deuteronomy 5.21)
5. Assault (Exodus 21:20-21, 26-27, 32
6. Sabbath (Exodus 20:10 = Deuteronomy 5:14)
7. Sabbatical Year (Leviticus 25:6)
8. Offerings (Deuteronomy 12:12, 18)
9. Feasts (Deuteronomy 16:11) (Feast of Weeks), 14 (Feast of Booths)

---

217   Gregory C. Chirichigno, *Debt-Slavery in Israel and the Ancient Near East* (Sheffield, 1993), 148.

10. Misc. (Leviticus 25:44-45 (note on permanent slavery) Deuteronomy 23.15-16 (escaped slaves).[218]

The New Covenant also supports the rules about slavery. However we must understand that not all "slavery" is the same. The slavery that took place in North America was not slavery in terms of indentured servitude. Instead, it was the result of "man stealing" (kidnapping) which the law of God in the Mosaic Covenant said was punishable by death (Deuteronomy 24:7). Africans were stolen from their home, robbed of their identity and their family and then sold in the market. The "slavery" that was practiced in United States of America prior to 1860 was the result of "man stealing." West Africans were kidnapped, put on ships, brought to America, sold at auction, and placed in forced labor. Contrary to some defenders of the American institution of slavery, the Gospel commands us to go to other nations and proclaim the gospel that brings liberty. It is a sin to support ungodly slave traders and then abuse men made in the image of God and seek to justify such slavery as being a "school for Christ" as some Christians asserted.

It may be said that what slave traders intended for evil, God in His providence intended for good so that they might hear the gospel and come to Christ, like Joseph being sold into slavery by his brothers (Genesis 50:20). Nevertheless the actions of these slaver traders was a crime in the Old Testament punishable by death (Exodus 21:16).

What must be kept in mind is that while slavery was a permissible socio-economic system (Leviticus 25:44), the Bible does not command anyone to have slaves as if it said, "Thou shalt take slaves." It merely recognizes and regulates a known economic situation without calling it "good" in order to protect slaves from being abused, "He who strikes a man so that he dies shall surely be put to death" (Exodus 21:12).

In Deuteronomy 24:7, the kidnapping of covenant members is particularly forbidden, but in Exodus 21:16, all man-stealing is prohibited. In the New Testament the apostles also recognized that slavery, as legislated by the Romans, as an economic reality without calling it "good." Christian slaves were exhorted to be good examples of the faith by being obedient to their masters (Ephesians 6:5; Colossians 3:22; 1 Timothy 6:2). But masters who were converted to the faith were exhorted to treat their Christian slaves as brothers (Ephesians 6:9; Colossians

218   Ibid, 147.

4:1; Philemon 1:16). When you condemn what God's law allows, you are a legalist and sin (Deuteronomy 4:3; Proverbs 30:6; Revelation 22:18–19). When you allow what God's law condemns, you are a law-breaker and sin (Exodus 20:1–17). When you cannot tell the difference, you cannot think as a Christian.

The Application of God's Law

Two of the most important issues for the Church in the 21st century concerns the *meaning* of the text of Scripture (the author's intended message to the original recipients) and the *application* of the text to subsequent generations. This requires readers to not only understand the text in its original context but also determine how the text's prohibitions, commands and warnings should be understood and followed in their own social and historical situation. In the remainder of this chapter we shall establish some basic guidelines for doing this by seeking to understand the structure of God's law and determine how they convey God's revealed will for mankind. We will then in subsequent chapters look at the so-called "clobber passages" in their original context, determine the normative moral principle of the text and apply them in our modern 21st century situation. We will ultimately find that the principle of the prohibitions of texts such as Leviticus 18:22 extend beyond the context of cultic worship of Molech and are to be universally applied to all same-sex behaviors.

One of the most crucial issues in dealing with the Bible and what it says concerning same sex acts and the relationship between Old and New Testaments is a proper understanding of the quantity, meaning and application of God's commandments. In opposition to this method of developing a system for understanding God's normative standard of ethics and means of discerning subsequent applications in various situations, Gay Theology apologist Rick Brentlinger asserts:

> God gave the Law to Moses and the Jewish nation, on Mt. Sinai, after the children of Israel left Egypt. The year was approximately 1450 BC. The Law of Moses contains 613 commandments... The 613 commandments of the Law of Moses cover everything from blood sacrifices to gardening

> to sexual worship of false gods to sewage disposal. I sus-
> pect no one alive today can even name all 613 of God's
> commandments in the Law. If you cannot even name the
> commandments, how could you ever hope to keep all
> 613? [219]

This is a misrepresentation of God's law and its purpose. Like many Dispensationalists and modern evangelicals who do not understand the law, speaking of it in this manner is intended to set forth an absurd notion that if a person can't remember, let alone perfectly keep, all of the laws then its purpose is simply to make the point that obedience to the law is impossible. This then is supposed to be what reveals a sinner's need for a Messiah who can and did remember and keep all the laws. Yet in a contradictory fashion they'll also state that Jesus and His disciples disobeyed God's law, particularly the 4th commandment and the penal sanctions for adultery, and in following Him we should do likewise. Subsequently, they assert that once you have faith in Christ obedience to any of the Old Testament laws is not required since Jesus kept them in your place or chose to do away with them by breaking them. They'll go on to insist that because we are living under grace the gospel does not require any act of obedience or faithfulness on our part.

It is certainly true that Jesus did keep all the laws perfectly and our righteousness that meets God's commands is His imputed righteousness. However, the notion that we are not required to obey any of the Old Testament laws contradicts the meaning of the phrase "not under law but under grace" and it ignores the explicit teaching of Scripture when the Lord declared, "For this commandment which I command you today is not too difficult for you, nor is it out of reach" (Deuteronomy 30:11).

The Mosaic Covenant was not a system of meriting salvation for it provided a means of atoning for sin. What was required in order to remain in good standing in the covenant was faith, humility, mercy and justice - in essence marital fidelity to YHWH as Micah declared, "He has told you, O man, what is good and what the LORD requires of you - to do justice, to love kindness, and to walk humbly with your God" (Micah 6:8).

---

219   Rick Brentlinger, *Gay Christian 101 - Spiritual Self-Defense For Gay Christians* (2007), 357.

The Structural Hierarchy of God's Law

To properly understand the law of God we need to see the relation-ship between the two Great Commandments, the Decalogue and their various applications throughout Scripture. The Law of God has two overarching commandments – "Love the Lord your God with all your heart and with all your soul and with all your mind" (Deuteronomy 6:5; cf. Matthew 22:36) and "Love your neighbor as yourself" (Leviticus 19:18; Matthew 22:39). But if we were to ask how we should love God and our neighbor, the answer lies in summary form in the Decalogue (Exodus 20:1-17). The Ten Commandments are not an exhaustive list of commands to be obeyed by the redeemed. Rather they are a short list of examples of how we should love God and our neighbor. The Decalogue is then explained and clarified by all the other moral laws in various hypothetical day-to-day scenarios throughout the Old Testament. We then find in the New Testament that Jesus and the apostles applied the principles of these Old Testament laws to their first century situations and thereby provided us with an example of how we too should seek to apply the same moral principles in our day.

Specifically, the 613 laws in the Old Testament were not intended to be steps in a ladder which God expected Israel to climb in order to merit their salvation. Rather, they are a detailed list of laws that help define the parameters of the Decalogue and the two overarching commandments which were to be obeyed because the LORD had saved them out of slav-ery. In addition, many of these laws are what we might refer to as "case laws" in which hypothetical scenarios are given to provide examples of how one might apply the various laws:

> The Scriptures are not catalogs of dos and don'ts on all matters of life topically arranged in alphabetical form. Instead, they consist largely of general and specific princi-ples stated in contexts to which they apply and exemplary incidents that are applicable to all of life.[220]

In fact, many of the general and specific principles are applications of the exact same law. Furthermore, because of the distinctive redemp-

---

220   Jay Adams, *A Theology of Christian Counseling* (Grand Rapids, MI; Zonder-van, 1979), 24.

tive-historic place of the Mosaic Covenant in comparing the Old and New Testament we discover that there is another two part overarching character of God's laws. First, there were those laws that revealed God's moral will for all people in every age. Second, there were those laws that had a designed obsolescence that were intended to end with the coming of Jesus Christ. The laws which had a designed obsolescence either prefigured Christ's office as prophet, priest and king and His work of redemption in the New Testament or they made a cultural distinction between Jews and Gentiles which ended with the ushering in of the Gentiles into the covenant by faith. These included such things as the Old Covenant signs of circumcision, the food laws, the clothing laws and the typological feast days.

With this in mind we can see that there were other laws given that relate to loving God and one's neighbor which are specified in the sixth commandment, "Thou shalt not murder" (Exodus 20:13). Many other laws are examples that explain the sixth commandment so that we can see that the principle of this law requires us to not merely refrain from wrongfully taking an innocent life but guard innocent life as well such as protecting an unborn child from quarreling men or a visiting house-guest from falling off of a patio on the rooftop (Exodus 21:22-23; Deuteronomy 22:8):

In addition, the other laws are examples that explain the sixth commandment in that while we may not take innocent life, we may justly take the life of a wrong doer in self-protection, "If the thief is caught while breaking in and is struck so that he dies, there will be no bloodguiltiness on his account" (Exodus 22:2). Likewise, the state government may also enact the penal sanction of death of a lawbreaker. This is not merely an Old Testament law for the Apostle Paul explicitly states that the civil magistrate is a minister of God to enact justice with the sword:

> Every person is to be in subjection to the governing author-
> ities. For there is no authority except from God, and those
> which exist are established by God. Therefore whoever
> resists authority has opposed the ordinance of God; and
> they who have opposed will receive condemnation upon

themselves. For rulers are not a cause of fear for good behavior, but for evil. Do you want to have no fear of authority? Do what is good and you will have praise from the same; for it is a minister of God to you for good. But if you do what is evil, be afraid; for it does not bear the sword for nothing; for it is a minister of God, an avenger who brings wrath on the one who practices evil (Romans 13:1-4).

Likewise, if we seek to understand how to apply the underlying principle of the commandment, "You shall not commit adultery" (Exodus 20:14) the solution would be found throughout the 613 commandments in the Old Testament including the sexual prohibitions found in Leviticus 18 and 20. In reading the other commandments, we would discover that the principle of loving one's neighbor by obeying the seventh commandment extends far beyond merely the act of a married man having sex with a woman who is not his wife. In general, the seventh commandment covers the category of all sexual sins which includes fornication, incest, bestiality and men having sex with other men. When the tenth commandment (which prohibits coveting) is paired with the seventh commandment we discover that the intent or spirit of the seventh commandment prohibits, as Jesus taught, lusting after a woman who is not your wife or by implication a woman coveting a man who is not her husband (Matthew 5:27-28). This is why Jesus said regarding the two overarching commandments of Deuteronomy 6:5 and Leviticus 19:18, "All the Law and the Prophets hang on these two commandments" (Matthew 22:4).

A teacher of the law posed a question to Jesus which was "Which commandment is the greatest?" The question was *not*, "What commandment can we live by so we can disregard all the rest?" In His teaching on the law of God Jesus responds in two ways. First, He quotes the Old Testament law (Deuteronomy 6:5; Leviticus 19:18) rather than giving the person who asked the question (a lawyer) a new law or commandment. Second, Jesus explicitly states that all of the rest of moral commandments "depend" on these two commandments. The word translated "depend" in the Greek is *krematai* which means "hangs" (as it is translated in the KJV). Just as a painting requires a hook in order to hang from a wall so too the rest of the commandments depend on these two laws in order to be observed. A person who is without love for God and his neighbor will not keep the rest of the laws such as not committing adultery, not fornicating, not committing same-sex acts and the other commandments in the law.

Of course a mere external observance of the law is not sufficient. The Pharisees often had a mere external superficial observance of the law and Jesus rebuked them for being hypocrites, likening them to being a cup that was clean on the outside but dirty on the inside (Matthew 23:25). In order for any act to be truly honoring to God it must be according to His Word just as Jesus quoted the law in response to Satan (Matthew 4:7, cf. Deuteronomy 6:16). It must be done in faith for without faith it is impossible to please God (Hebrews 11:6). The purpose for obeying must be to glorify God rather than merely for our selfish interests (1 Corinthians 10:31; Philippians 2:4), and it must be done with the motivation of love otherwise it is worthless (1 Corinthians 13:1-3).

The Old Testament law explained what it meant to love God and one's neighbor, and it provided a typological picture of the saving work of Christ. It also established the jurisdictions, roles and responsibilities of the elders of the family, the Church and the state. Only God Himself is without a limited jurisdiction for Jesus is King of kings and Lord of lords (Revelation 19:16). Contrary to what is commonly asserted, there was a distinction between what we might think of as the government of the Church, the government of the state, and the government of the family. This is why a king was not allowed to perform the role of a priest and the priest was not to perform the role of a king. The various governmental systems (self, family, church, and state) had different God-ordained jurisdictions that existed at the same time and place, affecting the same people, and God desired that they respect differences in jurisdictions. Consequently, when King Saul overstepped his jurisdiction by conducting the sacrifice that was within the jurisdiction of the priest alone he was subsequently rejected as king (1 Samuel 15).

What must be noted is that the apostles continue to cite the Decalogue (as in Ephesians 6:2) as well the two overarching commandments of God's law to love God and one's neighbor (Matthew 19:19; Romans 13:9; Galatians 5:14; James 2:8). They also cite portions of the case laws and apply their principle in a New Covenant context including

Deuteronomy and Leviticus passages that are found within the so-called "Holiness Code." The only commandments that the apostles do not continue to insist that all Christians obey are those which have been placed by a New Covenant antecedent (Passover/Lord's Supper, Circumcision/Baptism), were typological and tied to the sacrificial system of the Temple Worship, or made a distinction between Jews and Gentiles such as the food and clothing laws. In fact, even the principle or spirit of many of the non-bloody atoning sacrifices are observed in a New Covenant form (Exodus 29:18; Philippians 4:18).

Therefore, what we need to understand is not merely what the text explicitly states, but also the law's intent so that we'll understand its moral principles. If all we do is pay attention to the letter of the law we will repeat the error of some of the Pharisees who only had a static reading of text which ignored the heart of the law. Jesus, in His teaching on the law in the Sermon of the Mount, contradicts the errors of the man made traditions of the Pharisees in their antinomian treatment of the law:

> You have heard that the ancients were told, "You shall not commit murder" and "Whoever commits murder shall be liable to the court." But I say to you that everyone who is angry with his brother shall be guilty before the court; and whoever says to his brother, "You good-for-nothing," shall be guilty before the supreme court; and whoever says, "You fool," shall be guilty enough to go into the fiery hell (Matthew 5:21-23).

It was the Pharisees who believed that they could be obedient by only paying attention to a static letter-perfect reading of the text while ignoring the spirit and intent of the law. But Jesus also upheld God's holy law by applying it to the interior motives of human hearts such as when He declares:

> You have heard that it was said, "You shall not commit adultery"; but I say to you that everyone who looks at a woman with lust for her has already committed adultery with her in his heart (Matthew 5:27-28).

Elsewhere in the Sermon on the Mount Jesus contradicts not the law of God, but rather the tradition of the Pharisees who nullified the law of God with their teaching:

> You have heard that it was said, "You shall love your neighbor" and "hate your enemy." But I say to you, love your enemies and pray for those who persecute you, so that you may be sons of your Father who is in heaven; for He causes His sun to rise on the evil and the good, and sends rain on the righteous and the unrighteous (Matthew 5:43-45).

It was the law of God, specifically in the Holiness Code, that commanded God's people to love their neighbor (Leviticus 19:18) but it was the tradition of the Pharisees that taught the people "hate your enemy." This understanding of the Jesus' teaching on the law is completely antithetical to the antinomian assertions of Gay Theologians who argue that Jesus disobeyed the fourth commandment regarding the Sabbath such as when they assert, "Jesus says that His disciples, who broke the Law by harvesting grain on the Sabbath, are 'guiltless.' Matthew 12:1-7."[221] But Jesus and the disciples didn't violate the principle of the Sabbath for they were not harvesting grain, but only ate what was necessary for their immediate sustenance.

If Jesus had violated the Sabbath law He would have been a sinner and not worthy to be called the spotless Lamb of God who takes away the sin of the world (John 1:29). What Jesus does in His observance and teaching on the Sabbath is demonstrate its true intent. The Sabbath was ordained to be a means of rest for God's people (Mark 2:27), not a barrier to doing works of necessity or charity. Jesus pointed out the hypocrisy of the Pharisees who would judge Him for healing on the Sabbath while they wouldn't refrain from getting their animal out of a ditch (Luke 14:1-6). While it would have been a violation of God's law for a common man to partake of the show bread, because King David and his men were in a desperate situation and in need of food the necessity of preserving his life and uphold the sixth commandment

---

221   Rick Brentlinger, *Gay Christian 101 - Spiritual Self-Defense For Gay Christians* (2007), 364. For further reading on this subject see "The Lord of the Sabbath" in Joseph A. Pipa's book, *The Lord's Day* (Christian Focus, 1997).

took priority over the law regarding the showbread. Not all command-ments are equal as there are some laws that are "weightier" than others (Matthew 23:23). For example, the priority of preserving innocent life precedes the requirement to tell the truth to murderers (Exodus 1:17-19) or maintain the showbread in the temple. Jesus is not advocating that one may conduct a harvest of one's fields on the Sabbath, but rather in certain situations it may be necessary to eat a few kernels of wheat in order to obtain sustenance.

Rather than imposing a Dispensational hermeneutical grid which denies the ongoing implications of the law onto the text, we need to follow the apostolic example of citing Old Testament laws as the moral standard for Christians from the Decalogue, even for Gentile Christians living outside of Palestine (Ephesians 6:2). Then we need to apply the principle of the case laws in a New Covenant context (1 Corinthians 9:1-9; cf. Deuteronomy 25:49). In doing so we can derive from the entirety of God's written Word an objective universal normative stan-dard for ethics and morality. This is accomplished by carefully studying situationally applied case laws within the Old and New Testaments and then seeking to apply the same principle in similar situations in our modern era.[222]

Applying The Holiness Code In the New Covenant Era

One of the most important Old Testament texts on the issue of homo-genital acts are found in what is commonly referred to as the "Holiness Code" in which we read, "You shall not lie with a male as one lies with a female; it is an abomination" (Leviticus 18:22). This prohibition is then repeated later with the addition of a prescribed penal sanction, "If there is a man who lies with a male as those who lie with a woman, both of them have committed a detestable act; they shall surely be put to death. Their bloodguiltiness is upon them" (Leviticus 20:13).

The reason why these texts are important in our discussion on the issue of same-sex acts is that they do not use a single technical word to refer to the prohibition (such as Paul's term *arsenokoitai*), nor do they address the subjective psychological orientation of the person involved

---

222   For further reading on applying the Scriptures in a similar tri-perspectival man-ner see: John Frame, *Doctrine of the Knowledge of God* (P & R Publishing, 1987) and *The Doctrine of the Christian Life* (P & R Publishing, 2008).

such as the modern word "homosexual." Rather they descriptively tell us what is prohibited. There is absolutely no ambiguity whatsoever as to what is disallowed sexual behavior and Leviticus 18 and 20. Though these chapters are not exhaustive they sufficiently convey the God's ordained boundaries and prohibitions for sexual behavior.

There are two primary ways advocates of Gay Theology attempt to get around the clear meaning and application of these texts. The first is to avoid the implications of these texts, narrowly interpreting them as referring only to the prohibition of male cultic prostitution that took place in the worship of the Canaanite deities. Rick Brentlinger, borrowing from liberal Gay Theology advocates, states:

> Leviticus prohibits male cult prostitution, based on the precise wording... 'If a man also lie with mankind, as he lieth with a woman, both of them have committed an abomination: they shall surely be put to death; their blood shall be upon them,' Leviticus 20:13. Instead of saying 'If a man lie with a man' the prohibition says 'If a man also lie with mankind...' implying multiple sexual partners, precisely the situation a male cult prostitute would experience.[223]

Likewise, R.D. weekly states:

> God is dealing with the idolatry of the Canaanites, many of whom worshipped a false fire-god named Molech. Child sacrifice was one of the forms of Molech worship, and Moses began his list of proscriptions by dealing with this savage act. It would be a serious theological mistake to disconnect verse 13, which deals with male-male sexual activity, from the preamble of Molech worship.[224]

Brentlinger then states that the narrow context of the prohibitions clearly shows us that it can only be applied to the cultic worship of Molech or other equivalents by saying, "God carefully placed the prohi-

223   Rick Brentlinger, *Gay Christian 101 - Spiritual Self-Defense For Gay Christians* (2007), 83
224   R.D. Weekly, *Homosexianity* (Judah First Ministries, 2009), 18.

bitions of Leviticus 18:22 and 20:13 in the context of Molech worship, 18:3, 21 and 20:2-5, 23."[225] R.D. Weekly then wrongly concludes, "Clearly, God was not condemning same-sex activity in general, but the ancient idolatry that was taking place in the lands of Egypt and Canaan at the time."[226]

To see if they are correct in their narrow interpretation, we need to look at the entire context of the prohibition of a man lying down (a euphemism for having sex) with another man. Is this prohibition contextually associated with the worship of Molech such that it cannot be applied to any other context? If there are other sexual prohibitions within the same passage that also appear within close context that cannot be associated with cultic prostitution, then their narrow Gay Theological interpretation is unwarranted.

The Holiness Code is a list of sins practiced in the land of Canaan, some of which are associated with their cultic worship and others that are not. In fact, many of the sexual sins listed have been practiced in every non-Christian culture throughout history. These sins include incest (Leviticus 18:6), adultery, (Leviticus 18:20), and bestiality (Leviticus 18:23). These prohibitions against the practices of the Canaanites were not strictly associated with Molech worship and yet they are found within the same context as verses Leviticus 18:22 and 20:13.

In order to tie the prohibition specifically to cultic worship the passage would need to indicate the facilitator of the cultic homosexual act, namely the male cult prostitute. But this is not found within the text. Rather, the prohibition is found in the context of a list of other sexual sins not strictly tied to cultic worship. While it is also true, as Brentlinger points out, that there were male temple prostitutes (Hebrew: *qadesh*) in the land of Canaan (1 Kings 14:23; 15:12; 22:46; 23:7), there is no indication that Leviticus 18:22 and 20:13 refer only to this type of homosexual practice. Furthermore, there is evidence that *qadesh* and *qadesha* (sometimes transliterated in the plural form as *kedeshim*) refer to cultic cross-dressing androgynous priests, not homosexual cultic

---

225   Rick Brentlinger, *Gay Christian 101 - Spiritual Self-Defense For Gay Christians* (2007), 93.
226   R.D. Weekly, *Homosexianity* (Judah First Ministries, 2009), 19.

prostitutes, which is acknowledged by both opponents and advocates of Gay Theology.[227]

Even if *qadesh* does refer to cultic male prostitutes and were what Moses had in mind, this does not mean that the ethical principle of Leviticus 18:22 and 20:13 cannot be applied to other same sex unions, in other lands other than Israel, or in other eras in redemptive history. In fact, as we shall see in subsequent chapters, Gay Theology in all of its various forms is in fact a revival of pagan worship being blended with Christianity akin to ancient Gnosticism.

Rick Brentlinger argues that the commandments in Leviticus 17-26, particularly those on chapters 18 and 20, were only applicable to the nation of Israel, while in the land during a particular era of redemptive history. In doing so he argues that because God blessed Abraham who was married to his half-sister that therefore this was not a sin before the giving of the law at Sinai and it is not a sin in the New Covenant, "God richly blessed this forbidden brother-sister marriage and made an Eternal Covenant with Abraham while Abraham and Sarah were in the forbidden marriage relationship."[228]

Throughout Brentlinger's book, he repeats the assertion that if God blessed someone it must mean that He condones, approves and blesses everything that person does. However, the Scriptures teach that God is gracious and as a patient Father He blesses us *despite* the fact we are His sinful children. This is Paul's point when he wrote, "But God demonstrates His own love toward us, in that while we were yet sinners, Christ died for us" (Romans 5:8). In fact, the Lord had blessed the Corinthian church such that they did not lack in any spiritual gift:

> I thank my God always concerning you for the grace of
> God which was given you in Christ Jesus, that in everything
> you were enriched in Him, in all speech and all knowledge,
> even as the testimony concerning Christ was confirmed in

---

227   Peter Jones, "Androgyny: The Pagan Sexual Ideal" *Journal of the Evangelical Theological Society* 43/3 (September 2000), 448-449; See also Virginia Ramey Mollenkott, *Omnigender: A Trans-religious Approach* (Cleveland, OH: The Pilgrim Progress, 2007), 105-106.

228   Rick Brentlinger, *Gay Christian 101 - Spiritual Self-Defense For Gay Christians* (2007), 102.

you, so that you are not lacking in any gift… (1 Corinthians
1:4-7).

Yet Paul went on to rebuke them because there were factions and
various sins occurring including a man having sex with his father's
wife, a clear violation of law of God (Leviticus 18:8; 1 Corinthians 5:1).
It is the height of folly to conclude that because we are blessed by God,
or because He does not immediately punish people for their sin, that He
therefore condones, approves or is ambivalent towards rebellion.

Furthermore, as previously stated, the apostle Paul gives us an example of how a principle of Old Testament law given to the Jews, in the
land of Israel, under the Mosaic Covenant can be applied to a different
era, different nationality in a different cultural context when he argues
that according to the Law of Moses a worker deserves to benefit from his
labor, particularly those who minister in the gospel (1 Corinthians 9:1-9;
cf. Deuteronomy 25:4). If the Christians at Corinth were to interpret the
Bible as do Gay Dispensationalists they should have protested, "Paul,
we're Gentile Christians, not Jews, living in Corinth, not Israel, under
the New Covenant! That commandment is part of the Law of Moses and
we're not required to obey anything that is in the Old Testament. You're
trying to be like the Pharisees and put us under the law!" Yet this sort of
notion is exactly what Brentlinger asserts:

> …the Law of Moses does not apply to Christians today
> because the Law of Moses is not in force now. We are not
> under the Law of Moses today, Romans 6:14… Although
> the first century church, in Acts 15, settled the issue of
> whether Christians must keep the Law of Moses to be right
> with God (they decided we are not required to keep the
> Law), since nongay Christians in the twenty-first century
> keep trying to put gay Christians back under the Law, the
> question of sexual orientation is one which the church still
> wrestles.[229]

As we shall see in a subsequent chapter, the statement "not under
law" in Romans 6:14 does not mean that the ethical principles of the

229   Rick Brentlinger, *Gay Christian 101 - Spiritual Self-Defense For Gay Christians* (2007), 10-11.

law are no longer applicable today. In its context this phrase means that we are no longer under the dominion of sin and death and therefore free from the bondage of sin. It does not mean that we are free to disregard the entirety of law of God but only those which had a specific redemptive-historical and typological purpose that became obsolete with the death, burial and resurrection of Christ have ceased. The fact that the apostles in the New Testament clearly apply Old Testament laws to non-Jewish Christians outside of Palestine indicates that either Rick Brentlinger is blind, ignorant or self-deceived and is attempting to mislead his readers when contrary to the clear teaching of the apostles he states "God never applied these rules universally" and "God only applied the Holiness Code to Jews living in the land of Palestine, under the Law of Moses."[230] In fact, even within the context of the Old Testament the Lord judged the surrounding nations, who had witnessed the law of God given to Israel, for violating His commandments (Exodus 23:28; Leviticus 20:23).

Are we truly to believe that God is only concerned with His people not following the practice of the Canaanites and not these same behaviors conducted by Persians, Greeks, Romans and Americans? The assumption of the Gay Theologian is that there is something unique about the worship of Molech that does not exist in other sociological and religious cultural contexts and that the character of God is only concerned with it and not the behavior of other nations, cultures and religious practices that have many things in common with Canaanite religious practices. In fact, the worship of Molech did not even continue to exist during the time of the exile and yet God required His people to continue to obey the law while they were under the rule of the Assyrians, Babylonians, the Greeks, the Romans and throughout the regions of the Diaspora. No Jew, including Daniel, Jesus or the apostles, ever believed that once the temple was destroyed and his feet no longer walked on the land of their father Abraham that he was then free to disregard the entire Holiness Code. The reason for this is, while the names of the gods or goddesses may change in different places and eras, the underlying theological and spiritual nature of Molech worship is common in all pagan religions, including those by those practiced by people who call themselves, "Christian."

---

230   Ibid, 113.

The Gay Dispensational "static" reading of the Bible is the very essence of the hermeneutic of the Pharisees.[231] It fails to recognize the principle, intent or spirit of the law that transcends the immediate audience and the historical and cultural context. If we fail to recognize the essential transcultural attribute of Scripture then Paul's exhortation to Timothy to hold on to that which he has had from his children, the God-breathed Old Testament Scriptures, and use to them teach, exhort and rebuke so that the man of God may be equipped for every good work becomes meaningless (2 Timothy 3:14-17). Furthermore, if we adhere to a static reading and application of Scripture, modern Christians in the 21st century can likewise ignore the entire New Testament epistles since they are addressed to a particular people in a particular geographical location (Rome, Corinth, Thessalonica, Ephesus, Galatians etc.) and to particular people such as Timothy, Titus and Philemon.

Furthermore, throughout the New Covenant epistles the apostles paraphrase, allude to and directly quote Leviticus and Deuteronomy as the moral guide for Christian behavior. In doing so they do not merely repeat the commandments of the Old Testament but also cite the law authoritatively as the standard for Christian conduct. The two most common are "Be holy, for I am holy" (Leviticus 11:44-45; 1 Peter 1:16) and the "royal law" of liberty "You shall love your neighbor as yourself" which is a direct citation from Leviticus 19:18 which is from the very heart of the Holiness Code (see Galatians 5:14; James 2:8).

Because only the typological elements of the law are abrogated the apostle Paul is free to repeatedly quote Old Testament laws as the standard for ethical conduct such as Leviticus 19:18 (Romans 13:9), Deuteronomy 5:16 (Ephesians 6:2-3), Deuteronomy 25:4 (1 Timothy 5:18), as does the apostle James who quotes Deuteronomy 5:17-18 (James 2:11). Therefore, when Brentlinger states "The Holiness Codes is never affirmed in the New Testament as the standard for Christians" he is clearly contradicting what the New Testament actually states in numerous places. [232]

The second Gay Dispensational argument that these texts do not refer to "homosexuality as we know them today" is to assert that the

---

231   While I don't agree with all of his conclusions, for further reading on this matter I recommend: William J. Webb, *Slaves, Women & Homosexuals: Exploring the Hermeneutics of Cultural Analysis* (Downers Grove: IVP Academic, 2001)

232   Rick Brentlinger, *Gay Christian 101 - Spiritual Self-Defense For Gay Christians* (2007), 119.

entire Holiness Code of Leviticus chapters 17-26 was only applicable to Jews under the Mosaic Covenant and only while they were "in the land." According to Brentlinger, the prohibitions of the Holiness Code were never applicable to Gentiles and are no longer applicable to any Christian in the New Covenant era. The Gay Dispensational worldview asserts that the jurisdiction of the Holiness Code was limited to a particular place, a particular people, and a particular time period within history. It is therefore not applicable to anybody outside of those narrow boundaries as Brentlinger argues:

> Leviticus 18:22 & 20:13 forbids anal intercourse between two men during the time period the Mosaic Law was in force, in the Holy Land, for Jews. – a particular people in a particular land at a particular time for a particular purpose under a particular set of laws, approximately 1450 BC to AD 30.[233]

He then notes that this is "the dispensational view" and goes on to state that the jurisdiction of the law was restricted within very tight geographical boundaries and therefore they were not universally applicable to Jews outside those boundaries or anybody other than a Jew living under the Mosaic Covenant:

> God told Moses precisely where the Holiness Code would be in force. "In the Land" was where God intended His people to do the commandments, statutes and judgments of the Law. Moses wrote five times to make it absolutely clear to the children of Israel where the Levitical Holiness Could would be in force. The land of Israel was sacred ground which God treated differently than any place on earth.[234]

In other words, since the law was only applicable within "the land" of Israel that was promised to Abraham the law was not in force before they entered the land nor was the law applicable once a Jew or anyone else set foot outside those geographical boundaries.

---

233   Ibid, 85.
234   Rick Brentlinger, *Gay Christian 101 - Spiritual Self-Defense For Gay Christians* (2007), 86.

In contrast to his assertions, we can find Scriptural evidence that the prohibitions and requirements of the Holiness Code are applied to non-Jews, outside of the narrow geographical boundaries of national Israel. For example, we read in the New Testament that both Peter and Paul explicitly cite portions of the Holiness Code as the standard for Christian conduct. Paul quotes Leviticus 19:19 and applies it in a New Covenant context to exhort Christians to be holy (2 Corinthians 6:14). He also cites Leviticus 18:5 in Romans 10:5 and Galatians 3:12. Paul and James both quote Leviticus 19:18 as did Christ referring to the "Law of Love" (Romans 13:8-10; Galatians 5:14; James 2:8). Likewise, Peter cites Leviticus 19:2 as the standard of holiness as he exhorts Christians to abandon their "former lusts" (1 Peter 1:4-16). What must be noted is that the apostles do not merely repeat commandments from the Holiness Code, they cite the law as authoritative in matters of Christian conduct. Paul exhorted Timothy to hold on to what he had learned from him and what he had from his childhood, the Old Testament scriptures, in his ministry when evil doers arise.

Contrary to the assertions of Gay Theology proponents such as R. D. Weekly, the law is not merely a history lesson that is not to be applied to the New Covenant believer.[235] The Apostle Paul states that the law is "profitable for teaching, for reproof, for correction, for training in righteousness" which if believed and obeyed by faith has the intended result for the New Covenant believer of making him "adequate, equipped for every good work" (2 Timothy 3:14-17). What is clear from the teaching of the apostles is that the New Covenant did not abrogate every commandment in the Old Testament, nor the entirety of the Holiness Code. Rather, those aspects of the law which were mere types and shadows or had the purpose of distinguishing between Jews and Gentiles found their *telos*, their intended and designed end, in the New Covenant. Those aspects which were a reflection of the Holiness of God and His revealed will for all mankind were still to be obeyed.

Not only are the laws of the Old Testament (excluding only the types and shadows and similar laws) but the laws and covenant promises

---

235   R.D. Weekly states, "We needn't turn to the pages of the Mosaic Law in determining God's moral code. Let's simply accept and celebrate what Christ accomplished on Calvary, remaining faithful to our new husband by allowing the Mosaic Law to keep its rightful place – history, not establishing or informing Christian moral conduct." in *Homosexianity* (Judah First Ministries, 2009), 60.

given to Abraham and Moses are applied to believers and their children "in the land" outside of national Israel. Rick Brentlinger attempts to narrow not only the meaning of the Holiness Code, but also to whom it was applicable (Jews only) and the location where it was applicable (geographical Israel) as he asserts:

> God told Moses precisely where the Holiness Code would be in force. "In the land" was where God intended His people to do the commandments, statutes and judgments of the Law. Moses wrote this five times to make it absolutely clear to the children of Israel, where the Levitical Holiness Code would be in force. The land of Israel was sacred ground which God treated differently than any place on earth.[236]

Yet, what we find in the New Testament is the apostles applying the laws and promises to New Covenant Christians who are Gentiles by birth in congregations outside of national Israel, specifically citing laws that refer to "the land." For example, the fifth commandment given to Jews at Sinai tells us, "Honor your father and your mother, that your days may be prolonged in the land which the LORD your God gives you" (Exodus 20:12). Yet Paul cites this passage has being applicable and having accompanying promises for Gentile Christian children outside of the geographical land of Israel:

> Children, obey your parents in the Lord, for this is right. Honor your father and mother (which is the first commandment with a promise), so that it may be well with you, and that you may live long on the earth (Ephesians 6:1-3)

Notice that Paul quotes the Septuagint translation of the fifth commandment and applies it to Christians in the New Covenant living outside of "the land" of national Israel and in "the land" of Ephesus, which was located in what is now modern day Turkey. If the entirety of the Old Testament law is no longer required to be obeyed, if its restrictions and promises only are applicable to Jews in the Old Covenant era and only

---

236   Rick Brentlinger, *Gay Christian 101 - Spiritual Self-Defense For Gay Christians* (2007), 86.

within the geographical boundaries of national Israel, then the parents of these children at the church of Ephesus should have protested Paul's use of the law. The fact that there are so many passages from Leviticus chapters 17-26 applied by the apostles in the New Testament makes one wonder how Gay Theologians and Dispensationalists can make such assertions. Unfortunately their paradigm blinds them and keeps them from see anything that doesn't conform to their presuppositions.

The third argument that Gay Theology advocates use to deny that the prohibitions of Leviticus 18:22 and 20:13 condemn homosexual behavior is that such acts are not inherently sinful, but rather such conduct was merely a Jewish cultural taboo. They argue that an abomination was not an intrinsically sinful act but merely something that was so closely associated with Gentiles that it was considered grotesque by Jews. Hence it was something that was distasteful to the Jew like eating pork or shellfish but it should not be considered inherently sinful as John Boswell, and all other liberal Gay Theologians after him, asserted:

> The only place in the Old Testament where homosexual acts per se are mentioned is Leviticus... The Hebrew word 'toevah'... here translated 'abomination' does not signify something intrinsically evil, but something which is ritually unclean for Jews, like eating pork or engaging in intercourse during menstruation, both of which are prohibited in these chapters... The distinction between intrinsic wrong and ritual impurity is even more finely drawn by the Greek translation which distinguishes in 'toevah' itself the separate categories of law or justice (anomia) and infringements of ritual purity or monotheistic worship (bdelugma). The Levitical proscriptions of homosexual behavior fall into the latter. In the Greek, then, the Levitical enactments against homosexual behavior characterize it univocally as ceremonially unclean rather than inherently evil.[237]

Borrowing this false distinction from Liberal Gay Theology advocates, Dispensational Gay Theology advocates such as R. D. Weekly assert:

---

237   John Boswell, *Christianity, Social Tolerance, and Homosexuality* (University Of Chicago Press; 8th Edition. edition, 2005), 100, 101-102.

> The context of these verses [Leviticus 18:22, 20:13] clear-
> ly links the sexual behavior to the idolatry of Egypt and
> Canaan. Because of the connection with idolatry, the acts
> themselves should not be considered inherently sinful, just
> as planting mixed seed in the same field, working animals
> in two kinds, eating pork or shellfish, or wearing mixed
> fabrics are not inherently sinful. The purpose of these codes
> was to maintain the children of Israel as a sanctified people
> who were distinct in religion and lifestyle from the people
> surrounding them. Furthermore, even if these verses were
> a condemnation of all same-sex activity – which they are
> not – they do not apply to Christians.[238]

There are several problems with these assertions. First, in order to make this argument they have to reject their previous assertion that the prohibition only refers to a cultic sexual act of worship of Molech and Canaanite deities for one could hardly assert that such acts of idolatry are a mere cultural taboo and not inherently evil.

Second, as recognized even by some Gay Theology proponents, the New Testament passages that refer to same-sex acts are not treated as mere cultural taboos but heinous acts that stir up the wrath of God that will prevent a non-repentant violator from inheriting the Kingdom of God. Do they really want to argue that violating a first century equiva-lent to an Old Testament prohibition is another mere cultural taboo that has such dire consequences?

Third, a simple study of the word "abomination" and the penal sanction attached to the prohibition demonstrates that it does not merely refer to a simple culturally relevant taboo. Unfortunately some English translations have used the same word "abomination" to translate differ-ent Hebrew words which convey very different degrees of abhorrence. When we are trying to determine the meaning of a Hebrew word it is important to keep in mind that the Old Testament contains about 225 different Hebrew words that are used 200 times, the other words are either etymologically related or are rare words.[239] In contrast the basic vocabulary of the New Testament, a shorter collection of books, is about

---

238   R.D. Weekly, *Homosexianity* (Judah First Ministries, 2009), 102.
239   Jacques B. Doukhan, *Hebrew for Theologians* (University Press of America, 1993), xxii.

300 Greek words which make up 80 percent of all New Testament occurrences.[240] Consequently the Hebrew language in the Old Testament has a greater semantic range for words, since it has to convey the same ideas with a shorter vocabulary. For example, the Hebrew word *dabar* can mean "word," "thing," "history," or "prophecy" depending on the context in which it is used. Therefore, context becomes all the more important for determining the meaning of words when translating the Old Testament.

When we consider the meaning of *toevah* (translated as "abomination" in Leviticus 18:22 and 20:13) in relation to various other listed prohibitions, we find that they denote different degrees of abhorrence or loathsomeness. Then when we consider the penal sanction for violating the prohibition it becomes clear that not all violations are the same; hence same-sex acts are not considered to be in the same category as eating unclean animals.

For example, in Leviticus 11 we read that fish without scales, fowls that creep, flying creeping things (insects) which have four feet and every creeping thing that creeps upon the earth are unclean (*tameh*) and they shall not be eaten because they are *sheqets*. Some translations state that these are "disgusting" (Basic English Bible) or "detestable" (New American Standard Bible) and unfortunately it is translated as "abomination" in the King James Bible making it appear that eating such things is equivalent to committing the same sex acts prohibited in Leviticus 18:22 and 20:13. But this is not the case since it is an entirely different word which is used. The act of eating such things, incidentally, does not result in the death penalty.

When we then read Leviticus chapters 18 and 20 we find that only one act is singled out as being of *toevah* – a man having sex with another man. We also find that to violate this prohibition entails the death penalty for the individuals involved and if God's people tolerate the act then His judgment shall fall upon the entire nation. The conclusion we must come to then is that the highest degree of abomination is *toevah*. So while eating shellfish or having sex with a woman who is menstruating may make one unclean for a period of time and require undergoing a ritual washing (baptism) they are not in the same category of offences as adultery (Leviticus 20:10) or same sex acts (Leviticus 20:13).

240   S.M. Baugh, *A New Testament Greek Primer* (Phillipsburg, NJ: P & R Publishing, 1995), v.

Let us assume, for the sake of argument, that Gay Theology advocates are correct when they assert that Leviticus 18:22 and 20:13 only prohibit having sex with cultic male prostitutes which was merely a taboo. Let us also assume, for the sake of argument, that Dispensational Gay Theology advocates such as Rick Brentlinger and R.D. Weekly are correct that the Christian in the New Covenant is not required to obey any of the laws and prohibitions in the so-called Holiness Code. Since the New Covenant era began with the death, burial and resurrection of Jesus Christ in approximately 33 A.D. and Paul did not write the first chapter of epistle to the Romans until approximately 57 A.D., [241] 1 Corinthians 6:9 until approximately 57 A.D. [242] and 1 Timothy 1:10 until somewhere between 59-63 A.D. [243] are we to assume that Christians were free to have sex with cultic male prostitutes until then or that the only texts which prohibit such actions are these three passages? Ironically, those who affirm such an interpretation assert that Romans 1:26-27 and 1 Corinthians 6:9 are referring to the very same acts prohibited in Leviticus 18:22 and 20:13 are referring to the sin of having sex with cultic prostitutes as Rick Brentlinger states:

> Since shrine prostitution was commonly known in the first century... shrine prostitution is the primary though not necessarily the exclusive focus of Paul's argument.[244]

Likewise, R.D. Weekly asserts:

> As with the Leviticus and Deuteronomy passages, this condemnation [same sex activity in Romans 1:26-27] is directly related to idol worship, as clearly indicated by the context of the passage in question... because our modern culture no longer associates same-sex activity with idol worship, it would be wrong to hold Christians captive to

---

241   F.F. Bruce, *Romans* (Grand Rapids: Eerdmans, 1985), 18.
242   Charles Hodge, *Commentary on the First Epistle to the Corinthians* (Grand Rapids: Eerdmans, 1994), xii.
243   George W. Knight III, *The Pastoral Epistles* (Grand Rapids: Eerdmans, 1992), 53.
244   Rick Brentlinger, *Gay Christian 101 - Spiritual Self-Defense For Gay Christians* (2007), 288.

the ancient cultural perspective that informed Paul's worldview (particularly when the acts are not engaged in the
worship of idol gods).[245]

If the prohibition of having sex with cultic prostitutes in Leviticus
18:22 and 20:13 are not applicable to non-Jews, outside of Palestine in
the New Covenant era then how could Paul uphold the very same principle of Leviticus 18:22 and 20:13 in Romans 1, 1 Corinthians 6:9 and
1 Timothy 1:10? One cannot assert that Leviticus 18:22 and 20:13 are
not applicable to non-Jews, outside of Palestine in the New Covenant
era and then assert that the Apostle Paul is referring to these same acts
in his epistles.

Leviticus 18:22 and 20:13 are applicable in the New Covenant era
as applied by the Apostle Paul because the principle of the texts is applicable in other cultures, other redemptive historical eras and to non-Jews
as well. If this is so, then we as modern Christians can apply the same
ethical principles in the present day, even if the details of the forms
of worship (such as Molech worship or Greek and Roman cultic male
prostitution) have changed. As we shall see in the following chapters,
the entirety of our life is an act of worship, our bodies are the New
Temple in which the Holy Spirit dwells and our entire life is to be a
sacrificial act of worship which includes our sexual behavior.

Like his interpretation of Leviticus 18 and 20, Rick Brentlinger and
other Gay Theologians assert that Romans 1:26-27 is only narrowly
referring to unbelievers who participate in cultic homosexual sex with
male prostitutes. Therefore, they conclude, the text cannot be applied to
modern consensual homosexual relationships:

> Idol worship, Moloch worship and shrine prostitution
> were inextricably linked in the Jewish mind and in Paul's
> mind. No believing Jew would divorce Leviticus 18:21
> from Leviticus 18:22 or fail to see the connection between
> the verses... If Paul was not referring to every form of
> homosexuality in general when he wrote Romans 1, then
> Romans 1 cannot be referring to homosexuality in general
> now. If exclusive, monogamous homosexual relationships
> between Christians were not commonly known in the first

245   R.D. Weekly, *Homosexianity* (Judah First Ministries, 2009), 102

century, then exclusive monogamous homosexual relationships are not the focus of Paul's argument in Romans 1.[246]

But then Brentlinger admits,

Since shrine prostitution was commonly known in the first century... shrine prostitution is the primary though not necessarily the exclusive focus of Paul's argument.[247]

The issue at hand is not whether Paul specifically had in mind "monogamous homosexual relationships" but whether the principle can be *applied* to such sexual activity and persons today. If we look at all the various adjectives and behaviors that describe those whom Paul states are "suppressing the truth in unrighteousness" (Romans 1:18) we see that he describes them as having "exchanged the glory of the incorruptible God for an image in the form of corruptible man and of birds and four-footed animals and crawling creatures" (Romans 1:23). Yet we can apply this text to modern atheists who likewise suppress the knowledge of the existence of God even though, as Paul states "since the creation of the world His invisible attributes, His eternal power and divine nature, have been clearly seen, being understood through what has been made" (v. 20) even if they do not literally carve idols from wood or stone as did the pagans of the first century. While some might in third world nations behave this way, it can hardly be said that the average atheist who pays his taxes, is faithful to his wife, donates money to charity organizations, takes care of orphans, assists the elderly, and is friendly towards their neighbors meets the descriptions provided by Paul as if they are all "full of envy, murder, strife" (Romans 1:29) or participate in overt idolatrous activities or visit temple prostitutes. Let's face it, we have all met unbelievers who are really nice people who may even behave (at least outwardly in public) better than some Christians. Can we conclude then that because the idolaters described by Paul does match every aspect of modern unbelievers that therefore they are not "suppressing the truth in unrighteousness"? In fact, can we say that *all* unbelievers in Paul's day fit this description?

---

246   Rick Brentlinger, *Gay Christian 101 - Spiritual Self-Defense For Gay Christians* (2007), 287, 288
247   Ibid, 288.

The apostle Paul is giving us extreme examples that are the result of the noetic effects of sin, in denying that the God of the Bible exists. Yet, the principle or spiritual truth of the text is applicable to modern atheists and other types of unbelievers even if they bear some form of civil righteousness in being upstanding citizens in society. In a similar manner, even if Paul has specifically in mind the literal pagan idolaters of his day as seen in Athens (Acts 17:16) or in Rome the spiritual truth applies to the average modern civil unbeliever that does not exhibit such extreme behaviors. If he is not worshipping the one true God then he is an idolater since someone or something else is a "god" in his life even if he never steps one foot into a temple or shrine.

In a similar fashion, if the activity described in Leviticus 18:22 and Romans 1:26-27 takes place in non-cultic context the principle of the text still applies. The principle of the moral requirement of the commandment in Leviticus 18 and the description of the spiritual condition of the person who is "suppressing the truth in unrighteousness" is transcultural. Otherwise, nothing that anyone says about anything in the Bible applies to anyone or any other culture outside of its immediate cultural context.

Chapter 9
Marriage, Polygamy and Divorce Laws

Having discussed the various types of laws in the Old and New Testaments and introduced the apostolic method of applying Old Covenant laws in a New Covenant context, in this chapter we will address those commandants that specifically relate to the topic at hand – marriage, polygamy and same-sex acts. Gay Theology advocates make their case for homosexual relations and gay marriage on the fact that the Bible recognizes many means of becoming married and various forms of marriage other than the "husband of one wife" scenario such as polygamy. Based on a faulty liberation-theology/trajectory hermeneutic, as well as a misrepresentation of the relationships of people such as Ruth and Naomi and Jonathan and David, they assert that same sex marriages ought to be recognized by the Church as another option among many forms of marriage depicted within Scripture. This characterization on what the Bible teaches concerning polygamy is based on a misrepresentation of its existence and regulation in the Old Testament law of God. The basis for this caricature of what the Bible teaches concerning polygamy is the misconceived idea that if the law regulated an act it must be considered good because it was tolerated within certain parameters.

A second misconception is that if a person is blessed after committing a particular act then this must indicate the Lord's approval. However, as we shall see the Lord often blesses his children, including the kings who violate his prohibition against polygamy, *despite* the fact that they have sinned - not because their actions are approved of by God. One of the clearest examples of God blessing sinners is seen when the Lord asked Solomon, "Ask what you wish me to give you?" (1 Kings 3:3) This offer to grant a request comes immediately after we are told that the people of Israel were involved in forbidden sacrifices (1 Kings 3:1-2) and that Solomon loved the Lord and obeyed his commandments, "... except he sacrificed and burned incense on the high places" (1 Kings 3:3). Solomon then asks for wisdom so that he could lead the nation and the Lord blesses him with not only discernment but also riches and long life, "If you walk in My ways, keeping My statutes and commandments, as your father David walked, then I will prolong your days" (1 Kings 3:11-14).

The Origin and Model for Biblical Marriage

The first few chapters of Genesis describe the origin of the universe, the created order on earth, the origin of mankind made in the image of God as male and female and Adam's fall into sin followed by the consequences of the curse on creation. Both Jesus and the Apostle Paul appeal to the Genesis account as the basis for their teaching on marriage and the role of the husband and wife. Yet Gay Theology advocates argue that the Genesis account is not the defining text for the boundaries of God-ordained marriages: "In effect, Adam and Eve's marriage is *de*-scriptive, not *pre*scriptive. It describes the historical narrative, but does not demonstrate God's intentions for marriage."[248] According to Gay Theologians we should not look to Adam and Eve's relationship as the guidelines for the defining the boundaries of modern marriages as Rick Brentlinger argues, "The Genesis record is an explanation of origins. It is not a dissertation on marriage."[249]

But Scripture can not be justifiably read this way. Much of what is written in the first three chapters is not only descriptive but is also immediately prescriptive for all time or is the basis for later prescriptions in the Bible. For example, the regulations concerning the Sabbath are rooted in what occurred during the creation week (Exodus 20:8-11). Likewise, we read in Genesis a prescriptive statement concerning marriage:

> The LORD God fashioned into a woman the rib which He had taken from the man, and brought her to the man. The man said, 'This is now bone of my bones, And flesh of my flesh; She shall be called Woman, Because she was taken out of Man.' For this reason a man shall leave his father and his mother, and be joined to his wife; and they shall become one flesh (Genesis 2:22-24).

---

248   R.D. Weekly, *Homosexianity* (Judah First Ministries, 2009), 78.
249   Rick Brentlinger, *Gay Christian 101 - Spiritual Self-Defense For Gay Christians* (2007), 18.

Notice that this text is prescriptive ("You shall do this") not merely descriptive ("he did this") and that this prescription is for all time, even in a New Covenant context. Marriage is what most theologians refer to as a Creation Ordinance.[250] God took the woman from the man and subsequently a husband and a wife are to be a joined as "one flesh." Just as God is one (Hebrew: *achad*) so too a husband and wife are to be one (Deuteronomy 6:4; Matthew 19:4; 1 Corinthians 6:16; Ephesians 5:31). At creation fathers and mothers did not yet exist. Yet, at the institution of marriage, God ordained that future generations of sons were to leave their father and mother and cleave to their wife to form a new union and family.

However, contrary to some theologians this text does not teach that the image of God is only found in the binary nature of man, as if a single man cannot reflect the image of God without the woman. Adam was an image bearer before Eve was created and Christ did not need to be joined sexually to a woman in order to be an image bearer in His humanity. Unfortunately such notions often advocated by theologians, such as Robert A.J. Gagnon, who argue against Gay Theology by "borrowing… philosophical and moral arguments from Greeks" and interpreting the creation account through the lens of Greek philosophy.[251]

In mankind's original state before the fall, the human race was declared to be good (Genesis 1:31). As the image-bearer of God mankind was free from sin and death, free from slavery and free to obey God continuously with knowledge, original righteous and holiness (Genesis 1:27-28; Colossians 3:10). Had Adam not sinned against God, and we in him, his marriage and all of mankind would have progressed in order and without sickness and death. This distinction of the condition of man before and after the fall is extremely important since many Gay Theology proponents insist that if God created sex and man to have sex and declared it to be "good" then it follows that if some have the desire for same sex acts that they too must be good. In short, they argue that an "is" ("I am attracted to a man") implies an "ought" ("Therefore I ought to be allowed to have sex with a man.").[252]

---

250   John Murray, *Principles of Conduct* (Grand Rapids: Eerdmans, 1957), 27.
251   Robert A. J. Gagnon, *The Bible And Homosexual Practice (Nashville, TN: Abingdon Press, 2001), 182.*
252   Michael S. Piazza states, "…since every lesbian or gay person I know would tell you they were born gay, it is something God did… being lesbian or gay is a gift from God…" *Gay By God* (Dallas, TX: Source of Hope Publishing, 1998), 1, 6.

Marriage After The Fall of Mankind

The fall of mankind brought Adam not only spiritual death under the condemnation of sin but eventually physical death would follow. Not only was he cursed; all of creation would continue to fight him as he labored at the sweat of his brow (Genesis 3:17) and it would groan until the completion of his redemption at the resurrection (Romans 8:22). Where God had brought order out of chaos (Genesis 1:2), the fall into sin introduced disorder into creation so that death reigned (Romans 5:14).

Mankind was given a mandate, before and after the fall, to take dominion as God's stewards over the earth by being fruitful (Genesis 1:28; 8:17). But sin brought death and disorder with the result that creation would resist him. Sin not only affected mankind as individuals but corporately as a society as well. The fall brought into human society the existence of slavery, polygamy and divorce which God tolerated and permitted but would later regulate in His law. But the redemptive trajectory of the Bible, particularly the New Testament, is to return creation to God's original intent for man - freedom from slavery (of all kinds) and the one-man/one-woman marriage for life (Matthew 19:4-7).

What we find when we read the Bible is that after the fall of mankind into sin many economic and social customs developed as a result, which God later regulated amongst His people but did not explicitly prohibit. Two such practices were indentured servitude (slavery) and polygamy. Back then as well as today, in countries that have not been predominantly influenced by Christian practice, polygamy was a sign of economic prowess.

In His Law the Lord placed boundaries on these institutions in order to protect the slave and the first wife to keep them from being abused but He did not outlaw an economic situation that had some benefit for the wives and slaves. In other words, polygamy existed but rather than immediately prohibiting it God tolerated it within certain economic boundaries that protected the first wife from being neglected. Nowhere does God say that polygamy is "good" or command men to take multiple wives. Rather He insisted that men not use women as they wished for they had certain rights (Exodus 21:10-11) and not even a war captive could be deprived of those rights (Deuteronomy 21:10-14). While the law tolerated polygamy, according to God's pre-fallen created order monogamy between a man and a woman was the standard norm.

The first recorded incident of polygamy was in the life of ungodly Lamech (Genesis 4:19). Rick Brentlinger, like many other Gay Theology proponents, attempts to argue on the basis of this story for a misconstrued understanding of polygamy and marriage in the Old Testament:

> Our first example is Lamech's polygamous marriage, found in Genesis 4:19. Scripture informs us that Lamech had two wives, Adah and Zillah. We are only 44 verses past Adam and Eve, Genesis 2:24, and already Lamech has broken what traditionalists view as God's inviolable marriage template because he had two wives. And lest anyone think God was against polygamous marriages, consider Deuteronomy 21:15-17. God made provision in the Law of Moses for polygamy and set down rules to govern inheritance in polygamous marriage situations. God affirmed and blessed polygamy under the Law of Moses. After King David sinned with Bathsheba, God sent Nathan the prophet to confront David. Nathan points out David's blessings from the hand of God. Jehovah says: "*I gave thee thy master's house, and thy master's wives into thy bosom...*" II Samuel 12:8. Clearly, God was not against polygamy. A polygamous marriage is not a one man with one woman. Polygamy is substantially different from the Adam and eve model yet God blessed these marriages throughout the Old Testament.[253]

Then based on this misconception of polygamy in Biblical history as a supposedly God-approved and blessed viable alternate form of marriage he concludes, "Just as the dyadic (two person) nature of Adam and Eve's relationship was not used in Genesis to preclude polygamy, so the heterosexual nature of Adam' and Eve's relationship does not preclude homosexual unions..." [254]

In order to examine this caricature of polygamy in the Bible we need to first notice that this form of marriage did not begin until after the fall.

253   Rick Brentlinger, *Gay Christian 101 - Spiritual Self-Defense For Gay Christians* (2007), 21.
254   Ibid, 19.

The fall of mankind into sin brought slavery, polygamy and divorce, which God tolerated and permitted but regulated in His law as it fenced it in within certain limits to minimize its negative effect on society. But the trajectory of the New Testament is to return to God's original intent for man - freedom from slavery (of all kinds) and the one-man/one woman marriage for life (Matthew 19:4-7).

One of the most common misconceptions perpetrated by Gay Theology advocates (as well as traditional Mormons) is that God instituted, ordained and gave approval of polygamist marriages as a good practice. The intention of the Gay Theology proponents is to argue that it is not God's will that marriage be restricted to a one-man and one-woman relationship but rather that marriage can be defined a number of ways including a relationship between two men.

To rightly understand what Scripture teaches concerning marriage throughout Biblical history we need to first make a distinction between what God regulates and what God ordains or commands by His creative and decreed will. In the Garden of Eden God did not give Adam multiple wives but a single woman to be his helpmeet. To solve the problem of loneliness God gave Adam a wife, not a harem. This descriptive pattern was intended to be a model for all time as Thomas E. Schmidt rightly states:

> Of course these verses contain descriptions, not commands, so how can we know that it is appropriate to use them to help define sexuality? Four observations. First, the Bible is full of moral lessons conveyed in story form, so at least we *cannot rule out* the normativity of these verses. Second, the description here is given special significance by its *placement* before the rebellion, when the entire scheme of things is pronounced good by God. Third, the descriptions here are consistent with commands about sexuality given elsewhere, including many written at about the same time as Genesis. Fourth, and perhaps more important from a Christian perspective, we observe direct quotations of these verses in key statements about sexuality by Jesus and Paul.[255]

255   Thomas E. Schmidt, *Straight and Narrow? Compassion & Clarity in the Homosexuality Debate* (Downers Grove, IL: IVP Academic, 1995), 40.

In the context of Jesus' statement on the one-man to one-woman relationship He cites the Genesis account as precedence for His teaching against divorce (Matthew 19:3-9). Although Moses had given some latitude, God's will is that a man not leave his wife for another woman nor add more women to the marriage and the normative pattern for the monogamous lifetime marriage between a man and a woman is, "For this reason…" (Genesis 2:24) We find this relationship not only in Genesis but also affirmed by Jesus and upheld by Paul as a requirement for anyone who is to be in Church leadership as he must be "the husband of one wife" or more literally "a one woman man" (1 Timothy 3:2). In fact, we find this not only in the Genesis account, the teaching of Jesus and Paul but it is a pattern of God's redemptive design as Jesus is not a polygamist for He only has one wife, the Church (Ephesians 5:23, 25; Revelation 21:2). A husband is required to imitate Christ in serving his wife and he cannot do so by pursuing more than one woman or another man. To do so would exclude him from leadership in the Church (Titus 1:5-7).

Contrary to the assertion of Brentlinger, the first Biblical reference to polygamy is not that of a God-fearing man. Rather the first polygamist is a tyrant who comes from the line of Cain who goes beyond justice to boasting of his extreme acts of vengeance:

> Lamech took to himself two wives: the name of the one was Adah, and the name of the other, Zillah. Adah gave birth to Jabal; he was the father of those who dwell in tents and have livestock. His brother's name was Jubal; he was the father of all those who play the lyre and pipe. As for Zillah, she also gave birth to Tubal-cain, the forger of all implements of bronze and iron; and the sister of Tubal-cain was Naamah. Lamech said to his wives, "Adah and Zillah, Listen to my voice, you wives of Lamech, give heed to my speech for I have killed a man for wounding me and a boy for striking me. If Cain is avenged sevenfold then Lamech seventy-sevenfold" (Genesis 4:19-24).

It is this excessive violence and sexual promiscuity that sets in motion the depravity of the culture and society for which God later judged the world with a flood (Genesis 9). It can hardly be said then that Lamech's conduct is a case for an affirmation of polygamy. In fact, Lamech is far from a Godly example of rule. Rather than serving as God's vice regent as intended for man in the Garden of Eden in which man was to act as YHWH's representative exercising dominion over the earth he sets himself up as being holier than God. Lamech enacts not merely justice but tyranny as he is sings a song in which he boasts to his wives about how he will execute vengeance for bloodshed: "Listen to my voice, you wives of Lamech, Give heed to my speech, for I have killed a man for wounding me; and a boy for striking me. If Cain is avenged sevenfold, then Lamech seventy-sevenfold" (Genesis 4:23-24).Unlike the simple reciprocity implied in Genesis 9:6 and in the Mosaic law of *talion* (Exodus 21:23-25), the text depicts Lamech as an example of the tyranny of men who proclaimed themselves to be "elohim," formed for themselves a harem of women and produced a line of descendants known as the "sons of God" (Genesis 6:1-4), a lineage that was antithetical to the seed of the woman (Genesis 3:15). These elohim-kings were typified by their polygamy, tyrannical rule, and insistence on being worshiped as a "god." YHWH condemns the exercise of royal polygamy in which earthly kings ("sons of God") accumulating harems ("daughters of men") and He later prohibits His own kings from acting in like manner (Deuteronomy 17:17).[256] In fact, God later proclaims an ironic judgment upon such men (Psalm 82:6-17). Jesus later says, concerning Himself in citing this passage, that what they are referred to sarcastically, He is in reality – the one true God-King (John 10:34-38). Rick Brentlinger then goes on to make references to Abraham, Esau, Jacob, Gideon, Elkanah, Abijah, and Solomon as polygamists. [257] Likewise R.D. weekly asserts:

> ...rather than condemning polygyny, the Mosaic Law in-
> cluded provisions related to polygynous marriages (Deut.
> 21:15-17), serving as a de facto validation of the practice.
> The obvious question this raises is why God would accom-
> modate and facilitate practices that seem pretty untoward
> to our contemporary society, e.g. polygyny, the institution
> of slavery, the status and rights of women, the rules of war,

---

256   Meredith G. Kline, *Kingdom Prologue: Genesis Foundations For A Covenant-al Worldview* (Overland Parks, KS: Two Age Press, 2000), 185-189.

257   Rick Brentlinger, *Gay Christian 101 - Spiritual Self-Defense For Gay Christians* (2007), 22-23.

and even monarchism. There is but one answer, and it could not be more relevant to the discussion at hand. More than so many Christians realize, God is very flexible regarding changing social climates and His views on what comprises proper or acceptable behavior does, indeed change, depending on the culture in which we live.[258]

According to R.D Weekly, God is a cultural relativist who will condone other forms of marriage if the Church condones them, whether they are polygamous or same-sex unions. Arguing from a misconstrued understanding of polygamy in the Bible he then states regarding the Adam and Eve model for marriage:

> [God] didn't create polygyny in the Adam-Eve model, yet it was clearly an accepted practice for the Israelites, as well as for early Christians. If we are convinced that God's view of acceptable marriage models is unchanging, how can we reconcile that fact with the reality that God *gave* multiple wives to David (2 Sa. 12:8), and that even in the New Testament, He only restricted bishops, elders and deacons from polygynous marriage, not all Christians? Are we prepared to open the floodgates and support modern-day polygyny, given that God's perspective on marriage is supposedly unchanging?[259]

There are two very important questions that we must ask Brentlinger in response to his assertions. First, did God bless Abraham *with* polygamy or *despite* his polygamy? In fact, while Brentlinger, Weekly and others make general references to people being polygamists, if we take a closer look at the text we'll discover that often times they were not polygamists but rather adulterers.

Despite the assertions of Brentlinger, Abraham was an adulterer and not a polygamist. While Sarah was alive he never married any other woman. Abraham committed adultery and had an illegitimate son by Hagar because he listened to his wife and followed pagan customs of

---

258   R.D. Weekly, *Homosexianity* (Judah First Ministries, 2009), 75.
259   R.D. Weekly, *Homosexianity* (Judah First Ministries, 2009), 87.

the day, which allowed husbands to propagate through concubines when he listened to her advice to take her handmaid. It was Sarah, Abraham's own wife, who accused the Lord of preventing her from conceiving and subsequently brought to Abraham her servant handmaid, asking him to produce a child for Sarah by this servant woman (Genesis 16:2). Yet, Hagar is never referred to by God as Abraham's wife:

> Although Hagar was humanly regarded as Abram's wife, the narrator carefully records the contrast between human understanding and the divine perspective. Throughout the narrative, God never refers to Hagar as Abram's wife. Although God, in addressing Abram, emphatically speaks of Sarai/Sarah as "your wife" (17:15, 19: 18:9, 10), by contrast he refers to Hagar as "slave-girl of Sarai" (16:8) or "your slave woman" (21:12). Notably, when addressing Hagar fled from the presence of Sarah, God told her "Return to your mistress, and submit to her" (16:9). Nothing is said about returning to be Abram's wife...[260]

Abraham was a sinner who, despite his sin, was blessed because YHWH is a gracious God. Abraham committed adultery and lied twice about his wife being merely his sister (Genesis 12:12-13; 20:2) and yet the end result was Abraham left Egypt a wealthy man (Genesis 12:16, 20; 20:14). Are we supposed to believe that because Abraham lied about his wife and God subsequently blessed him with the wealth of Pharaoh and Abimelech that the blessing indicates approval of his behavior? Yet, that is exactly what Brentlinger would have us to believe as he goes to assert:

> If God held the traditionalist view of Adam and Eve, their God violated His own beliefs by blessing the marriages we listed. Because God richly blessed the marriages we listed, which do not fit the 'one man with one woman' paradigm, we conclude that God does not promote the traditionalist

---

260   Richard Davidson, *Flame of Yahweh: Sexuality in the Old Testament* (Peabody, MA: Hendriksen Publishing, 2007), 185

viewpoint and does not expect us to adopt the traditionalist viewpoint.[261]

Is receiving grace from God, being blessed by God, evidence that He approves of everything that you do? The Church of Corinth was blessed by the Holy Spirit and was given every spiritual blessing as Paul wrote:

> I thank my God always concerning you for the grace of God which was given you in Christ Jesus, that in every-thing you were enriched in Him, in all speech and all knowledge, even as the testimony concerning Christ was confirmed in you, so that you are not lacking in any gift, awaiting eagerly the revelation of our Lord Jesus Christ, who will also confirm you to the end, blameless in the day of our Lord Jesus Christ (1 Corinthians 1:4-8).

Yet, the Church of Corinth was riddled with sin in that there were divisions (1 Corinthians 1:10; 11:19), they were tolerant of a man who, in violation Leviticus 18:8, had sex with his father's wife (1 Corinthians 5:1), they sued each other in court (1 Corinthians 6:1), mature Christians stumbled weaker Christians over eating meat sacrificed to idols (1 Corinthians 8:1-13), and some sinned when they partook of the Lord's Supper with the result that were dying because of it (1 Corinthians 11:30). God is gracious and He blesses sinners despite their sin, not because of their sin. As Paul states, it is foolish to think that because where sin abounds grace often also abounds that we ought to therefore continue in sin so that grace may abound all the more (Romans 6:1ff.).

However, we see throughout redemptive history often times God allows His people to suffer the natural consequences of their sin rather than immediately judging them. Polyamory causes dissention in the home as the husband divides his love between the favorite wife and the not-so-favorite wife (1 Samuel 1:1-9). Abraham's sin resulted in strife in his house and so God ordered Abraham to listen to his wife and to send away the concubine Hagar and her son (Genesis 21:8-21). Incidentally, later the narrator states that at the time Isaac was weaned Abraham had

---

261   Rick Brentlinger, *Gay Christian 101 - Spiritual Self-Defense For Gay Christians* (2007), 23.

no more relations with Hagar and that Abraham's concubines' sons were also sent away (Genesis 25:6). We then read of Sarah's death and afterward Abraham lawfully married Keturah (Genesis 23:1-2; Genesis 25).

Both King David and Solomon, in violation of the law, had multiple wives (Deuteronomy 17:17; 2 Samuel 5:13). Polygamy was not considered on par with adultery, fornication, incest, bestiality or same-sex acts (Leviticus 18:22-24), but it did fall short of God's created order and was therefore not explicitly prohibited except for kings who were supposed to set an example for the people. What is clear from Scripture is that polygamy causes many problems (which is why God placed some boundaries around it) as it creates competition between the wives. It also inhibits a father's ability to rightly teach the multitude of children that would be produced from have a multiple wives at the same time (Genesis 29:30; Exodus 21:9-10; Leviticus 18:18; Deuteronomy 21:15-17). If polygamy is morally good there would be no reason to place any restrictions on it.

Even worse, just as the theological message of monogamy between a husband and a wife (especially between the king and his wife) reflects monotheism so too polygamy declares a theological message of polytheism. This is undoubtedly why traditional Mormons who are henotheistic polytheists are also polygamists and many Gay Theology advocates are also syncretistic polytheists. Just as monogamy mirrors monotheism so too polygamy mirrors polytheism:

> As in the beginning, the monogamous standard is ultimately rooted in the monotheistic nature of the biblical God and in the concept of the *imago Dei*. The Lord God, who is "alone" (Deut 6:4), is not engaged in promiscuous relationships within a polytheistic pantheon, and God's creatures are to be united in an exclusive relationship with God alone, and God with them alone (Exod 20:3). In the same way that humans should worship only one God – in a monotheistic relationship with God – so husbands and wives, created in God's image, are to be monogamous in their marital relationship with each other.[262]

---

262   Richard Davidson, *Flame of Yahweh: Sexuality in the Old Testament* (Peabody, MA: Hendriksen Publishing, 2007), 178.

Yet, Gay Theology proponents would have us believe that polygamy was a good and noble practice of an ancient culture that was blessed by God as Rick Brentlinger rhetorically asks:

> Did God really intend us to view Adam and Eve as the only permissible marriage model, prohibiting all other marriage relationships? Is 'one man with one woman' the only marriage relationship God will bless? Are there examples in scripture where God blessed a marriage relationship different from the Adam and Eve model?[263]

Rick Brentlinger then mentions that Esau "had at least three wives" (Genesis 26:24; 28:9).[264] However, we must keep in mind that Esau was rejected and hated by God (Malachi 1:3; Romans 9:13) so like Lamech he isn't exactly a model we want to follow.

Rick Brentlinger then refers to Jacob as a polygamist. However, Jacob did not choose to have two wives. In fact, Jacob only wanted to marry and was promised Rachel after he had worked for Laban for seven years. Laban deceived Jacob by disguising his elder daughter Leah whom Jacob thought was Rachel on his wedding night (Genesis 29:16-30). It was only after he had sex with Leah that he discovered that she was not the woman he vowed to marry. Rather than putting her away, which as a non-virgin may have stigmatized her for life and made her ineligible for marriage, he kept her and then worked another seven years for Laban to gain Rachel.

Furthermore, there is some indication that Jacob may not have been following in the faithful footsteps of his father Isaac and grandfather Abraham. Later we read that he undergoes a conversion (Genesis 32:24-30) at which time he puts all the idols out of his household (Genesis 35:2-4) and his name is changed from being "Heel Catcher" or "Supplanter" (Jacob) to being renamed Israel which means "Wrestles with God" or "Prevailer with God." Then the Lord reconfirmed with Jacob (Israel) the covenant promises given to his forefathers. Subsequently God took Rachel, his second wife leaving only his first and true wife Leah (Genesis 35:19). Following his conversion, Jacob (Israel) had but his

---

263   Rick Brentlinger, *Gay Christian 101 - Spiritual Self-Defense For Gay Christians* (2007), 21.
264   Ibid, 22.

one original wife and he did not seek another. Jacob had repented and no longer lived in polytheistic idolatry and polygamy after his conversion.

Rick Brentlinger goes on to refer to Gideon as a polygamist as if this was approved of by God. But if you actually read the text you will find that this fact is depicted much in the same way that the Bible talks about how Noah got drunk after he got off the ark (Genesis 9:21). It is mentioned at the end of his life followed by a statement of the consequences of these actions, that Noah was left in a state of being vulnerable to being abused by his own son (Genesis 9:22). Likewise, Scripture refers to Gideon being a polygamist at the end of his life with disastrous results in his family (Judges 8:30-35).

The sixth person that Brentlinger mentions as a supposed positive example of polygamy is Elkanah and he states that his polygamous marriage was blessed by God because he became the father of Samuel.[265] However, Scripture tells us that Elkanah's polygamy was the cause of dissention in his home as Peninnah and Hannah become rivals. Peninnah was able to give birth to children whereas Hannah was not which created a competitive strife between them. In fact, not being able to give birth to a child causes Hannah such great anguish that she is mistaken for being drunk by Eli when she is found to be in mournful prayer at the temple. Clearly, this polygamous marriage was not a benefit to Eli nor was it being blessed by God. Elkanah only becomes the father of Samuel because Eli blessed Hannah (1 Samuel 1:17-20). The Lord did not bless Elkanah's polygamous marriage which brought dissention and rivalry in the home. Rather, she was blessed because she petitioned God and was heard by the Lord. In other words, Hannah was blessed by God despite the sin of her husband.

The seventh person Brentlinger puts forth as evidence that polygamy is an approved alternate form of marriage is Abijah, the second son of Samuel (1 Samuel 8:2; 1 Chronicles 6:28). But what does the Bible say about him? Is he a hero of the faith who we should emulate and follow? This what Scriptures says of him, "And he (Abijah) walked in all the sins of his father, which he had done before him: and his heart was not perfect with the LORD his God, as the heart of David his father" (1 Kings 15:3). Abijah is far from being a positive example of marriage and Godly leadership. He is no more a model of what it means to be

265   Rick Brentlinger, *Gay Christian 101 - Spiritual Self-Defense For Gay Christians* (2007), 23.

righteous than Judas is a good example of what it means to be a follower of Jesus Christ.

Leaders are to be a representative of the Lord and all the Old Testament prophets, priests and kings are forerunners of Jesus Christ who has but one wife – the Church (Ephesians 5:25). This is why God forbade kings from multiplying wives in the Old Testament and He forbids elders from having more than wife in the New Testament:

> When you enter the land which the LORD your God gives
> you, and you possess it and live in it, and you say, `I will set
> a king over me like all the nations who are around me,'...
> He shall not multiply wives for himself, or else his heart
> will turn away (Deuteronomy 17:14, 17).

Brentlinger then lists David as a positive example of being a polygamist but what must be kept in mind is that David also sinned against the Lord by taking multiple wives (Deuteronomy 17:17) and taking a forbidden census (1 Chronicles 21). David had several wives and many concubines but after his committing adultery with Bathsheba and having her husband murdered (2 Samuel 11), David confessed his sin, repented and subsequently never repeated the sin (2 Samuel 12:13; Psalm 51). In fact, David did not just violate the commandment of God in committing adultery and murder, he actually despised God in his heart and took another woman to be his wife, "...because you have despised Me and have taken the wife of Uriah the Hittite to be your wife" (2 Samuel 12:10). His sin with Bathsheba and against Uriah was not the first sin against God, but it was the *grand finale* of the long line of sin of multiplying wives. This is evidenced by the fact that God takes all of his forbidden wives from him, "Behold, I will raise up evil against you from your own household; I will even take your wives before your eyes" (2 Samuel 12:11).

David then repented by ceasing to have sexual relations with the concubines and yet he did not leave them materially destitute:

> Then David came to his house at Jerusalem, and the king
> took the ten women, the concubines whom he had left to
> keep the house, and placed them under guard and provided

them with sustenance, but did not go in to them. So they
were shut up until the day of their death, living as widows
(2 Samuel 20:3).

David by keeping the ten concubines "living as widows" truly repented and ceased practicing polygamy. Unfortunately, he had already
set a bad example for his son to follow. As Rick Brentlinger notes, his
son Solomon became "the most extreme example of polygamy" with
seven hundred wives and three hundred concubines (1 Kings 11:3). But
what Brentlinger fails to mention, and conveniently leaves out of the
cited text, is the fact that the very warning that the Lord gave in His
prohibition against polygamy came to pass in Solomon's life:

When you enter the land which the LORD your God gives
you, and you possess it and live in it, and you say, "I will
set a king over me like all the nations who are around me."
you shall surely set a king over you whom the LORD your
God chooses, one from among your countrymen you shall
set as king over yourselves; you may not put a foreigner
over yourselves who is not your countryman. He shall
not multiply wives for himself, or else his heart will turn
away... (Deuteronomy 17:14-15, 17).

In the passage immediately following the one cited by Brentlinger
we then read concerning Solomon:

For when Solomon was old, his wives turned his heart
away after other gods; and his heart was not wholly devoted to the LORD his God, as the heart of David his father
had been. For Solomon went after Ashtoreth the goddess
of the Sidonians and after Milcom the detestable idol of the
Ammonites (1 Kings 11:4-5).

Is it astonishing that a Gay Theology apologist, who claims to interpret the Bible in its context and will accuse those who object to same-
sex acts of failing to do so, will cite the one verse regarding Solomon's
polygamy but fail to quote the following verse. There is someone else
in the Bible who does this very thing, quoting one verse but failing to

cite the following passage. We read about him in Matthew 4:5-6 when Satan tempted Jesus to jump off of the pinnacle of the temple and quotes Psalm 91:11-12:

> For He will give His angels charge concerning you, To guard you in all your ways. They will bear you up in their hands, That you do not strike your foot against a stone.

But, like Brentlinger, he fails to quote the following verse for obvious reasons:

> You will tread upon the lion and cobra. The young lion and the serpent you will trample down (Psalm 91:13).

The reason why Satan the serpent wouldn't want to cite that passage is obvious for it speaks of the fulfillment of the prophecy concerning the seed of the woman (Christ) crushing the head of the serpent which doesn't exactly fit in with his agenda (Genesis 3:15). Likewise, Brentlinger quotes 1 Kings 11:3 but fails to cite 1 Kings 11:4-5 because it doesn't support his theological agenda.

The most relevant data concerning polygamy is found in the words of Christ and the apostle Paul. What is clear from them is that God does not accept divorce except in the case of a spouse breaking the marriage covenant by adultery or the abandonment of a spouse by an unbeliever:

> Some Pharisees came to Jesus, testing Him and asking, "Is it lawful for a man to divorce his wife for any reason at all?"

> And He answered and said, "Have you not read that He who created them from the beginning made them male and female, and said, `For this reason a man shall leave his father and mother and be joined to his wife, and the two shall become one flesh'? So they are no longer two, but one flesh. What therefore God has joined together, let no man separate."

They said to Him, "Why then did Moses command to give
her a certificate of divorce and send her way?"

He said to them, "Because of your hardness of heart Moses
permitted you to divorce your wives; but from the beginning it has not been this way. And I say to you, whoever divorces his wife, except for immorality, and marries another
woman commits adultery" (Matthew 19:3-9).

The Pharisees want to base their views of marriage and divorce
on a static reading of the law, treating it as if every law is of equal
value and that because something is legal that it is therefore morally
just and right. This would be like people today arguing that because the
government regulates the use of cigarettes and alcohol and that being
addicted to smoking or getting drunk at home is legal it is therefore
morally justifiable to do so. In response Jesus takes His disciples back
to the foundation of marriage to see God's original intent and He asserts
that if a person marries a divorcee they are committing adultery because
the divorce is not recognized as being lawful. In short, if you marry
an unlawfully divorced woman you are having sex with another man's
wife. The marriage has not become polygamous; it is an act of adultery!
Likewise when people are married and they purposely add to their number of wives or take concubines they are committing adultery.

In the New Covenant, though a person who already who has multiple wives can become a Christian and join the Church along with his
wives, he may not hold a position of leadership (Titus 1:5-7; 1 Timothy
3:2). God is not merely being persnickety with those in leadership concerning polygamy, rather by being a "one woman man" they are to be an
example of righteousness to the men in the Church as Paul told Timothy,
"...show yourself an example of those who believe" (1 Timothy 4:12;
cf. Philippians 3:17; 2 Thessalonians 3:7, 9). Christian men ought not
to multiply wives for it goes against the created order and against the
teaching of Jesus Christ. Even more so same-sex acts goes against the
created order and it is declared to be a sexual sin along with fornication
and incest and those who live in this sin shall not inherit the Kingdom
of God (1 Corinthians 6:9).

One of the biggest misconceptions in the argument that God advocates diverse forms of marriage is the assumption that if His law allows

and regulates a behavior that it must therefore be good and promoted by God. But this is not how the law of God is written. There are many positive commandments in the law "Thou shalt do such and such," many prohibitions, "Thou shalt not do such and such," and there are a few fencing regulations which restrict undesirable behavior from getting out of hand or from causing further problems. For example, divorce is not a good thing and yet we see that the Law of God regulated it:

> When a man takes a wife and marries her, and it happens that she finds no favor in his eyes because he has found some indecency in her, and he writes her a certificate of divorce and puts it in her hand and sends her out from his house, and she leaves his house and goes and becomes another man's wife, and if the latter husband turns against her and writes her a certificate of divorce and puts it in her hand and sends her out of his house, or if the latter husband dies who took her to be his wife, then her former husband who sent her away is not allowed to take her again to be his wife, since she has been defiled; for that is an abomination before the LORD, and you shall not bring sin on the land which the LORD your God gives you as an inheritance (Deuteronomy 24:1-4).

The Pharisees took this text and twisted it to give them a free license for divorce and they assumed God approved of it:

> Some Pharisees came to Jesus, testing Him and asking, "Is it lawful for a man to divorce his wife for any reason at all?" And He answered and said, "Have you not read that He who created them from the beginning made them male and female, and said, 'For this reason a man shall leave his father and mother and be joined to his wife, and the two shall become one flesh'? So they are no longer two, but one flesh. What therefore God has joined together, let no man separate.' They said to Him, 'Why then did Moses command to give her a certificate of divorce and send her away?' He said to them, 'Because of your hardness of heart

Moses permitted you to divorce your wives; but from the
beginning it has not been this way. And I say to you, whoever divorces his wife, except for immorality, and marries
another woman commits adultery' (Matthew 19:3-9)

First, notice that Jesus appeals to Genesis 2:24 as the basis for the
original order for marriage. Whatever the law allowed was a post-fall
accommodation and not in accordance with the original intent and design for marriage. Second, the certificate of divorce was an accommodation to the sinfulness of man. This is the same purpose for regulation
of polygamy amongst the general population (Deuteronomy 21:15-17).
Jesus in His teaching on marriage and divorce is restoring in the New
Covenant God's original intent for marriage - one man and one woman for life, "'For I hate divorce,' says the LORD, the God of Israel"
(Malachi 2:16).

The law concerning divorce is not the only example of this sort of
tolerance and restriction of an undesirable practice. God put up many
hedges and fences to restrict other behaviors as well. Man was created
to be free: free from sin, free from suffering and free to be the head of
his own home. But after the fall men often resorted to selling themselves
into slavery in order to survive, their children became slaves due to
debt (2 Kings 4:1) or at times they became slaves due to being captives
of war. Going into debt is a form of slavery that people often found
themselves in due to living in a fallen world (Proverbs 22:7). The restorative laws restricted the consequences of slavery and provided some
freedoms by restricting who could be enslaved (Exodus 21:20, 26-27),
and how slaves could be treated (Exodus 21:20, 26-27). It enabled
runaway slaves to be freed from oppressive masters (Deuteronomy
23:15-16) and it created the year of jubilee in which slaves would be
freed from their debt (Leviticus 25:23-28). If the person was a member of the covenant he was to be treated as a hired worker, not a slave
(Leviticus 25:39-43) and he was to be freed after six years (Exodus
21:2, Deuteronomy 15:12) at which time he was to be liberally supplied
with grain, wine and livestock (Deuteronomy 15:12-15). Every fiftieth
year (the year of jubilee), all Hebrew slaves were to be freed, even those
owned by foreigners (Leviticus 25:10, 47-54). In special cases, slaves

could choose to remain with their masters if they felt it was in their best interest (Deuteronomy 15:16-17).

The situation and circumstances of slavery in the Bible was radically different than the slavery which took place in America, which was actually a form of man-stealing forbidden in the law and punishable by death (Exodus 21:16; Deuteronomy 24:7). Slavery is not God's desire for man for it would be best for each man to be the head of his own household and own his land. But since slavery was a given reality and at times an economic necessity the Lord in His perfect law protected the slave by regulating it. In doing so the slave was not to be mistreated by their master (they couldn't be forced work on the Sabbath) and they were to be included in the covenant (they received the sign of circumcision) and treated as part of the family, although not being the first in line for the inheritance. Slavery is a result of the fall of mankind into sin but God gave regulations concerning slavery in His perfect, good and righteous Law. The trajectory of the Old Testament, in contrast to forms of slavery in the surrounding nations, was away from the consequences of slavery by heavily restricting it and guarding the rights of slaves.

Likewise, the New Testament recognizes slavery as it was a common part of the Roman society. The apostle Paul exhorted slaves not to take their freedom in Christ as a means to rebel against their masters but rather as an opportunity to serve them as they do the Lord in order to be a good witness for the gospel (Ephesians 6:5-6; Colossians 3:22). But when Paul converted a runaway slave named Onesimus and his master Philemon to the faith, he appealed to the master to no longer treat Onesimus as a slave but rather as a brother in Christ for in Him we are all on equal footing (Philemon 16; Galatians 3:28; 1 Corinthians 12:13; Colossians 4:1). Like the Old Testament, the trajectory of the New Testament is away from slavery towards freedom by teaching us that Christ has set us free from the slavery to sin and therefore we ought to do the same for others. The Gospel of the New Testament establishes a trajectory away from slavery in order to restore man to his original state. In fact, sin is the chief form of slavery from which Christ came to set us free (Romans 6:6; 18; 1 Corinthians 7:23).

The Restoration of Marriage

The New Testament furthers the redemptive and restorative trajectory away from slavery and polygamy in that God requires those who are in leadership to set an example to the flock by meeting the highest standard, just as He required of the priests in the Old Testament. God requires that His under-shepherds, the leaders of the Church, provide an example of moral living and meet the criteria that every Christian man ought to seek. Specifically, elders and deacons are forbidden to have multiple wives:

> Here is a trustworthy saying: If anyone sets his heart on being an overseer, he desires a noble task An overseer, then, must be above reproach, **the husband of one wife**, temperate, prudent, hospitable, able to teach, not addicted to wine or pugnacious, but gentle, uncontentious, free from the love of money. He must be one who manages his own household well, keeping his children under control with all dignity (but if a man does not know how to manage his own household, how will he take care of the church of God?); and not a new convert, lest he become conceited and fall into the condemnation incurred by the devil. And he must have a good reputation with those outside the church, so that he may not fall into reproach and the snare of the devil (1 Timothy 3:2-7).

> For this reason I left you in Crete, that you might set in order what remains, and appoint elders in every city as I directed you, namely, if any man be above reproach, **the husband of one wife**, having children who believe, not accused of dissipation or rebellion. For the overseer must be above reproach as God's steward, not self-willed, not quick-tempered, not addicted to wine, not pugnacious, not fond or sordid gain (Titus 1:5-7).

The question at this point is, "What is Paul requiring when he says that the elder-shepherd is required to be 'the husband of one wife'?" In order to understand what Paul actually means by "the husband of one wife" we need to look at the phrase in the Greek text (*mias gunaikos andra*). The Greek structure of the statement "the husband of one wife" in 1 Timothy 3:2 and Titus 1:6 emphasizes the word "one." This would not be expected if being married were required, but rather Paul would have written that a man must be "the husband of a wife" and it is clear that neither Jesus (the chief Shepherd) or the Apostle Paul were married and yet apostles were also ruling elders as Peter referred to himself as a "fellow elder" (1 Peter 5:1). There is no distinct word in Greek for our word "husband." The word for "man" here is *aner* is the word for a male individual, not one that means "men in general." When this word is used in a context of marriage, it has the meaning of "husband." The words "wife/woman" (*gunaikos*) and "husband/man" (*aner*) are used without the definite article in the Greek, which emphasizes character or nature. Therefore the structure of this passage could easily be translated "one wife's husband" or "a one-wife sort of husband."

When examining the qualifications of an elder, it is important to look at the overall idea of the passage as well as the specific grammar and construction. These qualities were meant to show that a leader in the Church must be a godly man who mirrors Jesus Christ to the congregation. An elder-shepherd of the church is to act as an example, to the Church and the community, of Christ-like living. This is seen in Paul's first qualification, which is the key to all of the other specifications, "An overseer, then, must be above reproach." The overarching moral qualification of which the rest in the litmus test are supportive of this qualification. All the other moral prerequisites emphasize that idea. An elder-shepherd must be above reproach in his personal life, his social life, his family life, his neighborhood, his business life and his spiritual life. In Paul's requirement of being a "one woman man" he is saying that an elder who is married must be a man who is utterly single-minded in his devotion to his one wife as an example to the flock just as Jesus Christ is single-minded in his devotion to His one wife - the Church (Ephesians 5:25-30).

The fall of mankind into sin brought slavery, polygamy and divorce was tolerated and permitted but regulated in God's law. But the trajectory of the New Testament is to return to God's original intent for man - freedom from slavery (of all kinds) and the one-man/one woman marriage for life (Matthew 19:4-7). Ironically, the trajectory hermeneutics of Gay Theology and Liberalism takes us in the opposite direction - slavery to sin, a sky rocking divorce rate, polygamy and "Gay marriage."

Chapter 10
Purity Laws and Same Sex Acts

It is common for Christians to think of sin and its various synonyms entirely in terms of a volitional transgression of God's moral standards as The Westminster Shorter Catechism states, "Sin is any want of conformity unto, or transgression of, the law of God." As a result, when Christians read the purity laws in the Old Testament they conclude that these cannot have any relation to sin. Some of the laws, after all, do not entail a volitional act such as menstruation or the emission of seminal fluids which are part of the natural biological cycle (Leviticus 15:16-18, 32; Deuteronomy 23:10). Consequently a distinct classification of "ritual purity" is created and it is insisted that it has nothing to do with a sinful condition which prevents one from coming before God at His temple. However, to make such an assertion is to miss the point of the purity laws. The purity laws depict our inherent sinful condition inherited from Adam and the necessity of being cleansed of the moral impurity we refer to as "original sin." In fact in missing that these laws teach us that we are born unclean some will even go so far as to deny the doctrine of original sin and consequently the necessity for a substitutionary atonement.[266]

The Bible speaks of sin not only in terms of volitional acts against God's law, but it also portrays the human race as being born in a sinful condition, likened to a disease. The result of the sin that indwells our being is that we are like lepers in that we are born "unclean." Gay Theology proponents miss this point when they assert that the purity laws only refer to a mere form of "ritual cleanness" that had nothing to do with being in a state of sin, "Whatever rationale was behind the ancient Hebrew purity laws, such thinking certainly has nothing to do with ethics as we understand it. Indeed, such thinking is almost completely foreign to our own culture."[267] Many Gay Theology proponents then

---

266   Virginia Ramey Mollenkott, *Omnigender: A Trans-religious Approach* (Cleveland, OH: The Pilgrim Progress, 2007), 92.

267   Daniel Helminiak, *What the Bible Really Says About Homosexuality* (Estancia, NM: Alamo Square Press, 2000), 58

attempt to reclassify the prohibition of same sex acts in Leviticus 18:22 and 20:13 as not being sins but rather one of the "ritual purity laws":

> The distinction between intrinsic wrong and ritual impurity is even more finely drawn by the Greek translation which distinguishes in 'toevah' itself the separate categories of law or justice (*anomia*) and infringements of ritual purity or monotheistic worship (*bdelugma*). The Levitical pro-scriptions of homosexual behavior fall into the latter. In the Greek, then, the Levitical enactments against homosexual behavior characterize it univocally as ceremonially unclean rather than inherently evil.[268]

In making such an assertion the point of Scripture's close tie between ritual purity and moral purity is completely missed. They go on to wrongly assert that the purity laws have all been abrogated in the New Testament and therefore by reclassifying the prohibitions of same-sex acts as "purity laws" rather than a "moral law" they conclude that the laws against same-sex acts are no longer binding. This interpretation of same-sex acts does not want to appear to be disregarding the Bible's authority on morality or ethics and what it defines as sin. Rather, this argument attempts to reclassify homosexual behavior as part of the purity laws that along with the various food restrictions and the separation from the Gentiles that have been abrogated by the New Covenant:

> The context of these verses [Leviticus 18:22, 20:13] clear-ly links the sexual behavior to the idolatry of Egypt and Canaan. Because of the connection with idolatry, the acts themselves should not be considered inherently sinful, just as planting mixed seed in the same field, working animals in two kinds, eating pork or shellfish, or wearing mixed fabrics are not inherently sinful. The purpose of these codes was to maintain the children of Israel as a sanctified people who were distinct in religion and lifestyle from the people surrounding them. Furthermore, even if these verses were

---

268   John Boswell, *Christianity, Social Tolerance, and Homosexuality* (University Of Chicago Press; 8th Edition. edition, 2005), 101-102.

a condemnation of all same-sex activity – which they are not – they do not apply to Christians.[269]

However, these same Gay Theology advocates will also argue that the prohibitions against same-sex acts in Leviticus 18:22 and 20:13 only refer to forms of ritualistic cultic idolatrous acts of worship of Molech:

> As with the Leviticus and Deuteronomy passages, this condemnation [same sex activity in Romans 1:26-27] is directly related to idol worship, as clearly indicated by the context of the passage in question... because our modern culture no longer associates same-sex activity with idol worship, it would be wrong to hold Christians captive to the ancient cultural perspective that informed Paul's worldview (particularly when the acts are not engaged in the worship of idol gods).[270]

Are we to believe that such an act of idolatry was only a matter or ritual impurity and not an inherently sinful act? Furthermore, are we to believe that God imposed a penal sanction of death for a violation of an act of ritual impurity? (Leviticus 20:13) And do not these same authors argue that the homosexual acts mentioned in Romans 1:27 and 1 Corinthians 6:9 also refer to first century versions cultic forms of the same sex acts? Yet, Paul tells us that the wrath of God is upon them, that those who do such things are worthy of death (Romans 1:32) and that those who continue in such behavior shall not inherent the Kingdom of God (1 Corinthians 6:9). Gay Theology advocates are trying to make two different arguments as to how these passages ought to be understood, but by asserting both arguments (that the texts don't refer to sins but mere ritual impurity) and that the acts only pertain to cultic forms of idolatry (which are clearly sinful) they contradict themselves and each other. In fact, if the sexual prohibitions in Leviticus 18:22 and 20:13 only refer to purity laws, which Gay Theology advocates argue are no longer binding in the New Testament, how can they then argue that Paul is referring to these same acts in Romans 1:27 and 1 Corinthians 6:9, if such laws are not applicable to Gentiles or Christians? Clearly

---

269   R.D. Weekly, *Homosexianity* (Judah First Ministries, 2009), 102.
270   R.D. Weekly, *Homosexianity* (Judah First Ministries, 2009), 102.

Gay Theology proponents are grasping at straws in trying to find some way of getting around the clear moral implications of these texts which together unanimously condemn same-sex acts in both the Old and New Testaments.

The assertion that the prohibition of same-sex acts in Leviticus 18:22 and 20:13 only refers to ritual impurity fails to understand the purpose of the cleansing rites and purity laws. These laws were intended to be a picture of inherent inborn human defilement, not merely convey an idea of Jewish cultural boundaries to make them distinct from the surrounding nations as L. William Countryman asserts, "The human concern about dirt, moreover, can actually take many different forms. Even if the concern to avoid what is dirty is more or less universal, different cultures define what is dirty in quite different ways."[271]

Countryman's understanding of purity, morality and ethics is derived from reading the text through the lens of a cultural anthropologist. He then reads into the text an understanding of these issues rather than reading from the text what the Bible reveals to be the nature of morality, ethics and purity. The consequence is he asserts that purity, morality and ethics are entirely culturally relative determined by a larger community rather than by a transcendent God who reveals His will and an understanding of sin through law and the imagery of the language of the purity system in both the Old and New Testaments.[272] Instead of observing how the Bible develops purity language throughout the Old and New Testaments he borrows from cultural anthropology as he writes:

> What is this 'dirt,' which children are told to avoid, but which is neither literal, physical dirt nor anything threatening to health? Because anthropologists are used to examining such questions in a cross-cultural way, an anthropologist is probably the best person to help us gain perspective on it in our own culture… Mary Douglas, the cultural anthropologist, has argued that dirt can be understood

271   L. William Countryman, *Dirt, Greed & Sex: Sexual Ethics in the New Testament and Their Implications for Today* (Minneapolis, MN: Fortress Press; Revised edition, 2007), 9.
272   For a thorough response to L. William Countryman's book *Dirt, Greed & Sex* I highly recommend reading: Thomas Schmidt, *Straight & Narrow?: Compassion & Clarity in the Homosexuality Devate* (Downers Grove, IL: InterVarsity Press, 1995).

only in relation to a system that excludes it 'As we know it,' she says, 'dirt is essentially disorder'… 'the old definition of dirt as matter out of place.'… What is clean in one culture is dirty in another. Ancient Israel forbade the eating of pork (Lev. 11:7).[273]

He then traces what he considers to be "American purity law," sexual impurity, or what is considered "dirty" from the 1950's to the present day in which, "'Morality' – meaning, in this case, one's definition of sexual purity – came to be treated as a matter of private determination."[274] He then concludes in establishing the nature of the parameters of purity:

> Because of the complexity and incoherence of modern Western purity values, the reader of this book has to perform several difficult tasks to understand the topic at hand. One is to discover that what has long been seemed self-evident with regard to sexual ethics – namely, that certain acts are right or wrong in and of themselves – reflects purity values specific to our culture. The evident values of other cultures will often be significantly different. Another is to accept that purity systems change and that we cannot assume that ours is identical with that of our ancestral cultures.[275]

He then states concerning the prohibitions of Leviticus 18:22 and 20:13:

> …in literal translation 'lying with a male the lyings of a woman.'… scholars suggest anal intercourse – an interpretation accepted in what follows. The common practice of treating the text as a blanket prohibition of all sexual interaction between males or even between females goes beyond what it actually says. These two prohibitions appear as isolated rules, with the violations being described

---

273   L. William Countryman, *Dirt, Greed & Sex: Sexual Ethics in the New Testament and Their Implications for Today* (Minneapolis, MN: Fortress Press; Revised edition, 2007), 10-11.
274   Ibid, 14.
275   Ibid, 15.

as 'abominations' that is – 'disgusting things.' This language does not mean that they are exceptionally horrid in terms of the purity system. The Hebrew term *toebah* and its synonym *shiqquts*, both usually translated *bdelygma* in ancient Greek and 'abomination' in English, apply, in the Torah, to things as diverse as unclean foods (Lev. 11:10, 11, 12, etc. ; Deut. 14:3), the sacrifice of a blemish animal (Deut. 17:10), remarriage to a former wife (Deut. 24:4), and idols (Deut. 29:16, ET 17).[276]

However, Jesus Himself described what the ultimate goal of the purity laws involved. When Jesus told the scribes and Pharisees to clean both the outside and the inside of the cup, He used it as a metaphor for the necessity of being clean (from sin) on the inside of the human heart (Matthew 23:25-26). Jesus is not rebuking the Pharisees for failing to wash the inside of the cups, but for being concerned with the mere external appearance of righteousness while ignoring the impurity and uncleanness of their heart. True cleansing of the sinful condition, true circumcision, was always to be of the heart (Deuteronomy 10:16; 30:6; Romans 2:29). It is not that the Old Testament laws only referred to external physical purity and Jesus was only concerned with internal moral impurity as some interpreters assert. Rather Jesus, as He did with moral laws, taught the full implications of the law of God, that they go beyond mere external observance and point to the matters of the condition of the heart (Matthew 5:27-28).

The purity laws were related to the doctrine of sin in the Old Testament as a picture of the inherent inward depravity of mankind. A woman or a man could become unclean through various bodily discharges including menstruation or seminal ejaculation (Leviticus 12:2; 15:16). This did not indicate that they had committed a volitional act of sin. Instead, it indicated that the seed was in a condition of sin and uncleanness which is why after the discharge, or her period of uncleanness, they were required to provide an atoning sacrifice (Leviticus 15:15).

Under the Old Covenant believers needed to be repeatedly cleansed (baptized) with water and atoned for with blood (Leviticus 12:6-8). The priests also had to be repeatedly replaced (Hebrews 7:23-24) and animals had to be repeatedly sacrificed (Hebrews 10:1-4). This constant

276   Ibid, 24.

repetition of baptisms and sacrifices was one of the weaknesses of the Old Covenant. From the time of the giving of the law at Sinai, through the prophets and into the New Covenant the correlation between sin and uncleanness becomes closer and clearer. The New Covenant does not do away with the purity laws but rather consolidates them into a singular sacrament of baptism, a one-time act because Christ has died once for all (Ephesians 4:5; Hebrews 7:27; 10:10).

There are a number of different categories and types of purity laws in the Old Testament all of which typified sin, fallenness or being a Gentile outside of the Covenant Community. There were clean/unclean food laws (Genesis 7:2; Leviticus 11; Deuteronomy 14:9; Daniel 1:8), cleanliness in relation to sexual purity (Leviticus 15:16; 20:8), skin diseases (Leviticus 13-14), the discharges of certain bodily fluids (Leviticus 12:1-8; 15:25-30), and the touching of unclean things such as rotting animals or a human corpse (Leviticus 5:13; 7:19, 21; 11:24-28, 44).

The consequences of being unclean varied depending on whether it was a natural cyclical uncleanness (menstruation, childbirth, marital sexual intercourse), or whether it was a deliberate violation of the law. The result of being unclean sometimes required some sort of baptism, a period of being "unclean" or it may have required offering up a sacrifice (Leviticus 12:1-8; Luke 2:22-27). In the case of a disease such as leprosy it would require that the infected person remain outside the camp and if cured they would have to be declared clean by a priest. This was a law that Jesus Himself upheld (Luke 17:11-17). Ritual impurity did not denote that an act of willful sin or a social stigma but an inability to approach the temple or partake of certain feasts and festivals for a given time period because of the unclean condition the person was in. Yet, being unclean was associated with the common and universal condition of corruption, fallenness and the condition of sin. This is illustrated in King David's usage the language of the purity law when he declared guilt concerning his being born in sin and his subsequent personal acts of sin (Psalm 51: 5, 7).

We are not told specifically why some animals were considered "clean" and others "unclean" in the Old Testament. But when we come to the New Testament we find that the human purity laws pointed to the inborn condition of the person for what comes out of his heart and subsequently from his mouth is what truly makes him unclean (Matthew 15:11; Mark 7:20).

Some theorize that these laws had a pragmatic purpose to promote healthy eating and hygiene. It is recognized that pigs can transmit trichinosis, the hare can transmit tularemia, carrion birds can carry diseases and fish without scales burrow in the mud can cause disease as well.[277] Based upon this theory Gay Theology apologists then assert that while promiscuous homosexual and heterosexual sex can likewise cause health problems this is not so within committed relationships. Therefore, they argue, the prohibition of men having sex with other men was not a moral law but rather a purity law that is not binding on life-long sexual partners. Such observations can make this rationale for the purity laws plausible until it is recognized that there are far more poisonous plants than there are animals and yet there are no "unclean" plants mentioned in the Bible.[278] Also, the surrounding nations ate pork and apparently they were able to figure out that you needed to cook it long enough to kill the tapeworm that causes trichinosis. Furthermore, if health was the primary concern why would this dietary law be changed in the New Covenant? (Acts 10:15) While there may have been some secondary hygiene benefits to some of the purity laws it cannot be said that this was God's primary concern.

Other Gay Theology advocates argue that the purity laws are merely a reflection of local cultural taboo that does not apply to modern Christians.[279] This view states that the purity laws were due to the various prohibited items being associated with culturally disgusting practices or pagan rites, "...*toevah* is used most often as a religious or ceremonial 'abomination,' not an ethical condemnation. Put simply, the word means 'icky.'"[280] It is then argued by the Gay Theology apologists

277   Andrew Bonar commenting on Leviticus 11:9-12 wrote, "It is a well fact, that all fish have both scales and fins are at once wholesome and nutritious. This provision, therefore, secured to the people the free use of what was certainly profitable, and kept them from what might have injured them." *A Commentary on Leviticus* (Carlisle, PA: Banner of Truth, 1998), 217. See also Rousas John Rushdoony, *Leviticus* (Vallecito, CA: Ross House Books, 2005), 116-119.

278   For example the Oleander (Nerium Oleander) or "Harduf Hanachalim" is one of the most poisonous plants in Israel and it is commonly found in public parks, gardens, and schoolyards. A child can easily be poisoned by playing with the leaves and then his putting hands in mouth.

279   Daniel Helminiak, *What the Bible Really Says About Homosexuality* (Estancia, NM: Alamo Square Press, 2000), 64.

280   David W. Shelton, *The Rainbow Kingdom: Christianity & the Homosexual Reconciled* (Lulu, 2006), 51.

that same-sex acts were looked upon in a similar vein and were merely due to a cultural bias. Therefore such primitive notions ought not to be recognized by a more modern and enlightened people. The problem with this view of the purity laws is that there was no aversion to the hyrax (rock badger/coney) though it was an "unclean" animal (Leviticus 11:5) and a goat, which is a "clean" animal, can be rather disgusting in that it eats just about anything.

Some argue that those things that were declared "unclean" were associated with the religious worship of the surrounding pagan nations. This view often used by those who restrict the prohibited same sex acts as only that which was related to the pagan temple prostitution.[281] The problem with this argument, in addition to those already mentioned, is that the Israelites used some of the same animals (bulls) in their sacrifices as the surrounding nations such as the Egyptians and the Canaanites. Therefore, it cannot be consistently argued that the Israelites were only trying to avoid worshipping like their nations in every possible fashion.

The New Testament makes it clear that the purity laws were for a theological-typological distinction between the Godly seed and the ungodly seed, two lines of descendants - one of the woman and the other the serpent (Genesis 3:15). It is clear that one of purposes of the purity laws was to separate Israel from the Gentile nations to some degree in the manner in which they worshipped, ate, dressed and in their sexual ethics. Although Abraham was promised that he would be a father of many nations (Genesis 15:5; 22:18; Romans 4:18) the nation of Israel, after spending 430 years in pagan Egypt, had to be separated both in cult and culture from the perverse surrounding nations. Israel was far too prone to adapting its worship to mimic pagan forms of worship (Exodus 32) and desiring to imitate the surrounding nations in their polity (1 Samuel 8). Consequently the Lord had to make a clear visible distinction between His people and those that worshipped other gods and warned them what would happen if they failed to obey and instead played the role of a harlot.

The purity law system divided animals, people, and land into three categories. There were clean animals that could be sacrificed on an altar, clean animals that could be eaten but not sacrificed on an altar, and unclean animals that ritually defiled the eater and could not be sacrificed

281   John Boswell, *Christianity, Social Tolerance, and Homosexuality* (University Of Chicago Press; 8th Edition. edition, 2005), 100.

(Leviticus 11:10-13, 20, 23, 41; Deuteronomy 14:3). This categorizing of animals represents a covenantal distinction between people and the manner in which these people worshipped and how they lived ethically. The so-called "moral" commandments and the "ceremonial" laws are intertwined so that theologically the purity laws convey an ethical message. This is not to say that there is no distinction between the different types of commandments, only that in the Old Covenant the life of the believer was not to be divided but rather holistically devoted to obeying the law of God. These laws were a practical means of maintaining Israel as a morally holy people:

> You are therefore to make a distinction between the clean animal and the unclean, and between the unclean bird and the clean; and you shall not make yourselves detestable by animal or by bird or by anything that creeps on the ground, which I have separated for you as unclean. Thus you are to be holy to Me, for I the LORD am holy; and I have set you apart from the peoples to be Mine (Leviticus 20:25-26).

These purity laws, even those without any seemingly any inherent moral value such as not wearing blended fabrics (Leviticus 18:19), convey to Israel the concept of holiness. They served as theological and moral object lessons establishing Israel with an identity of a "separated" people.

Furthermore, the purity laws indicated to the believer that he too was born unclean and thus needed to be circumcised (a cleansing rite) and was frequently unclean throughout his life and thus needed to undergo various washings (baptisms). The cultural distinctions conveyed an ethical message such that, although the ethnic division is ended in the New Covenant (Galatians 3:28) along with the food laws (Acts 10:15; 11:9; Romans 14:14), the moral association of "clean" with that of holiness and devotion to the Lord remains. This is clearly seen in the New Covenant sacrament of baptism ("you were washed" 1 Corinthians 6:11) and the status of covenant children being declared "clean" (1 Corinthians 7:14). While the abolition of the food laws conveys the message of a breaking down of the ethnic barrier between Jews and Gentiles in Christ the principle that God's people are to be a separate (holy) from the world remains.

While it is common to categorize Old Covenant laws as moral, ceremonial and civil these distinctions are not always accurate or helpful. As previously stated, the laws might be more naturally understood in light of their covenant spheres (family, church and state) and the assigned leaders (elders). The goal then is not to determine a category that is no longer binding (such as ceremonial laws) but rather to discern which laws are still required to be obeyed in each category in the New Covenant.

All the laws of the Old Covenant were either explicitly moral in their purpose or they had an ethical component or were intended to theologically paint a picture of morality. Though we are not told explicitly the reasoning behind things being designated "clean" or "unclean," the purity laws are meant to promote ethical behavior particularly in relation to the preservation of life. For example, eating animals that have been torn by wild beasts not only defiles but it also demotes human beings to the level of a scavenger dog instead of being those who were called to take dominion (Exodus 22:31; cf. Matthew 7:6).[282]

A similar moral explanation could apply to some specific, repulsive species (pigs, snakes). Cooking a kid goat in its mother's milk was seen to be perverse because the kid was being cooked in that which was intended to give it life. Leaving a corpse of an executed man exposed on a tree overnight defiles the land because it is an act of excessive degradation and perhaps spare the family further emotional suffering (Deuteronomy 21:23).[283] Those involved in the slaughter of war (even at the command of God), became unclean hints at the moral defilement of war (Numbers 31:19-24). Laws concerning sexual emissions encouraged restraint and sexual self-control (e.g. avoiding sex during menstruation) and would rightly stigmatize violators such as prostitutes as social outcasts. The laws prohibiting same sex intercourse would then be seen in this manner as well. Rather than promoting life through the joining of the penis and the vagina, the act of male-to-male sex inserts the seed of the man into the anus - an orifice out of which dead matter and waste is excreted. This prohibition was both a matter of cleanliness and morality as the New Testament clearly teaches that same-sex acts

---

282   Rousas John Rushdoony, *Exodus* (Vallecito, CA: Ross House Books, 2004), 326.
283   Christopher Wright, *Deuteronomy* (Peabody, MA.: Hendriksen Publishers, 1996), 237.

are an act of unrighteousness, not merely a ceremonial uncleanness, that unless followed by repentance will bar the sinner from the Kingdom of God (1 Corinthians 6:9; 1 Timothy 1:10).

The command not to eat the flesh with the blood not only reminded the Israelite of God's use of blood for atoning sacrifice but also inculcated respect for animal life. The blood, symbolic of the life, had to be poured back to God even for non-atoning slaughter to symbolize that only by divine permission could even animal life be taken. In this manner, the blood prohibition (Genesis 9:3-6) taught the Israelite respect for animal life and for the Author of life whose permission was required to shed any blood, whether animal or human. This leads to a further moral implication: if taking mere animal life is not trivial, how much more serious is shedding human blood.

Uncleanness is used metaphorically to refer to deviations of morality hints also that there is a symbolic connection between so-called ceremonial and ethical uncleanness. In the Pentateuch, sexual acts such as rape (Genesis 34:5, 13, 27), adultery (Leviticus 18:20; Numbers 5:19), bestiality (Leviticus 18:23), and men having sex with other men (Leviticus 20:13) are all the various sins for which God judged the Canaanites (Leviticus 18:24-26). Immoral acts such as remarriage to a first husband after divorce and remarriage to a second husband (Deuteronomy 24:4), consultation with mediums (Leviticus 19:31), sacrificing one's children to Molech (Leviticus 20:3), and murder (Numbers 35:33-34) are all spoken of as acts of "uncleanness" which conveys the symbolic tie between ceremonial and ethical uncleanness.

This tie between the purity laws and morality is drawn closer together in the Poetical books and the Prophets. The language of ritual purity is used for ethical purity, such that a person with a skin disease being analogous to a sinner (Psalm 51:7 cf. Lamentations 4:13, 15). In the same way, prophets such as Isaiah and Ezekiel use the language of "clean" and "unclean" with ethical connotations. Ezekiel states that transgressions defiled Israel (Ezekiel 14:11), so that Israel is "unclean of name" because it has a reputation for (ethical) impurity (Ezekiel 22:5). Moreover, Ezekiel compares Israel's wicked deeds with that of the uncleanness of a menstruating woman (Ezekiel 36:17) and adds that the exile was due to Israel's (moral) uncleanness and transgressions (Ezekiel 39:24). Likewise, Isaiah states that he and his people have "unclean lips," because they are sinful (Isaiah 6:5). Later he states that no one who is morally unclean will travel on God's highway of holiness into the Kingdom of God (Isaiah 35:8). This language is borrowed by the apostle Paul when he states that the unrighteous will not inherit the Kingdom of God (1 Corinthians 6:9). Hence even if the same-sex acts prohibited in Leviticus 18 and 20 do belong to the purity laws, Paul clearly is in line with the prophets who see sexual impurity (fornication, adultery and men having sex with other men) as ethical violations of God's holiness as he equates the "lusts of their hearts" to "impurity" and "uncleanness" (Romans 1:24).

The theological-ethical message that is conveyed in both testaments is uniform: just as physical uncleanness can come from within (natural bodily functions) and from without (contaminating things), sin comes both from perverse human nature within and temptations without. Therefore, the sexual prohibitions in the New Testament regarding same-sex acts are conveying very strongly that such actions, regardless of their other associated circumstances, are unrighteous, in error, contrary to nature, and sinful.

There is Nothing Impure in Itself

Another argument used to reclassify the prohibition of same-sex acts as a defunct purity law and not a sin is that according to Paul in the New Covenant "there is nothing impure in itself" (Romans 14:14). It is then asserted that the manner in which an act is done is solely determinative as to whether or not it is a sin - not whether it is on a list of "thou shalt nots" in the Bible.[284] The argument then states that though Paul calls men having sex with men a sin and not a purity law, he is only arguing against a particular type of homosexual sex - one done as part of an overall life of rebellion against the one true God.

The problem with this argument is that if you actually read the text that is being cited you will find that Paul is specifically referring to the food laws and not unlawful sex acts (Romans 14:10-16). It is clear from the context that when Paul states that, "I know and am convinced in the Lord Jesus that nothing is unclean in itself" he is not using "nothing" to include every imaginable sex act. Rather he has a very specific category

284   Dan O. Via, *Homosexuality and the Bible: Two Views* (Minneapolis, MN: Fortress Press, 2003), 9.

of "things" in mind - namely food and those things that distinguished Jew from Gentile. He says the same thing in his letter to the church at Corinth:

> Now concerning things sacrificed to idols, we know that we all have knowledge. Knowledge makes arrogant, but love edifies... But food will not commend us to God; we are neither the worse if we do not eat, nor the better if we do eat (1 Corinthians 8:1, 8).

What are the "things" in verse 1? The rest of the chapter tells us - it is food that has been has been sacrificed to dumb idols (1 Corinthians 8:4) and is being sold in the market. Likewise, the context of the "nothing is unclean in itself" is specifically referring to food and not unlawful sex acts (fornication, adultery, incest or men having sex with other men) which he condemns elsewhere. In fact, in his epistle to the Colossians he specifically states that laws to abstain from certain foods are not to be followed for they are not helpful in fighting true sin - fleshly indulgences such as immoral sex acts (Colossians 2:16-23).

In the same manner many Gay Theology advocates assert that the ethical teachings of Jesus contradicted the moral and purity laws of the Old Testament. It is argued that if Jesus did not say that homosexual sex between "committed partners" was a sin, then neither should New Testament Christians. In support they cite Jesus' statement, "It is not what enters into the mouth that defiles the man, but what proceeds out of the mouth, this defiles the man" as an example of his doing away with the purity laws. [285] One thing that has become abundantly clear is that anytime a Gay Theology apologist quotes a small portion of the Bible you must always go to the text and read the passage in its context. Here is what this passage actually states:

> Then some Pharisees and scribes came to Jesus from Jerusalem and said, "Why do Your disciples break the tradition of the elders? For they do not wash their hands when they eat bread." And He answered and said to them, "Why do you yourselves transgress the commandment of God

285   Jack Rogers, *Jesus, The Bible, and Homosexuality* (Louisville, Kentucky; Westminster John Knox Press, 2006), 73.

for the sake of your tradition? For God said, 'Honor your
father and mother," and, "He who speaks evil of father or
mother is to be put to death." But you say, "Whoever says
to his father or mother, 'Whatever I have that would help
you has been given to God,' he is not to honor his father or
his mother." And by this you invalidated the word of God
for the sake of your tradition. You hypocrites, rightly did
Isaiah prophesy of you: "This people honors me with their
lips, but their heart is far from Me. But in vain do they worship Me, teaching as doctrines the precepts of men." After
Jesus called the crowd to Him, He said to them, "Hear and
understand. It is not what enters into the mouth that defiles
the man, but what proceeds out of the mouth, this defiles
the man." Then the disciples came and said to Him, "Do
You know that the Pharisees were offended when they
heard this statement?" (Matthew 15:1-12).

Gay Theology advocate, Dan O. Via, reads into the text that the
disciples must have touched something unclean and failed to adhere to
the purity laws by eating with unwashed hands.[286] But that is not what
happened. Jesus is not refuting the requirement of an Old Testament
cleansing rite. Jesus is responding to a man-made "tradition of the elders" to which He insists that they "...transgress the commandment of
God for the sake of your tradition." Jesus is not pitting His new teaching
against the Old Testament law. Rather He is pitting the Old Testament
law against their vain human traditions. In fact, in this text Jesus goes
on to uphold the penal sanctions of the law:

> "For **God said**, 'Honor your father and mother,' and,
> 'He who speaks evil of father or mother is to be put to
> death.' **But you say**, 'Whoever says to his father or mother,
> 'Whatever I have that would help you has been given to
> God,' he is not to honor his father or his mother.' **And by
> this you invalidated the word of God for the sake of
> your tradition**" (Matthew 15:4-6).

---

286   Dan O. Via, *Homosexuality and the Bible: Two Views* (Minneapolis, MN: Fortress Press, 2003), 9

The language of the purity laws continues into the New Covenant.[287] The reason why we do not follow the repetition of baptisms as they did in the Old Covenant is because of the finality of the baptism of Christ. This is why the Apostle Paul says of those who had repented of their homosexual acts, "Such were some of you; but you were *washed*, but you were sanctified, but you were justified in the name of the Lord Jesus Christ and in the Spirit of our God" (1 Corinthians 6:11).

Conclusion

To assert that any of the sexual prohibitions in Leviticus 18 and 20 are a purity law and not a moral law is a false dichotomy. All of the purity laws, even those that were only to be observed in the Old Covenant, conveyed an ethical and moral message. They either directly referred to an immoral act, they symbolized an ethical distinction between God's people and the pagan nations or they made it clear that we are born in a fallen and sinful condition and need to be cleaned of our inherent moral impurity. While some of the purity laws which required a ritual baptism in order to approach the temple are no longer required to be repeated it is because of the one perfect baptism of Christ. What we find in the New Testament is that the laws regarding sexual impurity continue to be upheld by the apostles. In fact, they not only repeat those laws they are followed by a warning, that those who continue in them will not inherit the Kingdom of God and will be judged.

---

287   Jesus did not do away with the cleanliness laws during His earthly ministry. On the contrary He was reacting against the traditions of the Pharisees. If Jesus thought cleanliness laws were meaningless and only the "heart" mattered, then why did He submit to baptism and baptize others? The New Covenant does not do away with the cleanliness laws - it changes them! The Old "washing" (baptism) laws have been reduced to the one sign of baptism which Jesus Himself underwent and requires of everyone who will call themselves His disciple (Matthew 28:19). While a superficial outward obedience is not sufficient it is not "just the heart" that matters apart from the outward actions and signs.

Chapter 11
Not Under the Law But Under Grace

When Gay Dispensationalists read the words "you are not under law but under grace" (Romans 6:14-15) they wrongly conclude that believers are not required to obey anything written in the Holiness Code, "… the simple fact is that the commands of the Levitical Code do not apply to Christians anyway."[288]Because of their presupposed hermeneutical paradigm, the lens through which they read the Bible, they interpret Paul's words to mean that Christians are not required to obey any commandment in the Old Testament:

> The law is also used by the Holy Spirit, to instruct believers in Jesus Christ yet those believers are not under the law in the sense of having to keep its statutes and judgments... If Christians are not required to keep the Law to be in right relationship with God, is it necessary to keep some parts of the Law, as a mark of spirituality? No. Christians are not required to keep any part of the Old Testament Law to be right with God. The Lord Jesus Christ perfectly kept every part of God's Law, in our place.[289]

This same assertion is made by Liberal Gay Theology advocates such as John Boswell who wrongly asserted:

> It would simply not have occurred to most early Christians to invoke the authority of the old law to justify the morality of the new: the Levitical regulations had no hold on Christians and are manifestly irrelevant in explaining Christian hostility to gay sexuality.[290]

---

288 R.D. Weekly, *Homosexianity* (Judah First Ministries, 2009), 23.

289 Rick Brentlinger, *Gay Christian 101 - Spiritual Self-Defense For Gay Christians* (2007), 367, 372.

290 John Boswell, *Christianity, Social Tolerance, and Homosexuality* (University Of Chicago Press; 8th Edition. edition, 2005), 105.

Such statements fly in the face of the clear teaching of the apostles who repeatedly cite the Old Testament (Leviticus and Deuteronomy in particular), in regards to sexual ethics. For the past century theoretical antinomian Dispensationalists have paved the way for Gay Theology as they assert, contrary to the teaching of the apostles, that one cannot make a distinction between the various types or uses of the law or various uses of the term "law." They then go on to insist that one cannot require that certain commandments from the Old Testament be obeyed while the others are not required to be followed. Norman Geisler provides us an example of this rationale when he states:

> The law of Moses was a unit. There were civil aspects to the moral law and moral dimensions of the civil law. Indeed, there were moral aspects of the ceremonial law, as is evident from the fact that it was said to reflect God's holiness (Lev. 11:45). Surely God's holiness is not an amoral issue. Nowhere in the Old Testament is there a separation made between the moral and the civil or between the civil and the ceremonial aspects of Moses' law. And nowhere in the Old Testament does it declare that only the ceremonial aspects of the law of Moses have been abolished.[291]

Dispensationalists following in his footsteps then conclude that since we are not required to obey the Old Testament laws regarding circumcision, kosher food laws and purity rites that the phrase "not under the law" means that the entire Old Testament has been abrogated as an objective moral standard for Christians. With this faulty assumption Gay Theology apologist R.D. Weekly then asserts, "One cannot keep a portion of the Mosaic law and not the rest. If we, as Christians, make decisions in obedience to the Law we are accountable to the entire Law (James 2:10)."[292]

Contrary to the assertion of Weekly, the Apostle James' point in the passage he cites is not that we do not have to obey the law of God and if we seek to obey some of its commandments we are required to keep the laws regarding circumcision, feast days, and the sacrificial system.

291   Norman Geisler, *Christian Ethics* (Grand Rapids: Baker Book House, 1989), 205.
292   R.D. Weekly, *Homosexianity* (Judah First Ministries, 2009), 57.

Rather James is arguing that if a person says they have faith but does not love their brother, shows favoritism and mistreats the poor (James 2:3) or fails to do good works such a "faith" cannot save. In fact, James goes on to teach that if you say you have faith and consequently obey the royal law (located in the center of the Holiness code which includes the prohibitions against same sex acts) that you are doing what is right, "If, however, you are fulfilling the royal law, according to the Scripture, 'You shall love your neighbor as yourself,' you are doing well." (James 2:8 cf. Leviticus 19:18)

Interpreting the phase "you are not under law" to imply that none of the Old Testament laws are applicable in the New Covenant contradicts the clear and repeated teaching of Jesus Christ and the apostles. In fact, Paul makes the point that Gentiles who obey the Old Testament commandments of God, thereby demonstrating that it has also been written on their heart, do not need to be physically circumcised because they are a true Jew and have the true circumcision (Romans 2:26-29).

Therefore, if when Paul says "you are not under law" he asserting that we do not have to obey *any* of the laws in the Old Testament then he is contradicting Jesus, Peter, James and even his own writings. They all uphold commandments from the Old Testament and apply them to Jewish and Gentile Christians in the New Covenant. Unless we want to insist that there are clear contradictions in the teaching of the apostles, before we go any further the one thing that is clear is that Christians are indeed required to obey the Old Testament commandments of God. The only exception are those which have been made obsolete by the New Testament. Let us now look at the phrase "not under law" in Paul's epistles to the churches at Rome and Galatia.

"Not Under the Law" In the Epistle to The Romans

In the Epistle to the Romans Paul refers to two categories of people: Jews who were born "under the Law" and Gentiles who are "without the Law" as he writes, "For all who have sinned without the Law will also perish without the Law, and all who have sinned under the Law will be judged by the Law" (Romans 2:12).

Elsewhere Paul uses the term "under the Law" to refer to people who are under the Mosaic Covenant - Jews who were still relying on the Old

Covenant types and shadows who are, as a result, consequently under the curse of Deuteronomy 27-30. He also uses the term "without law" as a reference to Gentiles who were never under the Mosaic Covenant and therefore never relied on the sacrificial system or came "under the curse of the Law" as he speaks to them as if he was one of them as a means of relating to them for the sake of the Gospel (1 Corinthians 9:20-21).

As we shall see, religious Jews were associated with the Mosaic Covenant via reception of the sign of circumcision. This administration was so inextricably bound up with the physical sign of circumcision that the reception of circumcision refers to being "under the law." To come "under the law" would then require not only being circumcised but also continue to obey the typological elements of the law and incur Israel's curses for apostasy as detailed in Deuteronomy 27-30. Paul then refers to those who insisted that Gentiles come under the law as "the circumcision" or "circumcision party" whom he characterized as "rebellious men, empty talkers and deceivers" (Titus 1:10; cf. Romans 15:8; Galatians 2:12; Ephesians 2:11). Likewise, when Paul states that those who "have sinned without the Law" he isn't asserting that people have sinned as defined by some other standard than God's holy character revealed in the moral code of the law. Rather these people sinned without have coming "under the Law" which was codified at the initiation of the Mosaic Covenant written on stone (Exodus 35:1-10):

> Now we know that whatever the Law says, it speaks to those who are under the Law, so that every mouth may be closed and all the world may become accountable to God (Romans 3:19).

It is essential then that the phrase "you are not under Law but under grace" be examined within its historical and literary context. In a previous chapter we looked at the various meanings of the term "law" and saw that it can refer to the Pentateuch as distinguished from the Prophets (Luke 2:22, 24:44; John 7:23), the moral commandments given at Sinai (Romans 7:7), and it can be a synonym for the entire Word of God including the Psalms and the Prophets (John 10:34; Psalm 82:36; 1 Corinthians 14:21; Isaiah 28:11).

However, this is not how Paul is uses "Law" in Romans 2:12 and 3:19. Here Paul is not referring to a set of abstract moral principles for how can a person be "under" a mere list of requirements and prohibitions. Rather, he uses the idea of being "under" as a matter of living within a particular jurisdiction, an administration and economic era. In other words, to be "under the Law" was a matter of citizenry, which in addition to being required to obey a legal moral code as a demonstration of faith and fidelity, one also had to bear the signs of citizenship (circumcision) and keep the national holy days as well as offer animal sacrifices for sin.

The fact that the apostles repeatedly quote and allude to portions of the law given at Sinai, particularly the Decalogue, indicates that the moral code of the Mosaic administration transcends this particular economy. While the types and shadows of the law had a particular purpose, with a designed obsolesce that would end with the new covenant which coincided with the ushering in of the Gentiles, the moral aspects of the law reflect the very character of God which does not change. This is why the apostles can rightly cite it as the objective standard for Christian conduct. What Paul then argues is that Jews and Gentiles will be judged by the same moral standard whether or not they were part of the Mosaic Covenant (i.e. the Law):

> For all who have sinned without the Law will also perish
> without the Law, and all who have sinned under the Law
> will be judged by the Law (Romans 2:12).

To commit idolatry, dishonor one's parents, murder, commit adultery, steal, lie, or covet your neighbor's wife is wrong for both Jews (who had the oracles of God and God's law written on stone tablets) and Gentiles even if they only knew the invisible attributes of God from that which was clearly revealed through creation (Romans 1:18-23). The Lord isn't a moral relativist. His standard for righteousness isn't different for Jews and Gentiles. Therefore the Jew will be judged according to the light given to Him found in the law and the Gentile without the law will be judged by the light given to Him in general revelation.

The advantage of being a Jew was that he had the oracles of God (Romans 3:1-2). The Law, the Mosaic Covenant, contained (in typological form) a means of atoning for sin. If you loved God, demonstrated your faith through a life of repentance and were not hard hearted, stiff necked, rebellious and consequently committed apostasy then you would be forgiven of your sin. The Gentile without the Law (the Mosaic Covenant) had no such opportunity. Under the Mosaic economy, the only way the Gentile could approach the Passover meal (which was typological of Christ cf. 1 Corinthians 5:7) was through the rite of circumcision (Exodus 12:48). Consequently, before the coming of Christ the only way the Gentile could be "clean" and approach God was by coming "under the Law" by bearing this sign.

To rightly understand Paul's use of the word "under" you must understand how he is using the term "Law" to refer to living within the jurisdiction of a distinctive redemptive-historical era that had some particular relation to the nation of Israel as a preparation for the coming of Christ which he refers to as an era of being "under grace." "Law" and "grace" in this context therefore are not a set of moral commands or an expression of God's favor; rather they are distinguishable epochs in redemptive-history. "Law" then is a reference to the chief mediator of the Old Covenant, Moses, whereas "Grace" is a reference to the New Covenant and its mediator Jesus Christ.

This is also how the Apostle John uses the terms when he states in the prologue of his Gospel, "For the Law was given through Moses; grace and truth were realized through Jesus Christ" (John 1:17). [293] Contrary to Gay Theologians, John is not asserting that "grace" is antithetical to "law" anymore than he is saying that "truth" is in opposition to "law."[294] Nor is he asserting that Moses didn't give the truth or that the Mosaic Covenant wasn't a gracious covenant. Rather, "Law" is being used as a synonym for "the revelation of the Old Covenant" in which Moses was

---

293   Douglas J. Moo likewise states, "As in John 1:17, then, "law" and "grace" contrast the od age of bondage and "tutelage" (cf. Gal. 3:25) with the new age of freedom and "sonship" (cf. Gal. 4:1-7; Rom. 8:14-17). "Under law," then, is another way of characterizing "the old realm"... To be "under law" is to be subject to the constraining and sin-strengthening regime of the old age; to be "under grace" is to be subject to the new age in which freedom from the power of sin is available." *The Epistle To The Romans* (Grand Rapids: Eerdmans, 1996), 389.

294   Theodore W. Jennings Jr. states, "The relativizing of Moses is further expressed in the initial references to Moses in the Gospel (1:17), in which Jesus and Moses are contrasted... We should notice that the law here is contrasted not only with grace but also with truth." *The Man Jesus Loved* (Cleveland, OH: The Pilgrim Press, 2003), 66.

the mediator through which it came and "grace and truth" is a synonym for "the revelation of the New Covenant" in which Jesus Christ was the mediator by which it came.[295]

This is the meaning of the term "Law" when Paul states to Christians, "For sin shall not be master over you, for you are not under Law but under Grace" (Romans 6:14). It is a reference to an era whose chief mediator was Moses during which sin and death was "master" or "reigned" (Romans 3:19; 6:14-15; 1 Corinthians 9:20-21; Galatians 3:23, 4:4-5, 21). Likewise, "grace" is not being used as merely God's favor (though it necessarily includes that) rather it is an era whose chief mediator is Jesus Christ and in which the Holy Spirit is reigning. Consequently the believer enjoys the benefits of God's grace in an entirely new and better way than in the Old Covenant of types and shadows and the reigning dominion of death. The transition from the Old to the New Covenant is a change from being in the first Adam who brought death to being in the second Adam who gives life (1 Corinthians 15:22; 45).[296]

What must be discerned when making distinctions between the Old and New Covenants is that the abrogated laws of the Old Testament, that became obsolete as a tutor to lead us to Christ, were the signs and symbols, the types and shadows that conveyed the notion reign of death through the repetition of dead sacrifices, the need for replacing dying priests, and the bloody rite of circumcision (Galatians 3:25). In fact, it was the hope of the person held up in the city of refuge that the chief priest would die (Joshua 20:6) whereas our hope is in the Chief Priest who lives and has passed through the heavens and is exalted (Hebrews 3:1; 4:14-15; 7:26). The weakness of this tutor is that the Law contained no concept of the resurrection to life. It is not until the era of the prophets that God's people began to receive hints of the concept of the resurrection in the form of prophecies but these were not part of the sacrificial system. It is for this reason that the Sadducees did not believe

295   In fact, in the passage John uses the term "Word" (Greek: *logos*) in verses 1-2 as a reference to the revelation of God which was previously found in the Torah. He then uses the term to refer to Jesus Christ who is the final, ultimate and superior source of revelation for He is God in the flesh (John 1:14) who is the one who reveals or "exegetes" (Greek: *exegesato*) Him (John 1:18).

296   As Rousas John Rushdoony states, "To be *under the law*, supremely, means to be born into the humanity of Adam, to be a member of the old human race. It means to be "in bondage" (Gal. 4:3)… under sentence of death as a member of Adam's fallen race." *Romans & Galatians* (Vallecito, CA: Ross House Books, 1997), 95.

in the resurrection because they only adhered to the Pentateuch and not the Prophets (Acts 23:8).

Prior to telling the Christians that they were "not under law but under grace" Paul states that sin no longer has dominion over them because the reign of death ("…death reigned from Adam until Moses…" Romans 5:12-24) had come to an end with the resurrection of Jesus Christ. This is why Paul writes in the preceding chapter "while we were enemies, we were reconciled to God through the death of His Son" but then he goes to state, "much more, having been reconciled, we shall be saved by His life" (Romans 5:10). That life to which Paul refers is the resurrection life of Jesus Christ that brought an end to the reign of death and the era of the Mosaic Covenant with all of its various repetitious bloody death rituals which were mere types and shadows that did not have the ability to atone for sin. If they could truly atone for sin then Christ died for nothing (cf. Hebrews 10:4). The pedagogue or tutor that we are no longer to follow are those elements of the law that continued until the "time of reformation" when they then ceased to be required to be obeyed (Hebrews 6:6-10).

In keeping with the teaching of Paul in Romans and Galatians, the entire theme of the Epistle of Hebrews is a demonstration of the superiority of Jesus Christ over angels and other old covenant mediators. It then warns, as Paul does in his epistles, of the folly of returning to the types and shadows of the Old Covenant, the old priesthood, the old sacrificial system, and the old temple. The issue of the Jerusalem Council (Acts 15) and Paul's epistles to the Romans and Galatians was the fallacy of thinking that circumcision of the flesh (which was part of an entry into the entire bloody system of the Old Covenant) could perfect what the Holy Spirit accomplished through the gospel who wrote the same content of the moral law on their hearts (Jeremiah 31: Romans 2:15). But there is absolutely no indication that the apostles asserted that Christians were subsequently free to disregard the moral elements of the law as an objective standard for Christian conduct. In fact Paul makes the point that when Gentiles keep certain portions of the law which have been written on their heart that their uncircumcision will be regarded as circumcision:

> If therefore the uncircumcised man keeps the requirements
> of the Law, will not his uncircumcision be regarded as

circumcision? And will not he who is physically uncircumcised, if he keeps the Law, will he not judge you
though having the letter of the Law and circumcision are
a transgressor of the Law? For he is not a Jew who is one
outwardly; neither is circumcision that which is outward in
the flesh. But he is a Jew who is one inwardly; and circumcision is that which is born of the heart, by the Spirit, not
by the letter; and his praise is not from men, but from God
(Romans 2:26-29).

If you cannot be a keeper of the law without keeping the laws regarding circumcision Paul's entire argument falls apart. The fact is that he can
and does make distinctions between various elements of the law. Some
commandments are universal and ethical in nature which transcend the
boundaries of particular redemptive-historical eras ("dispensations")
and others which were temporary with a designed obsolesce. If he could
not make such a distinction it would make no sense whatsoever to refer
to a person who has not kept the laws regarding circumcision as one
who "keeps the requirements of the law."

If we read the words "not under law but under grace" in their context
we see that Paul's argument is not that Christians are no longer required
obey anything in the Old Testament, but rather just the opposite. He is
telling them that they are no longer under the dominion of the reign of
sin and death because they are now under the dominion of the Christ
who reigns through the Holy Spirit and frees them from sin as defined
by the law (Romans 6:8-14).

Elsewhere Paul states that the Old Covenant was an "administration
of death" (2 Corinthians 3:7) in which death reigned and had dominion
from "Adam until Moses" (Romans 5:14). The Mosaic Covenant was
a glorious covenant for the Law and the sacrificial system reflected the
holiness of God and the consequences of sin. However, it was weak
in that in its typological character it could not atone for sin nor did it
provide a victory over death (2 Corinthians 3:5-11) and, as we shall see,
it was given to a stiff-necked people "in the flesh." The victory over sin
and death was accomplished by Jesus Christ who died for our sin and
was raised for our justification (Romans 5:1). The new and better covenant is one of the reign of life, resurrection, the coming of the Kingdom
of God and the dominating power of the Holy Spirit. However, this

change from the reign of death to the reign of life which put an end to the validity of the Old Covenant death rituals did not change God's ethical standard of obedience for His children. This is why the apostles can repeatedly cite the law as an ethical standard for living for not only Jewish Christians, but also for Gentile Christians living outside of the land of Palestine. The Old Covenant consisted of a repetition of sacrifices resulting in dead animals that were never raised (Hebrews 10:4). The sacrificial system was administered by the priests who had to offer a sacrifice for their own sin, would eventually die and were never raised and subsequently were replaced by another priest in a never ending cycle of death. Consequently they could never permanently take away sin (Hebrews 10:11). There was also the constant repetition of the cleansing rite of baptism or "washings" (Exodus 29:4; Leviticus 11:25; 15:13; Hebrews 9:10) because of the uncleanness associated with death.

Paul's point in his epistles is now that Christ the perfect Adam, the perfect priest, the perfect sacrifice has come, died for our sin and raised to life we are now no longer under the reign of death. Therefore, since we have been baptized into Christ and raised with Him we are under the reign and dominion of life in Christ and therefore we are not to continue in sin.

In the context of Romans chapter 6, to be "not under law but under grace" does not mean that God's standard for holiness revealed at Sinai has changed but rather the dominion of the reign of death and sin has ended. This is because there is a new King, a new High Priest, and that which was revealed in stone (the Ten Commandments) is now to be written on our hearts (Jeremiah 31:31; Romans 2:15). But the change in venue for this writing, from stone to hearts, did not alter the moral content of the law one iota. What was written on stone does not say anything different that what the Holy Spirit writes on our hearts. The subjective knowledge of the law in the heart and the Spirit empowered ability to obey it does not contradict the objective standard of the law that we now read on ink and paper.

"Under The Law" In The Epistle To The Galatians

Having considered Paul's use of the phrase "you are not under law but under grace" in Romans 6:14 we now turn our attention to Paul's teaching on the law in his Epistle to the Galatians, specifically his use of the phrase "works of the Law" (Galatians 2:16; 3:2-10) and "you are not under the Law" (Galatians 5:18).[297] Paul wrote to the Churches of Galatia because after he had preached the Gospel some Jews, specifically those teaching the doctrines of the Pharisees, from Jerusalem sought to convince them that they needed to be circumcised and keep the distinctively Jewish laws of the Mosaic Covenant in order to be saved (Acts 15:1, 5). After an uncharacteristically brief introduction, Paul then repeatedly warns anyone who would preach a Gospel contrary to the one He had already preached to them will be "cut off" or *anathema* (Galatians 1:8-9).

The false gospel that was being preached was not an assertion that Gentiles needed to merit their salvation through doing good works. Nor was he contending against an assertion that Gentile Christians are required to obey the moral requirements of the Decalogue or the sexual prohibitions of the Holiness Code (Leviticus 18:8 cf. 1 Corinthians 5:1). In fact, Paul and the other apostles insisted that *all* Christians, both Jew and Gentile, obey the moral elements of the law as they cite the authority of the Old Testament as a biding standard for Christian conduct (Deuteronomy 32:35 cf. Romans 12:19; Deuteronomy 25:4 cf. 1 Timothy 5:18; Exodus 20:13–15, 17 cf. Romans 13:9).

What these Jews insisted was that Christian Gentiles become Jews and keep the distinctively Jewish laws of the Mosaic Covenant and there was a lot of social pressure to do so. Yet Paul insisted that circumcision is not what mattered but rather obeying God's commandments (1 Corinthians 7:19). Since circumcision was one of God's commandments for Israel and Paul quotes the Decalogue as an objective moral standard of Christian conduct it is obvious the commandments Christians are to obey are the ones that were not distinctly Jewish in nature.

So pervasive was the teaching of the Pharisees that Paul states that even Peter and Barnabas had been duped by them for a time, such that when the Pharisees were around they reverted to their former Jewish ways of living as Paul states, "If you, being a Jew, live like the Gentiles and not like the Jews, how is it that you compel the Gentiles to live

---

297   I am indebted to the insights of Gabriel Wetmore in his unpublished paper, "An Exegesis of Galatians 3:10-14." Providentially I was studying the term "you are not under law but under grace" in Romans 6:14 when Gabriel was working on his paper on Galatians and we were coming to the same conclusions. What follows is an adaptation and synthesis of his paper with my own studies.

like Jews?" (Galatians 2:14) Was Paul upset because Peter was obeying the Ten Commandments or the sexual ethics of the Holiness Code? Of course not since there is nothing distinctly Jewish about the aforementioned Old Testament commandments. Rather, the laws that the party of the Pharisees were insisting on were "worthless elemental things" which included circumcision and the feast days associated with the Mosaic economy as Paul complains, "You observe days and months and seasons and years" (Galatians 4:8-10; Colossians 2:16).

The question at hand in the epistle to the Galatians is, "Did they receive the Holy Spirit by becoming Jews by being circumcised and keeping the feast days or by the hearing of the faith?" (Galatians 3:3) In other words, will becoming circumcised and acting like a Jew make them be more like Jesus Christ? The reception of the Holy Spirit, Paul states, was evidenced by the Gentiles in that they "do instinctively the things of the Law" which he refers to as the "precepts of the law" (Romans 2:26) and had been written on their hearts as promised in the New Covenant (Romans 2:15; Jeremiah 31:33). This reception of the Holy Spirit and the circumcised heart, evidenced by the obedience to the law, was the deciding factor at the Jerusalem Council, "And God, who knows the heart, testified to them giving them the Holy Spirit, just as He also did to us; and He made no distinction between us and them, cleansing their hearts by faith" (Acts 15:8).

The "yoke" that Peter refers to at the Jerusalem Council that ought not to be put upon the Gentiles was the undergoing of circumcision (Acts 15:10). For obvious reasons, circumcision was so overwhelming for an adult that two men alone could kill a debilitated army that had undergone the procedure (Genesis 34:25). God's moral standard is not burdensome or a heavy yoke (1 John 5:3), for his laws are a delight to the believer for they make him wiser than his foes and the Psalmist says they are preferred over riches, "The law of Your mouth is better to me than thousands of gold and silver pieces" (Psalms 119:72).

The center of Paul's argument in Romans and Galatians is whether Abraham was justified before or after circumcision, not whether it was before or after obeying one of the Ten Commandments (cf. Romans 4:10). It is true that no one can boast in the law and anyone who relies on his observance of the law for justification is then in debt (Romans 4:1-4). God justifies the sinner by faith (Romans 4:5-6) and therefore

Pharisaical boasting is excluded (Ephesians 2:8-9). However, the center of the crisis in the Church was focused on whether or not Gentiles needed to become descendants of Abraham by circumcision. Paul's response is that Gentile Christians are children of Abraham who was justified by faith before he was circumcised so that he would be the father of the faith for the Gentiles (Romans 4:11-12).

In making a distinction between the Old and New Covenant, Paul draws a clear line between the reception of the Spirit on the one hand, and the works of the law (such as circumcision) and the flesh on the other. In doing so Paul uses a flesh/Spirit distinction, in which he contrasts redemptive-historical epochs – the Old Covenant in which death reign from Adam to Moses verses the New Covenant in which the second Adam has conquered death by rising from the dead. For Paul, to be in the "flesh" is a description of man in the "old creation" or being in covenantal union with the first Adam. To be in or walk by the "Spirit" denotes the life of the new creation, the new man, inaugurated by the resurrection of the second Adam, Jesus Christ, as Paul teaches elsewhere (1 Corinthians 15:22, 45) as Herman Ridderbos wrote:

> ...'flesh' and 'Spirit' represent two modes of existence, on the one hand that of the old aeon which is characterized and determined by the flesh, on the other that of the new creation which is of the Spirit of God. It is in this sense that the difference is also to be taken between the first Adam as 'living soul,' i.e., flesh, and the second as life-giving Spirit. The contrast is therefore of a redemptive historical nature: it qualifies the world and the mode of existence before Christ as flesh, that is, as the creaturely in its weakness; on the other hand, the dispensation that has taken effect with Christ as that of the Spirit... It is within this redemptive-historical contrast of flesh and Spirit as the mode of existence of the old and new creation that Paul now views the life of Christ before and after his resurrection.[298]

Paul states that the Mosaic economy came to man while he was still in the "flesh," before the new creation had come into the world

---

298   Herman Ridderbos, *Paul: An Outline of His Theology* (Grand Rapids: Eerdmans, 1977), 66-67.

with Christ's resurrection and the giving of the promised Holy Spirit on Pentecost (Acts 2). In other words, it was before the age of the reign of Holy Spirit. The problem with the old economy was not merely in the typological elements but also in the fact that it was given to a people who were (with notable exceptions) fleshly, sniff-necked hard heart-ed people. Paul says that the Law cannot give the Spirit, because the Law was given to a people in the flesh. Paul's point is that the Gentile Galatian Christians have received the Spirit, they have already received the fullness of the new creation, which could not be attained under the law. They are heirs of Abraham who is their father according to the faith as he too was justified without circumcision (Genesis 15:6) and the giving of the distinctive Jewish laws that came five hundred years later at Mount Sinai.

The reason why many Christians, especially Gay Dispensationalists, fail to see that Paul's reference to being "under the Law" refers to being under the Mosaic Covenant with its types and shadows and that the "works of the law" refer to such things as circumcision and not the moral aspects of the law, is because of a misunderstanding of Paul's statement regarding the curse of the law when he states, "For as many as are of the works of the Law are under a curse; for it is written, 'Cursed is everyone who does not abide all things written in the Book of the Law, to perform them" (Galatians 3:10).

Traditional Protestant interpreters, reading the text through the lens of the dispute with the Roman Catholic Church in the 16th century, tend to take the view that "those of (who rely on) the works of the law" are those who embrace a principle of works righteousness and thereby rely on the merit of their good deeds for salvation.[299] They then go on to assert, as do Dispensational Gay Theology advocates, "God never intended us to keep the Law. He gave us the law to prove we could not keep it."[300] In other words, the Mosaic Law is a reinstitution of a supposed meritorious Covenant of Works that was given to Adam in the Garden, but with the purpose of making it clear that it was impossible to fulfill the laws demands, hence leading him to despair and total reliance upon a Savior.

---

299   Martin Luther, *Commentary on Galatians* (Grand Rapids, MI: Fleming R. Rev-ell, 1988), 161.

300   Rick Brentlinger, *Gay Christian 101 - Spiritual Self-Defense For Gay Chris-tians* (2007), 369.

According to this interpretation Paul is arguing from Deuteronomy 27:26 that anyone who does not keep every commandment of the law perfectly (i.e. without sin), at any point is under a curse. Therefore, according to their understanding of Paul, since neither Jews nor Gentiles have in fact kept the law perfectly (without sin) all who rely on their own meritorious law-keeping are under a curse.[301] This is exactly how Dispensational Gay theology advocates read the text such as when R.D. Weekly asserts:

> This [Galatians 3] is one of the most profound passages in the Bible regarding the purpose and duration of the Law. It teaches that the Law was given to show us that we sin. In other words, it served to reveal what a mess we are, and that we're in dire need of a savior. Paul wasn't saying that the Law was enduring, or that it shows us what God considers sinful under our new covenant. Indeed, he expressly stated the exact opposite in verses 10, saying, "Anyone who tries to please God by obeying the Law is under a curse." The Law was never intended to last forever. Once the prophesied seed of Abraham (Jesus) arrived and brought us into the era of faith, the Law ended (vs. 19, 25) So, then, the Law served a purpose, and that purpose was fulfilled in Christ. Now that He has come and brought us into the era of faith, "there is no more need to have the Law as a teacher" (v. 25). Paul's testimony brings Jesus' words in Matt. 5 into perfect focus. He didn't come to destroy the Law; but He *did* come to fulfill it. Why, then, 'stupid Galatians', are you still living under the outdated, obsolete commands of the Mosaic Law?[302]

They then conclude that since nobody can be justified by meritorious law keeping and that no one can insist on obeying just some of the laws (such as the moral elements of the law) without obeying all of them (including circumcision and the feast days), on the basis of a

---

301   F.F. Bruce, *Commentary on Galatians* (Grand Rapids, MI: Wm. B. Eerdmans Publishing Company, 1982), 159.
302   R.D. Weekly, *Homosexianity* (Judah First Ministries, 2009), 221.

wrong reading of James 2:10, that therefore Christians are not obligated to obey *any* of the commandments in the Old Testament whatsoever for they are all "outdated, obsolete commands of the Mosaic Law." In making such a statement Weekly fails to recognize that the apostles repeatedly cite the law as a moral standard for Christian living and read Galatians 3 in its redemptive historical context particularly the way in which Paul is citing Deuteronomy 27-30.

While it is theologically true that we cannot merit our justification by obeying the moral requirements of the law, this is it not the point Paul is making in his epistle. This line of interpretation removes Paul's understanding of law from its redemptive-historical context, and makes it into an abstract principle of meritorious law-keeping. However, Paul does not use the phrase "works of the law" to denote obedience to God's objective moral standard given at Sinai summarized in the Decalogue. Rather he is specifically referring to works which peculiarly belonged to the Mosaic administration. Furthermore, Paul says that those who are "of the works of the Law are under a curse" not those who rely on the law as if it were a Roman Catholic system of meritorious self-justification are under a curse. Paul says that Christ died for those under the curse, to deliver them from the curse (Galatians 3:13). This assumes that the curse is something that the law brings upon the objects of Christ's salvation, not on those who "falsely rely upon the law."[303] Jesus did not just come to die for people who are trying to save themselves.

The exegetical flaw of this interpretation is that the reader would have to conclude that Paul misinterpreted and misapplied Deuteronomy 27 for he would be using the text contrary to its original intent and context. Nowhere does the passage require sinless perfection. Rather, it threatens a curse upon Israel if they apostatize from God's gracious covenant by worshipping other gods. The Mosaic economy did not require sinless perfection in law keeping for it provided a (typological) means of atoning for sin in the sacrificial system. The Levitical system provided a

---

303   For example, R. L. Dabney states, "We must always remember that the Apostles are using, to a certain extent, an argumentum ad hominem: they are speaking of the Mosaic institutions under the Jewish view of them. They are treating of that side or aspect which alone the perverse Jew retained of them. Here is the key." *Systematic Theology*, (1871; reprint, Carlisle, PA: Banner of Truth, 1985), 458. Notice again the implications of this view, to be consistent Dabney must say that Christ came to deliver people from the curse that only comes about because of a misunderstanding of the law.

means of forgiveness and called the people to faith in the deliverance of God.[304] The curse threatened in Deuteronomy 27 is not a threat given to perfect people who might sin once and be cursed, but rather to a sinful people who had been delivered from bondage in Egypt by the LORD (YHWH) and are being told to have faith in His redeeming grace as a faithful bride. YHWH does not divorce His bride for committing any infraction of the law, but rather for committing adultery with other gods (Deuteronomy 28:14; 28:64; 29:18). The Law that Israel had to uphold by faith, under threat of a curse, was the entire Torah which graciously provided a means of atoning for sin through the blood of another. If Israel rejected God's grace, abandoned the Law to seek after other gods and followed their laws and ordinances (Ezekiel 11:12), then in effect they have returned to Egypt in their hearts and consequently the curse would come upon them.

The covenant stipulations of Deuteronomy 27-28 set before Israel a promise of blessing if they were faithful to the marriage and a curse if they abandoned God and His covenant. This is why Paul does not simply say that those who are of the works of Law are under *the threat of a curse*, but rather they are *under a curse*. How can Paul say this if Deuteronomy 27:26 merely threatens with a curse? After setting the blessing and curse before Israel (Deuteronomy 27-28), Moses prophecies that Israel will in fact fall under the curse of the Law and be exiled into a foreign land (Deuteronomy 29-30) and gives the reason:

> All the nations will say, "Why has the LORD done thus to this land? Why this great outburst of anger?" Then men will say, "Because they forsook the covenant of the LORD, the God of their fathers, which He made with them when He brought them out of the land of Egypt. They went and served other gods and worshiped them, gods whom they have not known and whom He had not allotted to them. Therefore, the anger of the LORD burned against that land, to bring upon it every curse which is written in this book; and the LORD uprooted them from their land in anger and

---

304   N. T. Wright, *The Climax of the Covenant: Christ and the Law in Pauline Theology* (Minneapolis, MN: Fortress Press, 1991), 145.

in fury and in great wrath, and cast them into another land,
as it is this day" (Deuteronomy 29:24-28).

As prophesied, Israel like an unfaithful wife will break the covenant
and inherit the curse because of apostasy and whoredom (Jeremiah 3:1).
Contrary to the traditional understanding of the phrase "as many as are
of the works of the Law are under a curse" that it refers to everyone, Jew
as well as Gentile who try to earn their own justification by meritorious
law-keeping, those outside of national Israel cannot not be in view in
Deuteronomy 27-30 because Gentiles were never part of the Mosaic
Covenant. Therefore Gentiles could never apostatize from a covenant of
which they were never a member of to begin with unless, as Paul warns,
they decide to become Jews by accepting the sign of circumcision. This
is why circumcision was the crucial issue because it was a sign that one
had come under the Law, that is the Mosaic Covenant, along with all of
its now obsolete types and shadows and Israel's accompanying curse for
having apostatized by rejecting their Messiah.

According to Deuteronomy 27-30 there is a prophesied inevitability
of the curse because the covenant was made with a stiff-necked people
of the flesh. As prophesied, Israel would be exiled and controlled by
foreign powers beginning with the Babylonian captivity (Deuteronomy
28:36, 49, 52). The actual experience of the curse took place in Israel's
history during the exile under the Babylonians, Assyrians, Persians,
Greeks and continued under the Romans during the first century. In
context, "the curse of the law" of Deuteronomy is Israel's exile to be
under the dominion of foreign nations and their foreign gods. In Paul's
time this was a present reality for Israel for, although they were in the
land, they were under the dominion of the Roman Empire. This would
continue to be so in the "times of the Gentiles" during which "Jerusalem
will be trampled underfoot by the Gentiles" (Luke 21:24). After the
rejection of the Messiah, the final judgment of this curse would entail
being utterly destroyed in 70 A. D. (Matthew 23:38 - 24:1-2). This is
a final historical recapitulation of the previous judgments described in
gruesome detail in Deuteronomy 28:52-57. This same type of event
fell upon Israel as prophesied by Christ and spelled out in the bowls of

judgment described by the apostle John in the Book of Revelation and recorded by the historian Josephus.[305]

However, the exile was not to be a permanent feature of Israel's identity; it would end and Israel would be restored. This glorious restoration came to pass with the arrival of the New Covenant in Christ (Jeremiah 31:31). Paul's argument in his epistles to the Romans and Galatians is that if the Gentiles want to submit to the Mosaic administration and become Jews by circumcision, then they would inherit the curse of Deuteronomy along with the Jews who were rejected Jesus as the Messiah.

Not only was the curse of exile a present reality at the time of Paul's writing to the Galatians as prophesied by Moses he assumed the *inevitability* of that curse. When Moses prophesied concerning Israel's fall under the curse, he did not merely predict the future concerning the nation, but because he firmly understood the stubborn, rebellious, hard hearted and stiff-necked nature of the Israel as they were quick to worship the golden calf and rebel in the desert (Exodus 32:9; 33:3, 5: 34:9). When Paul spoke of the curse he had in mind the contrast of Galatians 3:2-3, the flesh and the Spirit, and the Law as a covenant with people during the age of "flesh."

Paul speaks of the Mosaic Covenant ("the Law") as one that was made with those in the flesh with whom the curse of the law is inevitable due to their being in this sinful condition. The flesh/Spirit contrast is both redemptive-historical in that it speaks of the Old/New Covenant and it is anthropological in that it speaks of two ages of mankind's corporate existence. The age of the Spirit begins at the resurrection, because in the resurrection a new humanity came into being (Romans 8:3-13).

This takes us back to Paul writing on the same subject in his Epistle to the Romans. After stating that they we have died to sin in Christ and been raised again with Him and therefore, "sin shall not be master over you, for you are not under law but under grace" (Romans 6:14) he then very clearly makes this under law/flesh verses grace/spirit dichotomy

---

305   For further reading on this subject I recommend: David Chilton, *The Days of Vengeance* (Tyler, Texas, Dominion Press, 1987), Kenneth L. Gentry Jr., *The Book Of Revelation Made Easy* (Powder Springs, Georgia: American Vision Press, 2008), Kenneth L. Gentry, *Before Jerusalem Fell* (Powder Springs, GA: American Vision, 1988) and Keith A. Mathison, *From Age To Age: The Unfolding of Biblical Eschatology* (P & R Publishing, 2009)

(Romans 7:7-25). Paul, personifying the state of Israel with the first person "I", describes the situation of Old Covenant Israel as being sold into sin or in the "flesh."[306] The Law is good but the people are still the state of being in the first Adam, a people in the "flesh." This is why Paul states, "For we know that the law is spiritual, but I am of the flesh, sold under sin" (Romans 7:14). To be under the flesh, was to be sold under sin. The problem is not with the Law *per se*, rather the problem is that it comes to a carnal people therefore, "The very commandment that promised life proved to be death to me. For sin, seizing an opportunity through the commandment deceived me and through it killed me" (Romans 7:10-11).

Paul then speaks of Israel's hopeless condition under the law (in the flesh) issued in which he cries for deliverance, "Wretched man that I am! Who will deliver me from this body of death? (Romans 7:24)." But he also goes on to provide the answer to this plea, "Thanks be to God through Jesus Christ our Lord! So then, on the one hand I myself with my mind am serving the law of God, but on the other, with my flesh the law of sin" (Romans 7:25).

He then states that there is no condemnation for those who are in the new man, the second Adam, "For the law of the Spirit of life in Christ Jesus has set you free from the law of sin and of death" (Romans 8:1-2). The reason for this is that in Jesus, "God has done what the law, weakened by the flesh, could not do. By sending his own Son in the likeness of sinful flesh and for sin, he condemned sin in the flesh" (Romans 8:3). The Galatians' desire to be circumcised, and come under the Mosaic covenant, was nothing less than a desire to return to the former age of the flesh and reject what Christ had already accomplished (Galatians 3:2).

The state of being in the "flesh" is the very thing that made the curse of Deuteronomy inevitable, and that ultimately made it a reality. Thus, when Paul says that all those of the works of Law (the Mosaic Covenant) are under a curse, he assumes not only the present reality of that curse in Israel's history, but the fact that those of the works of the Law are in the flesh, and therefore are "sold under sin." This does not

---

306   This reading assumes that Paul is using "I" of Romans 7 to speak of Israel under the Mosaic Covenant as he describes their corporate experience in the flesh under the age of the Mosaic Covenant. For more reading see: N.T. Wright, *Paul For Everyone - Romans: Part One (Chapters 1-8)* (Westminster Knox Press, 2004), 124.

mean that the Spirit was in no way at work in the Old Covenant, but he was working on people in the "flesh." This is why Jesus declared in His lament over Jerusalem, just prior to His crucifixion, that they would soon be destroyed as a consequence of being under the curse:

> Jerusalem, Jerusalem, who kills the prophets and stones those who are sent to her! How often I wanted to gather your children together, the way a hen gathers her chicks under her wings, and you were unwilling. Behold, your house is being left to you desolate! (Matthew 23:37-38)

Likewise, as Stephen is about to be put to death by these same stubborn hard-hearted people he declares:

> You stiff-necked people, uncircumcised in heart and ears, you always resist the Holy Spirit. As your fathers did, so do you. Which of the prophets did not your fathers persecute? And they killed those who announced beforehand the coming of the Righteous One, whom you have now betrayed and murdered, you who received the law as delivered by angels and did not keep it (Acts 7:51-3).

The curse of the law comes upon a fleshly people under the demands of a spiritual law and the inevitable historical curse of exile and annihilation is the result. Paul then goes on to state regarding the law and justification, having introduced the curse in Galatians 3:10, "Now that no one is justified by the Law before God is evident; for, 'The righteous man shall live by faith.' However, the Law is not of faith; on the contrary, 'He who practices them shall live by them...'" (Galatians 3:11-12). He then provides the solution to the curse citing Deuteronomy 21:23, "Christ redeemed us from the curse of the Law, having become a curse for us for it is written, 'Cursed is everyone who hangs on tree.'" (Galatians 3:13)

The curse of the law was inevitable for it was given to a people under the dominion of the sinful remnant of the flesh. We see then that Jesus not only took the actual curse of exile upon himself, but He also took the inevitable aspect of the curse that comes from dominion of sin over the flesh and He nails it to the tree. Paul sees the Mosaic Covenant as bondage, because curse inevitably comes to a people who are ruled by the flesh. Humanity needed to be redeemed from the *situation* of being under the dominion of the sinful remnant of the flesh. Because blessing could not come to the people while they remained "in the flesh," they had to be brought into the new realm of humanity - in the Spirit. This is why Paul, after speaking of Christ redeeming His people from the curse, immediately says, "so that in Christ Jesus the blessing of Abraham might come to the Gentiles, so that we might receive the promise of the Spirit through faith" (Galatians 3:14). With this context in mind, we can look specifically at Paul's contrast between Law and promise from the perspective of his citations of Habakkuk 2:4 and Leviticus 18:5:

> Now that no one is justified by the Law before God is evident; for, "The righteous man shall live by faith." However, the Law is not of faith; on the contrary, "He who practices them shall live by them" (Galatians 3:11-12).

Protestants have traditionally taught the contrast Paul makes between faith and the Law in vs.11-12 is a contrast between believing and doing, between justification by faith and justification by meritorious law-works.[307] The consequence of this interpretation is that it asserts that there is a contradiction within in the Old Covenant itself. One part seems to teach justification by works/human effort, and another that seems to teach justification by faith. This line of thinking thinks of the unfolding of Old Testament as a record of God having His people go through various alternating dispensations of works-righteousness ("law) and grace with accompanying ethical intrusions in which God is more harsh in His dealing with people.[308] This pattern is particularly noticeable in those who speak of the Adamic Creation Covenant as a Covenant of Works understood as a Covenant of Merit and the Mosaic Covenant as a reinstitution of the Covenant of Works whose purpose was to make it clear that man cannot be saved by a Pelagian form of

---

307   William Hendriksen, *New Testament Commentary: Galatians and Ephesians* (Grand Rapids, MI: Baker Book House, 1968), 129.

308   This is evident in both classic Dispensationalism and Meredith Kline's "ethical intrusions" in which he asserts that there are various periods of theocracies in the Old Testament.

self-righteousness.[309] It is therefore concluded that to even seek to obey *any* of the Old Testament commandments obligates one to attempt to earn one's salvation by obeying all of the laws, including the types and shadows made obsolete by the New Covenant. This is exactly how Gay Theology proponent R.D. Weekly reads the text when he states:

> ...the Mosaic Law was a legalistic code by which the Israelites were required to live. Violation of many of these commands carried the penalty of death. Yet in all these commands and legal codes, the covenant of works, was wholly insufficient to justify the people in God's eyes... One cannot keep a portion of the Mosaic Law and not the rest. If we Christians make decisions in obedience to the Law we are made accountable to the *entire* Law (James 2:10); and because it's impossible to keep all points of the Law, we're brought under a curse – responsible for keeping the whole Law, but absolutely incapable of doing so.[310]

He then concludes:

> I can think of no reason except that people simply do not understand what Christ's death accomplished. They continue to reference the Mosaic Law as a standard for Christian moral conduct. But doing this is not simply a fruitless, but benign means of discerning God's will. It's actually quite dangerous since submission to any part of the Mosaic Law brings a curse, seeing as we cannot possibly keep all of it![311]

But the contrast Paul makes in this passage is not between meritorious human effort and having faith. Rather, Paul is making a very clear statement concerning the object of faith - specifically that no one is justified by the Law as their object of faith but rather in looking to the promises of God. He then supports this by citing Habakkuk 2:4 in which

309   For an example of this view see both Dispensational and modified Lutheran views of Wayne Strickland and Douglas Moo in *Law, Gospel, and the Modern Christian: Five Views* (Grand Rapids, MI: Zondervan, 1993).
310   R.D. Weekly, *Homosexianity* (Judah First Ministries, 2009), 52, 57.
311   R.D. Weekly, *Homosexianity* (Judah First Ministries, 2009), 57.

in the midst of evil the believer looks beyond his current circumstances and lives by faith. Paul previously stated concerning Abraham that he was justified by faith because he looked beyond his circumstances of being without a son to the heavens believing in the promise of God that his descendants would be more numerous than the stars (Genesis 15:5) and subsequently was justified by faith (Genesis 15:6; Galatians 3:6-9) and here he is making a reference concerning the blessing promised to Abraham (Galatians 3:14). In Galatians 3:6-9, Paul focuses on the fact that Abraham believed something particular and concrete, and not simply the fact of believing. He believed in the "gospel" that God preached to him (Galatians 3:8). The "gospel" that was preached to him was that all the nations would be blessed in him and that they would be his descendants. Abraham was justified because he believed that a day would come in which God would give a blessing to all the world, and that blessing would somehow come through Abraham's offspring despite the fact that he was at that time old and without a son. Therefore, since Abraham was not circumcised at that point he had to know that this gospel could not be fulfilled by the covenant of circumcision that was given to him. Furthermore, at the time that he received the sign of circumcision, it defined his own people distinguished from all the peoples of the earth (Genesis 17). So, how could Abraham inherit all the nations that are in one sense distinguished from his line marked by circumcision and also inherit what God had promised him - the whole earth? (cf. Romans 4:13). Paul's argument is that Abraham knew that a day would come when the covenant marked by circumcision would become irrelevant as God would fulfill the promise He gave to him, so Abraham looked for a day when uncircumcised Gentiles would be blessed in him (Galatians 3:8).

The point of Paul's epistles to the Romans and Galatians is that the gospel that Abraham believed could not be attained through the Mosaic Covenant which made distinctions between Jews and Gentiles because the promise to Abraham included the entire world. It was the Pharisees who falsely assumed that the Gentiles would be included in the covenant by becoming children of Abraham through circumcision.

Paul then makes his case that the blessing of Abraham could not come through the Mosaic Covenant ("the Law") because it brings a curse and not a blessing because the people are stiff necked and rebellious (Galatians 3:10). In doing so he proves that the Old Covenant itself shows that the blessing of Abraham would not come through the Law, but it would come to those who, like Habakkuk, look by faith to the future promise on the other side of the curse of exile.

In context, the curse of Habakkuk 2:4 is the curse of exile that was prophesied by Moses (Deuteronomy 27-30). The prophecy begins with Habakkuk crying out to God as he sees the apostasy of Israel and it seems to him as if the Lord is doing nothing about it. The Lord responds by assuring Habakkuk that He will bring the promised curse of exile upon the people by raising up the Babylonians against them (Habakkuk 1:6). Of course this is not the solution Habakkuk had hoped for so he then raises a second complaint in which he asks about how God could use an even more wicked nation to bring curse upon His people (Habakkuk 1:12-2:1). The Lord responds by assuring Habakkuk that the curse will come upon the people, but the righteous will yet live by faith by looking beyond the exile to a new and better covenant (Habakkuk 2:4). The righteous would look in faith beyond the exile, beyond the Mosaic covenant and find life as Moses prophesied:

> So it shall be when all of these things have come upon you, the blessing and the curse which I have set before you, and you call them to mind in all nations where the LORD your God has banished you, and you return to the LORD your God and obey Him with all your heart and soul according to all that I command you today, you and your sons, then the LORD your God will restore you from captivity... (Deuteronomy 30:1-10).

Moses says that after the curse of the law has been brought to pass and the people are in exile that the Lord would bring about a reformation and it would involve a changing of the covenant people. The people were exiled because they were stiff-necked, uncircumcised of heart, and consequently apostatized. Beyond the exile, however God will "circumcise your heart and the heart of your offspring, so that you will love the Lord your God with all your heart and with all your soul, that you may live" (Deuteronomy 30:6). When Paul cites Habakkuk 2:4 his point is not to argue that salvation isn't through meritorious law-keeping (however true that may be) but rather to make it clear that the Mosaic Covenant ("the Law") could not provide justification and bring about the blessing promised to Abraham that he would be a father to many nations, both Jew and Gentile. Instead the Mosaic Covenant ("the Law") brought a curse upon the rebellious while the righteous look beyond the curse brought by covenant stipulations of the Law to the blessing that God would yet bring.

When Paul then says "now the Law is not of faith" in Galatians 3:23 he uses "faith" not to refer simply to the act of believing but to the object of faith, that in which someone puts their faith.[312] This is the same way Paul uses the term when he says that Israel was under the pedagogue or tutor of the Mosaic Covenant ("the law") until Christ came with the result that, "…now that faith has come, we are no longer under a tutor" (Galatians 3:25). The Pharisees put their faith in the Law and Jesus pointed out this fallacy as it was intended to point people to put their faith Him, not in the Torah, "You search the Scriptures because you think that in them you have eternal life; it is these that testify about Me; and you are unwilling to come to Me so that you may have life" (John 5:38-39).

The faith just mentioned in Habakkuk is not derived from the Law. This is evident because in Habakkuk the Law brings a curse, not blessing. Therefore, faith must look beyond the Law to the coming Messiah. To prove this Paul cites Leviticus 18:5, "So you shall keep My statutes and My judgments, by which a man may live if he does them; I am the LORD."

Paul's citation of this passage is used to support the argument that the faith commended in Habakkuk 2:4 is not faith in the Law, but faith that looks beyond the Law for the blessing of life. In Leviticus 18:5 the Lord instructs Israel that since they are His people they are not to apostatize but be faithful to him. God commands Moses to remind the people that He is YHWH their God (Leviticus 18:1-2). Because He is their God, they are not to apostatize into the ways of the Egyptians and Canaanites and indulge in their deviant sexual practices which included men having sex with other men (Leviticus 18:3; 20). Instead, they are

---

312   The Greek preposition *ek* in "of faith" in the phrase "now the Law is not of faith" (*o de nomos ouk estin ek pistis*) according to the *Greek-English Lexicon of the New Testament* (BDAG) can be used as a "marker denoting origin, cause" and thus refer to "the source, from which something flows or comes" (Bauer-Danker Lexicon, 3.g).

to walk in His ways and obey Him for He is their God (Leviticus 18:4). If they remain faithful to God, then they shall experience covenantal blessing, covenantal life (Leviticus 18:5). The "do this and live" principle is repeated throughout the Old Covenant Scriptures has the idea of keeping covenant over and against apostasy. It is not a statement that if someone is sinless they shall meritoriously earn life.

Paul then concludes that the Mosaic Covenant codified in the Torah ("the Law"), is not the object or source of faith. Leviticus proves this as well, because the blessing of life promised in Leviticus would only come if the people kept faithful to the covenant and did not apostatize. But as we saw in Deuteronomy 27-30 this would not take place because the people were stiffed necked and rebellious and consequently the curse was inevitable, and it was on the brink of happening when Habakkuk was prophesying. Paul shows from Leviticus that the Law could not be the object or source of faith because Israel would have to keep covenant to receive it, which is something that would not only inevitably not happen, because Israel was in the flesh, but something that history has already shown did not happen. Israel under the Law is left in the state of the cursed exile. Therefore, if Gentiles seek to become Jews by receiving circumcision they too will come under the curse that Israel was under and would suffer in 70 A.D. which is a foretaste of the final judgment day in which all mankind will be judged (Acts 17:31).

The Curses of the New Covenant

At this point one might conclude that since to be "under the law" entails receiving circumcision and the "curse of the Law" refers to coming under the judgments of Deuteronomy 27-30 that therefore any Christian who does not seek to become a Jew is in the free and clear and that the New Covenant has no warnings for those who continue in sin or do not repent of sexual immorality. However, this is not the case. The New Covenant, like all covenants in the Bible, contains requirements not only of faith but also faithfulness to not apostatize by continuing in unrepentant sin. Some of the warnings of the New Covenant are addressed to Jews to discourage them from returning to the Mosaic Covenant (Hebrews 2:1-4; 3:12-15; 5:11-6:6; 10:26-39; 12:14-29). Others are addressed to Gentiles to not submit to the teaching of the

Pharisees and receive circumcision (Galatians 5:2). He also warns them to not return to their former Gentile manner of living, particularly in regards to sexual sin as defined by the Old Testament (Galatians 5:19-21). In the same manner the writer to the Hebrews warns, "Marriage is to be held in honor among all, and the marriage bed is to be undefiled; for fornicators and adulterers God will judge." (Hebrews 13:4)

Likewise, Jesus warned the Christian churches against sexual immorality in his epistles to the seven churches recorded in the Book of Revelation such as when He says to the Church at Smyrna, "Therefore repent; or else I am coming to you quickly, and I will make war against them with the sword of My mouth" (Revelation 2:16). He also says to the Church at Thyatira He will come and judge "the woman Jezebel" and that He will strike her with a severe judgment, sounding like something out of the Old Testament:

> I gave her time to repent, and she does not want to repent of her immorality. Behold, I will throw her on a bed of sickness, and those who commit adultery with her into great tribulation, unless they repent of her deeds. And I will kill her children with pestilence, and all the churches will know that I am He who searches the minds and hearts; and I will give to each one of you according to your deeds (Revelation 2:21-23).

Jesus then states why He issues such warnings and harsh judgments in His epistle to the church at Laodicea, "Those whom I love, I reprove and discipline; therefore be zealous and repent." (Revelation 3:19) This is why Paul had to warn those at Corinth:

> Do not be deceived neither fornicators, nor idolaters, nor adulterers, nor *malakoi* [a male performing the female role in homosexual relations], nor *arsenokoitai* [men who have sex with other men], nor thieves, nor the covetous, nor drunkards, nor revilers, nor swindlers, will inherit the kingdom of God (1 Corinthians 6:9).

Chapter 12
The Law of God, Temple Worship and Leviticus

The next three chapters shall consider the law's teaching concerning sexual ethics and worship in the Old and New Covenants. By seeking to understand the underlying principle of passages such as Leviticus 18:22, 20:13, Romans 1:26-27 and 1 Corinthians 6:9 we will be able to determine the transcultural application of these texts. In doing so it will be seen that even if the prohibitions and condemnation of same-sex acts in their original historical context were specifically tied to cultic worship that they are applicable to our modern era. Therefore the binding authority of these texts as they revealed the will of God transcend the narrow boundaries of a formal cultic worship of idols, pederasty, prostitution or sexual exploitation.

Worship, Idolatry and the Temple of God

Many people when they hear the word "idolatry" think of it only in terms of its most obvious sense - a formal ritualistic ceremonial cultic act towards a god, gods or goddesses in which the worshipper genuflects and performs various elaborate rituals around a carved image made of inanimate matter such as wood, clay or stone. Clear prohibitions of such obvious forms of idolatry are found throughout the Bible (Deuteronomy 4:15-16; Isaiah 42:8; 1 John 5:21). The Bible also tells of Paul's confrontation with the idolatry of Athenians, the Epicureans and the Stoic philosophers when he addresses their idol of the "unknown god" (Acts 17:16, 23). Paul also refers to this form of idolatry as being the result of suppressing the knowledge of the one true God (Romans 1:18-23).

Idolatrous practices were common amongst the pagan nations that surrounded Israel who worshipped the gods of Egypt and the Canaanite gods named Molech, Baal, and Asherah. Similar forms of overt idolatry exist today such as Hindus who worship statues of their gods (Brahma, Vishnu and Shiva). Idolatry is far more prevalent than in this most obvious form. It can be quite subtle, even occurring only in the mind and heart of the individual since, as John Calvin said, that our minds are, "a perpetual factory of idols."[313] This is why Ronald Nash states that everyone is a worshipper of some sort of god:

> ...there really is no such thing as an atheist. Someone named Jones may deny that the God of the Bible exists. He may even be foolish enough to believe that there is no god at all. But perceptive people will readily observe that there is something in life that functions as an object of ultimate concern for Jones... that something may be nothing more than the betterment of self. But whatever the object of ultimate concern is for us, that will be our god.[314]

An idol then is anything that has a place in our life where only the Triune God belongs whether that thing is an actual carved statue, another person, an occupation, social status or just an image in our thoughts. If we ascribe to it the honor and glory that is due only to God or put it in an undue place of priority in our life then it is an idol. Our career, our money ("mammon" personified as the god of wealth cf. Matthew 6:24), our spouse, our friends, our possessions, our hobbies and our forms of entertainment can all become a false god and an idol.[315]

In a similar fashion, many evangelicals tend to think of worship as the singing portion of a church service and those who lead the congregation in singing as "worship leaders." But worship incorporates much more that the singing hymns, psalms or praise choruses in the corporate

---

313   John Calvin, *Institutes of the Christian Religion*, (Volume 1), (Louisville, KY: Westminster John Knox Press, 1960), 107.

314   Ronald H. Nash, *Worldviews In Conflict* (Grand Rapids, MI: Zondervan, 1992), 27.

315   As Martin Luther wrote, "What does it mean to have a god? or, what is God? Answer: A god means that from which we are to expect all good and to which we are to take refuge in all distress, so that to have a God is nothing else than to trust and believe Him from the [whole] heart; as I have often said that the confidence and faith of the heart alone make both God and an idol. If your faith and trust be right, then is your god also true; and, on the other hand, if your trust be false and wrong, then you have not the true God; for these two belong together, faith and God. That now, I say, upon which you set your heart and put your trust is properly your god." *The Large Catechism* Translated by F. Bente and W.H.T. Dau Published in: *Triglot Concordia: The Symbolical Books of the Ev. Lutheran Church* (St. Louis, MO: Concordia Publishing House, 1921), 565-773.

service. It also includes the giving of tithes and financial offerings, the preaching of the Word and the sacraments of Baptism and the Lord's Supper. The Biblical concept of worship essentially has to do with ascribing *worth* to that which is most highly prized, valued and adored. In worshipping the worshipper is paying homage by attributing glory and honor in labor and service to that which is most valued as John Frame states:

> In Scripture, there are two groups of Hebrew [*abodah*] and Greek [*latreia*] terms that are translated "worship." The first group refers to "labor" or "service." In the context of worship, these terms refer primarily to the service of God carried out by the priests in the tabernacle and the temple during the Old Testament period. The second group of terms [*shacha* in Hebrew and *proskeneo* in Greek] means literally "bowing" or "bending the knee" hence "paying homage, honoring the worth of something else." The English term *worship*, from *worth* has the same connotation.[316]

This worship can take place in a formal setting as part of a community such as in a Church service on Sunday morning with the assembly of the saints in which we pray and sing to God while exhorting and encouraging one another (Hebrews 10:25). Or it can take place in an informal setting privately in one's own home (Daniel 6:10; Matthew 6:6). It can even take place when you are driving your car or sitting in front of your computer. The worship of God can be scheduled and planned or it can be spontaneous (Exodus 4:31).

Worship and ascribing glory to that which is ultimate in our life is part of everything that we do. In fact, the entire life of a Christian is to be an act of worship as we are to offer up our lives as Paul states, "I urge you, brethren, by the mercies of God, to present your bodies a living and holy sacrifice, acceptable to God, which is your spiritual service of worship" (Romans 12:1-2). This life of worship even includes the manner in which we eat our food which is why he tells the Church, "So whether you eat or drink or whatever you do, do it all for the glory of God" (1 Corinthians 10:31).

316   John Frame, *Worship in Spirit and Truth: A Refreshing Study of the Principles and Practice of Biblical Worship* (Phillipsburg, NJ: P&R Publishing, 1996), 1.

We see then that there is both a corporate form of worship and a private form of worship. There are also formal and obvious forms of worship and there are subtle and unseen forms of worship that take place in the heart. In essence, the entire life of the Christian is to be an act of worship. This worship can either bring glory to the one true God or it can be idolatrous in which we compromise and allow forbidden relationships, objects or experiences to be a part of our daily lives.

Many of us also tend to think of a temple only in terms of a building in which worship takes place and that the true last temple of God to exist on earth was destroyed in 70 A.D. in Jerusalem by the Romans as prophesied by Jesus Christ (Matthew 24:1-2, 34). What the disciples of Jesus did not understand at the time was that the temple in Jerusalem was designed to become obsolete. It was never intended to be a permanent means of worshipping God as Jesus told the Samaritan woman (John 4:21-24).

The original temple built by Solomon that was destroyed by the Babylonians (586 B.C.) and was later rebuilt by Herod was only a picture, a shadow, of the true temple in heaven where God dwells (Exodus 25:8-9; Hebrews 8:5). Some people might then assume therefore that in heaven there is a giant building that looks just like the one that Solomon first built. They might even go on to think that this building will come to earth like a flying saucer and land sometime in the future (Revelation 21:2). But such a notion fails to understand that a temple is where God dwells and manifests Himself whether it is the Garden of Eden, the meeting place with Moses on Mount Sinai ("holy ground" Exodus 3:5), a mobile Tabernacle that traveled through the desert or a building constructed by Solomon in Jerusalem. Ultimately, the physical temple building was but a type or shadow of Jesus Christ Himself as He told the Jews that He Himself is the true temple that would be destroyed and raised again in three days:

> Jesus answered and said to them, 'Destroy this temple, and in three days I will raise it up.' The Jews therefore said, 'It took forty-six years to build this temple, and will You raise it up in three days?' But He was speaking of the temple of His body (John 2:19).

The true temple is the body of Christ. When the Spirit descended upon Him at His baptism this was a fulfillment of the type when Solomon's temple was filled (Matthew 3:16; 2 Chronicles 7:1-2). After Jesus' death, burial and resurrection His physical body ascended into heaven where He was seated at the right hand of the Father and will remain until all of His enemies have been defeated (Psalm 110:1; Hebrews 1:13; 10:13). However, the people of God by means of their covenantal union with Christ are now referred to as the "body of Christ" (Ephesians 4:12) and each person is a different part of this body:

> For even as the body is one and yet has many members, and all the members of the body, though they are many, are one body, so also is Christ. For by one Spirit we were all baptized into one body, whether Jews or Greeks, whether slaves or free, and we were all made to drink of one Spirit. For the body is not one member, but many (1 Corinthians 12:12-14).

The literal physical body of Christ is in heaven but the New Covenant people of God, the bride of Christ who is one with her husband, is the body of Christ on earth (Ephesians 5:23-32). When Jesus foretold of His ascension into heaven He promised His people that He would not abandon them but rather He would send another to take His place:

> And I will ask the Father, and He will give you another Helper that He may be with you forever; that is the Spirit of truth, whom the world cannot receive, because it does not behold Him or know Him, but you know Him because He abides with you, and will be in you. I will not leave you as orphans; I will come to you (John 14:16-18).

On the day of Pentecost this Helper (*paraclete*) came and filled the New Covenant Temple who became the body of Christ here are on earth (Acts 2:1-4). This is the same sort of phenomenon occurred when the Temple of God was filled with the Holy Spirit (2 Chronicles 5:13-14) and when Jesus was baptized (Matthew 3:16; Mark 1:9-11; Luke 3:21-23).

The New Covenant Temple, the body of Christ, is also referred to as the Church. Many people think that a church is a building where the congregation meets, some speak of it a spiritual event "We're having church!" The Church (*ecclesia*) is actually the "assembly" (Acts 7:38) or "called out ones" or "the saints" who are none other than "the body of Christ." Each Christian is an individual member of Christ's body and is united with Him through the Holy Spirit (1 Corinthians 12:12-14). The Church is the body of Christ and the Temple of the Holy Spirit. Consequently, what we do with our body, which is the temple of the Holy Spirit, we do with the body of Christ. If you are truly a Christian then your physical body is a part of Christ's mystical body, the Church, the Bride of Christ, and it is a place of worship as well as a vessel of worship. What you do with it is an act of worship whether formally or informally, whether privately or with others.

With these concepts of idolatry, worship, the temple and the Church in mind we will now look at Leviticus 18:22, 20:13, Romans 1 and 1 Corinthians 6:9 in the next two chapters. In doing so we shall see how spirituality and sexuality are inherently tied together and yet are not to be intermixed.[317] They are to be treated as sacred but not confused as if God can be approached through a sexual act as was the case in Ancient Near Eastern cults.

The Redemptive-Historical Context of Leviticus

Gay Theology advocates rightly insist that the same sex prohibitions of Leviticus 18 and 20 can only be properly interpreted within their historical context, "In any thorough study of the Scriptures, we should be willing to look beyond the verse or text of a passage and into the Biblical literary context. We should also be willing to look beyond the literary context and into the historical context."[318] Subsequently they insist that Leviticus 18:22 and 20:13 in their historical context only refer to cultic forms of same sex acts which involve cultic prostitutes and

---

317   Richard Davidson states, "Sexuality is sacred not in the sense of the "sacraliza-tion/divinization of sex" practiced in the pagan fertility cults but in that it is hallowed by the divine approbation and presence." *Flame of Yahweh: Sexuality in the Old Testament* (Peabody, MA: Hendriksen Publishing, 2007), 52.

318   David W. Shelton, *The Rainbow Kingdom: Christianity & the Homosexual Reconciled* (Lulu, 2006), 25.

the worship of Molech as Brentlinger argues, "God carefully placed the prohibitions of Leviticus 18:22 and 20:13 in the context of Molech worship, 18:3, 21 and 20:2-5, 23." [319] However, as Richard Davidson points out, if we actually look at the context of these passages this argument immediately falls apart:

> ...it is pointed out that in Lev 18 the prohibition against homosexual intercourse immediately follows the prohibition of sacrificing children to Molech (18:21), this connecting homosexual practice with idolatry. This argument falters, however, when one recognizes that the repetition of this in Lev 20 does not follow the reference to child sacrifice but is placed between the prohibitions against incest and bestiality. [320]

Furthermore, what Gay Theology advocates fail to prove is that these passages can *only* refer to ritualistic same sex acts and they fail to consider how the Bible itself teaches us to apply the principles of Old Testament texts to other contexts by following the teaching of Jesus and the apostles. Therefore, it is not enough to merely assert "the text in its original historical and literary context meant such and such..." we must also consider how the principles of these passages may be applied in other historical and cultural contexts which is also a very important part of interpreting a text:

> Biblical texts originated in quite a different climate compared to the modern world in terms of values, norms and traditions. Applying the biblical texts to our time therefore is always a hermeneutical event, in which the differences between biblical and contemporary worlds are in some way smoothed out. In practice, the tradition of biblical interpretation, several thousands of years old, serves as a bridge, whether this is acknowledged or not. Internalized reading guided by this tradition is often unconscious to the

---

319   Rick Brentlinger, *Gay Christian 101 - Spiritual Self-Defense For Gay Christians* (2007), 93.

320   Richard Davidson, *Flame of Yahweh: Sexuality in the Old Testament* (Peabody, MA: Hendriksen Publishing, 2007), 152.

point that the readers of the Bible do not even notice that
they are constantly interpreting what they are reading…
Not only are the ancient sources culture-bound, reflecting the values of their own environment, but so also are
modern readers. To achieve a meaningful comparison and
to avoid anachronism and ethnocentricity, it is necessary
first to outline modern questions and then see how these
questions correlate with the old texts and their particular
issues.[321]

Let us then, keeping this in mind, consider the historical context of
Leviticus and the issues regarding cultic prostitution of the day. Then
we can examine the context in which the prohibitions of Leviticus 18:22
and 20:13 are given and seek to determine what, if any, contemporary
application of these passages may be made in our own day.

YHWH's Judgment of the Canaanites

In the Garden of Eden the Lord (YHWH) warned Adam and Eve that
if they if they should eat the forbidden fruit they would surely die that
day (Genesis 2:17). Though the prescribed penal sanction was death, after Eve had been deceived by the serpent and her husband subsequently
ate the fruit given to him, God in His mercy did not kill them that day
but instead cut them off from the land by exiling them out of the garden
(Genesis 3:23-24). He also cursed the ground and killed another animal
in their place to provide a covering (Genesis 2:17-19). Instead of an
immediate execution, they were given exile and purged from the land
and forced to live in a land that was cursed because of their sin. This tie
between a land being cursed because of the sin of its inhabitants is seen
throughout Scripture, such that those who worship false gods are said to
be "spewed out" by the land itself (Leviticus 18:28; 20:22).
As a consequence of their sin the world quickly became corrupt
with murder taking place within their own family (Genesis 4:8). Soon
thereafter the entire world became so corrupt with violence, idolatry
and sin that God in His grievance judged the world through a "natural"
disaster with a flood but saved Noah, "a righteous and blameless man,"

---

321   Martti Nissinen, *Homoeroticism in the Biblical World* (Augsburg Fortress Publishers, 1998), 4.

and his family (Genesis 6:5-8). In this judgment God cleansed the land and purged the people from it through a baptism (1 Peter 3:20-22) and thereafter gave the covenant sign of the rainbow to signify that He would never judge the world in this manner again (Genesis 9:12-17).

Generations later, the Lord began a new race of people through one man named Abraham who was promised the land of the Canaanites and to be a father of many nations (Genesis 12:1-3). But before the descendants of Abraham could occupy the land it would need to be purged from the corruption inhabiting it. This could not be done by Abraham alone, the Lord would have to build from him an entire nation that would come four hundred years later. During Abraham's life time YHWH judged the cities of Sodom and Gomorrah for their many sins including oppression of the poor, violence, adultery and homosexual rape (Genesis 19:5; Jeremiah 23:14; Ezekiel 16). To this city He sent His angels and thereafter it was also destroyed with the falling fire and brimstone (Genesis 19:24). Whereas the great flood of Noah's time was a cleansing of the land by water, this was a judgment by fire.

Hundreds of years later, after the children of Abraham had become an entire nation in the land of the Egyptians, the Lord was going to deliver His people from this bondage and fulfill the promise given to Abraham by having his descendants enter the land. In doing so, the Lord would judge the inhabitants using the Israelites and sending His angel before them:

> For My angel will go before you and bring you in to the land
> of the Amorites, the Hittites, the Perizzites, the Canaanites,
> the Hivites and the Jebusites; and I will completely destroy
> them (Exodus 23:23).

It was not that the Israelites were morally superior than the inhabitants for as history would prove they were, in general, a stubborn, rebellious, stiff necked people who were prone to apostasy (Exodus 32:9-10; Numbers 4:11; 2 Kings 17:14; Isaiah 48:4; Acts 7:51). Rather, the Lord was keeping His promise to Abraham and from these people He would eventually bring the Messiah.

Nor was the judgment of the Canaanites a simple genocide or a form of primitive religious intolerance as some liberal theologians and

Gay Theology advocates would claim.[322] The Canaanites worshipped
Molech, committed all sorts of abominations including idolatry, sacrificing their children alive, and committed various sexual sins as did
the people who were judged during the time of Noah and the occupants
of Sodom and Gomorrah, "They have built also the high places of
Baal, to burn their sons as offering to Baal" (Jeremiah 19:5). The land
was promised to Abraham but it was polluted by the gross immorality
of the inhabiting idolaters. But this time God's means of judging the
Canaanites would not be through the use of "natural" disaster using
water, nor through angels or fire from heaven but through the military
actions of the Israelites. The Israelites were chosen not because they
were more inherently righteous that the Canaanites. Rather, the earth
is the Lord's (Psalm 24:1) and because of His holiness sin cannot go
without being judged as we read:

> Do not say in your heart when the LORD your God has
> driven them out before you, "Because of my righteousness
> the LORD has brought me in to possess this land," but it is
> because of the wickedness of these nations that the LORD
> is dispossessing them before you (Deuteronomy 9:4).

By His sovereign decree, the Lord judged the Canaanites using the
Israelites as His means of carrying out His penal sanctions. This was
also a test of the faithfulness of Israel, to see if they would obey His
laws and avoid becoming like the people under the ban. Yet, as history
would prove they were constantly going after the gods of the pagan
nations:

> But it came about when the judge died, that they would
> turn back and act more corruptly than their fathers, in fol-
> lowing other gods to serve them and bow down to them;
> they did not abandon their practices or their stubborn ways.
> So the anger of the LORD burned against Israel, and He
> said, "Because this nation has transgressed My covenant
> which I commanded their fathers and has not listened to
> My voice, I also will no longer drive out before them any

---

322   L. William Countryman, *Biblical Authority or Biblical Tyranny?* (Harrisburg,
PA: Trinity Press, 1994), 12.

> of the nations which Joshua left when he died, in order
> to test Israel by them, whether they will keep the way of
> the LORD to walk in it as their fathers did, or not." So the
> LORD allowed those nations to remain, not driving them
> out quickly; and He did not give them into the hand of
> Joshua (Judges 2:19-23).

The problem was that the majority of the Israelites were a stiff necked, hard hearted and obstinate people who had a propensity to assimilate with pagan cultures. In fact, just after they had been delivered from Egypt they were already complaining, accusing God of bringing them out in order to kill them (Exodus 16:3) and they quickly turned to idolatry, worshipping what was either the Egyptian god Hapis or the Canaanite god Baal, while referring to it as the LORD who had brought them out of Egypt (Exodus 32). Sadly, though they had been repeatedly warned and suffered many disciplinary judgments they too eventually totally succumbed to total apostasy. The Lord then used the pagan nations of Babylon and Assyria to be His means of enacting His penal sanctions on Israel and purge them from the land just as He had done with the pagan nations:

> Hear this word which the LORD has spoken against you,
> sons of Israel, against the entire family which He brought
> up from the land of Egypt: "You only have I chosen among
> all the families of the earth; Therefore I will punish you for
> all your iniquities" (Amos 3:1-2).

Israel had falsely deduced that if we are they are the privileged people of God that they may look for His mercy and He will not punish them. The measure of our privilege in our covenant with Him is the measure of our responsibility. Therefore if we fail to fulfill that responsibility He will not pass over our sins, but rather will visit upon us all our iniquities. This was true of the nation of Israel, and it is true of the Church as well as Jesus Himself warned churches in a similar manner:

> To the angel of the church in Laodicea write: The Amen,
> the faithful and true Witness, the Beginning of the creation
> of God, says this: "I know your deeds, that you are neither

cold nor hot; I wish that you were cold or hot. So because
you are lukewarm, and neither hot nor cold, I will spit you
out of My mouth. Because you say, 'I am rich, and have
become wealthy, and have need of nothing,' and you do
not know that you are wretched and miserable and poor
and blind and naked, I advise you to buy from Me gold
refined by fire so that you may become rich, and white gar-
ments so that you may clothe yourself, and that the shame
of your nakedness will not be revealed; and eye salve to
anoint your eyes so that you may see. Those whom I love,
I reprove and discipline; therefore be zealous and repent"
(Revelation 3:14-19).

This is the historical context of the book of Leviticus. It was given
to Israel as God's holy law, to make them a holy set apart people. But
in order to do so, the Lord would have to make them culturally separate. They would need to look different (Leviticus 19:19; Deuteronomy
22:11; Numbers 15:38), eat different (Leviticus 11; Deuteronomy 14),
keep the Lord's assigned feast days such as Passover (Exodus 12-14;)
and not behave sexually as did the inhabitants of the land nor like the inhabitants of the land from which they had been freed – the Egyptians.[323]
Close cultural proximity tends towards a slow and subtle adaptation
such that one becomes like the company that one keeps. This is why the
apostle Paul warned the church at Corinth, "Do not be deceived: 'Bad
company corrupts good morals" (1 Corinthians 15:33).

The downward moral and spiritual decline of Israel is a foreshadowing of the direction of the modern church. As we shall see, sexuality
and spirituality are intrinsically tied together such that to deviate from
God's standard on the one will result in deviation on the other. In fact, so
closely are idolatry and prostitution connected that Israel's spiritual unfaithfulness to YHWH is likened to being a harlot. To be an idolater is to
be a whore and to be a whore (whether actually employed as a prostitute
or merely having sex outside of a God ordained marriage) likewise is
equivalent to idolatry as the Apostle Paul wrote, "consider the members

---

323   Richard Davidson writes, "In Egypt, as elsewhere in the ancient Near East outside Israel's monotheistic religion, sexuality was divinized as the many deities engaged in sexual activity." *Flame of Yahweh: Sexuality in the Old Testament* (Peabody,
MA: Hendriksen Publishing, 2007), 90.

of your earthly body as dead to immorality, impurity, passion, evil desire, and greed, which amounts to idolatry" (Colossians 3:5).

The Whoredom of Israel

There are two different words that are frequently translated "prostitute" in the Old Testament, *zonah* and *kedeshah* (feminine) or *kedeshim*
(masculine) (sometimes transliterated as *qedeshim*). The word *zonah*
refers to a woman who conducted sexual favors for money or it could
refer to a sexually fornicating or adulterous woman. The word *kedeshah*
(feminine) literally means "consecrated," from the root word *kedesh*
meaning "holy" or "set apart." Prior to the Israelites entering the land of
Canaan, the Lord in His Law warned them:

> None of the daughters of Israel shall be a *kedeshah,* nor
> shall any of the sons of Israel be a *kadesh.* You shall not
> bring the hire of a prostitute (*zonah*) or the wages of a dog
> (*keleb*) into the house of the Lord your God to pay a vow,
> for both of these are an abomination to the Lord your God
> (Deuteronomy 23:17-18).

The religious aspect of *kedeshah* is emphasized in the Septuagint as
it renders the first verse as a double prohibition. It prohibits both secular
prostitution and being an initiate of pagan cults:

> None of the daughters of Israel shall be a prostitute (*porne*),
> neither shall any of the sons of Israel be *porneuon*; none
> of the daughters of Israel shall be an initiate (*telespho-*
> *ros*), neither shall of the sons of Israel be a *teliskomenos*
> (Deuteronomy 23:17-18).

In the Bible the female form of *kedeshah* tends to accompany the
word *zonah*. For example we read in Hosea, in which we are told that
the men of Israel have not remained faithful to the Lord and have gone
whoring after foreign gods:

> I will not punish your daughters when they play the *zonah*
> or your brides when they commit adultery, for the men

themselves go apart with harlots and offer sacrifices with temple *kedeshot*; So the people without understanding are ruined (Hosea 4:14).

The two words are often translated in English as "harlot" and "temple prostitute." We see an even closer association between the *kedeshah* and the *zonah* in the story of Tamar in which the two words are used interchangeably. Tamar, a childless widow, disguises herself and tricks Judah into thinking she is a *zonah* to get herself pregnant (Genesis 38:15). But a few verses later Judah's friend the Adullamite, sent to find the woman again, asks the men of the place "Where is the *kedeshah*, that was openly by the way side?" And they reply, "There was no *kedeshah* in this place" (Genesis 38:21) which he then reports to Judah (Genesis 38:22). The *kadeshim* are also mentioned four times in the Books of Kings (1 Kings 14:24, 15:12, 22:46; 2 Kings 23:7).

The meaning of the male form *kadesh* may have been a counterpart to the *kedeshah*, that is a male cultic prostitute who likewise performed sex acts as a form of pagan worship. Consequently many English Bibles translate it as "cult prostitute" (NASB, ESV), "shrine prostitute" (NIV), or "whoremonger" (Douay-Rheims). What is not made clear is whether these male prostitutes would service women who were perhaps barren or other men in a homosexual act of cultic worship. If the Canaanite religion was a fertility cult, it is hard to imagine how same-sex acts would function as a fertility rite which had the purpose of obtaining sympathetic magic from the gods whose own sexual activity would produce rain for the crops:

> ...a foundational premise encountered already in Mesopotamian myths: the processes of nature are controlled by the relations of the gods and goddesses. In particular, the earth results from the sexual union of a male god and his consort, a female goddess. In the Baal cult, this (incestuous) sexual relationship is between the storm god Hadad (Baal) who dominates the Canaanite pantheon, and his sister, usually described as Anat (or Baal's consort Asherah)... Since the land is fertilized by the sperm (rain) of Baal, it is crucial that his sexual activity be stimulated. According to Canaanite fertility cult theology, when the

divine sex activity of the god is emulated at the earthly high place (a place of divine worship usually set on a hill, sometimes on a high or large altar), that same activity is further *stimulated* by means of sympathetic magic. Thus there appeared the cultic offices of "holy man" (*qades*) and "holy woman" (*quedesa*) – male and female personnel who, among other functions, engaged in sexual prostitution or, if not prostitution (sex for hire), at least ritual sex. Worshippers were encouraged to engage in ritual intercourse with the shrine devotees in order to emulate and stimulate the sex activities of the gods.[324]

However, others have argued that the women (*zonah*) mentioned are only common prostitutes and the *kadesh* and *kedeshah* are non-sexual pagan priests and priestesses.[325] But there is further evidence that what occurred in Canaan was similar to a more wide spread cultic phenomenon in which the cultus involved an androgynous priest who was a picture of both the supposed ideal original state of man as well as a picture of a future androgynous state of mankind. The *kedeshim* then are not merely sacred prostitutes for hire, akin to secular whores (*zonah*) but are androgynous priests in which all distinctions between male and female are broken down. This was a common phenomenon in throughout the ages in Mesopotamia, ancient Canaan, Syria and Asia Minor as Peter Jones states:

---

324   Richard Davidson, *Flame of Yahweh: Sexuality in the Old Testament* (Peabody, MA: Hendriksen Publishing, 2007), 93-94.

325   Jeffrey H. Tigay states, "There is probably no subject in the field of ancient Near Eastern religion on which more has been written, with so much confidence, on the basis of so little explicit evidence, than 'cultic prostitution.' It is a case of conjectures that have been repeated so often, without examination of the evidence, that they have turned into 'facts.' There is, in fact, no available evidence available to show that ritual intercourse was ever performed by laymen anywhere in the ancient Near East, nor that sacred marriage, even if it involved a real female participant, was practiced in or near Israel during the biblical period. There is a bit of uncertain evidence that may imply the practice of income-producing temple prostitution in Mesopotamia, and postbiblical evidence for the practice in Byblos, but no evidence that this is what the biblical *kedesha* did. There is little reason to believe that the women mentioned in Deuteronomy 23:18-19 are anything but common prostitutes." *The JPS Torah Commentary: Deuteronomy* (Jewish Publication Society of America; 1st edition, 1996), 481.

Throughout time and across space, the pagan cultus consistently, though not exclusively, holds out as its sexual representative the emasculated, androgynous priest. Mircea Eliade, a respected expert in comparative religions, argues that androgyny as a religious universal or archetype appears virtually everywhere and at all times in the world's religions. Much evidence exists to support his judgment.'

The clearest textual testimony in ancient times comes from nineteenth- century BC Mesopotamia. Androgynous priests were associated with the worship of the goddess Istar from the Sumerian age (1800 BC). Their condition was due to their 'devotion to Istar who herself had 'transformed their masculinity into femininity.' They functioned as occult shamans, who released the sick from the power of the demons just as, according to the cult myth, they had saved Istar from the devil's lair. '…as human beings,' says a contemporary scholar, '…they seem to have engendered demonic abhorrence in others; … the fearful respect they provoked is to be sought in their otherness, their position between myth and reality, and their divine-demonic ability to transgress boundaries.'

The pagan religions of ancient Canaan appear to maintain a similar view of spirituality and sexuality. The goddess Anat preserves many of the characteristics of Istar. Like the Syrian goddess Cybele, Anat is headstrong and submits to no one. She is both young and nubile but also a bearded soldier, so that many commentators conclude that she is either androgynous or bi-sexual. She thus symbolizes the mystical union, which was celebrated by her worshipers as a ritual enactment of the *hieros gamos* [sacred spiritual marriage]. The OT gives some indication that Canaanite religion included homosexual androgyny, against which Israel was constantly put on guard.[326]

---

326   Peter Jones, "Androgyny: The Pagan Sexual Ideal" *Journal of the Evangelical Theological Society* 43/3 (September 2000), 452.

This is recognized even by Virginia Mollenkot, who rather than being against such a practice today is seeking to revive it in the Church:

> In the New Revised Standard Version of the Bible (1989), Deuteronomy 23:7 is translated, 'None of the daughters of Israel shall be a temple prostitute; none of the sons of Israel shall be a temple prostitute.' This translation contradicts the findings of recent biblical scholarship that the *qadesh* was a male Canaanite priest, not a prostitute, and that the female *qedeshah* was in all probability also a priest, not a prostitute.[327]

These sacred androgynous priests (*kedeshim*) are a common theme in pagan religions and appeared throughout the ages. It was then revived in the pseudo-Christian Gnostic sect:

> Even though separated by many centuries, a historical and "theological" connection between the Mesopotamian *assinnus*, the Canaanite *qedeshim*, the Scythian *ennares*, and the Syrian *galli* is not difficult to imagine. They took on the same androgynous appearance, engaging in the same ecstatic behavior, including self-mutilation, were associated with occultic spirituality, and so in many ways occupied a similar liminal relationship to "normal" society. Such parallels suggest a profound and necessary connection growing out of the same ideological pagan root.

> Later in the second and third centuries of the Christian church, the gnostics were credited by their adversaries with mystery celebrations involving carnal knowledge. The charge is credible because 'Christian' Gnosticism was the attempt to Christianize pagan spirituality, even to the point of adopting some form of androgyny. Hippolytus (AD 170–236) reports that one particular gnostic sect, the Naasenes, who worshipped the Serpent (*Naas* in Hebrew) of Genesis, attended the secret ceremonies of the mysteries

---

327   Virginia Ramey Mollenkott, *Omnigender: A Trans-religious Approach* (Cleveland, OH: The Pilgrim Progress, 2007), 105-106.

of the Great Mother in order "to understand the 'universal mystery.' Like modern syncretists who are encouraged to cross over into other religions, the gnostics believed religious truth was one, to be found everywhere, and so they crossed over into pagan spirituality as a matter of religious principle. The most explicit testimony is from Irenaeus who says: Even though separated by many centuries 'They prepare a bridal chamber and celebrate mysteries.' A homosexual encounter is perhaps insinuated in the 'Secret Gospel of Mark.' At the very least, the final logion of the Gospel of Thomas appears to be an invitation to spiritual androgyny. All this would justify the judgment of Burkert that "certain Gnostic sects seem to have practiced mystery initiations, imitating or rather outdoing the pagans...[328]

It is important to keep this historical fact in mind for we shall see it again in a future chapter when we consider the spirituality of Queer Theology and Transgender Theology, particularly in the writings of Virginia Mollentkott, Robert Goss and Theodore W. Jennings Jr. all of whom appeal to the Secret Gospel of Mark and the Gnostic Gospel of Thomas. Gay Theology and the Metropolitan Community Church then is a revival of this ancient pagan worldview which, like Gnosticism, seeks to syncretize itself with Christianity.

The Hebrew word *keleb* (dog) may also signify a male prostitute (Deuteronomy 23:18). In the Septuagint it is rendered in Greek as *kinaidos* ("dog-like") and it was used for men who were flamboyantly effeminate and behaved as though they were in heat for homosexual advances. The term "dog" then may be a derogatory slang term for the male cult prostitute and it may also allude to the dog-like sexual position of a male mounting another male that reflects the manner in which a male dog mounts another dog.[329] This may be what the Apostle John

328   Peter Jones, "Androgyny: The Pagan Sexual Ideal" *Journal of the Evangelical Theological Society* 43/3 (September 2000), 452.

329   Jeffrey H. Tigay states, "Since the other clauses in verses 18-19 refer to humans, at least some of them prostitutes, it is often assumed that 'dog' is an epithet of some human professional, perhaps a male prostitute, perhaps a homosexual who performs in the stance of a dog." *The JPS Torah Commentary: Deuteronomy* (Jewish Publication Society of America; 1st edition, 1996), 216.

had in mind when he wrote, "Outside are the dogs and the sorcerers and the immoral persons and the murderers and the idolaters, and everyone who loves and practices lying" (Revelation 22:15). However, the term "dogs" also tends to be used throughout the New Testament merely as a derogatory term without any sexual connotations (Matthew 7:6; Mark 7:27; Philippians 3:2).

One of the most horrendous acts of pagan worship depicted in the Old Testament was conducted by the Canaanites in which they worshipped Molech, Baal and the Asherah pole, a fertility symbol. Accompanying this pagan culture were common prostitutes (*zonah*) and perhaps temple prostitutes (*kadeshim*), which often resulted in unwanted pregnancies. These unwanted children were then sacrificed by burning them alive in the arms of the Molech. In essence, sex outside of God's ordained boundaries of marriage leads to unwanted pregnancies, which results in unwanted children who are either disposed of by casting them away, as they did during the Roman era, or immediately killing them by burning them alive which was strictly forbidden in God's law, "You shall not give any of your offspring to offer them to Molech, nor shall you profane the name of your God; I am the LORD" (Leviticus 18:21).

This was an ancient equivalency to modern day abortions where the child is sacrificed unceremoniously, not in a formal pagan temple by a pagan priest, but within the boundaries of a clinic under the pretense of a medical procedure by a physician. We later read that Israel failed to heed the law; they whored after other gods and subsequently had a post-birth abortion of their children:

> Therefore, say to the house of Israel, "Thus says the Lord God, 'Will you defile yourselves after the manner of your fathers and play the harlot after their detestable things? When you offer your gifts, when you cause your sons to pass through the fire, you are defiling yourselves with all your idols to this day. And shall I be inquired of by you, O house of Israel? As I live,' declares the Lord GOD, 'I will not be inquired of by you. What comes into your mind will not come about, when you say: 'We will be like the

nations, like the tribes of the lands, serving wood and stone'" (Ezekiel 20:30-32).

Becoming like the surrounding nations, worldliness, failing to remain holy, is the root cause for incrementally succumbing to idolatry, sexual immorality and its subsequent outcome of murdered children. It is no wonder then why so many Gay Theology advocates such as Mel White are also proponents a "woman's right to choose" this modern form of Molech worship under the misnomer of "reproductive rights."[330] We see then in the Old Testament that the Lord forbids His people to imitate pagan ways of worship and the Israelites were commanded to remove the remnants of corrupt worship from their midst. They were commanded to destroy "all the high places" where the pagan nations served their gods and to purge the land of all the implements associated with idolatry:

> You shall utterly destroy all the places where the nations whom you shall dispossess serve their gods, on the high mountains and on the hills and under every green tree. You shall tear down their altars and smash their sacred pillars and burn their Asherim with fire, and you shall cut down the engraved images of their gods and obliterate their name from that place (Deuteronomy 12:2-3).

To the modern mind, this may sound strangely intolerant but the Lord warned His people against the danger of imitating the worship practices of the nations (Deuteronomy 12:4). The sexual prohibitions prohibited given in Leviticus 18 and 20 were not only prohibited in the public place of idol worship, they were prohibited from doing these acts in the privacy of their homes as well. Private idolatrous sex acts are no more tolerated by God in the home than they are in public in a temple. An idolater then is one "who sets up his idols in his heart" and how that person lives, particularly in their sexual behavior, is their act of worship of that idol (Ezekiel 14:4, 7; 20:16).

330   Mel White, *Stranger At The Gate: To Be Gay and Christian in America* (New York, NY: Penguin Books, 1994), 196-197.

Temple Worship in Leviticus

God is very concerned with what you do with your body sexually for whatever you do is a form of worship. This is taught in both testaments. This does not mean that all things are sacramental, means of grace or avenues for communing with God. In fact, there are numerous things which are sacred and yet are forbidden to be treated as sacraments, particularly sexual acts:

> God the creator is above and beyond the polarity of sex (See esp. Deut. 4:15-16); and thus sexuality is not divinized through intradivine sexual intercourse or sacralized through cultic ritual... Sexuality is part of the created order, to be enjoyed and celebrated between man and woman and not to be linked in any way with divine sexual activity or public rituals of the cultus... Because humans (and their sexuality) are created by God and are not part of divinity, any attempts to divinize or sacralize sexuality in Israel, as done in the pagan fertility myths and cult practices, is met with the strongest divine denunciation.[331]

Because sex is sacred, He has explicitly and without ambiguity told us what is allowed, what is commanded and what is forbidden in this act of worship whether formally or informally, privately or corporately in public with others. In Leviticus 18 the Old Covenant people of God are told that they are not to have sex with any close blood relatives (vs. 6), their parents (v. 7), their father's wife (v. 8), their sister (v. 9, 11), their grandchildren (v. 10), their aunt (v. 12-13), their uncle (v. 14), their daughter-in-law (v. 15), their sister-in-law (v. 16), nor have a *ménage à trois* with a mother and daughter (v. 17), two sisters (v. 18), sex with a woman while menstruating (v. 19), their neighbor's wife (v. 20), with an animal (v. 23), nor is a man to have sex with another man (v. 22). Nor were they to have a post-birth abortion by sacrificing their child as an act of worship to Molech (v. 21).

The law of God in Leviticus 18 and 20 is extensive as to what is forbidden and it says absolutely nothing that was distinctive of the Mosaic

---

331   Richard Davidson, *Flame of Yahweh: Sexuality in the Old Testament* (Peabody, MA: Hendriksen Publishing, 2007), 84, 85.

Covenant that is not applicable to Gentiles and ceased to be binding in the New Covenant such as offering animal sacrifices, circumcision, Old Covenant Feast Days, or Sabbaths all of which passed away with the coming of Christ (Colossians 2:16-17). Such commandments had a designed obsolescence as they were but mere types and shadows which passed away with the sacrifice of Christ and the end of the Old Covenant temple worship (Hebrews 10:1).

There are several ways that Gay Theology advocates attempt to argue that the sexual prohibitions of Leviticus 18-20 are not applicable to modern Christians. The most common is that this text is only applicable to ritualistic cultic forms of worship associated with the Gentile pagan nations.[332] The argument is that Leviticus 18:22 and 20:13 do not refer to same-sex acts in general, such as between two mutually committed men in a monogamous relationship. Rather, according to them, they only refer to male cultic sex. If this is so, then why doesn't the text specifically refer to the *kedesh* and wouldn't it also need to mention the *kedeshah* since the Canaanite religion was a fertility cult? Furthermore, none of the other sexual prohibitions are tied to cultic forms of sex so why should we conclude that the same-sex acts are strictly tied to ritualistic cultic sex? Are we to believe that mutual same sex acts are only a modern phenomenon? Surely if there are homosexuals today there were homosexuals then as well and the language of Leviticus 18:22 and 20:13 are clearly broad enough to include any type of same-sex activity whether consensual, exploitative, pederastic, cross generational, a form of street prostitution or part of a religious cultic form of worship. In fact, extra-biblical evidence also indicates that non-cultic forms of same sex acts also existed in Egypt.[333]

Another problem with such an assertion is that the entire life of a Christian is a religious act of devotion. Either your life is a holy sacrifice (Romans 12:1-2) or an act of idolatry. Only the "marriage bed" (a euphemism of the husband and wife having sex) as defined by Scripture is "undefiled" (a term borrowed from the purity laws) and all other sex

332   "The point is that The Holiness Code of Leviticus prohibits male same sex acts for religious reasons, not for sexual reasons. The concern is to keep Israel distinct from the Gentiles. Homogenital sex is forbidden because it is associated with Gentile identity." Daniel Helminiak, *What the Bible Really Says About Homosexuality* (Estancia, NM: Alamo Square Press, 2000), 54.

333   Robert A. J. Gagnon, *The Bible And Homosexual Practice* (Nashville, TN: Abingdon Press, 2001), 51-53.

acts will be judged (Hebrews 13:4). Since the Bible only recognizes a marriage between a man and a woman there is no means for two men or two women to have an undefiled marriage bed. The sexual union of two men or two women is therefore a violation of the seventh commandment and a sexual union that will be judged.

While some may point out that Leviticus only addresses men having sex with other men and not women with other women, throughout the law we repeatedly see prohibitions that are addressed to "man" that clearly are applicable to both men and women and therefore the prohibition against same sex unions applies to both genders:

> Even the Decalogue is addressed in the masculine singular, but this certainly does not mean that it applies only to the male gender. The masculine singular is the Hebrew way to express gender-inclusive ideas, much the same as it was in English until the recent emphasis on gender-inclusive language.[334]

A more common attempt to get around the prohibitions of Leviticus 18-20 is to assert that they were "under the law" and Christians are no longer "under the law" and therefore all of the moral commandments of the Old Testament are not applicable to the modern day Christian as Rick Brentlinger argues:

> Leviticus 18:22 & 20:13 forbids anal intercourse between two men during the time period the Mosaic Law was in force, in the Holy Land, for Jews. – a particular people in a particular land at a particular time for a particular purpose under a particular set of laws, approximately 1450 BC to AD 30.[335]

But as already discussed the term "not under the law" does not mean "free to disobey the moral elements of the law." Instead it means to not be under the Old Covenant, an administration of death and the curses

334   Richard Davidson, *Flame of Yahweh: Sexuality in the Old Testament* (Peabody, MA: Hendriksen Publishing, 2007), 150.
335   Rick Brentlinger, *Gay Christian 101 - Spiritual Self-Defense For Gay Christians* (2007), 85.

of Deuteronomy 27-30, as well as all of its distinctives in the types and shadows. These could not take away sin and therefore Gentiles are not required to be circumcised and come under the law.

Another attempt to get around the moral implications of the sexual prohibitions of Leviticus 18:22 and 20:13 is to assert that they do not refer to sexual sins, things that were inherently wrong, and to recategorize them as merely culturally repugnant. Homosexual acts then were amoral forms of ritual uncleanness or behaviors that were "dirty" according to the primitive Jewish culture as Daniel Helminiak states:

> When the Bible does talk about same-sex behavior, it refers to as it was understood in those ancient times. The biblical teachings will apply today only insofar as the ancient understanding of same-sex behavior is still valid.[336]

L. William Countryman, borrowing from cultural anthropology, uses this same line of argument. He asserts that an abomination was not something considered intrinsically evil by God. Rather it was merely a culturally repugnant behavior equivalent to the way in which modern parents tell their children that eating their boogers is "dirty" as he writes:

> What is this 'dirt,' which children are told to avoid, but which is neither literal, physical dirt nor anything threatening to health? Because anthropologists are used to examining such questions in a cross-cultural way, an anthropologist is probably the best person to help us gain perspective on it in our own culture... Mary Douglas, the cultural anthropologist, has argued that dirt can be understood only in relation to a system that excludes it 'As we know it,' she says, 'dirt is essentially disorder'... 'the old definition of dirt as matter out of place.'... What is clean in one culture is dirty in another. Ancient Israel forbade the eating of pork (Lev. 11:7).[337]

---

336   Daniel Helminiak, *What the Bible Really Says About Homosexuality* (Estancia, NM: Alamo Square Press, 2000), 39.
337   L. William Countryman, *Dirt, Greed & Sex: Sexual Ethics in the New Testament and Their Implications for Today* (Minneapolis, MN: Fortress Press; Revised edition, 2007), 10-11.

He then traces what he considers to be "American purity law," sexual impurity, or what is considered "dirty" from the 1950's to the present day in which, 'Morality' –meaning, in this case, one's definition of sexual purity – came to be treated as a matter of private determination."[338] He then concludes in establishing the nature the parameters of purity:

> Because of the complexity and incoherence of modern Western purity values, the reader of this book has to perform several difficult tasks to understand the topic at hand. One is to discover that what has long been seemed self-evident with regard to sexual ethics – namely, that certain acts are right or wrong in and of themselves – reflects purity values specific to our culture. The evident values of other cultures will often be significantly different. Another is to accept that purity systems change and that we cannot assume that ours is identical with that of our ancestral cultures.[339]

He then states concerning sexual prohibitions of the prohibitions of Leviticus 18:22 and 20:13:

> …in literal translation 'lying with a male the lyings of a woman.'… scholars suggest anal intercourse – an interpretation accepted in what follows. The common practice of treating the text as a blanket prohibition of all sexual interaction between males or even between females goes beyond what it actually says. These two prohibitions appear as isolated rules, with the violations being described as 'abominations' that is – 'disgusting things.' This language does not mean that they are exceptionally horrid in terms of the purity system. The Hebrew term *toebah* and its synonym *shiqquts*, both usually translated *bdelygma* in ancient Greek and 'abomination' in English, apply, in the Torah, to things as diverse as unclean foods (Lev. 11:10, 11, 12, etc. ; Deut. 14:3), the sacrifice of a blemish animal

---

338   Ibid, 14.
339   Ibid, 15.

(Deut. 17:10), remarriage to a former wife (Deut. 24:4), and idols (Deut. 29:16, ET 17).[340]

In other words, the sexual prohibitions against same-sex acts are not inherently evil but only "dirty" according to the Jewish outlook on the social norms of the surrounding nations. With this view in mind other Gay Theology proponents assert that same-sex acts were equivalent to eating non-kosher foods:

> The word 'abomination' in Leviticus was used for anything that was considered to be religiously unclean or associated with idol worship... Clearly, some foods that were once considered to be 'abominations' like shrimp or lobster, are now on buffets across the country. We can go to out favorite lobster restaurant and enjoy its succulent flavor without guilt [341]

What must be kept in mind when reading their books is that according to their worldview they believe that the Bible is full of errors, it was written by primitive, misogynistic ("woman-hating") men and consequently it does not reflect the mind of God but rather a patriarchal society that treated women as mere cattle. According to them the text must be understood as written by "a primitive and superstitious way of thinking."[342] This is the lens through which they look when they come to their understanding of "same-sex behavior... as it was understood in those ancient times." With this view of the text in mind they go on to assert that the Hebrew word translated "abomination" (*toevah*) that such an act is not something that is intrinsically evil but merely a local cultural taboo as Boswell argued:

> The only place in the Old Testament where homosexual acts per se are mentioned is Leviticus... The Hebrew word 'toevah'... here translated 'abomination' does not signify something intrinsically evil, but something which is ritually

340   Ibid, 24.
341   David W. Shelton, *The Rainbow Kingdom: Christianity & the Homosexual Reconciled* (Lulu, 2006), 49, 50.
342   Daniel Helminiak, *What the Bible Really Says About Homosexuality* (Estancia, NM: Alamo Square Press, 2000), 53.

unclean for Jews, like eating pork or engaging in intercourse during menstruation, both of which are prohibited
in these chapters.[343]

Borrowing from Boswell, Daniel Helminiak likewise asserts

The argument in Leviticus is religious, not ethical or moral. That is to say, no thought is given to whether the sex in
itself is right or wrong. The intent is to keep Jewish identity
strong. The concern is purity.[344]

This assertion fails to recognize how the purity laws were tied to the
inherent moral impurity of mankind which necessitated the cleansing
rite of circumcision and repeated washings. Boswell then goes on to
argue:

The distinction between intrinsic wrong and ritual impurity
is even more finely drawn by the Greek translation which
distinguishes in 'toevah' itself the separate categories of
law or justice (*anomia*) and infringements of ritual purity
or monotheistic worship (*bdelugma*). The Levitical pro-
scriptions of homosexual behavior fall into the latter. In the
Greek, then, the Levitical enactments against homosexual
behavior characterize it univocally as ceremonially unclean
rather than inherently evil.[345]

There are two flaws with this line of argument. First, the supposed
difference between impurity and morality is a false distinction. Even if
we were to interpret *toevah* as meaning "ritually impure" all the purity
laws had a moral connotation. They either referred to the inborn depravity of the fallen "seed" of the human race, which consequently made one
sinful from one's birth (Psalm 51:5), or they related to the reproducing
process, the menstrual cycle of a woman or the seminal emissions of a

343   John Boswell, *Christianity, Social Tolerance, and Homosexuality* (University
Of Chicago Press; 8th Edition. edition, 2005), 100.
344   Daniel Helminiak, *What the Bible Really Says About Homosexuality* (Estancia,
NM: Alamo Square Press, 2000), 55.
345   John Boswell, *Christianity, Social Tolerance, and Homosexuality* (University
Of Chicago Press; 8th Edition. edition, 2005), 101-102.

man which required a subsequent baptism (Leviticus 15:15-24). This repeated baptizing process only ended in the New Covenant because of the onetime perfect sacrifice and baptism of Jesus Christ. Christians are not required to receive repeated baptisms for now there is, "…one Lord, one faith, one baptism" (Ephesians 4:5).

Another problem with this argument that *toevah* does not refer to an inherently immoral act but something that was only deemed culturally disgusting is the various connotations with the term. Even if we were to interpret *toevah* as meaning "grotesque," this would not mean that all abominations are morally equal. It may rightly be said that eating balut (a fertilized chicken egg with a nearly-developed embryo inside that is boiled and eaten in the shell) and having sex with a corpse are both grotesque or disgusting, but it could hardly be said that the two are morally equivalent. Likewise, it may also said that a traffic violation and murder are both crimes, but it can hardly be said that the two are morally equivalent. Two different behaviors or conditions could both be referred to as *toevah* one clearly being *culturally* repugnant, such as an Egyptian eating with a Jew (Genesis 43:32), while the other is *morally* repugnant such as a man having anal sex with another man.

What signifies whether it is a cultural or moral *toevah* is the penal sanction, if there is one, assigned to it by God. It is the punishment or consequence of the act that indicates the grievousness of the crime and whether or not the grotesqueness is merely cultural or intrinsically evil. All one need do to discern God's repulsion of the act is to recognize the seriousness to which He punishes violators or what is required to rectify the condition. In this case, the minimal sentence for violating Leviticus 18:22 is expulsion (being "cut off" cf. Leviticus 18:29) and the maximum punishment is the death penalty as indicated in Leviticus 20:13. God does not ascribe the death penalty for mere cultural taboos.

Not only does the immediate context of the use of the word *toevah* go beyond that of a local cultural taboo but such an assertion contradicts other Gay Theological arguments. Many Gay Theology proponents assert that Romans 1:26-27 and 1 Corinthians 6:9 have the sexual prohibition of Leviticus 18:22 and 20:13 in mind. Therefore, even their own argument refutes that Leviticus 18:22 and 20:13 refer to mere cultural uncleanness and not an inherent moral evil since Paul asserts that the wrath of God is upon those who commit such acts (Romans 1:18, 27) and that they "shall not inherit the Kingdom of God" (1 Corinthians 6:9). You cannot argue both ways, that Leviticus 18:22 and 20:13 are a mere cultural taboo and not an intrinsic evil if Paul has these very same texts in mind which supposedly only refer to cultic male prostitutes. Paul declares that there is a heavy judgment upon people, as does Leviticus 20:13, who commit these acts and that such are "worthy of death" (Romans 1:32). Furthermore, do they really want to argue that having sex with a cultic male prostitute is not inherently evil and merely a cultural taboo? It would seem so for gay political activist advocate Mel White asserts that his encounter with a male prostitute was a "gift from God."[346]

One of the clearest passages that indicates that the word *toevah* can and indeed often does refer to sins is found in the Proverbs:

> There are six things which the LORD hates,
> Yes, seven which are an abomination (*toevah*) to Him:
> Haughty eyes, a lying tongue,
> And hands that shed innocent blood,
> A heart that devises wicked plans,
> Feet that run rapidly to evil,
> A false witness *who* utters lies,
> And one who spreads strife among brothers (Proverbs 6:16-19).

In this passage there are a number of sins that are declared to be *toevah*, none of which are mere cultural taboos or part of a ritualistic sacrifice. Therefore, it is the context of the use of the word clarified by the penal sanction attached to it that indicates whether the act is a mere cultural issue or a temporary prohibition to end with the New Covenant that determines whether or not the *toevah* is inherently sinful.

Another argument against the Levitical sexual prohibitions of same sex acts being applied to modern homogential relationships is an attempt to isolate Moses's use of the word *toevah* from the rest of the Old Testament. R.D. Weekly insists that Moses' understanding of the word can only be understood in the context of Leviticus, or at most within the Pentateuch. In doing so he argues that Moses *always* uses

---

346   Mel White, *Stranger At The Gate: To Be Gay and Christian in America* (New York, NY: Penguin Books, 1994), 133.

it in connection with idolatry, though during the time of Solomon who penned much of the Proverbs the word would have changed its meaning to include other sins as well. Therefore, the same sex acts prohibited in Leviticus can only refer to those which are tied to idolatrous worship. There are a two fundamental flaws with this argument.

First, since the law was to be read to the people at the Temple and in the Synagogue the liturgical use of the Hebrew language remained static much in the way that the Latin language remain static in the Roman Catholic Mass even after it was no longer the common tongue. The hearer of God's law and the Proverbs would not have understood the meaning of the word to have changed simply because they were penned in different times. The author of the later text could not dismiss the meaning of original use of the term as it had already been used in the Temple.

Second, while we may speak of differences between Classical Creek, Koine Greek and modern Greek this was not the case with Old Testament Hebrew as if we can speak of Mosaic Hebrew, Davidic Hebrew or Exile Hebrew. While the lexical meaning of a word may be expanded in time it would not lose its original meaning in the process. Therefore, in order to make his case stand Weekly would need to demonstrate that Moses' inspired use of the term *toevah* did not also include the lexical range of the author of Proverbs 6 and other later Old Testament passages.

One of the most absurd arguments against applying Leviticus 18:22 and 20:13 to same sex acts today is that supposedly the culture of the day was primarily concerned with increasing and maintaining the population. Therefore, the prohibition against same-sex acts was merely part of a larger concern for population growth. It is argued then that if increasing the population is not a concern in today's modern context that the "be fruitful and multiply" cultural mandate that motivated labeling same sex acts as an abomination no longer apply:

> The growth in the number of people within Israelite family
> unit was crucial to the survival of Israel... this is one of
> the chief reasons for the rules about sex and sexuality: the
> survival of the nation of Israel was at stake if it did not
> reproduce in appropriate numbers... Human beings are to
> be fruitful and multiply, and for a man to lie with a man as

with a woman is to 'sow seed where it cannot grow and produce its fruit.[347]

The problem with this argument is that even with the command to procreate in Genesis 1:28, nowhere in Scripture, particularly Holiness Code, is marital intercourse with a "closed womb" labeled an abomination or considered a waste of seed. Nor is *coitus interruptus* explicitly forbidden or condemned except when a man refused to uphold his duties in a Levirate marriage (Genesis 38:8-10). In fact, the book of Song of Solomon is a poetic display of the romantic sexual relationship between a husband and a wife and nowhere does it express any idea that the purpose of their love-making is primarily for the purpose of increasing the population.

The final attempt to assert that the prohibited same-sex acts do not apply to modern day relationships is that today homosexual behavior is based on mutual consent between social equals with no intent to humiliate or denigrate the masculinity of the one being anally penetrated. The intent of the text, according to them, is to maintain the man's grip of power and not be lowered to the inferior social class of the penetrated female and thus Leviticus 18 and 20 were written to maintain male power roles:

> Leviticus was written by and for a patriarchal-centered society, treating women as something less than their male counterparts; peripheral to society; as well as a threat to the purity of the priesthood cult. The androcentric mentality and the cultural and societal need to increase the population base of God's chosen people led the priestly authors of Leviticus to want to control women's bodies and their reproductive capabilities, as well as protect 'the seed' that sexual intercourse implants thereby increasing procreation... Women are treated as second-class citizens and the book treats their normal bodily functions [menstruating] in a degrading fashion and as something unclean. In ancient Israel it is believed that a woman was legally owned, and was the property first of her father and then of her husband.

347   John F. Dwyer, *Those 7 References: A Study of 7 References to Homosexuality In The Bible* (John F. Dwyer, 2007), 30.

> A woman had few to no legal rights of her own... The male-centeredness, the distinct quality with which the Israelite community was to be imbued, and the lack of standing of women, are all critical concepts to keep in mind when reading Leviticus.[348]

According to this view in the Ancient Near East same-sex acts, particularly anal intercourse, were an expression of male dominance. It is argued that the penetrator maintained his sense of masculine power while the passive receiver was viewed as being feminized, thus lowering a man to the status of a woman:

> Much of Leviticus presents directives and instructions *as if* God were speaking directly to the community about ritual and how social actions and activities can and do impact that ritual... The rules and laws of Leviticus were written for a people of a certain time and place related closely to a very particular society, in a very particular set of circumstances... This book comes from an era were much of sexual activity was exploitative, violent and in many cases connected with cultic practices... [and] was very much about power, domination, and strength. The language of Leviticus 18:22 and 20:13, 'a male lying with a male as with a female,' is indicative of this understanding and attitude toward sexual acts. For a man to act as a woman, to allow himself to be dominated, and taken, so to speak, went against the societal structures and understandings of roles and place in that society. To place oneself in that position was to step outside of a rigidly maintained hierarchy. Such action blurred what was considered appropriate dealings between society's hierarchal strata. When sex has to do with power and position in society, laws and rules were thought to be needed to keep that societal structure in place. Thus, much of Leviticus has to do with society for whom it was written. Add to this the need the priestly class felt to make the people of Israel 'holy,' multitudinous,

348   John F. Dwyer, *Those 7 References: A Study of 7 References to Homosexuality In The Bible* (John F. Dwyer, 2007), 31.

as well as separate and distinct from the societies that surrounded Israel, the rules about sexual activity, when placed in that context, make a certain amount of sense.[349]

John Dwyer then concludes:

> Another way to translate verse 22 is: 'to lie down in the place of lying a male shall not as with a woman.'... To lie down is to do something that is inappropriate, to act in a manner that is out of character for the culture of that time. For a man as a woman, 'lying down in the place of lying', as a woman, to act in a manner that did not keep, the power-center in the man, would be shameful. This action would be humiliation not only upon the man but on society and how power was structured and understood. This type of action would be challenging the patriarchal system that existed in that society and culture.[350]

When the text is read through the lens of liberation theology and a "hermeneutic of suspicion" then every prohibition is interpreted as a means of maintaining male heterosexual superiority. Consequently Dwyer can dismiss the commandment as only being relevant to "that society and culture." The argument that follows is that if the act is between social equals who alternately assume both positions, the penetrator and the penetrated, so that there is no power play then the text does not apply. Therefore, since the motivation of dominance and humiliation does not exist today in modern same sex relationships (unless that is what turns you on) as they are based on mutual consent between social equals the text does not apply.

The only way this argument can any validity is if the prohibition is derived purely from man and deny that the law reflects the holiness of God. It is absurd to assert that God is trying to maintain male domination over women or is merely prohibiting men taking a less than male power position in the sex act. But even if the origin of the text is from men seeking to maintain male dominancy with such narrow concerns, then we would expect a commandment that when a husband and a wom-

349   Ibid, 38-39.
350   Ibid, 29.

an have sex that he can only take the "missionary position" and that a woman may not mount her husband, i.e. be on top.

In conclusion, it is clear that the various prohibitions of Leviticus 18 and 20 cannot be relegated to a mere cultural taboo, as if they were akin to belching, farting in public or picking one's nose. Rather they are an intrinsically moral evil as are fornication and adultery. Nor can the life of the believer be sharply divided into "sacred" and "secular" as if what one does in one's private life is not also in some fashion an act of worship. Neither are the sexual prohibitions strictly tied to any cultic sex acts as cult prostitutes are not mentioned within the text. Furthermore, if the concern of the author was to maintain the male power position in the sex act then we would expect to see the prohibition of any sex act that does not maintain the "man on top." Finally, since the New Testament repeatedly cites and alludes to the sexual prohibitions of the Old Testament, as recognized by some Gay Theology advocates, one cannot dismiss the chapter entirely as an irrelevant obsolete standard for sexual ethics.

Chapter 13
The Law of God, Temple Worship and Romans

Romans chapter 1 reveals the consequences of suppressing the truth of God's revelation whether from creation or from His Word. If this suppression persists it results in a subtle erosive decline that develops into idolatry and other subsequent forms of unrighteousness. Unless there is repentance, this then incurs the wrath of God and the judgment of being "turned over" to the dominion of ever increasing forms of sinful depravity.

In examining this text I shall respond to the various attempts to dismiss Romans 1 as being irrelevant to understanding God's attitude towards modern same-sex acts. In doing so, we will also look at Romans Chapter 6, in which Paul's warns the Church of the danger of taking God's grace for granted and falling back into the bondage out which they had been delivered. To do so would be to repeat the way in which national Israel in the Old Testament took their deliverance from slavery from Egypt for granted and slipped into idolatry and subsequently committed gross sexual immorality resulting in their being "turned over" to the dominion of pagan nations (2 Kings 17). The Apostle Paul in his first chapter of his Epistle to the Church at Rome provides us a clear picture of where we are heading if we continue on this path and do not repent and heed his warnings in Romans chapter 6 (as well as 1 Corinthians chapter 10). If the Church (or at least certain segments of it) does not repent it will be in the same state of apostasy which will much look like the conditions described in Romans chapter 1. In fact, as we shall see, much of the Church today is proudly mirroring that state of depravity already.

In order to hear Paul's warning, we will need to understand his epistles in their original historical context that followed the decision made at the Jerusalem Council. Then we need to see how his statements parallel the condition of the Church today. In short, the redemptive-historical context of Paul's Epistles to the Churches at Rome and Galatia are primarily a response to errors of the Pharisees that were the point of contention at the Jerusalem Council (Acts 15:1, 5). These distorters of the Gospel insisted that Gentile Christians must "live like Jews" (Galatians 2:14) by doing such things as receiving circumcision, observing the food laws and keeping the feast days in order to be justified, i.e. be declared in a right standing with God. Paul responds to this heresy by arguing that the Gospel is the power of salvation for both the Jew and the Greek (Romans 1:16-17) who look by faith beyond the era of the Mosaic Covenant, as did Habakkuk (Habakkuk 2:4), to the work accomplished through the death, burial and resurrection of Jesus Christ who took upon Himself curse of the law (Galatians 3:10, 13), that was the inevitable outcome of the Mosaic Covenant because it was given to a people with hard hearts and stiff necks (Deuteronomy 27-30; Acts 7:51).

Romans chapter 1 then is a description of the life of a person before they had faith Jesus Christ whether a Jew, such as the Israelites who whored after pagan gods and broke covenant with YHWH, or the Gentiles who worshipped the Greek and Roman deities. In the history of Israel, when Jews became like their idolatrous Gentile neighbors they were involved in all sorts of heinous sins including various types of homosexual acts, which Paul says, according to the penal sanctions, are actions worthy of death (Romans 1:30; Leviticus 20:13). There is nothing in this chapter that indicates that Paul is *only* speaking of the Gentiles and not also of those who claim to worship YHWH. Read in this way, the contrast between the audiences of chapter 1 and 2 is between Jews who had co-opted to the Gentile culture, as had their Old Testament ancestors and their contemporary tax collectors, and Pharisaic Jews who thought that they were morally superior to others. Then in the latter half of Romans chapter 2 Paul speaks of Gentile believers who do the things of the law and thereby demonstrate that they have the law of God on their heart without circumcision proving that they are of the true circumcision (Jeremiah 31:33 Romans 2:14-15).

However if Paul is speaking exclusively of Gentiles in the first half of Romans chapter 1 and the latter half of chapter 2, as most commentators argue, then he is contrasting pagan Gentiles with believing Gentiles. The former have darkened hearts who are storing up wrath (Romans 1:21) and Paul has lumped in with them the Pharisees who have been circumcised but have an "unrepentant heart" and consequently are also "storing up wrath." These people are then contrasted with the believing Gentiles who have God's law written on their heart (Jeremiah 31:33 ; Romans 2:15). These Gentiles are then a spiritual Jew, a "Jew who is one inwardly" and has a "circumcision is that which is of the heart, by the Spirit, not by the letter and his praise is not from men, but from God" (Romans 2:29).

In the second chapter of his Epistle to the Romans Paul then turns to point his finger at the hypocritical Pharisees, who he knew so well having been one himself (Philippians 3:5), who held these non-Christian Gentiles in contempt while they themselves did the very same sort of sins by robbing temples (Romans 2:1-3). Paul goes on to argue in Romans chapters 2-3 that the Gentiles who have faith in Christ who are without circumcision, whom these Pharisees despised, give evidence that they are justified by faith in Christ apart from the distinctives of "The Law" (i.e. the Mosaic Covenant), such as circumcision (Romans 3:28-30), in that they have received the Holy Spirit the same way as the Jewish Christians - by faith (Acts 15:8-9). These Gentile Christians give evidence of the work of the Holy Spirit in their lives in that they now intuitively keep the commandments of God because the work of Law of God has been written on their heart as prophesied by Jeremiah concerning the New Covenant (Jeremiah 31:33; Romans 2:14-15). It is the person who has a genuine faith and keeps the moral law of God from the heart that is the true Jew and has the true circumcision (Romans 2:29). As he states elsewhere, "Circumcision is nothing, and uncircumcision is nothing, but what matters is the keeping of the commandments of God" (1 Corinthians 7:19).

Therefore, as Paul goes on to argue in Romans chapter 4, Abraham has become the father of the believing Gentiles as well for he too was justified before he was circumcised hundreds of years before the institution of the Mosaic Covenant (Romans 4:9-10 Galatians 3:7). Consequently, as Paul elsewhere warns the Church, if anyone should seek to come "under the law" (the Mosaic Covenant) by receiving circumcision that Christ will be of no use to them (Galatians 5:2) for they will be in the same state of condemnation as Israel who would soon be destroyed, as prophesied by Christ Himself, in 70 A.D. (Matthew 23:38-24:2).

Paul then goes on to declare in Romans chapter 5 that we now have peace with God having been justified by faith through Jesus Christ who died for our sin and was raised for our justification (Romans 5:1). The first Adam by his one act of disobedience brought an administration of death that reigned until the time of Moses. But the one act of redemption of the second Adam, Jesus Christ, brought the gift of grace and freedom to many (Romans 5:14-15; 1 Corinthians 15:22, 45).

However, lest anyone should confuse freedom for license to sin, Paul warns in Romans chapter 6 that this freedom in Christ should not lead us to licentiousness, for we are not "under the law" (Mosaic Covenant), an administration of death, but under grace, the new era of the resurrection and dominion of the Holy Spirit. Otherwise we will again become a slave to sin (Romans 6:7-16). Those who have been baptized into Christ's death have died to sin. But if you take your freedom for granted you will again become a slave to sin as did the Old Testament Israelite. They had been freed from Egypt but then took their freedom and marriage to YHWH for granted, sought after the gods of the foreign nations like an adulterous wife. Then after a series of judgments and refusal to repent they were turned over to their sin and went into captivity. This entailed going into exile under the dominion of pagan nations and their gods as a result of their committing all kinds of abominable acts of idolatrous sexual immorality. This is why Paul tells the Christians at Corinth that the consequences of Israel's rebellion is an example to Gentile Christians. If they do not repent they will also suffer the same consequences for one cannot be a partaker of the cup of the Lord and the cup of demons (1 Corinthians 10:1-14, 21). Therefore, Paul exhorts the Church to walk not according to the desires of the flesh, which produces all sorts of sin, but rather live in the power of the Holy Spirit and subsequently bear good fruit (Galatians 5:16-26).

Romans chapter 1:18-2:11 then speaks to the modern Church of the incremental decline that takes place when mankind, both Jew and Gentile, suppresses the truth of God's revelation. Likewise, Romans chapter 6 provides very clear warnings that if we take the gospel of grace for granted and return to our formers sins that we will become enslaved to the very bondage and the moral decay described in chapter 1. Christians in the Church who continue to sin like ancient Israel, turning to idolatry and sexual immorality, will be given over to depraved minds if they do not repent. The clear evidence of this pattern is seen in the fruit being born in the lives of Gay Theology advocates, the Metropolitan Community Churches and other like-minded denominations.

Romans 1 and Gay Theology

At this point, we will take a very careful look at this text and Paul's description of the effects of suppressing the knowledge of the truth and respond to the various attempts that various Gay Theologians use to get around its clear implications:

"For the wrath of God is revealed from heaven..."

What needs to be kept in mind as we read these verses is that God is angry and His wrath is being revealed against everything that Paul is going to go on to describe. If we are going to believe the Bible, the issue being addressed is not a matter of a violation of a cultural taboo or Jewish custom or a prejudicial misconception of Paul concerning the behaviors of idolaters and people who engage in same sex acts. Rather the one true Holy God who created the universe is *extremely* angry:

> ...against all ungodliness and unrighteousness of men, who suppress the truth in unrighteousness, because that which is known about God is evident within them; for God made it evident to them. For since the creation of the world His invisible attributes, His eternal power and divine nature, have been clearly seen, being understood through what has been made, so that they are without excuse. For even though they knew God, they did not honor Him as God, or give thanks; but they became futile in their speculations, and their foolish heart was darkened (Romans 1:18-21).

In these first three verses Paul states that the evidence of God's existence is known within those who deny and suppress the truth, for *since* the beginning of creation (not *from* creation) His invisible attributes have been clearly known, seen and understood so that those who deny the One true God's existence are without an excuse (*anapologetous*), literally "without an apology" or "without a defense." It is not that the existence of the one true God may be deduced from creation as if the universe provides the basis for a teleological or cosmological argument, but rather that the knowledge of God is known within mankind as he states, "that which is known about God is evident within them." The problem is what the rebellious heart and mind does with this knowledge – it suppresses it. Hence, all people know God exists but unless a person by faith repents and obeys the revelation of God given to him that knowledge is suppressed so that he cannot understand the things of God as Paul elsewhere states, "...a natural man does not accept the things of the Spirit of God, for they are foolishness to him; and he cannot understand them, because they are spiritually judged (Greek: *anakrinetai*)" (1 Corinthians 2:14).[351]

The consequence of suppressing this knowledge is that the natural man begins to speculate about the universe around him, inventing his own philosophies and religions to develop his worldview. The result is that not only does his thinking turn to folly but his heart becomes darkened. As the person increases his suppression of the truth it results in less restraint on their depravity which results in greater darkness which then, in a downward spiral, produces more depravity. The person who continues to suppress the truth, acting against the revelation given to his conscience stirs up guilt. The only way a person can become free from the feelings that follow is either to repent, or suppress the truth all the more which then leads to further depravity, more guilt and subsequently more suppression and greater depravity of sin as Peter Jones states, "....when conscience, provoked by guilt, is suppressed, it loses none of its force. The force is only redirected, driving a person into more and more wrong doing."[352]

This is true not only of those who respond wrongly to general revelation provided through creation but even more so of those who have received and reject God's special revelation codified in the Scriptures. The natural man left to his own with no moral restraints and given unrestrained power becomes beastly in nature. Inevitably he then turns to worship an idol that resembles himself:

---

351   Here "natural" (literally in Greek *psuchikos* "soulish") is used in contrast to *pneuma* "spiritual" (cf. 1 Corinthians 15:44)
352   Peter Jones, *The God of Sex* (Eastbourne, England: David C. Cook, 2006), 26.

> Professing to be wise, they became fools, and exchanged
> the glory of the incorruptible God for an image in the form
> of corruptible man and of birds and four-footed animals
> and crawling creatures (Romans 1:22-23).

The Greeks were known for their philosophers and their pantheon of gods, that the Romans inherited and renamed, which Paul Himself confronted on Mars Hill as we read, "Now while Paul was waiting for them at Athens, his spirit was being provoked within him as he was observing the city full of idols" (Acts 17:16). But lest we should think that this sort of rank idolatry could not happen amongst God's chosen people, Israel also fell into this same sin, even though they were given the oracles of God, as they failed to remain holy. Slowly and incrementally they became immersed in the pagan culture around them, even intermarrying with pagan wives, which eroded their sensibilities as their hard hearts suppressed the knowledge of the Lord who brought them out of Egypt.

> They mingled with the nations, and learned their practices,
> served their idols, which became a snare to them. They
> even sacrificed their sons and their daughters to the demons
> (Psalm 106:36-37).

It was not that Israel abandoned the temple of the sacrifices in Jerusalem altogether. Rather, they added to their religion the worship of idols thinking they could be Christians, if I may use the term anachronistically, and serve other gods as well, "They sacrificed to demons who were not God, to gods whom they have not known, new gods who came lately, whom your fathers did not dread" (Deuteronomy 32:17). Paul wrote elsewhere that this was true of Gentiles who are without the knowledge of the Lord and he warned the Church not to fall into their way of thinking and worshipping, "The things which the Gentiles sacrifice, they sacrifice to demons, and not to God; and I do not want you to become sharers in demons" (1 Corinthians 10:20).

Paul then goes on to describe in Romans 1 the result of suppressing the knowledge of the truth concerning God as eventually people are turned over to the enslavement of their sinful inclinations:

> Therefore God gave them over in the lusts of their hearts
> to impurity, that their bodies might be dishonored among
> them. For they exchanged the truth of God for a lie, and
> worshipped and served the creature rather than the creator,
> who is blessed forever. Amen (Romans 1:24-25).

Paul chronicles this process in terms that were the most obvious and clearly visible in the Gentile culture around him but this was also common in the history of His own people, "Has a nation changed gods, when they were not gods? But My people have changed their glory for that which does not profit" (Jeremiah 2:11).[353]

Paul then draws out the inevitable outcome of suppressing the truth in which we find our so-called "clobber passage":

> For this reason God gave them over to degrading passions;
> for their women exchanged the natural function for that
> which is unnatural, and in the same way also the men
> abandoned the natural function of the woman and burned
> in their desire toward one another, men with men commit-
> ting indecent acts and receiving in their own persons the
> due penalty of their error. And just as they did not see fit
> to acknowledge God any longer, God gave them over to
> depraved mind, to do those things which are not proper,
> being filled with all unrighteousness, wickedness, greed,
> evil; full of envy, murder, strife, deceit, malice; they are
> gossips, slanderers, haters of God, insolent, arrogant,
> boastful, inventors of evil, disobedient to parents, without
> understanding, untrustworthy, unloving, unmerciful; and,
> although they know the ordinance of God, that those who
> practice such things are worthy of death, they not only
> do the same, but also give hearty approval to those who
> practice them (Romans 1:26-32).

There are several ways that Gay Theologians attempt to get around the clear teaching of this passage that God does not approve of men having sex with other men or women having sex with other women. Some assert that the text only speaks of pagan idolatrous forms of homosexual

353   See also Jeremiah 10:1-15; Isaiah 44:9-20.

acts with temple prostitutes and so as long as their same sex acts are not conducted in a ritualistic manner it cannot apply to them. Others argue that Paul is not saying that same sex acts are inherently sinful but only that they are contrary to custom, while others assert that the text only condemns those who act contrary to *their* nature; i.e. heterosexuals acting like homosexuals. We'll examine each of these and see how none of these interpretations does justice to the text.

Romans 1 Only Refers to Pagan Idolatrous Sex Acts

The importance of Romans 1:26-27 is that, like Leviticus 18:21 and 20:13, it does not use any potentially ambiguous phrases (such as *aresenokoitai*) or any unclear psychological terminology to describe the subjective state of mind of a person (such as "orientation") nor any slang terms for persons who commit same sex acts (such as "gay" or "homosexual"). Rather it is descriptive in that it refers to the objective actions of people so that we are certain as to what sort of activity is being described. Nor is there any danger of mistranslating the passage. Subsequently, many Gay Theology advocates, such as John Boswell, who want to escape the clear implication of the passage argue that the same sex acts depicted in Romans 1 only refer to idolaters who do not worship the one true God and have sex with homosexual cultic prostitutes (*kadeshim)* prohibited in Deuteronomy 23:17-18[354]:

> The remaining passage, Romans 1:26-27, does not suffer from mistranslation... It is sometimes argued that the significance of the passage lies in its connection to idolatry: i.e., that Paul censures the sexual behavior of the Romans because he associated such behavior with orgiastic pagan rites in honor of false gods. This might seem to be suggested by the Old Testament condemnation of temple prostitution, both homosexual and heterosexual, and it is reasonable to

---

[354] "None of the daughters of Israel shall be a cult prostitute, nor shall any of the sons of Israel be a cult prostitute (*kadeshim*). You shall not bring the hire of a harlot or the wages of a dog into the house of the LORD your God for any votive offering, for both of these are an abomination to the LORD your God" (Deuteronomy 23:17-18).

conjecture that he is warning the Romans against the immorality of the *kadeshim*. [355]

This argument is repeated by Rick Brentlinger, R.D. Weekly, Jeff
Miner and John Connoley,[356] David W. Shelton[357] and others such as Jack
Rogers who states, "...Paul's statement is about idolatry, not sexuality
per se... and Paul's writings also reflect many of the cultural assumptions of his time."[358] Yet one must wonder how Paul could be referring to
"the immorality of the *kadeshim*" if in fact the prohibitions of Leviticus,
according to them, are no longer binding on Christians. Furthermore, if,
as they insist, the so-called Holiness Code is not applicable to Gentile
Christians outside of Palestine how could Paul, the defender of the
Gentiles, then turn around and allude to that very same text in his warning to the church at Rome? John Boswell himself goes on to point out
errors of such an interpretation, which more recent advocates of Gay
Theology who selectively repeat his arguments, fail to notice:

> Under close examination, however, this argument proves to
> be inadequate. First of all, there is no reason to believe that
> homosexual temple prostitution was more prevalent than
> heterosexual or that Paul, had he been addressing himself
> to such practices, would have limited his comments to the
> former. It is clear that the sexual behavior itself is objec-
> tionable to Paul, not merely its associations. Third, and

355   John Boswell, *Christianity, Social Tolerance, and Homosexuality* (University
Of Chicago Press; 8th Edition. edition, 2005), 108.
356   Jeff Miner and John Connoley assert, "The model of homosexual behavior Paul
was addressing here is explicitly associated with idol worship (probably temple prostitution), and with people who, in an unbridled search for pleasure (or because of
religious rituals associated with their idolatry), broke away from their natural sexual
orientation, participating in promiscuous sex with anyone available." *The Children
Are Free* (Indianapolis, IN: Jesus Metropolitan Community Church, 2002), 14.
357   David W. Shelton states, "It all sounds pretty bad, doesn't it?... but is it talking
about Christians? What's more, is it talking about gay people? The answer to both questions is, 'no.'... In word, this entire chapter deals with idolatry. And the 'gay-bashing'
verses are about pagan practices in temple rites... Can we seriously believe that this
chapter addresses Christians who might be gay?" *The Rainbow Kingdom: Christianity
& the Homosexual Reconciled* (Lulu, 2006), 33.
358   Jack Rogers, *Jesus, The Bible, and Homosexuality* (Louisville, KY; Westminster John Knox Press, 2006), 76.

possibly most important, Paul is not describing cold-blood-
ed dispassionate acts performed in the interest of ritual or
ceremony: he states very clearly that the parties involved
'burned in their lust one toward another... it is unreason-
able to infer from the passage that there was any motive for
the behavior other than sexual desire.[359]

Boswell then tries to deflect the implications of his own assertions
by going on to assert that the main point of the text is not to "stigmatize
sexual behavior of any sort but to condemn Gentiles for their general infidelity... the reference to homosexuality is simply a mundane analogy to
this theological sin; it is patently not the crux of the argument."[360] What
Boswell failed to recognize is that none of the various sins mentioned
in Romans chapter 1 (greed, envy, murder, strife, deceit, malice, gossip,
slander, insolence, arrogance, boasting, disobedience to parents) are the
"crux of the argument" as if Paul is focusing on any one sin in particular.
Rather, that all of these are characteristics of the downward spiral of
someone who, without restraint, continues to suppress the knowledge
of the one true God and put in His place another false god, even if that
god is falsely called YHWH or Jesus Christ.

Ignoring Boswell's refutation of the "cultic prostitute argument"
Rick Brentlinger and others assert that Romans 1 only narrowly refers to
people outside of the covenant who participate in cultic homosexual sex
with male prostitutes.[361] Therefore, according to them, the text cannot be
applied to modern consensual monogamous homosexual relationships:

Idol worship, Moloch worship and shrine prostitution were
inextricably linked in the Jewish mind and in Paul's mind.
No believing Jew would divorce Leviticus 18:21 from

359   John Boswell, *Christianity, Social Tolerance, and Homosexuality* (University
Of Chicago Press; 8th Edition. edition, 2005), 108.
360   Ibid, 108-109.
361   Jeff Miner and John Connoley assert, "The model of homosexual behavior Paul
was addressing here is explicitly associated with idol worship (probably temple prostitution), and with people who, in an unbridled search for pleasure (or because of
religious rituals associated with their idolatry), broke away from their natural sexual
orientation, participating in promiscuous sex with anyone available." *The Children
Are Free* (Indianapolis, IN: Jesus Metropolitan Community Church, 2002), 14.

Leviticus 18:22 or fail to see the connection between the
verses.[362]

However, in making this assertion Brentlinger is contradicting himself and R. D. Weekly who insist that nothing in the Holiness Code,
particularly Leviticus 18:22 and 20:13, is applicable to the Gentiles
outside of the land of Israel who are not in the Mosaic Covenant. How
could Paul have Leviticus 18:22 in mind when he wrote Romans 1:26-
27 if in fact that text is not applicable to anyone outside of the land of
Israel in another era? Rick Brentlinger goes on to argue, repeating his
fallacious axiom, that relevant texts cannot be applied to modern same
sex relationships:

> If Paul was not referring to every form of homosexuality in
> general when he wrote Romans 1, then Romans 1 cannot
> be referring to homosexuality in general now. If exclu-
> sive, monogamous homosexual relationships between
> Christians were not commonly known in the first century,
> then exclusive monogamous homosexual relationships are
> not the focus of Paul's argument in Romans 1.[363]

The issue at hand is not whether Paul specifically had in mind "monogamous homosexual relationships" but whether the principle can be
applied to such sexual activity and if we can see a similar pattern of
spiritual and moral decline described Romans 1 in the Gay Theology
movement. All the various adjectives and behaviors that of those who
are "suppressing the truth in unrighteousness" (Romans 1:18) describes
those have "exchanged the glory of the incorruptible God for an image
in the form of corruptible man and of birds and four-footed animals and
crawling creatures" (Romans 1:23). Yet, modern western atheists who
deny the existence of God even though, as Paul states "since the creation of the world His invisible attributes, His eternal power and divine
nature, have been clearly seen, being understood through what has been
made" (Romans 1:20), do not carve idols of beasts from wood or stone
as did the pagans of the first century. While Hindus or some idolaters in

---

362   Rick Brentlinger, *Gay Christian 101 - Spiritual Self-Defense For Gay Christians* (2007), 287.
363   Ibid, 288

animistic cultures might behave this way, it can hardly be said that the average American or European atheist who pays his taxes, is faithful to his wife, donates money to charity organizations, assists his elderly grandmother, is generally friendly towards his neighbors meets the description of Paul as being "full of envy, murder, strife" (Romans 1:29) or participates in overt idolatrous activities or visits temple prostitutes. The reality is there are many unbelievers who are really nice people who may even behave (at least outwardly in public) better than some Christians. This does not mean that because the idolaters described by Paul do not match every aspect of modern unbelievers that they are not "suppressing the truth in unrighteousness." More than likely, not *all* unbelievers in Paul's day fit this description and there are also Christians who at times commit some of the sins he mentioned such as being "full of envy, murder, strife, deceit, malice… gossip" (Romans 1:29). In fact, the apostle had to rebuke and warn the "saints" at Corinth who committed such sins, some of which "does not exist even among the Gentiles" (1 Corinthians 5:1).

The Apostle Paul is giving us the extreme and obvious result of the noetic effects of sin, in denying that the God of the Bible exists.[364] Yet, the principle or spiritual truth of the text is applicable to modern atheists and other types of unbelievers even if they bear some form of civil righteousness in being upstanding citizens in society. In a similar manner, even if Paul has specifically in mind the literal pagan idolaters of his day as seen in Athens (Acts 17:16) or in Rome the spiritual truth applies to the modern unbeliever. If he is not worshipping the one true God then he is an idolater for someone or something else is a "god" in his life even if he never steps one foot into a church, synagogue, temple or shrine. Therefore the theological and spiritual principle that Paul is discussing in Romans chapter 1, that those who do not worship the one true God are suppressing the truth, applies to *all* unbelievers even if the details depicted in this text does not describe their behavior to the letter. In fact, someone may even worship a god which they refer to as the One true God that brought Israel out of Egypt, and yet they are worshipping a false god as did the Israelites (Exodus 32; 1 Kings 12:28-21). They may even claim to worship Jesus Christ, and Paul made it clear that

---

364 The noetic effects of sin are the ways that sin negatively affects and undermines the human mind and intellect, particularly when the human mind suppresses the *sensus divinitatis* - the sense of knowledge of the Divine.

there were many false Christs in his own day (2 Corinthians 11:4). The Jesus of Mormonism and the Watchtower Bible and Tract Society is a different Jesus than that of the Bible and historical Christianity. As we shall later see, so is the Jesus Christ of Gay Theology.

Likewise, Paul's description of them becoming enslaved or "given over" to homosexual lust is applicable today. This is true whether homosexual sex is conducted with a shrine prostitute in a ritualistic form in dedication to a Canaanite deity, in worship of a Greek goddess, or between consensual partners in the Metropolitan Community Churches who also worship the goddess Sophia, incorporate Buddhism and Native American spirituality in their corporate worship. If the sexual activity described in Leviticus 18:22 and Romans 1:26-27 takes place in non-cultic context the principle of the text and what is taking place still applies. The principle of the moral requirement of the commandment in Leviticus 18:22 and the description of the spiritual condition of the person who is "suppressing the truth in unrighteousness" is transcultural. Otherwise, nothing that anyone says about anything in the Bible applies to anyone or any other culture outside of its immediate cultural context.

Furthermore, the Gay Theology argument assumes that Christians are immune from committing acts of idolatry by either wholeheartedly worshipping images or by incremental compromise blending the Christian faith with various forms of pagan idolatry. But history and the current activities that take place within Gay-affirming churches such as the MCC demonstrates just the contrary. This theology has already resulted in overt obvious acts of idolatry as well as the homosexual act being an act of rebellion against God's revealed will and thereby an idolatrous act in its very nature.

Finally, can we say that we are free to be involved in any of the various actions that Paul says are the result of being "given over" such as being "full of envy, murder, strife, deceit, malice… gossip" (Romans 1:29) so long as it isn't done in participation of a ritualistic act of pagan worship? Suffice it to say, there isn't one thing mentioned by Paul that is the result of suppressing the revelation of God that can be considered righteous or good in any context. Nor is there anything mentioned that a Christian is immune from falling into if he hardens his heart, suppresses the truth of God's Word or denies that Christians are obliged to obey the law of God. This very trajectory is taking place in the Gay Theology movement as its followers go from the historic Christian faith to a modern "spirituality" and subsequently engage in all sorts of devious same sex acts. This is why Paul had to warn the Christians at Corinth, "Do not be deceived…" (1 Corinthians 6:9).

Romans 1 Only Refers to A Cultural Taboo

Probably one of the weakest arguments concerning God's wrath upon idolaters who are given over to enslavement to homosexual lust is that such behaviors is not a sin but rather a mere cultural taboo. This same argument is made concerning same-sex acts in Leviticus 18 and 20, but then one would have to ask, "Why does God legislate the death penalty for a behavior if its abhorrence is merely a culturally bound taboo and not considered an inherently sinful act by God Himself?" Yet Daniel Helminiak asserts that, "Romans may refer to same sex-acts, but it intends no ethical condemnation of them."[365] He then goes on to argue that the word used to describe the appalling act indicates that such acts were less than sinful:

> …the Greek word translated as 'degrading' is *atimia*. It means something 'not highly valued,' 'not held in honor,' 'not respected.' 'Ill reputed' or 'socially unacceptable' also convey the sense of the word.
>
> That is the very same sense in which Paul commonly uses that word. For example, 2 Corinthians 6:8 and 11:21, Paul applies that word to himself. He notes that he is sometimes held in disrepute or shame because of his commitment to Christ. Evidentially, then, to be in *atimia* is not necessarily a bad thing.[366]

Whether *atimia* is to be considered a sin depends on who is making the judgment. To be considered *atimia* by the world because of Christ, such as in Paul's case in which he refers to himself in this manner is not a

---

365   Daniel Helminiak, *What the Bible Really Says About Homosexuality* (Estancia, NM: Alamo Square Press, 2000), 90.
366   Daniel Helminiak, *What the Bible Really Says About Homosexuality* (Estancia, NM: Alamo Square Press, 2000), 90.

sin (2 Corinthians 6:8; 11:21). However, concerning such people whose vile passions and behavior are *atimia* Paul says, "…that those who practice such things are worthy of death, they not only do the same, but also give hearty approval to those who practice them" (Romans 1:32). It is amazing how Gay Theology advocates beat the drum of interpreting a text within its context and yet they immediately go on to rip the meaning of a word out of its immediate context and insist on inserting a meaning of the word from a text where it is used differently.

Many Gay Theology advocates will also argue that *atimia* is a culturally bound word that only refers to something which is contrary to custom. Borrowing from Paul's use of the word in 1 Corinthians 11:14 they will point out that the issue of a man having long hair is also referred to as *atimia*, "…according to the biblical evidence, same-sex sex is more analogous to things like long hair on a man or women preachers than it is to moral wrongs like adultery or prostitution."[367] In doing so they miss the point. Paul's argument in 1 Corinthians 11:14 is concerning men looking like women as he states, "Does not even nature itself teach you that if a man has long hair, it is a dishonor (*atimia*) to him." The fact that both same-sex acts and having long hair which results in a man looking like a woman are *atimia* does not mean that these two things are morally equivalent. A person who violates a traffic speed limit and a person who commits rape are law-breakers. But it could hardly be said that the two are morally equivalent just because the two actions are both violations of the law. The one unlawful act, (murder) is inherently morally evil while the other is culturally relevant and determined by the state and therefore it is amendable, such as when California highway speed limits were changed from 55 to 65 miles per hour. The seriousness of the *atimia* of a man having longer hair may indeed be according to social custom. As to what constitutes excessive length of hair may be culturally bound just as "excessive" speed limits are locally determined and amendable. But this does not mean it is morally equivalent to engaging in homogenital acts. Men having sex with other men are an inherently immoral act for it does not merely disgust the Jew, the enslavement to such acts is a judgment of God. This lustful enslavement that one may be given over to is the result of suppressing the revelation of God, whether in the created order or in the Scriptures,

367   R.D. Weekly, *The Rebuttal: A Biblical Response Exposing Deceptive Logic of Anti-Gay Theology* (Judah First Ministries, 2011), 99.

which provokes the wrath of God. Therefore, like the Hebrew word *toevah* it is the context in which the word *atimia* is used that determines the seriousness of the act being considered dishonorable.

Taking the connotation of *atima* from 1 Corinthians 11:14, 2 Corinthians 6:8 or 11:21 and inserting it into Romans 1 is referred to as the hermeneutical fallacy of collapsing context. In committing this fallacy an interpreter takes two passages that use the same word, ignores the fact that the word is being used differently in the two passages and then imports that meaning from one text to the other. For example, if I were to read texts that spoke of a squirrel hiding a peanut in a trunk of a tree, a man putting a peanut in the trunk of his automobile and an elephant picking up a peanut with his trunk it would be erroneous to take the one meaning of "trunk" and import it into the other texts. Even though all three texts use the words "peanut" and "trunk" the context in which the words are used are radically different. The only thing that one can derive from these three texts is that "trunk" has a lexical range that can include the base of a tree, the front end of an elephant, and the back end of an automobile. But we are not free to read various dictionary meanings of a word and then pick and choose which one we think will best suit our argument. We must do justice to the meaning of a word within its own immediate context. From the context of Romans 1, it is clear that *atima* associated with homosexual behavior and the other sins mentioned results in not merely a social stigma but in coming under the wrath of God.

Romans 1 Only Refers to Acts Contrary to Jewish Cultural Custom

Another argument used to assert that same-sex acts depicted in Romans 1 are not inherently evil but rather they are mere contrary to cultural convention focuses on the phrase "contrary to nature" (Romans 1:26). It is argued that the Greek words *para physis* in this text often translated "against nature" (KJV) or "unnatural" (NRSV), again borrowing from 1 Corinthians 11:14, means "contrary to custom" or "out of the ordinary":

Since nature and against nature are cultural constructs in 1
Corinthians 11, is it possible natural and against nature are
cultural constructs in Romans 1 and not universal natural
laws?... Does against nature sometimes involve a cultural
component, as in 1 Corinthians 11:14? Clearly the answer
is Yes.[368]

Martti Nissinen likewise argues that "contrary to nature" does not
refer to that which is contrary to God's created order, but merely that
which is not in accord with Jewish custom:

In antiquity, *physis* expresses a fundamental cultural role
or a conventional, proper, or inborn character or appearance, or the true being of a person or a thing rather than
"nature" in a genetic biological sense, as a modern reader
would perceive it. Accordingly, "unnatural" is a synonym
for "(seriously) unconventional."[369]

The fallacy of this line of reasoning is that it borrows a meaning
of the word "nature" in one text in which it is being used differently,
even by the same author, than in the present text under consideration.
It is not enough to find other words in the two contexts that are similar;
one must determine the meaning in the use of the word by taking into
consideration the genre of the text and other factors as well. For example, if a word is being used metaphorically in one text and concretely in
another, one cannot immediately import a metaphorical use of the word
into the other text. Many Gay Theology advocates wrongly borrow the
use of the meaning of *physis* from 1 Corinthians 11:14 and import it into
Romans 1 such as R. D. Weekly when he states:

In making his argument against men with long hair, Paul
appealed to nature itself. He made the very same appeal
in Romans 1, when he called same-sex sexual activity

---

368   Rick Brentlinger, *Gay Christian 101 - Spiritual Self-Defense For Gay Christians* (2007), 298, 299.
369   Martti Nissinen, *Homoeroticism in the Biblical World* (Augsburg Fortress Publishers, 1998), 105.

"against nature" (v. 26) and opposite-sex sexual activity "natural" (v. 27). Yet, although nature has not changed in the 1,950 years since Paul wrote 1 Cor 11:14-15, we do not consider men with long hair unnatural in the vast majority of modern churches. In fact, we don't care how long a man's hair is, nor should we...

Interestingly, God Himself also did things "against nature"... He also did something "against nature" when He grafted Gentile believers into the covenantal tree (Ro 11:24); yet I don't hear anyone claiming that Gentile Christians (the vast majority) are an abomination simply because we are "against nature." Obviously, an appeal to nature in validation of an argument is not intended to apply an absolute expression of divine intentions. A cultural argument is still a cultural argument, even when nature itself is appealed to in making the argument.[370]

Again, just as in the case of the use of *atimia*, to take the connotation of the word "nature" as it is used in 1 Corinthians 11:14 and Romans 11:24 then argue that it means the same thing in Romans 1 is the hermeneutical fallacy of collapsing context. In Romans 11:24 Paul is talking about the inclusion of the Gentiles into the people God by using an agricultural metaphor, as if Gentiles were a wild vine being engrafted into Israel. But if Paul were referring to a literal engrafting of two olive trees or grape vines (one of which is wild), then *atimia* would indeed mean "contrary to the biological order" which would not support the Gay Theological argument. The only difference then would be that in Romans 11:24 God is doing a gracious act by engrafting the Gentiles in keeping with His promise of Abraham whereas in Romans 1:26-27 those who are being given over to the depravity of their mind and their unrighteousness have "abandoned the natural *function* of the woman" not that they have abandoned social customs.

Letha Scanzoni and Virginia Mollenkott likewise assert that Paul's use of the phrase "against nature" only refers to that which is out of the ordinary for the Jewish worldview, hence it refers to that which is against Jewish custom:

370   R.D. Weekly, *Homosexianity* (Judah First Ministries, 2009), 37.

What seems "natural" in any culture is often simply a matter of accepted social custom; and sometimes Paul spoke
of nature in that way... In the Greek and Roman culture
of the time in which Paul wrote, however, homosexual
conduct was to some extent an accepted social custom, and
it no doubt seemed neither "against nature" nor "against
custom" to some people. Thus, it would have made little
sense to speak of against nature in the sense of generally
agreed-upon social custom convention, unless Paul was
referring to a violation of Jewish custom and law.[371]

If Paul's use of "against nature" in only speaking of being contrary
to a Jewish custom, this begs the question as to why God's wrath against
idolatry would result in Gentiles being "given over" (*paradidomi*) to a
Gentile custom that was (according to the Roman-Greco culture) perfectly acceptable and "natural" to their inclinations. As Gay theologians
are quick to point out, the distinctively Jewish customs were not applicable to Gentiles who were outside the Mosaic Covenant and "without
the law." Furthermore, if the prohibition is part of what is commonly
referred to as a ceremonial law, why would God judge idolaters by turning them over to the enslavement to a transgression of a defunct purity
law that was never applicable to them in the first place?

Romans 1 Only Refers to Heterosexuals
Behaving Like Homosexuals

Another argument that Gay Theologians assert in order to dodge the
implications of Romans 1:26 is to argue that Paul is only referring to
heterosexuals who act contrary to their "natural" orientation and consequently behave like homosexuals. Whereas the last argument centered
on the word *atimia* this argument focuses on the Greek word *physis* in
which Paul asserts that the homosexual acts are contrary to "nature."
John Boswell asserts:

> Paul believed that the Gentiles knew of the truth of God
> but rejected it and likewise rejected their true "nature" as

371   Letha Scanzoni, Virginia Mollenkott, *Is The Homosexual My Neighbor?* (San
Francisco, CA: Harper, 1994), 68.

regarded their sexual appetites, going beyond what was "natural" for them and what was approved for the Jews. It cannot be inferred from this that Paul considered mere homoerotic attraction or practice morally reprehensible, since the passage strongly implies that he was not discussing persons who were by inclination gay and since he carefully observed, in regard to both the women and the men, that they exchanged or abandoned the 'natural use' to engage in homosexual activities.[372]

Gay Theology advocates often repeat Boswell's argument which asserts that Paul is not referring to people who were born homosexual but rather Paul is stating that those who are "naturally" heterosexual "exchange" their "natural" behavior for homosexual behavior which is not approved of by God. This entire argument revolves around the word "natural" (*physin*). The self-identified gay man feels like having sex with other men, then having classified such homoerotic desires as a biological variance within the created order he believes that such actions are "natural" to him. In fact, some Gay Theology advocates assert that it is wrong for a "natural" homosexually oriented person to act contrary to his homosexual "nature" by marrying or having sex with someone of the opposite sex claiming, "It would be unnatural for most homosexuals to have heterosexual sex."[373]

If Paul is merely stating that it is wrong for "natural" heterosexuals to engage in homosexual sex then how would anyone ever know if a person is "naturally" heterosexual if they are having homosexual sex? How would Paul ever know whether or not a heterosexual was acting "unnaturally" or a "natural" homosexual acting "naturally"? Sarah Ruden rightly observes that this is an absurd notion, "I'm trying as hard as I can to picture Paul standing outside the assembly, like a bouncer at a nightclub, scanning with his gaydar (keen or otherwise) for the mere metrosexuals."[374]

---

372   John Boswell, *Christianity, Social Tolerance, and Homosexuality* (University Of Chicago Press; 8th Edition. edition, 2005), 113.

373   David W. Shelton, *The Rainbow Kingdom: Christianity & the Homosexual Reconciled* (Lulu, 2006), 36.

374   Sarah Ruden, *Paul Among the People: The Apostle Reinterpreted and Reimagined in His Own Time* (New York, NY: Pantheon, 2010) 47.

Paul is not saying that they are acting contrary to their customary sexual desires, rather they are acting contrary to their nature of being man (*arsenes*) and woman (*thelias*) (Romans 1:27). The men have left the created order of sex with a woman and turned to having sex with a man. Earlier Paul refers to the revelation of God as being seen and understood having been revealed since the creation of the world (Romans 1:20). Clearly Paul has Genesis 1-3 in mind and he will soon again refer to this text in Romans chapter 5. In fact, Paul is alluding to the Septuagint translation of Genesis 1-3 as the two terms used here (*arsenes* and *thelias*) are reflective of the creation of man and woman as Robert Gagnon states, "…Paul was thinking of 'nature' not as 'the way things are usually done' (i.e. cultural convention) but rather as 'the material shape of the created order.'" [375]

Paul is not making an appeal to Natural Law as a means for making moral decisions, but to the natural revelation of God's attributes which when suppressed leads to the abandonment of the created order of Genesis 1-2. He is not referring to the subjective feelings of a person (his so-called "orientation"), but rather the objective actions of a person. Paul is talking about what a man does with another man and what a woman does with another woman, in that the male same-sex act is contrary to the "natural function of a woman" (Romans 1:27). Paul says absolutely nothing concerning the subjective orientation of a person but only addresses the desire for this form of sex as being "contrary to nature" which is that they "exchanged the natural function." There is nothing in this text to suggest he even recognized such a thing as a "true" homosexual versus a "false" homosexual. He simply describes the homogenital act as unnatural, no matter who is committing the sin. To read the subjective psychological disposition into the issue is to read into the text. Finally, in order to be consistent if the "orientation" interpretation is assumed then the other sins mentioned can only refer to those who do them contrary to their "nature" subjectively defined. Therefore, others sins such as "envy, murder, strife, deceit, malice…" are only prohibited if a person is doing them contrary to their natural inclination.

---

375   Robert A. J. Gagnon, *The Bible And Homosexual Practice* (Nashville, TN: Abingdon Press, 2001), 256.

Paul Was Ignorant of Modern Same Sex Relationships

Another closely related argument is that Paul was homo-ignorant of mutual non-exploitative or cultic same sex relationships and therefore in his mind he could only associate homogenital acts with idolatry due to his limited experience. R.D. Weekly insists that "...every time Paul referenced same sex sexual acts, he unfailingly conjoined them to idolatry... according to Paul, those particular acts were a result of idolatrous beliefs..."[376] He then equates Paul's association of homosexual acts with a black American's distain for the Confederate Flag because of its historical and cultural association with slavery and the cruel treatment of black Americans in the south. He then admits, "It's certainly true that in the text, the adjectives (*atimas*/degrading, *para phusin*/unnatural, and *aschemosunin*/indecent) described the acts themselves, not idolatry they flowed from..." but then still insists that "Paul hated idolatry and found same-sex intercourse sordid, at least in part, because of its association with idolatry."[377] Therefore, just as the flag isn't inherently wrong, it is only because of its association with slavery that many black people kind it offensive, so too same-sex acts are not offensive when disassociated with overt forms of idolatry.[378]

In making this argument, Weekly asserts that Romans 1 can only be understood in the light of Paul's limited knowledge of Roman Bacchanalia and that he had no knowledge of anything akin to modern-day homosexual relationships. He argues that because Paul had limited experience with same-sex relationships he would not have

---

376 R.D. Weekly, *The Rebuttal: A Biblical Response Exposing Deceptive Logic of Anti-Gay Theology* (Judah First Ministries, 2011), 114-115.

377 Ibid, 115.

378 R.D. Weekly states, "The connections Paul used when referencing same-sex sexual activity undeniable establishes that in his mind, idolatry and same-sex intercourse were inextricably linked. Even if the acts were not committed in Bacchanalia or other forms of idolatrous worship, he still believed that they were developed in a person's life as a result of his/her association with an idolatrous culture. He didn't see the acts as originating from inner desires that a person is born with, or otherwise develops outside of conscious choice, as those who understand the nature of sexual orientation realize today. It simply means that his perception was colored by his social context, much as it was when he opposed certain styles of women's dress (1 Ti. 2:9-10), women speaking in church or teaching men (1 Ti. 2:11-12), or even having long hair (1 Co. 11:14)." *The Rebuttal: A Biblical Response Exposing Deceptive Logic of Anti-Gay Theology* (Judah First Ministries, 2011), 111.

approved of any same sex acts, "The adjectives employed can only lead us to conclude that his concept was not isolated to acts within a particular context, but to the acts in general. Still, the context makes in abundantly clear that Paul didn't believe any other context existed."[379] In other words, according to Weekly, if Paul had experienced modern life-long homosexual committed relationships his perception of such acts would be changed. Therefore, according to him, the entirety of Romans 1 can be ignored as the perception of someone who was essentially homo-ignorant for, "Roman idolatry and Bacchanalia no longer characterize our culture. Consequently, Paul's view of the acts is now wholly obsolete..."[380]

However, Biblical evidence clearly indicates that Paul does not strictly link homogenital acts with idolatry. In 1 Corinthians 6:9 Paul lists idolaters in between fornicators and adulterers, not between the *malakoi* and *arsenokotai* ("men who have sex with other men"). Therefore, homogenital acts is no more strictly linked to overt forms of idolatry than is fornicating and adultery. In 1 Timothy 1:10 Paul lists *arsenokotai* ("men who have sex with other men") with those who kill their fathers or mothers, murderers, immoral men, kidnappers, liars and perjurers. Idolatry is not even explicitly mentioned in the text.

Similar to this argument, other Gay Theology proponents assert that Paul was a male chauvinist who was ignorant of modern "homogeniality." In other words, Paul wasn't homophobic but rather "homo-ignorant" due to being subject to a primitive pre-enlightenment worldview:

> Some people think the Bible and its writers were homophobic, especially Paul. To coin a word, I think they were homo-ignorant. Attempting to reconcile first and second century understanding of sexuality into a modern framework is virtually impossible. What the apostle Paul, his Christian contemporaries, and the society around him believed about sexuality would be rejected as ridiculous

---

379   R.D. Weekly, *The Rebuttal: A Biblical Response Exposing Deceptive Logic of Anti-Gay Theology* (Judah First Ministries, 2011), 111-112.
380   R.D. Weekly, *The Rebuttal: A Biblical Response Exposing Deceptive Logic of Anti-Gay Theology* (Judah First Ministries, 2011), 112.

myth by even the most conservative, prudish Christian today. Though homosexuality existed, it was not scientifically understood.[381]

They will then assert that since Paul was subject to the primitive understanding of sexuality of his time he mistakenly believed that God turned idolaters into homosexuals:

> These conducts which Paul condemns are the result of God's anger, not the reason for that anger [God turns idolaters into homosexuals]. In Paul's mind, the reason for sexual relations is a divinely constructed plan for males and females to reproduce. To Paul, sex has no other purpose. Pleasure was not part of Paul's vocabulary when it came to discussing sex. To his cultural mindset, the vices he lists are the manifestations of God's wrath for idolatrous behavior. Same sex activity, at least to Paul was 'so self-evidently contrary to God's creative purpose as to allow of such brief mention' allowing his readers to instant comprehension... Paul is simply highlighting a given, based on his worldview of society in which he lived and to which he wrote...[382]

As one whose understanding of sexuality was limited to the thinking of his time, Paul's only concern was for procreative sex and therefore he wrongly assumed that anything but procreative sex would make God angry. We can conclude therefore Romans 1 only refers to idolatrous homosexuality as understood in a paternalistic culture:

> In that society to which Paul is writing, there was a very strong link between idolatry and sexual conduct though to be pleasing to the 'gods' that were worshipped... Paul was also tapping into the concept of a paternalistic society

---

381   Samuel Kader, *Openly Gay, Openly Christian: How the Bible Really Is Gay Friendly* (San Francisco, CA: Leyland Publications, 1999), 69.

382   John F. Dwyer, *Those 7 References: A Study of 7 References to Homosexuality In The Bible* (John F. Dwyer, 2007), 52.

where gender and roles were interwoven, with females being dominated by males. Same sex relations would blur the lines of these gender role distinctions important to that societal culture, and would be easily recognized by the readers of Paul's letter as not fitting for the community they were trying to build and maintain... In that Greco-Roman world in which the community to which Paul was writing existed, same sex relations was a given. It was a part of the cultural life, the religious life, and the political life. In that surrounding culture, 'natural intercourse meant the penetration of a subordinate person by a dominant one.' Paul is aiming to affirm values of sex for purposes of 'pro-creation only' by pointing to the conduct of a community surrounding them which followed a different norm.[383]

They then conclude that the texts can be dismissed as the assertions of a primitive man who was unenlightened and was only reflecting his own ignorance, the prejudice of his own culture in a pre-scientific era:

> The kind of sexual activity that existed at the time Paul was writing from a patriarchal, male dominated viewpoint in a society severely stratified by class and role and status. Those in the lower strata of society were treated unequally and abusively: an important lens through which under-standing this text must be viewed. The loving natures of relationships that exist and underpin current understanding of relationships between people today, whether hetero-sexual or homosexual, were not known to Paul, but there existed a mindset that tolerated a taking of another individ-ual, of what we would consider rape and abusive misuse of others... This is a very different societal construct then the 21ˢᵗ Century understanding of the world and how healthy sexual relationships function...[384]

---

383   Ibid, 55.
384   John F. Dwyer, *Those 7 References: A Study of 7 References to Homosexuality In The Bible* (John F. Dwyer, 2007), 57.

Martti Nissinen operating from this same assumption concerning Paul then asserts, "...he was scarcely aware that he was participating in the making of Holy Scripture..." [385] and then he concludes:

> It would be most appropriate to let Paul be Paul – a human being, an educated Jewish theologian converted to faith in Christ... and who might have needed sexual therapy as much as any of us. Paul might be best contribute to today's conversation when understood in this way.[386]

The problem with this line of argument is that it contradicts their arguments for a positive presentation of supposed loving homosexual relationships that were known to Paul in the history of the Old Testament as well as his own day. If, as other Gay Theology proponents assert, Ruth and Naomi as well David and Jonathan were gays and lesbians then it cannot be argued that Paul was homo-ignorant of these supposed non-cultic, non-exploitative relationships. But even if some Gay Theology advocates disagree with their fellow LGBT theology advocates concerning the nature of these relationships, to assert that being homosexually inclined is genetic and that homosexual relationships are not contrary to the law of God then, assuming same sex attractions is not a new phenomenon, Paul must have known in his own day of Jews and Christians who were in such relationships. The reality is, if we understand Paul's writings with the Greco-Roman culture, as they insist, there is abundant evidence that there were in his own day relationships that were similar to that of modern gays.[387] All of which were condemned by the teaching of the Apostle Paul.

---

385   Martti Nissinen, *Homoeroticism in the Biblical World* (Augsburg Fortress Publishers, 1998), 103.
386   Ibid, 125.
387   Craig A. Williams states, "...the sources left to us from ancient Rome make it abundantly clear that Roman traditions fell squarely in line with the worldwide trend: homosexual behavior was not condemned per se, and a citizen could admit to sexual experience with males in certain contexts and configurations without fear of ridicule or reprisal, without the threat even of a raised eyebrow." *Roman Homosexuality* (Oxford University Press, USA; 2 edition, 2010), 17.

Romans 1 Only Refers to Acts Contrary to Natural Law

One of the most popular arguments *against* Gay Theology is that Paul's argument in Romans 1 is based on "natural law." According to those who make this argument the natural order provides us with a necessary ethic that reveals the will of God apart from Scripture. In short, it argues that one can derive an ethical "ought" from an ontological "is" from the created order without any transcendent Authority who reveals His will. From this line of argument, it is asserted that if we look to the anatomical design of the human body we find the intended purpose for its use. Therefore, even Gentiles who do not have the revealed moral law of God ought to be able to deduce from the created order that God exists and that homosexual behavior is contrary to how God has designed the human body and His intended purpose for it.

Robert Gagnon in his book *The Bible and Homosexual Practice: Texts and Hermeneutics* argues that Romans chapter 1 is grounded in the creation account of Genesis chapter 1 and a Greek notion of Natural Law, in which one is able to develop a justifiable system of ethics apart from God's divine revelation of His will as he states, "Even those who do not accept the revelatory authority of Scripture should be able to perceive the divine will through the testimony of the structure of creation."[388] He then later concludes that, "Acceptance of biblical revelation is thus not a prerequisite for rejecting the legitimacy of same-sex intercourse."[389] Most theonomists, such as R.J. Rushdoony, recognize the naturalistic fallacy of "Natural Law" and therefore reject it as a justifiable means of governing society. [390] However, there are some such as Greg Bahnsen who make a similar argument as Gagnon regarding Natural Law:

> ...it is incorrect to think that only Christians are aware of those moral standards by which the effects of homosexuality are evaluated. The law of God by which the Christians judges these matters is known, although not explicitly acknowledged, by *all* men whether they are Christians or

---

388   Robert Gagnon, *The Bible and Homosexual Practice: Texts and Hermeneutics* (Nashville, TN: Abingdon Press, 2000), 37.

389   Ibid, 488.

390   R.J. Rushdoony, "Natural Law and Canon Law" in *The Roots of Reconstruction* (Vallecito, Ross House Books, 1991), 249-253.

not, as Paul teaches in Romans 1:32 and 2:14, 15. God's standards reflect His moral character, and every man is the image of God; moreover every man lives in an environment through which God is continually, silently, clearly revealed. Therefore men are totally without excuse for failing to submit to the truth about Him and His moral demands; they have sufficient provision to acknowledge the standards of God's law, but perversely refuse to do so. It is incorrect to think that by going to God's Word in order to decide whether homosexuality is a crime, believers are trying to enforce a distinctly Christian ethic among unbelievers.[391]

Gagnon, like Bahnsen, then argues that behind Paul's argument is the idea of the Natural Law that provides "the simple recognition of a 'fittedness' of the sex organs, male to female."[392] Therefore, "Paul's own reasoning, grounded in divinely-given clues in nature" is the source for Paul's view of idolatry, the heinousness of same sex acts and the other consequences of suppressing the truth of God's existence.[393] He also states that the Old Testament Holiness Code also "was responding to the conviction that same-sex intercourse was fundamentally incompatible with the creation of men and women as anatomically complementary sexual beings."[394]

According to Gagnon, unbelievers, as well as Jews and Christians, find "the material creation around human beings and the bodily design of humans themselves, guiding us into the truth about the nature of God and the nature of human sexuality respectively."[395] Gagnon then follows his commitment to Natural Law consistently to its roots in Thomas Aquinas and Aristotle. He believes that Paul's reference to "by nature" in Romans 2:14 refers to "the natural faculty of reason implanted by the Creator in human bodies."[396] Paul, according to Gagnon, proclaims that

391   Greg Bahnsen, *Homosexuality: A Biblical View* (Grand Rapids, MI: Baker, 1978), 113.
392   Robert Gagnon, *The Bible and Homosexual Practice: Texts and Hermeneutics* (Nashville, TN: Abingdon Press, 2000), 364.
393   Ibid, 142.
394   Ibid, 157.
395   Ibid, 391.
396   Ibid, 371.

both God and ethical human behavior can be known through observing the created natural order.

As much as I appreciate many of Gagnon's exegetical observations and agree with his assessment that same-sex acts are contrary to the will of God, as I have stated elsewhere his view of the Scriptures undermines rather than bolsters the foundation of the Christian worldview. Likewise, his view of Natural Law undermines rather than bolsters Biblical ethics. Scripture points to God's revelation as our source for Biblical obligation for He is both fact and value, ontology and morality.[397] In other words, God *is* holy (as well as many other moral attributes) and is the essence of holiness for He is not deemed holy by a standard of holiness outside of Himself. Only in God does His "is" necessitate an "ought." Outside of Him one cannot derive moral obligations from natural facts because facts outside of God are not holy, good, just or righteous in and of themselves. Even before the fall Adam and Eve needed the Word of God in order to understand the moral obligation not to eat of the forbidden tree. If right and wrong can be determined according to Natural Law and apparent design, then given the design of the fruit of the tree it would have been right to assume that eating it would have been lawful. Furthermore, in a fallen creation one cannot assume that how things are reflect their intended design or original purpose as Gary North states:

> Cursed nature is not normative, any more than fallen man is. We cannot look to nature and discover absolute standards of thought, absolute standards of law, or absolute standards of judgment. Even if cursed nature were normative, perverse men would misinterpret nature. If Adam rebelled against the verbal revelation of God Himself, before he fell into sin, what should we expect from the sons of Adam, now that nature is cursed and no longer the same kind of revelation of God that was in the garden? It still testifies of God, as we read in Romans 1:18; man holds back the truth in active unrighteousness. But cursed nature is not the same open revelation of God that it once was, and we dare not use nature as an ethical, political, or any other kind of guidepost for building human institutions. We have to

397   John Frame, *Doctrine of the Christian Life* (Phillipsburg, NJ, P&R Publishing, 2008), 96.

abandon 'natural law' as a course of reliable information. Nature is cursed, and we are ethical rebels, spoiling for a fight or a misinterpretation. That is why we need the revelation of God in His word, the Bible and through His Word, Jesus Christ.[398]

In essence, Robert Gagnon has confused *natural revelation*, in which creation which reveals the existence of God, with *natural law* which is a flawed assertion that one can derive and justifiable ethical system of what *ought* to be from what *is* in existence. In fact, many Gay Theology advocates use this same form of argument for the "fittedness" of same-sex acts. They assert that the intended design for the human sexual organs is not merely procreation but also for pleasure and when homosexuals commit anal sex they may in fact be making use of that particular intended design:

> If biology indicates God's intentions, why do men (and men alone) have a sexual gland (the prostate) located within the body, flush with the inner anal cavity, which provides sexual gratification when stimulated through an anal probe? It seems that if any would be sexually stimulated through a probe of the inner body, it would be women, since they 'obviously' were the ones intended by God to be penetrated.[399]

In a similar fashion, a polygamist might also argue that it is very apparent that the human male is able to produce far more sperm that any single woman is able to make use of in child bearing. A woman's ability to give birth to children is set within a limited number of years (early teens to perhaps late-forties) whereas most men beyond the stage of puberty are able to continue to achieve arousal and produce semen for the rest of their lives. It might then be argued that according to the perceived design of the male anatomy as well the vitality of his libido would indicate that God intended for men to not be limited to one woman as a sexual partner.

---

398   Gary North, *Unconditional Surrender* (Institute for Christian Economics; 3 edition June 1983), 38.
399   R.D. Weekly, *Homosexianity* (Judah First Ministries, 2009), 217.

It also must be pointed out that the Song of Solomon, written by a polygamist, speaks a great deal concerning the pleasure of sexual love without a hint of mentioning an intention for bearing children. Consequently, it might be argued that since pleasure is more often than not accompanying the sexual act whereas procreation is only a limited function of the sexual act. This is keenly seen in the case of those who are infertile or beyond child-bearing years. In fact, even in heterosexual unions the consummation of the sex act does not always result in conception. We might deduce then, based on the design of the sexual organs, their capacity to function far beyond the capacity to produce children that the primary purpose for sex is pleasure, emotional bonding and other psychological benefits and not procreation. Therefore these other functions of the sex act are just as much if not more than a procreative function of sexual unions. Subsequently, it might be argued that while the homosexual sex act between committed partners cannot bear children, it does fulfill these other roles as much as heterosexual sex acts between committed partners; i.e. a husband and wife. In fact, many theologians who are not in support of Gay Theology assert that the primary purpose of marriage is to provide a solution to loneliness, not merely create an environment for the raising of children in a household. This problem of loneliness can also be met in same sex unions as much as it is in heterosexual marriages.

At this point it might seem that I am acquiescing to Gay Theology. On the contrary, I am pointing out this flaw in Gagnon's argument only to demonstrate where this line of reasoning leads and the fallacy of asserting that natural reason apart from God's law can possibly ever lead anyone to an epistemologically justifiable ethical system. His argument is the result of what is known as the naturalistic fallacy which is a confusion of categories, of metaphysics with ethics, thinking that one can derive an ethical "ought" from a metaphysical "is." The consequence of Gagnon's argument is that it bolster's the sufficiency of autonomous human reasoning, that man can know how to live rightly with his own judgments by observing the world around him. This flatly contradicts the testimony of the Bible as the Psalmist declares, "Your word is a lamp to my feet and a light to my path… Your word I have treasured in my heart, that I may not sin against You" (Psalm 119:105, 11).

In addition, Scripture is necessary to know God's will, to know right from wrong, because creation is fallen and the natural man left to His own suppresses the knowledge of God. Grace is therefore a prerequisite to knowing how to live. While the natural man may at times deem certain acts to be right or wrong that coincide with the law of God (such as the wrongfulness of theft and murder) his reason for not conducting such acts are not for the glory of God, a necessary condition for any act to be right. Rather, he avoids them because it best suits his wants and desires. Furthermore, the only reason why we know that creation reveals the invisible attributes of God is because the Scriptures tell us so, "The heavens are telling of the glory of God and their expanse is declaring the work of His hands" (Psalm 19:1; Romans 1:18, 25).

Therefore, we need to read Paul's introduction to his Epistle to the Romans without attempting to baptize Paul's theology in the Greek philosophy of the day or argue that any sort of natural moral law is being asserted. Paul's argument is that the created order (which includes our being created in the image of God) reveals the existence of God and therefore the sinfulness of worshipping idols. If this suppression goes unchecked it results in being turned over to enslavement to various heinous sins. This is evidenced in the history of Israel when they forsook YHWH to worship other gods and in the lives of the Greeks and Romans of Paul's day. Paul is not arguing we can then look to the created order to develop an epistemologically justifiable worldview to provide guidelines for sexual behavior. Rather the created order reveals the existence of God and therefore idolatry is contrary to the moral implications of that revelation.

Romans 1 Refers to Acts That Are Contrary to Natural Function

How then should we understand Paul's use of the term "contrary to nature" (*para physin*) if it does not refer to an act contrary to a person's subjective desires, social custom, Jewish taboo or a Greek notion of natural law? The term cannot be rightly understood if it is isolated from the context of the entire argument nor simply compared with another passage in which the phrase is being used in an entirely different context. What we need to understand is that Paul's argument is that since the creation of the world the existence of the one true God and His invisible attributes have been not only made known but also immediately perceived within the mind of man so that he knows God exists. But left to his own the natural man suppresses that knowledge which results in exchanging false gods for the one true God resulting in unrighteousness. Consequently the wrath of God is against him, such that he is judged by being given up to the depravity of his heart resulting in further degradation such as men exchanging the natural function of a woman for having sex with a man and likewise women exchange the natural function (*physiken chresin*) of a man for the same sort of lust for a woman. Clearly then *para physin* refers to that which is contrary to the natural function which is not determined by one's subjective feelings (contrary the inversion interpretation) nor by deducing from whether or not such actions produce pleasure (contrary to the Gay natural law argument) or whether the body parts "fit" (Robert Gagnon's natural law argument) or that the actions are only for procreation (contrary to Thomas Aquinas' natural law argument).

The question then is, "How do we determine the 'natural function' of a man and the 'natural function' of a woman in sexual behavior?" This cannot be answered by an appeal to our subjective feelings or from a teleological argument from a natural law apart from God's special revelation. The only place that we find the answer is within God's created order in Genesis 1-2 as upheld by both Jesus and the Apostle Paul who appeal to it as normative for marriage, and to God's moral law, which we find cited throughout writings of the New Testament authors and reflected in Romans 1 as Paul alludes to the Decalogue:

> The sins mentioned in Romans 1:26-30 also correspond
> to Exodus 20, but in this instance homosexuality replaces
> adultery. Both passages begin with a reference to idolatry,
> which is a violation of the first commandment (Ex 20:3),
> was considered the root cause of immorality.[400]

Like knowing whether or not it was permissible for Adam and Eve to eat from Tree of the Knowledge of Good and Evil, we can only know the natural function for the sexual organs of men and women by looking to God's revealed will found in His law. This includes the Genesis

---

400   Thomas E. Schmidt, *Straight and Narrow? Compassion & Clarity in the Homosexuality Debate* (Downers Grove, IL: IVP Academic, 1995), 52-53.

creation account of the women being created for the man as well as the sexual prohibitions found in both the Old and New Testaments.

Jesus vs. The Apostle Paul

There are some Gay Theology advocates, namely Queer apologists, who recognize that the passages of Scripture that condemn same sex acts cannot be "queered" to approve of modern homosexual behavior. The only solution then is to totally deny that Romans 1 has any authority over one's sexuality and dismiss it as an oppressive "text of terror" as Gary Comstock states:

> …two other passages have been used as frequently against lesbians and gay men and are, indeed, texts of terror for us. One is the story of Sodom (Gen. 19) and the other is Paul's letter to the Romans (1:18-32). Both speak of us in terms that are inaccurate, vicious, bombastic, and alarmist. These passages are not unlike the lies and stereotypes that are heaped upon us today. They are not unlike the numerous movies and televisions dramas in which the criminal, drug-dealing, villainous, less-than-desirable characteristics are lesbian and gay.
>
> And just as I know that these modern media presentations do not accurately reflect our social behaviors, but instead try to reinforce a limited view of us, so the 'wickedness' of the inhabitants of stumbling blocks that I try to temper; they are lies that I name and for which I offer no apology. I place judgment on the passage and not on myself.[401]

He then goes on to state concerning Romans 1:18-32:

> Paul's letter to the Romans (1:18-32) is similarly vicious and misleading in its description of us. Within the space of eight verses (24-32), it says we 'dishonor our bodies' and refers to 'our dishonorable passions,' 'our shameless

---

401   Gary David Comstock, *Gay Theology Without Apology* (Cleveland, OH: Pilgrim Press, 1993), 40.

unnatural acts,' 'our base mind and improper conduct'; it says 'we are filled with all manner of wickedness, evil, covetousness, malice, envy, murder, strife, deceit, malignity,' that 'we are gossips, slanderers, haters of God, insolent, haughty, boastful, inventors of evil, disobedient it parents, foolish, faithless, heartless, ruthless,' and that we persist even though we know 'God's decree that these who do such things deserve to die.'

Can there be any question as to what the writer and/or editor of this letter thinks of us? I am not convinced or soothed by claims that the letter targets a particular kind of homosexuality or that Paul attacks other kinds of sins, not just homosexuality, with the same enthusiasm.[402]

He subsequently, and perhaps more honestly, avoids trying to dance around the clear implications of the passage and attempts to make the text more palatable for active homosexuals as other Gay apologists have attempted to do. Instead, he judges the apostle for his supposed homophobia.[403]

Those who recognize that Romans 1 and 1 Corinthians 6:9 cannot be squared with the Gay Theological Worldview will then go on to pit Jesus against the Apostle Paul and assert, "We're Christians, not Paulinians and Jesus never said anything about homosexuality." Some will even deny that Paul wrote the epistles to the Romans and Corinthians. This view disregards the Bible as the standard for Christian ethics because it denies that the Holy Spirit is able to provide God's people with an

---

402   Ibid, 42, 43.

403   Gary David Comstock states, "It also makes little difference to me whether, as some scholars argue, Paul is against heterosexuals who violate their true nature by indulging in homosexuality or against homosexuals themselves; I do not feel that heterosexuals should be denied homoerotic experiences. What is important to see is that Paul associates turning away from God with same-gender erotic practices, i.e., that God gives up to same-gender sexuality those who turn away from him... [cites Romans 1:26-27] Not to recognize, critique, and condemn Paul's equation of godlessness with homosexuality is dangerous. To remain within our respective Christian traditions and not challenge those passages that degrade and destroy us to contribute to our own oppression.... These passages will be brought up and used against us again and again until Christians demand their removal from the biblical canon or, at the very least, formerly discredit their authority to prescribe behavior." Ibid, 43.

authoritative standard for all of life (2 Timothy 3:15-17) and superin-
tend His Word so that it is preserved for the Church through all time
(Isaiah 40:8 and 1 Peter 1:24-25). In contrast, Paul states concerning his
epistles:

> For this reason we also constantly thank God that when
> you received the word of God which you heard from us,
> you accepted it not as the word of men, but for what it
> really is, the word of God, which also performs its work in
> you who believe (2 Thessalonians 1:13).

What Paul wrote is the very Word of God and Peter referred to
Paul's writings as being Scripture which the unlearned twist to their
own destruction (2 Peter 3:16). As demonstrated, the Gay Theology
proponents are doing this as well.

Chapter 14

The Law of God, Temple Worship and First Corinthians

In the previous two chapters, we considered God's will for sexual ethics in the context of the believer's life as an act of worship in Leviticus 18 and 20 as well as Romans Chapters 1-6. We now want to understand the Apostle Paul's doctrine of worship and sexual ethics in his First Epistle to the Corinthians. In doing so we will focus on two controversial Greek words in a warning to the Church in which he states:

> Or do you not know that the unrighteous shall not inherit the kingdom of God? Do not be deceived; neither fornicators, nor idolaters, nor adulterers, nor *malakoi*, nor *arsenokoitai*, nor thieves, nor the covetous, nor drunkards, nor revilers, nor swindlers, shall inherit the kingdom of God (1 Corinthians 6:9-10).

The term *arsenokoitai* is found in only two New Testament vice lists and it isn't found in any contemporary Greek literature of Paul's time, nor any previous Greek literature (that we know of) and it doesn't appear again until approximately a hundred years after Paul's death in Theophilus of Antioch's *To Autolycus* and Hippolytus' *Refutation of All Heresies*.[404] It has been translated in various English Bibles as "homosexuals" (NASB), "homosexual offenders" (NIV 1978), "abusers of themselves with mankind" (KJV) "guilty of unnatural crime" (Weymouth), "sodomites" (Young's Literal) and along with the Greek word *malakoi* as "sexual perverts" (RSV), "men who have sex with men" (NIV 2010), and "men who practice homosexuality" (ESV). Probably one of the worst "translations" (it is more of a paraphrase than a translation) is found in *The Message* by Eugene Peterson:

---

404   However, it should be noted that if, as I shall argue, Paul is coining a term from the Septuagint then unless his contemporaries or previous writers were also alluding to or citing Leviticus 18 and 20, we shouldn't expect the find the term anywhere else.

> Unjust people who don't care about God will not be joining
> in his kingdom. Those who use and abuse each other, use
> and abuse sex, use and abuse the earth and everything in it,
> don't qualify as citizens in God's kingdom.[405]

The terms "use and abuse sex" are so vague and nondescript they can refer to just about anything and nothing in the Greek text corresponds to the idea of "use and abuse the earth and everything in it." It seems Peterson's intent is to avoid any potential controversy and while we certainly should not abuse the earth, this concept cannot be derived from the text itself. As we shall see, the most accurate translation of *arsenokoitai* is "men who have sex with other men" as it best reflects the source from which the word is derived – Leviticus 18:22.

In short, it is asserted by Gay Theology proponents that 1 Corinthians 6:9 and 1 Timothy 1:10 do not condemn Bible-believing Christians acting on their homosexual desires within a committed monogamous life-long relationship akin to a heterosexual marriage. Many of these commentators will argue that the text narrowly refers to either exploitative sex acts (cultic prostitution) or pederasty. Others insist that the term is too vague and has lost its meaning in time. Still others argue that even if we can know what he is referring to since Paul did not have a correct scientific understanding of the innateness of the "homosexual orientation" he could not have been referring to what we know today as the gay identity. Therefore, they argue, the text should not be given any consideration on modern day sexual ethics, in fact the passage should either be ignored or removed altogether from our Bibles.[406]

Contrary to these assertions, God has not left us with an inability to understand, translate and apply the relative normative principles of His Word. Therefore if these passages only refer to or can be applied to pederasty or prostitution, it will be clearly revealed trough a careful study of the text. Likewise, if this passage refers to or can be applied to male same sex acts in general, this too will be discovered by carefully examining the text within its historical and literary context and then

---

405   Eugene J. Peterson, *The Message: The Bible in Contemporary Language* (Nav-Press, 2002)

406   Daniel Helminiak, *What the Bible Really Says About Homosexuality* (Estancia, NM: Alamo Square Press, 2000),115.

seeking to apply any corollary normative principles from this passage written in the first century to our own.

If we are going to call our self "Christian" and take our faith seriously, we need to be willing to be obedient to the authoritative Word of God. In doing so we must humbly submit to it even if it demands that we act contrary to some of our emotional, relational and sexual desires as the gospel calls us to faithfulness in our sexuality as Wesley Hill states:

> From the gospel's point of view, then, there is no absolute right or unconditional guarantee of sexual fulfillment for Christian believers... If all Christians must surrender their bodies to God in Christ whenever they enter the fellowship of Christ's body, then it should come as no great shock that God might actually make demands of those Christians and their bodies – demands proving that God, and God alone, has authority over us... this kind of long-suffering endurance is not a special assignment the gospel gives to gay and lesbian persons. Many believers of all stripes and backgrounds struggle with desires of various sorts that they must deny in order to remain faithful to the gospel's demands... The sorrow and suffering we experience as homosexual Christians is that of saying good-bye to any sure hope of satisfying our sexual cravings. In choosing fidelity to the gospel, we agree to bear up under the burden for as long as it is necessary.[407]

In the previous chapters we looked at Leviticus 18 and 20, Romans 1, and the concept of worship as it pertains to the temple and our bodies. This chapter will take a closer look at 1 Corinthians 6:9 in relation to Paul's development of the entire epistle. In doing we shall see Paul's application of the Law of Moses, particularly the Book of Leviticus, and his use of the imagery of Old Testament feast days. We will also see the manner in which these contribute to his development of a theology of worship in which Christians, as Wesley Hill states, "surrender their bodies to God in Christ." In the process it will be demonstrated how Paul coins Greek terms using words from the Septuagint in order to draw a

---

407   Wesley Hill, *Washed and Waiting: Reflection on Christian Faithfulness and Homosexuality* (Grand Rapids, MI: Zondervan Publishing House, 2010), 70, 71, 75.

tie between the Exodus of Israel and the Gospel of the New Testament and the ethical demands of the New Covenant. Having determined the meaning and application of this passage from its context we will then be able to see how it is applicable to our modern era. Subsequently we will be in a better place to see the errors of the various arguments that Gay Theology advocates use to assert that this passage has no relevance to their advocacy that the Biblical understanding of sexuality, marriage and Christian liberty ought to lead the Church to support modern contemporary consensual monogamous same sex unions.

1 Corinthians in Its Historical and Literary Context

When the Apostle Paul arrived at Corinth during his missionary journey (49 - 50 A.D.), it was the capital of the province of Achaia. While dominated by Greek paganism it was a city of social, cultural, and religious diversity, including Jews who had been expelled from Rome (49 A.D.) and formed a synagogue where Paul first preached to the Jews before going to the Gentiles. While Paul stayed in Corinth he met with Jewish refugees from Rome in the synagogue but when they became hostile to the Gospel Paul set his attention to the local Gentiles. Paul also sought out two fellow tentmakers, Priscilla and Aquila, who became his coworkers in the Gospel (Acts 18:1-12, 1 Corinthians 16:19).

Most commentators note that Corinth was an especially licentious city; in fact one of the Greek verbs for "fornication" or "sexual immorality" was *korinthiazomai,* a word derived from the city's name.[408] It is reported that there were 1,000 sacred prostitutes in the temple of Aphrodite on the Acrocorinth, an 1886 foot hill that rises above the city to the south.[409] However, some assert that the charge was more likely an Athenian slander against the city before it was destroyed by the Roman Empire in 146 B.C. It was later rebuilt at the decree of Julius Caesar who reestablished the city as a Roman colony in 44 B.C., named it Colonia Laus Julia Corinthiensis and populated it with conscripted Italian, Greek, Syrian, Egyptian and Judean freed slaves.[410] While there were undoubtedly prostitutes, like other large port cities, at this time

---

408   Simon J. Kistemaker, *1 Corinthians* (Grand Rapids, MI: Baker, 1993), 5.
409   Simon J. Kistemaker, *Ibid*, 3.
410   Frederic Louis Godet, *Commentary in First Corinthians* (Grand Rapids, MI: Kregel Publications, 1977), 5.

Sacred Prostitution was a Middle East rather than Greek custom.[411] Therefore, any reference to prostitutes in Paul's epistles to the Church, though he refers to the body as a temple, are more than likely referring to a common prostitute for hire (1 Corinthians 6:15-16).

The Church of Corinth was blessed by the Holy Spirit and was given every spiritual blessing (1 Corinthians 1:4-8). Yet Paul's first letter to the Church might be described as a "problem epistle." He spends much of his time teaching, reproofing, and correcting the Christians for various ethical and theological errors using the Old Testament just as he would instruct Timothy to do (2 Timothy 3:16-17). The Church of Corinth was riddled with sin in that there were divisions (1 Corinthians 1:10; 11:19), they were tolerant of a man who, in violation Leviticus 18:8, had sex with his father's wife (1 Corinthians 5:1), they sued each other in court (1 Corinthians 6:1), mature Christians stumbled weaker Christians over eating meat sacrificed to idols (1 Corinthians 8:1-13), and the consequence for their sin was that when some of them partook of the Lord's Supper they were judged by God and subsequently died (1 Corinthians 11:30). They were also boasting in their spiritual gifts and those with more visible abilities were exalting themselves and saying that they had no need of others (1 Corinthians 12). The bottom line was that they were failing to love each other (1 Corinthians 13), and needed to be corrected as their order of worship was chaotic (1 Corinthians 14). There were also serious theological controversies in the Church as there were some who denied the resurrection of the body (1 Corinthians 15).

In Paul's letters to the Corinthian church he doesn't merely respond to these problems with a new list of rules, "Stop doing that, start doing this." Rather he addresses the issues in the context of the Christian life devoted to Christ as he develops a theology of the body as an instrument of worship.[412] In doing so he draws from the life of the Old Testament saints, appeals to the prophecies of Isaiah (1 Corinthians 14:21), and

---

411   Simon J. Kistemaker, *1 Corinthians* (Grand Rapids, MI: Baker, 1993), 5.

412   Throughout 1 Corinthians Paul uses "body" (*soma*) to refer to his own physical body which needs to be self-disciplined (5:3; 927), the physical body of the believer as the temple of the Holy Spirit (6:13, 16, 18-20), the physical body of the husband and wife in sexual relations (7:4, 34), the sacramental bread which represents the sacrificed body of Christ and His Church, which is also referred to as the body of Christ (10:16-17), the Church body which is made up of many members (12:12-17) and the resurrected body of Christ and our future resurrected body (15:35-44).

grounds their ethical requirements in the Law of God, particularly the books of Exodus, Leviticus and Deuteronomy.

Paul's Use of the Old Testament in 1 and 2 Corinthians

Some authors assert that the Apostle Paul was a Hellenistic Jew, mostly because he uses some phrases in common with the stoics. Thomas Schmidt for example writes, "Paul writes from the standpoint of Hellenistic (Greek-influenced) Judaism…" [413] However, the Bible tells us that he was a "Hebrew of Hebrews" and a former Pharisee (Philippians 3:5), who had been a strict adherent to the Mosaic Law and studied under Gamaliel (Acts 22:3). Paul was a Diaspora Jew from Tarsus (modern day Turkey), an educated man of his day who was familiar with the writings of the Greek philosophers, even citing them in his address to those in Athens (Acts 17:28). However, it is clear that he was a strict militant adherent to the Law prior to His conversion to the Christian faith as Bruce Metzger rightly states:

> Like other educated men of his day, the apostle Paul was acquainted with a certain amount of Stoic teaching… Paul's letters contain occasional phrases that have a Stoic ring… At the same time, however, the parallelism is more in the realm of words than basic ideas, for the theological presuppositions and the springs of Paul's actions were very different from those of a Stoic philosopher.[414]

While Paul may have been familiar with the words and terminology of the Greek philosophers of his day his way of thinking and writing, as we shall see, are interwoven with the history, language, customs and theology of the Old Testament as conveyed in the Septuagint. Therefore, when reading the Pauline Epistles we need to not only pay attention to the specific citations of the Old Testament, but also the ethos of his letters as he also alludes to Old Testament laws by lifting terms and ideas from the Septuagint, rather than try to read his writings through the lens of Roman Law or Greek Philosophy:

413   Thomas E. Schmidt, *Straight and Narrow? Compassion & Clarity in the Homosexuality Debate* (Downers Grove, IL: IVP Academic, 1995), 67.
414   Cited in David A Desilva, "Paul And The Stoa: A Comparison" (*JETS* 38/4 (December 1995), 549-564.

Historically... the Septuagint should be endowed with special significance considered as a translation, because, to some circles of Greek-speaking Jewry, it replaced the *Biblia Hebraica*, and thus became their Bible. Because it was accepted as conclusive evidence of the biblical revelations, it was used by the authors of the New Testament writings, and, accordingly, came to have a decisive impact on the theology of the New Testament. In a historical perspective, it became, to an even greater extent than the *Biblia Hebraica*, the Old Testament of the New Testament.[415]

If we then study and become familiar with the language, terminology, and imagery of the Old Testament as conveyed in the Septuagint when we read Paul's Epistles to the Corinthians we will see them in a different light. We will hear the religious life and ethics of the law permeating these letters which were, ironically, written to a congregation of believers who were primarily ethnically Gentiles. Paul expects these Gentile Christians to be familiar with the history and culture of the Old Testament and to consider themselves descendants of the Old Covenant saints as they were their "forefathers." As such, Paul informs these Gentile Christians who are now of the true Jews according to their faith and circumcision of the heart (Romans 2:28-29), that the rebelliousness and sinfulness and subsequent suffering of their forefathers serves as an example and a warning not to repeat their errors (1 Corinthians 10:1-6). In fact, Paul views the suffering of Corinthian believers as evidence of this sort of judgment in their own day (1 Corinthians 11:30). Since Paul is using the sin of Old Testament saints as an example we should expect to find Paul alluding to the law and citing it as that which defined their sin. In doing so, we should not be surprised to find throughout these epistles the exact words of the Septuagint as well as the formation of new terms created combining two words from the Greek translation of the law regarding idolatry and sexual sin.

In the third chapter Paul makes the first reference to the body as a temple. In doing so the Old Temple has been replaced with the New Temple, the body of Christ, which is made up of the members of the bride of Christ:

415   Mogens Müller, *The First Bible of the Church: A Plea for the Septuagint* (JSOT Supp 206; Sheffield: Sheffield Academic Press, 1996), 115-16.

> Do you not know that you are a temple of God and that the Spirit of God dwells in you? If any man destroys the temple of God, God will destroy him, for the temple of God is holy, and that is what you are. Let no man deceive himself. If any man among you thinks that he is wise in this age, he must become foolish, so that he may become wise (1 Corinthians 3:16-18).

In his second letter to this church he does so again stringing together quotations from the Old Testament including Leviticus 26:12: [416]

> Or what agreement has the temple of God with idols? For we are the temple of the living God; just as God said, 'I will dwell in them and walk among them; and I will be their God, and they will be My people [Leviticus 26:12];' Therefore, 'Come out from their midst and be separate,' says the Lord. 'And do not touch what is unclean [Isaiah 52:11]; and I will welcome you. And I will be a father to you, and you shall be sons and daughters to Me,' Says the Lord Almighty [2 Samuel 7:14] (2 Corinthians 6:16-18).

Clearly the imagery of temple worship and the ethics of Leviticus are on Paul's mind as he exhorts the Church to holiness in these passages. We then see in chapter 5 the Apostle Paul use the moral requirements of the law as the basis for correcting and rebuking the predominantly Gentile Christian church at Corinth. Again, it is self evident from Paul's use of the Old Testament that he believes that Gentle Christians are not free to disobey the moral requirements of the law. In fact, Leviticus chapters 18-20 are the basis of his exhortations in 1 Corinthians chapters 5-6 as he writes, "It is actually reported that there is immorality among you, and immorality of such a kind as does not exist even among the Gentiles, that someone has the wife (*gunaikos*) of his father (*patros*)" (1 Corinthians 5:1). This statement has obvious parallels to the prohibition in the law of God as the sin that was being tolerated in the church

---

416   Simon Kistemaker states, "Throughout his epistles Paul strengthens his discourse with quotations from the Old Testament Scriptures... In II Corinthians, he cites at least six Old Testament references; they appear to be linked together by the thought that God is a Father to his people, who are to keep themselves pure." *2 Corinthians* (Grand Rapids, MI: Baker, 1997), 231.

was a clear violation of the commandment, "You shall not uncover the nakedness of your father's wife (*gunaikos patros*) it is your father's nakedness" (Leviticus 18:8).

Yet, what also needs to be noted is the manner in which he addresses the violations of a sexual prohibition of the law interwoven with allusions to Old Testament worship in feast days, specifically the Passover. Rather than being ashamed of this sin the Christians are boasting in their tolerance of sinful sexual diversity between two mutually consenting adults:

> Your boasting is not good. Do you not know that a little leaven leavens the whole lump of dough? Clean out the old leaven so that you may be a new lump, just as you are in fact unleavened. For Christ our Passover [Exodus 12:21] also has been sacrificed. Therefore let us celebrate the feast, not with old leaven, nor with the leaven of malice and wickedness, but with the unleavened bread of sincerity and truth (1 Corinthians 5:6-7).

When Paul says to remove the leaven he is asserting that they need to remove the sinner from their midst as the Passover law required, "... there shall be no leaven found in your houses; for whoever eats what is leavened, that person shall be cut off from the congregation of Israel, whether he is an alien or a native of the land" (Exodus 12:19). Paul then states that he has judged the sinner who is violating Leviticus 18:8 and has been "turned over" (*paradounai* from *paradidomi*) to Satan for the destruction of his flesh so that his soul might be saved (1 Corinthians 5:6-7). This is the exact same terminology that he uses concerning God's judgment of those who persist in their idolatry and subsequently they are "turned over" (*paredoken* from *paradidomi*) to various sins including men having sex with men and women with women (Romans 1:26). He then cites the law concerning the penal sanction of "purging" or "cutting off" the flagrant sinner, "Remove the wicked man from among yourselves" (1 Corinthians 5:13; Deuteronomy 13:15). This injunction is the same punishment as the minimal penal sanction mandated in the Law, "For whoever does any of these abominations, those persons who do so shall be cut off from among their people" (Leviticus 18:29 cf. 1 Kings). Within his ecclesiastical jurisdiction and with the authority

given to him from Jesus Christ, Paul is carrying out the requirements of
the law by enacting what we commonly refer to as excommunication.

Paul says that having sex with your father's wife is not merely a
cultural taboo or the violation of an antiquated obsolete purity law. This
is an act of sexual immorality (*porneia*). Yet if the Christians at Corinth
were Gay Dispensationalists they would have asked Paul, "Why is it
wrong? Aren't we free to disobey the Old Testament law of God? What
if the son is more loving and caring than his father towards his mother-
in-law? Besides, didn't Ruth have sex with her mother-in-law Naomi?
They aren't blood relatives and they really care for and respect each
other. They're both mutually consenting adults who love each other!
Isn't that enough?"

In the next chapter Paul again applies the moral law in Leviticus
when he writes, "Does any one of you, when he has a case against his
neighbor, dare to go to law before the unrighteous, and not before the
saints?" (1 Corinthians 6:1) Paul, having addressed an issue of sexual
immorality, now turns to believers treating each other unjustly in court,
and in doing so he transitions from applying Leviticus chapter 18 to
applying Leviticus chapter 19 which states, "You shall do no injustice
in court. You shall not be partial to the poor or defer to the great, but in
righteousness shall you judge your neighbor" (Leviticus 19:15). Notice
how many laws from Leviticus 18-20 are in Paul's next exhortation:

> Or do you not know that the unrighteous shall not inherit
> the kingdom of God? Do not be deceived; neither forni-
> cators (Leviticus 18:4), nor idolaters (Leviticus 19:4),
> nor adulterers (Leviticus 18:20; 20:10), nor *malakoi*, nor
> *men who have sex with other men* [Greek: *arsenokoitai*]
> (Leviticus 18:22; 20:13), nor thieves (Leviticus 19:11, 13),
> nor the covetous, nor drunkards, nor revilers (Leviticus
> 19:16), nor swindlers (Leviticus 19:11, 35-36), shall inherit
> the kingdom of God (1 Corinthians 6:9-10).

It is even clearer that Paul is invoking the Old Testament moral
law, as we saw in chapter 5, as he alludes to the commandments which
are for the preparation for the Passover, "Clean out the old leaven"
(1 Corinthians 5:7, cf. Exodus 12:15; Leviticus 23:6). In this text the
"leaven" is being used a typology for sin as he does elsewhere with the

purity laws of the Old Testament. Since Paul explicitly cites Leviticus in regards to temple worship (2 Corinthians 6:16), he uses Old Testament history and imagery throughout his two letters to the Corinthian Church, warns them against repeated Israel's sins, who are their forefathers and so clearly Paul had Leviticus 18:22 and 20:13 in mind when he wrote 1 Corinthians 6:9. There is abundant evidence Paul is alluding to the Septuagint when he uses the Greek word *arsenokoitai* translated here as "men who have sex with other men" as we read, "If a man (*arsenos*) lies with (*koiten* = literally "goes to bed with") a male as he lies with a woman, both of them have committed an abomination" (Leviticus 20:13).

The prohibition here is in not in regards to two men who happen to sleep on the same bed, but rather the terms "lies with" or "goes to bed with" are euphemisms for sexual copulation. Paul has taken two Greek words from Leviticus 20:13 (*arsenos* and *koiten*) and combined them to create the singular adjective *arsenokoitai* which describes a person according to their actions. This is not unlike the job description "fireman" which refers to "a man who puts out fires." In essence the word *arsenokoitai* means "a man who lies [has sex] with another man." The fact that he has Leviticus in mind when addressing same sex acts whereas other writers before, during and after his time do not have Leviticus 18:22 and 20:13 in mind explains why they don't use the term *arsenokoitai*. Paul does not use a common word used by Greeks because he is not appealing to Roman or Greek law. He has coined a term from the Law of God that the Greeks did not have as a basis for ethics and morality until they too became children of Abraham and had the Israelites as their forefathers. This fact is even recognized by some Gay Theology proponents.[417]

But this is not the only verse in these two epistles in which he combines two Greek words from the Septuagint to form a new term. We find in Paul's writings Greek words that as they appear in the New Testament are not found in the Old Testament as such, but rather they are formed from the Septuagint by combining two words. For example the word *eidolon* in the Septuagint is found in combination with *latreuw* in the first and second commandments, "You shall not make for yourself an idol (*eidolon*)... You shall not worship them or serve (*latreuw*) them..." (Exodus 20:4-5). Paul then combines these words in 1 Corinthians to

417   John F. Dwyer, *Those 7 References: A Study of 7 References to Homosexuality In The Bible* (John F. Dwyer, 2007), 63.

form the word *eidololatria* (*eidolon* and *latreuw*) translated "idolater" in this same epistle (1 Corinthians 5:10, 11; 6:9; 10:7).

Of course one cannot determine a meaning of a word simply by looking at its component parts as if a "carpet" is a domesticated animal that rides in an automobile as Dale Martin points out:

> A common error made in such attempts is to point to its parts, *arsen* and *koites*, and say "obviously" the word refers to men who have sex with men… This approach is linguistically invalid. It is highly precarious to try to ascertain the meaning of a word by taking it apart, getting the meanings of its components parts, and then assuming, with no supporting evidence, that the meaning of the longer word is a simple combination of its component parts. To "understand" does not mean to "stand under."[418]

Martin's point regarding the fallacy of determining the meaning of a word by dividing it into parts is valid, but only if that is all we have for supporting evidence. However, while he goes outside of Scripture to texts written a century after Paul to try to determine the meaning of *arsenokoitai*, some of which were written by Gnostics, he avoids mentioning how Paul uses Leviticus throughout his epistles. Yet he also confesses that:

> I am not claiming to know what *arsenokoites* meant. I am claiming that no one knows what it meant. I freely admit that it *could* have been taken as a reference to homosexual sex.[419]

The fact is we do have very significant supporting evidence for the meaning of *arsenokoitai* being "men who have sex with men" from Leviticus 18:22 and 20:13. He also admits that there are later written extra-biblical texts in which *arsenokoitai* can refer to homosexual sex:

---

418   Dale Martin, *Sex and the Single Savior: Gender and Sexuality in Biblical Inter-pretation* (Louisville, Westminster John Knox Press, 2006), 38.
419   Ibid.

> There are two texts in which one might reasonably take
> *arsenokoitia* as referring to homosexual sex... The first
> occurs in Hippolytus' *Refutation of All Heresies* 5.26.22-
> 23... Since *arsenokoitia* is in parallel construction with
> *moicheia* [adultery] it would be reasonable for the reader
> to take its reference as simply homosexual penetration. [420]

There are several ways that Gay Theology advocates attempt to deny that 1 Corinthians 6:9 has any relevance to mutual sex acts between monogamous mutually consenting adults. Some will argue that *arsenokoitai* either only refers to Greek cultic prostitution or pederasty in which a man is in a sexual relationship or is exploiting a male youth.[421] They then insist that because they are not advocating pederasty (at least not openly) or homosexual prostitution (at least not up front) they insist that the texts are irrelevant to the modern day discussion on the issue of homosexuality.[422] Others, such as Jack Rogers, insist that the term *arsenokoitai* is too ambiguous to ascertain for certain what it means:

> ...the meaning of these words [*arsenokoites* and *malakos*]
> is not at all clear, and their reference to homosexuality as
> such has been challenged... Because the words occur in
> lists with no context, it is difficult to know exactly what
> they mean.[423]

Daniel Helminiak likewise asserts, "Nobody knows for certain what these words mean, so to use them to condemn homosexuals is really dishonest and unfair." [424] Jeff Miner and John Connoley agree and since

420   Ibid, 42.
421   Jeff Miner and John Connoley, *The Children Are Free* (Indianapolis, IN: Jesus Metropolitan Community Church, 2002), 20.
422   However, their arguments for the legitimacy of same sex acts based on the (false) assertion that Ruth and Naomi, David and Jonathan, Jesus and Jonathan and the Centurion and his servant are all positive examples of homosexual relationships in the Bible, none of these present an example of a monogamous homosexual relationship but rather they would (if they were homosexual relationships) be examples of incest, adultery, fornication and pederasty.
423   Jack Rogers, *Jesus, The Bible, and Homosexuality* (Louisville, Kentucky; Westminster John Knox Press, 2006), 73-74.
424   Daniel Helminiak, *What the Bible Really Says About Homosexuality* (Estancia, NM: Alamo Square Press, 2000), 107.

we can't know the meaning of these texts God has failed to preserve not only the text but left His Church without any possibility of understanding His Word:

> A similar phrase appears in a list of sins in 1 Timothy 1:10. Both phrases are derived from a single word, *arsenokoitai*, which is quite rare. In fact, these two Biblical examples [1 Corinthians and 1 Timothy 1:10] may be the first examples we have of this word being used in the literature of the time. Because the word is so rare, its exact meaning is probably lost forever.[425]

Daniel Helminiak, likewise states:

> ...male homosexuality – which, according to contemporary scientific understanding, implies a normal variation in sexual attraction that inclines men to emotional and genital intimacy with each other. It may not be altogether possible to translate in one or two English words what *arsenokoitai* really means. So, caught in a distorting time warp, the Christian testament may ever continue to support homophobic and unchristian attitudes and behavior. Maybe some passages of the Bible just ought to be deleted – or at least never read in public![426]

However such an assertion would mean that the Holy Spirit lead Paul choose a word that would be unknown to his readers and He moved Paul to write an inspired text that would be useless to future generations. The understanding and obeying of this text is crucial for to fail to repent of these sins will result in being cut off from the Kingdom of God. The issue is not adiaphorous - a mere cultural taboo or an issue of conscience such as eating meat sacrifice to idols (1 Corinthians 8:8). The issue concerns a matter of eternal life or death.

---

425   Jeff Miner and John Connoley, *The Children Are Free* (Indianapolis, IN: Jesus Metropolitan Community Church, 2002), 18.
426   Daniel Helminiak, *What the Bible Really Says About Homosexuality* (Estancia, NM: Alamo Square Press, 2000), 115.

In a similar fashion, R.D. Weekly argues that the meaning of these terms is too vague and cannot be proven to refer specifically to homo-genital acts:

> In Koine Greek (common Greek dialect used during Paul's day), *arsenokoitai(s)* appears to be a compound, combining *arsen* ("male") with *koitai* ("beds"). Literally translated, *arsenokoitas* means "male beds"; or, considering the verb form "bed", it means "those who have sex with men." It's important to note that every compound word cannot be defined by its constituent words. For example, a butterfly is not a stick of butter that flies, or a fly made of butter... So we cannot necessarily assume that *arsenokoitai(s)* can be understood by defining its constituent words... I think it's relatively safe to literally translate the word as male-bed-ders. But, even if we do, we don't know exactly to whom Paul is referring. Wives are male-bedders, for instance. How can we assume a same-sex aspect to the activity?[427]

The flaw of this argument is that it totally ignores the source for the term which may have been coined by Paul. Frequently throughout his epistles he cites the Mosaic Law (contrary to the dispensational assertion that it is no longer applicable) and within the immediate context Paul is specifically alluding to the Septuagint translation of Leviticus 18:22. In fact, within the immediate context Paul had already mentioned fornica-tors and adulterers so if *arsenokoitai* could refer to a woman having sex with a man (albeit outside the bounds of marriage) he would be repeat-ing himself. Clearly Paul has something in mind other than women, let alone wives having lawfully ordained sex with their husband. To assert that *arsenokoitai* could refer to wives being "male-bedders" with their husband who will not inherit the kingdom of God is absurd.

Others argue that the term *arsenokoitai* combined with *malakoi* only refers to an exploitative form of homosexual sex such as that between a prostitute and his customer as John Boswell asserts:

---

427   R.D. Weekly, *The Rebuttal: A Biblical Response Exposing Deceptive Logic of Anti-Gay Theology* (Judah First Ministries, 2011), 126.

The second word, 'arsenokotai,' is quite rare, and its application to homosexuality in particular is more understandable. The best evidence, however, suggest very strongly that it did not connote homosexuality to Paul or his contemporaries but meant 'male prostitute' until well into the fourth century, after which it became confused with a variety of words for disapproved sexual activity and was often equated with homosexuality.[428]

Ever since John Boswell wrote his book *Christianity, Social Tolerance, and Homosexuality* other Gay Theology advocates have repeated this argument. Although under the guise of being evangelical Brentlinger asserts, "Arsenokoites is never used in antiquity, to describe a committed, faithful, noncultic relationship between two men of equal status."[429] It is fallacious to assert that just because a prohibited action is being done in a different venue and between two mutually consenting people that such an act is thereby permissible. Can two people justifiably commit adultery or fornicate in a "committed, faithful, noncultic relationship between two people of equal status"? And what criteria are you going to use to determine whether or not both parties have equal status? Is it a matter of financial income, political power, social standing, age, or health?

Others argue that the term *malakoi* refers to a male sex slave and *arsenokoitai* refers to the user of that sex slave and not any sort of homosexual practice. Jeff Miner and John Connoley argue:

> ...most of the times when *arsenokoitai* is used in early Greek literature, it occurs in a list of sins (just like in 1 Corinthians 6). Common experience tells us list-makers tend to group similar items together... In these lists *arsenokoitai*, is often placed at the end of the list of sex sins and the beginning of the list of economic sins or vice versa. For example, we find malakoi (which may refer to male prostitutes) and 'thieves.' In 1 Timothy 1:10, the word appears

---

428   John Boswell, *Christianity, Social Tolerance, and Homosexuality* (University Of Chicago Press; 8th Edition. edition, 2005), 107.
429   Rick Brentlinger, *Gay Christian 101 - Spiritual Self-Defense For Gay Christians* (2007), 356.

between 'fornication' and 'slave traders.' This is consistent with the meaning suggested above – that *arsenokoitai* describes a male who aggressively takes sexual advantage of another male. Examples of this type of behavior would include a man who rapes another... or a man who uses economic power to buy sex from a male prostitute who sells his body to survive. This latter example is an especially neat fit if *malakoi* is understood to be a reference to a prostitute, to which Paul's list would include a reference both to the male prostitute (*malakoi*) and the man who takes advantage of the prostitute (*arsenokoitai*)... Thus we conclude that *arsenokoitai* is best understood as a reference to men who force themselves sexually on others.[430]

This argument only seems plausible if the source from which Paul derived the term *arsenokoitai* is ignored as well as his repeated citation of the Old Testament. You also have to ignore Paul's other references to same-sex behavior when he states that they "burn for one another" which clearly indicates that the sex act is consensual and mutual, not exploitative (Romans 1:27).

It is clear that *arsenokoitai* cannot refer to pederasty for the text Paul is alluding to in Leviticus 18 and 20 refers to sex acts between men, not boys. If he wanted to refer to the common practice of Greek adult male sex with boys there were known words such as *paiderastia*[431] which referred to the social custom of these sex acts or the verb *paiderasteuein* which is "to be a lover of boys."[432] He could have also referred to the two parties in the relationship using the words *erastes* (the adult participant) and *eromenos* (the boy lover). Also, if he wanted to refer to an effeminate passive homosexual he could have used the terms such as *pedico, pathicus, cinaedus, catamitus*, or *malacus* which well-known words to the Romans. These Greek-borrowed Latin terms related to the one who would play the passive role in homosexual acts and failed to be

---

430   Jeff Miner and John Connoley, *The Children Are Free* (Indianapolis, IN: Jesus Metropolitan Community Church, 2002), 20-21.
431   Craig A. Williams, *Roman Homosexuality* (Oxford University Press, USA; 2 edition, 2010), 11, 14,
432   Henry George Liddell and Robert Scott, *A Greek-English Lexicon* (Oxford: Clarendon Press, 1940 9th ed., with 1968 supplement in 1985 reprinting), 1286.

truly masculine in his mannerism and manners of clothing. Also, if Paul wanted to use a term that referred to the Greek love of youths, pederasty, he could have used the general term *stuprum*, but only if the boy were freeborn. [433]

Because the evidence for Paul's usage of Leviticus is overwhelming some Gay Theology proponents such as John Dwyer concede that Paul did in fact derive the term from Leviticus:

> This [*arsenokoites*] appears to be a rendering into Greek of a standard rabbinic phrase that literally means 'one who lies with a male (as with a woman)' or more specifically 'sleeper with males.' Paul apparently took the words utilized in Leviticus 18:22 and 20:13… and created a word that would be descriptive and understandable to his readers. This word *arsenokoites* would have been used to describe men who were more 'active' member of a same sex male sexual relationship.[434]

Having considered the term *arsenokoitai* we now turn our attention to the meaning of another hotly debated word in 1 Corinthians 6:9 - *malakoi*. This Greek word has been translated or mistranslated in various ways in English as "effeminate" (NASB, KJV) "homosexuals" (NKJV), "male prostitutes" (NLT), "who make women of themselves" (Darby Translation) and "a male who submits his body to unnatural lewdness" (Thayer's Greek-English Lexicon). By itself *malakoi* (plural from *malakos*) is a very broad word that requires an immediate and larger context in order to determine what the author is intended to covey by this term. This is not unlike the various ways in which the term "gay" may be understood in the late 19th and 20th century. Consider for example the well-known Christmas Carol "Deck the Halls" (1881):

> Deck the halls with boughs of holly,
> Fa la la la la, la la la la.
> Tis the season to be jolly,

---

433   Craig A. Williams, *Roman Homosexuality* (Oxford University Press, USA; 2 edition, 2010), 197.

434   John F. Dwyer, *Those 7 References: A Study of 7 References to Homosexuality In The Bible* (John F. Dwyer, 2007), 63.

Fa la la la la, la la la la.
Don we now our **gay** apparel,
Fa la la, la la la, la la la.

Or the theme song of the Flintstones (1960) cartoon:

Flintstones... meet the Flintstones,
They're a modern stone age family.
From the town of Bedrock,
They're a page right out of history.
Let's ride with the family down the street.
Through the courtesy of Fred's two feet.
When you're with the Flintstones,
have a yabba dabba doo time,
a dabba doo time,
we'll have a **gay** old time!

It would be fallacious to assert that the authors of these two tunes were homosexuals and that "gay apparel" refers to the clothing that men might wear in a Gay Pride parade, or that "yabba dabba doo" and "gay old time" were intended to indicate that Fred Flintstone and Barney Rubble were Gay Pentecostals speaking in tongues. Yet during the time in which the Flintstones song was written "gay" was frequently, and perhaps more commonly, used to refer to men who experience same-sex attractions. In fact one the definitions of "gay" in most modern dictionaries is "indicating, or supporting homosexual interests or issues" and according to Dictionary of American Slang it was used as such as early as 1920. Yet as far back as the 1700's a "gay woman" referred to a prostitute, a "gay man" was a womanizer and a "gay house" was a brothel. However, as it is commonly known the term "gay" can also mean "merry, lively, bright or showy" which most people today would agree is the intended meaning of the previously cited songs.

Imagine someone 2,000 years from now, in a time in which people no longer read or speak 20th century American English, were to read of the "gay parade" that began on June 27, 1969, in New York City. This person then finds within the lexical meaning of "gay" that the word can refer to something which is "merry, lively, bright or showy" and then immediately conclude that the "gay parade" was an event that merely included people in colorful costumes traveling on colorfully decorated floats. On the other hand, someone might also read an ancient newspaper article from 1935 of someone referring to the Macy's Thanksgiving Day Parade, an event also held in New York City since 1927, as a "gay parade." Reading from the same lexicon that "gay" refers to "indicating, or supporting homosexual interests or issues" this person concludes that the annual Macy's Parade was a celebration of homosexuality. So, now we have two ancient "gay parades" that were conducted in New York City in the 20th century. Are the people of the future left without any means of determining which of these events were of homosexual interest and which was a merry, lively and showy event? Without any further context written or visual evidence it would seem that they would be left to speculate concerning the nature of these parades. But they would not be free to pick and choose which definition they wanted to use to determine the meaning of "gay parade." Nor could they rightly determine the meaning of "gay" as it refers to one parade and immediately infer that it must also mean the same thing when referring to the other parade, simply because both events occurred in the exact same city during the exact same time in history.

This is the difficulty that all translators and interpreters face when handling any document and sorting through ancient texts and lexicons composed by linguistic scholars. In order to be honest and credible one needs to do justice to the text in its various contexts (literary historical, cultural) by not seeking to force the text to meet the goal of one's predetermined agenda nor throw up one's hands and assert "We can't really know what it meant!" when we discover that the meaning of the passage doesn't suit our ends. This is particularly true when handling the Word of God which has been promised to never pass away (Isaiah 40:8; 1 Peter 1:25) and to always be able to equip the man of God for every good work (2 Timothy 3:16-17). Nor should we despair or become lazy in our efforts merely because the text is a difficult one to understand. The Apostle Peter, the Apostle Paul's contemporary, admitted that at times Paul was difficult to understand and the untrained and uneducated twist his words, as they do the rest of the Scriptures to their own destruction (2 Peter 3:16-18).

While the term *malakoi* can mean "illness" (Matthew 4:23, 9:35, 10:1), or when referring to clothing it can mean "soft" or "extravagant" (Matthew 1:8) we cannot justifiably lift these definitions from these texts out of their context and freely insert their meaning into Paul's epistle. Yet, this is exactly what a multitude of Gay Theology authors in fact do. Arguing that *malakoi* literally means "soft" in 1 Corinthians 6:9 is just like arguing that "Gay Theology" literally means "Happily Carefree Doctrine." This isn't scholarly and it isn't honest. Today nobody has any illusions what "gay" really means in reference to gay parades. Similarly in Paul's day nobody misunderstood what he was referring to when he used the term *malakoi* in 1 Corinthians 6:9.

What is clear is that Paul is not using the term in a neutral or positive sense as Jesus did when referring to clothing. Rather he is using it in the midst of sexual sins as he refers to those who shall not inherit the kingdom of God as "sexually immoral *(pornoi)*... adulterers *(moichoi)*... *malakoi*... nor men who have sex with other men *(arsenokoitai)*" to a church in an epistle in which he repeatedly cites, alludes to and quotes the Law of God including Exodus (1 Corinthians 5:6-7; cf. Exodus 12:21), and Leviticus (2 Corinthians 6:16-18; cf. Leviticus 26:12). It is in this sexual context that we must determine the meaning of the word.

In the Bible the Greek word *pornoi* from *porneia* has an extended semantic range, particularly when it is followed by other specifically named sexual sins including adultery (Matthew 5:32, 19:9), fornication (Matthew 15:19), incest (1 Corinthians 15:1) prostitution and, as we shall see, same-sex acts. The noun form, *pornos,* covers practitioners of pederasty as well as men who use male and female prostitutes, in both male commercial and ritual prostitution (Ephesians 5:5; 1 Timothy 1:10), and when specifically spelled out in a list of sins such as 1 Corinthians 6:9 it includes "men having sex with other men." The feminine form *pornes* is used to refer to a woman who engages in prostitution (1 Corinthians 6:15).

It follows then that if we read the term in the context of sexual sins that the word *malakoi,* contrary to Gay Theology advocate's assertions, is not impossible to identify. If Paul were giving us a laundry list there would be no need for an argument that Paul is using the term to refer to soft or luxurious clothing. What then needs to be asked is, "What connotation can 'soft' have in the context of a list of sexual sins when preceding a coined word from Leviticus 18:22 which means 'men who have sex with men'?" The adjective *malakos*, here used substantivally, is clearly a male performing the "soft" role in sexual relations. In such a context immediately following the *moichoi* (adulterers) and preceding the word *arsenokoitai* (men who have sex with men) no-one would have read it to mean anything other than what was typical perceived to be the feminine role in sex, that is, one who submits their body to being penetrated by a male.

One of the most common arguments against this understanding of the text is to point out that English Bibles have translated the word *malakoi* in 1 Corinthians 6:9 various ways and then assert that such variation is due to previous generations not knowing what the word meant. Then in light of such seeming historical uncertainty it is asserted that we too should also conclude that we really cannot be sure what Paul was referring to and therefore not charge modern same sex actions as being a sin based upon this passage.

There are two problems with this line of reasoning. First, even if previous translators were not sure how to understand the term it does not follow then that modern scholarship with greater access to various textual resources and further study of the passage cannot have a better understanding of the term. There are many words in older English translations that are not translated differently because the art of making dynamic equivalencies has improved as well as a better understanding of Pauline theology. Furthermore, unless previous generations had a singular term in English that is equivalent to *malakoi* then they would either have to invent an English word or use its approximate equivalency that would be understood by English readers.

Second, such an assertion fails to take into consideration that previous generations often were "polite" in their translations such that to give a more literal and upfront meaning of the term might have embarrassed or shocked the sensibilities of the readers of their day. For example, the Greek word *skubala* (Philippians 3:8) has also been translated in various polite ways "rubbish" (NASB) "garbage " (NIV) "dung" (KJV) "refuse" (RSV) "filth" (Darby) so as to not shock modern readers. The fact is *skubala* literally means human excrement. But what pastor would want to read such a translation to a congregation that is mixed with women and children? A better way to determine as to whether or not translators knew what the word meant is to read ancient scholarly commentaries.

For example, John Calvin thought the word *malakoi* referred to people who "...do not openly abandon themselves to impurity..." but rather "... their unchastity by blandishments of speech, by lightness of gesture and apparel, and other allurements." He then goes on to vaguely refer to *arsenokoitai* as "that monstrous pollution which was but too prevalent in Greece."[435] In writing this he assumes everyone knows what he is referring to and so he does not spell it out for as the Apostle Paul states, "...for it is disgraceful even to speak of the things which are done by them in secret" (Ephesians 5:12). In other words, while the subject of homosexual acts such as anal and oral sex is openly displayed in the media and promoted in modern government schools, previous generations in their translation of the Bible had to talk around the subject so as to only politely refer to the act without actually discussing it in detail. It was not until the Church was confronted by this issue that we began to publicly address the issue so that we can now find it being discussed in sermons, books, and magazine articles. Therefore politeness and not ignorance by in large accounts for the various ways in which the word *malakoi* and *arsenokoitai* have been translated.

The problem is all too often such politeness and the subsequent use of euphemisms often obscures the meaning to those who don't know what the translation is implying or the commentator is inferring. Unless the issue was a pressing matter in their own day or there is a specific reason to look deeper into the meaning of the term it may have been misunderstood or politely passed over altogether. It is only because homosexuality is a "hot topic" in our own day that we are spending so much time and research in trying to determine the meaning and most accurate translation of these seldom used sexual references. In short, if we were to put aside all politeness and not concern ourselves with offending sensitive ears, we would translate *skubala* as "shit" and the term *malakoi* as "male recipients of anal penetration."

435   John Calvin, *The Epistles of Paul The Apostle To The Corinthians* (Vol. 1) in *Calvin's Commentaries* (Vol. XX) (Grand Rapids, MI: Baker Publishing, 2003), 208-209.

The question then is, does *malakoi* refer to any passive member in a same sex act or does it specifically refer to a male prostitute or "catamite" (a boy kept for homosexual purposes) and if so can it also be applied to male participants in anal sex in general? If Paul wanted to specifically refer to men having sex with boys there were words used at the time and specifically refer to the *erastes* (the older man) and the *eronomos* (the younger boy). Hence he could have written, "Or do you not know that the unrighteous will not inherit the kingdom of God? Do not be deceived; neither fornicators, nor idolaters, nor adulterers, nor *erastes*, nor *arsenokoitai*…will inherit the kingdom of God."

However, even if Paul specifically has male prostitutes in mind the moral principle equally applies to all same-sex acts involving anal penetration for nowhere in Scripture do we find any precedence for any sexual behavior outside the boundaries of marriage between a man and a woman. In fact, even some Gay Theology advocates readily admit that there were ancient equivalents to modern day homosexual relationships during Paul's day:

> The homosexual identity was certainly known to Plato and Aristotle; recent scholarship has unearthed examples of it as recently as New York in the 1920s and as long ago as the Stone Age. It has existed in Native American tribes and Roman Catholic monasteries.[436]

If the homosexual identity has been widely known throughout the ages and in various cultures, then how can anyone claim that Paul was ignorant of it? If there were specific words in Paul's day that were used to refer to pederastic relationships and that is what Paul is narrowly referring to in 1 Corinthians 6:9, then why didn't he use such terms? The reason is simple, he is using very broad yet polite words that refer to same sex acts – the one who is passively penetrated in the anus by another man (*malakoi*) and a reference to the descriptive terminology derived from Leviticus 18:22 (*arsenokoitai*) to refer to any man who actively has sex with another man as a man has sex with a woman, i.e. he penetrates another man.

---

436   Andrew Sullivan, *Virtually Normal* (New York, NY: Vintage, 1996), 30.

1 Corinthians 8 - Cultic Context

One of the most common arguments put forth by Gay Theology advocates is that Leviticus 18:22, Romans 1:26-27 and 1 Corinthians 6:9 only prohibit or condemn homosexual behavior that is conducted in a pagan cultic context in which it is associated with worshipping the gods of the Canaanites, Greeks or Romans. It is then argued that they cannot be applied apply to modern same-sex acts outside of such a context, particularly if they are within a committed monogamous relationship, since the cultic connotations have been removed.[437] Therefore these passages do not condemn same-sex acts in general. Is there a Biblical precedence for an activity being sinful within a cultic context but clearly not sinful outside of that context? If so, can we apply the principle of the text to same sex relationships?

One example of an action being allowed or prohibited based upon its common or cultic context in the first century was the issue of eating meat that had been sacrificed to a pagan idol. There are passages in the New Testament that seem to indicate that it is a sin to eat meat that has been sacrificed to pagan idols and there are other passages that seem to indicate that Christians are free to eat such meat. At first it may seem that there is there a contradiction in the New Testament until we take into consideration the context in which this meat is eaten.

The first passage that seems to prohibit eaten sacrificed meat regardless of context is in a letter from the apostles to the Gentile Christians. After the apostles, along with the Holy Spirit, at the Jerusalem Council determined that the Gentiles do not need to be circumcised in order to be saved, it was declared to them in an epistle:

> For it seemed good to the Holy Spirit and to us to lay upon you no greater burden than these essentials: that you abstain from things sacrificed to idols and from blood and from things strangled and from fornication; if you keep yourselves free from such things, you will do well. Farewell (Acts 15:28-29).

Another is found in two epistles from Jesus Himself in the Book of Revelation in which He rebukes two churches:

---

437   R.D. Weekly, *Homosexianity* (Judah First Ministries, 2009), 18.

> But I have a few things against you, because you have
> there some who hold the teaching of Balaam, who kept
> teaching Balak to put a stumbling block before the sons
> of Israel, to eat things sacrificed to idols and to commit
> acts of immorality… But I have this against you, that you
> tolerate the woman Jezebel, who calls herself a prophetess,
> and she teaches and leads My bond-servants astray so that
> they commit acts of immorality and **eat things sacrificed
> to idols** (Revelation 2:14-20).

It would seem from these passages that regardless of context it is a sin to eat food that has been "sacrificed to idols." However, when we come to Paul's first epistle to the Corinthians we have two seemingly contradictory statements regarding this matter. The first seems to indicate that Christians, who are theologically informed, who know that there is only one God and that an idol is nothing may freely eat meat sacrificed to an idol (1 Corinthians 8:8). The second passage seems to condemn such practice as having a divided loyalty between Jesus Christ and demons (1 Corinthians 10:20). However, if we take a closer look at both passages we find the distinction between the venues in which the food is eaten becomes the deciding factor as to whether or not Christians may in good conscience eat such meat.

In the first passage Paul is discussing meat that has been sacrificed in a pagan temple, is being sold in the open market and eaten in a non-sacramental fashion. Paul's point is that there is nothing inherently wrong with the meat, the person who purchased the meat is not participating in the cultic ritual and therefore he is free to eat the meat if his conscience allows him to do so. However, he also exhorts the Christians "with knowledge" not to use this liberty to offend other Christians whose conscience may not be able to dissociate the meat from its source and consequently to them it is still, in their mind, a pagan sacramental meal. Therefore, when Christians are eating in the presence of a "weaker brother" they should not eat the meat (1 Corinthians 8:1-9).

In the second passage in this epistle Paul clearly refers to the sacramental consumption of the Lord's body in the loaf and partaking of His blood in the cup as an act of worship. He then refers to the forbidden consumption of that which has been "sacrificed to idols," the cup of demons, which refers to partaking of it within a cultic context (1 Corinthians 10:16-21). Essentially, the statement, "you cannot partake of the table of the Lord and the table of demons" is a reference to serving two masters and blending both Christian and pagan worship. This is the same context of the prohibition given by the Jerusalem Council and the act which Jesus condemns (Revelation 2:14-20). But then Paul says when dining with a Gentile that you are not ask where the meat came from, lest an unbeliever think Christians are free to worship pagan gods:

> If one of the unbelievers invites you to dinner and you are disposed to go, eat whatever is set before you without raising any question on the ground of conscience. But if someone says to you, "This has been offered in sacrifice," then do not eat it, for the sake of the one who informed you, and for the sake of conscience. I do not mean your conscience, but his. For why should my liberty be determined by someone else's conscience? (1 Corinthians 10:27-29)

We see then that eating food "sacrificed to idols" is only sinful when it is done within a cultic context as a participant in idol worship.[438] The question is, "Can we make this same argument in regards to same-sex acts?" If, for the sake of argument, the authors of Leviticus 18:22, Romans 1:26-27 and 1 Corinthians 6:9 only have cultic same sex acts in mind, is the Christian be free to engage in same-sex behavior in a manner that is equivalent to a Christian eating sacrificed meat outside of a cultic context? Although I have yet to come across an argument for such a principle from these specific passages, the Gay theological argument if logically followed would be in the affirmative:

> As with the Leviticus and Deuteronomy passages, this condemnation [same sex activity in Romans 1:26-27] is directly related to idol worship, as clearly indicated by the context of the passage in question... because our modern culture no longer associates same-sex activity with idol worship, it would be wrong to hold Christians captive to

---

438   Similar parallels are drawn between the Biblical prohibition of the cultic use of tattoos and modern use of tattoos for merely body-art (Leviticus 19:28). R.D. Weekly, *Homosexianity* (Judah First Ministries, 2009), 85.

the ancient cultural perspective that informed Paul's worldview (particularly when the acts are not engaged in the worship of idol gods).[439]

There are several criteria that we can use to evaluate such an argument. First, can we find other actions within Leviticus 18, Romans 1 or 1 Corinthians 6 that are clearly tied to a cultic context and when disassociated from that context are permissible? The only act in Leviticus 18 that is specifically related to a cultic act of worship is, "You shall not give any of your offspring to offer them to Molech" (v. 21). This act when disassociated from a cultic context is murder in the form of a post birth abortion which is clearly prohibited (Exodus 20:13). In Romans 1 none of the other sins listed (greed, evil; envying, murder, strife, deceit, malice, gossiping, slandering, hating of God, insolence, arrogance, boasting, disobedience to parents) have any relation to an act of cultic worship and they cannot be rightfully indulged in any context whatsoever (vv. 29-30). Likewise, none of the other sins listed in 1 Corinthians 6:9-11 (fornicating, idolatry, adultery, thieves, coveting, drunkenness, reviling, swindling) have any relation to an act of cultic worship and they cannot be rightfully indulged in any context. Nor are there any other sexual acts within these texts that may be justifiably indulged in a non-cultic context. Therefore we have no clear precedence that the prohibited same-sex acts are only a sin due to their distinctively idolatrous associations.

Second, we need to ask, "Were there known same-sex acts that were non-cultic and not a form of prostitution during the time that these passages were written?" If there were the fact that they do not specify cultic acts or prostitution indicates that the prohibitions and condemnations of same-sex acts are universal and not just cultic sex, pederasty or prostitution. There is clear extra-Biblical evidence that non-cultic and mutually consenting adult same-sex acts were widely known during the time that Leviticus, Romans 1 and 1 Corinthians were written though the "penetrated male" was often viewed as a feminized person of ridicule and scorn.[440]

---

439   R.D. Weekly, *Homosexianity* (Judah First Ministries, 2009), 102
440   Craig A. Williams, *Roman Homosexuality* (Oxford University Press, USA; 2 edition, 2010), 3, 18-19

It must be asked then, "If consensual non-cultic same sex relation-ships were known at the time and only cultic or prostitution forms of same sex acts are prohibited, then why are we not given a scenario, akin to 1 Corinthians 8, in which we may see that there are contexts that one may participate in homosexual acts?" The answer is clear, Paul knew of non-cultic consensual same sex acts that were not pederastic in nature that did not involve prostitutes and there are no allowances for such act provided in the Christian worldview.

Third, are there proscriptive boundaries provided within the Bible which provide the positive parameters for sexual relationships? If so, is there any allowance given within those boundaries for anything outside of sex between one man and woman in marriage? The short answer to this question is, "No."

Conclusion: The Law of God, Temple Worship and Same Sex Acts

There is not one text in the entirety of Scripture that provides a qualified approval of homosexual conduct or expression. Same-sex acts are not merely a Jewish taboo but are such an offence to God that they are deemed being worthy of death (Leviticus 20:13; Romans 1:32). Along with adultery it belongs to a category of genital sin that violates a marriage covenant (Matthew 5:31-32; 19:3-12) and it inwardly defiles its participants (Matthew 15:1-20). Engaging in homogenital acts is one sign of having turned away from the worship of the Creator, even if one claims to be a follower of YHWH or Jesus. Consequently those who do not repent are not to be deceived into thinking that they will still inherit the kingdom of God (1 Corinthians 6:9). Along other habitual gross sins such as having sex with your father's wife, if chosen and persisted in it breaks covenant obligations for time and eternity (Leviticus 18:8; 1 Corinthians 5-6). Same-sex acts defy the moral code of the Law of God which is still binding upon the people of the New Covenant (1 Timothy 1:10). Finally, same-sex acts directly contradict all the implications of the created order (Genesis 2:24) as well as Jesus' and Paul's personal example and teaching on sex and marriage (Matthew 19:4-6; Mark. 10:1-12). There is no Scriptural or historical warrant for the Christian Church to allow it. The body of the Christian, which is the temple of the

Holy Spirit, belongs to the Creator who made it and to the Redeemer who bought it back from slavery to sin, "You were bought at a price. Therefore honor God with your body" (1 Corinthians 6:20).

Chapter 15
The Law of God and Penal Sanctions

In the previous chapters we thoroughly looked at various aspects of the law and some of the relevant passages in the Old and New Testament related to homosexual behavior. We now come to one of the most sensitive and controversial issues regarding the law of God and the prohibition of same-sex acts. According to the Bible, not only is homosexual conduct a sin but also under the theocratic state of Israel the consequence for violating the commandment as a crime was subject to the death penalty:

> If there is a man who lies with a male as those who lie with a woman, both of them have committed a detestable act; they shall surely be put to death. Their bloodguiltiness is upon them (Leviticus 20:13).

In light of the New Testament upholding the Law of God and its continuing obligations (with the exception those that were distinctively Jewish in nature in the Mosaic Covenant) and having studied various issues related to the Law of God in redemptive history the question that remains then is "Should Christians seek to have the state enforce the penal sanctions of the law, as prescribed in the Old Testament, today?" There are several ways in which honest Christians have differed in answering this question.

As we shall see, each view tends to be tied to not only an ethical system but also closely related to an eschatological paradigm. These eschatological frameworks concern not merely a certain expectation of the future and an interpretation of the "millennium" (Revelation 20:4). They each have a different understanding of the unfolding of redemptive history, the continuity of the Old and New Testaments and the extent of perpetuity of the laws of the Old Covenant in a New Covenant era. More importantly and relevant to the topic at hand, they differ in their expectations of the impact that the preaching of the gospel will have on the world and the subsequent change it will bring on society. If an eschatological perspective has no or very little anticipation of the world being converted but instead expects the Church and its influence to dwindle to a mere remnant of faithful believers (or soon be removed from the earth in a "rapture") then there may be little concern as to how Biblical principles ought to be applied outside of the individual Christian life. To even ask, "How or should the penal sanctions of the Bible be applied to modern judicial systems?" becomes an absurd question. It is like asking whether or not Christians should polish the brass on a sinking ship. On the other hand, if an eschatological paradigm antici-pates an eventual incremental conversion of the majority of the human population through the preaching of the gospel resulting in a change in the culture, then how a Christianized culture ought to be governed by law becomes paramount. Of course, since the majority of the world has not been converted to the Christian faith any theorizing of how to apply Biblical law on a national level becomes purely hypothetical at this point in time.

Penal Sanctions and Eschatological Perspectives

The Dispensational Premillennial view of eschatology insists that the entire Old Testament law and its penal sanctions are no longer appli-cable as they were only required to be observed during in an era of "law" whereas we are now living in an era of "grace" though they will be rein-stated to the fullest during a future millennium. Some Dispensationalists state that while some laws are repeated in the New Testament we do not find with them any penal sanctions. However, they then go on to assert that during a future millennium, a golden era in which Christ is ruling on earth for a thousand years after a seven year tribulation in which the Antichrist is ruling on the earth, God's redemptive plan will return to dealing with National Israel as they existed in the Old Testament. This will include the rebuilding of the earthly temple, the return to animal sacrificial system (albeit as a memorial) with Jesus ruling all the nations on earth from Jerusalem with a "rod of iron." [441] According to this view, it is only during that time that the penal sanctions as prescribed in the Old Testament will be reinstated. If you were to ask a Dispensationalist,

---

441   J. Dwight Pentecost, *Things to Come* (Grand Rapids, MI: Zondervan, 1958), 393.

"Do you think the state should uphold the penal sanctions of the Old Testament *today* in the present age?" their answer would be, "No, for we are living during a dispensation of grace. But they will be reinstated during a return to an age of law during the millennium. In the mean time, the Civil Magistrate should govern by Natural Law."

By Natural Law they do not mean an autonomous type of law that mankind may to some degree have in common. Rather, they believe that the law of God has been written on the hearts of Christians and non-Christians alike which, though obscured by man's sinful depravity, nevertheless remains "the work of the law." This is based on a faulty understanding of Romans 2:14. The problem with this view is that the law being written on the hearts of men is a promise for the believer in the New Covenant (Jeremiah 31:31). The Gentiles who do not have the Law who instinctively do the things of the Law are believers who are physically uncircumcised, yet because they keep the law it is counted as "circumcision of the heart, by the Spirit" demonstrating that they are true Jews (Romans 2:27-29). While unbelievers may to some degree act in accordance with God's standard this does not mean that they have God's law written on their heart. At times the self-interests of man may, at the civil level, correspond to the law of God (not murdering, stealing, etc.) but this does not mean that God's law is written on their heart. Nowhere in Scripture does it say that God's law is written on the unbeliever's heart.

The Amillennial "general equity" (also called the "Two Kingdom") view to answering this question is to assert that while the moral principle of Leviticus 18:22 is still applicable in the New Covenant era the maximum penal sanction prescribed in 20:13 should not be followed due to the cessation of the unique Church/state connection in Old Testament theocracy. This view often cites the Westminster Confession of Faith in support of their position:

> To them also, as a body politic, He gave sundry judicial laws, which expired together with the state of that people, not obliging any other, now, further than the general equity thereof may require (WCF 19.4).

In other words, the penal sanction is only applicable to the unique religious-sociopolitical setting of Israel in which the Church and state "as a body politic" were closely related and the Kingdom of God was tied to the earthly realm. This view then asserts that since the Kingdom of God is not of this earth and our citizenship of Jerusalem is above (Galatians 4:26), so too the theocratic state is now in heaven from where Christ rules as King over the Church and will continue to do so until He has placed all His enemies on earth at His footstool (Psalm 110; Luke 20:43; Acts 2:35; Hebrews 1:13; 10:13). This view asserts that the civil law and its penal sanctions were given to the people who lived in the theocratic context of national Israel, not to the people of the United States, Britain, Uganda or any other now existing earthly government. Rather it was given to a nation in which the Church and the state were intertwined. It is then argued that since we are now not under such a theocracy (and it is argued that one should not be sought after) the penal sanction is no longer applicable in the state, though the moral principle is applicable in the Church because it is alone is a theocracy, a society governed by God. In the New Covenant era, the Church's sword is spiritual (Ephesians 6:17; Hebrews 4:12), not physical and therefore the only sword that the Church should seek to use entails either exclusion from the Church or an act of excommunication for unrepentant baptized Christian who engages in same-sex acts, fornication or adultery. It may also be added that Paul specifically stated that the Church was not to take their issues to the civil magistrate but rather to handle such issues in an ecclesiastical court (1 Corinthians 6:1-8).

This view of the penal sanctions has much agreement with the Dispensational view as it asserts that the commandments of God in Old Testament were in an era of "law" as a "Covenant of Works" principle. Therefore they are not applicable in a New Covenant era of "grace" and severe judgments (such as the destruction of Sodom and Gomorrah), were eschatological intrusions, foretastes of the final judgment. This theological scheme argues that redemptive history fluctuates between eras of "law" or theocratic epochs (The Garden of Eden, in Noah's Ark during the flood, the Mosaic Covenant) and eras of "grace" (Abrahamic Covenant, the New Covenant). Since the New Covenant is an era of "grace" to insist that the penal sanctions be upheld would then be a failure to recognize that such judgments are now suspended until the final judgment. This view is asserted by adherents of "Intrusion Ethics."[442]

Intrusion ethics has a lot in common with Dispensationalism in that it denies that God's revealed law is applicable to all people in all places as they assert that Israel was a type and the law doesn't apply to those outside the covenant with whom it was made. They will then assert a view of natural moral law, as taught by Thomas Aquinas, that is supposedly written on the heart of all men that is deemed to be sufficient as a moral standard for governing a society. The problem with this line of reason is, even if we were to grant the existence of such a law it too would be a reflection of God's holy character. Consequently it would not be any different in substance than what is also revealed in His written law. If it is, and it differs with its commands at the same time in history then we have two different standards that are contradictory ethical norms within the Godhead. But if it is impossible for God to have two different moral standards then His natural moral law cannot be any different than what is more clearly made known in His written revealed law. Another problem with this view is that God's law is deemed culturally relative and if it is a reflection of his character, then God Himself is a moral relativist. Finally, I would argue that the "intrusions" they refer to are not ethical, but epistemological in that the progressive nature of His revelation was a process of continuing to make known to the world His holy will for all mankind. God does not change His standard of justice throughout history but rather He incrementally reveals His will for mankind redemptive-historically giving greater light and thereby greater responsibility throughout time.

If you were to ask an adherents to this view, "Do you think the state should uphold the penal sanctions of the Old Testament?" their answer would be, "No, and they never should be. The Civil Magistrate should govern by Natural Law."[443]

There are others who insist that regardless of the covenant or circumstances, the maximum penalty may be justifiably upheld to the

442   Meredith Kline writes, "It will only be with the frank acknowledgement that ordinary ethical requirements were suspended and the ethical principles of the last judgment intruded that the divine promises and commands to Israel concerning the Canaanites come into their own." *The Structure of Biblical Authority* (Grand Rapids, MI: Wm. B. Eerdmans Publishing Company, 1972.), 163.

443   David VanDrunen, *Natural Law and the Two Kingdoms: A Study in the Development of Reformed Social Thought* (Wm. B. Eerdmans Publishing Company, 2010)

letter in every case by any civil magistrate *today* and Christians ought
to urge such penalties via their sphere of influence in the political arena.
This view sees the underlying principles of the law (though not "to the
letter") of the Old Testament as ideal for developing civil, familial,
and ecclesiastical laws that if they were employed today would bring
about a more just and God honoring society. This understanding of
the law is commonly referred to as a Theonomic view that is closely
associated with Christian Reconstruction and it tends to also be tied to a
Postmillennial eschatology.[444] According to their primary works on the
subject, if you were to ask an adherent to this view, "Do you think the
state should uphold the penal sanctions of the Old Testament?" there
answer would be, "Yes, and the civil magistrate will be judged for not
doing so." The conclusion of this view, when asked, "Do you believe
that the state should uphold the penal sanction of death penalty for homosexual acts *now*?" they tend to answer in the affirmative.[445]

Rather than arbitrarily choosing a theological paradigm with which
we are most comfortable, we need to look at what God has ordained and
to what extent and by what means He Himself has throughout redemptive history enacted various degrees of penal sanctions. In observing
God's judgments in history we also want to note that there is often a
range of punishment for a sin or crime depending on the circumstances,
from excommunication to the death penalty. Then we will examine the
New Testament epistles to determine how the apostles used the terminology of the Old Testament penal sanctions within their ecclesiastical
jurisdiction in the New Covenant era. After we have accomplished this
task we will be better suited to address the question as to whether or not
the civil magistrate today is morally culpable before God for not seek-

444   John Frame provides a helpful definition of Theonomy when he writes, "Theonomy, sometimes called Christian reconstruction, is a movement of Reformed thinkers
dedicated to encourage observance of the Mosaic law by Christians. The patriarch of
the movement was the late Rousas J. Rushdoony, who set forth his position in many
writings, especially *The Institutes of Biblical Law*. This position is also espoused in
many writings by economic historian Gary North, Rushdoony's son-in-law. The most
cogent exponent of theonomy was the late Greg L. Bahnsen, author of *Theonomy in
Christian Ethics*." *The Doctrine of the Christian Life* (Phillipsburg; P & R Publishing,
2008), 217.
445   R.J. Rushdoony, *The Institutes of Biblical Law* (Vol. 1) (P & R Publishing,
1980), 425.

ing to enforce the civil penal sanctions against same sex acts. Finally, we need to determine the moral duty of the Christian who is called to be faithful to the Word of God and the Christian worldview while serving vocationally within the civil government.

Sins and Crimes

To rightly address this issue we need to first understand the distinction between a sin and a crime, the variations of penal sanctions in the law and the various ways in which God has upheld them directly and through His servants throughout Biblical history. Then we will examine the degree to which such penal sanctions can be rightly applied today within the Church and the civil government.

Within the law of God there is a distinction between sins and crimes. While all acts of sin are a violation of God's law and all sins have a penal sanction tied to them ("the wages of sin is death" Romans 6:23), not all sins are classified as crimes punishable by the state according to God's law. Sin can incur a verbal rebuke or a temporal punishment that is designed to correct the behavior of the offender. Such punishments are not purely punitive for they are a form of discipline that has restoration as their goal.

The primary difference between a sin and a crime is whether or not the action is punishable within the jurisdiction of the state, the Church or the family or any combination of the three covenantal spheres of society. Both parents and Church leaders address the sins of those under the charge of their care but they do not address them as a crime. Furthermore, there are many sins that only take place in the heart but they are only addressed by God for neither the state, the Church nor family leaders can look into the heart of an individual and judge their interior motives or sinful thoughts. While parental and ecclesiastical correction is always to verbally address the heart, they can only look at the outwards actions of a person. For this reason, only God can look into and judge the sins of the heart, "...for God sees not as man sees, for man looks at the outward appearance, but the LORD looks at the heart" (1 Samuel 16:7). For example, coveting is an inward disposition that often precedes other sins and crimes but the state was not required to judge and punish people for coveting or lusting.[446]

According to some theonomists, the civil penal sanction is not primarily intended to deter crime or correct the behavior of the offender. Rather it is purely punitive in the form of "an eye for an eye."[447] The corrective and deterrent nature of the civil enforcement of the penal sanctions of the law then is secondary, indirect and consequential instead. However, in Scripture we find the same language that is used to exhort parents to correct their children is also used in the procedures for the civil court. For example, the Proverbs tell us that corporal punishment is designed to bring wisdom to the fool by showing him the consequences of his actions (Proverbs 10:13).

When we see this understanding of corporal punishment implemented by the civil justice system in Scripture this is what we find:

> If there is a dispute between men and they go to court, and the judges decide their case, and they justify the righteous and condemn the wicked, then it shall be if the wicked man deserves to be beaten, the judge shall then make him lie down and be beaten in his presence with the number of stripes according to his guilt. He may beat him forty times but no more, so that he does not beat him with many more stripes than these and your brother is not degraded in your eyes (Deuteronomy 25:1-3).

While the penal sanctions at times act as an emergency stopgap measure to preserve a society clearly one of the intended purposes of penal sanctions is corrective and not purely punitive for there is an expressed concern for the dignity of the offender. The motive of the punishment is parental for the state is to bring wisdom to the adult fool who is acting childishly in his sin. The reason why a sinner finds himself in court being punished by the state is because the foolishness of his childhood

446   As Greg L. Bahnsen states, "It is perhaps helpful to distinguish between 'sin' and 'crime.' While all crime is sinful, not every sin is a crime. An offense against God's law is a crime when it is a social misdeed punishable by the governing authorities; sin on the other hand, is always judged and punished by God" *Theonomy in Christian Ethics* (Covenant Media Press; Third Edition, 2002), 422.

447   Greg L. Bahnsen states, "The main underlying principle of scriptural penology (whether civic or eternal) is not reformation or deterrence, but justice." *Ibid*, 423.

is still bound up in his heart. When a person grows up and is no longer under the jurisdiction of his parents, the state then becomes a means of external discipline. For the state not to uphold this form of correctional discipline is to spare the childish adult (Proverbs 22:15; 23:13-14).

What we are concerned with in this chapter is the fact that the Word of God considers many sexual acts not only a sin, but also a crime that was punishable by the civil magistrate. The key to determining whether an act is not only a sin but also a crime is whether or not the action has a prescribed capital penal sanction in God's law, a punishment that was to be a carried out by the state as distinguished from familial or ecclesiastical authorities. While only God can punish sins that have not been atoned for, the state in both the Old and New Covenants has been given the authority by God to use the sword to punish evildoers in order to administer justice (Romans 13:1-7).

Covenant Conditions and Obligations

To rightly understand the relationship between God's law and the various assigned penal sanctions we must keep in mind when reading the progression of redemptive history in the Scriptures that faith and obedience has always been required in all of the covenants between God and His people. The failure to maintain fidelity always incurred some form of penal sanction that may be enforced by God directly or through His ordained representatives in the family, Church or state. For example, we read that all of the covenants require faith and a subsequent faithful walk with Him:

> Abrahamic Covenant – "**Walk** before me and be blameless" (Genesis 17:1).

> Mosaic Covenant – "You shall **walk** in all the way which the LORD your God has commanded you, that you may live and that it may be well with you, and that you may prolong your days in the land which you will possess" (Deuteronomy 33:4).

> The New Covenant – "Therefore I, the prisoner of the Lord, implore you to **walk** in a manner worthy of the calling with which you have been called" (Ephesians 4:1).

Furthermore, all of the covenants contain promises of life, conditions and obligations. These are the "if" statements which are to be kept which are accompanied by warnings of being "cut" off" "vomited out" or "purged" (Leviticus 18:25; Revelation 3:16) should the covenant member seek to follow other gods or not live in repentance of sin:

> Abrahamic Covenant – "This is My covenant, which you shall keep, between Me and you and your descendants after you: every male among you shall be circumcised.... But an uncircumcised male who is not circumcised in the flesh of his foreskin, that person shall be **cut off** from his people; he has broken My covenant" (Genesis 17:10, 14).

> Mosaic Covenant – "'For whoever does any of these abominations, those persons who do so shall be **cut off** from among their people" (Leviticus 18:29).

> The New Covenant – "Behold then the kindness and severity of God; to those who fell, severity, but to you, God's kindness, if you continue in His kindness; otherwise you also will be **cut off**" (Romans 11:22).

There are many who assert that the Creation Covenant and Mosaic Covenant were conditional being a covenant of law whereas the Abrahamic Covenant and the New Covenant in Christ is "unconditional" being covenants of grace.[448] But this is not the testimony of Scripture. The New Testament contains many warnings to not be deceived and exhortations to persevere in faith and not turn back to one's former way of life. Specifically, there were Christian Jews who were tempted to "drift away" and return to the types and shadows of the Old Covenant (Hebrews 2:1-2) and Gentile Christians who were tempted to return to

---

448   Dwight Pentecost, *Things To Come* (Grand Rapids, MI: Zondervan, 1958), 68; Michael Horton, *God of Promise* (Grand Rapids, MI: Baker Books, 2006), 10, 33.

pagan philosophies and the subsequent way of life (1 Corinthians 6:9; Ephesians 4:17).

Of course, what also must be noted in the transition of the covenants is that the warning that one will be "cut off" in the Mosaic Covenant applies to an earthly kingdom in which the offender or apostate will be exiled from the land and in the New Covenant it ultimately applies to the heavenly kingdom. Hence apostasy in the Mosaic Covenant has civil sociopolitical as well as eternal ramifications whereas the New Covenant currently only has ecclesiastical and eternal consequences unless a state were to become thoroughly Christianized and begin upholding these laws as well.[449]

Minimum to Maximum Penalties: From Exile to The Death Penalty

While the death penalty for any sin or crime may seem to some to be extreme, cruel and contrary to the love of God the Bible tells us the payment that is due for sin, any and *all* sin, is death (Romans 1:32; 6:23). Receiving anything less than the death penalty from God is an act of leniency in which the sinner is given time to repent so that his soul might be saved through the atoning death and resurrection of Jesus Christ. When God enacts anything less than death for a particular sin it is a nonobligatory act of grace and mercy on His part. Furthermore, the Lord often withholds an immediate sentence to death for a sin because He is allowing the person to store up wrath for themselves for the Day of Judgment (Romans 2:5) or He has given the sinner time to repent and He has provided a substitutionary death to bear the punishment of the sin in the place of the offender (2 Peter 3:9).

Closely associated with death, or at times in place of the death penalty, the Lord often enacts or commands a form of exile from the land or the covenant community (i.e. the land of Israel or the Church). There are various terms that are used through the Old and New Testaments to convey this idea including "cast out" (Kings 9:7; Jeremiah 7:15; Matthew 8:12), "purge" (Ezekiel 20:38; 1 Corinthians 5:7), "vomit out"

---

449   By "Christianized" I do not mean the Church rules over the state, the state rules over the Church or that there is a mixture or confusion of Church and state jurisdictions. A "Christianized" society would be one in which a society becomes predominently Christian through the Church preaching of the gospel and the discipling of the nations and consequently the law of the state reflects the Church's influence on culture.

(Leviticus 18:28; Revelation 3:16), "removed" (Deuteronomy 28:25; 2 Chronicles 7:20) "accursed" or "anathema" (Romans 9:3; Galatians 1:8-9) all of which refer to what we would call "excommunication," a religious censure used to deprive or suspend membership in the covenant community. While excommunication may not entail physical death, to be "cut off" from the covenant community and from the Lord Himself is often equated with spiritual death. To be received and restored back into the community after a confession of sin and repentance is to be returned to life as the father said concerning the return of his prodigal son, "… for this son of mine was dead and has come to life again; he was lost and has been found" (Luke 15:24; 32).

Whatever we may think about a punishment fitting a crime, the first sin and crime worthy of the death penalty was for eating a piece of forbidden fruit as we find the very first commandment (law) that had a prescribed death penalty in the Creation Covenant. After creating the earth and all that it contains in six days, resting on the seventh, the Lord said to Adam, "From any tree of the garden you may eat freely; but from the tree of the knowledge of good and evil you shall not eat, for in the day that you eat from it you will surely die" (Genesis 2:16-17).

In the Hebrew text the penal sanction is quite emphatic as it literally states, "…in dying you shall surely die." We know that Adam did break this commandment and yet he did not "surely die" "in the day" that he ate from it. In his place an animal died and was used to cover his nakedness (Genesis 3:21). Subsequently a lesser penalty was given in that he was cast out of the Garden of Eden, a penalty that is synonymous with later sanctions of being "cut off," "vomited out," "purged" or "ex-communicated." Being cut off and barred by the angel with the sword, Adam was prevented from partaking of the Tree of Life which would have given him eternal life (Genesis 3:24). Being mortal and unable to partake of the Tree of life, eventually Adam's body would die but the destruction of his flesh occurred slowly in time. This extended time of death introduced into the world a redemptive-history that provided the opportunity for his soul to be saved through the One that would crush the head of the serpent (Genesis 3:15). After Adam sinned the Lord mercifully held back from fully enacting the full extent of the penal sanction upon him. Instead He provided a substitute death as a type of Christ, purged Adam out of the garden, and turned his body over to decay so that his soul might be saved. We also see the affect of his sin as the sword enters his own household when Cain slays Abel (Genesis 4:8). This exact same pattern is repeated throughout redemptive history on numerous occasions in which the Lord withholds the full sentence allowable by His law for an act of sin, the death penalty, and yet the sin has an enormous impact on the individual, the family, the tribe or nation.

Another case in the Bible in which we see the Lord not fully carry out the prescribed penal sanction and the provision of a substitute was when King David committed adultery with Bathsheba and then murdered of her husband Uriah (2 Samuel 11:2-27). Even before the giving of the law in written form at Sinai, the Lord had already commanded the death penalty for the sin of murder (Genesis 9:6). In the law the Lord states if someone did not accidentally kill someone but actually plotted to take his life he is to be excommunicated and then put to death, "If, however, a man acts presumptuously toward his neighbor, so as to kill him craftily, you are to take him even from My altar, that he may die." (Exodus 21:14) This precisely describes King David's sin and crime.

Some theonomists argue that the death penalty was required to always to be upheld regardless as to the identity of the criminal:

> Not only was punishment according to an equitable standard in the Older Testament, but such punishment (in order to remain just) had to be certain (Prov. 11:21) and without mercy or pity to the criminal – no matter who he was (Heb. 10:28; Deut. 19:13, 21; 25:12; cf. James 2:13)… **All** those who committed capital crimes (as defined by God's law) had to be executed or else the magistrate would be sinfully judging *against the victim* and *in favor of the defender*; this is the sign of wicked judgment.[450]

Yet, this is not what we find in the Scriptures. Upon confession of his sin this is what Nathan, the prophet of the Lord, said to David:

> The LORD also has taken away your sin; you shall not die. However, because by this deed you have given occasion to

---

450   Greg L. Bahnsen, *Theonomy in Christian Ethics* (Covenant Media Press; Third Edition, 2002), 425.

the enemies of the LORD to blaspheme, the child also that
is born to you shall surely die (2 Samuel 12:13-14).

In David's place, the son-of-David would die as a type of Christ and
yet the impact of his sin would affect his entire household. Out of mercy
the Lord held back from enacting the full penal sanction upon David.
Yet David, like Adam, would see the sword within his own household
(Genesis 4:8; 2 Samuel 12:10).

It must be noted then that when the Apostle Paul states that men
having sex with other men and women with other women are conducting acts "worthy of death" that he also includes those sinners who are
greedy, full of envy, murder, deceit, gossips, slanderers, haters of God
who "know the ordinance of God" and yet "practice such things" and
"also give hearty approval to those who practice them" (Romans 1:32).
Greg Bahnsen cites this passage to legitimize the upholding of the death
penalty today for, among other things, homosexuality:

> When God says homosexuality (for instance) warrants
> capital punishment, then that is what social justice de-
> mands; that is how heinous with respect to social relations
> the crime is in God's judgment. Those who are put to death
> according to the law of God are described in Deuteronomy
> 21:22 as ones who have "committed sin worthy of death."...
> Even the Gentiles know the judicial commandment of God
> that they who commit certain things (homosexuality in
> particular) are "worthy of death" (Rom. 1:32).[451]

But in doing so Bahnsen has ripped Paul's statement out of its context. The apostle has used the penal sanction of Deuteronomy 21:22
to refer to *all* sins including those which were not punishable by the
state (envy, greed, gossip) under the Mosaic Covenant, not to argue for
the legitimacy of capital punishment. As Paul will go on to argue in
Romans chapter 2, he makes the point that both Jew and Gentile are
under the same condemnation for sin because those without the law will
be judged and those with the law will be judged (Romans 2:12) because
"all have sinned and fall short of the glory of God..." (Romans 3:23).

451   Greg L. Bahnsen, *Theonomy in Christian Ethics* (Covenant Media Press; Third
Edition, 2002), 427.

In fact, if you read Deuteronomy 21:22 in light of the New Testament we find that it points us not to the legislation of the death penalty but to the work of Christ, "If a man has committed a sin worthy of death and he is put to death, and you hang him on a tree" (cf. Galatians 3:13). To assert then that Romans 1:32 is a justification for the state to enforce the penal sanctions of the law is to then insist that the civil magistrate put to death those who are envious, gossipers or greedy which even the Mosaic Covenant did not require. I dare say that if they did this there wouldn't be anyone alive in the Church!

The Prohibitions and Penal Sanctions of Leviticus 18 and 20

Leviticus chapters 17 through 26 are often referred to as the "Holiness Code" due to the repeated use of the word "holy." In chapter 18 there is a list of prohibited sexual activities ("you shall not uncover the nakedness") with the warning that should they violate the law the land will "vomit you out" (v. 24) and the person will be "cut off from his people" (v. 29). This is synonymous with being exiled, purged or excommunicated as were Adam and Eve from the Garden of Eden. The following is a summary of the Lord's sexual prohibitions in Leviticus 18:

> Do not be have sex with your father (v. 7)
> Do not be have sex with your mother or step-mother (v. 8)
> Do not be have sex with your sister (v. 9)
> Do not be have sex with your granddaughter (v. 10)
> Do not be have sex with your sister (v. 11)
> Do not have sex with your aunt (on your mother's side) (v. 13)
> Do not have sex with your uncle (on your father's side) (v. 14)
> Do not have sex with your daughter-in-law (v. 15)
> Do not have sex with your sister-in-law (v. 16)
> Do not sexually involved with a woman as well as her daughter (v. 17)
> Do not marry a woman as well as her sister (v. 18)
> Do not have sex with a woman during her menstrual impurity (v. 19)

Do not have sex with your neighbor's wife (v. 20)
Do not give any of your offspring to offer them to Molech, nor
shall you profane the name of your God; I am the LORD. (v. 21)
Do not have sex with a man as you would with a woman (v. 22)
Do not have sex with an animal (v. 23)

This list of forbidden sex acts are listed again in chapter 20 with
the same admonition against following the practices of the Canaanites
along with the warning that if they disobey they will be exiled out of
the land. While Leviticus 18 presents them as a simple list, Leviticus
20 presents them according to the seriousness of the offence and the se-
verity of the penal sanction (punishment) deemed appropriate for each
violation. These range from excommunication to execution or what we
might think of as turning the person over to the executioner for "the
destruction of his flesh" (1 Corinthians 5:5). The reason given for the
prohibition and the penalty is because God is holy and they are His
people whom He is sanctifying (Leviticus 18:7-8).

If someone offers their son as a sacrifice to Molech, he shall be put
to death by the people (vv. 2-3). But if the people fail to carry out the
death penalty on the violator then the Lord Himself will carry out the
penal sanction (v. 5). In other words, penal sanctions cannot be avoid-
ed. We will see this pattern again in the New Testament as the Father
(Romans 1:26), the Son (Revelation 3:16), and the Holy Spirit (Acts
5:1-11) each carry out the penal sanction judgments. If anyone consults
mediums or spiritists such an act is considered spiritual whoredom and
the Lord Himself will "cut him off" from among the people (v. 6). If
there is anyone who curses his father or his mother, he shall surely be
put to death (v. 9). If this punishment seems excessive we should keep
in mind that this is a law that the Pharisees had set aside for the sake
of their tradition and Jesus rebuked them for it, thereby upholding the
commandment (Mark 7:9-10). However, it is clear that we not talking
about a toddler having a temper tantrum but rather an obstinate rebellious juvenile delinquent who defies all authority as we read elsewhere:

If any man has a stubborn and rebellious son who will not
obey his father or his mother, and when they chastise him,
he will not even listen to them, then his father and mother

shall seize him, and bring him out to the elders of his city at the gateway of his hometown. They shall say to the elders of his city, "This son of ours is stubborn and rebellious, he will not obey us, he is a glutton and a drunkard." Then all the men of his city shall stone him to death; so you shall remove the evil from your midst, and all Israel will hear of it and fear (Deuteronomy 21:18-21).

If anyone commits adultery they are to be put to death and yet at times the full punishment is withheld, such as in the case of King David (v. 10). This same death penalty is stated for having sex with your father's wife (v. 11), a sin Paul confronted in the church of Corinth and upheld the lesser penalty of being "purged" or "cut off" for the slow death, the destruction of the flesh, which gave the man time to repent and be restored (Leviticus 18:29; 1 Corinthians 5:13). Then when the man repented Paul exhorted the church to restore him to life and fellowship in the body (2 Corinthians 2:6-8).

Greg Bahnsen in his book *Theonomy in Christian Ethics* states, "… the death penalty for certain crimes is not simply a suggestion from God but a formal *command*."[452] However while the penal sanctions of the law were definitely prescriptions and not suggestions we should not jump to the conclusion that such the death penalty by the state was always mandatory. One of the first things that need to be recognized is that the penalties attached to the various sins and crimes in the Old Testament are often examples of the maximum punishment that may be applied. This is not unlike fines and penalties today in which an offender can be fined, serve time in jail or both. As previously stated, the law of God frequently provides a range of punishment from a form of exile which may be referred to as "excommunication," "purged," "removed," "put away," "impeachment," or "cut off" (Leviticus 18:29) all the way up to an actual execution. Such executions may be carried out directly by God or one of His agencies including angels, the domestic head of the civil government who is His minister of wrath (Romans 13:1-7), or foreign kings in the judgment of His own people who are also referred to as His

---

452   Greg L. Bahnsen, *Theonomy in Christian Ethics* (Covenant Media Press; Third Edition, 2002), 433.

minister or servant of wrath (Jeremiah 25:9).[453] Or in His providence He may carry out His judgment through "natural disasters" or the person may simply be allowed to suffer the "natural consequences" of their actions such as deadly venereal diseases and other somatic illnesses. We see an example of this range of enforcement of penal sanctions enacted when Asa "put away" the cult prostitutes who are banished rather than executed:

> Asa did what was right in the sight of the LORD, like David his father. He also put away the **male cult prosti-tutes** (Hebrew: *kadeshim*) from the land and removed all the idols which his fathers had made. Likewise, he also impeached his mother because of her idolatry, He also removed Maacah his mother from being queen mother, because she had made a horrid image as an Asherah (1 Kings 15:11-13).

In light of this, it is fallacious to conclude that when the penal sanction of the death penalty is read in the law of God that it *always* had to be carried out to its fullest extent by the state as some theonomists assert, "Such are the demands of justice of the civil judgment; a crime *always* receives what it, with respect to the context of social life, deserves as equitable for the nature of the offense." [454]

This is the result of a "static" reading of the text in which only the narrow context is read without also taking into consideration the law's principles in the full range of God's Word in prescribing and upholding penal sanctions throughout redemptive history. Therefore, to argue that in order to uphold the moral principle of the sexual ethics of the Holiness Code requires the upholding of the death penalty is inaccurate as James R. White and Jeffrey Niell point out:

---

453   "'Behold, I will send and take all the families of the north,' declares the LORD, 'and I will send to Nebuchadnezzar king of Babylon, *My servant*, and will bring them against this land and against its inhabitants and against all these nations round about; and I will utterly destroy them and make them a horror and a hissing, and an everlasting desolation...'" (Jeremiah 25:9)

454   Greg L. Bahnsen, *Theonomy in Christian Ethics* (Covenant Media Press; Third Edition, 2002), 426. (emphasis mine)

...we see that they were not summarily executed, but over an extended period of time – through the reigns of his father and into his own reign – they worked on ridding the land of this sinful practice. Those who wanted to remain among the covenant people of the Lord were required to repent.[455]

Contrary to the assertion of some theonomists the death was the *maximum* penalty to be carried out by the state, not the *required* penalty for committing acts of sexual sins and crimes. This is found even in the Old Testament as the law could be upheld regarding men who had sex with other men in a cultic context without fully carrying out the death penalty. Asa obeyed the law by expelling (which is synonymous with "vomiting out" "purging," "removing the leaven," and "excommunicating") the male cult prostitutes even though the law states that the maximum punishment for the sin is death. This is the same punishment listed for the remainder of the sins in Leviticus 20 such as having sex with one's sister (v. 17) or having sex with a menstruating woman (v. 18).

At the end of the list of prohibitions and penal sanctions we find the warning is that failure to obey will result in the people of God being expelled rather than receive their inheritance:

> You are therefore to keep all My statutes and all My ordinances and do them, so that the land to which I am bringing you to live will not spew you out. Moreover, you shall not follow the customs of the nation which I will drive out before you, for they did all these things, and therefore I have abhorred them. Hence I have said to you, "You are to possess their land, and I Myself will give it to you to possess it, a land flowing with milk and honey. I am the LORD your God, who has separated you from the peoples" (Leviticus 20:22-24).

We also need to take notice that the Old Testament promises and warnings of obtaining or losing one's inheritance (which are typological of inheriting the Kingdom of God) are maintained and carried over to

---

455   James R. White, Jeffrey Niell, *The Same Sex Controversy* (Minneapolis, MN: Bethany House Pub., 2002), 88.

the New Covenant as well. This is why Paul exhorts the children in the church, "Children, obey your parents in the Lord, for this is right. Honor you father and your mother (which is the first commandment with a promise), so that it may be well with you, and that you may live long on the earth" (Ephesians 6:1-3; cf. Exodus 20:12). This is also why, after judging the man who violated Leviticus 18:8, Paul then cites a list of sins from Leviticus 18 and 20 and warns those who would assume to be free to commit such acts because they call themselves Christians, "Or do you not know that the unrighteous will not inherit the kingdom of God?" (1 Corinthians 6:9)

What is extremely important to keep in mind is that in the middle of Leviticus Chapters 18-20 we find the Great Commandment that is upheld in the New Covenant and deemed to be the heart or summary of the law in which the believer to commanded, "You shall love the LORD your God with all your heart and with all your soul and with all your might" (Deuteronomy 6:5) and "love thy neighbor as thyself" (Leviticus 19:18). In fact, Jesus Himself regarded these as the two most important commandments for by following these two commandments you would then seek to obey all the others as well (Mark 12:30-31).

Covenant Jurisdiction and The Law

Before we continue to look at the New Testament's use of the law of God and the Old Testament penal sanctions we need to understand the law's prescribed jurisdictional boundaries for the various types of leaders within a society. The prescribed spheres of jurisdiction limits the authority delegated to these rulers by God and it informs them of their responsibilities and duties towards God and man.

The Lord in creating the ordered universe structured the sea and its creatures, the land and its creatures, the sky and its creatures, and the heavens with its ruling lights. In the created order of the universe we see various spheres along with their governors or rulers, "God made the two great lights, the greater light to govern the day, and the lesser light to govern the night" (Genesis 1:16).

The Lord also created mankind and gave them the mandate to subdue, govern and rule the earth as His representative on earth (Genesis 1:28). However, mankind's rule or governing had jurisdictional boundaries that were prescribed to Him by God as they were commanded not to eat from the tree of knowledge of good and evil (Genesis 2:16-17). In subduing the land we see a foreshadowing of the role of a king in which Adam was to act as a ruler. But, he needed someone to rule with him, a help-meet and so God gave him a queen to rule with him having been taken from his side (Genesis 2:21-23).

Just as there was a created order with various spheres (land, sea, sky) with various metaphorical rulers (animals, fish, birds) with the sun to rule the day and the moon to rule the night, so too mankind was in a familial covenantal sphere in which Adam after he was given the commandments of the Lord, before the woman was created, was to pass on to his wife. In this way Adam also served as a priest. We know that he did so for when she is later confronted by the serpent she is able to repeat to the serpent the commandments of the Lord (Genesis 3:2).

Mankind was also created within a household. In the household the husband and wife are ontologically equal as they are created in the image of God and are on equal par with each other before God (Genesis 1:27; Galatians 3:28). Yet in the economy of the covenant household they have different roles and responsibilities for the husband is the head of the wife just as Christ is the head of the husband and the Father is the head of the Son (Genesis 3:16; 1 Corinthians 11:3). The relationship of the husband, wife and children reflect the economic Trinity of the Father, Son and Holy Spirit in which there is ontological equality but differing responsibilities and roles within the Godhead. So too, while there is ontological equality in the household there is an economic sub-ordination in the family in which the wife is to submit to the husband as the Church submits to Christ (Ephesians 5:22-24). In turn the husband is to love, lead, shepherd his wife and family as Christ does for the Church and children are to submit to their parents (Exodus 20:12; Ephesians 6:1-3). We see then from the beginning that the jurisdictional function of king, priest, and father existed together and that all of these roles were to be carried out under the rule of the Word of God.

One of the first things that the crafty serpent did to undermine God's order, what He had instructed Adam to do, was to undermine Adam's headship over His wife. Both the husband and the wife are to be under God's revealed Word by which they were to live and interpret creation. They were not to use the scientific method to find out whether or not eating from the tree of the knowledge of good and evil would cause them to die, but rather by faith they were to trust and obey God's Word.

The serpent in order to undermine God's authority sought to disrupt the order of creation by undermining Adam's authority as head of his wife. He did this by directly addressing her and calling her to question the truthfulness of God's Word. It is at that point that the entire order of God's creation was being undermined and the rest is history. The woman heeded the word of the serpent and then gave the forbidden fruit to her husband. From that point, all of creation was fallen from its original order. Rather than man having dominion over the land, the land would have dominion over the man as it would swallow him in the grave.

However, the dominion mandate did not end with the Adam's rebellions. Man still has the command to rule over the earth but now that the human race is fallen, there is a battle for rule between the seed of the serpent and the seed of the woman to see which of them will have dominion. The story of redemption involves God restoring the order of creation by redeeming man by means of the covenant of redeeming grace that will find its *telos* in the seed of the woman (Christ) who crushes the head of the seed of the serpent (Satan) (Genesis 3:15). Ultimately the restoration of the created order culminates at the time of the resurrection, when the earth will no longer groan with the sons of God (Romans 8:18-23). This task is made sure by the second Adam keeping God's law and paying the price for man's sin. Having accomplished the work of redemption through being raised from the dead, the Second Adam reinstates the dominion mandate according to His authority (Matthew 28:18-20).

The means by which this second dominion mandate is accomplished is through God's means of grace - through the preaching, baptizing, and teaching new disciples to obey Christ's law. However, in order to rightly disciple the nations Christ's commandments must be rightly observed. We must not impose our own taxonomy on God's law, and therefore seek to interpret it according to our order. Rather, we must seek to understand Christ's commandments according to how He has always ordered things. That is, according to the covenant and their respective jurisdictional responsibilities and boundaries. Just as there is an order in creation, so too there is an order in the covenant. In God's covenant with man, like the creation spheres and rulers, He has ordered three social covenantal spheres with their respective heads.

The first covenantal sphere that we see in the Garden of Eden, is the family with the husband whose job it is to lead the wife. After the fall we see the parents over the children (Exodus 20:12; Ephesians 6:1-2). The other two spheres that grew out of the nucleus of the family are the church and the state with their respective heads the priests/elders and the king/civil magistrate.[456] In relation to these latter two, there is a certain degree of continuity from the Old Mosaic economy to the New Covenant but there is also clearer distinction and separation. For example, under the Old Covenant in Israel the leader of the civil magistrate (the king) had to also be a member of the Church. Under the New Covenant the civil magistrate does not have to be a member of the Church even though he is still referred to as a "minister of God" (Romans 13:1). We also see this in the Old Testament as well as the foreign kings during the exile were also referred to as a minister of God (Jeremiah 25:9). The authority of the civil ruler (king, prime minister, president) does not come from his own might but rather from God who, in His providence, delegates authority to them, "It is He who changes the times and the epochs; He removes kings and establishes kings; He gives wisdom to wise men and knowledge to men of understanding" (Daniel 2:21). This is why Jesus said to Pilate, "You would have no authority over Me, unless it had been given you from above" (John 19:11).

Many contend that there was no distinction between the Church and state in the old economy but such an assertion hardly can be supported by the evidence. The king in the old economy had clear jurisdictional limits as he was not to perform temple sacrifices as Saul did and for breaching his jurisdictional boundary he was rejected by God as king (1 Samuel 15). While there were at times exceptions to the rule, this is no different from the possibility of that same rule today. For example, though it is the role of the civil magistrate to conduct war in the protection of a nation, if such a country were under attack by an invading army a ruling elder or pastor would not be prohibited from taking up arms as a citizen to defend the country. However, it is not normative for ecclesiastical rulers to be involved in such activities, neither were the actions of the priests who administered the civil sword.

It is common today for pornographers, gay activists and pro-abortionists to boastfully declare, "You can't legislate morality!" To them "morality" is narrowly defined as the sexual conduct which takes place between two people and the consequence thereafter, i.e. an unwanted pregnancy and A.I.D.S. However, morality cannot be so narrowly

---

456   John Frame, "Toward A Theology of the State" *Westminster Theological Journal* 51:2 (Fall, 1989), 199-226.

defined. Morality is a system of ideas of right and wrong conduct and
ethics is a set of principles of right conduct.[457] If morals cannot be legislated, then neither can the prohibition of certain activities be declared
illegal which is an absurd assertion. In short, those who want to be free
to conduct their sexual perversions want to say, "I want to be free from
any and all laws!"[458]

457   Ethics is the study of the general nature of morals and the rules or standards
governing the conduct of a person. Therefore, all laws have a moral and ethical component to them and together they convey God's standard for justice and mercy. The
prohibition against murder and stealing is a moral law. Therefore the person who advocates an imposed social acceptance of homosexual behavior or the legalization or
prostitution to declare, "You can't legislate morality!" is a self contradictory statement
for in essence they are saying, "It is immoral to legislate morality!"

458   In a similar manner, it is absurd to assert that the fifth commandment, "Honor
your father and your mother" is a moral law whereas the first four commandments are
religious laws, much less to relegate the fourth commandment to being a "ceremonial
Law." The Bible gives us no warrant for imposing such categories on the Decalogue.
Therefore, to insist that the penal sanctions of the death penalty of the law should be
upheld today by the state would also entail the state upholding the death penalty for
breaking the first four commandments. How then should we categorize God's Law? In
order for a law to be upheld and enforced it needs an officer, a covenantal head, who
is responsible to uphold that law. Without anyone to uphold a law, it is unenforceable.
Therefore, God has assigned authorities to uphold His Law according to their respective covenantal spheres; the family, the Church, and the state. The parents uphold
familial laws, the church elders uphold ecclesiastical laws, and the civil magistrate is
God's minister to uphold civil laws (Romans 13:4). Seen in this light, we might then
argue that the first four commandments (and all their various applications) in the Old
Covenant had civil, familial, and ecclesiastical applications, as the father was required
to ensure that everyone within the jurisdiction of his household kept the Sabbath: "…
the seventh day is a Sabbath of the LORD your God; in it you shall not do any work,
you or your son or your daughter, your male or your female servant or your cattle or
your sojourner who stays with you." (Exodus 20:10) The law of God ought not to be
categorized as moral laws, ceremonial laws, and civil laws, but rather according to
their respective covenantal heads. In doing so we see in Scriptures various familial
laws, ecclesiastical laws, and civil laws. We also need to see that many of the laws
had familial, ecclesiastical and civil applications. In a nation that is culturally and religiously unified these three spheres of society will be unified in their understanding and
application of the law. Without such a cultural uniformity, it is not possible to expect
there to be a uniform upholding of God's law which creates a great deal of tension
within a nation as civil leaders tend to overstep their jurisdictional boundaries and
impose the will of the state over the family and the Church. Or, when ecclesiastical
rulers gain civil political power, men tend to seek an office within the Church in order
to gain such political advantage as they think spirituality is merely a means for gaining
great political and financial gain.

It is therefore our task in conducting sound exegesis of God's Law-word to determine which familial, ecclesiastical, and the civil laws remain binding and which do not in the New Covenant and whether or not they can be rightly applied today by existing governments. However, since God alone is Lord over His Word, only He may state which laws remain binding and which do not. But in seeking to discern from God's Word when and how Biblical principles ought to be applied, as we shall later see, what is required is not merely cherry-picking of God's laws but rather a formal system of justice that is applied to the civil sphere.

When we read the New Testament we find that the apostles maintained a continuity of God's law until it was revealed to them that they were to do otherwise. An example of this is when God told Peter concerning eating non kosher foods and associating with Gentiles, "What God has cleansed, no longer consider unholy" (Acts 10:15). Therefore, our presumption should favor not the expiration of any law but its eternal validity, unless we have evidence to believe otherwise. In each category (familial, ecclesiastical, civil) there are laws that remain and those that were both typological and found their end in Christ. There are some laws that remain but are now observed differently. Not only is God's Law divisible according to covenantal spheres with its respective authorities (parents, elders, civil magistrates) but each sphere has its own delegated jurisdiction. Just as a covenant consists of promises, obligations for obedience and warnings of curses for disobedience so too each covenantal head has his own rights, privileges, and responsibilities.

It is the responsibility of the civil magistrate, as God's minister of wrath, to uphold justice in the civil sphere and to defend his citizens from foreign invasion. But here is where continuities and discontinuities between ancient civil governments and modern civil governments complicate the manner of not only what governing authorities *ought* to do, but what they are *able* do in their public office.

Throughout the Old and New Testaments we see that in the surrounding nations is essentially a monarchical form of government in which the king's word was law (Daniel 9:15). In Israel the word of the king was limited as he was under obligation to abide by God's law which was not given to the surrounding nations. If this were still the manner of civil government today, from a Biblical perspective we would assert that the civil magistrate has the right to create laws that are in accord with an epistemologically justifiable ethical system in which he could use his delegated authority to make the principles of God's Word, including its civil penal sanctions, the basis for law of the land.

However, civil rulers today are comparatively limited in power and consequently they are required, by oath of an allegiance to their state's constitution, to uphold and enforce laws within the system of government that they have inherited from their predecessors. To assert then that the Prime Minster of England or the President of the United States is required to enforce laws that are contrary to, say the Constitution of the United States, because such a law was required of the Kings of Israel is contrary to the context of Romans 13 and the faithful actions of God's servants who served in the Civil sphere in governments with a non-Biblical system of law throughout redemptive history.

For example, both Joseph and Daniel who served as vice-regents under pagan forms of government had to work to the best of their ability within their given limited authority. Likewise, in the first century Roman soldiers who were God-fearers had to serve to the best of their ability to do justice within their given limitations of serving under not only a totalitarian form of government, but one that was militantly hostile towards God's law (Luke 3:14). To assert that modern Christians are morally obligated to uphold penal sanctions that are not permissible within their given government constitution would be like asserting that an ostrich is required to be able to fly. This is why it is fallacious to assert that a Christian serving in the public area in state government ought to uphold the penal sanctions of God's law when he lacks the authority to do so. Yet, theonomists such as Greg Bahnsen have asserted this very thing:

> Therefore, civil magistrates **today** are under obligation to execute all those who commit capital crimes as defined by God's authoritative law. Paul's word in Romans 13 is sufficient to demonstrate to us that the magistrate does have the obligation and authorization to inflict the death penalty upon certain violators of God's law.[459]

Again, Bahnsen has ripped Paul's words out of their historical context. Paul is exhorting Christians for the sake of the Gospel to pay what

459   Greg L. Bahnsen, *Theonomy in Christian Ethics* (Covenant Media Press; Third Edition, 2002), 428. (emphasis added)

we would deem according to God's law as unjust taxes in submission to the civil ruler who has the God-given authority to execute those who resist their will. This does not mean that the laws of Caesar were in accordance with God's law, but rather *for the sake of the gospel* and for *the sake of conscience* the apostles exhorted the Church to not use their freedom in Christ as an excuse to rebel against the tyranny of the occupying Roman government, as the Jews did in the revolts that took place in 66-70 A.D. Rather they were to comply and submit to their masters and governing authorities so that their good deeds would act as a witness of the gospel:

> Keep your behavior excellent among the Gentiles, so that in the thing in which they slander you as evildoers, they may because of your good deeds, as they observe them, glorify God in the day of visitation. Submit yourselves for the Lord's sake to every human institution, whether to a king as the one in authority, or to governors as sent by him for the punishment of evildoers and the praise of those who do right. For such is the will of God that by doing right you may silence the ignorance of foolish men (1 Peter 2:12-15).

The civil magistrate may not justifiably interfere with the role of the elders of the Church, but he is to guarantee the freedom of the leaders of the Church to perform their respective responsibilities. The civil magistrate alone has the physical sword to perform his tasks. Should the civil magistrate go beyond his sphere and interfere with the rights and responsibilities of fathers and elders they are to resist him according to a higher law - the Law of God. In such cases they are to obey God, rather than men for the civil magistrate is not to be followed blindly as Martin Luther wrote:

> But if, as often happens, the temporal power and author-ities, or whatever they call themselves, would compel a subject to do something contrary to command of God, or hinder him from doing what God commands, obedience ends and the obligation ceases. In such cases a man has to

say what St. Peter said to the rulers of the Jews, "We must
obey God rather than man."[460]

There are several cases throughout Scripture of God's people dis-
obeying the civil authorities. For example, as Luther quoted, Peter's
response of the command from the high priest who ordered the Apostles
not to teach in the name of Jesus (Acts 5:27f). In addition, we read
concerning the midwives who disobeyed the command of Pharaoh:

> The king of Egypt said to the Hebrew midwives, whose
> names were Shiphrah and Purah, "When you help the
> Hebrew women in childbirth and observe them on the
> delivery stool, if it is a boy, kill him; if it is a girl, let her
> live" (Exodus 1:15-16).

At this time the nation of Israel was in slavery to the Egyptians and
was under their governing authority. If the midwives strictly followed
the governing authorities they would have killed Moses as well as all
the other Israelite children. But then we read, "The midwives, however,
feared God and did not do what the king of Egypt had told them to do;
they let the boys live" (Exodus 1:17).

The midwives rightly disobeyed the secular authority because of a
higher law for if they had obeyed the king of Egypt they would have
been committing murder. Although it had not been written down yet we
read that the law of God says, "Whoever sheds the blood of man, by man
shall his blood be shed; for in the image of God has God made man"
(Genesis 9:6) and later Moses writes as one of God's commandments
"Thou shall not murder" (Exodus 20:13). Thus, the law of the kingdom
of God was seen as higher than the authority of the civil magistrate.

In the book of Daniel we read of several other examples. King
Nebuchadnezzar has an image of himself made and has it declared to all
the people, "...the moment you hear the sound of the horn, flute, lyre...
and all kinds of music, you are to fall down and worship the golden
image that Nebuchadnezzar the king has set up. But whoever does not
fall down and worship shall immediately be cast into the midst of a furnace of blazing fire." (Daniel 3:5-6) However, three God fearing Jews

460   Martin Luther, "Treatise on Good Works" in *Luther's Works* (Vol. 44) in J. At-
kinson (ed) *The Church in Society* (Philadelphia, PA: Fortress Press, 1966), 81.

rather than dishonoring God, disobeyed the command as the Chaldeans reported to the king, "There are certain Jews whom you have appointed over the administration of the province of Babylon, namely Shadrach, Meshach, and Abednego. These men, O king, have disregarded you." (Daniel 3:12) They are then brought before the king who states, "If you will not worship, you will immediately be cast into the midst of a furnace of blazing fire, and what god is there who can deliver you out of my hands?" (Daniel 3:15) In the minds of the three God fearing Jews was the prohibition of idol worship (Exodus 20:3-5). This is why they reply to the king:

> O Nebuchadnezzar, we do not need to give you an answer
> concerning this matter. If it be so, our God whom we serve
> is able to deliver us from the furnace of blazing fire; and
> He will deliver us out of your hand, O king. But even if He
> does not, let it be known to you, O king, that we are not
> going to serve your gods or worship the golden image that
> you have set up (Daniel 3:16-18).

Later, the commissioners and satraps tried to set king Darius against Daniel by coercing the king to make a law that he could not revoke, "King, Darius, live forever! All the commissioners of the kingdom... have consulted together that the king should establish a statute and enforce an injunction that anyone who makes a petition to any god or any man besides you, O king, for thirty days, shall be cast into the lion's den." (Daniel 6:7)

While Daniel could have easily prayed in secret and avoid the conflict with the secular authority he instead continued his normal practice of praying in which, if someone wanted to, could see him, "Now when Daniel knew that the document was signed, he entered his house (now in his roof chamber he had his windows open toward Jerusalem); and he continued kneeling three times a day, praying and giving thanks before his God, as he had been doing so previously" (Daniel 6:10). Clearly, the civil magistrate whether in a Christianized country or not may not justly institute laws which requires its citizens to sin against God's law.

While Jesus Christ is Lord of the Church, the family and the state and Christians are members of all three, the Church is to have its jurisdictional freedom from the state. While the relation of Church to the state is to be declarative, making known God's will in all matters of life, the state is to have its own work distinct from the Church. The state is to derive no authority from the Church and should exercise its authority free from Church interference within its respective jurisdictional boundaries.

What we find in the Scriptures is the concept of "three kingdoms" each with its own respective jurisdiction and earthly ministers who are required to work in a cooperative manner under the Lordship of Christ. These kingdoms are not earthly verses heavenly but rather in accordance with the three covenantal spheres that the one Lord has established - the Family Kingdom, the Church Kingdom and the Civil Kingdom.

It is not the civil magistrate's role to preach the gospel, to administer the sacraments, or other functions of the ecclesiastical rulers. Likewise, it is not the primary role of elders of the Church or the father of a family to police society. In addition, it is not the primary role of the ecclesiastical elders to feed, clothe, and raise the children of families. It is the parent's role to govern their own home and do such things as feed and educate their children (Deuteronomy 6:7; Proverbs 22:6; Ephesians 6:4). While the Church may conduct acts of mercy in helping families, it is not to take over the God-given responsibility of the family. It is also not the role of the head of the family to administer sacraments, conduct Church discipline, and other tasks assigned to the ecclesiastical elders. When a father conducts such activities, it must be because he is performing them not as the head of a household, but rather because he also holds the office of a presbyter (an elder). Likewise, when the civil magistrate conducts roles of a familial head, he is not doing so in his kingly role but rather as the head of his own house. Therefore when he tells his children to do something he may not say, "Do this because I am the President of the United States (or a policeman, judge, etc.)." Rather the reason for obeying him is, "Because I am your father to whom you are to submit under the Lordship of Christ." In a real sense a father's home is his castle, his dominion, in which he is to serve as the shepherd, king and priest along with his wife who also serves in a cooperative manner as his help-meet.

To summarize, Scripture teaches that there are three basic God-ordained covenantal spheres in society: the family, the Church, and the state. Each sphere has its covenantal heads (ministers) who are responsible for upholding the duties of such roles. Civil authorities are to perform their duties justly as God's ministers (Romans 13:1-7), ecclesiastical leaders (elders) are to teach and rule the Church well (Ephesians 4:1-13; 1 Timothy 5:17), and fathers (and mothers) are to train the children (Proverbs 22:6; Ephesians 6:4).

Penal Sanctions Within the New Covenant
Ecclesiastical Jurisdiction

What we now need to do is determine whether the New Covenant has abrogated the penal sanctions of the Old Testament within either the familial, ecclesiastical or civil jurisdictions. We cannot rightly presume that they have been, for God alone is sovereign over His law. Therefore we need to look to the writings of the apostles to see if they uphold any of the Old Covenant penal sanctions *within their covenantal jurisdiction.* This is an important key distinction since they were not civil rulers but rather they lived as sojourners under the civil rule of a pagan king. Furthermore, unless the culture in which the apostles lived was within a unified Christianized nation (a nation which is predominantly Christian with a culture that reflects its population) we should not expect to find *any* of the penal sanctions as prescribed in God's law being upheld by the state nor any of the apostles seeking to have the state meddle in ecclesiastical affairs in the New Testament. While the pagan kings may at times enforce penal sanctions that coincide with God's law, such as executing murderers, they do so for their purposes, for political expediency and to maintain their hold over the people. They do not do so because they think God's law requires them to do so or because they have deduced such a requirement from a notion of Natural Law. In fact, history bears witness that they will frequently violate God's law in order to maintain and protect their own political interests. A perfect example of this is when Pilate had Christ crucified at the demand of the Jews even when he found Jesus to be innocent of any crime. He did so to appease the hostile Jews and maintain some level of civility in the land (Matthew 27:17-27). When their laws at times formally agree with God's Law their motive is not because they believe the Decalogue requires it. Rather, they are executing murders or providing protection for their citizens because they believe it will suit their political agenda and self-interest that is best suited by maintaining some semblance of civil order.

During the first century the Roman Empire was in control over the state and served (however unjustly) as the minister of God in that sphere and it was the duty of the Christian to submit to the lawful orders of the king. In contrast, in the early days of the Church the apostles only ruled within the ecclesiastical jurisdiction and only wielded the sword of Spirit in Christ's name who is Lord of Lords, and King of kings, and King of the nations with authority and dominion over heaven and earth (Matthew 28:18; Revelation 15:3; 17:14; 19:16). We then find in the New Testament that the apostles upheld the law, specifically from Leviticus 18, and they enforced the penal sanctions even going so far as to turn over a violator to be punished by Satan for the destruction of his flesh so that his soul might be saved (1 Corinthians 5:5). Paul did not enlist the aid of the state or take the violator to a civil court. In fact, he rebuked the Church for seeking to have the civil magistrate meddle in ecclesiastical affairs (1 Corinthians 6:1-5). The shame of the Church today is that Christians take each other to secular courts because they lack wisdom and jurisprudence to handle affairs amongst Christians and they are constantly seeking to use the strong arm of the state to accomplish what is essentially a matter of spiritual warfare. It is particularly true within Liberal Scripture-denying denominations and the Metropolitan Community Churches that see tolerance of what God clearly forbids as a virtue rather than a matter of shame.

Paul makes it clear in Romans 3:31 and 1 Corinthians 6:9-11 that with the exception of the distinctives of the Mosaic Covenant era (circumcision, Old Covenant feast days, food laws) that law keeping is a continuing obligation for Christians as he states, "I am not free from God's law but am under Christ's law" (1 Corinthians 9:21). The "Law of Christ" is not a different set of moral laws than that given to Moses at Sinai. Jesus upheld the law of God and corrected the errors of the Pharisees and then warned that anyone who would do away with the law or teach other otherwise shall be least in the kingdom of heaven (Matthew 5:17-19). If you argue that Christians are not required to keep or obey any of the law given at Sinai then you have to disregard every New Testament text that not merely repeats the law but cites the law as a justification for a call to repentance and standard for living in obedience to Christ.

The Israelites thought they could worship the image of Egyptian god Hapis and Baal if they only renamed it YHWH and so Aaron formed for them a golden calf as he declared to the people, "This is your god, O Israel, who brought you up from the land of Egypt" (Exodus 32:4). In the same way Gay Theology tells people that if they worship in the name of Jesus that Romans 1:25-28 doesn't apply to them. But just as the people of God in the Old Testament would claim to worship YHWH and yet fall into grievous sin to too Christians did this in the first century, even those who have every spiritual blessing imaginable (1 Corinthians 1:7, "...you are not lacking in any gift..."), when they condoned a man having sex with his father's wife, a clear violation of Leviticus 18:8.

The Corinthians may have even protested, "But they love each other.... Besides all things are lawful because we're not Jews or under the law!" Yet Paul told the Church at Rome that not being under the law was the very reason for them *not* to give themselves over to the slavery of sexual sin, "For sin shall not be master over you, for you are not under law but under grace. What then? Shall we sin because we are not under law but under grace? May it never be!" (Romans 6:14-15)

He then went on to uphold Leviticus 18:29 as recorded in 1 Corinthians 5:13, "Remove the wicked man from among yourselves." Repeatedly throughout the Old Testament and the New Testament if people commit these acts and do not repent they are removed like yeast at Passover or otherwise be, "vomited out," or "cut off." He then states concerning the man who is having sex with his father's wife, "In the name of our Lord Jesus, when you are assembled, and I with you in spirit, with the power of our Lord Jesus, deliver such a one to Satan for the destruction of his flesh, so that his spirit may be saved in the day of the Lord Jesus" (1 Corinthians 5:4-5).

This is the exact same thing that God did with Adam and Eve in the Garden of Eden when they violated His law. Though the penal sanction stipulated the death penalty, in God's mercy He provided time to repent in the form of exile. The Lord warned Adam and Eve that the day they ate the forbidden fruit they would surely die. Yet, in His mercy He turned them over for the "destruction of their flesh" (physical death) and then exiled (vomited out, cut off) them from the Garden of Eden and then provided a substitute, the death of an animal, for a covering of their nakedness as a foreshadowing of Christ. The penal sanction warranted death on the day that they sinned, but God in His mercy gave them time for redemption. Paul did the exact same thing when he commanded that the offender be "purged" from the Church.

The Lord did this on another occasion when King David had sex with Uriah's wife Bathsheba, a clear violation Leviticus 18:20 which stated, "You shall not have intercourse with your neighbor's wife, to be defiled with her." What David deserved was death but instead God killed the son-of-David in his place, another foreshadowing of Christ. Yet, David also suffered a lesser consequence as well as his sin would affect his entire household the way yeast leavens an entire lump of dough. This is why Adam was exiled. His sin would have affected paradise if he was allowed to eat from the Tree of Life and live forever. This is also why all the sins mentioned in Leviticus 18 required exile or even possibly death, because the worshippers of Molech were being vomited for the same sins. Paul required that the man violating Leviticus 18:8 be "vomited out" "purged" or exiled, for the "destruction of his flesh" (1 Corinthians 5:4-5) because his sin would permeate the Church the way yeast affects an entire lump of dough (1 Corinthians 5:6). Such acts are akin to worshipping Molech or Hapis rather than truly worshipping YHWH, our Lord Jesus Christ. These sorts of sins are a violation of Christian temple worship, because our body is the temple of the Holy Spirit (1 Corinthians 6:19). This why Jesus was judging the Church at Laodicea and warned them that if they didn't repent He would "vomit them out" (Revelation 3:16).

Penal sanctions allowed for different degrees of application depending on the degree of willfulness and unrepentance of the violator. The death penalty was a maximum sentence, not a required sentence, in the Old Testament. The minimal penal sanction for violating Leviticus 18:8 in Leviticus 18:29 is to be "cut off" which Paul carries out on the man who violated that law (1 Corinthians 5:1, 11-13). The Church does not execute unrepentant adulterers, those who commit same-sex acts and so forth because it is not within its jurisdiction to do so. But, under the Roman law Paul could have sought to have the man put to death by the Romans just as the Jews had Jesus put to death if he had petitioned the state to do so. Yet he did not call the state to meddle in the Church's affairs. What the New Testament teaches is that the Church is to have ecclesiastical trial (Matthew 18:15-18) and then excommunicate, "cut off," "purge," "vomit out" and "remove the leaven" from our midst the unrepentant sinner lest the world think that we condone habitual unrepentant sin. If we do not, then Jesus will vomit us out just as YHWH stated that if a church condoned various abominations that He Himself would judge the church (Revelation 3:16).

Furthermore, we find in the New Covenant when His people are under a non-Christian civil jurisdiction that He Himself carries out the death penalty as a penal sanction for violating His law so that fear will come upon the Church and people will repent of their sin (Acts 5:1-11; 1 Corinthians 11:30). We also cannot assume that if we commit these sins and are not under the jurisdiction of the Church elders that we are free from God's direct judgment as we read of the gruesome death of Herod:

> On an appointed day Herod, having put on his royal apparel, took his seat on the rostrum and began delivering an address to them. The people kept crying out, 'The voice of a god and not of a man!' And immediately an angel of the Lord struck him because he did not give God the glory, and he was eaten by worms and died (Acts 12:21-23).

This is why the Apostle Peter warned the Church not to think that God is slack concerning His promises or that He has completely suspended His judgment on those who mock the law of God and follow their own lusts (2 Peter 3:3-12).

The Corrective Character of Penal Sanctions

As previously said, we see an example of Paul upholding his ecclesiastical jurisdiction and enacting Old Testament penal sanctions within that covenantal sphere when he confronts the issues concerning the man who was who was violating Leviticus 18:8 in having sex with his step-mother. Paul rebukes the church for tolerating this flagrant sin and subsequently says that he has turned him over to Satan for the destruction of his flesh so that his soul might be saved. He then goes on to exhort the church to not even eat with a person who calls himself a "brother" but lives a life of heinous sin (1 Corinthians 5:5-11). However, in his next letter to the same church he states that because this sinning brother has confessed and repented of his sin they are to restore and affirm their love for him lest the punishment be too severe:

But if any has caused sorrow, he has caused sorrow not to me, but in some degree - in order not to say too much - to all of you. Sufficient for such a one is this punishment which was inflicted by the majority, so that on the contrary you should rather forgive and comfort him, otherwise such a one might be overwhelmed by excessive sorrow. Wherefore I urge you to reaffirm your love for him. For to this end also I wrote, so that I might put you to the test, whether you are obedient in all things. But one whom you forgive anything, I forgive also; for indeed what I have forgiven, if I have forgiven anything, I did it for your sakes in the presence of Christ, so that no advantage would be taken of us by Satan, for we are not ignorant of his schemes (2 Corinthians 2:5-11).

The goal of Church discipline of this manner is always recovery of the fallen brother through confession, repentance and restoration. Jesus has given the keys of the Kingdom to His Church for this purpose:

So it is not the will of your Father who is in heaven that one of these little ones [a person who as a humble child is to be received and sought after like a straying sheep Matthew 18:1-13] perish. If your brother [the forenamed child/sheep] sins, go and show him his fault in private; if he listens to you, you have won your brother. But if he does not listen to you, take one or two more with you, so that by the mouth of two or three witnesses every fact may be confirmed. If he refuses to listen to them, tell it to the church; and if he refuses to listen even to the church, let him be to you as a Gentile and a tax collector. [i.e. someone cut off from the community] (Matthew 18:1-17).

The Father does not want any of his children, the stray sheep, to perish and so if we see a brother sinning and straying from the fold, we are to go to him in private (in a non-hypocritical fashion cf. Matthew 7:1-5) and correct him, seeking his repentance. But if that person will not listen, then in accordance with the law of God Jesus says we are to bring a witness to again seek his repentance. But if he will not listen he is to be excommunicated from the community. What must be noted is that the law that Jesus cites and applies to being "cut off" "purged" "turned over" or "excommunicated" is a reference to convicting someone of a crime and the requirements for enacting the death penalty:

> On the evidence of two witnesses or three witnesses, he who is to die shall be put to death; he shall not be put to death on the evidence of one witness. The hand of the witnesses shall be first against him to put him to death, and afterward the hand of all the people. So you shall purge the evil from your midst (Deuteronomy 17:6-7; cf. 19:15).

Yet Jesus is clearly applying the principle to a sin, which may or may not also be a crime, and the punishment He sanctions is less than a literal bodily execution. Why does He desire less than the physical death penalty? He goes on to tell us that His goal and the Father's goal is to seek and save that which is lost (Matthew 18:11) so that "if he listens to you, you have won your brother" (Matthew 18:15). The civil government that wields the physical sword may indeed put criminals to physical death, and that is the civil magistrate's ordained purpose as a minister of God (Romans 13:1-4). But Jesus' goal in the New Covenant is to save the lost and stray sheep and so He only applies the law to its minimal requirement, excommunication or banishment.

It might be argued that Paul did not enact the full extent of the penal sanction for the man having sex with his father's wife because the Romans, not the Christians, were in power and so he could only enact within his limited ecclesiastical jurisdiction. However, if a nation became predominantly Christian through the preaching of the Gospel, such that the leaders of the country reflected the worldview of the Christian citizens, then that nation's laws would consequently reflect God's law. Subsequently the penal sanctions for same sex acts, however rare, could be justifiably carried out. But the question needs to be asked, "Could Paul have petitioned the Roman court to uphold the penal sanctions of Leviticus and weren't the actions of this man not also a crime against Roman law?" If so, then why did Paul not do so? What must be clear is that the Church's goal, mission, and calling does not correspond to that of the state and civil magistrate. While the primary focus of the state is to administer justice the primary mission of the Church is to administer mercy. Justice and mercy are not exclusive categories but they are different in their emphasis. Yet, even under what most people would refer to as a "theocracy" we see a form of justice and mercy provided to open sinners in violation of God's law.

According to many theonomists the penal sanction of death was *always* to be upheld. But this isn't the case. As we have already seen Asa "put away" the cult prostitutes who are banished rather than execute them. Likewise, Solomon, who served as the minister of justice as judge in settling disputes, showed great leniency towards a prostitute and yet was considered wise for doing so. During this time, two prostitutes came before him asking him to settle a custody dispute over a child. These women lived together openly in violation of God's laws and committed crimes against the state came before him because the one woman had accidentally crushed her child to death by rolling over him in her sleep (1 Kings 3:19). She then stole the child of the other woman by swapping her dead child for the other's child, claiming him as her own (1 Kings 3:20). What we have here are several violations of God's law that were not just private sins, but crimes punishable by death or banishment. They were violating God's laws concerning prostitution (Leviticus 19:23; Deuteronomy 23:17) and one of them bore false witness in court (Exodus 20:16). What is amazing about this passage is not only Solomon's wisdom in devising a means to determine who was the true mother of the child, but also the fact that he did not enact the penal sanctions against these women for their crimes. Yet, Solomon is extolled as the wisest king in all the lands (1 Kings 3:12). Clearly, even under the Mosaic Covenant there was room for compassion on the most heinous of sinners in a court of law.

Penal Sanctions In the New Covenant Within the Civil Jurisdiction

There are numerous arguments that might be made to assert that the civil magistrate ought not to enforce the death penalty on anyone, let alone for sinful sexual acts between mutually consenting adults. There are two responses to such an assertion. If the civil magistrate's duty is to uphold justice, by what standard can one assert that what the law of God prescribes is unjust, extreme or unfair? Second, the New Testament has not put to an end to the God ordained role of the civil magistrate nor removed the lawful use of the sword to punish evil doers as Paul wrote:

> Every person is to be in subjection to the governing author-
> ities. For there is no authority except from God, and those
> which exist are established by God. Therefore whoever
> resists authority has opposed the ordinance of God; and
> they who have opposed will receive condemnation upon
> themselves. For rulers are not a cause of fear for good
> behavior, but for evil. Do you want to have no fear of au-
> thority? Do what is good and you will have praise from the
> same; for it is a minister of God to you for good. But if you
> do what is evil, be afraid; for **it does not bear the sword
> for nothing**; for it is a minister of God, an avenger who
> brings wrath on the one who practices evil. Therefore it is
> necessary to be in subjection, not only because of wrath,
> but also for conscience' sake… (Romans 13:1-5).

Paul then tells the Church to pay their taxes to Caesar and then quotes the Law of God including the prohibition of a sexual sin that was punishable by death, "…you shall not commit adultery…" (Romans 13:9) and exhorts the church "let us behave properly as in the day, not in carousing and drunkenness, **not in sexual promiscuity** (*koitais*; "bed-ding" a euphemism for sexual sin) and **sensuality** (*aselgeiais*; a wanton violence, wantonness, lewdness), not in strife and jealousy. But put on the Lord Jesus Christ, and make no provision for the flesh in regard to its lusts" (Romans 13:13-14).

While we see Paul at times exerting his rights as a Roman citizen, even appealing to Caesar, what we do not find is Paul or the other apostles petitioning the state to uphold the penal sanctions of the Mosaic Law. It is arguable then that if it was within the Christian agenda, part of the New Covenant dominion mandate given in the Great Commission, that he could have done so yet he did not use his opportunity to do so when standing before the Roman Emperor. The only thing he did plead was that he personally had not violated either the laws of the Mosaic Covenant or the law of the Roman Empire (Acts 22:28; 25:11).

Did Jesus Abolish the Death Penalty for Sexual Crimes?

One of the most common arguments against the penal sanctions being upheld is the assertion that when Jesus was confronted with a violator of a capital offense according to the Law of Moses He dismissed the law. However, such an assertion fails to recognize all the stipulations that the law required in order to enact the death penalty.

What must be kept in mind is that both parties in the various listed sexual sins (a man with a man, a man with a woman and her mother, bestiality, and incest vv. 13-16) are accountable for their actions such as when Leviticus 20:12 states, "If there is a man who lies with his daughter-in-law, both of them shall surely be put to death; they have committed incest, their bloodguiltiness is upon them." Yet, when the mob led by the Pharisees brought the woman caught in adultery before Jesus to be judged (in order to trap him) they only brought the woman as we read:

> Early in the morning He came again into the temple, and all the people were coming to Him; and He sat down and began to teach them. The scribes and the Pharisees brought a woman caught in adultery, and having set her in the center of the court, they said to Him, 'Teacher, this woman has been caught in adultery, in the very act. Now in the Law Moses commanded us to stone such women; what then do You say?' They were saying this, testing Him, so that they might have grounds for accusing Him. But Jesus stooped down and with His finger wrote on the ground. But when they persisted in asking Him, He straightened up, and said to them, 'He who is without sin among you, let him be the first to throw a stone at her.' Again He stooped down and wrote on the ground. When they heard it, they began to go out one by one, beginning with the older ones, and He was left alone, and the woman, where she was, in the center of the court. Straightening up, Jesus said to her, 'Woman, where are they? Did no one condemn you?' She said, 'No one, Lord.' And Jesus said, 'I do not condemn you, either. Go. From now on sin no more.' Then Jesus again spoke to them, saying, 'I am the Light of the world; he who follows

Me will not walk in the darkness, but will have the Light of life.'" (John 8:19-52)[461]

Jesus does not do away with the death penalty, contrary to the assertions of Gay Theology advocates, but knowing the hypocritical hearts of men he turned the tables on them with the result that none of her accusers remained. In doing so He upheld the law's requirement to have two or more witnesses (Deuteronomy 17:6) and since there were none, He did not condemn her in accordance with the law.

A simplistic reading of the text leads many to say, "See! Jesus didn't require that the woman be stoned for her adultery! Jesus revoked the penal sanction of the law while still requiring its moral obedience and therefore, the seventh commandment is only binding on us as a personal ethic, not as a civil law with its penal sanctions!" For example, R. D. Weekly states:

> Consider Jesus' actions when He stopped the mob from stoning the adulterous (Jn. 8:3-11). The law required that she be stoned for her sin, so the mob was correct in asserting that her sin required condemnation under the letter of the law. Now we're very familiar with Jesus' response to the people. He simply said, "Let he who is without sin cast the first stone." Unwilling to lie about the reality of sin in their own lives, the mob dispersed, leaving on Jesus and the adulterous standing there. What many people don't consider are the implications of what happened next. Jesus was the only one present who was qualified to stone this woman. The requirement to carry out her condemnation, then fell squarely upon Him. Yet, in a move contrary to the letter of the law, Jesus chose to forgive the woman and let her go her way uncondemned. He broke the letter of the law by refusing to condemn this adulterous to death. What compelled Him to condemn this adulterous to death? Love – the overriding *spirit* of the law.[462]

---

461   I recognize that there is much debate whether or not this passage was in the autographa, but it is often cited by Gay theology advocates as justification for dismissing the Old Testament law.

462   R.D. Weekly, *Homosexianity* (Judah First Ministries, 2009), 67.

If you don't pay any attention to the details of the text this view can seem very reasonable. But let us take a closer look at the text. First, we see that a lone adulterous woman has been brought before Jesus. The last time I checked, it takes two people to commit adultery. So, where is the man who was involved in this sin and crime?

Second, notice John's comments as to why they brought the woman before Jesus - "They were saying this, testing Him, so that they might have grounds for accusing Him." If you read through the gospels of Jesus' interactions with the Pharisees you will find that He never responds to their questions and comments the way they expect. He knows that when they come to him they are trying to trap Him and set Him up in order to have grounds to accuse Him of violating God's Word and be subsequently executed. But, Jesus is wisdom incarnate (1 Corinthians 1:30). Therefore He never answers these fools according to their foolishness. Rather He knows that this is a trap and so He turns the table on them to show them their folly (Proverbs 26:5-6).[463] In this case, if Jesus should say that she should be put to death then He is making a judgment that would require an action without the sanction of those in power - the Roman Empire. This might give the Romans a just cause for putting Him to death as an insurrectionist. On the other hand, if He says she should not be put to death then He would appear to be contradicting the law of God and therefore be disqualified as a teacher of Israel and the Messiah. Therefore, rather than responding in the manner that they expected He writes something on the ground and the accusers depart.

But that is not the end of the story. Jesus still has before Him this guilty woman who was caught in a sin worthy of death. The law of God requires at least two credible witnesses when bringing a plaintiff before a judgment seat (Deuteronomy 17:6). Jesus is in court with this woman but then He turns to the defendant and asks, "Woman, where are they? Did no one condemn you?" She said, "No one, Lord." And Jesus said, "I do not condemn you, either. Go. From now on sin no more." Jesus didn't violate the law or disregard it in order to grant her forgiveness. But like Boaz who redeemed Ruth, He upheld the law of redemption and required that those who wanted to quote part of the law uphold all of the God's commandments. Jesus upholds both of the justice of the law and the grace of gospel as they work hand in hand. We cannot conclude

463   For example see Luke 11:14-23, "Others testing Him... But He, knowing their thoughts..."

on the basis of this story that Jesus was opposed to the state executing violators of the sexual prohibitions of the law.

Sins, Crimes and the Law of God in a Pluralistic Society

What we need to keep in mind is not only the distinct jurisdictions and purposes of the civil, familial and ecclesiastical spheres of society but the also the place and time we are living at this juncture in redemptive history. Here is where we are confronted with some difficulty when applying penal sanctions outside the Church in a pluralistic society that seeks to some degree protect the private beliefs of individuals to worship according to their worldview. For example, in the United States of America the civil government seeks to neither endorse nor prohibit the free exercise of any religion as the Establishment Clause of the First Amendment to the Constitution of the United States declares, "Congress shall make no law respecting an establishment of religion, or prohibiting the free exercise thereof…"

However, even this apparent allowance for the free exercise of religion has its limits as to what the government of the United States will allow. Should someone seek to revive the post-abortion worship of Molech under the guise of "freedom of religion," the laws of the United States of America, as they currently stand, would more than likely "prohibit the free exercise thereof." Likewise, should someone wish to revive the native religions of the Mayans and Aztecs which also involved human sacrifice as part of the consecration of new leaders or temples it is doubtful that the Supreme Court would consider such acts as being protected forms of worship under the First Amendment to the Constitution. Clearly the leaders in the jurisdictions of the Church or religious organizations are not completely sovereign in their own sphere. Nor are fathers completely free to run their homes as they wish without being subjected to the law of the state. Nor are Church members free from having to submit in some matters to the ecclesiastical authority of the elders of the church who are not over stepping their jurisdictional boundaries.

The question that needs to be asked then is, "Who then has the final word on such matters in a seemingly pluralistic society?" The civil magistrate in a non-theocratic nation has the "sword" and alone can physically punish those who resist the will of the state. The truth is in the United States of America (and other similar nations) the citizens are living in a poly-theocracy (a nation of many gods) in which people are free to worship (or abstain from worshipping) any god they wish so long as at the end of the day they bow to the will of the state. Like the Roman Empire, the state in a Democracy has the final word in all matters and in essence its rulers govern as if Caesar is lord. The Roman Empire did not care which Greek or Roman god that the citizens worshipped in their heart so long as such worship was not viewed as a competing authority. The primary difference between a Democracy and a tyrannical empire is the constraint on the President's power by the Supreme Court and the Congress as well as their need to please their constituents in order to get re-elected.

The Christian living under a poly-theocracy is required by Scripture to obey the civil magistrate, even paying seemingly unjust taxes, so long as the state does not require the Christian to overtly violate the Word of God such as worshipping a false god, profane the Sabbath, or turn his children over to the state to be indoctrinated by the worldview taught in government schools. What then is the duty of the Christian who serves in such a society? What is the duty of the President of the United States if he truly is a Bible-believing Christian in regards to God's law and its penal sanctions? Are Christians serving as the governing authorities in pluralistic democratic governments, such as those found in Europe or the United States of America, morally required by God to uphold every jot and tittle of the moral law as revealed in the Mosaic Covenant *today*? My short answer to that question is, "No." The second question that naturally follows this one is, "What then, according to Scripture, is the moral duty of the Christian serving today in public office?"

According to Greg Bahnsen "*In this present age* the civil magistrate ought to follow the law of God and its commandments pertaining to punishment for social crimes."[464] When contemplating the issue of homosexual acts and penal sanctions what we must keep in mind is that such acts were not the only offence that was potentially punishable by death in the law of God. Nor were same-sex acts isolated or unrelated to the other sins that had a prescribed death penalty. Sexual ethics and religious worldviews have always been and always will be closely

464   Greg L. Bahnsen, *Theonomy in Christian Ethics* (Covenant Media Press; Third Edition, 2002), 439 (emphasis mine).

associated with each other. According to the law of God proselytizing within the nation in order to convince the citizens to worship a god other than YHWH was also punishable by death. To advocate worshipping another god was equated with the sexual sin of prostitution as well as treason against the law of the nation. This is why the law set very distinct boundaries to hedge out the influence of foreign religions and their sexual practices:

> Now concerning everything which I have said to you, be on your guard; and do not mention the name of other gods, nor let them be heard from your mouth... You shall not worship their gods, nor serve them, nor do according to their deeds; but you shall utterly overthrow them and break their sacred pillars in pieces... You shall make no covenant with them or with their god. They shall not live in your land, because they will make you sin against Me; for if you serve their gods, it will surely be a snare to you (Exodus 23: 13, 24, 32-33; cf. Deuteronomy 12).

Not only were foreign religions and their sexual practices not to be allowed, but as Israel entered the land promised to Abraham they were to physically remove their places of worship by force and violence:

> Watch yourself that you make no covenant with the inhabitants of the land into which you are going, or it will become a snare in your midst. But rather, you are to tear down their altars and smash their sacred pillars and cut down their Asherim - for you shall not worship any other god, for the LORD, whose name is Jealous, is a jealous God - otherwise you might make a covenant with the inhabitants of the land and they would play the harlot with their gods and sacrifice to their gods, and someone might invite you to eat of his sacrifice, and you might take some of his daughters for your sons, and his daughters might play the harlot with their gods and cause your sons also to play the harlot with their gods (Exodus 34: 12-16).

The punishment for proselytizing in the land, to urge the people to follow a god other than YHWH, was death ("...that prophet or that dreamer of dreams shall be put to death...") and any city that tolerated such actions was to be utterly destroyed (Deuteronomy 13:1-16). The commandments that required the physical removal of foreign religions and their sexual practices are tied together such that it is not possible to prohibit or remove the one without the other. The worldview of the person who is advocating that people ought to be free to worship according to another religion also entails a sexual ethic. To tell someone that they are free to practice Baal worship but not participate in the sexual practices that accompanied it would be a contradiction. This would be like telling Christians that they can worship Jesus Christ but they are not allowed to perform baptisms or partake of the Lord's Supper.

Not only were same sex acts and proselytizing for a foreign religion considered worthy of death, so was breaking the Sabbath:

> Therefore you are to observe the Sabbath, for it is holy to you. Everyone who profanes it **shall surely be put to death**; for whoever does any work on it, that person shall be cut off from among his people. `For six days work may be done, but on the seventh day there is a Sabbath of complete rest, holy to the LORD; whoever does any work on the Sabbath day shall surely be put to death (Exodus 31:14-16).

Then we read again:

> For six days work may be done, but on the seventh day you shall have a holy day, a Sabbath of complete rest to the LORD; whoever does any work on it **shall be put to death**. You shall not kindle a fire in any of your dwellings on the Sabbath day (Exodus 35:2-3).

Lest we should think that being put to death for kindling a fire on the Sabbath was a mere hypothetical possibility we then read of a man who purposely violated the Sabbath by gathering wood to make a fire:

Now while the sons of Israel were in the wilderness, they found a man gathering wood on the Sabbath day. Those who found him gathering wood brought him to Moses and Aaron and to all the congregation; and they put him in custody because it had not been declared what should be done to him. Then the LORD said to Moses, 'The man shall surely be put to death; all the congregation shall stone him with stones outside the camp.' So all the congregation brought him outside the camp and stoned him to death with stones, just as the LORD had commanded Moses (Numbers 15:32-35).

Some might argue that the state today should uphold only the "second table" of the law, that is the last six commandments of the Decalogue that do not include what may seem to be the more overly religious statutes. However, as Greg Bahnsen states, according to the theonomic-reconstruction system, to remove any of the penal sanctions is to pull the thread of a seamless garment that will result in anarchy:

I submit that *any legitimate principle* which is used to endorse the Mosaic law **today** will endorse *its penal injunctions at the same time.* Contrawise, any principle (aside from question-begging) used to *eliminate* the Mosaic *penal* sanctions will also cover the other commandments. God's moral law is a garment without seams... Because all sin is defined by God, all sin must receive the punishments assigned by God, for this Judge will certainly do right. A smorgasbord approach to penology is just as wrong as personal selectivity in one's personal obedience to God's commandments... if rulers are to follow the whole law of God as they are responsible to do, then they must execute the punishments God prescribed. In this way the law of God can act as a restraining force on the unrighteousness of society.[465]

If the full extent of the penal sanctions of the Old Testament are to be upheld by the state today, as Greg Bahnsen states, then violating the first

465   Greg L. Bahnsen, *Theonomy in Christian Ethics* (Covenant Media Press; Third Edition, 2002), 449, 450, 451.

four commandments are required to be punished by death as well. These laws include the prohibition of worshipping a God other than YHWH, not creating or bowing down to idols, not taking the Lord's name in vain and keeping the Sabbath (Exodus 20:3-11). Under these laws not only are proselytizers of foreign religions (Muslims, Jews, Buddhists, Hindus) subject to the death penalty but potentially so are Christians. Most Protestants believe that the Roman Catholic and Eastern orthodox use of icons is a violation of the second commandment. Some denominations, such as the Reformed Presbyterian Church in America, assert that singing anything other than the inspired Psalms in corporate worship is a violation of the second commandment. There are also Christian denominations that believe that the Sabbath continues as an obligatory day of observance on the seventh day (Seventh Day Adventists) and there are those that believe that full Sabbath observance now resides on the first Day of the week corresponding to the day of resurrection of Jesus Christ. [466] There are those who believe that the Sabbath was part of the "ceremonial law" that points to the finished work of Christ and therefore Christians have no obligation observe it. [467] If Christians are going to insist that the penal sanction of the death penalty of the Old Testament be upheld by the state, according to the Theonomic construct they are not justifiably free to arbitrarily "cherry pick" which ones they want to be upheld and those that are to be ignored. As Greg Bahnsen observed, Sabbath breaking as well as same-sex acts are equally capital offenses punishable by the state according to the law of God:

> Scripture lists the following as capital offenses against God: murder (Deut. 13:5, 11), **adultery** and unchastity

---

466   "As it is of the law of nature, that, in general, a due proportion of time be set apart for the worship of God; so, in his Word, by a positive, moral, and perpetual commandment, binding all men in all ages, he hath particularly appointed one day in seven for a Sabbath, to be kept holy unto him: which, from the beginning of the world to the resurrection of Christ, was the last day of the week; and, from the resurrection of Christ, was changed into the first day of the week, which in Scripture is called the Lord's Day, and is to be continued to the end of the world as the Christian Sabbath." Westminster Confession of Faith Chapter 21.7 "Of Religious Worship and the Sabbath-day"

467   Michael Horton, *The Law of Perfect Freedom* (Chicago: Moody Press, 1993), 124-125.

(Lev. 20:10; Deut. 22:21, 23), sodomy and bestiality
(Lev. 18:23; 20:15; Ex. 22:19), **homosexuality** (Lev.
18:22; 20:13), rape (Deut. 22:25), incest (Lev. 20:11, 14),
incorrigibility in children (Ex. 21:15, 17; Deut. 21:20f.),
Sabbath breaking (Ex. 31:14; Num. 15:32 ff.; Ex. 35:2),
kidnapping, (Ex. 21:16; Deut. 24:7), apostasy (Lev. 20:2;
Deut. 13:6-17), witchcraft, sorcery, and false pretension to
prophesy (Ex. 22:18; Lev. 20:27; Deut. 13:5; 18:20), and
blasphemy (Lev. 24:10-16).[468]

If Christians are going to petition the state to uphold the death penalty for same sex-acts because of Leviticus 20:13, to be consistent we will
have the Seventh Day Adventist seeking to have First Day observers
put to death and both sixth and seventh day observers will seek to have
those who believe that the Sabbath is an abrogated commandment put
to death. The law of God did not provide an exception for those in the
land who were not part of the covenant community, everyone including
the "sojourner in the land" was required to observe the Sabbath (Exodus
20:10). So not only will Christians be seeking to have non-Christians
put to death but each other as well. This is not mere a hypothetical
possibility, it is a very long and sad part of the history of the Church.
Do we really believe that God wants Christians to *again* start killing
each other because of differences in theology such as Roman Catholics
killing Protestants or Protestants killing Roman Catholics?[469]

According Greg Bahnsen in his book *Homosexuality: A Biblical
View* the repentant sinner who has committed a capital offense, such as a
homosexual act, would receive forgiveness from God and be welcomed
into the church:

> The church's two-fold responsibility toward the homosexual
> is this: (1) to proclaim God's just judgment on homosexual

468   Greg Bahnsen, *Theonomy in Christian Ethics* (Covenant Media Press; Third
Edition, 2002), 431.
469   Examples of this would include the over 500 year persecution of the Waldensi-
ans, the execution of John Huss (*1369 – July 6, 1415*) a predecessor of the Protestant
Reformation who was who was burned at the stake, and the "Thirty Years War" (1618-
1648) Williston Walker, *A History of the Christian Church* (4th Edition) (New York;
Scribner, 1985), 300-310, 382, 530.

perversion, excluding the impenitent from the congregation; and (2) to announce the gospel as the power of God
unto salvation, so that as repentant believers homosexuals
may become fellow-members in the body of Christ. To this
may be added a third obligation, to support and encourage
them in a transformed lifestyle. The church must not only
require a change in direction, but extend aid to the former
homosexual in his Christian growth and in resisting temptation. The son of homosexuality will not completely stop
tempting the new convert any more than any other habitual
sin immediately loses influence over a young believer. The
problem will not necessarily disappear easily; it may take
time, and it certainly will require pastoral counseling.[470]

However, this assertion is at odds with his view on penology in his
book *Theonomy in Christian Ethics.* According to Bahnsen not only
would those advocating other religions, violators of Sabbath regulations, homosexuals and murderers be put to death by a civil government
system, but so would repentant homosexuals. This is because, according
to Bahnsen, the civil magistrate would still be obligated to carry out the
death penalty for the act as a social offense:

> The civic punishment upon a man's crime could not be
> eliminated even though he was required to make atone-
> ment and find God's ultimate forgiveness of sacrifice for
> sin. Social restitution (the penal sanction) was not incom-
> patible with being forgiven by the trespass offering (Lev.
> 6:4-7; Num. 5:5-8). Therefore, the civil punishment was
> required to be executed upon every criminal uncondition-
> ally – without consideration of his status, without mercy,
> without cancellation through atoning sacrifice. Such are the
> demands of justice of the civil judgment; a crime *always*
> receives what it, with respect to the context of social life,
> deserves as equitable for the nature of the offense... When

---

470   Greg Bahnsen, *Homosexuality: A Biblical View* (Grand Rapids, MI: Baker,
1978), 96.

God says homosexuality (for instance) warrants capital punishment, then that is what social justice demands; that is how heinous with respect to social relations the crime is in God's judgment.[471]

For Greg Bahnsen, the enforcement of the penal sanctions and observing the Decalogue in the civil sphere is an "all or nothing" enterprise. According to him, one cannot seek to uphold the sixth commandment that prohibits murder and not also uphold the laws against same sex acts and their accompanying penal sanction for, as he says, they are all part of the same garment of God's law:

> I submit that *any legitimate principle* which is used to endorse the Mosaic law today will endorse *its penal injunctions at the same time*. Contrawise, any principle (aside from question-begging) used to *eliminate* the Mosaic *penal* sanctions will also cover the other commandments. God's moral law is a garment without seams.[472]

If the Theonomic thesis is put into place the conclusion one comes to from reading Bahnsen's *Theonomy in Christian Ethics* is inescapable; the civil magistrate is required *today* to execute homosexuals as well as Sabbath breakers, even those who have found forgiveness in the Church:

> ...we should conclude that crimes which warrant capital punishment in the Older Testament continue to deserve the death penalty today... Therefore, civil magistrates today are under obligation to execute all those who commit capital crimes as defined by God's authoritative law.[473]

Lest anyone should think that the above reading of Bahnsen's *Theonomy in Christian Ethics* is a caricature of theonomy, John's Frame offers the following helpful perspective, "Bahnsen and other

---

471   Greg L. Bahnsen, *Theonomy in Christian Ethics* (Covenant Media Press; Third Edition, 2002), 426-427 (emphasis mine).
472   Ibid, 449.
473   Ibid, 428

theonomists insist that the penalties for civil crimes in the Pentateuch are normative for modern civil governments, including the death penalty for adultery, homosexuality, and blasphemy…"[474] He then points out:

> There is some confusion in theonomy between present and future application of the law. The rhetoric of theonomy is often calculated to arouse immediate action, and at least some of the appeal of the movement is that people see in it a practical political program for today's society. But others are horrified by the idea that theonomists, taking over government in these confused times, would immediately proceed to execute homosexuals, adulterers, and so on. Confronted with this objection, Bahnsen argues that the Mosaic laws should *not* be enforced today. They presuppose, he says, a people who understand and believe the law and who are committed to being God's people.[475]

John Frame does not offer any documentation as to why he believes "Bahnsen argues that the Mosaic laws should *not* be enforced today." In what is deemed by theonomists to be *the* quintessential text on the subject, Bahnsen repeatedly asserts that the death penalty *should* be enforced today. Frame then goes on to say that theonomy is more accurately understood as a political theory as a "…future ideal, rather than a present-day political program, it becomes less radical and more theoretical."[476] The truth is, Greg Bahnsen is not alone in his rhetoric. I have been living in the company of theonomists since my freshman year in seminary in 1996 and this sort of "kill the homosexuals now" rhetoric is not uncommon. While Bahnsen may have had a government in the future in mind when he wrote his penology in *Theonomy in Christian Ethics* this is not how many of his successors have taken it. I have been in many theonomically influenced congregations and without exception not only do members of these congregations talk this way, so do their pastors. Because of this I have to agree with John Frame when he states:

---

474   John Frame, *The Doctrine of the Christian Life* (Phillipsburg; P & R Publishing, 2008), 218.
475   Ibid, 222.
476   Ibid, 223.

I have come to the conclusion that theonomy is a good case study of how theological ideas should *not* be introduced. The sharp polemics of the theonomic movement... have been, in my view quite unnecessary and indeed counter-productive to its own purposes."[477]

God Upholds The Penal Sanctions

What must be kept in mind is that, according to Paul, "the wrath of God is revealed from heaven" not against people who violate social taboos or social customs. Rather His judgment is "against all ungodliness and unrighteousness of men" which is the fruit of those "who suppress the truth in unrighteousness." The result of the wrath of God is not that these people then commit various acts of sin or unrighteousness, but rather that they have been "given over" (*paredoken* from *paradidomi*) to the enslavement of these sins, "Therefore God *gave them over* in the lusts of their hearts to impurity, so that their bodies would be dishonored among them" (Romans 1:24). In other words, it is the refusal to repent and the hardening of the heart that results in being turned over to one's own devices and the lusts of the heart. This is the same word Paul uses to describe the one whom He has judged for having sex with his father's wife, "...*deliver* (*paradounai* from *paradidomi*) such a one to Satan for the destruction of the flesh..." The term *paradidomi* means to be handed over in judgment, such that the man who calls himself a "brother" and yet violates God's law in such a manner, or the idolater, is being "handed over" to his own devices to suffer the wrath of God. In a parallel manner, in the place of the sinner for whom Christ died, God "delivered up" (*paredoken* from *paradidomi*) His own Son to suffer His wrath on the cross for our sin (Romans 8:32). The handing over of idolaters to the enslavement to sin, the person committing incest to the destruction of the flesh and Jesus being "delivered" or "handed over" to suffer the wrath of God for our sin are parallel judgments of God. The term used for the handing over of the Son for sinners is the same verb (*paredothe*)

---

477   Ibid, 223.

which also describes the manner in which Jesus was handed over for our trespasses, and raised for our justification (Romans 4:25).

Do Christians at times sin? The apostle John says that we deceive ourselves and the truth is not in us if we say that are without sin and subsequently states that if we confess our sins He is faithful and just to not only forgive of us but also, using the language of Old Testament purity laws, cleanse us from all unrighteousness (1 John 1:8-9). The Christian then who has same-sex attractions or a "homosexual orientation" should not think that he has been "given over" or that God has rejected him, anymore than the Christian who wrestles with the temptation to envy or gossip which are also mentioned (Romans 1:29). He should also take great comfort in that fact that though he may battle against this sexual sin all his life, he has not been "given over" to it and when he does sin he can in faith repent and remember that Christ was "handed over" to the cross in our place so that we will not suffer the wrath of God by being be handed over to the enslavement to sin. But, the truth of Christ's being "handed over" and suffering on our part is not a license to continue to sin, as Paul exhorts:

> ...consider yourselves to be dead to sin, but alive to God in Christ Jesus. Therefore do not let sin reign in your mortal body so that you obey its lusts, and do not go on presenting the members of your body to sin as instruments of unrighteousness; but present yourselves to God as those alive from the dead, and your members as instruments of righteousness to God. For sin shall not be master over you, for you are not under law but under grace (Romans 6:11-14).

However, lest we should think that one can sin or commit crimes worthy of death without ever suffering its immediate and full consequences, throughout history God does at times enact the death penalty either directly or through His agents. In fact, He does so for what may seem to us "small" sins and crimes in both the Old and New Testaments such as picking up sticks on the Sabbath (Numbers 15:32-36), lying to the Holy Spirit (Acts 5:5, 10) and causing division in the Church (1 Corinthians 11:30). Yet He also withholds punishment for what, in our eyes, seems to be a much greater offence such as adultery and murder. What must be kept in mind is that every sin deserves death but God is free to have mercy upon whom He chooses to have mercy and to show divine justice upon whom He sovereignly chooses on individuals or upon nations (Exodus 33:19; Romans 9:15; Lamentations 3:39; Jeremiah 21:14). He can choose to wipe out the Amalekites who worshipped pagan gods and sacrificed their children to Molech (1 Samuel 15:3) or have mercy on Nineveh when they repent (Jonah 3:7-10). Yet some Gay Theologians argue that such judgments are the genocidal assertions of the "seer" such as Samuel and not of God. Therefore such accounts ought to be considered morally repugnant.[478] Clearly, the god of Gay Theology is not the righteous sovereign holy God of the Bible.

The Lord also uses various means of enacting judgment including a direct enforcement of the penal sanctions with His invisible hand even in the New Covenant era (Acts 5; 1 Corinthians 11). However, such judgments may not be perceivable as they may appear to be the result of "natural" disasters or diseases such as when the Lord judged Herod, "And immediately an angel of the Lord struck him because he did not give God the glory, and he was eaten by worms and died" (Acts 12:23). God also at times tests and then enacts judgment on His own people when they are unrepentant of their sin through secondary means, including the use of using foreign military forces such as the Canaanites, Philistines, Moabites, Ammonites, Midianites, and Amalekites (Numbers 14:44; Judges 3). Then when they repented and cried out He sent them a deliverer. But eventually because of the constant whoredom He would send them into exile and cut them off from the land just as He had warned, as He had when He sent Adam and Eve out of the Garden of Eden (Jeremiah 44:8, 11). The Lord also judges people, cities and nations through the use of angels (Genesis 19; 2 Samuel 24:16; Isaiah 37:36), pagan kings whom He refers to as His ministers (Jeremiah 43:10; Romans 13:1-6), and through "natural" disasters, plagues and pestilences (Exodus 7-11).

---

478   L. William Countryman, *Biblical Authority or Biblical Tyranny* (Harrisburg, PA: Trinity Press, 1994), 12.

Furthermore, at times the Lord enacts the death penalty or various others forms of punishment on an individual violator. When His leaders are in rebellion or have committed a great sin His judgment may be only on that particular leader, such as His otherwise faithful servant Moses who misrepresented God when he struck the rock and was consequently forbidden to enter the Promised Land (Numbers 20:12). This too was a form of excommunication or being "cut off" from the land. But an individual's sin does not affect merely himself since God often punishes not only the individual sinner but also his family, the Church or the nation that are under the person's jurisdiction (Joshua 22:20).

What we find in the New Testament is that God Himself upholds the penal sanctions of the death penalty as He wills, on both the unbeliever and on the Church that harbors sin. As previously stated, Paul asserts that God is presently carrying out His penal sanction on all those who suppress the knowledge of the truth and subsequently become idolaters and commit subsequent sexual sins. His punishment is that He "gives them over" (Romans 1:26) to it in the same manner that Jesus was "given over" to the state to be crucified on the cross (Romans 8:32). This is the same language that Paul uses when he "turns over" the violator of Leviticus 18:8 to Satan for the destruction of his flesh. To assert then that if the state does not uphold the penal sanction of the death penalty according to Leviticus 20:13 that the person committing same sex acts is somehow evading God's standard of justice is mistaken. God's penal sanctions are not being pushed off until the final judgment at the eschaton and if the violator of God's law is not punished by the state He and the culture that condones or promotes his sin is not escaping the wrath of God. The family, state or denomination that turns a blind eye to gross immorality and gives approval of those who do such things will eventually, within history, suffer the consequence as individuals, ecclesiastical denominations and entire nations are turned over to their depravity and its consequences. This includes pandemic diseases, economic depression and the death of a generation of children.

Conclusion

I am in agreement with the presuppositions of the theonomic view but I have not found the majority of its proponents to be consistent or thorough in the handling of the subject of penology in light of what the entirety of Scripture says on the matter. While the theonomic view rightly seeks to uphold God's law many of its adherents tend to simply read the prohibitions and the penal sanction and then insist that they ought to be upheld. The problem is that though the view rightly views God's holy law as the only epistemologically justifiable system of ethics for mankind, it often fails to do justice to the *system* of law that needs to be implemented as well as the Church and the state's current status at this eschatological juncture in history. What needs to be implemented is not a piece meal collection of laws but rather an entire system of law that can only be implemented when the worldview of a culture and society has been changed via the preaching of the gospel and the discipling of the nations. Therefore, if you were to ask me, "Do you think the state should uphold the penal sanctions of the Old Testament?" my answer would be, "Not yet. The penal sanctions as a component of implementing the law are part of an entire *system* (worldview) and ought not to be isolated from that system that can only be brought about by a transformation of a society through the gospel into a distinctly Christianized culture."

At our current stage in history to implement the penal sanctions "as is" would be like giving three-year-old child a kitchen knife and expecting him to handle it rightly. Our development of cultural maturity in the eschatological timeline needs to precede our full development and implementation of theonomic principles. Included in that timeline would be the development of a more Biblical means of addressing the issue of same-sex attractions than what is currently being offered by modern psychology.

We need to recognize the jurisdictions of the law, the current secularized status of earthly governments as well as the allowable range of penalties within the law. It is my contention that such this view does more justice to the manner in which God himself placed expectations on the civil governments in the Old Testament. I contend that in our discussion on the matter, eschatological development precedes full Biblical civil penology. It should also be recognized that should a society become predominantly Christian in which citizens will be followers of the laws of Christ, the need to enforce penal sanctions would rarely ever actually be carried out since the people will have been converted. Of course, any reader who does not adhere to the postmillennial expectations of history will conclude that my view can be dismissed as a mere theoretical impossibility.

When adherents of theonomy discuss penology more often than not they fail to maintain their eschatological framework in their discussion on their expectation of the state to be able to uphold the law of God. They also fail to see that the civil laws were not bits and pieces of laws but part of an entire judicial system which contained such things as rules of evidence and many commandments that were unique to the socio-political status of ancient Israel.

Chapter 16
The Law of Christ and Situation Ethics

It is frequently said today, even by some preachers, that the New Covenant and the Christian life is not about "thou shalt nots" like the Old Covenant, it is governed by the new law of Christ - the law of love. What they fail to see is that the royal law of love comes from the heart of the Holiness Code found in the Mosaic Law that they wish to abrogate in its entirety. The result of this misperception is that many Christians have a rather negative view of the law of God as if the Lord gave His people the Ten Commandments in order to oppress them at Mt. Sinai. But did the Lord really deliver His people from bondage only to then turn around and put them under His own yoke of slavery in being required to keep an overbearing set of commandments?

At times these preachers, teachers and theologians sound almost like Marcion as they speak of the moral component of the law as if it needed to be quenched by the gentler and kinder God of the New Testament. Borrowing from Luther's commentary many Christian pastors have taught that the "tutor" (pedagogue) of Galatians 3:24 was God's assigned task master to drive His people to despair for their moral failures and thereby recognize their need for Jesus Christ. [479] But, Scripture teaches that this "tutor" was not a harsh taskmaster beating a child, but rather a guardian-protector until the child had matured at the coming of Christ. Then once He had come, this protector-tutor was no longer needed because the elementary portions of the Law, the types and shadows, were fulfilled in Christ. [480]

479   See Martin Luther, *Commentary on Galatians* (Grand Rapids, MI: Baker House, 1988), 27. An example of a Lutheran view of the law taught by a Reformed Christian can been found in the theology of Michael Horton such as when he says, "Also called the pedagogical use, taken from Paul's reference to the law as God's tutor, leading us to faith in Christ (Galatians 3:24), the law shows us how hopelessly we fall short of the righteousness God requires. Just when we think we are not quite as bad as the guy down the street living with so-and-so, the law puts us on trial and compares us - not with other fallen men and women, but to God." *The Law of Perfect Freedom* (Moody Publishers, 1993), 32.

480   For a historical Reformed view, in contrast to a Lutheran view, of the law and the tutor of Galatians 3:24 see Wilhelmus á Brakel, *The Christian's Reasonable Service* (Vol. 3) (Phillipsburg, NJ: Soli Deo Gloria Pub., 1984), 62-63.

It is true that we cannot merit our salvation through our observance of the moral requirements of the law and to think that our own self-righteousness can put us in a right standing before God is one of the many fallacies of the first century Pharisees. But is the law of God really something that ought to be thought of as that overly harsh standard from a bygone era that has now somehow been replaced by a new standard that is more loving and less demanding? Has Christ really abolished the requirements of the Decalogue? Are the moral requirements of the New Covenant any less difficult than that of the Old? Try reading 1 Corinthians 13 and each time you read the word "love" insert your own name and see if you are living up to the requirements of the text, *"Erik is patient, Erik is kind and is not jealous; Erik does not brag and is not arrogant..."* I find it difficult to even read verse 4 like this and honestly say that love is the motive for all my actions.

Another misunderstood and misused term is Paul's phrase "the law of Christ." It is often argued that this law is some other standard for our Christian living than the one given at Mt. Sinai. Here are two passages in which we find this term:

> For though I am free from all men, I have made myself a slave to all, so that I may win more. To the Jews I became as a Jew, so that I might win Jews; to those who are under the Law, as under the Law though not being myself under the Law, so that I might win those who are under the Law; to those who are without law, as without law, though not being without the Law of God but under **the law of Christ**, so that I might win those who are without law" (1 Corinthians 9:19-21).

> Brethren, even if anyone is caught in any trespass, you who are spiritual, restore such a one in a spirit of gentleness; each one looking to yourself, so that you too will not be tempted. Bear one another's burdens, and thereby fulfill **the law of Christ**" (Galatians 6:1-2).

A similar phrase to "the law of Christ" is John's repeated use of the term "a new commandment" found in his Gospel account as well as in his epistles which refers to the same moral requirement:

A new commandment I give to you, that you love one another, even as I have loved you, that you also love one another. By this all men will know that you are My disciples, if you have love for one another" (John 13:34-35).

Beloved, I am not writing a new commandment to you, but an old commandment which you have had from the beginning; the old commandment is the word which you have heard. On the other hand, I am writing **a new commandment** to you, which is true in Him and in you, because the darkness is passing away and the true Light is already shining. The one who says he is in the Light and yet hates his brother is in the darkness until now. The one who loves his brother abides in the Light and there is no cause for stumbling in him (1 John 2: 7-10).

Now I ask you, lady, not as though I were writing to you **a new commandment**, but the one which we have had from the beginning, that we love one another (2 John 1-5).

In order to understand the newness of the commandment, it has to be understood it in light of the newness of the covenant. God's commandments are tied to His redemptive acts, as we read in the Decalogue, "I am the LORD your God, who brought you out of the land of Egypt, out of the house of slavery" (Exodus 20:2). The old commandment for God's people was to love the LORD and our neighbor in light of His work of redemption of bringing them out of Egypt. The Israelites were to love the sojourner for they too were once slaves and aliens (Deuteronomy 10:19).

In the same way, the New Covenant is a new redemptive act in history, it is part of the "last days" (Hebrews 1:2). In light of this new stage in redemptive history the old commandment is given new meaning. We are to love others as Christ loved us. Husbands are to love their wives as Christ loved the Church (Ephesians 5:25). As friends we are to lay down our lives for each other as Christ laid down His life for us (John 15:13). The law of Christ is the law of His love revealed in this act of redemption in which He demonstrated the Father's love towards us

(John 3:16). It is the Gospel that makes the old commandment "new." Likewise, it is Jesus' death, burial and resurrection that makes the old Psalms "new" as we now understand and sing them in the light of His love declared to us at Calvary (Psalm 96:1).

To be a disciple of Jesus is to be baptized and taught to keep His commandments, the law of Christ (Matthew 28:20) which is none other than His interpretation of the Decalogue which He Himself gave to Moses (Matthew 5:21-48). To love Jesus Christ is to love His law for love is defined by His commandments. This is why we can sing along with the Psalmist, "O how I love Your law! It is my meditation all the day" (Psalm 119:97).

As Christians we are to reach out to sinners with the Gospel - the story of the death, burial and resurrection of Jesus Christ and what this act in history accomplished - the substitutionary atonement for our sin which is defined by God's law (Leviticus 16; 1 Corinthians 15:3-4). The call of the Gospel is to believe on the Lord Jesus Christ, confess and repent of our sin, be baptized and as His disciple learn to obey His commandments (Matthew 28: 20; Acts 2:38-39).

The call of the Gospel has a lot of "doing" involved and the Lord to whom we submit and follow has a lot of marriage-covenant laws. It is inaccurate to say we don't have to follow any laws as a Christian. If there are no commandments to submit to, then Jesus is not our Lord and Master. Yet, you cannot have Jesus as your Savior without Him also being your sole Lord and Master (Matthew 6:24; Romans 10:9-10). The laws or commandments that we are required to follow as a Christian (as a part of the bride) is not an overbearing list of "thou shalt nots" for his law is not burdensome (1 John 5:3). In fact, the Lord specifically told Israel concerning His law, "For this commandment which I command you today is not too difficult for you, nor is it out of reach" (Deuteronomy 30:11).

Due to the impact of theoretical antinomianism many Christians think of the Ten Commandments as a burden that God gave to crush us. The Scriptures clearly teach that, while we cannot justified by our obedience, the law itself included the gospel in the form of typological animal sacrifices. In the Christian faith there is no antithesis between the Law and the Gospel anymore than there is between a hammer and a screwdriver. While we cannot be made right with God through our obedience to His commandments; to keep the law of God is the Church's wedding vow to the Kinsmen-Redeemer!

The requirement of the law that was given to the people of God did not say to them, "You're damned if you can't keep these perfectly." Rather, in light of His work of redemption He said to her, "You're my wife, love me and keep your marriage vows." The grace of the Lamb of God saves us from our sin so that we can do the works He has prepared for us (Ephesians 2:8-10). They are not a means to gain His favor, nor were they ever intended to be so. Rather because we have already been saved by His grace we are to love Him and seek do be a submissive and dutiful bride. The Holy Spirit uses the commandments of Christ to convert our soul, to change us from a whore to a beautiful bride, and His law is sweet to those are redeemed by His grace and who love the Lord:

> The law of the LORD is perfect, restoring the soul; the testimony of the LORD is sure, making wise the simple. The precepts of the LORD are right, rejoicing the heart; the commandment of the LORD is pure, enlightening the eyes. The fear of the LORD is clean, enduring forever; the judgments of the LORD are true; they are righteous altogether. They are more desirable than gold, yes, than much fine gold; sweeter also than honey and the drippings of the honeycomb (Psalm 19:7-10).

The very heart of the law of Christ is the love of the wife (Israel/ the Church) for her husband Jesus Christ (Ephesians 5:22-33). Does anyone believe that there are no rules that have to be followed in order to become a wife? If not, then why take a vow? Yet, the bond of a marriage is love. Many Roman Catholics and Protestants have become quite confused about the nature of the law and the Gospel. One wants to give you a ladder to climb in order to get to heaven (Rome) and the other often thinks that the New Covenant (a marriage covenant!) has no conditions or requirements.

If we are to rightly understand the Ten Commandments, in light of the law of Christ and the Great Commandments to love God and our neighbor, we would read them through the lens of 1 Corinthians 13 and think of them in the following manner:

Then Jesus spoke all these words, saying,
I AM the LORD your God, who brought you out of the land of
Egypt, out of the house of slavery.
Love has no other gods before Me.
Love does not make for oneself an idol.
Love does not take the name of the LORD your God in vain.
Love remembers the Sabbath day and keeps it holy.
Love honors your father and your mother.
Love does not murder.
Love does not commit adultery.
Love does not steal.
Love does not bear false witness against your neighbor.
Love does not covet your neighbors possessions.

In this way we see that the heart's motivation to obey God's law revealed in both covenants is love. This is why Paul states that in the New Covenant, "For in Christ Jesus neither circumcision nor uncircumcision means anything, but faith working through love" (Galatians 5:6). He then goes on to quote the Holiness Code of Old Testament as the standard by which we are to live, "For you were called to freedom, brethren; only do not turn your freedom into an opportunity for the flesh, but through love serve one another. For the whole Law is fulfilled in one word, in the statement, 'You shall love your neighbor as yourself'" (Galatians 5:13-14; Leviticus 19:18). What is new about the law of Christ is this commandment has been taken to the ultimate level by His own example, "A new commandment I give to you, that you love one another, even as I have loved you, that you also love one another" (John 13:34; 15:12).

The Law Written On Our Heart

The promise of the New Covenant was that the Lord would write the law of God on the heart of His people (Jeremiah 31:31-34). It is because of this promise that the Epistle of Hebrews warns those who would wish to commit apostasy by returning to the types and shadows of the Old Covenant:

By this will we have been sanctified through the offering
of the body of Jesus Christ once for all. Every priest stands
daily ministering and offering time after time the same
sacrifices, which can never take away sins; but He, having
offered one sacrifice for sins for all time, sat down at the
right hand of God, waiting from that time onward until His
enemies be made a footstool for His feet. For by one offering He has perfected for all time those who are sanctified.
And the Holy Spirit also testifies to us; for after saying,
"This is the covenant that I will make with them after those
days, says the Lord. **I will put my law upon their heart**,
and on their mind I will write them," He then says, "and
their sins and their lawless deeds I will remember no more.
Now where there is forgiveness of these things, there is no
longer any offering for sin" (Hebrews 10:10-18).

The laws that God promised to write on their heart are no different
that what was revealed at Sinai for He says that in this New Covenant
He would not remember their "lawless deeds" no more. By forgiving
their sins through the final sacrifice of Christ their violation of the law
given at Sinai would be forgiven and this same law would then be written on their heart.

The Apostle Paul said that Gentiles without circumcision who are
doers of the law demonstrate that the moral law has been written on their
heart (Romans 2:15), which is a promise of the fulfillment of the New
Covenant promised (Jeremiah 31:31-33). In keeping the moral requirements of the law they demonstrate that they are Jews inwardly and yet
without circumcision (Romans 2:28-29). The result is that on Judgment
Day their faith will be justified by their works, as was Abraham and
Rahab the Harlot (James 2:24-26), because their obedience demonstrates
the validity of their faith. Jesus will separate the sheep from the goats
on the basis of their works which demonstrate whether or not they are
a true disciple of Christ (Matthew 25). To have the law of God written
on your heart is to obey the law by the power of the Holy Spirit, out of
a new nature having been born again and made a new creation in Christ.

The Law, Love and Situation Ethics

When Gay Theology advocates are pressed for a basis for right and wrong and a reason for their assertion that sexual behavior is morally justifiable between "monogamous committed same sex couples," especially those claiming to be evangelicals, they will appeal to a form of situation ethics with a vague notion that "Christians are to live by love, not law" as Rick Brentlinger asserts:

> Because Jesus satisfied the righteous demands of God by keeping the Law in our place, we are no longer required to keep the Law ourselves. Christians have a higher standard, the Law of Love, which guides us as we walk in the spirit.[481]

Consequently any appeal to the law of God, His commandments, ordinances or rules are flatly rejected even if they come from the New Testament as RD. Weekly states, "Love is the overriding commandment of God... It usurps every rule and regulation, and holds together the entire covenant we're living under."[482]

In essence, they argue that the only law for Christians is the "law of love" or the "Law of Christ" which they wrongly assert is not to be equated with anything written in the Old Testament. While the New Testament certainly speaks of love as the "royal law" (James 2:8) and the "Law of Christ" (1 Corinthians 9:21; Galatians 6:2) it roots these laws in the Old Testament, specifically the very heart of the Holiness Code found in Leviticus 19:18. These Gay Theology proponents then assert that when making moral and ethical decisions they are to "walk in the spirit" rather than search the Scriptures to discern God's will on the matter at hand.

Of course this begs the question as to how you know whether or not you are "walking in the spirit," which Paul states that to do so is to "crucify the flesh with its passions and desires" (Galatians 5:25). And how can you know whether or not you are living according to the "law of love" while rejecting the Old Testament as any objective standard for Christian morality, which is the very source for the New Testament's "law

---

481   Rick Brentlinger, *Gay Christian 101 - Spiritual Self-Defense For Gay Christians* (2007), 373.
482   R.D. Weekly, *Homosexianity* (Judah First Ministries, 2009), 64.

of love" (Galatians 5:14)? In essence, Gay Theology proponents want to use the Old Testament's law of love found in Leviticus 19:18, which is repeatedly upheld by the New Testament, like climbing Wittgenstein's ladder only to then throw God's law away once they have arrived.

What Gay Theology advocates actually assert in their use of the term "law of love" is not in accordance with what the New Testament means by this term, but rather an ethical philosophy known as "Situation Ethics." This doctrine asserts that, "The ruling norm of Christian decision is love: nothing else" and hence "love is the only norm" for ethics as "love replaces law."[483] In Gay Theology this "love" is eroticized. Gay Theology advocates consequently will dismiss even the New Testament's appeal to the Old Testament commandments when they conflict with their new morality which eschews any objective standard for Christian conduct. This is due to a misconceived notion that the New Covenant emphasizes relationship over the objective law of God contained in the vows of the covenant which are the binding stipulations for that relationship, "Built upon the foundation of faith in Christ, our new covenant is about enjoying a personal relationship with the Lord, rather than obligatory obedience to a moral code written on tablets of stone – or even on pages of tree sap, for that matter."[484]

This idea "relationship" over objective morality, or "love" pitted against "law," was popularized in the 1960's by Joseph Fletcher in his book *Situation Ethics: The New Morality*. Although it has been refuted on numerous occasions it continues to be a popular idea, particularly amongst experienced oriented evangelicals and theoretical antinomian Dispensationalists.

When situation ethics are used in Christian morality it sets the subjective, personal and social context for relationships against the rightness or wrongness of specific acts as stated in Scripture. This is an untenable means of establishing a justifiable system of ethics for although the context (the situation) may affect the degree of culpability for a wrong act, and determine which commandments are applicable, an objective normative standard for morality is needed in order to establish any justifiable universal standard for what may be called "right" or "wrong." In fact, situational ethics is rooted in an attempt to avoid a

---

483   Joseph Fletcher, *Situation Ethics: The New Morality* (Louisville, KY: Knox Press, 2006), 69.
484   R.D. Weekly, *Homosexianity* (Judah First Ministries, 2009), 63.

system of ethics, a moral code, set of rules and principles and instead appeals to philosophical pragmatism, that the desired ends is the sole basis for justifying one's actions. It subsequently asserts that any appeal to *any* objective standard for Christian ethics, particularly the Old Testament, is tantamount to legalism.

The problem with situational ethics is that the Bible reveals a God to whom some acts are wrong whatever context is associated with them. Sexual acts (whether heterosexual or homosexual) that are outside the heterosexual marriage covenant come into that category. Heterosexual fornication is a sin regardless of the inner disposition and mutual consent of those involved. Likewise, same-sex acts are a sin regardless of the inner disposition and mutual consent of those involved. The entirety of Scripture upholds the pattern of nature in creation in Genesis 1-2, Matthew 19:5-6 and Romans 1 as the norm for human sexuality. Both heterosexual fornication and same-sex acts are outside of God's created order and to participate in such sins is an act of rebellion against God.

A loving motive - as important as it is - cannot override God's objective standard (the moral requirements of the law) for right and wrong which reflects His holy character. Therefore, while homosexual behavior feels "natural" to someone who identifies themselves as being "gay" it is contrary to God's set boundaries for human sexual expression. God has repeatedly throughout history judged those who violated His holiness whether or not they were in covenant with Him.

While I understand that restricting sexual behavior to a heterosexual marriage may sound severe and even burdensome to those who have homosexual inclinations and temptations, nevertheless right and wrong is determined by God and not our subjective emotional or fleshly desires. If situational ethics were to become determinative for Christian morality then any form of seemingly "natural" inclination will become acceptable and tolerated in the Body of Christ as it has in the Metropolitan Community Churches.

Chapter 17
Outing Closeted Gays in The Bible

In order to justify engaging in homosexual relations Gay Theology advocates not only deny that the well known prohibition passages apply to them, they also argue that the Bible contains examples of God-approved "committed faithful same sex unions." R.D. Weekly states that the Church's failure to see such approval is in its failure to recognize the homosexual relationship of David and Jonathan:

> If God intended for people of the same sex to be together, we would see examples in the bible. The only people who make this claim are those who are not aware of a same-sex couple – David and Jonathan. Enough evidence exists to come to an almost certain conclusion that David, one of the great heroes of our faith, had a very intimate, loving relationship with another man – a relationship that carried the heights of love he never had with a woman.[485]

In searching for such supposed affirmations, it is claimed that there are numerous homosexual relationships in the Bible that are blessed by God or that at least hint that they entailed a male/male sexual relationship or a female/female sexual relationship. These include the relationship between Naomi and Ruth, King Saul and David, David and Jonathan, Jesus and the Beloved Disciple (John or Lazarus), the Roman Centurion and his servant as well as numerous eunuchs in the Old and New Testaments. By reading between the lines Gay Theology advocates purport that they are "outing" closeted gays in the Bible. We will examine each of these relationships in their textual context and then address the issue as to whether a "eunuch" in the Bible is a close equivalent to modern concept of a "gay" man.

---

485   R.D. Weekly, *Homosexianity* (Judah First Ministries, 2009), 227.

Mother and Daughter: Were Naomi and Ruth Lesbians?

One of my favorite stories in the Old Testament is found in the Book of Ruth. It was the first book I ever translated from Hebrew into English and as I did so I found myself absolutely captivated by its literary style including the drama of the main characters, the sudden shifts in plot and its use of paranomasia (word play). Yet in doing so and when paying such a close attention to the details of the text it never occurred to me to translate or interpret the text as conveying a mother – daughter lesbian love affair. Yet, when reading the works of Gay Theology proponents that is exactly what they assert is the central nature of the relationship of two of its main characters, Naomi and Ruth.

To rightly understand the story we need to see how it begins and ends, how the author develops the narrative, the relationships of the people within it and how their lives provide us with the message that the author is seeking to convey to his hearers. One of the unique features of the Book of Ruth is that it ends with a genealogy, not of Israel's first king, Saul, but rather of one of the greatest Old Testament Kings – David (Ruth 4:17-22). In doing so the Book of Ruth also provides us with one the most important persons in the genealogy of Jesus Christ:

> The record of the genealogy of Jesus the Messiah, the son of David... Boaz was the father of Obed by Ruth, and Obed the father of Jesse.... Jesse was the father of David the king (Matthew 1:1, 6).

Genealogies appear in most books in the Bible either at the beginning (Genesis, The Gospel of Matthew) or they appear in transitional point that begins a new story within the book. The fact that the Book of Ruth ends with a genealogy is a tell-tale sign that the author's purpose of the book is to provide historical background for King David and subsequently for the Messiah. If we lose sight of the fact that the book serves as a Messianic prologue to the New Covenant the story will be misunderstood and misrepresented by commentators.

The overall theme of the Book of Ruth is that of redemption as the word "kinsmen-redeemer" (Hebrew: *goel*) appears repeatedly in the climax of the story in chapter 4 and the need for redemption is made known in its introduction. The timing of the story is during the period of the judges (Ruth 1:1) in which we read that Israel was in national decline for although they had promised to keep the covenant (Joshua 24:16-18), they repeatedly sought after other gods during a time in which "everyone did what was right in his own eyes" (Judges 17:6; 21:25). This is a pattern that we see throughout Biblical history – the exchange of the one true God for another (such as a golden calf falsely called YHWH), leads to an exchange in true spirituality that then leads to sexual perversion (Exodus 32; Romans 1:25-26). Consequently the nation of Israel went through twelve cycles of sin, repentance, delivery and a return to sin. Each cycle resulted in a judgment from God in the form of coming under siege by a pagan nation, which brought about a temporary repentance during which the Lord showed them mercy by delivering them through a judge.[486] Then as soon as that judge died the cycle would begin all over again.

It is during one of these cycles that the story of Ruth and her mother-in-law Naomi takes place. Having lost her husband and her sons, she subsequently loses the land of her inheritance due to indebtedness which is later redeemed by a near kinsmen-redeemer named Boaz who marries her daughter-in-law. The culmination of the Book of Ruth ends with a genealogy not of Israel's first king, Saul, but one of their greatest rulers King David. The author's purpose for this book then is to show the providence of God in redeeming His people through the kinsmen-redeemer Boaz, a foreshadow of the Messiah, and to establish the line of King David and ultimately King Jesus. The story of the Book of Ruth provides us with a picture of the redemptive work of Jesus Christ the kinsmen-redeemer who paid the redemption-price for His bride the Church, not with gold or silver but with His very blood (Leviticus 25:25; 1 Peter 1:18). If we do not keep this theme in our mind we will lose focus on the intent, purpose and nature of the relationship between

---

486   1. Othniel, the son of Kenaz from the tribe of Judah (3:7-11). Ehud, the son of Gerah from the tribe of Benjamin (3:12-30) 3. Shamgar, the son of Anath from the tribe of Levi (3:31)4. Deborah (and Barak) (4:1-5:31) 5. Gideon (also named Jerubbaal), the son of Joash from the tribe of Manasseh (6:1-8:32) 6. Tola, the son of Puah from the tribe of Issachar (10:1-5) 7. Jair, from the tribe of Gilead (10:1-5) 8. Jephthah, the son of Gilead from Gilead (10:6-12:7) 9. Ibzan, from the tribe of Judah (12:8-15 10. Elon, from the tribe of Zebulun (12:8-15) 11. Abdon, the son of Hillel, the Piratoni, from the tribe of Ephraim (12:8-15) 12. Samson, the son of Manoah, from the tribe of Dan (13:1-16:31)

Naomi and Ruth and more importantly the relationship between Ruther and Boaz, her kinsmen-redeemer.

In the opening of the story we read of the death of Naomi's husband and her two sons as they are away from their homeland in Moab (Ruth 1:2-5). Naomi's sons had married Moabite women, Ruth and Orpah, and upon her sons' death she hears that the Lord is providing during a time of famine back in her homeland (Ruth 1:6). She then urges her daughter-in-laws to return to their homeland and their gods for they cannot wait around for her to find another husband, bear two more sons and then wait for them to become old enough to be their husbands. What must be kept in mind is that the only thing Naomi has in mind for her daughter-in-laws is for them to find another heterosexual relationship. So, she urges them to return to the only place that she believes that they might find husbands and be able to bear children – in Moab. In doing so she refers to them in familial terms, "Return, my daughters. Why should you go with me? Have I yet sons in my womb, that they may be your husbands?" (Ruth 1:12) Orpah then returns to her homeland and her gods while Ruth clings to her mother-in-law and vows to be of her people and her God YHWH:

> Do not urge me to leave you or turn back from following you; for where you go, I will go, and where you lodge, I will lodge. Your people shall be my people, and your God, my God (Ruth 1:16).

It is extremely important that we pay attention to the familial nature of the relationship between Naomi and Ruth as the text explicitly states that Naomi repeatedly refers to Ruth as her daughter (Ruth 2:2; 2:8; 3:10; 3:11; 3:16; 3:18), the narrator of the story refers to Ruth as Naomi's daughter-in-law (Ruth 1:7; 2:20; 2:22; 3:1) and Naomi is repeatedly referred to as Ruth's mother-in-law even after her sons had died (Ruth 1:14; 2:11; 2:18; 2:19; 2:23; 3:1; 3:6; 3:16; 3:17; 4:15). Clearly the context and nature of this love and devotion is between that of a mother and daughter.

Upon returning to her homeland with her daughter-in-law, Naomi, whose name means "sweet" or "pleasant" insists on being referred to as "Mara," which in Hebrew means "bitter" for as she says, "The Lord has dealt bitterly with me" (Ruth 2:20). She has not only lost her husband

and sons, but as far as she knows this is the end of her family line, her genealogy, and consequently the possession of land of her inheritance. In her mind, her family has been blotted out of the national roll and consequently she has no hope for the future of her husband's family line. Consequently, Naomi is in mourning because of the loss of her husband, sons and family's future. But, in her mourning she does not know that Providence would bring her daughter-in-law a husband, a near kinsmen-redeemer and she would soon be holding her grandson in her arms.

In the second chapter Ruth goes out into the field to glean after the harvesters as allowed by the law (Deuteronomy 24:19). It turns out that the field providentially "just so happens" to belong to Boaz, who is later revealed to be a near relative (*goel*) of Naomi and her deceased husband Elimelech. Boaz takes note of Ruth's graciousness towards Naomi and then shows her favor by telling her not to glean elsewhere. He then provides more than what she was able to harvest according to the gleaning laws and he says to her:

> May the LORD reward your work, and your wages be full from the LORD, the God of Israel, under whose wings (Hebrew: *kanaph*) you have come to seek refuge (Ruth 2:12).

Ruth then returns home with her bountiful harvest and informs her mother-in-law where she had gleaned and then Naomi responds:

> May he be blessed of the LORD who has not withdrawn his kindness to the living and to the dead. The man is our relative, he is one of our closest relatives (Ruth 2:20).

Naomi then gives Ruth a plan to reintroduce herself to Boaz and claim him as their kinsmen-redeemer according to the provisions in the law and seek him as a husband under the principle of the levirate marriage. After Boaz and his workers have finished the day's harvest, eaten and laid down for the night, Ruth, at the advice of Naomi, goes and uncovers his feet and pulls his garment (Hebrew: *kanaph*) over herself. When he awakes at his astonishment he finds her at his feet. She then asks him to be her cover as her kinsmen-redeemer and says to him:

> I am Ruth your maid. So spread your wing (Hebrew:
> *kanaph*) over your maid, for you are a close relative (Ruth
> 3:9).

What we see in the Hebrew, which is often missed in English translations, is that the "wing" (often translated "cover" in Ruth 3:9) of the
Lord that Boaz had prayed would cover her is fulfilled by Boaz himself
as he would fulfill the law's cultural mandate for preserving family lines
through the levirate (Hebrew: *yibbum*) marriage. A levirate marriage
is one in which the nearest relative, usually a brother, of a deceased
man is obligated to marry his brother's widow in order to preserve his
family line and his name in the family genealogy. Through the law's levirate marriage the firstborn child is then treated as that of the deceased
brother in order to preserve the deceased man's name in the family tree,
(Deuteronomy 25:5-6; Genesis 38:8) which renders the child the heir of
the deceased brother and not the biological father.

Boaz in turn expresses his thankfulness that she has chosen him
to be her redeemer rather than a younger man (Ruth 3:10). However,
there was one hitch in the situation, which was that there was another
closer relative (Ruth 3:12) that the text only identifies in Hebrew as
Ploni Almoni, which most English translates as "friend" (NASB, NIV),
"such a one" (KJV) or they do not translate it and leave it out of the
text (Douay-Rheims) (Ruth 4:1). In order for Boaz to take the place of
the *goel*, Ploni Almoni would have to relinquish his duty as the nearest
kinsman. The law had another provision known as *halizah* which states
that if a man refuses to carry out this "duty" the woman must spit in
his face, take one of his shoes, and the others in the town must always
call him "the one without a shoe" (Deuteronomy 25:9-10). We see this
played out in Ruth Chapter 4 in which we find a conversation between
the two men in which Boaz challenges him to redeem the land of Naomi
through marrying Ruth. But if he doesn't want to do so, let him know so
that he may marry Ruth. In this chapter the verb and noun form of *goel*
is repeated 10 times ("redeem" and "redeemer") which is often missed
in English translations.

Most "pictures", types or analogies of Christ that we tend to think
about in the Old Testament are very bloody, especially the Passover and
sacrificial system as they portray Jesus, as John would later say, as the

"Lamb of God who takes away the sin of the world" (John 1:29). But there are other non-bloody types of Christ as well, such as the prophets, priests and kings who in their imperfections prepare the way for the Prophet, Priest and King. But Ruth gives us a picture of Christ in a different way, through a story of redemption of the Kinsmen-Redeemer.

Let us now look at the climactic moment in the story. In doing so I will offer a translation of Ruth 4:1-6 that I believe emphasizes what the reader ought to hear:

> And Boaz went up to the gate and sat there and behold the [legal] redeemer passing by of whom Boaz had spoken and he said, "Ploni Almoni, sit here." And he turned and sat down (Ruth 4:1).

There are several key features in this pericope, namely the repetition of *goel* in both noun and verb form. The author of the text is urging the ear to hear an emphasis on the role of the redeemer and who was to be redeemed. However, most English translations render the noun form *goel* as "kinsman" rather than "redeemer."[487] This is most likely due to the fact that while all redeemers had to be a near kinsmen, not all kinsmen performed the role of a redeemer. But unless the emphasis on the repetition and contrasting of the two redeemers is made the English reader will not notice that "kinsmen" and the one to be "redeemed" is a variation of the same word which indicates the central theme of the book. As we shall see the first "redeemer" introduced in Ruth 4:1 is but the potential legal redeemer, and is not the actual redeemer in redemptive history. For clarification the difference between the first potential role of the person being addressed by Boaz ought to be identified as the "legal redeemer" or "redeemer-by-law." In addition to the repetition of phrases in this text there is also the air of a courtroom. The first of which is the mentioning of the "gate" in Ruth 4:1. This gate is not merely an entranceway, but is the venue of legal transactions as we read concerning the trial of a rebellious youth (Deuteronomy 21:19).

Most commentators recognize the fact that the gate of the city was the center of the social life of the city where important issues were discussed and judgments were made. The venue of the discussion

---

487   NKJV and NASB "a close relative"; KJV "kinsman"; Basic English Bible "near relation."

between the competing redeemers may therefore be likened to that of a courtroom. In addition, we also see the establishment in what might be considered a jury:

> And he took ten men from the elders and said, "Sit down here." And they sat down (Ruth 4:2).

The elders of a city, not merely elderly men, are to serve as witnesses of the evidence of the case to be presented by Boaz. This too was a requirement of a legal court case as we read concerning the trial of a rebellious son (Deuteronomy 21:2). The author of Ruth has now added to the courtroom venue a jury. Now all that awaits in this court room is an appeal to the law:

> And he said to the [legal] redeemer [*goel*], "The portion of the field that belonged to our brother to Elimelech, Naomi who has returned from the fields of Moab" (Ruth 4:3).

Here we see the opening case of Boaz as he addresses "the [legal] redeemer," that is the one who by law ought to redeem Ruth and Naomi:

> And he said, "I will open your ears to say 'purchase it' before those sitting and before the elders of my people, if you will redeem [*goel*] redeem. [*goel*] and if you will not redeem [*goel*] tell me so I may know because there is no other than you to redeem [*goel*] and I am after you." And he said, "I myself will redeem [*goel*]" (Ruth 4:4).

While not seen in this passage, earlier in the book we see the grace and kindness of Boaz toward Ruth in his abundant provision for her in allowing her to glean to which Ruth asks, "Why have I found grace in your eyes, that you would take knowledge of me, seeing I am a stranger?" (Ruth 2:10) In Ruth 4:4, however, we see the call for the law in the form of the legal redeemer, the closest relative, to redeem Ruth and Naomi. At first the legal redeemer, Ploni Almoni, seems willing to redeem as he states "I myself will redeem." But then a further stipulation is made by Boaz in the court room drama:

> And Boaz said, "In the day you purchase the field for the
> hand of Naomi and for Ruth, the Moabite, the wife of the
> dead, you have to purchase it, to raise up the name of the
> dead upon his inheritance" (Ruth 4:5).

Now the redeemer-by-law is told that he must also "raise up the
name of the dead." Ploni Almoni, the legal redeemer, is faced with a
problem. If he redeems Naomi's field he must also marry Ruth in order
to carry on the lineage of the departed husband. But can the Law, metaphorically, raise the dead? Is a glorified resurrection to be found in the
Law (Ploni Almoni), or in the gospel of grace (Boaz)? Ploni Almoni
wasted no time in expressing his willingness to acquire the land but then
he learns that it has strings attached. His motive for redeeming is not
that of grace, unlike Boaz, but rather out of perhaps either sheer legal
obligation, or personal gain, so he responds:

> And said the [legal] redeemer, "I am not able to redeem
> otherwise for myself otherwise I will ruin my inheritance.
> You for yourself redeem because redemption I am not able
> to redeem" (Ruth 4:6).

The redeemer-by-law does not merely state, "I do not *want* to redeem" but rather "I am not *able* to redeem." In this we find a picture of
a clear distinction between redemptive grace (Boaz) and the law (Ploni
Almoni). The law, though good and holy, does not have the power to redeem as the Apostle Paul states, "For if the inheritance is based on law,
it is no longer based on a promise; but God has granted it to Abraham
by means of a promise" (Galatians 3:18). The law (as typified by Ploni
Almoni) was not able to obtain the inheritance of Naomi and Ruth.
Consequently, their inheritance had to be based on promise, the promise
of Boaz who not only purchases the field for the "hand of Naomi" but
also purchases Ruth's hand in marriage and then we read:

> So Boaz took Ruth, and she became his wife, and he went
> in to her. And the LORD enabled her to conceive, and
> she gave birth to a son. Then the women said to Naomi,
> "Blessed is the LORD who has not left you without a

redeemer [*goel*] today, and may his name become famous
in Israel. May he also be to you a restorer of life and a
sustainer of your old age; for your daughter-in-law, who
loves you and is better to you than seven sons, has given
birth to him." Then Naomi took the child and laid him in
her lap, and became his nurse. The neighbor women gave
him a name, saying, "A son has been born to Naomi!' So
they named him Obed. He is the father of Jesse, the father
of David" (Ruth 4:13-17).

The land that was redeemed belonged to Naomi's natural family line
but because Ruth remained a loyal daughter-in-law, Boaz was able to
redeem "the field for the hand of Naomi" whereas the unnamed competing kinsmen was not (Ruth 4:1). This is why it was a time of rejoicing
for not only Ruth, but also for Naomi whose legal line of descendants,
a son of Naomi and her deceased husband, and inheritance of the land
would continue through Boaz and Ruth. In the Bible "son of" can connote the direct son, the grandson, the great-grand son or even in the case
of Jesus who was referred to as the "Son of David" even though He was
the great-great-great-great... grandson of King David (Matthew 1:1).

Were Naomi and Ruth Lesbians?

Many Gay Theology advocates assert that although the text does not
explicitly state that Naomi and Ruth her lesbians, they believe that there
is enough textual evidence to affirm that the story of the Book of Ruth is
about a loving committed lesbian affair. This is despite the fact that they
were both married and Ruth was remarried to a man. In order to do so
they must read the text through the Queer lens of Liberation Theology.
In doing so they read into the text that Naomi and Ruth were the victims
of a misogynistic society in which two Lesbians could not possibly live
out their lives together in peace. They therefore had to capitulate to
the "man on top" patriarchal heterosexist culture of the day by using a
man in order to survive. Supposing that the author is a closeted lesbian
telling a story of secret lesbian love with a hidden "code" that provides
indicators of the true nature of the relationship Michael S. Piazza poses:

If, however, the author of the book of Ruth was a woman, it is possible that she understood precisely what was happening here. She would have known that, although they were almost utterly dependent on men for their physical survival, women of that day often turned to one another for the tenderness, affection and companionship they longed for and needed. Notice, in verse 14, how the author recorded Ruth clinging to Naomi. The physical point of contact had probably become an important part of their survival in the face of brutal sexism and personal grief... the idea of sex being part of a relationship between two women is not something that would occur to the average male Biblical scholar. Combine sexism and homophobia and you have a most powerful silencer. Why wouldn't their love have found intimate expression?[488]

Ignoring the mother-daughter nature of the relationship Jeff Miner and John Connoley likewise assert:

Here then is the story the Bible tells us: Ruth gave up everything so she could be with Naomi; she put her own life at risk, so she could spend it with Naomi; and, even after she married a man, her most significant relationship remained the one she shared with Naomi. These actions and emotions are difficult, almost impossible, to explain as mere friendship. If we set aside our preconceptions of what is possible in the Bible, the book of Ruth reads like the story of two women in love.[489]

According to Piazza the only reason then for Naomi to seek a husband for Ruth is for pragmatic survival in a an oppressive male dominated culture, "Unfortunately, because of the social structure of their day women would still need a man to help them if they were to survive."[490]

488   Michael S. Piazza, *Gay By God* (Dallas, TX: Source of Hope Publishing, 1998), 58.
489   Jeff Miner and John Connoley, *The Children Are Free* (Indianapolis, IN: Jesus Metropolitan Community Church, 2002), 31.
490   Michael S. Piazza, *Gay By God* (Dallas, TX: Source of Hope Publishing, 1998), 60.

Contextually, what then is the *supposed* justification for Gay Theology advocates for turning this story into a secret Lesbian love affair? It is found in the covenantal oath which Ruth made to Naomi after she had urged her daughter-in-law to return to Moab to find another husband:

> But Ruth said, "Do not urge me to leave you *or* turn back
> from following you; for where you go, I will go, and where
> you lodge, I will lodge. Your people shall be my people,
> and your God, my God. Where you die, I will die, and there
> I will be buried. Thus may the LORD do to me, and worse,
> if anything but death parts you and me" (Ruth 1:16-17).

There have been some modern heterosexual couples who have taken the words of this passage out of context and used them for wedding vows. Gay Theology advocates insist this is because the text cannot be read but with romantic overtones. Still, this does not justify reading the text as if it were a homosexual marriage vow. The Apostle Paul's statement concerning love in 1 Corinthians 13 has also been used out of context in heterosexual marriage ceremonies. But neither text is speaking about the romantic relationship of a husband and wife and so to do so is to use these passages in a manner contrary to their original context. To then argue that because some heterosexuals have used such texts in a modern marriage ceremony somehow justifies as reading it akin to being Lesbian marriage vows is unjustified.

Having considered the story in its entirety and examined the relationship of Naomi and Ruth and the subsequent relationship with Boaz, her second husband, it is abundantly clear that the relationship between these two women is that of a mother and daughter. Furthermore, it is the heterosexual union between Boaz and Ruth that not only is the Lord's means of providing a cover ("wings") for Ruth, but also raises up the name of the dead, Elimelech, and establishes the genealogy for King David and the Son of David, the King of kings Jesus Christ. A Queer interpretation of this book absolutely destroys the true beauty of the story as it presents to us a perfect picture of the relationship between Jesus Christ and His bride the Church.

In this story there is absolutely no mention of any sexual relations between the mother Naomi and her daughter-in-law Ruth and the only interest Ruth has is to find another husband. The expressions of loyalty and devotion are made completely within a familial context and to assert otherwise would be to lead modern women into believing that they too could justifiably have a husband to be used as sperm bank while maintaining a lesbian love affair with not only another woman but one's mother-in-law. Yet that is exactly what Gay Theology proponents would have us believe:

> It is a story of the love between women, celebrating faithfulness, passionate care, commitment, devotion, and loyalty. We now know that many women such as Ruth and Naomi exist, and have exited throughout the history of the world, as emotionally intimate lesbians and that genital expression is not necessarily the defining quality of lesbianism… And, of course, lesbianism does not exclude motherhood. The biological urge and the psychosocial desire to perpetuate the human race continues to remain strong. Women are discovering more and more resources for obtaining sperm. Naomi instructed Ruth how to become impregnated by her kinsmen Boaz. Once Ruth had given birth to a son, the women in the village gathered, saying, "A son has been born to Naomi" (Ruth 4:17).[491]

According to Queer Theology advocates, the story of Naomi and Ruth using Boaz and "tricking him" into marriage is a model for modern day lesbians to likewise use men (albeit via a sperm bank) in order to have child and maintain a lesbian relationship:

> Catholic theologian André Guindon also points to Ruth and Naomi as the patron saints for the procreative strategies of same-sex couples. Their story becomes very appropriate, especially given the artificial insemination strategies frequented by queers. Ruth is looking for a legal inseminator

---

491   Irene S. Travis, "Love Your Mother: A Lesbian Womanist Reading of Scripture" Robert E. Goss, Mona West (ed.) *Taking Back The Word: A Queer reading of the Bible* (Cleveland, Ohio, Pilgrim Press, 2000), 38-39.

to present a child to Naomi, with whom she made an earlier covenant. With Naomi's guidance, she seduces Boaz into a levirate marriage to become pregnant with a child. Upon the birth of the child, the village women acknowledge Ruth's son as her covenanted partner's son, declaring "A son has been born to Naomi." (Ruth 4:17) The two women risk everything within a patriarchal structure to create a family visible only to other women.[492]

Brothers and Comrades: Were David and Jonathan Homosexual Lovers?

It is common for men with same-sex attractions to sexualize their male-to-male relationships, turning friendships into objects of sexual desire, and then read into other close male friendships their own personal experiences. An example of this is seen in the way in which Gay Theology proponents read the story of the brotherly friendship of David and Jonathan and the relationship of fictional characters such as Frodo Baggins and Samwise Gamgee. By reading these narratives through the lens of their own experiences they subsequently become homosexualized because they cannot imagine two men having such a close relationship without it being expressed sexually. This is largely due to their tendency to think of love primarily as a feeling which is ultimately expressed in a sexual union with whoever is willing. The Gay Theological interpretation of the relationship between Jonathan and David then is that these were two warrior-lovers who infuriated Saul because of their sexual relationship.

One of the most prominent books which asserts such a view is Tom Horner's *Jonathan Loved David: Homosexuality in Biblical Times*. Like most Gay Theology advocates, he views the Biblical culture of Israel not as one that was to be antithetical to the surrounding cultures but one that arose up out of and was formed by the culture of the day. Hence the stories of the Bible are to be read like any other near Ancient Near Eastern text, "The Bible, the book that has been venerated by Western

---

492   Robert E. Goss, *Queering Christ: Beyond Jesus Acted Up* (Eugene, OR: The Pilgrim Press, 2007), 99-100.

civilization throughout history, was produced by the Ancient Middle Eastern World and was part and parcel of that world."[493]

The Bible is a book that is God-breathed which records the sinful acts of people in the Ancient Near Eastern world. It was written to reveal the holy will of God in order to sanctify, instruct and correct a group of people to think and live differently than the surrounding nations. In contrast to this view of Scripture, Horner instead sees the Bible as the product of a primitive misogynistic culture whose sexual ethics as prescribed in the law wasn't any different than the Gentiles nations as he states:

> And how could Israel not have been influenced by these cultures? How could it have adopted an entirely different sexual ethic, living as close as it did to foreign influences?[494]

Horner completely misses the point of the law, particularly Leviticus 18-20, which forbade Israel from imitating the abominable sexual practices of the surrounding nations. He also ignores the fact that that David as the Psalmist declared that he loved God's law (Psalm 119:97). He also conveniently leaves out the fact that David, his son Solomon and grandson Rehoboam suffered the consequences of violating that law, particularly when he committed adultery and accumulated wives contrary to the explicit commands of God's law (Deuteronomy 17:17).

Horner goes on to cite various extra-Biblical pagan homosexual hero narratives of the Ancient Near East such as the Gilgamesh Epic and interprets the relationship of David and Jonathan as being just another pagan homosexual liaison. This is the fundamental error of revisionist Gay Theological reading of the Bible and is it repeated by Virginia Mollenkot who likewise asserts:

---

493   Tom Horner, *Jonathan Loved David: Homosexuality in Biblical Times* (Philadelphia, PA: Westminster Press, 1978), 15.
494   Ibid, 20.

Although many interpreters are at pains to explain away
the passionate details of the David and Jonathan story,
their love is in the tradition of great warrior-lovers such as
Gilgamesh and Enkidu or Achilles and Patroclus. And their
presence in the Bible renders untrue the often-repeated
assertion that the Bible has nothing good to say about same
sex love.[495]

The result is that they read into the close brotherly friendship of
David and Jonathan their own homoerotic experiences and conclude,
"There can be little doubt, however, except on the part of those who
absolutely refuse to believe it, that there existed a homosexual relationship between David and Jonathan."[496] Rick Brentlinger, borrowing from
the Liberal Gay and Queer Theology advocates, likewise states, "...the
most famous gay relationship in scripture, Jonathan and David, provides a positive Biblical witness indicating this famous couple enjoyed
an intimate sexual relationship over a fifteen year period, with God's
approval."[497]

In contrast to this homosexualized understanding of the text, the
story of Jonathan and David is *not* about competing sexual loves between two friends and a jealous father. Rather, it is an epic story of
two men who become brothers through times of adversity. It is about a
man's loyalty to the chosen anointed king over his father who has been
rejected by God as the ruler over Israel. In this heroic story Jonathan
chooses the interests of his brother David over the self-seeking interests
of his father Saul, even to the detriment of his own life. The camaraderie
and brotherly love of David and Jonathan and the violent reaction of his
father cannot justifiably be read as a sexual love affair, either explicitly
or by reading "between the lines." This is a story of a jealousy triangle
caught between two allegiances; Jonathan's relationship to Saul as his
father and to David as his brother. The preference of David over his own
father provokes in Saul a jealousy and hatred for David because he fears

495   Virginia Ramey Mollenkott, *Omnigender: A Trans-religious Approach* (Cleveland, OH: The Pilgrim Progress, 2007), 109.
496   Tom Horner, *Jonathan Loved David: Homosexuality in Biblical Times* (Philadelphia, PA: Westminster Press, 1978), 20.
497   Rick Brentlinger, *Gay Christian 101 - Spiritual Self-Defense For Gay Christians* (2007), 8.

losing his dynasty to David.

To make their argument that the friendship between Jonathan and David was more than familial there are a number words and phrases throughout the text which if read in the light of very limited and carefully chosen word studies can be made to sound seemingly homosexual. But a more careful and honest study of these words in their immediate and larger context will prove that such a reading of the text is the worst case of Scripture twisting imaginable.

First, let us take a look at the relationship of Jonathan and David in comparison to their forefathers and how they also had similar close ties with other men that are expressed in a familial fashion. To rightly understand the nature of the love of Jonathan for David we must examine the lives of Abraham, Ishmael and Isaac. Then we must look to Jacob, his sons and Joseph and finally we must see the corollary between the relationship of David and Jonathan and Jesus (the Son of David) and His disciple Jonathan.

When Abram (later named Abraham) was seventy-five years old he was told by the LORD that He would make him a great nation and that through him all nations would be blessed (Genesis 12:1-3). After waiting ten years for the promises to be fulfilled, at the advice of his wife, Abram takes matters into his own hands and has a child named Ishmael by Hagar, Sarai's handmaid (Genesis 16). Later God met with Abram again at which time He told him that his name would be changed to Abraham, for he would become a father of many nations and that Sarai would be called Sarah because she would become a mother of nations. Abraham had loved Ishmael for he thought he was the fulfillment of God's promise as he proclaimed, "Oh that Ishmael might live before You!" (Genesis 17:18) But then the Lord tells Abraham that he will indeed have a son named Isaac through his wife Sarah and that his descendants would come from him (Genesis 17:15-19). Years later God met with Abraham again and asked him to do the unthinkable, to sacrifice his son of promise:

> Now it came about after these things, that God tested Abraham, and said to him, "Abraham!" And he said, "Here I am." He said, "Take now your son, your only son, whom you **love** (Hebrew: *ahab*) Isaac, and go to the land

of Moriah, and offer him there as a burnt offering on one
of the mountains of which I will tell you" (Genesis 22:1-2).

Even though Abraham had a son named Ishmael through Hagar, the
Lord refers to Isaac as the "only son" (Hebrews 11:17). He is the one
who is favored over the other son and it is here that we see for the first
time the Hebrew word *ahab* (sometimes transliterated as *ahav*), which
is translated "love." This is a very important term for we shall see it
many times in which there is a familial love between Jacob who favors
his son Joseph over his other sons, Jonathan who favors David as a
brother over his father, and Jesus who favors John as a brother who will
care for his mother Mary after his death. While the term can also be
used of marital love with sexual connotations, it is significant to see that
the first time it is seen in the Bible it is used in a familial context and
that these other relationships are spoken of in familial contexts as well.
It is the context of the word, not the frequency of its use in a particular
manner that determines its meaning.

Our next example of familial love (*ahab*) is seen in the relationship
between Jacob (Israel) and his preference of Joseph over his other sons:

> These are the records of the generations of Jacob. Joseph,
> when seventeen years of age, was pasturing the flock with
> his brothers while he was still a youth, along with the sons
> of Bilhah and the sons of Zilpah, his father's wives. And
> Joseph brought back a bad report about them to their father.
> Now Israel **loved** (*ahab*) Joseph more than all his sons,
> because he was the son of his old age; and he made him a
> varicolored tunic. His brothers saw that their father **loved**
> (*ahab*) him more than all his brothers; and so they hated
> him and could not speak to him on friendly terms (Genesis
> 37:2-4).

Notice how such love can stir up jealousy and contention when one
is loved over the other such as in the case between Ishmael and Isaac,
Joseph and his brothers, and as we shall see between David and Saul.
Jacob loves his son Joseph over his other sons and gives evidence of this
by giving him a special tunic. We see this same action in the brotherly
love of Jonathan for King David and King Jesus, the son of David, for

Jonathan the Beloved when he gave him the honor of caring for His mother. First, we see that Saul had first loved David as his own son:

> Then David came to Saul and attended him; and Saul loved (*ahab*) him greatly, and he became his armor bearer" (1 Samuel 16:21).

Then later we see that Jonathan, the son of Saul, came to love David as his own brother:

> Now it came about when he had finished speaking to Saul, that the soul of Jonathan was **knit** (Hebrew: *qashar*) to the soul of David, and Jonathan **loved him as himself.** Saul took him that day and did not let him return to his father's house. Then Jonathan **made a covenant** with David because he loved him as himself. Jonathan stripped himself of the robe that was on him and gave it to David, with his armor, including his sword and his bow and his belt (1 Samuel 18:1-4).

There are three very important textual clues that indicate the nature of the relationship between David and Jonathan. First, we find that their souls were "knit together." The idea is that their lives are intertwined so that they are of the same mind, heart and soul. Gay Theology advocate Richard Brentlinger sexualizes the text when he asserts that the phrase "refers to being romantically in love with someone" and that it speaks of "the intense romantic, emotional attachment which bound these men."[498] Likewise David W. Shelton asserts:

> Jonathan "became one in spirit with David," it says. The constant bond between the two is clear, and is just the first of four major points that establish their relationship as being one of romance, not just "friendship." [499]

---

498   Rick Brentlinger, *Gay Christian 101 - Spiritual Self-Defense For Gay Christians* (2007), 152.
499   David W. Shelton, *The Rainbow Kingdom: Christianity & the Homosexual Reconciled* (Lulu, 2006), 71.

However, the same phrase is used throughout Scripture in male-male relationships that are very close but non-sexual so that they speak of each other familial terms. For example, Jacob's love for his youngest son is said to be "knit together" or "bound up" with his youngest son:

> Now therefore when I come to thy servant my father, and the lad be not with us; seeing that his life is **bound up** (*qashar*) in the lad's life (Genesis 44:30).

The Hebrew term *qashar* also refers to making a political or strategic allegiance, which is exactly how Saul uses the term to refer to the friendship of Jonathan and David:

> For all of you have **conspired** (*qashar*) against me so that there is no one who discloses to me when my son makes a **league** (Hebrew: *karath*: to covenant, make an alliance) with the son of Jesse, and there is none of you who is sorry for me or discloses to me that my son has stirred up my servant against me to lie in ambush, as it is this day (1 Samuel 22:8).

Again we read:

> Saul then said to him, "Why have you and the son of Jesse **conspired** (*qashar*) against me, in that you have given him bread and a sword and have inquired of God for him, so that he would rise up against me by lying in ambush as it is this day?" (1 Samuel 22:13)

It is clear that Saul perceives the nature of the relationship between Jonathan and David as that of a political allegiance, not a homosexual love affair. Ever since the people began to love David and sing his praises Saul has been paranoid about losing his throne. Now Saul thinks that his worst nightmare has come true, that his own son has made an allegiance with David against him to overthrow the throne.

Another important concept in the description of the relationship between Jonathan and David in 1 Samuel 18:1-4 is the idea of being of two men "knit together." Contrary to the assertion of Gay Theologians this term does not have any homosexual overtones. In fact, it is more often used to describe political allegiances or familial relationships. For example, in the New Testament where we find similar language such as when Paul says of his "son" Timothy:

> But I hope in the Lord Jesus to send Timothy to you short-ly, so that I also may be encouraged when I learn of your condition. For I have no one else of **kindred spirit** (Greek: isopsychos - the same life-soul) who will genuinely be concerned for your welfare. For they all seek after their own interests, not those of Christ Jesus. But you know of his proven worth, that he served with me in the furtherance of the gospel like a child serving his father (Philippians 2:19-20).

Likewise, Paul speaks of his relationship with the Christians at Colossae using the same phrase "knit together" and "love" that describe the relationship David and Jonathan:

> That their hearts might be comforted, **being knit together in love** (Greek: *sumbibasthentes en agape*), and unto all riches of the full assurance of understanding, to the ac-knowledgement of the mystery of God, and of the Father, and of Christ (Colossians 2:2).

Second, we see that Jonathan loved David "as himself." Jonathan was married but he does not love David as his wife. Rather, the nature of this love is a fulfillment of the great commandment to love your neigh-bor as yourself (Leviticus 19:18; Mark 12:28-31).

Third, we notice that Jonathan and David made a covenant with each other, which is followed by the giving of gifts. This was a common expression of fidelity between men without having any sort of sexual connotation to it as we read of Abraham and Abimelech:

> Abraham took sheep and oxen and gave them to Abimelech, and the two of them made a covenant (Genesis 21:27).

Then the relationship between David and Saul took a turn for the worse. Not only did Saul and Jonathan love David, but because of his military victories the people of Judah came to love him too and shout the praises of his victories as being greater that of Saul (1 Samuel 18:5-9).

Jonathan loved David as a brother and Saul had loved him as a son. But then David began to receive the love of the people and Saul grew jealous and suspicious of his popularity as a potential political rival. This jealousy and fear of losing his own throne was so intense that Saul attempts to kill David:

> Now it came about on the next day that an evil spirit from God came mightily upon Saul, and he raved in the midst of the house, while David was playing the harp with his hand, as usual; and a spear was in Saul's hand. Saul hurled the spear for he thought, 'I will pin David to the wall.' But David escaped from his presence twice. Now Saul was afraid of David, for the LORD was with him but had departed from Saul. Therefore Saul removed him from his presence and appointed him as his commander of a thousand; and he went out and came in before the people. David was prospering in all his ways for the LORD was with him. When Saul saw that he was prospering greatly, he dreaded him. But all Israel and Judah **loved** (*ahab*) David, and he went out and came in before them (1 Samuel 18:10-15).

Saul's son Jonathan has chosen to be loyal and make an allegiance with David through a covenant signified by the giving of his royal robe and sword. The Lord has prospered David so that now the people, Saul's subjects, love David. In all these relationships the same word for love (*ahab*) is used and all within the same non-sexual context.

Rick Brentlinger recognizes that the same word *ahab* is used for the Saul's love for David, as well as Michal's love for David and all Israel and Judah.[500] He also recognizes that the relationship between Saul and David was not sexual. However, some Gay Theology apologists who are more consistent in their queer reading of the text go on to assert that there was a jealous romantic triangle going on between Saul, David

---

500   Rick Brentlinger, *Gay Christian 101 - Spiritual Self-Defense For Gay Christians* (2007), 147.

and Jonathan.[501] Brentlinger then attempts to make the case that because there was a covenant between Jonathan and David that the context of that relationship indicates it was a romantic and sexual relationship akin to a Gay marriage. Like liberal Gay Theologians, he then argues that the Jonathan and David's relationship paralleled pagan homosexual-warrior relationships. Yet, as we have already seen non-sexual covenants between men, such as Abraham and Abimelech, where mutual interests were confirmed was common (Genesis 21:27). There is no contextual reason why the same word *ahab* used in relation to different people in the same context has changed its meaning, that one use is sexual whereas the others are familial or friendly.

As the text tells us Saul feels threatened on every side, even within his own home. So out of fear and anger he attempts to kill the man he once loved as a son. But David escapes the attempt to take his life. Saul then makes a few political moves in an attempt to minimize the threat of David taking his popularity all the way to the throne. First, he gets David to become his son-in-law as a means to do what the Chinese general and military strategist Sun-Tzu (400 B.C.) once said, "Keep your friends close to you, but keep your enemies even closer." Saul makes David one of his chief military officers with the hope that David might be killed in battle:

> Then Saul said to David, "Here is my older daughter Merab; I will give her to you as a wife, only be a valiant man for me and fight the LORD's battles." For Saul thought, "My hand shall not be against him, but let the hand of the Philistines be against him." But David said to Saul, "Who am I, and what is my life or my father's family in Israel, that I should be the king's son-in-law?" So it came about at the time when Merab, Saul's daughter, should have been given to David, that she was given to Adriel the Meholathite for a wife (1 Samuel 18:16-19).

---

501   John Boswell states, "...intense love relations between persons of the same gender figure prominently in the Old Testament – e.g. Saul and David, David and Jonathan, Ruth and Naomi – and were celebrated throughout the Middle Ages in both ecclesiastical and popular literature as examples of extraordinary devotion, sometimes with distinctly erotic overtones." *Christianity, Social Tolerance, and Homosexuality* (University Of Chicago Press; 8th Edition. edition, 2005), 105.

Again Saul's plan is foiled as David rejects the offer, not out of spite or unthankfulness or because he isn't attracted to women. Rather he has such a humble heart that he does not see himself worthy to become the king's son-in-law. But then one of Saul's younger daughters comes to love David and so Saul tries this plan again to have David killed, this time by the Philistines (1 Samuel 18:20-30).

This time David accepted the offer to become his son-in-law and though it could have cost him his life he paid the dowry that he won in battle. David was willing to put his life on the line in order to have Michal as his wife. This is not the reaction you would expect from a man who wants to have sex with Jonathan.

Saul's plan to have David killed in battle did not work and so Saul tells his men, including his son, that there is a bounty on the head of David. Here is where we see the righteousness of Jonathan in that he is willing to go against the wicked plans of his own father while being true to David by informing him of his father's intent (1 Samuel 19:1-6). For a moment Saul relents of his anger, jealousy and wrath towards David, his own son-in-law. But then Saul, because of the wickedness of his heart, repeatedly seeks to kill David even as he is making music for the house of Saul. David manages to flee when Saul throws a spear at him and later Mical, David's wife and Jonathan's sister, helps David escape out of the house and covers for his absence from Saul by stating that he is sick (1 Samuel 19:7-15).

Both Jonathan and Michal, who love David, protect him. David refuses to return to the king's table, which is a great insult, because Saul's invitations are only a cover to have the opportunity to kill him. David is puzzled over Saul's anger for he has no intent to conduct a coup and take over the throne (1 Samuel 20:1). Jonathan then shows his loyalty and friendship towards David in a manner that no other person, including his own wife, had ever done. He puts his life on the line and does a recognizance mission to discern whether Saul is still intent on killing David. This is a very dangerous mission because they know that David has found favor, or grace, in the sight of Jonathan rather than taking up his father's anger towards him. David does not say, "Because we are lovers" but due to Jonathan's loyalty and allegiance with David which was consigned by an oath and covenant like Abraham and Abimelech (1 Samuel 20:1-4).

David then devises a plan for Jonathan to investigate the attitude of Saul towards David, to determine if he considers him a threat and is bent on killing him, and a means of sending a secret signal to him out in the field. In doing so, Jonathan and David make a familial covenant so that when David ascends to the throne David will not cut off or extinguish Jonathan's house as if he were an enemy like Saul, "So Jonathan made a covenant with the house of David, saying, 'May the LORD require it at the hands of David's enemies'" (1 Samuel 20:5-16).

Jonathan makes a covenant with David in which he vows to show towards him the love of the LORD, not the love of a sexual partner. He is exemplifying the requirement of the law, the same "Holiness Code" that condemns men having sex with other men, to "Love your neighbor as yourself'" (Leviticus 19:18; Mark 12:28-31; John 13:34-35). This is not a marriage covenant, an act which is a public declaration followed by the celebration with family and friends. Rather this is a political alliance between two friends and households to treat one another as brothers.

Jonathan then tells David what the sign will be that will indicate David's status in the house of Saul (1 Samuel 20:18-23). Returning to his father's house Jonathan finds that Saul is still angry and jealous towards David. Saul is a rejected king who recognizes that David is in the LORD's favor and yet he is trying to hold on to his dynasty. When David doesn't come to the table Saul is angry even though Jonathan has given him an excuse for his not appearing.

In contrast to this understanding of the relationship between Jonathan and David, Gay Theology proponents Jeff Miner and John Connoley assert that when Jonathan gave David his possessions that his disrobing also has sexual implications.[502] But nothing could be farther from the truth. In context, we see that Saul tried to kill David several times (1 Samuel 18:6-11, 17; 19:1; 20:31), because he wanted his son Jonathan to be next in line for the crown. He knew, however, that David had already been chosen by God (1 Samuel 16:1-13). Even Jonathan knew that David was to be the next king (1 Samuel 23:16-17). This is why Jonathan gave David his robe, armor, and weapons. These gifts from Jonathan signified his knowledge that David was God's chosen king. Jonathan was, in a sense, giving the crown to David, since the robe refers to kingship (1 Samuel 15:27 - 28).

502   Jeff Miner and John Connoley, *The Children Are Free* (Indianapolis, IN: Jesus Metropolitan Community Church, 2002), 35.

Saul was then outraged because Jonathan had recognized and chosen David as the next king instead of himself. If we continue reading the text we note that Miner and Connoley should not have stopped at verse 30 for we go on to read:

> You son of a perverse, rebellious woman! Do I not know that you are choosing the son of Jesse to your own shame and to the shame of your mother's nakedness? **For as long as the son of Jesse lives on the earth, neither you nor your kingdom will be established.** Therefore now, send and bring him to me, for he must surely die (1 Samuel 20:30-31).

This is a very important text for understanding the context of the animosity of Saul towards David. It is one which many Gay Theology apologists such as Tom Horner try to argue confirms that David and Jonathan were homosexual lovers:

> The expression "uncovering the nakedness" is an allusion to sexual relations throughout Leviticus 18:1-9; and in the still older story of Ham's (or Canaan's') seeing his father's (or grandfather's) nakedness there may be a bowdlerized reference to Canaanite homosexual orgies.[503]

There are several problems with this argument. First, if such laws as found in Leviticus 18-20 only prohibited cultic forms of homosexual relationships (as many Gay Theology proponents argue) then the supposed homosexual relationship would have been religiously, morally and socially acceptable for it did not take place in a cultic, pederastic or exploitative context. Therefore Saul would have no grounds for chastising Jonathan and be angry with David. Second, if Jonathan and David's plan was to rule the kingdom together as gay lovers then Saul's assertion about Jonathan's kingdom not being established would be in error, for his kingdom would have been established with David as Gay Theology proponents assert. In either case, if the Gay Theology interpretation is correct Jonathan could have simply responded to his father by pointing

---

503   Tom Horner, *Jonathan Loved David* (Philadelphia, PA: Westminster Press, 1978), 32

out that their sexual relationship is neither forbidden by the law of God because it was not done in an exploitative, pederastic or ritualistic cultic fashion to Molech nor was it a threat to his dynasty.

What then is the meaning of Saul insulting Jonathan's mother and the reference to his mother's nakedness? First, notice that Saul is not making an accusation concerning Jonathan's nakedness, as if the phrase is meant to insinuate that he had a sexual relationship with David. In the context Leviticus 18 the phrase "you shall not uncover the nakedness" refers to committing a shameful act by having sex with that person. Therefore, the text states that "you shall not uncover the nakedness" of your father (have sex with your father) for to do so would be to uncover the nakedness of your mother (v. 8). The same prohibition is applied to your father's wife (step mother), sister (v. 9), granddaughter (v. 10), step sister (v. 11) and other near relatives. If Saul is using the phrase "to the shame of your mother's nakedness" to mean that Jonathan had committed a sexual act then he would be implying that Jonathan had sex with his mother, not with David.

Furthermore, the Hebrew word for "shame" (Hebrew: *bosheth*) is often an expression of embarrassment, humiliation, disgrace, and dishonor without any sexual connotations (2 Chronicles 32:21; Job 8:22; Psalms 35:26; 40:15; 44:15; 69:19; 70:3; Isaiah 30:3 - 5; Jeremiah 3:24 - 25; 7:19; Habakkuk 2:10; Zephaniah 3:5, 19). When Saul says to Jonathan, "You son of a perverse, rebellious woman!" by insulting his mother in the same fashion as we might say to someone, "You son-of-a-bitch!" or "You bastard!"

We see then that the subject of the quarrel concerns kingship - not sexuality. Jonathan's choice was shameful for him and his mother (according to Saul), because it meant that the crown had left him and his family line. It is also quite apparent, even apart from the fact that the gift of the robe was in reference to the kingship, that the fact of being unclothed often has nothing at to do with sexuality. Over and over again, we see in the Bible that someone has torn their clothes because of distress. Indeed, in the very same story, we find that, "the Spirit of God was upon him [Saul] also, and he went on and prophesied until he came to Naioth in Ramah. And he also [like the men he had sent previously] stripped off his clothes and prophesied before Samuel in like manner, and lay down naked all that day and all that night" (1 Samuel 19:23-

24). This again just supports, from another angle, what we saw above. The story in question has nothing to do with sexuality. Instead it deals with Jonathan's recognition and transfer of kingship to David and Saul's outrage over Jonathan's actions.

We then read of Jonathan's response to his father Saul in which his father attempts to kill him as he had David:

> But Jonathan answered Saul his father and said to him, "Why should he be put to death? What has he done?" Then Saul hurled his spear at him to strike him down; so Jonathan knew that his father had decided to put David to death. Then Jonathan arose from the table in fierce anger, and did not eat food on the second day of the new moon, for he was grieved over David because his father had dishonored him (1 Samuel 20:32-34).

Jonathan then returns to meet with David to send him a secret signal that would indicate whether or not his father was still intending on killing him:

> Now it came about in the morning that Jonathan went out into the field for the appointment with David, and a little lad was with him. He said to his lad, "Run, find now the arrows which I am about to shoot." As the lad was running, he shot an arrow past him. When the lad reached the place of the arrow which Jonathan had shot, Jonathan called after the lad and said, "Is not the arrow beyond you?" And Jonathan called after the lad, "Hurry, be quick, do not stay!" And Jonathan's lad picked up the arrow and came to his master. But the lad was not aware of anything; only Jonathan and David knew about the matter. Then Jonathan gave his weapons to his lad and said to him, "Go, bring them to the city" (1 Samuel 21:35-40).

Following this event Gay Theology advocates assert that David and Jonathan had a sexually charged rendezvous:

When the lad was gone, David rose from the south side and fell on his face to the ground, and bowed three times. And they kissed each other and wept together, but David wept the more. Jonathan said to David, "Go in safety, inasmuch as we have sworn to each other in the name of the LORD, saying, 'The LORD will be between me and you, and between my descendants and your descendants forever.' Then he rose and departed, while Jonathan went into the city (1 Samuel 21:41-42).

Far from being a sexual encounter in an open field, this is a sorrowful moment in which two brothers kiss each other. This was a common practice in the culture seen throughout Scripture without any sexual implications whatsoever (Genesis 27:26; 31:28; 2 Samuel 15:5; 1 Kings 19:20; Luke 7:45; Romans 16:16; 1 Peter 5:14).

The final passage which Gay Theology proponents cite as a supposed reference to Jonathan and David's gay affair is David's lament over the death of Saul and Jonathan:

Your beauty, O Israel, is slain on your high places! How have the mighty fallen! Tell it not in Gath, Proclaim it not in the streets of Ashkelon, Or the daughters of the Philistines will rejoice, the daughters of the uncircumcised will exult. O mountains of Gilboa, let not dew or rain be on you, nor fields of offerings; For there the shield of the mighty was defiled, the shield of Saul, not anointed with oil. From the blood of the slain, from the fat of the mighty, the bow of Jonathan did not turn back, and the sword of Saul did not return empty. Saul and Jonathan, beloved and pleasant in their life, and in their death they were not parted; They were swifter than eagles, they were stronger than lions. O daughters of Israel, weep over Saul, who clothed you luxuriously in scarlet, who put ornaments of gold on your apparel. How have the mighty fallen in the midst of the battle! Jonathan is slain on your high places. I am distressed for you, **my brother** Jonathan; You have been very pleasant to me. Your **love** (*ahab*) to me was more wonderful

than the **love** (*ahab*) of women. How have the mighty fall-
en, and the weapons of war perished! (2 Samuel 2:19-27)

First, notice that Jonathan is spoken of in familial terms, "my brother
Jonathan." As previously stated, the Hebrew word for love, *ahab*, used
in this passage does not inherently possess the sexual overtones as Gay
Theologians assert. It is used variously to denote a man's love for his
wife (Genesis 24:67), a man's love for his son (Genesis 25:28), a woman's love for her son (Genesis 25:28), the Lord's love for His servant
(2 Samuel 12:24), the Lord's love for His people (2 Chronicles 2:11), a
servant's love for the Lord (1 Kings 3:3), all of Israel's and Judah's love
for David (1 Samuel 18:16), the love of God's commandments (Psalms
119:47), and the wicked's love of cursing (Psalms 109:17). While it certainly can and does refer to love between individuals who are sexually
intimate, it does not, in any way, imply sexuality *per se*.[504] Context, not
frequency of use determines the meaning of the word and in this context
it is being used in a lament over the death of a brother. We see a parallel
relationship between King David and Jonathan and Jesus (the Son of
David) and His brotherly for his disciple Jonathan:

> There was reclining on Jesus' bosom one of His disciples,
> whom Jesus loved... Peter, turning around, saw the disciple
> whom Jesus loved following them; the one who also had
> leaned back on His bosom at the supper... (John 13:23;
> 21:7, 20).

The Hebrew translation of John 13:23 uses the word *ahab* in these
texts as well, "...reposing in the bosom of Yeshua whom Yeshua *ahab*."
Not surprisingly, many Gay Theologians sexualize this relationship as
they assert that Jesus was a practicing homosexual. Jonathan's love
was greater than that of women not because David had more intense
orgasms with Jonathan than he did with his wives, but as Jesus said it
was because he sacrificed his seat on the throne and his own life for
another, "Greater love has no one than this, that one lay down his life
for his friends" (John 13:15).

---

504   Daniel A. Helminiak, *What the Bible Really Says About Homosex*uality (Alamo
Square Distributors, 2000), 104.

The love of Jonathan was greater because it was a brotherly sacrificial love in laying down his life for David, a love which surpassed the love of any woman or any other man for that matter. Furthermore, this song was to be taught to the children of Judah (2 Samuel 2:18). Are we to believe that they were to sing about a gay romance to their children? Gay Theologians read the text with a homoerotic mindset because they themselves are accustomed to looking at men in that manner. Hence they are reading their own experiences into the text. Sadly this inhibits their ability to love another man as a brother in a nonsexual manner and to read the story of David and Jonathan such that not reading it as a gay-affirming relationship, "…asks us to put an interpretation on the story that is completely at odds with our own experience of human behavior."[505] As a result they completely miss the main point of the story, which is the Christ-like sacrificial nature of Jonathan's love (he gave up the crown and then died for his people) and in its place they insert a homoerotic concept of love into the text.

The reality is that if David and Jonathan were sexual lovers they would both be adulterers. If God approved of or blessed such a relationship then Christians could then seek to justify imitating their behavior. Gay Theology advocates would then argue that gay men could justifiably have a wife "on the down low," in order to have children, and have a gay lover on the side "…because David and Jonathan did it!" This same argument is used by traditional Mormons and other polygamists who wrongly assert that God approved of polygamy in the Bible. Yet, I can think of nothing crueler to a woman than for a man to use her in such a fashion so that she essentially becomes a "fish wife." Yet, that is in essence what Gay Theology advocates assert that both David and Jonathan did!

Father and Son: Were Saul and David Homosexual Lovers?

As previously stated, the Bible tells us that when Saul first met David and before he viewed him as a potential political threat, he loved David as his own son (1 Samuel 16:21). Yet, David Helminiak wants to turn this father-son relationship into a sexual one as he asserts that the word translated "attended him" or "stood" before him could mean that

505   Jeff Miner and John Connoley, *The Children Are Free* (Indianapolis, IN: Jesus Metropolitan Community Church, 2002), 35.

David had a spontaneous erection in front of Saul. Saul then supposedly seduced David so that they became homosexual lovers as well:

> 1 Samuel 16:21 could read, "When David came to Saul and he [David] had an erection in his presence, he [Saul] loved him greatly." Later the prophet Samuel accused Saul of having an affair with David. Samuel protested to Saul, "Surely, thrusts in the rear are an offense" (1 Samuel 15:23).[506]

Helminiak attempts to justify this claim by asserting, "with one vowel change that makes the verb reflexive, mean 'had an erection (*wa yye' amodh*) before him.'" [507] There is absolutely no justification for asserting that the author is telling the reader that when David stood before Saul that he suddenly had an erection. Here is what every other translation of the text states:

> And David came to Saul, and stood before him: and he loved him greatly; and he became his armourbearer.

Likewise, here is what every translation of 1 Samuel 15:23 states:

> For rebellion is as the sin of divination, and insubordination is as iniquity and idolatry. Because you have rejected the word of the LORD, He has also rejected you from being king.

Yet Helminiak then states that:

> You will not find this rendition of the story in any of the current biblical translations. Scholars have not yet responded to this novel and controversial reading about Saul, though detailed textual evidence does support this fascinating interpretation.[508]

---

506   Daniel Helminiak, *What the Bible Really Says About Homosexuality* (Estancia, NM: Alamo Square Press, 2000), 125.
507   Ibid, 125.
508   Ibid, 125.

There is nothing in the context that would support such a translation or this "rendition of the story" because there is no textual evidence to support it. The reason why Saul was rejected as king was because he had rejected the word of the Lord, failed to carry out God's commands to utterly wipe out the Amalekites and instead he kept their livestock as spoils of war, not because he had anal sex with David (1 Samuel 15:22-26).

How then should we understand the closeness of the relationship between David and Jonathan that may seem unfamiliar to many men today? Martti Nissinen rightly states:

> Nothing indicates that David and Jonathan slept together "as one sleeps with a woman." Neither of the men are described as having problems in their heterosexual sex life. David had an abundance of wives and concubines (2 Sam. 5:13) and suffered impotence only as an old man (1 Kings 1:1-4). The text thus leaves the possible homoerotic associations to the reader's imagination.[509]

He then states that the nature of the relationship and displays of affection were not homosexual, in their fact as he goes on to write:

> This was hardly considered particularly inappropriate, and it raises the question whether a modern reader is more prone than an ancient to find a homoerotic aspect in the story... Modern readers probably see homoeroticism in the story of David and Jonathan more easily than did the ancients. In the contemporary Western world, men's mutual expressions of feelings are more restricted than they were in the biblical world. Men's homosociability apparently was not part of the sexual taboo in the biblical world any more than it is in today's Christian and Islamic cultures around the Mediterranean. Physical expressions of feelings belong to homosocial contacts and seem strange to Western people, who understand eroticism and gestures in their own way categorizing people accordingly as homosexuals or heterosexuals.[510]

509   Martti Nissinen, *Homoeroticism in the Biblical World* (Augsburg Fortress Publishers, 1998), 56.
510   Ibid, 56.

Elsewhere he defines "homosociability" as "…a collective name for an important set of relationships, referring not simply to the preference of men for each other's company, but for the location of the relationship in public or semipublic regions… and for the particular set of exchanges and interdependencies that grow between men.'"[511] In other words, "homosociability" refers to close non-erotic social interactions between men. The closest counterpart today might be men on a football team who, as a form of camaraderie, slap each other on the ass or socialize in a stream room at a gym.

Brother and Friend: Were Jesus and The Beloved Disciple Gay Lovers?

Our next consideration of potential positive stories of gay lovers in the Bible is found in none other than the supposed homosexual relationship between Jesus and one of His disciples. One of the chief proponents of this reading of the text is Theodore W. Jennings in his book *The Man Jesus Loved.* Queer Theology advocates assert that even if the text does not clearly teach that Jesus was gay, for their purposes they must assume that God not only became human flesh, in doing so He also must have assumed a solidarity with active homosexuals:

> This reconfiguration is not only a spiritual experience of connecting with Jesus on a quest for personal perfection but also a passionate identifying born concretely from love-making extended to others. Solidarity includes an imaginative reading and contemplation of Jesus' ministry. Whether or not we are able to prove that Jesus was sexual with either Mary Magdalene or the Beloved Disciple, in order to counter with erotophobic forms of Christian practice that now dominate in the early twenty-first century we must assume that God has not only become flesh but also sexually active. Imaginative solidarity with Jesus means active prayer of the Gospels… Queer Christians discover that the God Jesus preached is, in fact, also the God of queers.[512]

---

511   Ibid, 17.
512   Robert E. Goss, *Queering Christ: Beyond Jesus Acted Up* (Eugene, OR: The Pilgrim Press, 2007), 30-31.

While some within the Gay Theology advocates may wish to disassociate themselves from such an assertion, if we come to understand the way in which Gay and Queer Theology proponents read the text we will see that Robert Goss and Theodore Jennings are not mavericks in the Gay Theological movement. Rather they have merely taken the Gay and Queer hermeneutical trajectory to its logical conclusion. For example, like his fellow Gay Theology proponents, Jennings reads Jesus as setting aside the law of God, particularly in regards to the Sabbath:

> This relativizing of Moses is further expressed in the initial reference to Moses in the Gospel [of John] (1:17), in which Jesus and Moses are contrasted: the law came through Moses but 'grace and truth' through Jesus. We should notice that the law here is contrasted not only with grace but also with truth… the law is understood as something that applies to Jesus' opponents, and not Jesus and his followers. The most telling is the assertion that Moses gave the law to Jesus' opponents yet they didn't keep the law (7:19-24). Their attack on Jesus is thus unwarranted. This passage seems to admit that Jesus does not himself keep the law, but that fact places him in no worse condition that his opponents. What is at issue here is Jesus' nonconformity with the law regarding the Sabbath. But Jesus' reply here is exactly parallel to his defense of the woman taken in adultery…. Jesus certainly could not be understood as being the exemplar of literal conformity to the law. He and his followers are "above the law." Thus, even if the law of Moses were correctly understood as proscribing same-sex relations, neither Jesus nor his followers would necessarily find that in itself a sufficient reason for applying it to themselves.[513]

He goes on to write:

> Jesus is portrayed as disregarding the commandment regarding the Sabbath, the commandment generally viewed

---

513   Theodore W. Jennings, Jr., *The Man Jesus Loved: Homoerotic Narratives From the New Testament* (Cleveland, OH: Pilgrim Press, 2003), 66.

as definitive of Judaism (5:9-10, 16; 7:23; 9:14) Moreover, Jesus is viewed as violating the first commandment, which protects the sanctity and uniqueness of God (10:30-31, 39) When Jesus is accused of blasphemy he does not simply pull rank by claiming divinity but, in effect, compounds the problem by referring to the biblical suggestion that all are gods (Psalm 8:2:6); hence for him to say that he is a god cannot be blasphemy (10:35).[514]

Like all of his fellow Gay Theology advocates, he also reads Jesus as being more relaxed concerning sexual mores, or at least He sets aside the Law of Moses in regards to the woman caught in adultery, "...Jesus has a relaxed attitude toward sexual impropriety, he either wants the woman [caught in adultery] to avoid the behavior that would result in her being stoned if he were not there to protect her in the future, or Jesus does disapprove of adultery but is not prepared to make a big deal about it."[515]

In the same manner as all of his fellow Gay Theology advocates Jennings wrongfully dismisses the relevance of all of the law of the Old Testament, especially the well known passages in the Holiness Code, "...the legislation regarding homosexuality is precisely found in the part of the law most radically rejected by early Christianity."[516]

My point in drawing attention to all this is that Jennings' reading of the Bible is in line and consistent with the worldview of his fellow Gay Theology advocates. In fact, as this movement continues we will undoubtedly see more of his colleagues come to the same conclusion, particularly given their reading of the relationship between David and Jonathan, in which the "easiest" reading of the Gospels through the Gay hermeneutical lens is:

> The simplest explanation for the presence of the beloved [the disciple John] in the narrative is that Jesus was the lover of a beloved, that this beloved was wholly identified with the one who loved him and so claimed nothing for himself, wanted only to 'testify' concerning his lover.[517]

514   Ibid, 66.
515   Ibid, 61.
516   Ibid, 67.
517   Ibid, 74.

The primary emphasis of Jennings' book is the insistence that there is a sublimated "hidden history" of the Gay life of Jesus of which only subtle glimpses and clues are remain in John's Gospel from what has been supposedly eliminated from the synoptic gospels. Yet there still remains other supportive texts from them as well. The idea of a conspiracy of the power mongers in the Church to suppress the true Jesus by editing out the gay positive aspects of His teaching and that He had a sexual relationship with Mary or Jonathan is inherently Gnostic. Theodore W. Jennings, Robert E. Goss, Virginia Mollenkott and many others assert that in order then to fill in the supposed gaps left by the editors of the canonical Gospels, information concerning Jesus from other resources such as the Gnostic "Gospel of Thomas" and the "Secret Gospel of Mark" needs to be read into the account:

> The Secret Gospel of Mark represents an alternative tradition of make homodevotionalism to Jesus that has countered the dominant sexless constructions of Jesus. Today, gay men have reclaimed the text for themselves and Jesus as a paradigm for make same-sex relationships.[518]

It is then argued that it was the Apostle Paul's homophobic influence on the Church that set it in a direction away from the same-sex affirming ethics of Jesus Christ:

> The fear of the body and sexuality in the first and second century Christians led to the social construction of the celibate Jesus. The beginnings of such sexual negativity can be seen in the writings of Paul [who was a self-hating closet homosexual] and his sexual asceticism... For Paul, Jesus is certainly devoid of sexual desire and is an exemplar of self-mastery. Underlying Paul's theology of self-mastery is his notion of Christ as the enabler of the restored and disciplined self.[519]

---

518   Robert E. Goss, *Queering Christ: Beyond Jesus Acted Up* (Eugene, OR: The Pilgrim Press, 2007), 122.
519   Ibid, 116.

The argument then is that erotic Jesus was edited from the Gospels to suit the attitudes of Roman Empire:

> Were their erotophobic currents that affected the portrayal of Jesus in the four canonical Gospels? How much of the canonical gospels were edited to portray a theological image of Jesus suited for the Roman Empire? All attempts to reconstruct Jesus' sexuality and his teaching on sexuality need to recognize that the narrative accounts have been filtered and edited through a screening by each evangelist. It is similar to Log Cabin Republicans who try to present the gay community in the most positive fashion so its members can fit into society. They edit out the least desirable information of queer lifestyle... The silence of the Gospels about Jesus sexuality is deliberate. Traditionally Christianity has argued for Jesus' celibacy. Is this really the case, or is it a process of representing Jesus as a sage or divine man?[520]

This influence then supposedly lead the Church to expunge from the Gospel accounts any overt indications that Jesus and John were homosexual lovers. This then leaves us with only a "hidden memory" that needs to be revived and brought out of the closet if the Church is to recover from its 2,000 history of homophobia. Jennings then concludes:

> The tragic history of the church offers plenty examples of church finding itself in clear opposition to the way of Jesus as that way is attested in the Gospels. But the marginalization and denigration of persons who engage in same-sex relationships in the church is especially ironic, given the clear tendency of the Gospel of John to suggest that Jesus was himself involved in an analogous relationship.[521]

As previously stated regarding the relationship between David and Jonathan, the love that is "more wonderful than the love of women" is not homosexual sex with another man who is married to a woman.

520   Ibid, 116, 117.
521   Theodore W. Jennings, Jr., *The Man Jesus Loved: Homoerotic Narratives From the New Testament* (Cleveland, OH: Pilgrim Press, 2003), 93.

Rather, what David was referring to was the sacrificial love of a friend as Jesus taught, "Greater love has no one than this, that one lay down his life for his friends" (John 15:13). With this in mind we need to examine the Gospels and Jesus' relationships with the disciples and His love for them to determine the identity and nature of His relationship with the "disciple whom Jesus loved."

References to the disciple "whom Jesus loved" are limited to five passages from the Fourth Gospel including him being at the Last Supper (John 13:23-25), at the foot of the cross (John 19:25-27), at the empty tomb with Peter (John 20:2-10), in the boat with the other disciples (John 21:7) and finally following behind Peter and the resurrected Jesus at the shore of the Sea of Galilee (21:20-23). The two primary candidates for being the "disciple whom Jesus loved" are John the Son of Zebedee, the brother of James, who one of the original twelve disciples and Lazarus, the brother of Mary and Martha of Bethany, who Jesus raised from the dead.

The strongest evidence is that the disciple John is the author of the Gospel and the "whom Jesus loved" which comes from the ties between the Epistles of John which read like a commentary on the Gospel as they use many of the same themes and phrases, [522] and the Apocalypse (Revelation) in which we find the author's identity as the one who was exiled:

> I, John, your brother and fellow partaker in the tribulation
> and kingdom and perseverance which are in Jesus, was on
> the island called Patmos because of the word of God and
> the testimony of Jesus (Revelation 1:1).

---

[522] For example both the gospel and the first epistle start with "the beginning" as we read, "In the beginning was the Word…" (John 1:1) and "What was from the beginning…" (1 John 1:1) and tie in the notion of the Word (*logos*) who is the provider of life as we read in the gospel, "…was the Word… In Him was life" (John 1:1, 4) and the epistle, "concerning the Word of Life" (John 1:1) who is also the light as we read in the gospel, "The Light shines in the darkness, and the darkness did not comprehend it" (John 1:5) and the epistle, "This is the message we have heard from Him and announce to you, that God is Light, and in Him there is no darkness at all" (1 John 1:5) which is then tied in with the concept of truth in the gospel, "…grace and truth were realized through Jesus Christ" (1 John 1:17) and in the first epistle, "if we say that we have fellowship with Him and yet walk in the darkness, we lie and do not practice the truth" (1 John 1:6)

The links in the authorship of these New Testament books are found various similarities such as the "I am" statements found throughout the Fourth Gospel [523] as well as in the Apocalypse, "I am the Alpha and the Omega" (Revelation 1:8, 17, 18; 21:5, 6; 22:13) and the author's use of *logos* (Revelation 1:2, 9; 19:13) as well as other similarities in diction (Revelation 2:2, John 16:2; Revelation 20:6, John 13:8; Revelation 22:15, John 3:21; Revelation 22:17, John 7:37). If the disciple John is identified as the one wrote the Book of Revelation and the internal evidence points towards the same author penning the epistles and the Fourth Gospel then we have significant internal evidence. We also have significant external evidence from the early church fathers that the disciple John wrote the Fourth Gospel and is the "disciple whom Jesus loved" who was closest to Jesus at the Last Supper and stood at the cross along with the women and subsequently became the "son" and caretaker of Jesus' mother Mary.

Identifying John as the "disciple whom Jesus loved" we then find that there is a striking similarity between the relationship of King David and Jonathan and King Jesus (the Son of David) and His relationship with His disciple Jonathan. This fact is not missed by many Gay Theology advocates. As this movement grows the idea of Jesus being a homosexual is gaining popularity in their circles such that where John Boswell hinted at the notion of Jesus and John being gay lovers, others have openly made the argument that not only did was Jesus in a homosexual relationship with John but had a sexual rendezvous with a call-boy just prior to his crucifixion.[524] In fact Robert Goss points out:

> Biblical scholar Sjef Van Tilborg views John's portrayal
> of the relation of Jesus and the Beloved Disciple. As the
> pederastic relationship of the older male as lover (*erastes*)

---

523   "I am the bread of life" John 6:35 "I am the Light of the world" John 8:12, "…
before Abraham was born, I am" John 8:58; ""I am the door" John 10:9; ""I am the
good shepherd" John 10:11; "`I am the Son of God" John 10:36; "I am the resurrection
and the life" John 11:25; "You call Me Teacher and Lord; and you are right, for so I
am." John 13:13; "I am the way, and the truth, and the life;" John 14:6; "I am the true
vine" John 15:6; "I AM" which resulted in the solders falling down in John 18:6.
524   John Boswell, *Christianity, Social Tolerance, and Homosexuality: Gay People
in Western Europe from the Beginning of the Christian Era to the Fourteenth Century*
(University Of Chicago Press; 8th Edition. edition, 2005), 115, 225.

the beloved younger male (*eromenos*), similar to the relation depicted in Plato's *Symposium*. This pederastic relation
of older male to younger male was an educational model in
the Greco-Roman world of the first century C.E..[525]

While most Gay Theology advocates might not take the trajectory
of their hermeneutics this far (at least not in print) if they are consistent
this is in fact where the lens of their hermeneutics will naturally lead
this movement. In fact, while some Gay Theology advocates may insist
that Theodore W. Jennings Jr. is on the fringe of their movement, his
book *The Man Jesus Loved* appears on many recommended reading
lists along with their books. The truth is writers such as Robert Goss
and Theodore Jennings are simply being consistent and in a sense more
open and honest with their theology. In the introduction of his book
Jennings writes:

> If one surfs the Internet, one may find a number of sites
> through key words like "gay Jesus." But does that sug-
> gestion have any solid biblical support? This book is an
> attempt to carefully and patiently explore texts from the
> Gospels that suggest something about Jesus' own erotic at-
> tachments and attitude towards same-sex relationships that
> may be fairly extrapolated from the traditions about Jesus.
> What emerges is evidence for the "dangerous memory" of
> Jesus as the love of another man and as one whose attitudes
> toward such relationships, as well as toward gender and
> what are today called "marriage and family value," are
> incompatible with modern heterosexism and homophobia.
> I hope this study will provide change in church and soci-
> ety toward affirmation of gay, lesbian, transgendered and
> bisexual people.[526]

Like his fellow Gay Theology advocates he adopts the same
presupposed hermeneutical lens. Specifically he uses a liberationist

---

525   Robert E. Goss, *Queering Christ: Beyond Jesus Acted Up* (Eugene, OR: The
Pilgrim Press, 2007), 120.
526   Theodore W. Jennings Jr., *The Man Jesus Loved: Homoerotic Narratives From
the New Testament* (Cleveland, OH: The Pilgrim Press, 2003), ix.

trajectory hermeneutic of suspicion, through which he, like his fellow Gay Theology advocates, read the Bible:

> Now this case can only be made by rereading the biblical materials. The issue is not just a matter of the five isolated verses that presumably disqualify persons who engage in same-sex erotic behavior. It is a question of rereading the biblical witness much more broadly and appropriating the Bible for a gay-positive perspective. This kind of rereading of the Bible is related to the sort of rereading that has gone on in a variety of liberationist contexts.[527]

This method of reading the Bible includes reading the text from a presupposed "pro-gay" perspective that entails "...reading the texts from the perspective of contemporary gay or queer sensibility. Here the aim is to discover how the texts appears when it is read from a standpoint affirmative of gay or queer reality – that is, what the text means now, when viewed from this perspective."[528] Then, once this lens is adopted it becomes very easy to read "in between the lines" of the text for a "hidden history" of the homosexual relationship that Jesus had with "the beloved," which he claims is revealed in the Gospel of John, hinted at in Mark but suppressed in Matthew and Luke's gospels:

> As we shall see, the least forced reading of the texts that concern the "beloved disciple" is one which supposes that they refer to a relationship of love expressed by physical and personal intimacy – what we might today suppose to be a homoerotic or "gay" relationship... Thus we will look at material in the Gospel of Mark that seems to confirm what we have seen in the Gospel of John: that Jesus was remembered as having an erotic relationship with another man.[529]

Not only does Jennings assert that Jesus and the "disciple whom Jesus loved," were Gay lovers, but because the disciple was much

---

527   Ibid, 3.
528   Ibid, 7.
529   Ibid, 9.

younger this was in fact a pederastic relationship. This is also asserted concerning the Roman Centurion and his slave whom Jesus healed:

> In same-sex relationships, the 'lover' is typically the older of the pair, often associated with the one who takes the active part in wooing or in lovemaking. The beloved in such a case is the younger, the pursued, the object of desire, or the 'passive' partner where sexual practices are specifically in focus. The ideal that stands behind this linguistic convention is that of a pederastic relationship.[530]

He then reads the same prominent persons in the genealogy of Jesus, such as Ruth and King David, in the same manner as all other Gay Theology advocates and in a similar fashion weaves into his reading of the Bible numerous extra-biblical resources to make his case. These include the so-called Gospel of Thomas, which is actually a second century Gnostic text, and the "Secret Mark" which provide us with the "hidden memory" which is the supposedly suppression and forgotten gay life of Jesus Christ:

> Morton Smith discovered the material called 'Secret Mark' in an eighteenth-century copy of previously unknown letter of Clement of Alexandria (ca. 200 C.E.) found in 1958 in the Orthodox monastery of Mar Saba outside of Jerusalem. Subsequently Smith published the letter together with extensive analysis and commentary. Although the text has been the subject of intense scholarly debate, many scholars (including those of the Jesus Seminar), take it to be authentic and even to represent an earlier version of the Gospel of Mark than the one that is found in the New Testament.[531]

However, if we read the Bible without the presupposed Gay lens we find throughout the gospels a number of references to Jesus loving others, particularly His disciples, without any sexual connotations at all. Jesus had what might be thought of as concentric circles of disciples in which we see that as the circle grows larger the degree of closeness and

---

530   Ibid, 56.
531   Ibid, 114.

familiarity becomes more distant. This is a common social phenomenon as many of us have friends who are as close to us as brothers, those who may be very dear to us but we have infrequent contact and others who may be more thought of as associates and acquaintances. In a similar fashion Jesus had three disciples (Peter, James and John) who were of the "inner circle" and consequently privy to more insider information such as when they were with Him on Mount of Transfiguration (Matthew 17:1-9).

Peter, though he wavers at times, often acts and speaks for the Twelve and in doing so takes a dominant role as one of the inner three along with the sons of Zebedee - James and John. Sometimes he speaks rightly (Matthew 15:10-17; Matthew 16:16) and at other times he speaks out of place, "He did not know what he was saying" (Luke 9:33), especially when he denied knowing Christ three times (Matthew 26:69-75). Yet we also find Jesus reaffirming His love three times after His resurrection in which He asks Peter, "Simon, son of John, do you love Me more than these?" (John 21:15) Are we now to postulate that perhaps Peter and Jesus had a romantic relationship because Jesus asks Peter if he loved Him more than John?

We also find in the Gospels that there are a number of disciples who are not within the Three or the Twelve that Jesus loved, including the inquisitive rich man, "Looking at him, Jesus felt a love for him…" (Mark 10:17-22) When Lazarus was on his deathbed his sisters went to Jesus and informed Him, "Lord, the one you love is sick" (John 11:3). Then upon arriving after Lazarus had died and weeping at his tomb the Jews respond, "See how He loved him!" (John 11:36)

It is clear that, like the relationship between King David and Jonathan, Jesus' relationship and his disciples is that of a mentor, a teacher and a brother as we read elsewhere, "He had to be made like His brethren in all things, so that He might become a merciful and faithful high priest in things pertaining to God, to make propitiation for the sins of the people" (Hebrews 2:17). We see then in the Gospels that Jesus said that His true family were His followers and sought to do the will of His Father, "For whoever does the will of My Father who is in heaven, he is My brother and sister and mother" (Matthew 12:50). It is in this familial context that Jesus says to His mother and the only male disciple at the foot of the cross:

...standing by the cross of Jesus were His mother, and His mother's sister, Mary the wife of Clopas, and Mary Magdalene. When Jesus then saw His mother, and the disciple whom He loved standing nearby, He said to His mother, "Woman, behold, your son!" Then He said to the disciple, "Behold, your mother!" From that hour the disciple took her into his own household (John 19:25-27).

It shouldn't surprise us then that the author of John's Gospel refers to himself as, "the disciple whom Jesus loved" since love is a reoccurring theme throughout the Fourth Gospel. The word love (*agape*) appears 34 times in the Gospel of John, the first time it is mentioned we read of the Father's love for the entire world (John 3:16) and love is central to the commandments of Christ (John 15:12). Yet not once does the John's Gospel ever use of *agape* to convey any sexual connotations. It is used to describe Jesus' laying down His life all of His disciples (John 13:1, 34; 15:9, 12-13) who obey His commandments (John 14:21, 23; 15:10). We also read of Jesus' love for Martha, Mary, and Lazarus (John 11:5), His love for God the Father (John 14:31) and the Father's love for His Son (John 3:35; 15:9; 17:23-24, 26) because the Son obeys His will by laying down his life (John 10:17) and obeying the Father's commandments (John 15:10). Likewise it is Jesus' disciples loving of one another that manifests to the world that they are His followers (John 8:42; 14:15, 21, 23-24) as they obey His commandments (John 14:28), which is revealed by following His example of love by sacrificial love for "one another" (John 13:34-35; 15:12-13, 17) and in feeding Jesus' sheep (John 21:15-16).

The observation that *agape* does not refer to sexual love in the John's Gospel is made clearer when we see it is often used synonymously with the Greek verb *phile*, which refers to the love of a friend and the related noun *philos* (friend). These terms are used interchangeably with *agape* and *agapa* in John's Gospel thus proving the non-erotic character of this love. In fact, we see in a context in which there is mention of more than one disciple whom Jesus loved, "So she ran and came to Simon Peter and to the other (*allon*) disciple whom Jesus loved (*philei*)..." (John 20:2)

Likewise, when Mary and Martha inform Jesus that Lazarus is ill we read, "Lord, see, the one whom you love (*phileis*) is sick" (John 11:3) and we then read that Jesus "loved (*agapa*) Martha and her sister and Lazarus" (John 11:5). Jesus loves Mary and Martha and Lazarus and yet he, like John, is referred to as "the one whom you love (*phileis*)." Clearly Jesus' love for Lazarus was not any more sexual than it was for Mary and Martha. We then read that when the Jews saw how Jesus wept for Lazarus they respond, "See, how he loved (*ephilei*) him," and they obviously were not asserting that Jesus was in a sexual relationship with Lazarus. Rather, Jesus loved him as though Lazarus were his own brother. The same applies to the references to the beloved disciple.

We seen then in the description of the relationship "the disciple whom Jesus loved" John uses both *agapa* (John 13:23; 19:26; 21:7, 20) and *phile* (John 20:2) which in their context reveals that the nature of this love is friendship and not homosexual romance. This interchangeability of the two different words translated "love" is also seen in the well known dialogue between Peter and Jesus after His resurrection:

> Jesus said to Simon Peter, "Simon, son of John, do you love (*agapas*) Me more than these?" He said to Him, "Yes, Lord; You know that I love (*phile*) You." He said to him, "Tend My lambs." He said to him again a second time, "Simon, son of John, do you love (*agapas*) Me?" He said to Him, "Yes, Lord; You know that I love (*phile*) You." He said to him, "Shepherd My sheep." He said to him the third time, "Simon, son of John, do you love (*phileis*) Me?" Peter was grieved because He said to him the third time, "Do you love (*phileis*) Me?" And he said to Him, "Lord, You know all things; You know that I love (*phile*) You." Jesus said to him, "Tend My sheep" (John 21:15-17).

While it is common to hear preachers assert that *agapas* in this text is some sort of higher love than *phile* the fact is both words are used in the Septuagint to translate the same word (Genesis 37:3). Theodore Jennings acknowledges the interchangeability of *agape* and *phile* but then he ignores their usage in the context of the Gospels and instead reads into them their usage in the Song of Solomon from the Septuagint. This is telling for it becomes clear that he doesn't want to read and understanding the love of Christ as revealed in the Gospels so he reads into the text the meaning of *agape* and *phile* from an erotic love story from the Old Testament. Therefore, like the relationship between King David and Jonathan this love is familial, not sexual, and to constantly read into such accounts of love one's own homoerotic tendencies, as Jennings clearly does, is to pervert the text.

According to Jennings, not only were Jesus and the "disciple whom Jesus loved," in a gay lover relationship but He also had homoerotic lust after the rich young ruler in which it is said that, "looking at him loved him" (Mark 10:17-22):

> An erotic reading of this episode then would recognize in this gaze the beholding which awakens desire and antici-pates delight. This response to the combination of exem-plary character and physical appearance would be entirely consistent with the literary traditions of same-sex eroticism in the Greek and Hellenistic worlds where inward and out-ward moral and physical beauty were supposed to coincide in the beloved.[532]

Borrowing from Jeremy Bentham and the "hidden history" of a gay-positive reading of the relationship between Jesus and the disciple He loved, not only does Jennings assert that Jesus and the beloved dis-ciple had a homosexual love affair but He also had a pederastic sexual encounter as well. According to Jennings, just prior to Jesus' arrest and crucifixion there is "…another incident of gay in the Jesus tradition" of a suggested "homosexual relationship" in the incident "…of the youth who escapes naked from Gethsemane after the arrest of Jesus, as briefly described in the Gospel of Mark":

> And they all forsook him and fled. And a youth (*neaniskos*) accompanied him, clothed in a linen cloth (*sindona*) over his nudity. And they seized him. And he, leaving the linen cloth (*sidona*), fled nude (*gymnos*) (Mark 14:50-52).

---

532   Theodore W. Jennings, Jr., *The Man Jesus Loved: Homoerotic Narratives From the New Testament* (Cleveland, OH: Pilgrim Press, 2003), 108.

Supposedly this text suggests that this youth "...was a *cinaedus* (*kinaidos*) or boy prostitute."[533] This reading of the text asserts that Jesus was quite the bed-hopper who, if He had been a member of the Corinthian church, would have come under the condemnation of the Apostle Paul (1 Corinthians 6:9). The "makeshift covering" (*sidona*) is supposedly not a normal attire but rather is a piece of linen which was the clear sign of the nature of the boy's relationship to Jesus:

> ...the *sidona* that covers while drawing attention to the nudity of the youth and to the reader's gaze, not only suggests that the youth is the object of homoerotic attention but also serves to place the youth in relation to the institution of prostitution, which was one of the principle ways which homoeroticism was legalized and institutionalized in the Roman Empire.

He then goes on to assert:

> The narrative, in effect, undresses him even before the mob does by referring to his nudity first as covered and then as uncovered. The term for nudity here is gymnos, which refers not simply to body (*soma*) or flesh (*sarx*) but to the nudity that gave its name to the gymnasium (or nuditorium) where hellenized youth honed and displayed their athletic prowess in the nude. In classical Greece and in the subsequent hellenistic world, the gymnasium is the privileged site for homoeroticism and for the making of pederastic liaisons. The nudity (*gymnou*) of the youth (*neaniskos*) is the local point of the homoerotic gaze of men. None of this could have been lost on Mark's hellenistic, gentile readers.[534]

Jennings goes on to mention the tradition of the custom of "naked baptism" and a hypothesis for an explanation of the text but then he states:

---

533   Ibid, 109.
534   Ibid, 111.

If the baptismal practices cannot be established, then we are left with an apparent allusion to the typical recipient of homoerotic attention (the nude youth) in hellenistic pederastic culture at a decisive moment in the passion of Jesus, and with the suggestion of a particularly close relationship between Jesus and this youth. The scene rather precisely parallels the situation of the disciple Jesus loved in the Gospel of John.[535]

What are we to make of this story of this young man fleeing? Was Jesus alone with the fellow having a romp with a boy prostitute just prior to his arrest? Hardly, if we read the text in its context the weight of evidence points to this boy not fleeing alone but was with the other disciples, who in his haste, having been awakened in the night by the commotion, follows Jesus and His captors and then is almost taken prisoner himself. So in fear he breaks free without his garment and flees for his life, which accounts for his being naked as we read, "But he pulled free of the linen sheet and escaped naked." Being one of the disciples, most likely John Mark himself, this "naked youth" was a Jew, not a Greek boy-prostitute. To read into the text elements from a "hellenistic pederastic culture" is unjustified.

What will seem obvious to most readers is that it is absolutely absurd to assert that Jesus had sex with anyone for there are no explicit or even suggestive texts that He ever did, so he then states:

> I am not presuming knowledge of whether or how the people involved 'had sex,' but rather that the relationship is the sort in which we may suppose, in analogous circumstances, that some or another sexual practice would be involved. We suppose that sex is or would be "natural" or likely extension (in private presumably) of what offers itself to be seen in public. In this sense I call the relationship between Jesus and the man he loved (and that between the centurion and his "lad") "homoerotic." [536]

---

535   Ibid, 113.
536   Ibid,11.

This is the exact sort of twisting of the text that Gay Theology advocates do with other Biblical narratives which also do not provide any explicit or implicit refers to Ruth and Naomi or David and Jonathan having sex. In order to come to their conclusions the "gay reader" has to read the text through his own sexual desires and his own homoeroticism of same sex relationships in order to come to such conclusions.

The Roman Centurion and His Pais

While most Gay Theology advocates will not go so far as to assert that Jesus Himself was a homosexual, most attempt to argue that Jesus healed the lover-servant of a homosexual Roman centurion. They then insist that in doing so without calling him to repentance, and in fact commending him for his faith, that such an action indicates that Jesus approved of same-sex acts (Matthew 8:5-13; Luke 7:1-10). Rick Brentlinger argues:

> ...traditionalists cannot prove their contention, that the centurion and his *pais-servant* were not same sex lovers. It is equally impossible to prove absolutely, that the centurion and his *pais* were same sex lovers.[537]

The "traditionalist" does not need to prove that the centurion and his *pais* were not same sex lovers because we are not asserting anything that is not clearly indicated from the text. If, however, we wanted to assert that the centurion and his *pais* were aliens from another planet then the burden of proof would be upon us to make the case that that they were from outer space. Any assertion that they were extraterrestrials would be pure conjecture. What Brentlinger and any other Gay Theology advocates must do is make the case that they were gay lovers but until they can prove that they were any such conclusions from the text is merely reading into the text what they wish to find. This in fact has been the practice Gay Theology proponents who out of their own wishful thinking assert that Ruth and Naomi were Lesbians and that David and Jonathan were homosexual lovers. Rick Brentlinger goes on to state:

537   Rick Brentlinger, *Gay Christian 101 - Spiritual Self-Defense For Gay Christians* (2007), 193.

> Gay Christians tend to ignore the passage [Matthew 8]
> because they fear nongays will view them as child mo-
> lesters... It is interesting that modern Christians shy away
> from the historic meaning of *pais* because they cannot
> imagine Jesus condoning a same sex relationship. Yet
> modern Christians have no problem accepting that Jesus
> condoned the master-slave relationship in this story[538]

There are several revealing points about this statement. First, as we
shall see, the assertion that the centurion and his *pais* were same-sex
lovers and that Jesus approved and condoned such a relationship does
indeed result in the conclusion that He approved of men having sex with
a child for a *pais* is a term which, "...can be used for a boy 7- 14 years
old as distinct from one not yet 7 (*paidon*) or the adolescent (*meirakion*)
of 14 - 21."[539]

Second, if the Gay Theology apologist argues that slavery is wrong
regardless of the circumstances, in order to be consistent, he would have
to conclude that Jesus by his not condemning the master-slave relationship approved of slavery. Or he would have to admit that just because he
healed the servant without addressing other peripheral issues does not
mean that Jesus sanctioned slavery or the same-sex lover relationship, if
in fact they had one. What we shall see in this text and others is that just
because a king does not address a particular sinful relationship or action
does not mean that he condones or sanctions it.

Much of the argument regarding the relationship of the Roman
Centurion to his servant revolves around a single Greek word *pais*. Gay
Theology advocates such as Rick Brentlinger insist that the servant was
not merely a valued slave but a young gay lover:

> Had God in His wisdom used only the word *doulos*,
> meaning servant instead of *pais*, which sometimes means
> servant and sometimes same sex lover, in the two passages
> [Matthew 8:5-13 and Luke 7:1-10] under consideration,
> this chapter would be unnecessary... The Greek word

---

538   Ibid, 194.
539   Alfred Oepke, *Theological Dictionary of the New Testament* (Vol. V) Gerhard
Kittel (ed.) (Grand Rapids, MI: Wm. B. Eerdmans Publishing Co., 1965), 637.

pais, was used in Greek literature for centuries prior to Mathews Gospel with idiomatic meaning of *beloved* or *same sex lover*. *Beloved* or *same sex lover* is the common understanding of first century, Greek speaking Jews and Gentiles would have of its usage in this context.[540]

A common practice of Gay Theology advocates is to find a word in a text, cite a lexicon's various meanings for the word and then pick the term that best suits their agenda. Yet, Brentlinger goes on to admit:

> Luke uses *pais* to refer to Jesus at age twelve, 2:43, and to Jarius' daughter, 8:51, and to menservants, 12:45. The meaning of *pais* is determined by the context in which it is used.[541]

If Brentlinger is correct that *pais* means "*beloved* or *same sex lover*" then we would have to conclude that Luke is referring to Jesus, Jarius' daughter and menservant as "beloved or same sex lover" for there is just as much reference to sexual activity in these texts as there is in Matthew 8:5-13 and Luke 7:1-10. There is no contextual evidence to prove that the centurion's *pais* was anything other than a valued servant and all that the word *pais* means in all these texts is simply a young person without any reference to participating in any sexual activity whatsoever.

Brentlinger then goes on to provide a list of sources with various meanings of *pais* from extra-Biblical resources most which are from non-Biblical cultures centuries before or after the time of Christ. What he has not done is consider the Biblical culture's use of the term in the Old Testament (LXX). He then cites one source and states:

> ...the younger partner in a homosexual relationship is called *pais* or *paidika*. The younger partner ranged in age from a teenage boy to an adult in his thirties.[542]

---

540   Rick Brentlinger, *Gay Christian 101 - Spiritual Self-Defense For Gay Christians* (2007), 195, 197.
541   Ibid, 198.
542   Ibid, 201.

According to the *Theological Dictionary of the New Testament* a *pais* was 7-14 years old and that an adolescent (*meirakion*) was between 14 – 21. However, Brentlinger changes the age range for the meaning of the word *pais* in order to avoid being accused of advocating pederasty. Given the age of the other persons referred to as *pais* in the gospels (including Jesus himself) what is clear is that Brentlinger is asserting that Jesus not only did not condemn a supposed homosexual relationship with a child but He gives approval of it and that such a relationship would have included at the oldest a 14 year old teenage boy.

Brentlinger then wrongly asserts that Jewish life was regulated by Roman Law and therefore anything that was legal or sanctioned by Roman Law was then considered legal or proper in Jewish custom.[543] There are several problems with this assertion. First, while the Jews were under Roman Law in Palestine there was great resistance to many Roman Laws which contributed to their destruction in 70 A.D. Second, the Roman government in an attempt to appease the Jews often gave them exceptions to having to obey Roman Laws that conflicted with their Jewish Law. Therefore, to assert that because something was legal or permissible under Roman Law would have been lawful or condoned by Jesus is patently false. What needs to be kept in mind when reading the New Testament, particularly the Gospels, is that the historical and culture background for the text is Jewish, not Greek. The Old Testament is the history that lays the foundation for how the writers of the gospels used the Greek language. Therefore, before looking to any ancient Greek sources for the etymological root meaning of the word, the reader needs to consider the fact that the writers are repeatedly quoting the Septuagint and deriving their use of language from the Bible and not Plato, Thucydides, or Eupolis.

Another word that supposedly indicates that the servant was a sexual lover of the Roman Centurion is the Greek word *entimos*, which simply means "held in honor, prized, precious" and it is translated "dear" in Luke 7:2 (KJV).[544] The word can be variously translated "valued highly," (NRSV) "highly regarded," (NASB), "in reputation" (KJV), "honor" (NASB) (Philippians 2:29) or "precious" (1 Peter 2:4, 6). Daniel

---

543   Ibid, 201.
544   Joseph H. Thayer, *Thayer's Greek-English Lexicon of the New Testament* (Hendrickson Publishers, 1996)

A. Helminiak states that he believes there are various possible meanings for the term and then admits, "Then what was the relationship between the centurion and the servant? There is no way to know for certain."[545] Even granting that the word should be translated "precious" or "deeply cared for" as opposed to "dear," "honorable," or "valuable" would not necessitate that the nature of the relationship is sexual and to assert that it was is pure conjecture. None of the biblical usages of the word *entimos* even hint at having a sexual content so to try to make such an argument from the text is to be grasping at straws, it is *eisogesis* (reading into) rather than *exegesis* (reading out from) the text.

If we pay close attention to the arguments of Gay Theology advocates what becomes clear is that they argue, on a twisted understanding of Scripture, that the Christian worldview supports men having sex with young boys (so long as it isn't "exploitative"). All that is needed for such practice to become acceptable within the Church is for Gay Theology to radically transform the way the Church views same sex acts, to view it as did the ancient Greeks:

> Greek and Roman culture greatly influences our New Testament. In ancient Greece, for six centuries before Christ, it was common for young men in their teens to enter same sex relationship with an older man. In the Roman Empire, which ruled Israel at the time Matthew wrote his gospel, Roman women generally married in their early teens but Roman men usually waited for heterosexual marriage until their mid to late twenties. Roman law set the legal age of marriage for a girl at twelve years old... For a boy, the ancient Romans regarded fourteen as the legal age for marriage... prior to these heterosexual marriages, pederastic relationships were sometimes arranged by the father of a teenage son, were begun with the father's permission and were regulated by law and custom...While pederasty is not accepted today in western culture, it was common and generally accepted in the first century Roman Empire.[546]

545   Daniel A. Helminiak, *What the Bible Really Says About Homosexuality* (Alamo Square Distributors, 2000), 128-129.
546   Rick Brentlinger, *Gay Christian 101 - Spiritual Self-Defense For Gay Christians* (2007), 206.

Brentlinger then goes on to state:

> Greek culture had a centuries long history of a practice known as pederasty. An older male would mentor a younger male, teaching him philosophy and science, the art of war and his place in Greek society. Pederastic relationships frequently included a sexual relationship between males involved. Our modern culture would rightly reject pederastic relationship between a man and an underage boy. We certainly do not argue for pederastic relationships in the modern world. We merely point out the cultural situation Matthew and Luke addressed and the way first century Roman culture understood the Greek word *pais* and the relationship it frequently indicated.[547]

Brentlinger argues that the Roman centurion and his servant had a pederastic sexual relationship. Consequently, Jesus by failing to rebuke the centurion gave approval of the homosexual pederastic relationship, "If the *pais* was no more important to the centurion than his other *doulos*-slaves, why did Mathew, Luke and the Holy Spirit so carefully use a different word with a common meaning of same sex lover, to describe this special slave?"[548] He the states that Jesus, by not rebuking this supposed pederastic homosexual relationship, gave consent and approval of it by his silence:

> Jesus is straightforward in dealing with sinners... Yet, when confronted with a Roman centurion asking healing for his beloved *pais*. Jesus does not rebuke their relationship or their master-slave relationship but instead, compliments the great faith of the centurion.[549]

While he states that we "certainly do not argue for pederastic relationships in the modern world" this only because "modern culture" rejects such relationships and, according to the Gay Theological interpretation

---

547 Ibid, 208.
548 Ibid, 211.
549 Ibid, 213.

of Matthew and Luke's Gospel, such relationships are wrong from a cultural perspective today and not inherently wrong.[550] Therefore, all that would need to take place for such relationships to again be considered acceptable would be for our culture to change, beginning with the culture and theology of the Church, which is exactly the agenda of Gay Theology advocates, "It's obvious that a change of thinking is going to have to invade the Church if we are going to see this truth [of Gay Theology] come to light in the pews across the world."[551]

Brentlinger then goes on to assert that if Jesus approved of a sexual relationship between a man and a servant, who may have been as young as fourteen years old, then we need to realign our thinking to be more like the homosexuality approving Jesus:

> If Matthew and Luke's use of *pais* means the centurion and his servant [who according to Brentlinger may have been as young as fourteen] enjoyed a loving, gay relationship, how does that affect your personal relationship with Jesus Christ?... The sexual aspect of the story is a minor issue. Jesus, Matthew and Luke do not respond negatively, to a loving, gay relationship [which Brentlinger states may have been with a fourteen year old boy]. They respond positively. When will the modern Christians emulate the example of Jesus and respond with affirming love to committed gay relationships [including between men and fourteen year old boys].... What would you do if you were Jesus?... The centurion comes to, admits he is in a loving, gay partnership [with a fourteen year old boy] and asks for healing for his sick [fourteen year old] partner. Would you heal the centurion's sick partner?... If your reaction is different than Jesus' reaction, who needs to change, you or Jesus?[552]

---

550   Ibid, 208.
551   R.D. Weekly, *Homosexianity* (Judah First Ministries, 2009), 116.
552   Rick Brentlinger, *Gay Christian 101 - Spiritual Self-Defense For Gay Christians* (2007), 215-16.

Brentlinger tries to fence his argument by insisting that we should not approve of pederasty (adult males have sex with minor boys). He then asserts that the *pais* of this centurion may have been as young as fourteen, that Jesus approves of this supposed man-boy sexual relationship and then questions if we would respond any differently than Jesus. Despite his personal reservations and assertions that he does not advocate man-boy sex, what other conclusion can one come to that he does want his readers to believe that such a relationship was approved of by Jesus and should likewise be approved of by the Church? The truth is man-boy sexual relationships are advocated by other Gay Theologians who insist that so long as the nature of this sexual relationship is not oppressive or coerced that it should be allowed and promoted within certain guidelines as Gary Comstock asserts:

> Perhaps we need to look at other cultures in which children sexuality is permitted and integrated into the life of the community. Instead of practicing flat restriction and complacent ignorance, we need to take on the more complicated task of facilitating and protecting privacy, autonomy, mutuality, and reciprocity, of permitting expression and restricting imposition... [he then cites a poem of a seemingly playful sexual encounter between a child at an adult in a bath]... I would also offer my own practical suggestion for changing the quality of touching between adults and children and for giving children power to control it... as a basis and resource for physical interactions and for forming sexual and affectional relations between adolescent and adults.[553]

The truth is NAMBLA (North American Man Boy Love Association) has always marched in the back of the gay parade. I am not asserting that all Gay Theology advocates promote the idea of men having sex with young boys is morally justifiable nor does everyone with same-sex attractions have such proclivities. But both liberal and so-called evangelical Gay Theology advocates do indeed make such assertions.

---

553   Gary David Comstock, *Gay Theology Without Apology* (Cleveland, OH: Pilgrim Press, 1993), 29-32.

Once objective authoritative Biblical standards have been abandoned and all constraints on human sexual expression have been removed in the place of a purely subjective feelings-oriented definition of love, the lowering of the legal age of consent to engaging in sex with an adult will undoubtedly be lowered.

But, let us assume for the sake of argument say that indeed the relationship between the centurion and his *pais* is that of a gay man with a fourteen-year-old boy. Does Jesus silence of the immorality and commendation of the faith of the centurion mean that He gave approval of it or sanction homosexual relationships? Jesus as a wise and righteous person addresses the issue at hand (the sick *pais*) without addressing other issues such as when two harlots bring their case of a disputed custody of a child before Solomon.

Solomon as king (in order to discern the identity of the true mother) orders the child to be cut in half, knowing that the real mother would rather give up the child than see the infant die. Then the true mother protests, "Oh, my lord, give her the living child, and by no means kill him." But the other said, "He shall be neither mine nor yours; divide him!" Then Solomon in his wisdom says, "Give the first woman the living child, and by no means kill him. She is his mother." However, Solomon never addresses the fact that these women who lived as harlots were in violation of the law and yet the text goes on to tell us, "When all Israel heard of the judgment which the king had handed down, they feared the king, for they saw that the wisdom of God was in him to administer justice" (1 Kings 3:16-28). Should we conclude that Solomon's silence on the issue of their prostitution means that he approved of their behavior or that God approved of their behavior because the text tells us that "the wisdom of God was in him to administer justice"? Solomon did not address the fact that they were harlots because it was not the issue at hand. In a similar fashion even if in fact the Roman centurion and his *pais* were had homosexual relationship Jesus did not address it because it was not the issue at hand. The fact is, Jesus gives grace to sinners despite their sin not as a means of granting approval of their sin.

Is "Eunuch" An Ancient Equivalency to "Gay"?

Although the modern English language has developed terms to describe people in regards to their sexual inclinations, orientation and behavior the Bible contains no word that is equivalent to the psychological term "homosexual" or various slang terms such as "gay" or "queer," except perhaps the euphemistic use of the Greek term *malakoi*. This being the case, one might wonder what term the authors of Bible might have used for people who acted out on these inclinations. Gay Theologians have rejected that the terms *arsenokoitai* or *malakoi* (1 Corinthians 6:9) refer to homosexuals "as we know them today" because such terms entail condemnation. They then look for another term for a category of person who was once excluded from access to the temple (Church) but now is included in the New Covenant. In doing so they insist that, "Perhaps the situation in the Bible that most closely parallels the lesbian and gay community is the story of the eunuch."[554]

In other words, since men being sexually attracted to other men is not a recent phenomenon and cultures of the Ancient Near East, including those recorded in the Bible, would have been aware of it one would have to ask, "Did they have a term for it? If it was not referred to in descriptive terms such as those found in Leviticus and they did not use the term *arsenokoitai*? What is the ancient equivalency to the modern term 'homosexual' or 'gay'?" Gay Theologians insist that when we read the word "eunuch" we should think of it as the ancient equivalency to our idea of a "gay man" as Jack Rogers argues, "In ancient time, there were no doubt people who were incapable of heterosexual activity, and thus were considered 'eunuch.'"[555]

The word "eunuch" in the Old Testament referred to an officer who was a man who may have been emasculated or was impotent and those who held their office came to be known as a eunuch whether physically castrated or not (Isaiah 56:3-4). The Hebrew word *saris* is translated "officer" 12 times (Genesis 37:36; 39:1) and "chamberlain" 13 times (2 Kings 23:11) and translated "eunuch" 17 times (2 Kings 9:32). The Hebrew word is commonly identified with the Akkadian word *sa-resi*

---

554   Michael S. Piazza, *Gay By God* (Dallas, TX: Source of Hope Publishing, 1998), 69.

555   Jack Rogers, *Jesus, The Bible, and Homosexuality* (Louisville, Kentucky; Westminster John Knox Press, 2006), 82.

(courtier, dignitary official) around 1,000 B.C. There were married eunuchs (Genesis 39:1,9 rendered "officer") and although castrated eunuchs were excluded from entering the temple (Deuteronomy 23:1) they often obtained high position and great authority. The captain of the guard of Pharaoh and his chief butler and his chief baker were eunuchs (Genesis 37:36; 40:2, 7 translated "officer") and they ministered at the court of Babylon (Daniel 1:3). They served in the presence of the Persian king, acted as gatekeepers of his palace (Esther 1:10; 2:21). A eunuch was a guard over his harem (Esther 2:3, 14) and appointed to attend his queen as well (Esther 4:5). They also served in the court of Ahab and his son Jehoram and waited upon Jezebel (1 Kings 22:9; 2 Kings 8:6; 9:32). In Judah most if not all eunuchs were foreigners (Jeremiah 38:7). According to Josephus, the cupbearer of Herod the Great was a eunuch and was the officer that brought him food and assisted him to bed; and his favorite wife was served by a eunuch.[556] A eunuch was also over the treasure of Queen Candace of Ethiopia and was subsequently included into the New Covenant and baptized by Philip as prophesied by Isaiah (Acts 8:27, 27; cf. Isaiah 53:3). Jesus refers to various means in which a man may become a Eunuch (by birth, made so by men or by choice in Matthew 19:12) and such men are referred to as "virgins" (chaste men) in Revelation 14:4.

Ironically, whereas Gay theologians wish to claim the eunuch as a first century counterpart, Transgender Theology advocates do so as well such as Justin Tanis who believes:

> Eunuchs are the closest biblical analogy we have to trans-gendered people… Eunuchs are analogous to modern transgendered persons since they were considered to have crossed gender lines.[557]

and Elisabeth Anne Kellogg states:

> [T]he post-operative transsexual is not just a male eunuch. She has passed over to the female side, but with one important

556   Josephus, *Antiquites* xv. 7, 4; xvi. 8, 1.
557   Justin Tanis, *Transgendered: Theology, Ministry and Communities of Faith* (Cleveland, OH: The Pilgrim Press, 2003), 69, 78.

exception. She will never be able to give birth to any
children, a burden for any woman whether genetic or neo.
Even after SRS when you have ceased to be a man and
have become a barren woman, the Lord will still have
words of encouragement for you.[558]

The primary text that Gay Theology proponents use to make their
case for Jesus giving approval of homosexuality is found in the context
of His conversation on the subject of divorce:

> For some are eunuchs because they were born that way;
> others were made that way by men; and others have re-
> nounced marriage [or have made themselves eunuchs] be-
> cause of the kingdom of heaven. The one who can accept
> this should accept it (Matthew 9:12).

For example, Rick Brentlinger asserts:

> The definition of eunuch also includes a man incapable of
> marriage, not sexually attracted to women or unwilling to
> marry a woman. Incapable of marriage could mean same
> sex attracted and thus, not interested in heterosexual mar-
> riage. Or, it could mean asexual, without sexual attraction
> to either sex or it could, in rare cases, refer to one born with
> genital defects which make siring children impossible. A
> eunuch for the sake of the kingdom of heaven is a man who
> voluntarily abstains from marriage.[559]

Yet transgenderists want to claim this passage as well:

> Jesus knows that some people are born outside of the bina-
> ry gender system and people whose lives lead them beyond
> it. He speaks of multiple ways in which someone might

---

558   Elisabeth Anne Kellogg, "Transsexualism from the Perspective of the Biblical
Eunuch and the barren Woman." Cited in Justin Tanis, *Transgendered: Theology, Ministry and Communities of Faith* (Cleveland, OH: The Pilgrim Press, 2003), 71.
559   Rick Brentlinger, *Gay Christian 101 - Spiritual Self-Defense For Gay Christians* (2007), 223.

become gender variant, and he does so with compassion and clarity. We are called to do likewise.[560]

Rick Brentlinger then goes on to assert that there were three different types of eunuchs as asserted by Jesus:

> Jesus recognized three classes of Eunuchs... According to Jesus, a eunuch is one who cannot receive His teaching on heterosexual marriage according to the Adam and Eve model.[561]

According to Brentlinger and other Gay theologians, one of the types of eunuchs were those who were "not sexually attracted to women." These types of eunuchs were free to have sex with men because they are not bound by the Biblical confines of marriage of the "Adam and Eve paradigm" or what others refer to as the "social gender binary construct" of a one man and one woman marriage.[562] Therefore, according to Gay Theology advocates, the modern Church ought to hold in high regard active homosexuals and view them as the modern equivalency to a "eunuch," one granted good moral standing in the Church:

> Because scripture mentions eunuchs 45 times in the Old Testament and 10 times in the New Testament, usually in an overwhelmingly positive light, we conclude that God considers eunuchs – gay people, to be vitally important part of humanity and His church. Believers throughout scripture worked with, worshipped with, interacted with eunuchs-gay men, in an honorable way. God, as the Ultimate Author of scripture, presents eunuchs as men of integrity, worthy of respect.[563]

This is clearly a twisting of the text. In context Jesus says that there are those who have difficulty in accepting his teaching on divorce, that

---

560   Justin Tanis, *Transgendered: Theology, Ministry and Communities of Faith* (Cleveland, OH: The Pilgrim Press, 2003), 75.
561   Rick Brentlinger, *Gay Christian 101 - Spiritual Self-Defense For Gay Christians* (2007), 226.
562   Ibid, 225.
563   Ibid, 226.

Moses only gave the authorization of the certificate of divorce because of the hard hearts and that God's original design for marriage was a one man and one woman relationship for life. He then goes on to make an argument from the lesser to the greater, that if they thought His teaching on marriage and divorce based on the original created order was difficult they should consider the fact that there are some who have chosen (referring to Himself) not to marry for the sake of the Kingdom of Heaven. In other words, Jesus is one who has chosen such a role and thus is a voluntary eunuch. This same category of "eunuch" also describes the Apostle Paul (1 Corinthians 7:7, 32) .

The Greek word translated "eunuch" (*eunouchos*) is a compound word made up of two words - *eune* and *echein*. The word *eune* means "bed" and specifically refers to the marriage bed. The Greek word *echein* means "to have" or "to hold" and it can mean either "to be in charge of" or "to keep away from." In this context *eunouchos* means "the one who keeps away from the marriage bed." There is only one kind of eunuch, broadly speaking, which is a non-procreating man. However, there are according to Jesus three different ways, means or reasons why a man becomes non-procreating – he was born with the inability to procreate, he was made unable to procreate or he chose not to procreate for the sake of the Kingdom of God. This third reason for being a eunuch would include Jesus and the apostle Paul (1 Corinthians 7:6-9), neither of whom (contrary to Gay theologians) were homosexuals. The fact that some eunuchs were employed to be "keepers of the bed" does not define the term such that every eunuch is one who is employed to safeguard a harem. One can hardly imagine being a guard of a harem for the Kingdom of Heaven! Rather, like many other terms, the fact that such guardians did not bear children the term eunuch came to be a simple term meaning "not bearing children." This is similar to the way in which the Greek term *monogene*, which originally meant "first born" or "only begotten," came to be associated with the idea of "one who receives the inheritance" and hence a person who is preeminent, whether or not the person is actually the first to be born. Connotatively *monogene* means "son of inheritance" or "son of privilege" or "son of promise" because the first-born son was the one who had had special privileges and an inheritance, even if he wasn't actually born first such as Isaac and Jacob (Hebrews 11:17). In a similar fashion, the term eunuch came simply to

mean "one who does not bear children." It was not a synonym for a homosexual, although some active homosexuals my have been employed
as eunuchs. We cannot therefore justifiably read "homosexual" into the
word "eunuch" when used by Jesus as if He said:

> For some are *homosexuals* because they were born that
> way; others were made *homosexuals* by men; and others
> have made themselves *homosexuals* because of the king-
> dom of heaven. The one who can accept this should accept
> it (Matthew 9:12).

The context of Jesus' statement is within a teaching on marriage and
divorce. Jesus states that the only lawful cause for divorce is infidelity
and the only reason why Moses allowed for a certificate of divorce was
because of the hardness of hearts. He then says that if anyone divorces for any other cause then they are committing adultery (Matthew
19:1-11). The disciples then responded by saying, "If the relationship
of the man with his wife is like this, it is better not to marry." Jesus
then responds by essentially saying, "If you think having such stringent
rules for divorce is difficult - and not everyone can accept this - trying
remaining single for the Kingdom of God." Jesus of course is the very
person He is speaking of who is living the more difficult life.

Jesus is not discussing three different classes of eunuchs, but rather
three different *ways* men become eunuchs. Brentlinger is asserting there
are three different *types* of eunuch, one of which is a gay man who was
born a homosexual. However, this is not what the word means or what
Jesus is teaching. The word "eunuch" means the exact same thing in
each of these three cases though there are various means by which person becomes one – born biologically incapable of siring children, made
incapable of bearing children or choosing not to sire children for the
sake of the Kingdom God Heaven. The one who chooses to be a eunuch
does so presumably so that they can be totally devoted to serving God
without the double duty of having to also be concerned with providing
for a family (1 Corinthians 7:32).

Because Brentlinger reads into the text three classes of eunuchs,
each with a distinctly different definition, and one of these classes cannot
accept the Adam and Eve paradigm for marriage, such a person must be

an equivalence to a modern homosexual. Yet, according to Brentlinger, such a person is not required to abstain from sexual relationship:

> ...Jesus, implies that born eunuchs are not required to abstain from sexual relationships... Jesus did speak to the issue of homosexuality, clearly excluding born eunuchs or gay people, from the Adam and Eve marriage paradigm, which is the norm for nongay people.[564]

If there is no precedence for gay marriage in the Bible, one would then conclude that while heterosexuals are required to confine their sexual activity to the covenant marriage relationship that homosexuals are not. Hence according to Gay theologians, homosexuals who are married to women are free to have sex with men outside of marriage with other men, if we are to believe that King David and Jonathan were homosexual lovers and that God approved of and blessed their homosexual activity.

Therefore, far from supporting the idea of "monogamous homosexual relationships" if we were to read all the texts that Gay Theology advocates suggest make a positive case for same sex relationships, they actually support practicing incest (Ruth and Naomi), adultery (David and Jonathan), fornication (Jesus and Jonathan) and pedophilia (the Roman Centurion and the servant).

---

564   Rick Brentlinger, *Gay Christian 101 - Spiritual Self-Defense For Gay Christians* (2007), 228-229.

Chapter 18
The Confusion of Gay Marriage

One of the most heated debates today related to the issue of homosexuality is the issue of whether or not two people of the same gender
in life-long committed monogamous sexual relationship should be
recognized and granted legal status that is recognized by the general
public, the state and the Church. Some may refer to this relationship
as a "gay marriage." Others will argue that it should only entail the
recognition of the civil government and not forced upon the Church
and therefore be referred to as a "same-sex civil union." In essence,
there are two jurisdictions for this debate; one is with the ecclesiastical
sphere (the Church) as it pertains to people who identify themselves as
Christians and the other is in the civil sphere (the civil government) for
those outside the Church.

In democratic civilizations this is set in a political framework in
which the issue is argued as a matter of public ethics and "civil rights."
In this context an argument needs to be won and a decision needs to be
made in a religiously pluralistic society. What we see then is a clash of
worldviews in which various social groups and special interest parties
vie for political power grabs. This is done not merely through persuasion
in debating the issues to convince the public that their cause is right, but
more often than not a manipulation of public opinion and the coercion
of elected officials. When the desired end is not achieved through democratic vote, the complainants then take the matter to court to force upon
society through the legal system what has not been achieved through
persuasion.

Within the ecclesiastical sphere the issue of Gay Marriage is seen by
GLBT advocates as an extension of "equal rights" that have been historically denied to other minority or oppressed groups within the Church
such as woman and people of African descent, particularly within the
United States. They then argue that since in many denominations wom-
en and people of African descent may now be ordained and serve as
pastors, by extension the right to be ordained and married ought to now
be extended to another minority group within the Church – to active

homosexuals. In doing so, Gay Theology advocates do not merely argue for recognition from the state, but from the Church and God Himself.

In this chapter I shall first address the issue of Gay marriage within the Church and then in a limited fashion address "same sex civil union" in the civil sphere of society. In doing so I shall focus on the ethical issues regarding the public sphere of the state, particularly in the realm of politics, and the jurisdiction of who may define marriage.

The Complementarian Theory

The most common response against the Gay Theological interpretation of same-sex acts in relation to the issue of marriage is what is commonly referred to as the Complementarian Theory or what feminists refer to as the Gender Binary Construct.[565] An essential component of this theory is that together man and woman reflect the *imago dei* (image of God) and are complimentary halves of what it means to be fully human.

Some proponents of this theory even go so far as to argue that without the woman, the man falls short of fully bearing the image of God and thus he needs a wife in order to complete himself.[566] When Eve was created from Adam, he became incomplete and is only again made whole when the man and woman become "one flesh" as their compatible parts (the penis and the vagina) are rejoined in the sexual union as well as other aspects of the covenantal bond. If this view is followed to its logical conclusion, single men and women become second-class citizens in the Kingdom of God as they are indicted with being less than an image bearer, including Jesus Christ and the Apostle Paul. This view is not derived from a careful exegesis of Scripture but is borrowed from a Platonic dualistic worldview.

To conclude that Adam was not fully an image bearer without Eve is to assert that no man is whole without a woman and no woman is whole without a man. But Scripture tells us, "Whoever sheds man's blood, by man his blood shall be shed, for in the image of God He made man" (Genesis 6:9). The text does not tell us that both a man and a woman

565   Virginia Ramey Mollenkott, *Omnigender: A Trans-religious Approach* (Cleveland, OH: The Pilgrim Progress, 2007), 9.
566   Robert A. J. Gagnon, *The Bible And Homosexual Practice* (Nashville, TN: Abingdon Press, 2001), 58.

must be murdered in order to violate the image of God, nor does it say that both a man and a woman need to be involved in the punishment of the murderer because only together are an image bearer carrying out the penal sanction. Likewise, James says that when we curse another person we are defacing someone who is "made in the likeness of God" (James 3:9). To assert that only men and women together in a sexual union are fully image bearers of God is not only a sociological *faux pas*, but it is also a Christological heresy since Jesus is fully an image bearer of God who represented and paid the penalty for Adam's defacing the image of God.

Having said this, according to the creation account the wife is a compliment to the husband and for this purpose Eve was given to Adam. This was not because he was less than whole without her or needed a wife in order to bear the image of God. Rather, it was so that together they could cooperatively carry out the commands given to them by God. If we read the two creation accounts of Genesis 1 and 2 together, we find in Genesis 1 there are a series of commands, some of which were first given to the animal kingdom in the created order, specifically to "be fruitful and multiply" (Genesis 1:22). Adam then is charged with naming the animals but in doing so he finds that none are comparable to him. God concludes, "It is not good for man to be alone" (Genesis 2:18). After creating Eve from Adam's side the same command to "be fruitful and multiply" is given them (Genesis 1:28). The point then of Eve being a help-meet to Adam is not so that he will fully reflect the image of God, but so that together they too can "be fruitful and multiply." While reproduction is not the sole reason for sex, *it is a primary reason*, especially at creation.

While many theologians in the past have sought to purely allegorize the Song of Solomon, the truth is that this book is God's handbook on the blessedness of marriage and sex. It poetically displays the blessing of sexual intercourse between a man and a woman without ever mentioning bearing children. Likewise a husband and wife can continue to have sex and enjoy its pleasures after the childbearing years. Still, biological reproduction is a central part of the original design of marriage. It is only after the fall that the problems of infertility arise in marriages due to age, low sperm counts or numerous other causes.

The ontological issues regarding marriage and the complimentary nature of the husband and wife relationship is not so that man may become an image bearer of God. Rather the ontological nature of the husband and the wife along with their children is to reflect the nature of the ontological and economic Trinity as well as the relationship between Jesus Christ and His bride the Church (Ephesians 5:22-6:4). Therefore, the primary objection to the Church's recognition of Gay marriage then needs to be seen in the Biblical concept of marriage that reflects the doctrine of the Trinity in which we assert the ontological equality and economic subordination of the Father, Son and Holy Spirit in the relationship of husband, wife and children.[567] Before we can understand this paradigm for understanding a Biblical marriage some essential doctrines of the historical Christian faith need to be reviewed.

In Biblical theology it is important to keep clear that there is only one God (Deuteronomy 6:4; Isaiah 44:6-8; 45:5-6; 1 Timothy 2:5; 1 Corinthians 8:4). Yet, there are three persons within the Godhead as this God is also a complexity within unity (Genesis 2:24; 11:6; 1 Corinthians 3:6-8) as taught in the Church's Athanasian Creed, "We worship one God in Trinity, and Trinity in unity; neither confounding the persons nor dividing the substance." All three persons within the Godhead are ontologically the same essence but they differ in person and function, and all three persons within the Godhead are completely equal. This is what is referred to as the "ontological trinity."

Ontologically there is no "chain of authority" with the exception of the voluntary submission of God the Son to God the Father while He was on earth. This is referred to as the "economic" Trinity in which the Son in history is submitted to the Father who is economically greater as Jesus said, "...the Father is greater than I" (John 14:28). Because the Father is greater than the Son this does not make Jesus ontologically inferior to the Father and the Son does not insist on having the right to be in the same redemptive role as the Father. Likewise, the Holy Spirit is sent by the Father and the Son to accomplish His role in redemptive history as well, which is different yet not less significant than that of the Father and the Son as Jesus said, "I will ask the Father, and He will give

---

567   Of course we need to keep in mind that this paradigm for understanding the covenant relationship of the family is an analogy that should not be pressed too far. Most analogies break down at some point, that is why we say the economic relations within the family is *like* the relationships in the Trinity, not an exact representation. What is clear is that the issue gender roles within the family plays an essential component of this analogy such that this will not work within a same sex relationship.

you another Helper, that He may be with you forever that is the Spirit of truth" (John 14:16-17).

In a similar fashion, the husband and wife are of equal substance since they are both created in the image of God (Genesis 1:27). Yet, in the household the husband is the head of the wife and she is to submit to His God-given authority (Ephesians 5:22-24; 1 Corinthians 11:3). Likewise, the children in the household are ontologically equal with their father and mother and yet they are subordinate to them until they leave and cleave to their spouse to form a household of their own (Genesis 2:24; Matthew 19:5; Ephesians 5:31).

Feminism, egalitarianism and Gay Theology strike at the heart of this Biblical concept that is found in both the Old and New Testaments which is a cardinal doctrine of the historic Christian faith. Gay Theology proponents do not deny this fact, but they reject it for they assert that this teaching is the result of the authors of the Bible, including the Apostle Paul, being culturally bound to the primitive male dominated mindset of their day.[568] According to feminists and the Gay Theological Worldview, as moderns we need to reject the teaching of Paul and what he says concerning the place of women in the home and in the Church in the name of libertine "freedom." But to deny the reality of the economic subordination in the household is to deny an essential doctrine of the Trinity. Paul grounds his view of the relationship between the husband and wife not in the culture of the day, but in the created order and in the relationship between the Father and the Son. This is why R.D. Weekly complains, "...many traditionalists still believe that the man is the head of the house; and it is difficult to prove them wrong theologically because a face value reading of the Bible supports that view."[569]

When the family and the Church lose its God given form of leadership in which men abdicate their responsibility women seek to perform the tasks mandated to men. When this happens the family and the Church does not become feminized and matriarchal. Rather, when taken to its logical end the family and the Church become disorderly, confused and

---

568   Jack Rogers states, "Both the Hebrew and Greek cultures were patriarchal. Men were and were intended to remain, dominant over women. Paul assumes the conventions of these cultures that he is addressing." *Jesus, The Bible, and Homosexuality* (Louisville, Kentucky; Westminster John Knox Press, 2006), 78.

569   R.D. Weekly, *The Rebuttal: A Biblical Response Exposing Deceptive Logic of Anti-Gay Theology* (Judah First Ministries, 2011), 51.

eventually the culture becomes androgynous. From the book of Genesis we learn that in the beginning God created the universe. He made the earth formless and void, chaotic and out of order (Genesis 1:1-2). Then God set the world in order and placed on it various kinds of plant life and creatures, each in their own sphere and without confusion (Genesis 1:6-25). God not only put the universe in order but also continues to sustain it as well by His own power. Should this order be disrupted it would, to some degree, fall back into disorder and chaos.

At the end of the creation week God created man in His own image, Adam as the head of all creation and from him a wife (Genesis 1:27). God created an order in this family that follows the economic Trinity such that God the Father is the covenantal head of God the Son, He in turn is the head of man and the husband is the covenantal head of the woman (1 Corinthians 11:3). As her covenantal head Adam named his wife and together they were the first parents of mankind. All of creation, including the family of man, was in order and without confusion. Adam was clearly the federal head (Christ-like leader in the covenant household) and Eve as his help-meet had a clearly defined and orderly role (Genesis 2:21-25). The man as the head of the household is to be the provider, protector and leader in the family. This is why Paul says that if a husband does not provide for his family he is worse than an unbeliever (1 Timothy 5:8). The wife, as the help-meet, is to aid him in his task by being a co-homemaker, co-caregiver and co-nurturer of children and a multitude of other ways in which she can be a co-laborer in furthering the Kingdom of God.[570] While both the father and mother are to instruct and guide the children (Proverbs 1:8), it is the father who bears the ultimate responsibility for managing his household well in a manner in which he mirrors Christ's management of His household (1 Timothy 3:4; Ephesians 6:4; Hebrews 3:2-6).

God has designed both the man and the woman physically and mentally for these tasks. He also designed the husband and wife for each other. The physical design of the husband and the wife reflects the fact

---

570   I recommend reading the following books on this subject: Stuart Scott, *The Exemplary Husband* (Focus Publishing, MN: 2002); Martha Peace, *The Excellent Wife* (Focus Publishing, MN: 1999); Jay Adams, *Christian Living in the Home* (Phillipsburg, NJ: P & R Publishing, 1972); Philip Lancaster, *Family Man, Family Leader* (The Vision Forum, Inc., 2003). John Piper and Wayne Grudem, *Recovering Biblical Manhood & Womanhood* (Crossway Books: Wheaton, IL, 2006)

that they were created for each other for marital relations. Not because their bodily parts "fit" together, but that (barring the effects of the fall) as originally intended they bring forth life. Man was not created for man or woman for woman in this manner. Should the husband/father abandon his responsibility to be the federal head of the family, this created order of would be disrupted with the result that confusion would arise.

After Adam and Eve were created, the family order was established. They were given the dominion mandate and a prohibition to not eat from the Tree of the Knowledge of Good and Evil. But the deceiver's plan was rather simple: he wanted to disrupt the order of God's creation and bring confusion and disharmony to the husband/wife relationship and mankind's fellowship with God. Similar to today's revisionist interpreters, Satan did so by first bringing into question the reliability, trustworthiness of God's Word by "queering" it (Genesis 3:1). Adam failed to take dominion over the serpent as commanded by God (Genesis 1:26, 28) and consequently Eve was deceived by the lie of the serpent. She then took and ate that which was forbidden, then gave it to her husband and he sinned by eating it as well (Genesis 3:1-6).

The result of the sin of Adam was the fall of mankind into confusion, hostility toward God's order and all of creation became a hostile environment for mankind (Genesis 3:18). While God continues to sustain the universe, bringing some degree of environmental balance in the world, the order of creation has become futile and confused so that where there was once harmony there is now conflict (Romans 8:20). Rather than man taking dominion over the earth, the earth now physically takes dominion over man as he eventually dies and is buried in the ground (Genesis 3:17-19). As a result, mankind will continue to return to dust and be swallowed by the earth until the resurrection (Genesis 3:19; Romans 8:21).

Due to the fall, disorder and confusion spread in the family the way that yeast permeates dough or the way a disease infests the body (1 Corinthians 5:6; Deuteronomy 29:22). Brother now rises against brother as the holy seed seeks to worship in truth while the seed of the serpent seeks to worship according to his own will and wages war against the true worship of God (Genesis 3:15). This is first seen in the death of Abel by the hand of Cain (Genesis 4:8), followed by the rise of a confused worship of false gods formed in the image of animals and beasts

(Romans 1:23). One of the chief characteristics of disorderly worship is a confusion of the Creator/creature distinction in which creation is worshiped rather than God. In judgment for exchanging the truth for a lie, God has given such worshippers over to their folly so that their thinking devolves into utter depravity. Men and women exchange what is in accordance with the order of creation for that which is confused and contrary to their being designed in the image of God (Romans 1:26-27). Consequently, if people choose disorder and confusion they will be given over to more in the same manner.

This sinful disorder then affects the way in which men abuse their authority and power. Rather than conducting their roles as leaders reflecting God's order and justice in Christ-like service, the heads of households and governments became tyrannical. This is seen when the civil magistrate goes beyond justice to a Nero-like revenge such as when Lamech said to his wives, "Listen to my voice, you wives of Lamech, Give heed to my speech, for I have killed a man for wounding me; And a boy for striking me; If Cain is avenged sevenfold, then Lamech seventy-sevenfold" (Genesis 4:23-24).

In essence, such tyrants set themselves up as gods (*elohim*) gathering for themselves harems in polygamous marriages and concubines. In this sinful form of patriarchy rather than the men being the servants of all under their care, they became oppressors of women and servants. This is what happens when brutish men want the power and authority given to them but not the responsibility to serve in a self-sacrificing humble fashion. This is why the law of God given at Sinai had to begin to reign in these horrendous behaviors and provide some protection for women and slaves (Exodus 21:2, 20, 26-27). Contrary to the assertions of Gay Theologians, the law given to Moses was not the product of a tyrannical culture but the beginning of fencing in of such a culture and was antithetical to that of the surrounding nations. To see what a tyrannical kingship was like all one needed to do was look outside of the nation of Israel to the pagan kings. This is why Samuel warned Israel that if they wanted a king like the other nations they would receive a tyrant who would take their wealth, their sons and daughters as slaves with the result that, "Then you will cry out in that day because of your king whom you have chosen for yourselves, but the LORD will not answer you in that day" (1 Samuel 8:18).

It was not until the first advent of Jesus Christ that we begin to see God's original intent for the role of male leadership and the ideal for the Christian husband, as He loved His bride the Church. In essence what the New Covenant calls for is not a "patriarchy" in the negative sense of the word, but rather, if I may coin a term, a "Christarchy" in which men serve their wives and children in a Godly manner and wives then respond to their husbands as the Church ought to respond to Christ her husband.

Likewise, homosexual behavior, androgyny and pagan worship (like all other forms of sinful thinking) are the result of a confused and disorderly mind. Men who have sex with other men are not feminized, but confused and out of order. A feminine mother, wife, daughter or sister does not act like a gay man and so we should not think that homosexuals are feminized men. The stereotypical affectations and passive sexual behavior of gay men is not feminine, rather it is a learned caricature of feminine behavior that is confused and out of order. Likewise, lesbians who dress and mimic the sexual behavior of men are not masculine for they do not truly act like men. Rather they are confused in their thinking and their behavior is out of order. If to think God's thoughts after Him is orderly thinking, then all sinful thinking is the result of a disorderly mind which needs to be renewed and transformed (Romans 12:1-2). This disorderly thinking is intensified in people who are confused not only in their sexual roles but in their sexual identity, such as when a so-called transsexual man perceives himself to be a woman in man's body.

The consequence of the fall is that there is disorder and confusion in the family, Church and state. There is not one iota of creation that is free from the affects of the fall. Even Christ's bride, the Church, is tainted by sin as she awaits the completion of her sanctification and glorification (Ephesians 5:27). We see today and throughout history, elders in the Church abdicating their responsibility to be shepherds of Christ's flock and failure to equip the saints to do the work of ministry (Ephesians 4:11-12). In similar fashion, we see that contrary to their calling as a minister of God (Romans 13:4), leaders of governments resist His revealed will as the standard for justice as they seek to enforce their own will which is contrary to God's law. Consequently, we see civil magistrates constantly trying to over step their boundaries and infringe on the responsibilities and roles of the elders in the Church and in the family. Throughout history civil leaders have repeatedly become a tyranny over the people they govern. Far too often they accomplish this task by promising a reward to parents and Church leaders if they will only turn over their responsibilities to the state. All too often parents and elders of the Church are willing to abdicate their responsibilities for the promise of an easier life if they will just allow the government to be their provider from cradle to grave. We see this when Christian parents send their children to government schools where they are indoctrinated with Darwinism and the Church refuses to train men for the ministry by turning them over to liberalizing institutions that receive their seal of approval by a government accreditation committee. The role of the headship of the father in the family is constantly being abdicated by men and the ordained role of men in society in general is under a barrage of attacks from the culture around us. The result of family, Church and civil leaders abdicating their responsibilities or seeking to encroach on the responsibilities of other leaders is a confusion of the family, Church and state and total disorder in each of these covenantal social spheres.

The father or Church elder that abdicates his role and duty contributes to the confusion and disorder of those who they are supposed to shepherd. In essence, fathers and elders in the Church that fail in their duty may be contributing to the confusion and disorder in the thinking of Children who then, as a result, turn to idol worship and homosexuality. If the father in the home fails to be a role model as a husband and father for his son he should not expect his sons to be equipped for the task of being a Christ-like leader in his own home when he comes of age.

Confused and disorderly role models produce confused and disorderly thinking in the minds of their children. The result is often rebellion against God, their parents and any other type of authority. Frequently this leads to sexual promiscuity either in various forms of heterosexual fornication or in being overcome with confusion in one's sexual identity and gender role that leads to homosexual behavior. This confusion can even begin at an early elemental stage of development if the father fails to provide an example for what it means to be a Godly man.

For the past century there has been an incremental and systematic break down of the family unit and an attack on the Biblical role of men and women in the family. To make matters worse, this has occurred in the Church as well. The same arguments and hermeneutical system that has been used for the past century to get around clear texts that prohibit the ordination and leadership of women in the Church are now being used to interpret the classic texts in the Bible concerning same sex acts. Consequently, not only are churches today sanctioning homosexual "marriages" but they are also ordaining active homosexual men and women as pastors in the church.

The breakdown of the Biblical family unit results in chaos and disorder in every sphere of life. If the Church is to be obedient to the Word of God and seek to stop the erosion of society Christians must begin in the home. Fathers and husbands must accept the responsibility to perform their God-given role and mothers and wives must likewise see that the Lord has given them a very important and distinct task as the nurturers of the family.

To combat this downward trend many good Christian writers, preachers and teachers are seeking to stem the tide of the erosion of the family and restore the place of the father/husband as a Christ-like leader. These Christian leaders lament the loss of godly men who will lead their wives and children and they rightly rebuke men who have turned over their God ordained role as fathers/husbands to the State. They also point out how in many churches, liberal and evangelical, the leadership of the men has been abandoned as women have become ordained ministers in the Church. However, as much as I agree with their assessment of the cause and solution for the decay of the leadership of the husband, I have to disagree to some extent with their diagnosis of this ill in society. Most writers and teachers on this subject state that we have seen a feminization of men in society and particularly of fathers. The result, according to these Christian writers, is the rise of a matriarchy in the place of a patriarchy.

Indeed, in the so-called feminist movement there has been a denouncement of "patriarchy" in the push for egalitarianism in all of society. But egalitarianism does not create a feminine order or a matriarchy. Egalitarianism argues that all people should be regarded as economically equal in every way so that differences, even between the sexes, should be eliminated as far as possible. A closer look at this movement will reveal that it is not feminine. There is nothing ladylike about this growing trend whatsoever. What we see in the media, on television and in protest marches is not the promotion of feminine over masculine but

rather the promotion of disorder, chaos, confusion and the androgeniza-
tion of society.

In fact, so-called "feminist" writers and critics use the term "androgyny" to refer to the so-called "Women's Movement" which is largely led
by lesbians. Androgyny is then celebrated as a liberating vision of the
blurring or breakdown of gender categories. It is no wonder then that to
these people Eve, in breaking God's law, is championed as the first feminist to abandon God's order and overthrow the role of the patriarchy.[571]

The result of forsaking God's law and the ordained role for men
in the Church, the state and the family is not feminization or the rise
of a matriarchy. To be feminine is to be clearly and distinctly female.
In a matriarchy, the identity of the feminine role is clear, distinct, and
orderly like a queen bee in a hive. But such a role in the hive is ordained
and ordered by God. What we see in society is not clearly feminine, but
rather it is confusion and chaos that results in androgyny or Virginia
Mollenkott's "Omnigender." When men become confused in their thinking in this manner and then behave accordingly, they do not become
like women. Rather they become homosexual activists, cross dressers,
transsexuals, "transgendered" and every other sort of abomination that
is commonly seen today in Western Civilization. Likewise, when wom-
en become confused in their thinking and abandon femininity they do
not seem like real men. Rather there is sexual ambiguity in the manner
in which they dress, talk and relate to other people.

We see then that masculinity and femininity, the roles of the husband
and wife, are not merely descriptive but also prescriptive according to
the divine order. Both Jesus and Paul when speaking on marriage go
back to the original design, not to the state of marriage as it is after the
fall. It is sin that leads men to behave like brutes towards their wives
and daughters and it was the law of God that first began to fence in their
behavior by putting restrictions on how they could treat their wives. But

571   The term "androgyny" is a blending of two Greek words (*andras* with *gyne*)
which describes the confusion of the identity of male and female. There are two Greek
words which are translated "man." The first is *anthropos* (from which we get the word
"anthropology") which can mean "male" or "mankind" in general. The second word
is *andras* which can either specifically mean "male" or "husband." The Greek word
for woman or wife is *gyne* (from which we get the word "gynecology"). Androgyny,
therefore, is a confusion of the roles and identity of masculine and feminine with the
result that the order and defined boundaries of God's creation is disrupted or abandoned.

it was because of the hardness of hearts that such laws were necessary. If husbands truly loved their wives as Christ loved the church, then such laws would not be necessary. If they obeyed Leviticus 19:18 to "love your neighbor as yourself" then the commandments regarding slavery and divorce would not be needed.

When Jesus and Paul speak on marriage, they do not refer back to the restrictions of the law that limited the brutish behavior of men, but to the original role of husbands and wives before sin entered the world. Jesus Christ came to remove the curse of sin and put back into order what had been made chaotic by man's sin and rebellion. He does so by His own example of His love for His bride the Church and then laying down His life for her. This is why Paul then appeals to this new world order and not merely the original order that existed before the fall. Christian men are not to imitate the brutish behavior of pagan patriarchal cultures in which men act as tyrants over women. Rather they are to lead their homes as humble servants, setting aside their own selfish desires for the needs of their wife and children.

What is lacking then in the fallacious concept of "gay marriage" is not merely the failure to obey God's revealed will for sexual ethics but a total disregard for the very ontological nature of men and women as revealed in Genesis and upheld by Jesus Christ, the second Adam. While it is understandable that non-Christians would disregard God's Word and seek to undermine God's order and revealed will for husbands and wives revealed in both testaments, it is absolutely deplorable that anyone who identifies as a "Christian" would seek to do so as well.

Gay Marriage as a Right

According to the Gay Theology proponents what they are seeking is not special rights but equal rights. Within their worldview, homosexuality is an ontological reality as same-sex attractions are not merely an emotional or sexual proclivity, but an aspect of their very essence. They view this as a reflection of their biological makeup that is a minor sexual variation that exists within the animal kingdom. It is argued that while the majority of the created order is either male or female and heterosexual there are also God-designed minor variations of gender within the created order such that we see species that are neither male nor female or are even able to change their gender. According to this paradigm, homosexuality exists within the animal kingdom as a universal but minor subset of sexual behavior within the created order. The human race being at a more highly developed stage on the created order, or the evolutionary ladder, is expected then to contain some variances so that we see not only homosexual behavior among lower life forms but also naturally within the human race as well.

While in most debates this issue might be come down to an argument between Christianity and Darwinian Evolution, what we find in many works of Gay Theology proponents is the assertion of theistic evolution that seeks to accommodate both the purely naturalistic interpretation of the created order and the Bible's record of the order of creation. If then homosexuality, bisexuality and "transgender" is a naturally occurring variation within God's created order as He originally intended it to be, then to fail to recognize and accommodate the place of God's creation in society and within the Church might be viewed not merely a necessity of upholding human rights, but a discernable mandate of God's revealed will in General Revelation. This, in essence, is a natural law argument for the sanctioning of Gay marriage.

The second argument in favor of same sex marriages by Gay Theology advocates is dependent on the misrepresentation of polygamy in the Old Testament and the false assertion that David and Jonathan were gay lovers which has been refuted in the preceding chapters. It is then argued that one of the purposes for marriage is to provide an outlet for one's "sexual needs" (not just desires) and prevent fornication (1 Corinthians 7:2).[572] Since, according to Gay Theology advocates, we see in the Bible various forms of marriage outside the "one man, one woman" paradigm then Gay Marriage is simply another permissible form of marriage that is analogous to heterosexual marriage.[573]

It is then asserted that since people who are not attracted to the opposite sex are not psychologically designed to be in a heterosexual marriage that self-identified gay people ought to be allowed to have monogamous life-long commitments that are legitimized by the Church and the state so as to corral homosexual behavior within the confines of

---

572   R.D. Weekly, *Homosexianity* (Judah First Ministries, 2009), 94.
573   Rick Brentlinger, *Gay Christian 101 - Spiritual Self-Defense For Gay Christians* (2007), 23.; R.D. Weekly, *Homosexianity* (Judah First Ministries, 2009), 86.

monogamy.[574] This is often proposed as a solution to homosexual pro-miscuity and the spread of A.I.D.S.. To fail to allow such a relationship is not only a violation of civil rights, but a prohibition that is cruel which in essence says to gay people, "Thou shalt not love."[575]

There are several problems with this line of reasoning, as even argued by some proponents of Gay Liberation Theology. First, once the Biblical boundaries of the husband/wife definition of marriage are abandoned there are no limitations as to why homosexual monogamy should not also be abandoned as a mere copycat of the binary gender construct ("patriarchal dyads") of the heterosexist majority.[576] For that matter, there is no reason why marriage should be confined to adults for if, as Gay Theology advocates assert, Jesus approved of a Roman Centurion's homosexual relationship with his *pais*, a child servant, then there would be no reason why we modern Christians should not also argue for "cross generational" marriages between male adults and young boys. If a homosexual orientation is but one "natural" variation within sexual norms then one must consider whether or not there are also others within an even smaller minority who are likewise born with a proclivity to being attracted to and falling in love with prepubescent children, adolescents and teenage boys.

Second, if marriage were an obstacle to sexual promiscuity then adultery would be an unknown phenomenon. While it might be argued that heterosexual couples have some advantage over the single person, the reality is married couples also experience times of the unavailability of the spouse so they too must practice self-restraint. Self-control, not marriage, is the solution to preventing fornication and adultery. To deny that self-control is possible for a single person is to deny the power of the Holy Spirit and the means of grace for the fruit of the Spirit is, "love, joy, peace, patience, kindness, goodness, faithfulness, gentleness and self-control" (Galatians 5:22-23). For the Christian who either cannot find a suitable spouse or is not inclined towards remaining within the Biblical boundaries for marriage needs to follow Jesus Christ as the

---

574   David G. Myers and Letha Dawson Scanzoni, *What God Has Joined Together: The Christian Case For Gay Marriage* (New York, NY: Harper Collins, 2005), 115.

575   Mary E. Hunt, *Fierce Tenderness: A Feminist Theology of Friendship* (New York, NY: Crossroad, 1991), 137, 139.

576   Patrick M. Chapman, *"Thou Shalt Not Love": What Evangelicals Really Say to Gays* (New York, NY: Haidukpress, 2008), 298.

supreme example of what it means to remain single and yet content with his calling and station in life. We may be tempted to think that because we do not have sexual relations that somehow we are less than others or we are not getting all our "needs" met. But to make such an assertion flies in the face of the gospel and the very words of Christ to another single man, "My grace is sufficient for you" (2 Corinthians 12:9). To think that remaining a virgin or maintaining celibacy is some form of social stigma is to succumb to the carnal philosophy of this world. Jesus Christ, the virgin, said to His disciples, "A pupil is not above his teacher; but everyone, after he has been fully trained, will be like his teacher" (Luke 6:40).

It is claimed that to require people with same-sex attractions to restrict sexual behavior within the boundaries of a heterosexual marriage or celibacy is a form of cruelty and oppression of a minority within the Church as R. D weekly asserts, "…it's nothing short of cruel to demand that those not gifted with celibacy endure a lifetime of emotional and physical sexual denial."[577] I do not want to be come across as seeming unsympathetic to the plight of those who long to have a soul-mate. In fact as I write this I know exactly how it feels to want to be "one flesh" with someone in every way imaginable; emotionally, relationally and sexually. I also know what it is like to feel like a second-class citizen in a family centric church that overlooks the needs and struggles of single people. While they may look out for the orphans and widows and seek compatible spouses for their own children more often than not once the single person graduates the "college age" group at church it is not uncommon to suddenly find oneself feeling like a vestigial organ in the body of Christ. But the solution is not to violate God's Word by seeking a sexual relationship which His Word forbids. Nor should we become bent inwards such that one begins to think that having an orgasm with another person is a civil right which the Church and society must allow, or even provide, if one does not feel like confining such activity within the confines of Biblical matrimony.

Third, since-same sex acts are inherently sinful to argue for gay marriage is merely to assert that it is a lesser evil than homosexual promiscuity, not that such a relationship could be considered good, holy or approved of by God. It is argued that "marriage grows a person up, stabilizes a person emotionally, and forces a person to be responsible

577   R.D. Weekly, *Homosexianity* (Judah First Ministries, 2009), 97.

toward someone else" and that "civil same-sex marriage would benefit society by helping to curb promiscuity and to civilize gay men."[578] This is essentially an argument from pragmatism, that a desired (though by no means guaranteed) ends justifies the means. We must keep in mind that monogamy, which is a necessary element of God glorifying marriage, is not a sufficient grounds for marriage. We cannot legitimately argue for incestuous sexual relations to be declared holy merely because they are monogamous nor same-sex unions for by their very nature they defy the revealed will of God. Likewise, while it might be argued that same-sex acts that are confined within monogamy are a "lesser evil" than rampant promiscuous homosexual acts, they are still a defilement that will be judged by God, "Marriage is to be held in honor among all, and the marriage bed is to be undefiled; for fornicators and adulterers God will judge" (Hebrews 13:4).

Jurisdiction: The Church, The State and the Family

Having discussed a Biblical model for marriage and the roles of husbands and wives that the Church is called to follow, we need to address the issue of the boundaries marriage for those outside the Church. This is has been one of the most heated debates in recent years. The questions that most Christians are asking are, "Should Christians seek to have the state restrict the definition of marriage to include only one man and one woman?" While most Christians would probably answer, "yes" to this question there have been some who have argued that conservative Bible-believing Christians should support same sex civil unions even if we believe that homosexual behavior is a sin.

Once such argument is made by Misty Irons in her paper, "A Conservative Christian Case for Civil Same-Sex Marriage."[579] The conclusion that one comes to from her argument is that there should be a distinction between what the Church recognizes and what the state recognizes. Then when a person gets married they can have a state marriage which could recognize same-sex civil unions as well as a Church marriage which, in accordance with the religious views of the Church they could choose not to perform or recognize gay marriages. The

---

578   Misty Irons, "A Conservative Case for Civil Same-Sex Marriage." November 19, 2000 MusingsOn.com © 2000, 2004 http://www.musingson.com/ccCase.html
579   Ibid.

Christian then, according to Misty Irons, should defend gay people's desire to have a recognized marriage by the state. In short, her argument equates the freedom to have a civil marriage (which is distinct from an ecclesiastical marriage) with the freedom of religion. She asserts that Christians who do not want their own freedom to worship as their conscience dictates should not only refrain from infringing on the freedom of others to practice a religion with which we disagree, but we should in fact support their freedom to practice their religion (such as Buddhism). Only by supporting such freedom do we also guarantee our own freedom to worship without any hindrance from the state. She then asserts that in a similar fashion that though we may disagree with same-sex unions, by supporting the freedom of gay people to have recognized marriages by the state we likewise ensure our own continuing freedom to marry how we choose. This line of reasoning is akin to an argument for the freedom of speech often attributed to Francois-Marie Arouet de Voltaire who supposedly asserted, "I disapprove of what you say, but I will defend to the death your right to say it."

According to this line of thinking, by defending other's right to complete freedom of speech (including blaspheming God) we are defending our own right to free speech. The freedom to marry, practice a religion and speak freely are then viewed as "civil rights." It is then argued that the best way to guarantee one's own "civil rights" in such matters is to guarantee the protection of other people to speak, worship and engage in sex acts even if they differ from our own. The basic philosophy behind this line of reasoning is not Christian, but rather a modern notion of "enlightened self-interest" as discussed by Alexis de Tocqueville in his work *Democracy in America*.[580] This line of reasoning asserts that by voluntarily joining together in associations to further the interests of the group, even with those whom we disagree, we in turn serve our own interests in spreading the gospel which is the only real way to truly convert a culture that does what is right from the heart rather than due to the use of external force as Misty Irons states:

> It is high time that we grow up and learn to play fair. Freedom for us means freedom for someone else too, even our fellow Americans in the gay and lesbian community.

---

580   Alexis de Tocqueville, *Democracy in America* (Signet Classics, 2001)

Is that too high a price to pay? Of course not. Civil lib-
erties is what gives Christians the freedom to pursue our
moral convictions in this country in the first place. It is
what guarantees a future for ourselves and our children in
which we will be able to practice our religious beliefs free
of harassment and fear. It is what paves the way for us to
make a true moral impact on our culture, not by trying to
legislate the Bible as if that will change people's hearts,
but through leading by example as Jesus commanded us:
"Let your light shine before men in such a way that they
may see your good works, and glorify your Father who is
in heaven" (Matthew 5:16).[581]

While I appreciate Misty Iron's genuine concern for the freedom
of the Gospel, her fair treatment of her gay neighbors and her distain
for bullying power politics there are several problems with this line of
argument. The first is the Christian is required to define "freedom" in
Biblical terms. Can we justifiably assert that we want to *promote* the
freedom to do be enslaved to sin? It is one thing to argue for one's own
freedom as defined by the Bible and demand of the state that it not
violate the boundaries of its jurisdiction by stepping into the jurisdiction
of the family or the Church. But Misty Irons doesn't even tackle the
issue of sphere responsibility or what the New Testament states concerning the role of the civil magistrate. I would argue that we should
let the Buddhist make his case for his desire to be free to practice his
religion. The Christian cannot rightly come to his side and deny the
Lordship of Christ over every sphere of life. While we certainly should
not seek to dissolve the boundaries of the Church and the state into
Erastianism we cannot justifiably defend Buddhism and be true to the
Lord Jesus Christ at the same time. Let the Buddhist or the homosexual
fight for his own worldview. While the law of God provides numerous
common protections for the "stranger within the gate" we cannot take
the next step to then conclude that we ought to defend the Muslim who
wants to uphold Sharia law, the evolutionist who wants to practice eu-
genics or the self-identified homosexual who wants to have the "how
to" of same-sex acts taught to impressionable youths in public schools
as Andrew Sullivan, Misty Iron's mentor on this issue, insists on "...

581   Ibid.

inclusion of the facts about homosexuality in the curriculum of every government-funded school." [582]

As stated in the opening chapter, "facts" are not observed in a neutral fashion and the "facts about homosexuality" will be conveyed and interpreted according to a particular worldview. Can the Christian then in good conscience advocate that the state uphold the teaching of the "facts about homosexuality" according to a homosexual worldview or the even the "Gay Christian" worldview? What Misty Irons is essentially arguing for is not a neutrality towards the things of Christ in the public arena (for that is not even possible). Rather she is advocating a public policy that is hostile towards the Lordship of Christ in what is tantamount to a poly-theocracy in which the citizen is free to worship any god he wishes from the menu of the pantheon so long as in the end in his actions he declares, "Caesar is lord."

Furthermore, if Misty Irons is consistent with her own theology she would then have to also support not only gay civil unions but also polygamy, cross generational marriages (pederasty), and incestuous marriages. Since she has set aside the law of God as the only epistemologically viable standard for the ethics of the state in favor of a fallacious "natural law," her view has no objective standard for voicing any objection to such marriages from being legalized. Furthermore, marriage is a "creation ordinance" which historically has been universally observed all over the globe by even non-Christian societies for thousands of years. How can we then justifiably so quickly abandon the boundaries of the institution for what is in reality is a modern fad.

In contrast to Misty Iron's view there are others who have argued that Christians are obligated to seek to have the state institute laws that would define marriage to only include heterosexual couples. Entire books and lengthy papers have been written on this subject and it is not my intent to enter into the debate as it has been stated. What I would challenge is the grounds of the very notion that it is within the jurisdiction of the state to define marriage. What God has ordained and defined the state has no authority to redefine. Therefore, rather than seeking to urge the state to define marriage Christians should seek to have the state get out of the business of issuing marriage licenses altogether. It has no more authority to define marriage than it does to define the Church. Yet most Christian churches and denominations in America today have

582   Andrew Sullivan, *Virtually Normal* (New York, NY: Vintage, 1996), 172.

abdicated their right to define themselves on the basis of the Bible by surrendering their ecclesiastical jurisdiction in order to gain an identity as a 501(c)(3) non-profit organization. What I am suggesting then is not upholding what was called "Proposition 8" in California, but rather what we might called "Proposition 86" – the ceasing of state issued marriage licenses. Rather than seeking to have the government define marriage, we should be arguing that defining marriage is not within their jurisdictional prerogative.

Chapter 19
The "T" in GLBT

In the preceding chapters we focused on what a consistently developed Biblical Christian worldview teaches on the boundaries for
sexual behavior and marriage. In doing so we considered the foundational *epistemological* issues related to the authority of Scripture and
hermeneutical issues which form the lens through which we read God's
Word, understand our experiences and interpret the world around us.
We then examined the redemptive-historical nature of the law of God
revealed in the Old Testament and the apostolic interpretation of it in
the New Testament as the basis for Christian *ethics*. Having done so, it
was argued that the only justifiable conclusion is that the Bible only approves of sexual acts within the boundaries of a marriage between one
man and one woman. Polygamy, incest, fornication, adultery, bestiality
and same-sex acts are prohibited regardless of the subjective disposition
of its participants or the degree of mutual consent or life-long commitment of the persons involved. In this chapter we shall consider the
metaphysical issues related to human ontology, particularly in relation
to our gender identity and sexual attractions.[583] We will then have a final
look at the trajectory of the GLBT theological movement as manifested
in the Metropolitan Community Church.

Having read several books on transgenderism, listened to their
own stories and what they have wrestled with it would be unloving to
address this issue in a clinical, abstract, philosophical fashion without
acknowledging the real suffering these people have experienced. People
who refer to themselves as *transsexuals*, those who feel that their gender
identity does not match their biological gender, often suffer with a lot

583 Whereas epistemology concerns a theory of knowledge and ethics addresses
moral issues, metaphysics *is a branch of philosophy concerned with explaining the
fundamental nature of being and the world.* Within this study there are two types of inquiry. The first focuses on a general investigation into the nature of reality. The second
type of inquiry seeks to uncover what is ultimately real, frequently offering answers in
sharp contrast to our everyday experience of the world. Understood in terms of these
two questions, metaphysics is very closely related to ontology, which is usually taken
to involve both "what is existence (being)?" and "what (fundamentally distinct) types
of things exist?"

of confusion, depression and rejection from others. They have sought to find a resolution to the perceived conflict between the birth gender of their body and their perceived gender identity, often beginning at a very young age.

Then there are various types of *intersexuals,* people with Disorders of Sex Development (DSD), commonly referred to as "hermaphrodites," who have an actual anatomical phenomenon in which they are born with genitals or chromosomes that are not distinctly male or female. Frequently, choices are made for an intersexed person by their parents at the time of their birth. Medical professionals often recommend that these children undergo a multitude of reconstructive surgeries that often causes physical and psychological trauma. Adults that underwent sex assignment surgery as a child often feel as if their body was violated without their consent, leaving them physically and emotionally scarred.

There is a great need for research on how to best Biblically counsel people who perceive themselves to be transsexuals. A Christian worldview of biomedical ethics needs to be developed that would indicate what counsel should be given to parents who have a child born with DSD, particularly if the condition does not pose any immediate health risks. But such a task is beyond the purpose of this chapter, which is to examine how two sectors within Gay Theology are creating an entire worldview based on their experiences and anatomical anomalies.

The Queer/Transgender Worldview

Before we can go on to address the claims of the Transgender Theology, we need to define some terms and make some distinctions between homosexuality and the claims of transgenderism and Transgender Theology. We then need to see how Transgender Theology affects the interpretation of self that then creates an existentialist lens through which they interpret the created order, the world around them, the Bible and then redefine God, Jesus Christ and the Christian faith.

Most of this book has been about what the Scriptures teach concerning sexual behavior. The issue of transgenderism is somewhat different. This issue isn't primarily about sexual attractions or how one behaves sexually in a relationship with another person. Rather transgenderism concerns how a person perceives their own gender identity and expresses their biological gender as Virginia Mollenkott states, "Strictly speaking, *sexual orientation* is one thing, *gender identity* is another, and *gender expression* is still another."[584] Unlike same-sex attractions, transgenderism is not primarily a matter of who one feels emotionally and sexually attracted to but how one feels and perceives one's own gender or sexual identity:

> Transgendered people are those individuals who do not fit comfortably into society's traditional understanding of sex and gender. We occupy a space beyond and/or between the standard categories of female and male. Some do so knowingly, deliberately, and as a statement against the binary gendered system. Others feel that they have no choice in the matter and were born as they are.[585]

"Transgender," then, is an umbrella term for various groups of people that think and feel that they don't, for a variety of reasons, fit neatly into the categories of male or female:[586]

> At first, the term transgender referred only to people who had changed their gender but not their genitals – for instance, a man who uses estrogen, lives as a woman, but has no plans to undergo sex-reassignment surgery. (Now, such a person would be called a non-operative transsexual.) But gradually, the term has been extended to include intersexuals, transsexuals, cross-dressers, drag-queens and kings,

---

584   Virginia Ramey Mollenkott, *Omnigender: A Trans-religious Approach* (Cleveland, OH: The Pilgrim Progress, 2007), 77-78.

585   Justin Tanis, *Transgendered: Theology, Ministry and Communities of Faith* (Cleveland, OH: The Pilgrim Press, 2003), 18.

586   Lisa Mottet and Justin Tanis define "Transgender" as, "An umbrella term for people whose gender identity, expression or behavior is different from those typically associated with their assigned sex at birth, including but not limited to transsexuals, cross-dressers, androgynous people, genderqueers, and gender non-conforming people. Transgender is a broad term and is good for non-transgender people to use. "Trans" is shorthand for "transgender." "Opening The Door to the Inclusion of Transgender People: The Nine Keys to Making Lesbian, Gay, Bisexual and Transgender Organizations Fully Transgender-Inclusive" http://www.thetaskforce.org/reports_ and_research/opening_the_door page 6.

androgynes, and anyone else who feels 'otherwise' from society's gender assumption. Those assumptions would also define homosexuals, bisexuals, and non-conforming heterosexuals as transpeople, whether or not they saw themselves that way.[587]

The various categories (intersexual, transsexual, cross-dressers etc.) may at times get lumped into the category of "transgender." However, the truth is there are very distinct differences between these self-identities based on their self-perception and their interpretation of reality, particularly the biological order and the categories of male and female. Some of these, such as cross-dressers and drag queens, are not a confusion concerning biological sexual identity. Rather these categories reflect a psychological, emotional and sexual proclivity to have a fetish towards occasionally transgressing customary social indicators (clothing, hair style, make up etc.) of one's biological gender.

For example, a *transvestite* man may be completely heterosexual in his sexual desires, even be married with children, and yet he occasionally dresses as a woman:

> Transvestites (who prefer the term *cross-dresser* because it sounds less clinical) dress in the clothing of the 'other' gender for emotional satisfaction, for erotic pleasure, or for both. On the deepest, cross-dressing is an attempt to live the full truth of one's nature in which the cross-dresser feels profoundly identified both with her/his own and with the 'other' gender... Sometimes, but not always, the cross-dressing involves a sexual fetish.[588]

What needs to be noted is that the act of cross-dressing is based on a *perception* of one's nature. Cross-dressing is an act, a masquerade, based on self-perception, or what we may refer to as a self-interpretation, of their true gender identity. Yet they do not desire to undergo Sex Reassignment Surgery (SRS).

---

587   Virginia Ramey Mollenkott, *Omnigender: A Trans-religious Approach* (Cleveland, OH: The Pilgrim Progress, 2007), 43.
588   Ibid, 62.

The truth is that, based on a Biblical Christian Worldview, they need to realize that the mental processes that they are using to interpret their perception of gender and sexual identity is distorted. In other words, they are looking at themselves in the mirror through a cracked colored lens and the consequence is their perception of themselves does not correspond with reality. What needs to be corrected then is their thinking, their mind, and consequently their actions and behaviors rather than demanding that the world around them capitulate to transvestism by ethically or psychologically defining it as a normal variance within the created order.

There are also those who self-identify as *transsexuals.* Such persons say that they feel like they are a man living in a woman's body or a woman living in a man's body. They often believe that inwardly they are a different gender than their given biological birth gender and therefore their sexual organs need to be changed in order to come in line with their perceived gender identity. Psychologists refer to this as Gender Identity Disorder (GID) and it is also known as Gender Dysphoria. Some transsexuals may take hormones and undergo a medical operation to change their biology to appear as the opposite gender while others, for various reasons, may only dress as the opposite gender. Depending on what stage such a person is in, a self-identified transsexual may be a non-op, pre-op or post-operational transsexual. Like self-identified gays, lesbians and cross-dressers, these people are also interpreting themselves and the world around them through their feelings and perceptions of their body and desires.

This phenomenon of feeling like there is something wrong with one's body is not unique to transsexualism as it also occurs in a number of body-image perception disorders. One similar psychological malady is referred to as *aptomnophilia* in which a person self-interprets and self-identifies as an amputee even though all of their limbs are present and healthy. This is also similar to *somatoparaphrenia* in which a person denies the ownership of one of their limbs. This may seem insulting to some people who identify as transsexuals and they may think that the real problem is I am not really hearing them in their own story and consequently I am just not sympathetic enough with their plight. But, for a moment, I would ask anyone who is prone to go along with the transsexual interpretation of the world to read a fascinating, albeit disturbing,

564 Do Not Be Deceived

article by Carl Elliott "A New Way To Be Mad" in the December 2000 edition of *The Atlantic Monthly*.[589] The language of self-perception as "this is the real me" of "wannabe amputees," people that want to have a limb removed because they believe being an amputee is their true identity, mirrors the way in which transsexuals describe themselves and subsequently seek to have their physical body altered to make it coincide with their perception of reality:

> I have been struck by the way wannabes use the language of identity and selfhood in describing their desire to lose a limb. "I have always felt I should be an amputee." "I felt, this is who I was." "It is a desire to see myself, be myself, as I 'know' or 'feel' myself to be."[590]

But this self-perception is not just a matter of body-image; it often carries over into their sexual desires or sexual orientation as well:

> Even wannabes who describe their wish for amputations as a wish for completeness will often admit that there is a sexual undertone to the desire. "For me having one leg improves my own sexual image," one of my correspondents wrote. "It feels 'right,' the way I should always have been and for some reason in line with what I think my body ought to have been like." When I asked one prominent wannabe who also happens to be a psychologist if he experiences the wish to lose a limb as a matter of sex or a matter of identity, he disputed the very premise of the question. "You live sexuality," he told me. "I am a sexual being twenty-four hours a day." Even ordinary sexual desire is bound up with identity, as I was reminded by Michael First, a psychiatrist at Columbia University, who was the editor of the fourth edition of the American Psychiatric Association's *Diagnostic and Statistical Manual*. First is undertaking a study that will help determine whether apotemnophilia

589   http://www.theatlantic.com/magazine/archive/2000/12/a-new-way-to-be-mad/4671/
590   Carl Eliott, "New Way To Be Mad" in *The Atlantic Monthly* (December 2000), 74.

should be included in the fifth edition of the *DSM.* "Think of the fact that, in general, people tend to be more sexually attracted to members of their own racial group," he pointed out. "What you are attracted to (or not attracted to) is part of who you are."[591]

Carl Eliott goes on to state that there is a strong correlation between the way in which aptomnophiliacs perceive themselves who often seek the amputation of their limb and transsexuals who seek an inversion of the penis into a vagina in order to provide a perceived solution to feeling that they are in the wrong body:

> One of the issues we have struggled with is how to un-
> derstand people who use the language of self and identity
> to explain why they want these interventions: a man who
> says he is "not himself" unless he is on Prozac; a woman
> who gets breast-reduction surgery because she is "not the
> large-breasted type"; a bodybuilder who says he took ana-
> bolic steroids because he wants to look on the outside the
> way he feels on the inside; and -- perhaps most common
> -- transsexuals whose experience is described as "being
> trapped in the wrong body."[592]

He then goes on to state that, much like the testimonies of self-iden-tified transsexuals, the issue of body-image and the all consuming perception of not being in the right body often leads to depression and various forms of self-harm with a result that they become, "...a man whose discomfort in his own body is so all-consuming that he begins to think of suicide."[593] In fact, the early stages of behavior of an aptomno-philiac parallel the behavior of the pre-operational transsexual. Just as the pre-operational transsexual man begins by dressing as a woman, or the woman dresses as a man, prior to actually going through with sex reassignment surgery so too the aptomnophiliac begins by behaving like an amputee hobbling around on crutches or riding in a wheel-chair. In addition, they report that the inclination to think, feel and behave in this

591   Ibid, 78.
592   Ibid, 74.
593   Ibid, 74.

manner began at an early age which leads them perceive that they were "born that way."

> It is clear that for many [amputation] wannabes, the sexual aspect of the desire is much less ambiguous than many wannabes and clinicians have publicly admitted. A man described seventeen years ago in the *American Journal of Psychotherapy* said that he first became aware of his attraction to amputees when he was eight years old. That was in the 1920s, when the fashion was for children to wear short pants. He remembered several boys who had wooden legs. "I became extremely aroused by it," he said. "Because such boys were not troubled by their mutilation and cheerfully, and with a certain ease, took part in all the street games, including football, I never felt any pity towards them." At first he nourished his desire by seeking out people with wooden legs, but as he grew older, the desire became self-sustaining. "It has been precisely in these last years that the desire has gotten stronger, so strong that I can no longer control it but am completely controlled by it." By the time he finally saw a psychotherapist, he was consumed by the desire. Isolated and lonely, he spent some of his time hobbling around his house on crutches, pretending to be an amputee, fantasizing about photographs of war victims. He was convinced that his happiness depended on getting an amputation. He desperately wanted his body to match his self-image: "Just as a transsexual is not happy with his own body but longs to have the body of another sex, in the same way I am not happy with my present body, but long for a peg-leg." [594]

The argument to then have the medical industry sanction and provide amputations for aptomnophiliacs borrows from the exact line of reasoning of those who identify themselves as transsexuals. Both aptomnophiliacs and transsexuals want to remove a perfectly healthy part of their anatomy:

---

594   Ibid, 78.

> Transsexuals want healthy parts of their body removed in order to adjust to their idealized body image, and so I think that was the connection for me," the psychiatrist Russell Reid stated in the BBC documentary *Complete Obsession.* "I saw that people wanted to have their limbs off with equally as much degree of obsession and need and urgency." The comparison is not hard to grasp.[595]

This is not unlike another type of disordered thinking that is a result of a faulty interpretation of self, known as anorexia nervosa. An anorexic person looks in a mirror and has a distorted perception of their body. They think they are over weight even when they are malnourished and extremely thin, pinching an inch of skin while thinking, "I'm fat." Anorexia, like Gender Dysphoria, is an emotional and psychological disorder except that it focuses on food. Yet it is actually an attempt to deal with a faulty notion of perfectionism and a desire to control things by strictly regulating food and weight. However, unlike Gender Dysphoria no one is arguing that anorexia is a normal, healthy perception of reality or self.

Another similar distorted body-image phenomenon is the modern preoccupation of "plastic surgery addiction." As seen in some of the most well known cases of Michael Jackson and the infamous Jocelyn "Cat Woman" Wildenstein, those who experience this disorder become obsessed with a distorted perception of their "true self" and then seek to achieve it by repeatedly undergoing plastic surgery. Often times this is a consequence of a fear of growing old and faulty sense of body-perfection. They will then prescribe for themselves a solution in the form of body modification in which they continually undergo plastic surgery and yet never really achieve the perception of perfection because like the transsexual the problem is in their mind, not their body.

The truth is Gender Dysphoria, aptomnophilia, anorexia and "plastic surgery addiction" are all various forms of what psychologists refer to as a Body Dismorphic Disorder (BDD), none of which can be truly resolved by either the medical field or the Church capitulating to their distorted self-perceptions. It should be noted that in all of these groups there is nothing biologically wrong with their bodies, particularly their <u>sexual organs.</u> Rather, the real problem lies in the confusion of their

595   Ibid, 78.

mind and they are in desperate need of our understanding and empathy. But neither the Church nor the medical field should be offering them a false hope which offers body mutilations as a solution. The only thing that is different between these various groups is that anorexics and aptomnophiliacs do not develop a theology or worldview from their distorted sense of self, and yet this is exactly what self-identified gays and transgendered people have done.

The Anatomical Anomaly of Intersexuality

I have chosen to address the issue of *intersexuality* separately from the others which reside under the umbrella of "transgender" since this issue concerns an actual biological condition of the body and is not merely a matter of self-perception. However, like the other issues discussed, the phenomenon of intersexuality/DSD needs to be understood and interpreted through the lens of an epistemologically justifiable worldview – Biblical Christianity. The biological facts of intersexuality are not in dispute, but the interpretation of them and the ethical response to this rare condition is a serious matter.

An *intersexual* is a person who has been born with intermediate or atypical combinations of physical features that usually distinguish male from female. When occurring in insects this is often referred to as gynandromorphism.[596] This is usually understood to be congenital, involving chromosomal, morphologic, genital and/or gonadal anomalies, such as diversion from typical XX-female or XY-male presentations, e.g., sex reversal (XY-female, XX-male), genital ambiguity, sex developmental differences. Consequently, an intersex individual may have biological characteristics of both the male and the female sexes. An intersexual then is a person whose biological sex cannot by external observation be easily classified as clearly male or female. There are a variety of biological manifestations that often get categorized under the general label of "intersexual" such as Androgen Insensitivity Syndrome

596   Gynandromorphism is a rare abnormal condition in which both female (gyn) and male (andr) characteristics are displayed in one individual. The term gynandromorph is mainly used in the fields of Lepidopterology (butterfly/moth study), entomology (all insects) and ornithology (birds). Other terms used to describe a mixture of male and female characteristics in an individual organism are sexual mosaic, intersex and hermaphrodite. Hermaphrodite is used to describe animals, including humans, having both male and female sexual characteristics and organs.

(AIS),[597] Progestin Induced Virilization (PIV),[598] Congenital Andrenal Hyperplasia (CAH)[599] and Klinefelter's Syndrome.[600]

There are three important issues in regards to intersexuality. The first is an ontological issue, whether this is a natural healthy variant within the created order of genders as intended by God or whether this phenomenon is one of many potential biological deformities that a person may suffer as a result of the fall of mankind due to the sin of Adam. The second is an ethical issue, whether the parents of an intersex child should have them undergo an operation or allow the child to remain as they are and allow themselves to choose to undergo an operation later in life. I would argue that there is only an ethical *necessity* of sex assignment surgery if the condition creates a potential health hazard. To argue any further on the issue is beyond the scope of this chapter.

The third is a psychological issue in regards to the identity of a person born with this condition for one's gender is an important factor in developing a perception of self. Like many people with same-sex attractions, some people with DSD have chosen to not see intersexuality as an

597   Androgen insensitivity syndrome (AIS) is when a person who is genetically male (has one X and one Y chromosome) is resistant to male hormones called androgens. As a result, the person has some or all of the physical characteristics of a woman, despite having the genetic makeup of a man.

598   Progestin-Induced Virilization ('PIV'), which results from an abundance of male hormones in an otherwise normal XX female. PIV is caused by exposure in-utero to progestin that has been taken by the mother during pregnancy. Like individuals with CAH, PIV women will frequently have clitoral hypertrophy. In all other respects, however, they have completely female gonads.

599   Congenital adrenal hyperplasia (CAH) refers to any of several autosomal recessive diseases resulting from mutations of genes for enzymes mediating the biochemical steps of production of cortisol from cholesterol by the adrenal glands (steroidogenesis). CAH is one of the possible underlying synthesis problems in Addison's disease. Most of these conditions involve excessive or deficient production of sex steroids and can alter development of primary or secondary sex characteristics in some affected infants, children, or adults.

600   Klinefelter syndrome is a disorder that affects only males. Males normally have an X chromosome and a Y chromosome (XY). But males who have Klinefelter syndrome have an extra X chromosome (XXY), giving them a total of 47 instead of the normal 46 chromosomes. People with this disorder develop as males with subtle characteristics that become apparent during puberty. They are often tall and usually don't develop secondary sex characteristics, such as facial hair or underarm and pubic hair. The extra X chromosome primarily affects the testes, which produce sperm and the male hormone testosterone.

identity but rather as a condition that they *have*, not a defining characteristic of who they *are* as a person. In other words, they see themselves as male or female and yet one with a biological variance as Susannah Cornwall points out, "…plenty of intersexed people feel unremarkably male or female even if their genitals appear unusual."[601] She goes on to write, "Saying that the child *has* a DSD rather than that the child *is* intersexed sidesteps this problem [of social stigma due to labeling] and also avoids identifying the child entirely by their condition…"[602] Therefore, it may be unnecessary to have a child undergo sex assignment surgery for the sake of supposedly make them appear "normal" when in fact such a procedure may actually have other negative emotional, psychological and physiological side effects.

In regards to the first issue of whether being born with DSD is God-designed variance within the created order, what we must keep in mind is that one of the consequences of the fall is that quite often people are born with malformed limbs and organs. Frequently people are born with missing or malformed eyes, ears, noses, palates, arms, or legs. Infants may also be born with missing or malformed internal organs, respiratory and cardiovascular systems and tragically even with malformed brains. Why then should it be expected that a person would never be born with malformed sexual organs? And if a person does have a malformed sexual organ, why should society construct a third gender rather than see the phenomenon merely as one of many that occur along with other malformed limbs and organs?

There is of course a significant difference here in that being born intersexual creates a potential serious social and psychological challenge as well a physical handicap. Being born blind, deaf or with a missing limb, while creating various lifelong physical challenges does not carry with it a social stigma such that the individual is looked upon as a "freak." Nor does being born blind or deaf affect ones perception of self and identity in how one relates to men and women. In contrast, males tend to understand their own masculinity and identity as a boy or man in how they relate to being like other males but also in how they are not like females, "I am a man, she is a *woman*." A person who is born intersexual however finds himself/herself in a category that our

---

601   Susannah Cornwall, *Sex and Uncertainty in the Body of Christ: Intersex Conditions and Christian theology* (Sheffield, England: Equinox Publishing, 2010), 6.
602   Ibid, 46.

culture and society does not provide a box to check in a survey, a job application or on a driver's license. The consequence is that such people may understandably feel like a misfit and suffer wrongly from a social stigma attached to this condition.

One of the indicators that intersexuality in humans is a result of the fall and not a normal gender variance originally designed by God is the fact that it often results in a life-threatening situation that needs to be corrected by a surgical operation. This biological problem is recognized even by Virginia Mollenkott as she writes:

> According to the best estimate of the Intersex Society of North America, "about five intersexed children have their genitals cut into in U.S. hospitals every day for cosmetic reasons, a procedure performed by accredited surgeons and covered by all major insurance plans." Some operations may be necessitated by life-threatening conditions because systems of urination and defecation are situated close to human genitals.[603]

Therefore, there is a bio-ethical justification for performing operations on some children who are born intersexual. If a life-saving operation is necessary, then this condition is a consequence of the fall and not part of God's intended "variety of creation." Instead of recognizing that intersexuality is like many other malformations of body organs, Mollenkott insists that such an assertion is somehow degrading to people who are born with this condition "…the drastic disrespect involved in implying that intersexuals may be the defective results of human sinfulness."[604] While babies born male or female can have other types of medical complications, they are incidental to being born male or female. Furthermore, whereas intersexuality (Gynandromorphism) exists in the animal kingdom, such as in crustaceans, wasps and butterflies, it is often a symptom of environmental pollution.[605]

---

603   Virginia Ramey Mollenkott, *Omnigender: A Trans-religious Approach* (Cleveland, OH: The Pilgrim Progress, 2007), 45.
604   Ibid, 7.
605   Allen W. Olmstead and Gerald A. LeBlanc, "The Environmental-Endocrine Basis of Gynandromorphism (Intersex) in a Crustacean" *International Journal of Biological Science* (2007), 3.

There are, of course, also fully productive varieties of non-binary gender forms in the animal kingdom in which an organism that has reproductive organs normally associated with both male and female genders. These are commonly known as simultaneous (or synchronous) hermaphrodites. There are also sequential hermaphrodites (dichogamy) in which the creature is born as one sex, but can later change into the alternate sex and it is common in some species of fish and gastropods.[606] Transgenderists, by way of analogy, then argue that if such a phenomenon exists in the animal kingdom that the human phenomenon of intersexuality is a rare but healthy variance in human gender.

There are two Biblical responses to such an assertion. The first is that the creation account in Genesis 1-2 does not speak of the animal or plant kingdom as being created male and female. It only states that the various types of animals (flying creatures, sea creatures, creeping things and beasts) were created, where they were to dwell (sky, sea, land) and that they subsequently reproduced after their own kind (Genesis 1:20-25). It does not state that they are all created distinctly male and female. While in the story of Noah's Ark the collection of animals entails the command to collect male and female animals so that they may reproduce and fill the earth after the flood, the text does not say that all animals *only* exist in male or female or that synchronous or dichogamist animals were not to also be collected (Genesis 7:2-3, 9, 16). God's primary concern was that Noah be sure to collect a cow *and* a bull and not just two heifers.

Second, with the exception of those that are a result of environmental change and ecological pollution and a contamination of the environment, the hermaphroditic phenomenon in various species is the norm as it functions as part of their ability to reproduce. Such is not the case with humans. In fact in humans, like gynandromorphism in animals that are a result of environmental pollution, intersexuality frequently causes sterility and many other health complications.

The reason why Mollenkott and transgenderists insist that intersexuality is part of God's intended created order is because, as we shall see, she denies the fall, original sin and the historicity of the Genesis account of creation. Instead, she asserts what she refers to as an Omnigender view of theistic evolution and that the Genesis account is merely a mythical

---

606   These are referred to as protandry in which an organism is born as a male but then changes sex to a female and protogyny in which the organism starts as a female, and then changes sex to a male.

poem tells us *that* God created the universe, not *how* God created the human race:

> One non-controversial rule of hermeneutics is that a reader must pay attention to the genre or literary type of whatever is being interpreted. A historical treatise should not be read as if it were a lyric poem, a novel, a letter, or a doctrinal treatise. By this standard, chapters 1 and 2 of Genesis belongs to the genre of creation accounts, stories intended to describe origins and reassure people who are feeling threatened and endangered world. Genesis 1:1-2:4 is an elegant poem or hymn of creation; Genesis 2:5-24 is an older account, an earthy folktale of creation emphasizing the interests of peasant society. Neither account is a scientific treatise. Both are religious statements intended to glorify God and to suggest God's involvement with humankind.

> The efforts of 'creationists' to exclude the teaching of evolution from public schools (citing genesis 1 and 2) are violations of the rule that, like any other piece of literature, biblical passages must be read in accordance with their own genre... Poems and folktales of creation must not be treated as scientific textbooks... Genesis 1-2 affirms *that* God created without stating *how* God created. Similarly, Genesis 1 and 2 do not address the astonishing biodiversity of human gender and sexuality.[607]

This is a seriously flawed understanding of how the poetic genre operates in Biblical or general hermeneutics. In fact, if we followed this line of reasoning, based on a faulty understanding of the function of the poetic genre, we would have to conclude the entire story of Paul's Revere's ride is a myth, because Henry Wadsworth Longfellow (1807-1882) speaks of the event in the form of a poem in "Paul Revere's Ride":

> Listen my children and you shall hear
> Of the midnight ride of Paul Revere,

---

607 Virginia Ramey Mollenkott, *Omnigender: A Trans-religious Approach* (Cleveland, OH: The Pilgrim Progress, 2007), 96.

On the eighteenth of April, in Seventy-five;
Hardly a man is now alive
Who remembers that famous day and year…

Using Mollenkott's understanding of the limited function of the poetic genre, that poems cannot convey historical facts, then not only must we dismiss Genesis 1-2 as a historical account, but also Jonah's prayer from the belly of the great fish (Jonah chapter 2), the prologue of the Gospel of John (which also starts with the phrase, "In the beginning…"), the kenotic hymn of Christ's incarnation, humility and crucifixion (Philippians 2:5-11) and many other passages as being non-historical poetic myths written to convey only "theological truth." The fact is the Bible employs a multitude of genres to convey actual historical events. The truth is, within historic Christianity all of the commonly held views regarding the creation week while they debate the nature of the sequence of days they all uphold the historicity of the creation of Adam in that it tells us not only *that* God created Adam and Eve from his side, but also *how* He did so.

The phenomenon of conjoined twins (also known as Siamese twins) is another example of a biological anomaly that entails individual and personal sexual identity. Would it be unethical to separate conjoined twins after birth (if they can survive the process) or should we allow them to grow up as they are and treat them as a third category of human because they too are outside the box of the "social binary construct"? Are we being presumptive and imposing a social norm on them if we separate them at birth or are we giving them a freedom to function according to biological norms as much as possible given the circumstances? These types of questions are not dissimilar to the issues related to babies born intersexual. Disorders of Sex Development may be a biological anomaly, an exception to the human male/female gender, but we cannot then justifiably reinterpret the created order by making the exceptions the determining factor in how we understand human gender and sexuality.

The Queer/Transgender Culture War

In light of what Scripture teaches in both testaments concerning the human race being created male and female I am convinced that self-identified transsexuals are misinterpreting the world around them through the lens of their experiences. Their self perception does not coincide with either science or the clear teaching of Scripture. Like the Queer Theologian who constructs a worldview from his homo-emotional desires, sexual attractions and homoerotic experiences with which he subsequently reinterprets the Bible and the created order, so too the self-identified transsexual, even those who claim to be Christian, interprets their reality through the lens of their existential experience. When they then adopt a Queer Theology they then interpret the Scriptures, especially the creation account and the incarnation of Jesus Christ, through this paradigm.

In most books on Gay Theology the issue of transgenderism is not addressed with the exception of those advocating Queer Theology. Although the "T" of "transgender" appears at the tail end of the acronym GLBT (or LGBT) more often than not the concerns, needs, questions, struggles and worldview of those who identify themselves as such are left to ride in the back of the Gay, Lesbian, and Bisexual bus. If the trajectory of Gay Theology is consistently followed, the Omnigender Worldview will be the inevitable conclusion of this growing movement in order to become truly all inclusive and affirming of every sort of sexual proclivity and self-perceived gender identity. Such a worldview seeks to put an end to the historical Biblical understanding of human gender as being either male or female as recorded in Genesis 1:27, the binary definition of marriage and sexual expression belonging strictly within the one man and one woman relationship. But, as Peter Jones points out, this is not a new worldview at all. It is a revival of an ancient form of spiritual monism (what he refers to as "One-ism"). This worldview existed in pagan cults such as the ancient Canaanite religion, the androgynous priesthood of Mesopotamia and pseudo-Christian Gnosticism. It consists of the breaking down of Biblical binary categories of male and female as well as the Creator/creature distinction and it rejects the Biblical distinctions of what Peter Jones refers to as "Two-ism": [608]

> Two-ism believes that God placed distinctions in the natural world, whereas One-ism rejects those distinctions.

[608] Peter Jones, "Androgyny: The Pagan Sexual Ideal" *Journal of the Evangelical Theological Society* 43/3 (September 2000), 443–469.

> Two-ism believes that the main distinction is the one
> between the Creator and His creatures, whereas pagan
> One-ism confuses the two, making nature divine… In the
> sexual arena, Two-ism respects the "natural" order of the
> marriage union with its heterosexual distinctions, whereas
> One-ism erases sexual distinctions and produces, in the
> name of freedom, a culture of pansexuality.[609]

There are several reasons why issues of transgender are seldom addressed by Gay Theological authors. First, within sexual minorities those who identify as gay men outnumber women who identify as lesbian. Consequently the issues and concerns of self-identified gay men are more frequently addressed than the issues of lesbians. Those who claim to be bisexual or identify as transgender are even fewer in number. These last two sexual minorities tend to be a lost as a minority within a minority with little voice of their own.

Apparently, the Gay Theological movement is not without its own form of social hierarchy and subsequent oppression (as they define the term). In the Liberation Theology construct that stems from a Darwinian/ Marxist worldview in which everything is viewed as an oppressor/ victim power struggle of the bourgeoisie and proletariat, there is a perceived tier of oppression in which homosexuality is competing against heterosexuality. In this social and political battle of the survival of the fittest, a sub-minority group such as transgendered people cannot compete in the sexual culture war. As a result, these sexual minorities have a tendency to step on each other in order to overthrow what it views as a patriarchal heterosexist "man on top" social order. The only hope then for a transgenderist within a Liberation Theology social construct is to attempt to tag along for the ride up the social ladder along with gays, lesbians and bisexuals. Or, attempt to convince the GLBs that they are politically stronger if they unite with the Queer Theology perspective and the transgender cause rather than pursue their own agenda without it. This is exactly what is taking place in the Metropolitan Community Churches and an increasing number liberal gay-affirming mainline denominations.

---

609   Peter Jones, *One or Two: Seeing A World of Difference* (Escondido, CA; Main Entry Editions, 2010), 80.

The problem is that the Gay and Lesbian Worldview is dependent on what transgendered people see as a flawed essentialist binary gender (male/female) and sexual social construct (hetero/homosexual). Yet without this essentialist binary social construct the Gay and Lesbian Worldview loses its foundation for their assertion that the homosexual orientation is a fixed biological variation of the created order. In other words, for GLBs to accept the transgender notion of sexual fluidity is to acquiesce to the idea that sexual orientation is flexible and can change. GLBs assert that their sexual desires are essential to their humanity and therefore change is *not* possible. In contrast, Queer and Transgender Theology advocates insist that change *is* possible and it is part of God's (or the goddesses') original plan for humanity. They insist that people are free to transgress and bend sexual identities and gender modalities even so far as to biologically change their sexual organs. In short, to accept the Omnigenderism is to put an end to the essentialist homosexual identity:

> If gender is as fluid as the facts of intersexuality, transsexuality, and human experience would seem to indicate, then sexual orientation may not be as rigidly fixed as some of us used to believe. D. Travers Scott questions, 'How can you be rigidly 'oriented' toward something that is amorphous, shifting, fluid, tricky, elusive?' And he warns, 'basing your identity on sexuality is like building a house on a foundation of pudding... Fixed, strictly policed identities are a right-wing project. For mature lesbian women and gay men, as Travers Scott dramatizes it, 'Homosexuality's over,' that 'Queers are not a distinct minority group neatly parallel to ethnic, religious, or biologically based groups,' and that the issue 'isn't identity, it's ideology. It's about ideology. It's about freedom, responsibility, and values.[610]

As we shall see, one of the ways in which transsexuals attempt to further their worldview is to affiliate themselves with people who are born intersexual so that they can claim to have a biological justification

---

[610]   D. Travers Scott, "Lefreak, C'est Chic! LeFag, Quelle Drag!" *PoMoSexuals*, 66-67. Citied by Virginia Ramey Mollenkott, *Omnigender: A Trans-religious Approach* (Cleveland, OH: The Pilgrim Progress, 2007), 83.

for their worldview. In doing so, they point out the anatomical anomaly of intersexuals and then assert that this phenomenon provides evidence that the binary construct of male/female genders is not true to the created order. They then conclude that their perception of themselves as transsexuals ought to also be recognized as just another variation within the created order akin to intersexuality/DSD.

Another reason why transgender issues are ignored or overlooked in the GLBT culture war is that while many self-identified gays and lesbians may be sympathetic to the cause of those who identify as transgender, others see them as a hindrance to their own cause for public social acceptability. Even within some gay-affirming churches that purportedly support GLBT causes many transgendered people find themselves sitting (figuratively speaking) on the back pews. This is because they are viewed as an inauthentic gender identity and consequently suffer from what Lisa Mottet and Justin Tanis refer to as "transphobia":

> One of the most significant challenges LGBT organizations face is that transgender (and bisexual) labels have often been added in name (the addition of the 'B' and 'T' to LGBT) without any authentic effort to integrate transgender and bisexual people and experiences into the organization. While often well-intentioned, changes in name only render the impact of adding those letters almost meaningless, as transgender people have learned the hard way. Because the addition of the 'T' only sometimes translates into concrete programs or even a genuine welcome, trans people may view the 'T' with suspicion or simply ignore it altogether. Transgender people have also encountered overt hostility in some LGBT organizations. Some people—regardless of their sexual orientation—are uncomfortable with transgender people because of the transphobia that they have learned from the larger society. Sometimes lesbian and gay people recycle the homophobia they have heard and use it against transgender people, saying things like, 'that's not natural,' or 'it's just a phase.' Not intending to be hostile, some LGB people have pointed out the real differences between being LGB and T, and the different ways in which

people experience discrimination, and have said that their organization should treat these issues differently. Whatever the reasoning, the result is that transgender people have learned, through painful experience, that lesbian, gay and bisexual spaces are not always welcoming, safe environments for them.[611]

The queer and transgender response to essentialist gay and lesbian's attempt to gain public social acceptability is that they are dependent on the so-called "gender binary construct" of what they deem to be "heterosexism." Therefore, they argue, GLBTs should not seek to accommodate themselves to the "straight world." Rather, by political and physical force they ought to disrupt the perceived oppressing system of the dominant paradigm in Western culture through the means used by activist groups such as "ACT UP" or "Queer Nation." The primary *focus* then of seeking to force change in our culture is the Church. The primary *means* of subverting the Church is by queering Biblical doctrine and terminology such as what it means to be "evangelical," the creedal and confessional doctrines of the Trinity, the incarnation, as well as redefine the definition of sin, salvation and the sacraments.

A second reason for the issues of transgenderism being seldom discussed is that the demographics of sexual orientation are difficult to establish. This is due to some people not being willing to divulge such personal information or they are not clear about the definitions. Consequently some sexual-identity minority groups may exist without being recognized which makes it is difficult to calculate what percentage of society identifies as gay, lesbian, bisexual or transgender.

The third reason why transgenderism as a sexual minority is rarely discussed is that they have not produced much in the form of written material to compete with the voices of the dominating gay and lesbian sexual proponents. What they do write tends to be more anecdotal and full of personal testimonies rather than any serious philosophical, theological or exegetical work. Consequently this minority-within-in-a-minority is being out-shouted by the competing gay/lesbian rights

---

611   Lisa Mottet and Justin Tanis, "Opening The Door to the Inclusion of Transgender People: The Nine Keys to Making Lesbian, Gay, Bisexual and Transgender Organizations Fully Transgender-Inclusive." http://www.thetaskforce.org/reports_and_research/opening_the_door, page 4.

organizations and they offer very little for serious scholarly theological interaction. The primary argument for transgenderism then comes not from a distinctively Transgender Theology, but as an application of Queer Theology.

Fourth, in an age of sexual confusion and ambiguity, people are often left pondering which block to check on a sexual survey or they may not see their sexual desires as being a definitive aspect of their identity. The goal of omnigenderism is to remove from language the gender box which makes any sort of definitive gender distinctions. It then argues for a "new" paradigm for gender and sexuality in the form of gender fluidity with androgyny being the original state of perfection in the human race. This is the same objective of Queer Theology advocates who seek to undermine ("queer") the very Bible that other Gay Theology advocates seek to base their arguments upon as being "gay friendly":

> Queer theory is a set of ideas based around the notion that identities are not fixed and do not entirely determine who we are. As a field of inquiry, queer theory shifts the emphasis away from specific acts and identities to the myriad ways in which gender and sexualities organize and even destabilize society. Queer theory claims that sexual categories shift and change. It differs from earlier gay/lesbian identity politics by arguing that sexual identity and even gender templates are not fixed but elastic... Postmodern sexualities demolish the neat social categories of sexuality and gender with multiple subjectivities and fluid desires.[612]

Queer Theology then goes on to promote a new paradigm for interpreting human biology in which there is a fluidity of human sexuality and gender, including that of Jesus Christ.[613] While all these various groups (Gay Theology, Queer Theology, Transgender Theology, Omnigender Theology) which claim to be Christian may have similar interpretations

612   Robert E. Goss, *Queering Christ: Beyond Jesus Acted Up* (Eugene, OR: The Pilgrim Press, 2007), 226-227
613   Robert Goss states, "I want to expand further the dimensions of the Queer Christ to include the Bi/Christ and the Trans/Christ... The construction of Christ need not be exclusive, for fluid categories enable Jesus to become the Drag Christ, the Leather Christ, the Heterosexual Christ, the Drag Christ, and the Lesbian Christ." Ibid, 170, 175.

of the supposed "closeted gay" relationships in the Bible and the Roman Centurion and his servant as well the so-called "clobber passages," the reality is there is a division within the GLBT community on the understanding of gender. Virginia Mollenkott interprets this division accordingly:

> Frankly, I suspect that the acceptance of gender fluidity and pluralism will be difficult for many homosexuals and bisexuals as for many heterosexuals. Unfortunately, les-bi-gay people can sometimes be as rigid and labeling as anybody else, defining our sexualities through binaries like active and passive, top and bottom, butch and femme. Sometimes stereotypes of 'masculinity' and 'femininity' control gay lives almost as much as heterosexual lives.[614]

It is for this reason that one of the primary goals of the transgenderist is to form a greater unity to the GLBT movement by bringing transgender issues and theology to the forefront with greater awareness in the GLB side of the cause. If the transgenderist is successful in achieving their goals and the trajectory of the Gay Theological movement is followed through consistently, this will undoubtedly cause a shift in the Gay Theological paradigm towards Mollenkott's Omnigender Worldview. This is none other than a revival of the pseudo-Christian cult of Neo-Gnosticism.

The Queer/Transgender Paradigm Shift

According to Mollenkott the problem with transsexuals and inter-sexuals desiring to have a sex change operation is that they, like the heterosexual/homosexual perspective, are rooting their decision in an essentialist binary gender social construct or what Susannah Cornwall refers to as the "sexually dimorphic model."[615] According to Mollenkott because the transsexual and intersexual thinks in binary categories they see no other option other than to change from one gender to the other or

---

614   Virginia Ramey Mollenkott, *Omnigender: A Trans-religious Approach* (Cleveland, OH: The Pilgrim Progress, 2007), 81.
615   Susannah Cornwall, *Sex and Uncertainty in the Body of Christ: Intersex Conditions and Christian theology* (Sheffield, England: Equinox Publishing, 2010), 7.

choose either male or female rather than remain androgynous or simply as they are, a gender male on the outside and a female gender on the inside, "...I hope that if and when gender pluralism becomes a fact, fewer people will feel the need to seek gender reassignment surgery, although some will and should have the right to do so."[616]

Mollenkott asserts that if they were to understand gender as fluid or on a grading scale they would see that they do not have to be either/or male or female but may exist in a variety of different categories:

> Transsexuality is a function of the binary gender construct, because when only two alternatives exist, a person is forced to choose one and then do whatever is necessary to present herself or himself in a way that is culturally appropriate.[617]

Transgenderists rightly see skin pigment categories of "black" or "white" as artificially constructed for in reality there is a long range of shades in skin color pigmentation. However, they then wrongly assert that gender likewise exists in a range of biological expression in the natural order of various genders with different degrees of masculinity and femininity in the human species. Subsequently they fallaciously assert that the either/or construct of human male and female genders, as recorded in Genesis 1:27, are to be dismissed in favor of a transgender or omnigender worldview of gender variation. If adopted, this worldview would require that the human language and public restrooms change in order to accommodate the new genderless paradigm and cease the use of pronouns such as "he" or "she" and society would have to be reconstructed to reflect a gender neutral culture.

Like most proponents of Gay Theology, transgenderists believe that the Old Testament is the product of an oppressive male dominating patriarchal social construct and therefore it is to be read with a "hermeneutic of suspicion."[618] Mollenkott in fact states that whatever may have broken from this oppressive mold in the New Testament was edited out of the Bible in a conspiracy of second century scribes who sought to maintain male dominance in the Church:

616   Virginia Ramey Mollenkott, *Omnigender: A Trans-religious Approach* (Cleveland, OH: The Pilgrim Progress, 2007), 59.
617   Ibid, 55.
618   Susannah Cornwall, *Sex and Uncertainty in the Body of Christ: Intersex Conditions and Christian theology* (Sheffield, England: Equinox Publishing, 2010), 22.

The idol of male primacy has been around for a very long time. Bart Ehrman describes the significant and public, high-profile role women played in the early Christian church, and explains that by the second century the battle lines were drawn between those who adhered to the early policy and those who wanted to subordinate Christian women. So important were these conflicts that the scribes who were copying texts that later became Scripture sometimes changed those texts in order to reflect their own views... Since the scribes were aware that what they were copying would be received with reverential awe, keeping women subordinate mattered enough to them to motivate their deliberately changing the texts that were to become sacred Scripture. And these texts in turn have been used to provide religions validation for the gender binary hierarchy ever since.[619]

In other words, she acknowledges that the "binary gender construct" is present in the New Testament canon, but she asserts that it was added to the text by second century scribes. Virginia Mollenkot, Theodore Jennings, Robert Goss and other Queer Theologians who assert this type of conspiratorial thinking believe that Jesus established a Church which was later reconstructed by Paul or second century Church leaders. They then go on to assert that in order to rediscover the true life and teaching of Jesus we must read the Gnostic "gospel" accounts that were "suppressed" from the canon of Scripture such as The Gospel of Thomas [620] and the Secret Gospel of Mark at the Council of Nicaea.[621]

This supposed secret and suppressed knowledge of the real Jesus, like the androgynous view of Adam and supposed sexual conduct

---

619   Virginia Ramey Mollenkott, *Omnigender: A Trans-religious Approach* (Cleveland, OH: The Pilgrim Progress, 2007), 20.

620   Patrick M. Chapman, *"Thou Shalt Not Love": What Evangelicals Really Say to Gays* (New York, NY: Haiduk Press, 2008), 105; Theodore W. Jennings Jr., *The Man Jesus Loved* (Cleveland, OH: The Pilgrim Press, 2003), 157-160; Virginia Ramey Mollenkott, *Omnigender: A Trans-religious Approach* (Cleveland, OH: The Pilgrim Progress, 2007), 120.

621   Theodore W. Jennings Jr., *The Man Jesus Loved* (Cleveland, OH: The Pilgrim Press, 2003), 114-130, 233-234.; Robert Williams, *Just as I Am, A Practical Guide to Being Out, Proud, and Christian* (Perennial, 1993), 118–20.

of Christ, has its roots in ancient Gnosticism. It was also part of the
Canaanite religion that had an androgynous priesthood that occupied
the land promised to the descendants of Abraham, which YHWH judged
and forbade the Israelites to imitate, the religion of the Roman Empire
of the first century, as well as a multitude of other pagan religions as
Peter Jones point out:

> Even though separated by many centuries, a historical and
> "theological" connection between the Mesopotamian *as-*
> *sinnus*, the Canaanite *qedeshim*, the Scythian *ennares*, and
> the Syrian *galli* is not difficult to imagine. They took on
> the same androgynous appearance, engaging in the same
> ecstatic behavior, including self-mutilation, were associat-
> ed with occultic spirituality, and so in many ways occupied
> a similar liminal relationship to "normal" society. Such
> parallels suggest a profound and necessary connection
> growing out of the same ideological pagan root.

> Later in the second and third centuries of the Christian
> church, the Gnostics were credited by their adversaries
> with mystery celebrations involving carnal knowledge.
> The charge is credible because "Christian" Gnosticism
> was the attempt to Christianize pagan spirituality, even to
> the point of adopting some form of androgyny. Hippolytus
> (AD 170–236) reports that one particular gnostic sect, the
> Naasenes, who worshipped the Serpent (*Naas* in Hebrew)
> of Genesis, attended the secret ceremonies of the mysteries
> of the Great Mother in order "to understand the 'universal
> mystery.'" Like modern syncretists who are encouraged to
> cross over into other religions, the Gnostics believed reli-
> gious truth was one, to be found everywhere, and so they
> crossed over into pagan spirituality as a matter of religious
> principle. The most explicit testimony is from Irenaeus
> who says: "They prepare a bridal chamber and celebrate
> mysteries." A homosexual encounter is perhaps insinuat-
> ed in the "Secret Gospel of Mark." At the very least, the
> final logion 114 of the *Gospel of Thomas* appears to be an

invitation to spiritual androgyny. All this would justify
the judgment of Burkert that "certain Gnostic sects seem
to have practiced mystery initiations, imitating or rather
outdoing the pagans ..." [622]

Mollenkott's ultimate goal then is to deconstruct, what Robert Goss
refers to as "queering," the text. This entails reading back into the text
what was supposedly removed in order to create a basis for a new egalitarian gender fluid understanding of humanity and a new paradigm for
society.[623]

The Revival of Gnostic Androgyny

The importance of the Genesis creation account for the Biblical
Christian Worldview cannot be overstated. While a sequential 24 hour
view of the days in the six-day creation week is not essential to Historic
Christianity (as orthodox Christians might also argue for a day-age or
literary view), the Genesis record as a historical account of the origin
of man is foundational for the Christian faith.[624] Genesis chapters 1-3
as a historical record provides us with an essential understanding of the
created order. It also provides a basis for a Biblical understanding of
the biological and spiritual condition of the human species, the original
covenant between God and mankind, and a proper understanding of
God's intention for marriage. It is in this text that we see the breaking
of the first covenant which resulted in sin and death in the world as well
as the reason why the Son of God became flesh in order to ratify a new
covenant that atones for sin, provides redemption for the human race
and will restore the entire created order.

622   Peter Jones, "Androgyny: The Pagan Sexual Ideal" *Journal of the Evangelical
Theological Society* 43/3 (September 2000), 452.
623   Virginia Ramey Mollenkott, *Omnigender: A Trans-religious Approach* (Cleveland, OH: The Pilgrim Progress, 2007), xi.
624   It must be noted that there are many who hold to a young earth 6-day creation
week, an old earth day-age creation week and those who hold to a literary framework approach committed to the infallibility and inerrancy of Scripture that are in
agreement concerning the historicity of Adam, Eve, the serpent and the fall. For more
reading on this issue see: J. Ligon Duncan III (Author), David W. Hall (Author), Hugh
Ross (Author), Gleason L. Archer (Author), Lee Irons (Author), Meredith G. Kline
(Author), David G. Hagopian (Editor), *The Genesis Debate: Three Views on the Days
of Creation* (Global Publishing Services, 2000).

To negate, deny, undermine or "queer" the historicity of Genesis 1-3 is to attack the very foundation of the historic Christian faith. It is no wonder then why so many assaults on the Biblical Christian Worldview at one point or another seek to undermine the historicity of this text. We also see in Genesis 3 that this was the very thing that the serpent sought to undermine. He challenged the woman to question God's interpretation of the created order, particularly the Tree of the Knowledge of Good and Evil, and queer it with his own interpretation, "The serpent said to the woman, 'You surely will not die! For God knows that in the day you eat from it your eyes will be opened, and you will be like God, knowing good and evil'" (Genesis 3:4-5).

The exaltation of the autonomous self to become as God, determining for oneself what is good and evil is at the very heart of the Gay, Queer and Trans/Omnigender worldview that, as we shall see, defies the God of Scripture. According to Queer/Trans/Omnigender Theology, the Bible teaches that Adam was originally androgynous before Eve was created. In order to convince his readers of the androgyny of Adam, Justin Tanis mistranslates "man" as "earth-being" in his rendering the creation account:

> Then God said, "Let us make an earth-being in our image, after our likeness; and let them have dominion over the fish of the sea, and over the birds of the air, and over the cattle, and over all the earth, and over every creeping thing that creeps upon the earth." So God created humanity in God's own image, in the image of God, God created humanity in God's own image, in the image of God, God created them; male and female God created them. And God blessed them" (Genesis 1:26-28a).[625]

Based on this faulty interpretation and translation of the text Tanis goes on to assert that God's true nature reflects an androgynous image from which the human race was created:

> ...the word *Elohim*, is a plural form and the use of 'our' is simply consistent with the noun form. The use of the plural

---

625   Justin Tanis, *Transgendered: Theology, Ministry and Communities of Faith* (Cleveland, OH: The Pilgrim Press, 2003), 55.

could refer to the plurality of God's own being – male, female, and beyond – which is broader than what can be understood in a single term of gender. Holly Boswell states in her article 'The Spirit of Transgender,' 'Adam mirrored an androgynous God before the split into Eve.[626]

Consequently, not only are transsexuals confused about their gender identity so is YHWH:

> God 'himself' is unsure whether he is plural or singular... Significantly the slippage extends from the God(s) to the human(s) created in his/their image... Thus despite the appearance of a world ordered and sustained by exclusive and fixed definitions, God's own blurred and slipping self-definition suggests that things might be otherwise. This world might in fact be as inherently indeterminable as the identity that creates it.[627]

It is faulty to assert that if God is referred to in the male gender as "Father," as some feminists do, that this then means that male is God.[628] The Bible does not teach that God has male genitalia for God is spirit (John 4:24). God is not in essence male and so the eternal Father and the eternal Son are not male in their divine nature. Nor is the Holy Spirit a gendered male in His divine essence. Yet, God has told us how to understand the Trinitarian relationship of the Godhead using the analogy of familial human language and so that we can know how we are to relate to God using male personal pronouns. Likewise, the feminine gender references to Israel and subsequently the New Testament Church are a familial metaphor to help us understand how the people of God are to relate to their God and Savior. Individually all Christians are metaphorically "sons of God" (Romans 8:14-15, 19, 23) and corporately we are "the bride of Christ." (Ephesians 5:27). Feminist and Transgender Theology advocates are confused on this point when they see "sons" as somehow excluding them and insist on saying, "sons *and daughters* of

---

626   Ibid, 56-57.
627   Ibid, 57.
628   Mary Daly, *Beyond God the Father: Towards a Philosophy of Women's Liberation* (London: The Women's Press, 1986), 19.

God" or that the New Testament gender-bends as if it refers to men as "brides of Christ." The New Testament does not refer to any individual as a bride of Christ for Jesus is not a polygamist with many wives. Instead, He has a single spiritual bride that corporately consists of all believers by means of the New Covenant.

Transgender Theology advocates misconstrue the metaphorical use of gendered familial language to refer to God and subsequently androgynize Him. They then go on to assert the original state of Adam before the creation of his wife Eve was androgynous as well:

> The earth-being (*adam*) created originally is both male and female, created in the image of God. This view is strongly supported by the Hebrew text, which uses the term *adam*, not as a name as is currently familiar in English, but in description of this being created from the earth. The word *adam* is a play upon the Hebrew word for earth, *'adamah.* Rather than translating the word as a proper name, a more accurate rendering of the word would be 'earthling' or 'earth-being.' Originally the earthling was one without gender differentiation, encompassing both male and female.[629]

Virginia Mollenkott likewise asserts:

> When this hermaphrodite earthling is later placed under a deep sleep, he/she is divided into the human male and female. From this perspective, intersexuals are not only part of God's original plan, they are primarily so... From this angle, hermaphrodites or intersexuals could be viewed as reminders of Original Perfection.[630]

There are several reasons why "earth-being" is an illegitimate rendering for Adam before the creation of Eve and the subsequent assertion that he was androgynous, a hermaphrodite or intersexual. First, through-

---

629   Justin Tanis, *Transgendered: Theology, Ministry and Communities of Faith* (Cleveland, OH: The Pilgrim Press, 2003), 58.
630   Virginia Ramey Mollenkott, *Omnigender: A Trans-Religious Approach* (Cleveland, OH: Pilgrim Press, 2001), 91.

out the entire narrative, the first human is referred to as the man (Hebrew: *ha-adam*) and after the creation of the woman in Genesis 2:23, the first one created continues to be referred to as *ha-adam*. In other words, the text does not say, "...and when the woman was created Adam became a male..."[631] Later that same human male is unambiguously referred to as "Adam" in Genesis 3:17 (i.e., as a proper name; without the definite article). Second, in the immediate context the *adam* that was created in Genesis 1 and was told to till the ground in Genesis 2:15 is the same *adam* that is male and said to be the one who will after the fall till the ground by the sweat of his brow in the midst of thorns and thistles in Genesis 3:17-18. In other words, the sexual and gender identity of the first one created remained the same before and after the creation of the woman. Third, later in redemptive-history the Apostle Paul tells us that the woman came from the man ("...the woman originates from the man..." 1 Corinthians 11:12), not that the man and the woman are the product of the splitting of an androgynous creature into two separate sexual identities.[632]

---

631   As Richard Davidson states, "A second facet of human sexual theology emerging from Gen. 1-2 is that God created the bipolarity of the sexes from the beginning. The popular idea that Gen 1:27 presents *ha adam* as an ideal androgynous (or hermaphroditic) being later split into two sexes cannot be sustained from the text. "The plural in v. 27 ('he created them') is intentionally contrasted with the singular ('him') and prevents one from assuming the creation of an originally androgynous man." This is confirmed by the following verse (1:28), where God blessed *them* and commanded *them* to be fruitful and multiply; only a heterosexual couple, not a bisexual creature, could fulfill this command. Further confirmation of an original duality of sexes and not an androgynous creature is the parallel passage of 5:2, where the plural "them/they" is again employed: 'Male and female he created *them*, and he blessed them and named them 'Humankind' when *they* were created." *Flame of Yahweh: Sexuality in the Old Testament* (Peabody, MA: Hendriksen Publishing, 2007), 19.

632   As Richard Davidson states, "Regarding Gen 2, a number of more recent studies have revived an older theory that the original *ha adam* described in this chapter was androgynous, one creature incorporating two sexes, or "a sexually undifferentiated earth creature." But such a hypothesis is not supported by the text. According to 2:7-8, 15-16, what God creates before woman is called *ha adam*, "the man," better translated as "the human." After the creation of the woman, this creature is denoted by the same term (vv. 22-23). Nothing has changed in the makeup of "the human" during his sleep except the loss of a rib." Ibid, 20.

But this view of an androgynous Adam is not new as it is rooted in pseudo-Christian Gnosticism and later reappeared in theosophy.[633] Theosophy, or *divine wisdom*, refers either to the mysticism of philosophers who believe that they can understand the nature of God by direct apprehension, without revelation, or it refers to the esotericism of eclectic collectors of mystical and occult philosophies. Proponents of Theosophy, like the Gnostics before them, claim to be handing down the great secrets of some ancient wisdom. As Peter Jones points out, the antithesis between esotericism and exotericism is a key distinction between the Biblical Worldview (Two-ism) and the pagan or Neo-Gnostic Worldview of Transgender Theology (One-ism/Monism):

> One-ism (all-is-one) is an esoteric ["a quest for the divine within the self"] read on reality. It maintains that everything can be explained by everything else. There are no qualitative distinctions to be found in the universe. The world creates itself and humans are "co-creators" along with everything else. In this system, reality is One. Two-ism (All-is-two) is an exoteric ["a quest for a divinity that stands outside the self and outside human reality"] read on reality. It maintains that the world is made by a Creator who is uncreated and radically different from his creatures. There are two forms of existence: the created and the one who created it. The two, while deeply related, are qualitatively distinct.[634]

The One-ism of Theosophical mysticism is rooted in the philosophy of Plato (427-347 B.C.), Plotinus (205-270 A.D.) and other neo-Platonists such as Jakob Boehme (1575-1624) and Franz von Baader (1765– 1841). Long before Transgender Theology came on the scene Franz von Baader postulated that the androgyne had existed at the beginning (Adam) and would appear again at the end of time.[635]

---

633   Peter Jones, *The Stolen Identity: The Conspiracy to Reinvent Jesus* (Eastbourne, England; David C. Cook; New edition, 2005), 99-102.

634   Peter Jones, *One or Two: Seeing A World of Difference* (Escondido, CA; Main Entry Editions, 2010), 87, 88.

635   Peter Jones, "Androgyny: The Pagan Sexual Ideal" *Journal of the Evangelical Theological Society* 43/3 (September 2000), 453

The Revival of Gnostic Christology

According to the Apostle Paul, Jesus Christ fulfilled the role of a second Adam. Whereas the first Adam brought sin and death through his transgression, the second Adam brought life through His one act of obedience on the cross and the resurrection (Romans 5:19; 1 Corinthians 15:22, 45). According to Queer and Transgender Theology it follows then that if the first Adam before the creation of Eve was androgynous that transsexuals and intersexuals (hermaphrodites) are a "throw back" to the original perfection of the human race. Therefore, the perfect man and second Adam, Jesus Christ, would likewise be born intersexual or androgynous:[636]

> Edward L Kessel... explained if we believe Scripture that Mary had never been with a man when she conceived Jesus, then "Jesus' conception, gestation, and birth were parthenogenetic." He cites the views of several research scientists who separately reached the conclusion that virgin birth is "probable among humans." He also explains that virgin-conceived offspring are always chromosomal females, and that "because human beings have the same X-Y kind of sex determination found in other mammals, with the female... possessing two X chromosomes, Jesus was conceived as a chromosomal female." And because "no animal can change the genotype that it receives at conception, Jesus remained female always in this chromosomal sense."

How then to account for Jesus' maleness according to the gospel witness? Kessel explains that Jesus underwent a

---

636   Patrick S. Cheng states, "Theologians have also started to write about the intersex Jesus Christ, or the Jesus Christ who has physical attributes (either genitalia or chromosomes) of both sexes... So to the extent that Jesus Christ is a product of parthenogenesis and is traditionally depicted with male genitals Jesus Christ is actually an intersex person! This observation is important because intersex theology is an emerging area of queer theology, just as the LGBT community is becoming more aware of the intersex political movement and organizations like the Intersex Society of North America." *Radical Love: An Introduction to Queer Theology* (Seabury Books; 1 edition, 2011), 83, 91.

sex reversal to the male phenotype, adding "biologists are generally agreed that sex reversal, like parthenogenesis, may sometimes occur in human beings as it does in lower animals." He describes several scenarios by which the sex reversal might have occurred, and several genetic scenarios concerning the probable genotypes of Mary and Jesus. But for our purposes, the important factor is Kessel's conclusion: "The female embryo Jesus of the Virgin Conception and Incarnation became the two-sexed infant of the Virgin Birth who was the androgynous Christ, bearing both the chromosomal identification of a woman and the phenotypic anatomy of a man."

...A chromosomally female, phenotypically male Jesus would come as close as a human body could come to a perfect image of a God... it seems to me that from the perspective of his findings, intersexuals come closer than anybody to a physical resemblance to Jesus... any church that worships in Christ's name should be willing to let go of an inaccurate and unjust binary gender construct that does not allow room for a Christ Himself who is also Christ Herself![637]

This is a classic example of what happens when the Bible is interpreted through extra-Biblical resources and the reader seeks a naturalistic understanding of the supernatural. The parthenogenetic conception and birth of Jesus Christ is a completely naturalist attempt to understand and explain the virgin birth of the Messiah.[638] In the Scriptures when Mary asks the angel, "How can this be, since I am a virgin?" (Luke 1:34) she is specifically told that the conception of the Son of God will take place, not through a natural process like parthenogenetic fungi or plants, but through the means of the Holy Spirit, "The Holy Spirit will come upon you, and the power of the Most High will overshadow you;

637   Virginia Ramey Mollenkott, *Omnigender: A Trans-religious Approach* (Cleveland, OH: The Pilgrim Progress, 2007), 115-116.
638   Parthenogenesis derives from the Greek for "virgin birth," *parthenos*, meaning "virgin" and *genesis* meaning "birth," and is the means of reproduction among all fungi and many plants and animals, including lizards, bees and some fish.

and for that reason the holy Child shall be called the Son of God" (Luke 1:34). Likewise, her husband was told, "Joseph, son of David, do not be afraid to take Mary as your wife; for the Child who has been conceived in her is of the Holy Spirit" (Matthew 1:20-21). While there is a great deal of mystery to the incarnation of the Logos as the Bible does not explain how metaphysically God can take on a human nature, it remains that what did not happen is an event that is common place in the animal kingdom. The result of this exegetical monstrosity is a feminized Christ (or Christa) that becomes the deconstructed savior of feminist theology which assumes that a distinctly male Jesus cannot represent the spiritual needs of women.

The idea of the original man and subsequently Jesus Christ being androgynous comes out of a recognition that if Adam was always distinctly male then the creation story supports a binary construct which is not friendly towards the transgender worldview and a feminist misconceived notion of patriarchy. It is then argued by some feminist writers that if Jesus is only male and not feminine or androgynous then He cannot be the savior of women. What women then need is a savior who as a woman can identify with women can subsequently be sympathetic to their unique causes, struggles, trials and tribulations.[639] This notion that Jesus must be a woman (or at least a half woman intersexual) in order to be sympathetic of the plight of women and their savior is nonsensical. Jesus was a Jewish male and yet Gentiles do not need a Gentile Messiah, nor do Northern Europeans need a Northern European (or African, Asian etc.) messiah in order to have a human savior who understands their plight. Indeed, despite not being specialized in the way these theologians would seem to prefer, Jesus sympathizes with our weaknesses (Hebrews 4:15). When we look at the specifics of Jesus' temptation we actually find that they are far weightier than what any of us have had to contend with in our battles. Who of us have been tempted to turn stone to bread after fasting for forty days or to avoid the cross and be given the kingdoms of the world by bowing down and worshipping the devil? (Matthew 4:1-11)

"... there is no longer male and female..."

639   For an excellent response see: Micah Daniel Carter, "Reconsidering the Maleness of Jesus" in *The Journal for Biblical Manhood & Womanhood* Volume 13 No. 1 (Spring 2008) http://www.cbmw.org/Vol-13-No-1/

Egalitarian feminists insist that the Apostle Paul's phrase "there is no longer male and female" (Galatians 3:28) indicates an end to all social role distinctions. Transgender advocates likewise assert that it presents a new ideal of an end to the ontological gender distinctions of men and women of the original created order.[640] It is argued that the social role distinctions between husbands and wives is intended to be put to an end. Accordingly, the phrase "no longer male and female" is to be understood *economically* so that there are no longer any social roles or ethnic classes.[641]

Queer Theology advocates on the other hand interpret the phrase *ontologically*, that the new age is ending sexual and gender distinctions as Patrick S. Cheng states:

> Jesus Christ is the embodiment of radical love because Jesus crosses gender boundaries. As Paul writes in his letter to the Galatians, "there is no longer male and female" in Christ Jesus. To that end, a number of theologians have written about the transgender Jesus Christ, or the Jesus Christ who dissolves the boundaries between "female" and "male."[642]

640   Many Gay Theologians also want to add to Paul's words by asserting that it also implies "…there is neither heterosexual or homosexual…" although such an assertion cannot be justified either directly or by inference from the text as Rick Brentlinger states, "Since the first century church changed her mind and accepted saved Gentiles as equal members in the body of Christ, this analogy concludes that the twenty-first church should change her mind and accept saved homosexuals as equal members in the body of Christ." *Gay Christian 101 - Spiritual Self-Defense For Gay Christians* (2007), 122; See also R.D. Weekly, *Homosexianity* (Judah First Ministries, 2009), 132.

641   Virginia Mollenkott states, "It is worth noticing that the three statements in Galatians 3:28 about the New Creation's transcendence of race/ethnicity, class and gender are not precisely parallel. This lack of parallelism is reflected in the New Revised Standard Version translation: 'There is no longer Jew or Greek, there is no longer slave or free, there is no longer male and female; for all of you are one in Christ Jesus.' If there is anything to be found in that grammatical shift from *or* to *and*, what might it be? Does it reflect a belief that women and men are so necessary to one another that *or* cannot be spoken, because without either could be no humankind, a fact Paul emphasized in 1 Corinthians 11:11-12? And does it point toward a time when instead of separate gender obligations, both physical maleness-femaleness and masculine-feminine social roles locate themselves comfortably and without fear of reprisal?" *Omnigender: A Trans-religious Approach* (Cleveland, OH: The Pilgrim Progress, 2007), xii.

642   Patrick S. Cheng, *Radical Love: An Introduction to Queer Theology* (Seabury Books; 1 edition, 2011), 82.

Likewise, Transgenderist Justin Tanis concludes from these words that Paul is asserting the end of gender distinction in the new economy in Jesus Christ:

> This verse of Scripture calls into question, and ultimately into accountability, the human-divisions of race, class, and gender... Galatians 3:28 signified for me a radical shift in my understanding of what it meant to be in Christ. I was no longer bound to the divisions of gender, or to the roles our society assigns to women, but was set free by Christ... If those of us who are Christians would follow this mandate, such a change would have a profound impact on how we live and are. Among other things, transgendered people would not be excluded from or just tolerated in communities of faith but welcomed as equals; nor would distinctions be placed on the roles of women and men in our religious bodies.[643]

According to Liberation Theology Feminists and Gay/Queer/ Transgender Theologians the Apostle Paul was a product of his age – a misogynistic self-hating (even closeted!) homophobe since in numerous other places he upholds the gender role distinctions in the family and the Church along with the Apostle Peter (1 Corinthians 11:2-16, Ephesians 5:22-31, 1 Timothy 2:8-15 and 1 Peter 3:1-7). Yet they also assert that Galatians 3:28 (written by Paul) puts an end to all sex and gender roles in society and suggest that Paul is speaking of an eschatological age in which there will no longer any gender differentiation in the human race. This inconsistency is embraced by transgenderist Susannah Cornwall, who concludes from her reading of the text:

> The end of male-and-female is the end of an exclusive, heteronormative system wherein humans are completed as humans only by so-called sexual complimentary system...
> This is particularly interesting in thinking through visions of a society where sex and gender do not work as a binary

---

643   Justin Tanis, *Transgendered: Theology, Ministry and Communities of Faith* (Cleveland, OH: The Pilgrim Press, 2003), 80.

but rather as a continuum or a multiplicity, and where anatomy (particularly genital anatomy) is not unproblematically
used as a cipher for identity. If male-and-female is passing
away, then it need not stand for or encompass everyone;
human bodies need not be altered to 'fit' it, particularly
before those who live in them (like neonates with intersex/
DSD conditions) can express an option... The end – the
cessation – of male-and-female is the end – the *telos* – for
humanity.[644]

The only logical conclusion is that either Paul is in conflict with his
own worldview or the Gay/Queer/Transgender Theology advocates are
misreading and misapplying this passage entirely. To rightly interpret
Paul's statement that there is "no longer male and female" we need
to look at it in its larger literary and Redemptive-Historical context.
If we notice what precedes and follows our passage we find that Paul
is referring to a transitioning from being "under the law" (the Mosaic
Covenant) in the first Adam to being in Christ the second Adam (the
New Covenant), which brings God's people from being in a status of
slave under a pedagogue to the status of a son who has received his
inheritance (Galatians 4:4:1-9).

In short, the thrust of the passage does not concern a fundamental shift in the *social* (master-slave) relationships in society since the
apostles do not abolish institutional slavery. Instead they exhort slaves
to obey masters for the sake of the gospel and for masters to treat their
Christian servants as brothers (Ephesians 6:5,9; Colossians 3:22; Titus
2 2:9; 1 Peter 2:18). Nor do the apostles advocate a radical change in the
current or future *biological* or *ontological* state of humans for they exhort husbands to treat their wives honorably as the "weaker vessel" who
is "a fellow heir of the grace of life" (1 Peter 3:7). In its redemptive-historical context Paul is commenting in this text on the *soteriological* and
hence *ecclesiastical* status of various persons in that there has been a
fundamental change in *who* and *on what basis* a person has access to
God. For example, in Herod's Temple there were various divisions such
as the court of the Gentiles which divided Jews from Greeks as well as

644   Susannah Cornwall, *Sex and Uncertainty in the Body of Christ: Intersex Conditions and Christian Theology* (Gender, Theology and Spirituality) (Sheffield, England:
Equinox Publishing, 2010), 73, 74.

barriers for the common Jew to gaining access to the throne of God, since only the High Priest could pass through the veil and enter the Holy of Holies once a year (Exodus 26:33; Hebrews 9:7). Now that all have been made one in Christ they now have equal access to God (Ephesians 2:13-14).

Paul goes on to state that historically even the sons of Israel had the status of slaves as they were kept under the tutelage of the pedagogical function of the law. But now by faith in Christ, who has entered the temple made without hands with His own blood (Hebrews 9:11-12), all have been made mature sons with the full rights to the throne of grace as co-heirs with Jesus (Galatians 3:23-29). This is the fundamental change that has taken place in the New Covenant which Paul is addressing both in his epistle to the Galatians and the Romans as he states, "For I am not ashamed of the gospel, for it is the power of God for salvation to everyone who believes, to the Jew first and also to the Greek" (Romans 1:16).

Of course, such a fundamental soteriological and ecclesiastical changes also carry with them various social changes as well within the body of Christ such as when Paul exhorted Philemon to receive Onesimus, his runaway slave, "...no longer as a slave but more than a slave, as a beloved brother" (Philemon 16). But this by no means put an end to the different roles, responsibilities and distinctions in God's economy in which ontological equality does not mean that there are no role responsibilities as the apostles teach elsewhere. Just as the Father, Son and Holy Spirit have different roles in redemptive history, so also do husbands and wives within the family and men and women within the Church.

In fact, Paul in making his point borrows the language from the creation account, as the phrase "male and female" is an allusion to Septuagint translation of Genesis 1:27 ("male and female He created them"). Thus the New Covenant restores the creation of the original human (Adam) having been made one in Christ (one person) which brings about a unity in the Church akin to the unity between a husband and wife ("Therefore a man leaves his father and his mother and cleaves to his wife, and they become one flesh") as Paul also uses this language to refer to relationship between Christ and His bride (Ephesians 5:31-2). The idea then is that the New Covenant brings about a restoration of the

original state of mankind, which specifically designates differences between "male and female" rather than obliterating the distinctions within
the oneness of humanity established in Genesis 1:27. Elsewhere Paul
speaks of the various roles and gifts within the body of Christ, some
of which are more visible and others less so and yet all are required to
perform their function and just because some parts of the body receive
less prominence (a foot, an internal organ etc.) than the face or the eye,
"…it is not for this reason any the less a part of the body" (1 Corinthians
12:15-16). So also it is with the role of the husband and the wife within
the family and men and women within the Church. The phrase "there
is no longer male and female" then means that in Christ there is a soteriological equality between men and women as both have equal access
to grace.

Sexual and Gender Differentiation:
The Prohibition of Cross-Dressing

One of the most misconstrued concepts in Queer/Transgender
Theology is the denial that human gender categories of male and female
was created by God. They insist that this is entirely a human social
construct. In their rejection of the clear teaching of Genesis 1:27 they
put forth three primary reasons why the Biblical understanding of binary gender ought to be rejected. First, they point to the anomaly of
intersexuals which we have also noted is not a normal, healthy variance
but merely one of many potential birth defects that affect human limbs
and organs.

Second, they argue for egalitarianism in which they confuse ontological equality with social and role differentiation. As previously
stated, this argument flies in the face of the doctrine of the Trinity in
which we see an ontological equality with an economic subordination
in the Godhead as well as multiple Biblical passages that teach that the
husband is the head of the wife just as Christ is the head of the Church
(Ephesians 5:23; 1 Corinthians 11:3).

The third argument is to point to various types of culturally determined signs of gender such as forms of clothing, household tasks and
so forth, what we might think of as gender signifiers, which change
in different climates, societies and eras. They then conclude that since

these signifiers are not universal but culturally derived, then all des-
ignations of gender are merely manifestations of particular culturally
relative constructs. They then conclude that there are no significant
biological or God ordained role distinctions between men and women,
"Such variations are enough to prove that there is no universally innate
'masculinity' and 'femininity' and, therefore, that those concepts neither
follow any universal law nor constitute the will of God."[645]

The primary text that addresses this issue is Deuteronomy 22:5
which states, "A woman shall not wear man's clothing, nor shall a man
put on a woman's clothing; for whoever does these things is an abomination to the LORD your God." Virginia Ramey Mollenkott notes:

> Religious leaders often condemn transvestites under the
> rubric of Deuteronomy 22:5... Or they might refer to
> David's curse upon the house of Joab, wishing Joab's
> family might always contain someone with gonorrhea,
> someone leprous, someone violent, someone hungry, and
> someone who holds a spindle [that is, a man who enacts
> female behaviors, a transgender person]' (2 Sam. 3:29).[646]

She then goes on to state that this passage (like all the other passages
which condemn same-sex acts) cannot be applied to modern people in
a different culture:

> It would appear that in ancient Judaism and in the early
> Christian Church, there were people whom we would
> call transgender. And apparently they were surrounded by
> social disapproval. But does this mean that all these cen-
> turies later, and in entirely different cultures, God is dead-
> set against people who cross-dress or enact gender roles
> that do not match their bodies of birth?... Any sincerely
> religious person who believes that women and men are
> equally created in God's image should think twice before
> invoking biblical prohibitions against cross-dressing and

---

645   Virginia Ramey Mollenkott, *Omnigender: A Trans-religious Approach* (Cleveland, OH: The Pilgrim Progress, 2007), 4.
646   Ibid, 103.

same-sex love. Because these prohibitions are associated with the attitude that femaleness is a pollutant, they have no place within a democratic and fair-minded society, let alone in a contemporary church, synagogue, or mosque.[647]

Contrary to this reactionary feminist assertion, nowhere is Scripture is there any indication that "femaleness is a pollutant" anymore than maleness was a pollutant because they *both* had to periodically undergo a ritual baptism (washing) due to bodily ejaculations (Leviticus 15:16-17; Deuteronomy 23:10). What needs to be understood concerning a passage such as Deuteronomy 22:5 is that while what constitutes "man's clothing" or "woman's clothing" may change depending on the climatic environment or cultural shifts in fashion, this text indicates that the function of clothing is more than a means of maintaining modesty. Scripture gives us numerous examples of how clothing served as a role signifier so that a person's religious, social, or vocation was often designated by their clothing. Just as the High Priest had a garment that designated his function (Exodus 28:6-14), men and women were likewise to provide some form of designation of their gender. In a similar fashion, while there may be some variances from city to city, modern police officers wear a uniform that designates their roles and responsibilities as do civil judges and many clergy. Clothes act as markers for how the wearer is to live and function and how others are supposed to respond to that person. While the specific form may be culturally determinative the underlying principle is universal. The clerical garb of the high priest, the uniform of a police officer or the clothes of a man or woman send a signal as to who they are, their role in society and how others are to respond to them and what their duties are in a given culture. What is crucial is that the distinctions be maintained, not whether the husband or the wife does the gardening or takes out the garbage and clearly both have a part in instructing children (Deuteronomy 6:7; Proverbs 1:8; Ephesians 6:4).

The prohibition of Deuteronomy 22:5 then reveals God's will that men and women in some form or fashion have clear gender distinctions and that their clothing serve as a signifier. To do otherwise is to drift into the androgyny that is a common phenomenon in pagan cultures. C.F. Keil rightly states that God's created order entails distinctions and the

647   Virginia Ramey Mollenkott, *Omnigender: A Trans-religious Approach* (Cleveland, OH: The Pilgrim Progress, 2007), 104, 105.

prohibition against cross-dressing is intended to maintain what pagan cultures obliterated, the distinction between man and woman:

> As the property of a neighbor was to be sacred in the estimation of an Israelite, so also the divine distinction of the sexes, which was kept sacred in the civil life by the clothing peculiar to each sex, was not to be less but even more sacredly observed... The immediate design of this prohibition was not to prevent licentiousness, or to oppose idolatrous practices... but to maintain the sanctity of that distinction of the sexes which was established by the creation of man and woman, and in relation to which Israel was not to sin. Every violation or wiping out of this distinction – such even, for example, as the emancipation of a woman – was unnatural and therefore an abomination in the sight of God.[648]

Gender is created, not eternal. God created it and has told how we are to relate to each other differently and how we are to refer to the Almighty. God the Father of Jesus is a "He" not a "she", not that He has male genitalia but rather God has told us how to refer to Him as a means for us to understand how we relate to Him. The husband/wife relationship is a familial mirror of the relationship between God and His people as well the father/son relationship. The economic (not ontological) subordinate gender paradigm is created and mandated in the created order and is maintained throughout Scripture in both Testaments.

Conclusion

Gay/Queer/Omnigender Theology proponents object to the argument that self-identified transgendered people are confused concerning their gender identity. To grant the possibility that transgender is the result of a developed mental and emotional disorder is to be willing to admit that their interpretation of their feelings is wrong. Sadly, many people when they experience distress and anxiety as a result of a desire to be a member of the opposite sex such that they feel like "a woman

648   C.F. Keil, *Keil & Delitzsch, Commentary on the Old Testament: Volume 1 – The Pentateuch* (Peabody, MA; Hendrickson Publishers, 2001), 945.

in a man's body" undergo sex reassignment surgery (SRS) through a medical operation and consume hormone supplements which alters their physical sexual characteristics in an attempt to realign their bodily characteristics to reflect their perceived psychological/social gender identity. While the focus of this book has been on same-sex acts the fact is the Gay Theological movement also includes lesbians, gays (male homosexuals), bisexuals (people having sex with both sexes) and the so-called transgendered.

Gay Theology proponents insist that being homosexual is a "gift from God" and to attempt to change one's sexual attractions is to reject a gift from God insisting, "God makes no mistakes." While it is true that God does not err, such an assertion fails to take into consideration the consequences of the fall. It is hypocritical to tell one segment of their own movement "change is not possible" and the other that "change is preferable" rather than living according to the objective moral standard of God's revealed will.

Chapter 20
The Cult of the
Metropolitan Community Church

The *foundation* of the historic Christian Church is Jesus Christ and the apostles (Ephesians 2:20). The *only* authorized epistemologically authoritative starting point of the Church then is the Word of God found solely in the canon of Scripture which was completed by the apostles and confirmed by the Church. The entirety of the Christian faith then rests on a correct understanding of and humble submission to, both the written and incarnate Word of God who alone is the final revelation of the Father (John 1:1, 14, 18; 14:9). If we deviate from either one of these we will slide into apostasy. Throughout the history of the Church false teachers, wolves in shepherd's clothing, have arisen from time to time spreading their destructive heresies in the congregation seeking to lead people astray. But we are not left without a means of discerning false prophets and heretical teaching as Jesus exhorted the disciples:

> Beware of the false prophets, who come to you in sheep's clothing, but inwardly are ravenous wolves. So every good tree bears good fruit, but the bad tree bears bad fruit. You will know them by their fruits. Grapes are not gathered from thorn bushes nor figs from thistles, are they? So every good tree bears good fruit, but the bad tree bears bad fruit. A good tree cannot produce bad fruit, nor can a bad tree produce good fruit. Every tree that does not bear good fruit is cut down and thrown into the fire. So then, you will know them by their fruits (Matthew 7:15-20).

It is in the fruit, the teaching and practices of the false prophets, that the trajectory of a heretical movement can be clearly seen. As we shall see, the Gay Theological Movement is no different.

Since the time our first parents stepped foot in the Garden of Eden the serpent has sought to undermine both the trustworthiness and meaning of God's Word (Genesis 3:3:4-5). His goal is to subvert mankind's devotion to the One True God who revealed Himself in the Old Testament through the prophets but "…in these last days has spoken to us in His Son, whom He appointed heir of all things, through whom also He made the world (Hebrews 1:1-2). Throughout history every heresy that has confronted the Church has involved the authority, meaning and application of God's written Word and every false gospel that it has opposed has consisted of either a full frontal attack on the *person* or *work* of Jesus Christ.

The seriousness of the increasing popularity of Gay Theology in all of its various forms is that it is not merely about sexual ethics. Nor is this a matter in which faithful Christians can "agree to disagree" on and remain in fellowship with one another and be faithful to the historic Christian faith. The Gay Theological movement is antithetical to Biblical orthodoxy (right teaching) and orthopraxy (right conduct). The doctrines and practices of its adherents, especially the leaders of the Metropolitan Community Church, are nothing less than an attempt to seduce Christians into a paganized version of the faith. Whether it is the subtle revival of theoretical antinomianism of Montanism under the guide of Dispensationalism or the more overt forms in Liberal and Queer Theology, the entire Gay Theological movement is a cultic revival of ancient Gnosticism.

In this chapter we shall take a closer look at Gay and Queer Theology and see, like many other modern cultic paradigms, that it seeks to redefine (or in their terms "queer") the identity of God as well as the person and work of Jesus Christ. In doing so it seeks to bring the Church into the pagan captivity of sacramental pansexual idolatry. If successful, it will bring the Church under the judgment of God by enticing her to the bondage of the abominations of Jezebel (Revelation 2:20).[649] This is most keenly seen in the doctrine and practices of the leadership of the

---

649   According to the Bible, Jezebel was responsible for paganizing the worship of God (1 Kings 21:25-26). Yet, Feminist/Lesbian/Queer Theology advocates "queer" the Biblical account and turn Jezebel into a sexual liberator and then urge Christians to look to "the Spirit of Jezebel" as a model for Christian conduct. For an example, see Tina Pippin, "Jezebel Re-Vamped": Semeia, no. 69-70 (1995), 221-233.

Metropolitan Community Church, particularly in the writings of Robert E. Goss and Patrick S. Cheng.[650]

Orthodoxy, Orthopraxy, Heresy and The Nature of A Cult

The Apostle Paul told the church at Ephesus that Christians are not unaware of the tactics of the devil (2 Corinthians 2:11). Scripture reveals to us not only the history of God's redemptive work, but also a pattern of the ways in which the enemy of His people, the Father of Lies, seeks to deceive and lead them astray into apostasy particularly through idolatry. While he has been worshipped in diverse places under masculine (Baal, Molech, Quetzalcoatl) and feminine names (Artemis, Asherah, Diana, Ishtar, Isis, Gaia, Sophia) the nature of enticements to idolatrous forms of worship have essentially remained the same. All these identities are simply a mask for the demonic as Paul states, "...the things which the Gentiles sacrifice, they sacrifice to demons and not to God" and then he states "...and I do not want you to become sharers in demons" (1 Corinthians 10:20).

The most deceptive tactic that the serpent uses comes in the form of religious syncretism. That is, to blend the truth with lies and the worship of demons all the while calling them "YHWH" or "Jesus." Throughout history he deceived God's people to engage in worshipping the Egyptian god Hapis and the pagan god Baal through pagan sexual orgies (Exodus 32; 1 Corinthians 10:8) and then in the New Covenant era, to worship the androgynous Christ of Gnosticism. The most seductive means that Satan, the deceiver, leads them into apostasy is through lust. This includes the lust for power, material wealth and sinful forms of sexual pleasure. It is no wonder then why idolatry is so closely associated with sexual and spiritual adultery throughout the Bible (Numbers 25:1; Ezekiel 16:15; James 4:4).

The craftiness of the serpent enables him to creep into the congregation of God's people without notice. Consequently he is able to

650   Patrick S. Cheng is an ordained minister in the *Metropolitan* Community Church (MCC) and the Associate Professor of Historical and Systematic Theology at the Episcopal Divinity School in Cambridge, Massachusetts. Robert E. Goss was ordained a Jesuit priest in 1976, and he resigned the Society of Jesus as an unlaicized priest in 1978. He transferred as clergy to the Universal Fellowship of Metropolitan Community Churches (MCC) in 1995 and has been a part-time theologian/clergy on staff with MCC of Greater St. Louis.

slither his way into places of leadership spreading his lies by teaching in the seminary, pastoring in the Church, and spreading his twisting of Scripture through popular media. Where the Church has lost its spiritual discernment he is able to present his message boldly and blazingly - openly defying the Word of Truth. Like a wolf he preys on wandering sheep when the shepherds are not alert to guard and protect them. But where he is yet to gain a foothold, he must first approach them slyly as an ophidian approaches its prey. This is why the so-called "conservative evangelical" form of Gay Theology is so deceptive. Under the guise of evangelicalism this form of Gay Theology becomes more difficult to recognize since, on the surface, it appears to proclaim a genuine Gospel. However, in its affirmation of Jesus as Savior it denies His sovereign Lordship and the ruling standard of His law over every sphere of life. In its emphasis on grace, it has denied the Gospel's requirement to be obedient to the call of discipleship and in its rejection of the law of God it is a revised form of the ancient Gnostic heresy of Marcionism.

In seeking to deceive the Church, the Gay Theology advocate is not hesitant to twist ("queer") the Word of God and Biblical terms to achieve his ends. Having convinced unlearned and untaught lay people to buy into the queered hermeneutic under the guise of evangelicalism, the followers are then hooked to begin the steady erosion into apostasy. But this queered evangelicalism has gone beyond its liberal and Dispensational roots as it is now making steady inroads Reformed confessional churches and seminaries as well. A new accepted reinterpretation of the law via another theoretical antinomianism has laid the groundwork for the theological and ethical erosion of historically conservative churches as Reformed Theologian Hendrik Hart asserts, "Most churches can now make use of legitimate and accepted hermeneutical approaches to the Bible that would enable to consider that these texts [such as Leviticus 18:22, 20:13; Romans 1:26-28; 1 Corinthians 6:9] do not directly apply to our modern situation."[651]

---

651   D.T. Maurina, *Reformed Believers Press Service*, June 16, 1994, 2. Hendrik Hart taught systematic philosophy at the Institute for Christian Studies, Toronto since its founding in 1967 until his retirement in 2001. Prior to that he was head of the philosophical Institute of the Free University in Amsterdam, where he studied under D. H. Th. Vollenhoven.

Some people may follow the trajectory of Gay Theology further than others. There are those who will go all the way to liberationist Queer Theology while others will abandon any claim to be Christian and fall into open paganism. The consistent course of action once you buy into the Gay Theological Worldview, sometimes referred to as "Side A" Gay Christianity, is to then believe that this theological and moral corruption is something to be tolerated within the boundaries of the Church.

But this type of baptized sexual paganism is not new. The early Church was confronted with two primary forms of syncretism. The first was primarily a Jewish Christian problem influenced by the Christian Pharisees, who although they thought of themselves as a church they were actually a synagogue of Satan (Relation 2:9). This false form of worship denied the sufficiency of Christ's saving work on the cross as it attempted to hold on to the defunct form of temple worship, its animal sacrifices, holidays and the requirement of circumcision.

The second was a result of the inclusion of the Gentiles into the covenant who did not want to leave their former ways of thinking and living behind. While many trouble making Jewish Christians would not leave behind the Old Covenant, the syncretistic Gentile Christians sought to blend their former worldview and its pagan practices with the Christian faith. The apostles had to confront both of these errors in their epistles. With the destruction of the temple in 70 A.D. and the majority of the population of the Church becoming non-ethnic Jews the influence of Greek philosophy with its roots in Platonism escalated for the next few centuries, seeking to add new "gospels" to the Canon and new pseudo-apostolic epistles to the writings to the New Testament. By the time of the second century this movement became what we now refer to as Gnosticism. Until the discovery of the Nag Hammadi Library most of what we knew of these was from the early church father's response to these heresies. Now with the rediscovery of these texts liberal and gay-affirming churches are fully endorsing them, claiming that they were wrongly suppressed from the canon of Scripture.

The ancient forms of Gnosticism came essentially in two forms, an anti-material asceticism and another that advocated licentiousness. Peter Jones provides us with a helpful short sketch of Gnosticism:

Just as our culture offers a choice of secular or Christian liberalism, so the second century allowed both secular and Christian Gnosticism. A long and complex development of the political, social and religious mega-trends of the pre-Christian Mediterranean world molded ancient Gnosticism. This pagan spirituality began when East met West in the fourth century B.C. Alexander the Great took Greek (Western) culture to the Eastern ends of his far-flung empire. In that meeting, the rational culture of Greece was significantly modified by the great religions of the East (Hinduism, Manichaeism, Zoroastrianism, Babylonian astrology, the Egyptian goddess worship of Isis, and Judaism, whether orthodox, mystical or apostate). The blending of these great traditions produced the intellectual and religious syncretism of the so-called Hellenistic age (4th century B.C. – 4th century A.D.). This is the thinking alluded to in New Testament books such as 1 Corinthians, Colossians, 1 and 2 Timothy and the Johannine epistles... Knowledge of the self as divine is essential pillar of Gnosticism, however elaborate and "Christian" the outer dress. Gnosticism became a full-blown, appealing, religious system in the second century A.D. when certain so-called Christian thinkers (Marcion, Basilides, Valentinus et al) re-interpreted their faith to make it more palatable. They did what liberals have always done – reinterpret the faith by the pagan philosophy of the day, claiming such an amalgam to be the truest form of Christianity. Unconvinced, the Church saw in Gnosticism a Christianized form of paganism.[652]

These heretical doctrines had serious implications for understanding epistemology, ethics and the material universe. The most obvious ethical deviations from Scripture came in the form of the understanding of lust and sex.

---

652   Peter Jones, *Spirit Wars: Pagan Revival in Christian America* (Escondido, CA; Main Entry Editions, 1996), 65-66.

Following the Church's triumph over Gnosticism there were various other assaults on the person and work of Christ, namely Arianism[653] and Pelagianism.[654] Unfortunately, as much as the early Church fathers fought well against these destructive heresies, they were not totally immune from introducing their own errors stemming from Neo-Platonism. For example, Augustine, the Bishop of Hippo, borrowed from his previous Neo-Platonic worldview and subsequently misconstrued Scriptures teaching on sexuality. Daniel Heimbach is worth quoting at length to illustrate this error:

> Augustine was schooled in Platonic Philosophy, which blamed evil on material existence and thought purity was a matter of removing pleasant sensations. In regards to sex, Augustine believed the Platonic idea that sexual passion (the feeling itself) corrupts the soul regardless of marriage. So on becoming a Christian, this former teacher of Platonic philosophy decided sexual purity meant giving up sex

---

653   Arianism was a 4th Century Christian heresy named for Arius (c.250 - c.336 A.D.), a priest in Alexandria. Arius denied the full deity of the preexistent Son of God who became incarnate in Jesus Christ. He held that the Son, while divine and like God ("of like substance"), was created by God as the agent through whom he created the universe. Arius said of the Son, "there was a time when he was not." Arianism became so widespread in the Christian church and resulted in such disunity that the emperor Constantine convoked a church council at Nicaea in 325 A.D.. Led by Athanasuis, bishop of Alexandria, the council condemned Arianism and stated that the Son was consubstantial (of one and the same substance or being) and coeternal with the Father, a belief formulated as *homoousios* ("of one substance") against the Arian position of *homoiousios* ("of like substance"). Nonetheless, the conflict continued, aided by the conflicting politics of the empire after the death of Constantine (337 A.D.).

654   *Pelagianism, named after a British monk named* Pelagius *(354 A.D. – 420/440 A.D.)* whose reputation and theology came into prominence after he went to Rome sometime in the 380's A.D. views humanity as basically good and morally unaffected by the Fall. It denies the imputation of Adam's sin, original sin, total depravity, and Christ's substitutionary atonement. It simultaneously views man as fundamentally good and in possession of libertarian free will. With regards to salvation, it teaches that man has the ability in and of himself (apart from divine grace) to obey God and earn eternal salvation. Pelagianism was opposed by Augustine (354-430 A.D.), the Bishop of Hippo, and it was condemned as a heresy at Council of Carthage (418 A.D). These condemnations were summarily ratified at the Council of Ephesus (A.D. 431).

completely. It also led him to think that warnings in scripture against lust referred to sexual arousal whether it occurred in marriage or not. That assumption created a dilemma, because Augustine knew God did not order Adam and Eve to sin when he told them to "be fruitful and multiply" (Gen. 1:28).

Augustine therefore struggled to explain how husbands and wives could have sex without getting passionate and how Adam and Eve could have followed God's order without feeling aroused. Augustine's attempt to resolve this unnecessary "problem" led to some of the strangest writing he ever did. In discussing the morality of sex in marriage, Augustine wrote,

> What friend of wisdom and holy joys, who, being married... would not prefer, if this were possible, to beget children without the lust, so that this function of begetting offspring the members created for this purpose should not be stimulated by the heat of lust. [655]

And, when he tried to understand how Adam and Eve could have had sex without feeling aroused, he said,

> The man, then, would have sown the seed, and the woman received it, as need required, the generative being moved by the will, not excited by lust. [656]

> Of course, Augustine meant well. But his dilemma did not come from scripture, rather it came from Greek philosophy. Yet the mistake he made influenced Christian teaching on sexual morality for centuries. Some decided, if Augustine was right, it meant Christians could not live holy lives (be saints) without renouncing marriage, and that getting married was a lower moral state than remaining unmarried.

---

655   Augustine, *City of God* VIV. 16.
656   Augustine, *City of God* VIV. 24.

> Monks and priests took vows, in which they renounced not
> only immoral sex but sex in marriage as well...[657]

Various forms of the paganism of the Canaanites have existed throughout Biblical history and in various places around the globe. Unfortunately, these destructive doctrines continue to rear their head and challenge the Church under new names. Just as the third century heresy of Arianism that denied the deity of Christ was revived by the Watchtower Bible and Tract Society, so too the ancient heresy of Gnosticism has been reincarnated in postmodern liberal theology as well as liberationist, feminist and Gay theology.

Historically pseudo-Christian sects (cults) have three things in common: They all want to claim to be tied to the historical Jesus Christ of the Bible, their literature contains a twisting of Scripture in which it is obvious that they are misquoting sources and taking Biblical texts out of context and what they tell you up front about their beliefs and practices is only a facade. They do not tell you what they really believe until you get deeper into the organization as they want to appear as if they are just another Christian denomination.

In a similar fashion, the Metropolitan Community Church (MCC), founded by Troy Perry, on the surface, according to their statement of faith on their web sites, seem as though they uphold all the historic Christian creeds and essential historic doctrines such as the redemptive work of Christ and the doctrine of the Trinity. But, in reality they are pouring a completely different meaning into these terms. On the surface they seem like they have an evangelical statement of faith. In fact, they appear as if they are an evangelical church which only differs from others in that they affirmed consensual, monogamous life-long committed same sex unions. This deception is so convincing that they managed to fool sociologist Michelle Wolkomir into believing that they are a conservative Christian denomination.[658]

---

657   Daniel Heimbach, *True Sexual Morality: Recovering Biblical Standards for a Culture in Crisis* (Wheaton, IL; Crossway Books, 2004), 136.
658   Michelle Wolkomir states, "MCC is a theologically conservative, evangelical Protestant denomination that there is one triune God, that the Bible is the divinely inspired Word of God, that Christ is the route to salvation, and that the Holy Spirit indwells the believer." *Be Not Deceived: The Sacred and Sexual Struggles of Gay and Ex-Gay Christian Men* (New Brunswick, NJ; Rutgers University Press, 2006), 21.

Regardless of the statement of faith on their web site the MCC is so "inclusive" that just about any doctrine, pagan practice, or sexual fetish can be taught, practiced and celebrated as a sacrament as one of their theologians states:

> In 1968, Troy Perry founded the UFMCC as an alternative to the established churches. The UFMCC is unlike the mainline denominational groups or independent churches in that it is a postdenominational church, representing and blending the diverse traditions of a number of Christian denominations... UFMCC is a postdenominational church in that it does not start with the principle of doctrinal adherence but rather begins with doctrinal diversity, allowing for a wide range of ecumenical interpretation of doctrine and a blending of a variety of worship practices... In 1996, twenty years to the day of my ordination of a Jesuit priest, the UFMCC reaffirmed my original ordination, my call to service... I am currently an openly queer clergy in a church, the Metropolitan Community Church of greater St. Louis, affiliated with the UFMCC (Universal Fellowship of Metropolitan Community Churches) where approximately 52 percent of the clergy are women and where the majority of clergy are gay, lesbian, bisexual, and transgendered... it is also a church where gender-inclusive language is normative, where a variety of expressions of cross-gender identifications are celebrated as natural and where the integration of sexuality and spirituality is practiced. There is little communal anxiety over a butch dyke, a transvestite male, a leather man, a stone butch, a male-to-female or a female-to-male transsexual clergy, or any other fluid expression of gender.[659]

The heresy of Gay Theology is quickly moving beyond the confines of the Metropolitan Community Church and is invading many mainline denominations such as the Presbyterian Church USA, the United Church

659   *Robert E. Goss, Queering Christ: Beyond Jesus Acted Up (Eugene, OR: The Pilgrim Press, 2007), 29-30, 54-55.*

of Christ, the Evangelical Lutheran Church and the United Methodist Church. The MCC and its supporters use the same theological terms as historical Biblical Christianity but then pour different meanings into them. The result is that people like David G. Myers and Letha Dawson Scanzoni, authors of *What God Has Joined Together,* argue that the Church should be inclusive of sexually active homosexuals and endorse gay marriage assert:

> We Christians come in many varieties – mainline and evan-
> gelical, Pentecostal and Catholic, liberal and conservative.
> But on the big-ticket items we are discussing here, follow-
> ers of Jesus pretty much agree. Whatever our differences,
> we stand on common ground. Most of us not only agree on
> the basics of our faith but also have found some common
> ground in emerging understanding of sexual orientation...
> Despite this considerable and growing common ground,
> differences remain. But by reaching across to one another
> in Christian love, we can view our differences as spring-
> boards for conversation rather than contention. Friends of
> kindred faith wrestle with their lingering differences...[660]

Do Bible believing Christians and liberal Christians really agree on what they call the "big-ticket items"? Can we consider each other "fol-lowers of Jesus" who "stand on common ground"? Liberal Christianity and the Metropolitan Community Church, like the ancient Gnostics, want to appear as if they are just another Christian denomination or another segment of the Church with the same foundation as Peter Jones points out:

> The foundations of modern liberalism are the supremacy
> of human reason and the right to follow "truth" wherever
> it may be found. Scripture is not the norm for truth, but
> must be subjected to human reason. Today's liberalism
> treats Scripture as it would any ancient writing. The same
> "spirit" is present in ancient Gnosticism.[661]

660   *David G. Myers and Letha Dawson Scanzoni, What God Has Joined Together (San Francisco, CA: Harper Collins, 2005), 54-56.*
661   Peter Jones, *Spirit Wars: Pagan Revival in Christian America* (Escondido, CA; Main Entry Editions, 1996), 66-67.

The truth is while we may all use the same language of the historic Christian faith, in reality these heretical deviations pour a completely different meaning into it. The Jesus of liberalism and the MCC is a completely different Christ than of the Bible and the historic Creeds. These movements use the very same deceptive tactics of Gnosticism in redefining Christology using Gnostic texts as they view it as a suppressed expression of genuine Christianity as Peter Jones points out, "Today liberals claim that ancient Gnosticism is an alternate authentic expression of early Christianity."[662]

Organizations that orthodox Christians usually refer to as cults, as well as many mainline liberal "Christian" denominations, want to use the words of the Bible, the confessions and the historical creeds. But then they insist that are free to use such terms in a manner completely different than what the Church has historically meant by them. The revival of this tactic of shifting the meaning of Biblical and theological terminology can be seen in such documents as the Auburn Affirmation of 1923 of the Presbyterian Church (USA) which states:

> ...We all hold to these great facts and doctrines. We all believe in our hearts that the writers of the Bible were inspired of God. That Jesus was God manifested in the flesh. That God was in Christ reconciling the world to Himself and through Him we have our redemption. That having died for our sins He rose from the dead and is our ever living Savior. That in His earthly ministry He wrought many mighty works and by his vicarious death and unfailing presence He is able to save to the uttermost. Some of us regard the particular theories contained in the deliverance of the General Assembly of 1923 as satisfactory explanations of these facts and doctrines. But we are united in believing that these are not the only theories allowed by the Scriptures and our confessions as explanations of these facts and doctrines of our religion and that all who hold

---

662   Ibid, 72.

to these facts and doctrines, whatever theories they may employ to explain them are worthy of all confidence and fellowship.

This is the significant mark of liberalism, that Christianity is not about theology but "loyalty to Jesus Christ and united work for the kingdom of God" however that may be defined. There is also a certain dishonesty in distinguishing "theories" from "facts." They are playing word games in which they assert that people are free to say the same thing in referring to the Bible, the creeds and doctrines of the confessions of the faith (facts) but mean something completely different things by those words (theories). This is exactly how every pseudo-Christian cult seeks to deceive others into believing that they are teaching the historic Christian faith. They want to be free to use words such as "virgin birth" "incarnation" "resurrection" "inspired" "atonement" but then mean something completely different by these terms. As we shall see, the doctrines and practices of the Metropolitan Community Church and other like minded organizations are a hybrid of liberal theology and monistic paganism that is preaching a different Christ, a different Gospel and promoting its Gnostic spirituality through sacramental sex.

Dissolving Distinctions: The Queer Hermeneutical Matrix

Having declared that the sexual morality of the Old Testament is irrelevant to the Christian life and that the Bible is a collection of historically, theologically and morally flawed oppressive patriarchal documents to be usurped, the Gay Theological movement proceeds to attack every essential doctrine of the historic Christian faith. The ultimate goal is then is to put an end to any distinction between pagan sexualized idolatry and worship of YHWH under the guise of radical love,"…defined as a love that is so extreme that it dissolves existing boundaries."[663]

They include in these "dissolved boundaries" the ceasing of distinctions between Creator/creature, Christian/pagan, good/evil, male/

---

663   Patrick S. Cheng, *Radical Love: An Introduction to Queer Theology* (Seabury Books; 1 edition, 2011), 44.

female and love/erotic. In the "queering" of Scripture the Biblical understanding of God, morality, love, justice, holiness, sin, salvation, gender and sex are all redefined. In doing so Gay Theology does not simply seek to throw out the Christian faith, but to replace it with a new paradigm by subverting all ecclesiastical authority and that which upon it is based, sacred writ. When this common tactic of the second century Gnostics is employed, "…the Bible is turned to serve falsehood rather than truth."[664]

The underlying religious philosophy girding this paradigm is not Christian, but hyper-sexualized paganism that was commonly found in Ancient Near Eastern (ANE) religions. One example of Gay Theology's queering of the doctrine of God can be found in Michael S. Piazza's assertion that, "God is Gay." As the pastor at The Cathedral of Hope, the flagship congregation of the Universal Fellowship of Metropolitan Community Churches, he tells his congregation:

> Our church strongly believes that being lesbian or gay is a gift, that it is something of which we should be proud. We teach and preach that lesbian and gay people are created in the image and likeness of God. Having said that it was interesting to watch people wince a bit or snicker the first time I announced that I was going to teach on the topic of the 'homosexuality' of God. Why should that idea make us so uncomfortable? If we believe there is 'nothing sinful' about being lesbian or gay, why should the idea of God being homosexual bother us? What is wrong with a God who has lesbian tendencies? Shouldn't there be at least a one-in-ten chance that God is gay?[665]

Likewise Patrick S. Cheng, an ordained minister in Metropolitan Community Churches, rejects the omnipresent and omniscient God of Biblical theism and in His place inserts the pagan sexualized feminine

---

664   Peter Jones, *Spirit Wars: Pagan Revival in Christian America* (Escondido, CA; Main Entry Editions, 1996), 113.
665   Michael S. Piazza, *Gay By God* (Dallas, TX: Source of Hope Publishing, 1998), 95.

goddess who is the "divine lover."[666] He goes on to queer the attributes of God:

> Perhaps a more satisfying way of thinking about God's divine attributes, however, is that such attributes are actually a matter of performativity. Thus, like gender, God's divine attributes are simply a matter of divine performance—a parody or divine drag show—as opposed to characteristics that are "natural" or "essential" for God. This view of God's divine attributes would allow God to take on other "omnis" such as being omnisexual, omnigendered, or omniqueer. As B.K. Hipsher, an ordained minister with the Metropolitan Community Churches, has argued, "We are compelled to image God in the ever-changing, shifting, diverse and multiple transgender realities that human beings embody."[667]

The consequence is that although Queer Theologians claim to adhere to the doctrine of the Trinity as taught in the creeds, they then go

---

666   Patrick S. Cheng writes, "...the doctrine of God can be viewed as radical love to the extent that it dissolves the boundaries that prevent us from rethinking God's divine attributes in queer ways. The God of classical theism is described as having all-powerful "omni" characteristics such as omniscience (all-knowing), omnipotence (all-powerfulness), and omnibenevolence (all-goodness). For some queer theologians, this traditional understanding of God is toxic. For example, Robert Williams encouraged LGBT people to "fire" the God of their childhood, which often can be abusive and demonic. Instead, Williams argued that we must try on new models of God, including God as female, as grandmother, as divine lover, and as the one who suffers with us. As an HIV-positive man, Williams rejected the view of an omnipotent and all-powerful God, which Dorothee Sölle has described as "sadomasochistic" spirituality (and not in a good way). Williams refused to believe that an all-powerful God could allow the horrific suffering of HIV/AIDS to exist. To think otherwise—that is, to worship a God who doesn't need humans and is unmoved by our sorrows and joys—is "psychologically and spiritually unhealthy." J. Michael Clark, an openly gay theologian living with HIV/AIDS, also has wrestled with such questions of theodicy (that is, how evil can exist with an all-powerful and all-loving God). Clark also documents his battle with HIV/AIDS and challenges the classical theistic understanding of God. Malcolm Edwards, a self-described gay post-liberal theologian, has suggested that LGBT people should rethink the God of classical theism." *Radical Love: An Introduction to Queer Theology* (Seabury Books; 1 edition, 2011), 53-54.
667   Patrick S. Cheng, *Radical Love: An Introduction to Queer Theology* (Seabury Books; 1 edition, 2011), 54.

on to "queer" this doctrine so that it supposedly indicates a ceasing of the distinctions between God and man.[668] This denial of the Creator/creature distinction is at the heart of pagan monism. The sexual implications of the queering of God and the breaking down of distinctions is the elimination of the boundaries not only between God and man, but also between husband and wife as well as friend and lover. Consequently what are normally and ethically considered to be non-sexual relationships now become an opportunity for "friends with sexual benefits" ending all pretense to maintaining monogamous sexual relationships.[669]

God is then viewed not metaphorically a husband to His bride (Israel/the Church) but as an ontologically transgendered sexual partner.[670] This transgendered god then plays the role of either being the penetrator or penetrated in a spiritual orgy which then provides a new

668   Patrick S. Cheng writes, "The doctrine of the Trinity is a manifestation of God's radical love because it is an internal community of radical love. That is, the Trinity breaks down a number of categories, including the self and the other. Because God is an internal community within God's very being, this collapses the usual difference between the self and the other (that is, otherness as being "external" to one's self). Thus, God consists of both the "self" and the "other." *Ibid*, 56.

669   Patrick S. Cheng writes, "For Elizabeth Stuart, the Trinity is worth reclaiming by queer theologians because, at its heart, the Trinity represents God as passionate friendship. This principle of passionate friendship should be at the core of queer theology and ethics because it breaks down the artificial divide between sexual relationships and nonsexual relationships. In other words, passionate friendship displaces pair-bonded, monogamous, reproductive sexuality as the norm for Christian relationships. According to Stuart, we Christians are called to be promiscuous with our friendship." *Radical Love: An Introduction to Queer Theology* (Seabury Books; 1 edition, 2011), 57.

670   Patrick S. Cheng writes, "Gavin D'Costa, a theologian at the University of Bristol, has a similar view of the relational nature of the Trinity. D'Costa argues that, metaphorically speaking, queer relationships are at the ontological heart of the Trinity... [This] view of the Trinity has some very radical implications. First, both transgender and "switch" (that is, "versatile" or both "top" and "bottom") relationships are at the very heart of the Trinity. That is, each person in the divine three-way is both male and female as well as top and bottom. Thus, queer relationships are divinely sanctioned as long as such relationships also represent an overflowing love to the wider community. Second, the transgender nature of the Trinity means that, as an ontological matter, women should be permitted to be ordained Roman Catholic priests. That is, Roman Catholic theology traditionally asserts that only men can be ordained priests because Jesus Christ was ontologically male. However, under D'Costa's view of the Trinity, the second person of the Trinity—Jesus Christ—is ontologically both male and female. Therefore, there would be no theological bar to ordaining women as Roman Catholic priests." *Ibid*, 57, 58.

model for human pansexuality as the Trinity is to be "understood as an orgy" of a "polygendered being."[671]

This form of Gay Theology then proceeds to deconstruct Christology by queering the person and work of Jesus Christ, in not only asserting that He was born androgynous but also denying that God so loved the world that He sent His only-begotten Son to make an atonement and ransom for sin. According to Queer Theology, Jesus was merely a politicized victim as Robert E. Goss asserts:

> It was not God's will that Jesus died to ransom those with sin. This was a Christian interpretation of the death of Jesus. Rather, the cross symbolized the violent and brutal end of Jesus in the context of his political praxis for God's reign. Jesus was executed by the political infrastructure of Jewish Palestine as a political insurgent.[672]

Having deconstructed Jesus Christ, Patrick S. Cheng then is left to ask:

> Who is Jesus Christ for LGBT people today? In some ways, this question is at the very heart of Christian theology. Many queer people see Jesus Christ as a great teacher or prophet who lived two thousand years ago, but they generally have difficulty in thinking about Jesus Christ as one

---

671 Patrick S. Cheng states, "...the Trinity needs to be understood as an orgy, which breaks down the privileging of binary or pair-bonded relationships. Initially, the Trinity appears to be an example of "restricted polyfidelity" in which the three persons of the Godhead are themselves in a closed, or faithful, sexual relationship. However, Althaus-Reid argues that each person of the Trinity has her/her own closet of lovers and "forbidden desires" (for example, Jesus' relationships with Mary Magdalene and Lazarus), which in turn results in the death of the "illusion of limited relationships. As such, the Trinity can be a model for individuals who are polyamorous because the Trinity deconstructs the binary relationship model of marriage and domestic partnerships. Indeed, the radical love of the Trinity dissolves the boundaries between coupledom and singleness. Also, to the extent that each of the three persons of the Trinity are multigendered... then Trinity is actually a polygendered or polysexual being itself." *Radical Love: An Introduction to Queer Theology* (Seabury Books; 1 edition, 2011), 58-59.

672 Robert E. Goss, *Queering Christ: Beyond Jesus Acted Up* (Eugene, OR: The Pilgrim Press, 2007), 158.

being, or substance, with God. They also have difficulty
with christological doctrines such as the virgin birth, the
miracles, the resurrection, and the ascension.[673]

He then asserts that the social-political androgynous Jesus puts an
end to the distinctions between God and man, biological genders and the
created sexual order.[674] This Gnostic intersex[675] Queer Jesus then crosses
all sexual and gender boundaries[676] who then becomes the Bi/Christ and

673   Patrick S. Cheng, *Radical Love: An Introduction to Queer Theology* (Seabury
Books; 1 edition, 2011), 78.
674   Patrick S. Cheng states, "Jesus Christ is the boundary-crosser extraordinaire,
whether this relates to divine, social, sexual, or gender boundaries.... The story of
Jesus Christ as told in the four gospels—that is, the narrative of Jesus Christ's incarnation, ministry, crucifixion, resurrection, and ascension—can be difficult to fathom
from a post-Enlightenment perspective. What rational and educated person could ever
believe in the virgin birth, the miracles, or the resurrection? However, I believe that
these events make perfect sense if they are understood as showing how the boundaries
between the divine and the human are forever dissolved in the person of Jesus Christ.
Thus, the incarnation and miracles can be understood as the crossing of the divine into
the human realm. Conversely, the resurrection and ascension can be understood as the
crossing of the human back into the divine realm. Indeed, the story of Jesus Christ
fundamentally changes the relationship between God and humanity. That is why, for
Christians, Jesus Christ is considered to be the axis around which all of salvation history turns. No longer are "God" and "humanity" mutually exclusive categories, but
they come together in the person of Jesus Christ, the God-human, who is fully divine
and fully human *Radical Love: An Introduction to Queer Theology* (Seabury Books; 1
edition, 2011), 79.
675   Patrick S. Cheng writes, "Theologians have also started to write about the intersex Jesus Christ, or the Jesus Christ who has physical attributes (either genitalia
or chromosomes) of both sexes... So to the extent that Jesus Christ is a product of
parthenogenesis and is traditionally depicted with male genitals Jesus Christ is actually an intersex person! This observation is important because intersex theology is
an emerging area of queer theology, just as the LGBT community is becoming more
aware of the intersex political movement and organizations like the Intersex Society of
North America." *Radical Love: An Introduction to Queer Theology* (Seabury Books; 1
edition, 2011), 83, 91
676   Patrick S. Cheng writes, "Jesus Christ is the embodiment of radical love because—in addition to crossing divine and social boundaries— Jesus also crosses sexual boundaries. That is, Jesus' life and ministry can be viewed as dissolving the rigid
line between "heterosexual" and "homosexual." Bisexuality is significant because it
demonstrates what queer theory, as well as the Kinsey report, has argued—that sexuality is not a binary construct, but rather it is a fluid and evolving phenomenon." *Ibid*,
79-80.

Trans/Christ with various sexual fetishes, "I want to expand further the dimensions of the Queer Christ to include the Bi/Christ and the Trans/Christ... The construction of Christ need not be exclusive, for fluid categories enable Jesus to become the Drag Christ, the Leather Christ, the Heterosexual Christ, the Gay Christ, and the Lesbian Christ."[677]

The Revival of The Gnostic Gospel

Having distorted the creation account, the nature of God, the doctrine of the Trinity, the person of Jesus Christ and the human race, Queer Theology advocates then go on to queer the gospel. In doing so they deny the fall of humanity, original sin and consequently the need for reconciliation to God through the substitutionary atoning blood of Jesus Christ:

> ...the disagreement [is] between those who believe that creation remains good because God's sovereign and loving will cannot ultimately be controverted by human agency, and those who believe that in the Fall, human sinfulness succeeded in creating a real separation between creation and Creator. (This separation can be overcome only through individual repentance and faith in the saving work of Jesus' death on the cross, which is interpreted as paying the penalty for human sinfulness in order to assuage God's anger).[678]

Scripture teaches in the first two chapters of Genesis that God created everything good. It then tells us that because of the sinful act of the man, Adam, that the created order is cursed and was subjected to corruption (Genesis 3:17; cf. Romans 8:19-20). But Scripture also tells us that all of creation is waiting to be restored, resurrected, as it will be set free from the effects of sin, slavery and death along with the sons of God who await the redemption of their body (Romans 8:21-23). It is this truth that explains not only sin, sickness and death but also why we have various sinful inclinations as well as why some people are born

677   Robert E. Goss, *Queering Christ: Beyond Jesus Acted Up* (Eugene, OR: The Pilgrim Press, 2007), 170, 175.
678   Virginia Ramey Mollenkott, *Omnigender: A Trans-religious Approach* (Cleveland, OH: The Pilgrim Progress, 2007), 92.

with birth defects, including malformed sex organs. In contrast to this Biblical truth, Virginia Mollenkot asserts what she refers to as "creation spirituality":

> Those who subscribe to 'creation spirituality,' as I do, hold that God's connection to the creation is just as unalterable as a mother's relationship to her child – mother and/or child could deny their connection all they liked, but the fact of their relationship would remain. If Ephesians 4:6 is correct that the eternal God is 'above all, and through all, and in you all,' then there is no eternal or real separation between Creator and creation. Indeed, if the traditional or transgender sexuality is as sacred as anyone else's sexuality, because God's presence inhabits every entity.[679]

This "creation spirituality" is a common theme in Ancient Near Eastern religions (Paganism) and Gnosticism. In this worldview the patriarchal Heavenly-Father-God of the Bible is supplanted by the Earth-Mother-Goddess and it is being revived by Feminists, Queer Worldview advocates and leaders of the MCC. Like the syncretistic apostasy of Israel in the Old Testament, when promoted as if it is acceptable within Christianity it becomes a return to the ancient heresy of Gnosticism. This then becomes a spiritual A.I.D.S spreading throughout the Church when it is advocated in Christian seminaries and popular media as a Christian virtue:

> When pagan ideas masquerade as *Christian* values, the assault is more insidious and more deadly, for it is difficult to see that the velvet glove conceals the iron fist. Earth-centered monism has slipped into the pew beside transcendent Christian theism.[680]

How then does Mollenkot explain away what the Bible teaches is the result of the curse on creation? According to her, it is modern man and his lack of environmentalism that is the cause of not only air pollution but for natural disasters:

679   Ibid, 93.
680   Peter Jones, *Spirit Wars: Pagan Revival in Christian America* (Escondido, CA; Main Entry Editions, 1996), 34.

As for natural disasters such as earthquakes, destructive storms, avalanches, and so on, the sheer intensity of them may originate in a similar problem: a cavalier use of natural resources, including nuclear testing and accidents, or careless about carbon emissions, with little concern for the outcome to others and to the environmental as a whole.[681]

If this is the case, then what was the cause of earthquakes, volcanic eruptions, destructive storms, avalanches and so forth during the thousands of years in which modern man made pollution was non-existent? The logical conclusion of Queer creation spirituality is, the created order is as it should be except for mankind's lack of environmentalism. This denies the very root cause of actual sin by denying the inborn original state of sin inherited from Adam that causes a divide between God and man. The result is the need for redemption, atonement, and reconciliation and any separation between God and the sinner is purely illusionary:

> So, then, there is a great theological divide within Christendom. The doctrine of Original Sin interprets Genesis 3 as describing the real objective perversion of God's original plan by human disobedience and sinfulness. Salvation then comes from a Jesus who is uniquely divine among human beings and who must be invited to enter the human heart; and millions of beautiful lives have lived within that belief system. By contrast, Christians who believe that the goodness of God's creation could not be subverted see Genesis 3 as describing body-identified *imagined* separation from God. It is the terrifying sense of separation that sets every body against every other body and pits humankind against the natural environment as well.[682]

The truth is there is no "great theological divide within Christendom" on this issue as historical creedal Christianity upholds the doctrine of original sin. The ultimate divide here is between Christianity and a revived pseudo-Christian Gnostic paganism.

---

681   Virginia Ramey Mollenkott, *Omnigender: A Trans-religious Approach* (Cleveland, OH: The Pilgrim Progress, 2007), 93.
682   Ibid, 95.

Having denied the fall of mankind and the subsequent curse on creation, Gay Theology then proceeds to queer the doctrine of sin by redefining it as the failure to cease from making any sexual/gender distinctions and labeling any adherence to God's holy law as "legalism."[683] Patrick S. Cheng for example asserts that sin is accepting the Biblical essentialist binary gender construct of sexual relationships.[684] In contrast, the Scriptures define sin in relation to God's law. The theologians of the

683   Patrick S. Cheng writes, "Sin is a very difficult topic for many LGBT people. Many of us have grown up being told that we are sinners and that we will go to hell for our nonconforming sexualities and/or gender identities. It is not surprising, therefore, that the doctrine of sin has not received a lot of attention in queer theology to date.1 Indeed, much of the discussion around sin and LGBT people has been focused on biblical interpretation and the handful of "texts of terror" relating to same sex acts and nonconforming gender behavior. This approach is what I call the legalistic approach to sin: if you break God's biblical or natural law, then you will be punished for it. In contrast to the legalistic approach to sin, this section proposes that sin can better be understood as the rejection of radical love. That is, if God is radical love (in other words, a love so extreme that it dissolves all kinds of boundaries), then sin is what opposes God, or what opposes radical love. Sin is the resistance to dissolving boundaries and divisions. Specifically, we sin when we reinforce existing divisions with respect to sexuality, gender identity, or other factors." *Radical Love: An Introduction to Queer Theology* (Seabury Books; 1 edition, 2011), 70-71.

684   Patrick S. Cheng states, "In the context of radical love, we can understand sin as humanity's rejection of the radical love that God has given to us. In other words, if radical love is understood as a love so extreme that it dissolves existing boundaries, then the rejection of radical love is essentialism, or the reinforcing of the boundaries that keep categories separate and distinct from each other... Sin in this context (that is, a rejection of radical love) would be the refusal to challenge these two binary categories and to reinscribe the essentialist notions of sexuality as being either homosexuality or heterosexuality! ...Put differently, sin can be understood by queer theology to be *sexual and gender essentialism*. That is, whenever we understand sexuality and gender identity to be fixed and unchangeable (that is, by limiting sexuality to only homosexual and heterosexual, or by limiting gender identity to only female and male), we commit the sin of essentialism by failing to recognize the constructed nature of these categories. In creating and perpetuating these false dichotomies, we reinforce—rather than erase—sexual and gender categories. By contrast, whenever we challenge the essentialist nature of these categories, we experience the grace of constructivism.... In sum, sin can be understood as our refusal to accept God's radical love for us. This can take a number of forms, but especially the form of refusing to dissolve or even challenge existing boundaries that limit our views of sexuality, gender identity, and/or race. Sin can also take the form of refusing to see the interrelatedness of social oppressions; for example, continuing to maintain the lines of division between racism and heterosexism." *Radical Love: An Introduction to Queer Theology* (Seabury Books; 1 edition, 2011), 74, 77.

MCC reject this definition and go on to redefine sin as anything but what the law of God teaches. [685]

The theologians of the MCC and their fellow Queer theology advocates have queered the doctrine of God, the Trinity, the person and work of Jesus Christ and redefined sin as any objection to homosexual behavior. It should come as no surprise then that they reject the gospel of salvation which consists of Christ's substitutionary, propitiatory and atoning death on the cross and His bodily resurrection. In the place of the Biblical gospel they proclaim a message self-salvation through the self-realization that humans are divine.[686]

It follows then that once the gospel has been distorted that they would go on to queer the visible means of conveying the gospel – namely the sacraments. While various denominations understand the sacraments differently,[687] they universally view the various ordinances as a means of presenting the benefits of Christ's saving grace.[688] Only in paganism do we find that intimacy with God is obtained through sexual ecstasy, homosexual intercourse and various sexual fetishes as Daniel Heimbach notes:

685   Patrick S. Cheng writes, "The traditional doctrine of sin is a legalistic one. That is, sin is defined as disobedience with respect to God's divine commands. Under this view, original sin is attributed to the fall of Adam and Eve, who disobeyed God's command not to eat of the Tree of the Knowledge of Good and Evil. As a result, God punishes Adam and Eve by expelling them from Eden and by introducing death into the world." *Ibid,* 71.

686   Virginia Ramey Mollenkott states, "*Salvation comes from recognizing that the Sacred Presence within the human core of ourselves and all other creatures and learning to abandon the ego in favor of communion with that Presence. To the degree that we become fully human, we become divine and to the degree that we realize our divinity, we become fully human. From my Christian perspective, as the first born of many* sisters and brothers, Jesus led the way and made all this possible for the rest of us." *Omnigender: A Trans-religious Approach* (Cleveland, OH: The Pilgrim Progress, 2007), 95.

687   Protestantism is unanimous in numbering the quantity of Sacraments to two (Baptism/Lord's Supper) whereas Roman Catholicism includes seven (Baptism, Confirmation, Holy Communion, Confession, Marriage, Holy Orders, and the Anointing of the Sick).

688   For example, the Westminster Confession of Faith states, "Sacraments are holy signs and seals of the covenant of grace, immediately instituted by God, to represent Christ and His benefits; and to confirm our interest in Him: as also, to put a visible difference between those that belong unto the Church and the rest of the world; and solemnly to engage them to the service of God in Christ, according to His Word." (Chapter 27.1) Roman Catholicism likewise states, "The Sacraments are outward signs of inward grace, instituted by Christ for our sanctification." (Catechismus concil. Trident., n. 4, ex St. Augustine, "De Catechizandis rudibus")

...sexual pagans believe that unrestrained sex puts them in contact with spiritual powers running the universe. It is what makes them gods and goddesses. And they believe that experiencing sexual ecstasy gives the spiritual power they can use however they wish.[689]

This paganized sexuality then becomes a new means of redefining spirituality. Rather than water, bread and wine being the elements of Christian sacraments the new "means of grace" is the exchange of bodily fluids and achievement of orgasms, "This *jouissance* ('pleasure in orgasm') in anal intercourse represents an important element in the spirituality of many gay males, for it effaces self-boundaries in a communion open to spiritual possibilities for gay men."[690] The human body then becomes the central focus, the pagan temple, in which this "sacrament" is enacted in a new worship experience:

> Spirituality includes body, sexuality and self. That sexuality is intrinsic to our experience of God as men and as gay men should hardly be surprising to us, though erotophobic religion has tried to separate sexuality from spirituality. Sexuality expresses ineffable meanings between people that cannot adequately be expressed in any other fashion. This may be one of the gifts of gay spirituality to erotophobic. Many gay men view sexuality as a necessary and authentic part of their spirituality, for sex brings not only a group solidarity but also a sense of transcendence. The power of sex is a strong drive (and I might add a spiritual instinct) within gay men.[691]

This is the very essence of pagan sexual spirituality that was practiced by the nations such as the Sumerians,[692] Mesopotamians,[693]

---

689   Daniel Heimbach, *True Sexual Morality: Recovering Biblical Standards for a Culture in Crisis* (Wheaton, IL; Crossway Books, 2004), 56

690   Robert E. Goss, *Queering Christ: Beyond Jesus Acted Up* (Eugene, OR: The Pilgrim Press, 2007), 79.

691   Ibid, 78.

692   Richard Davidson, *Flame of Yahweh: Sexuality in the Old Testament* (Peabody, MA: Hendriksen Publishing, 2007), 87.

693   Ibid, 89-90.

Egyptians,[694] the Hittites[695] and the Canaanites[696] that surrounded ancient Israel which was a constant source of enticement to lure them away from faithfulness to YHWH. The end result is that any and every sexual experience is redefined in religious, even Christian, spiritual terms as Daniel Heimbach points out:

> Ultimately, sexual indulgence is justified in *spiritual* terms, and sensual *spirituality* leads to a pagan faith in sex. Sensual pagan spirituality then becomes a driving force that not only excuses but even demands sexual indulgence, and rituals are added to celebrate the *spirituality* of sexual sin.[697]

In worshipping God through sex, the exchange of bodily fluids becomes the new means by which Christ dwells and is communicated in gay men's semen.[698] The homosexual act then becomes the new vehicle for spirituality and the level of orgasm is the new standard of achieving

---

694   Ibid, 90.

695   Richard Davidson states, "As with all other polytheistic religions surrounding Israel, the Hittite documents reveal a divinization of sex, as the relationships among the deities include references to sexual activity."*Flame of Yahweh: Sexuality in the Old Testament* (Peabody, MA: Hendriksen Publishing, 2007), 92.

696   Richard Davidson, *Flame of Yahweh: Sexuality in the Old Testament* (Peabody, MA: Hendriksen Publishing, 2007), 93-94.

697   Daniel Heimbach, *True Sexual Morality: Recovering Biblical Standards for a Culture in Crisis* (Wheaton, IL; Crossway, 2004), 114.

698   Robert E. Goss states, "Michael Kelly, a former Franciscan presents a six-volume video series, *The Erotic Contemplative*, where he voices the Catholic tradition of erotic contemplation of nuptial mysticism, merging it with explicit physical love-making... Kelly is quite explicit in recovering the social shame of anal intercourse as the point of gay male communion with Christ. Christ is within gay men's semen, entering the body of another man, being absorbed by the body, and transforming the shameful stigma of anal intercourse into divine love-making. Gay men enter into the body of Christ, and Christ penetrates gay men in anal intercourse. Gays forbidden to love, are invited by God to become Christ's lover. But perceiving Jesus as a penetrated male subverts penetrative, heterosexist masculinity that eschews mutuality for self-pleasure and power. The penetrated Christ provides gay bottoms with an icon of alternative masculinities, subverting heterosexual phallocentrism." *Queering Christ: Beyond Jesus Acted Up* (Eugene, OR: The Pilgrim Press, 2007), 137.

higher levels of spiritual consciousness.[699] Rather than meeting Christ at the Communion Table of bread and wine, the new sexualized sacrament entails condomless sex with other men as it intensifies the spiritual experience.[700] But this act does not include just two men, for the worshipper through his act also seeks to engage in homosexual *ménage à trois* with the androgenized transsexual (Gnostic) Christ as Robert Goss, a Queer Priest in the MCC, testifies concerning penetrating his A.I.D.S infected lover:

> We engaged in erotic prayer and love-making. Our sex was eucharistic, intensely passionate, and intensely spiritual. During our sessions, I felt Christ in a way that I only experienced in solitary erotic prayer. I felt Christ in our love-making and did not want to give it up... Each Sunday morning we made sexual love, followed by eucharist at the dining room table for the two of us... There were times that I saw Christ's face within Frank's face as I penetrated him in intercourse. As I was penetrated I felt penetrated by Frank and Christ. As I tasted Frank's body, I tasted Christ's body. We experienced a ménage à trois and the inclusionary love of God. We made love and extended that sexual love into our weekly celebrated eucharist. Both were intense

---

699   Andrew Sullivan states, "Sexual experience, from the beginning, seemed to me almost a sacrament of human experience, a truly transforming experience in the adventure of being human; an insight into both what love may possibly be and what death almost certainly is... And to physically invade another person, and to be invaded, to merge with another body, to abandon the distance that makes our everyday lives a constant to save me. Far from seeing them as a simple negation of spirituality, I instinctively found them to be windows into it."Andrew Sullivan, *Love Undetectable: Notes on Friendship, Sex, and Survival* (New York, NY: Alfred A. Knopf, 1998), 57. Cited in Robert E. Goss, *Queering Christ: Beyond Jesus Acted Up* (Eugene, OR: The Pilgrim Press, 2007), 78.

700   Scott O'Hara states, "Feeling a man's dick inside me, condomless – that's when the sex becomes spiritual in its intensity. Communion, in the truest sense. Integral to that closeness is the knowledge that he intends to leave a piece of himself inside me; his cum, like sex itself, has a psychological value, beyond anything physical. Recognizing that power is one of the ways to defy this virus, I believe in exchanging bodily fluids, not wedding rings" "Viral Communion," *POZ* (November 1997): 69. Cited in Robert E. Goss, *Queering Christ: Beyond Jesus Acted Up* (Eugene, OR: The Pilgrim Press, 2007), 77.

experiences of love-making with God. There is no more intense spiritual experience than to make love with your lover and see Christ's face in your lover's face while in the throes of passion. The letting-go was carried into our prayer around the table as we broke bread and shard the cup of Christ's love. The communion intimacy was found equally in the bedroom for us in word and sacrament. Eating the consecrated bread and drinking the wine were as intense communion as our intimate love-making.[701]

Of course to the faithful Christian such assertions are not only shocking but utterly blasphemous. To this MCC leaders respond that our revulsion of their assertions are simply another indication of our "erotophobia" as they worship Christ as the penetrated male.[702] Since orgasms are sacramental and the more intense experience brings about a more heightened spirituality, anything that might potentially lesson that experience and the experience of flesh on flesh contact in the same-sex act is viewed as a barrier to true spirituality. The conclusion then is that "barebacking" (anal sex without condoms) becomes an important spiritual experience:

---

701   Robert E. Goss, *Queering Christ: Beyond Jesus Acted Up* (Eugene, OR: The Pilgrim Press, 2007), 22.

702   Robert E. Goss writes, "Some Christian erotophobes would claim that my above genealogical analysis of homoerotic constructions of Jesus is perverse and obscene. I would counter their homophobic judgments by saying that we find traces of erotic grace in these passionate constructions of Jesus. They have been lifelines for pious Christian men attracted to the same sex, helping them to find meaning from their prayer closets and perhaps a limited self-acceptance of their sexual attractions to men and Christ. For two millennia, many Christian men have read the story of Jesus with a homoerotic gaze and devotion. For them, Jesus remained a cipher for homoerotically connecting with God and accepting themselves. They have long recognized Jesus as one of their own. He is claimed as the penetrated male, a bottom violating the masculine code of penetration and phallic domination. He is an outsider, transgressing the normative borders of heteronormavity and experiencing forbidden love between men... I and many other Catholic men, priests and laymen, have found the naked Jesus utterly sexually desirable, calling us to pursue a relationship, and many of us have discovered that we were utterly desirable to Jesus." *Ibid*, 138-139.

Many men are barebacking for no other reason than it holds significant meaning in their lives even with all its incumbent risks. Are they willfully and proudly risking their lives for the better orgasm?... I will suggest that barebacking has spiritual dimensions for some segments of the gay community.[703]

So central is this act to gay and queer spirituality they are willing to continue doing so even if it means putting oneself and one's partners in danger of contracting a potentially fatal disease.[704] This explains why Robert Goss was more than willing to forego so-called "safe sex" as he resented doing so with his infected sexual partner:

Unprotected sex may also embed primal desires to love another man in ways that feel powerful, intimate, and spiritual. I would argue that... the spirituality of love-making that renders protected sex less important than the risk of contracting the HIV virus. For many gay men, anal intercourse is an important expression, even a spiritual expression, of intimacy... Though Frank [who was HIV-positive] generally refused to engage in condomless sex with me, I was only too willing to engage in condomless sex.[705]

The god of Gay Theology is not content to be worshipped through prayer, Scripture and the sacraments of baptism and communion in the Lord's Supper. Rather communion with this god is through the

---

703   Ibid, 76.
704   Stephen Gendlin states, "A year and a half ago at a conference, I heard a talk by a really cute positive guy on the fun of unsafe sex with positive guys. He was beautiful, the subject was exciting, and I soon ended up getting fucked by him without a condom. He then came inside me, I was in heaven, just overjoyed. I'd had unsafe sex before, but never intentionally. Those experiences were guilt-ridden because I worried during the sex and afterward – about exposing my partner to HIV." "Riding Bareback," *POZ* (June 1997): 66; Cited in Robert E. Goss, *Queering Christ: Beyond Jesus Acted Up* (Eugene, OR: The Pilgrim Press, 2007), 77.
705   Robert E. Goss, *Queering Christ: Beyond Jesus Acted Up* (Eugene, OR: The Pilgrim Press, 2007), 81.

ecstatic experiences in a ritualized sexual act.[706] This is nothing less than a modern form of the practices of the ancient pagan sex cults which were prohibited in the law of God in the so-called "clobber passages" and "texts of terror." So insistent on the spiritual importance of this sex act and its use as a form of practicing "hospitality" with strangers, that to assert that any sort of moral argument for monogamy or the use of condoms becomes a form of "homophobia."[707]

The Revival of The Gnostic Divination of Self

The monistic Gay/Queer/Transgender worldview as promoted within the MCC seeks to break down any sort of distinctions not only between genders but also between the Creator and the creation:

> Queer theologians have used queer theory to challenge not only the fluidity of sexual and gender boundaries, but also the boundaries relating to Christian theology itself. These boundaries include the divine vs. human, soul vs. body, life vs. death, heaven vs. earth, center vs. margins, and numerous other boundaries that are dissolved or erased by radical love [the erotic] as we approach the eschatological horizon.[708]

---

706   Robert E. Goss explains, "Let me candidly speak about the spirituality of our love-making. We found God in the midst of ecstatic sex or our love-making anal intercourse disrupted the boundaries of ourselves; we felt the spiritual charge of the love of God in the *jouissance* of our bodies entangled in pleasure and choreographed in a union that embodied transcendent possibilities. We both resented condoms; they formed a latex barrier to personal and spiritual communion that we so often felt in condomless love-making. Barebacking [anal sex without condoms] had been part of our spiritual prayer and our union form its very beginning I certainly longed for viral communion with Frank, to share his fate [to become HIV-positive and die of AIDS]... We made a conscious to engage in unprotected sex to sustain our union and our experience of God, and those were moments of deep spiritual love, trust, vulnerability and giving." *Ibid*, 83.
707   Robert E. Goss states, "...to abandon anal sex (including anal sex with condoms) and promiscuity entirely, I believe expresses an internalized homophobia (if not a form of biological fundamentalism)." *Ibid*, 79.
708   Patrick S. Cheng, *Radical Love: An Introduction to Queer Theology* (Seabury Books; 1 edition, 2011), 18.

Consequently, according to Mollenkott, not only was Jesus androgynous and born of a natural parthenogenetic conception He was not uniquely divine. Rather, like the Jesus of Gnosticism, he led the way to show us our divinity and how we can obtain salvation through our divine self-knowledge.[709] This then brings a universal salvation for everyone so that, although there are many paths, each person is lead to the actualization of the divine self as we realize that we are a manifestation of God's divinity which can be accomplished through a variety of religions.[710] As Peter Jones points out, the lure for humans to become gods is part of the original lie promoted by the serpent, which is quite contrary to the very meaning of divinity.[711]

This realization of the Divine Self entails seeing that not only are humans created in the image of God, but so is all of creation. In this Gay/Queer/Omnigender theological worldview all people are incarnations of God that reflect the diversity within God through the plurality of genders as Virginia Mollenkott states:

> ...I agree with Chicana Gloria Anzaldúa, who argues
> that when people are 'queer' – gay, lesbian, bisexual,

709   Virginia Mollenkott, states, "Salvation comes from recognizing that the Sacred Presence within the human core of ourselves and all other creatures and learning to abandon the ego in favor of communion with that Presence. To the degree that we become fully human, we become divine; and to the degree that we realize our divinity, we become fully human. From my Christian perspective, as the first born of *many* sisters and brothers, Jesus led the way and made all this possible for the rest of us." *Omnigender: A Trans-religious Approach* (Cleveland, OH: The Pilgrim Progress, 2007), 95.

710   Virginia Mollenkott, "...I believe that everyone has his or her own life-path chosen for purpose of maximum spiritual growth. If a person is born transsexual, intersexual, or homosexual, for instance, then precisely those experiences are perfect for the development of that particular soul. But that fact does not indicate that I should sit back passively while bigotry exacts huge penalties from such people. Because I, as a child of God, am manifestation of God's self, a part of God's process, I am to do whatever I can do to lighten human burdens, confident that I could not deflect any soul from its authentic path even if I tried. I believe that eventually every created being will give heartfelt assent to the glories of the New Creation as embodied in the Christ (Phil. 2:9, 11)), known by other religions by other names: the corporate Messiah, for instance, or the Buddha nature. So every one of us will eventually come home." *Omnigender: A Trans-religious Approach* (Cleveland, OH: The Pilgrim Progress, 2007), 16.

711   Peter Jones, *One or Two: Seeing A World of Difference* (Escondido, CA; Main Entry Editions, 2010), 74-75.

transgender, *or off-form in any fashion* – it is because real gods, goddesses, and/or spirits have chosen those people to embody or incarnate them. Although I believe in only one Divine Source, not a multiple of gods and goddesses, I have certainly noticed that One Source likes variety and has chosen to be incarnated in millions of diverse ways. I therefore assume that the ultimate reason for 'queerness' does not lie in concepts constructed by society, or some eternal essence like 'male' or 'female' or 'bi-gendered,' but rather the fact that God has chosen to embody Himself/Herself/Itself in just this person's particularities at just this time and place.[712]

Transgenderists will add to this assertion that part of the process of discovering the revelation of the divine self is to also become one's own co-creator. Having interpreted the Bible through their own experiences and distorted perception of their sexual identity which results in recreating their god and the original man as androgynous, one is then left to wonder, "Why would God create a person to be a man and then intend for them to be something other than their birth-gender?" Their answer is, God has called them to be their own co-creator:

We can argue, then, that from the beginning humanity has been invited by God to participate in the creation process. The development of our lives, our minds, our bodies, and our spirits, over the course of our lifetimes, has been given to us as a responsibility from God. Therefore, the ways in which we have learned to modify our bodies to reflect our spirits could be part of this creative process that has been ongoing from the origins of humanity. We share, with God, the responsibility for creating our lives; God designed creation in this process.[713]

According to the transgender interpretation of Genesis 1-2, God purposely gave them a body that does not match their inner gender so

---

712   Ibid, 17-18.
713   Justin Tanis, *Transgendered: Theology, Ministry and Communities of Faith* (Cleveland, OH: The Pilgrim Press, 2003), 59.

that they live a life of confusion until such a time that medical technology has developed a means to align their inner and outer genders. This confusion then can only be resolved and the co-creator process accomplished thousands of years after the creation of the human race. Only when modern science has developed a method to correct this mismatch of gender can the supposed co-creator plan of God become actualized as it requires that the post-operative transsexual to continually consume hormones in order to complete the transition and never will the post-op be able to bear a child. Therefore, this supposed co-creator plan entails being able to do anything *but* pro-create.

Yet contrary to Justin Tanis, Virginia Mollenkott asserts that not all transsexuals are intended to re-create themselves through sex reassignment surgery and the consumption of hormones. According to her, some transsexuals are able to determine God's will for their bodies by discovering whether or not their body will adapt to the process:

> I met one transsexual who discovered that estrogen made him so desperately sick and depressed that he was forced to give up transitioning, deciding that apparently God wanted him to remain within a male body. Because he graciously united his will with God's, he is remarkably contented to remain outwardly male, inwardly female.[714]

If transitioning entails uniting one's body with one's true natural God-given inner gender, then how can the body demand otherwise, unless of course the process itself is inherently foreign to the human body? And how does he know that it is God's will to be an inner woman with an outer man's body and not God's will for him to live a life of estrogen induced sickness? Isn't it more likely (and Biblical) that there is nothing wrong with his manly body and the real problem is the thought in his head that his true inner identity is that of a woman?

What must be kept in mind is that the Gay Theological Movement is not content to merely promote their heretical doctrines and practices within their own circles. Their mission is to change the theological and sexual paradigm for all of society through redefining the Church, the family and our culture, "It's obvious that a change of thinking is going

714   Virginia Ramey Mollenkott, *Omnigender: A Trans-religious Approach* (Cleveland, OH: The Pilgrim Progress, 2007), 58.

to have to invade the Church if we are going to see this truth [of Gay Theology] come to light in the pews across the world."[715]

Queer Eschatology: Spiritual Monism

The Gay theological movement has a vision for the future, an eschatological objective that is not only transgender and pansexual but transreligious with a radical ecumenicalism of all religions. The only faith excluded from this paradigm is historical orthodox Christianity:

> Where is queer theology headed in the future?... Some queer theologians of color who have addressed issues of intersectionality and hybridity include Renée L. Hill, Elias Farajajé-Jones, and myself. Hill, a lesbian African American Episcopal priest, has written about developing a "multireligious, multidialogical" process that arises out of her own "multiply intersected life." For Hill, this means examining sources from other religions in the African Diaspora, including Islam, Santeria, Akan, Yoruba, Vodun, Buddhism, Judaism, and Humanism.... Like Hill, I cite the importance of reclaiming other religious traditions—for example, Buddhism, Confucianism, Daoism, and Hinduism— as well as other rites, rituals, and sacred spaces.[716]

The eschatological objective then is a singular universal religion:

> For me, the second-century theologian Origen had it right in terms of his doctrine of *apokatastasis*, or the restoration of all things. According to this doctrine, if God is truly sovereign, then good must decisively triumph over evil in the end, which would mean that even Satan is saved. This does not mean that people will not need to be purified before reaching heaven—just as gold needs to be refined

---

715   R.D. Weekly, *Homosexianity* (Judah First Ministries, 2009), 116.
716   Patrick S. Cheng, *Radical Love: An Introduction to Queer Theology* (Seabury Books; 1 edition, 2011), 39, 40.

by fire—but, in the end, all will reach heaven... According
to the doctrine of *apokatastasis*, all things will be restored
because of the ultimate triumph of God over evil and death.
As we have seen, the boundaries between female and male,
life and death, and punishment and reward will be subject
to eschatological erasure at the end of time. Indeed, even
the boundaries between the different world religions will
be erased.[717]

One of the theological means of accomplishing this task is to univer-
salize the precious promises of the Gospel for everyone. This includes
even those who are utterly opposed to it and worship Buddha, feminine
goddesses and so forth in her trans-spirituality.[718]

Peter Jones rightly points out that the One-ist trajectory of Feminist/
Gay/Queer Theology is towards ontological and spiritual monism – the
end of the gender differences, the end of the Creator/creature distinction, and the unification of all forms of religions in a "new" paradigm of
spirituality with androgyny as the eschatological ideal:

> We surely must conclude that sexual perversion, and in
> particular the elimination of sexual distinctions, is not
> an incidental footnote of pagan religious history, of mere
> passing interest, but represents one of its fundamental ideo-
> logical commitments. That the pagan priesthood would be
> so identified, across space and time, with the blurring of
> sexual identity via homosexual androgyny indicates, be-
> yond a doubt, the enormous priority paganism has given,
> and continues to give, to the undermining of God-ordained

717   Ibid, 135, 136.
718   Virginia Mollenkott states, "Christians who believe the Fall brought about an
utter separation from our Source feel that the gulf can be crossed only through faith in
the redeeming death and resurrection of Jesus. Salvation is something God provides
from the outside; it is external to any human effort other than acceptance. Although St.
Paul testifies that there is nothing that can ever separate us from the love of Christ (the
Anointed One), Christians who emphasize the Fall as an objectively real sundering
would say that Romans 8:38-39 applies only Christians who interpret the Scriptures
as they do." *Omnigender: A Trans-religious Approach* (Cleveland, OH: The Pilgrim
Progress, 2007), 93.

monogamous heterosexuality, and the enthusiastic promotion of androgyny in its varied forms.[719]

Queer Theology is a wholesale abandonment of the God the Bible and the Christ of the New Testament, an apostasy into a syncretistic pagan revival of the ancient Roman Empire. Peter Jones describes well the repercussions of the Gay/Queer/Omnigender worldview in his book *The God of Sex* in which he outlines this incremental downward decline that is the eventual outcome of suppressing the knowledge of the truth which leads to radical exchanges in three critical domains:

Theology (Rom. 1:23): "They exchanged the glory of the immortal God for images made to look like mortal man and birds and animals and reptiles."

Spirituality (Rom. 1:25): "They exchanged the truth for the lie and worshipped and served the creature rather than the creator."

Sexuality (Rom. 1:26): "They exchanged natural sexual relations for unnatural ones." [720]

Paul's description of the decline that comes from suppressing the knowledge of the truth and being given over to degrading homosexual acts is already evident in the Metropolitan Community Churches (MCC) as well as other like-minded denominations, demonstrating over acts of pagan forms of worship. Their leaders advocate Gay prostitution, patronizing Gay masseurs for receiving manual "releases," pedophilia and all sorts of sexual activity outside monogamous heterosexual marriages.

Jesus warned His disciples that they would not be the only ones in the market place of ideas and claims to be bearers of the truth. He told them that when they would go out to teach that they would be followed by false teachers and preachers disguised as pastors and prophets. But He also told them that they would know these heretics by what their teaching and lives produced (Matthew 7:15-23).

Granted, there are no perfect churches and wolves are probably to be found in just about every denomination. The difference is in the Metropolitan Community Churches (MCC) and other like-minded

719 Peter Jones, "Androgyny: The Pagan Sexual Ideal" *Journal of the Evangelical Theological Society* 43/3 (September 2000), 464-465.
720 Peter Jones, *The God of Sex* (Eastbourne, England: David C. Cook, 2006), 142.

denominations, the bad fruit is indicative of the denominationally en-dorsed doctrines and practices. Most of the MCC congregations have a statement of faith which sounds Biblical and orthodox that upholds the doctrine of the Trinity and the saving work of Jesus Christ. The result is what they assert on one side of their mouth they then deny with the other side. This is the chief characteristic of false teachers. They always mix lies with the truth in order to make their false doctrine more palatable as they twist the Scriptures to their own destruction (2 Peter 3:16-17). For example, consider the following statement from an MCC congregation:

> Love is our greatest moral value and resisting exclusion is a primary focus of our ministry. We want to continue to be the conduits of a faith where everyone is included in the family of God, and where all parts of our being are welcomed at God's table (MCC Home Page).[721]

The problem is when a so-called "love" abandons the truth of God's Word in doctrine or practice, particularly in regards to His moral law in both testaments, it ceases to be truly the love of God regardless of how they might feel about each other, themselves or do charitable deeds. For example, it is not uncommon to find MCC congregations that deny the exclusivity of Jesus Christ. They deny that He is *the* way, the truth and *the* life and that no one will come to the Father but through Him (John 14:6). The MCC of San Francisco advocates the very sort of idolatry described in Romans 1 and endorses doctrines and religions that are antithetical to the teachings of Jesus Christ, "We come from a variety of spiritual backgrounds and believe there are many paths to the holy."[722] This "variety of spiritual backgrounds" includes a gay Buddhist minis-try in their church called "Q Sangha":

> The 'Q' in Q Sangha refers to Queer, which includes les-bian, gay, bisexual and transgender people. Sangha is the Buddhist term of spiritual community. Our practice helps us to be present and accepting and to calm our bodies and minds. From this place, it is easier to live with greater

---

721   http://mccdc.com/mccdc-church-history/ufmcc-statement/
722   http://www.mccsf.org/visitor.html

compassion, understanding and happiness. (MCC of San Francisco)

The Metropolitan Community Church of Northern Virginia practices Native American (or Indigenous People) pagan worship practices.[723] This is done in the name of "Elastic Theology," which incorporates a multitude of doctrines and practices from outside of historical Christianity.[724]

Many MCC congregations also teach doctrines explicitly contrary to the teachings of Jesus Christ who taught us to refer to God in the masculine and pray, "Our Father..." (Matthew 6:9). In doing so they abandoned the language of Scripture in order to endorse a feminist theology[725] as they state:

> Because we want to exclude no one, we use inclusive language for persons. Because we believe that any one metaphor is inadequate when speaking of the Divine, we use inclusive language for God in our worship services. This

---

723   http://www.mccnova.com/Worship/specserv.htm
724   "One of our Core Values is Elastic Theology. This means that we affirm a variety of faith expressions and experiences. One of the ways in which we live out of this core value is to respectfully explore the lessons others have to teach us. All of us gain when we come to know and understand more about what nourishes and inspires the spirits of our sisters and brothers. MCC NOVA presents a sacred/community drumming circle each quarter, around the time of the solstice. All are welcome. No experience is required. Bring a favorite drum / rhythm instrument, or use those provided. Drumming has been used by indigenous people all over the world for thousands of years as a powerful spiritual tool. In recent years, thousands of Community Drumming Circles have come into an existence as a way for people in our time to capture some of the concepts and practices of the ancient tradition and experience the benefits of it. These circles typically borrow some of the concepts and traditions of the ancient traditions, but are more flexible and require no special training or talents to participate. Our circle is based on this concept." http://www.mccnova.com/Worship/alternative.htm
725   "UFMCC seeks to be open to all people and to include all of God's people in every aspect of Church life, and not to use wording that excludes any group of God's people... One aspect of inclusive language is not to limit our understanding of God by addressing God in any single gender term. We do this primarily by using non-gendered terms such as 'Creator' or 'God" instead of 'Father'. http://www.mccdetroit.org/index.php?option=com_content&view=article&id=48&Itemid=54

means that you may hear many different metaphors, and pronouns referring to Deity may be masculine, feminine, or neutral."[726]

Jesus wasn't limiting our understanding of God when He told us to refer to God as "our Father." But the MCC isn't alone in such heresies as other pro-Gay Theology congregations also endorse the worship of female deities and "Christ-sophia" rather than Jesus Christ the incarnate Son of God as one Lutheran church announces, "The Lutheran Feminist/Womanist/Mujerista Movement exists to celebrate the feminine persona of God/dess and dimensions of the sacred as expressed in faith, worship, learning, mutual care, and acts of justice."[727] Like the MCC, this gay Lutheran congregation called "Her Church" teaches to pray "Our Mother who is within us" rather than "Our Father who is in heaven" contrary to the teaching of Jesus Christ.[728]

These churches and denominations have abandoned the one true God as He has revealed Himself and turned to pagan idolatry. The very spiritual whoredom for which Israel was judged and is described in Romans 1 is being advocated and practiced in these congregations. While the MCC makes bold claims that they strive for "justice" and against "oppression" since they deny the law of God as the absolute standard for right and wrong and the exclusive claims of Jesus Christ, they have abandoned the only justifiable standard for justice.

What must be clearly understood is that there is a huge difference between being hospitable to unbelievers who are visiting and actually incorporating into the church the doctrines and worship practices of anti-Christian religions in the name of "love" and "inclusion." While some notable "bible-thumping televangelists" have preached against homosexuality only to see them be exposed as adulterers, patrons of prostitutes or have homosexual liaisons with gay masseurs these men have proceeded to publicly confess their actions as sin. In contrast, many leaders of the Gay Theology movement have not only committed adultery and made use of homosexual prostitutes, rather than such

726   Tree of Life MCC of Ann Arbor, Michigan: http://www.treeoflife-mcc.org/brochure.html
727   http://www.herchurch.org/
728   Michael S. Piazza, *Gay By God* (Dallas, TX: Source of Hope Publishing, 1998), 84.

actions being highlighted in the media as a scandal, they have gone on to call their actions virtuous claiming in their books that such actions are a blessing of God with the praise of worldly media.

I am convinced that the growing apostasy of the Gay Theological movement is *the* greatest threat to the 21st century Church whose foundation was established generations ago. The creation of the Metropolitan Community Church and other like-minded organizations is the result of over a century of the gradual erosion of doctrines being taught or tolerated within the Church, most of which have their roots in the seminaries. Unless truly orthodox Bible-believing churches and seminaries denounce this movement and become equipped to refute it, eventually we will see an increasing number of denominations join their ranks.

Conclusion

1. Recapping the Arguments

Throughout this book we have examined the various components of the Gay Theological Worldview. Liberal Gay Theology denies the inerrancy, infallibility and the supreme authority of the Scriptures. They subsequently argue that the various debated passages (Leviticus 19 and 20, Romans 1, 1 Corinthian 6:9, 1 Timothy 1:10) ought to be deemed irrelevant to the matter of modern ethics and sexuality. According to them, these passages are the product of the author's primitive misogynistic homo-ignorant culture or that the prohibitions and condemnations only refer to cultic acts or exploitative forms of same sex acts such as homosexual prostitution and pederasty. The Dispensational Gay Theological arguments borrow the exegetical arguments of Liberal Gay Theological proponents and they dismiss the entirety of the Old Testament law as having any applicability to the New Testament believer. Finally, Queer Gay Theology apologists argue that the Scriptures cannot be interpreted to be "gay friendly" and subsequently rather than make an argument *from* the text, they intentionally seek to subvert ("queer") the text for their own political agenda.

As demonstrated, the Liberal Gay Theology has no justifiable epistemological ground to stand on. Its challenge to the reliability of Scripture is unwarranted and the applicability of the relevant passages within their context cannot be limited to cultic or merely exploitive sexual relationships. The laws in Leviticus do not mention the cultic prostitutes and they are listed with other sexual prohibitions that were not tied to the cult of Molech and Baal. Paul's statement in Romans 1 cannot be limited to cultic sex, pederasty, or exploitation as the burning for one another is mutual (Romans 1:27). Nor can the text be limited to heterosexuals acting like homosexuals for Paul states that the acts are contrary to nature, not contrary to *their* nature. Paul describes the objective acts, not the subjective psychological disposition ("orientation") of the participants for it would be impossible to determine whether a person was a true homosexual acting in accordance with his "natural" desires or a heterosexual acting contrary to his "natural" inclinations.

The Dispensational Gay Theological assertions that Old Testament laws are no longer binding in the New Testament era are clearly fallacious. They contradict Jesus' upholding the correct understanding of the moral elements of the law (Matthew 5:17) as well as the apostle's repeated appeal to the laws of Moses as the standard for Christian conduct (Romans 7:7; 1 Corinthians 9:9; Galatians 5:14; James 2:11). This includes the prohibition of a man having sex with his father's wife and a man have sex with another man (Leviticus 18:8, 1 Corinthians 5:1; Leviticus 18:22, 1 Corinthians 6:9). The "all or nothing" argument, that asserts if *some* Old Testament laws are abrogated then *all* of them are obsolete, contradicts Paul referring to Gentile's ability to keep the law and yet without having to keep the obsolete commandments which were distinctly Jewish, such as circumcision and the feast days (Acts 15:29; Romans 2:26). They lift Paul's phrases "not under law" and "law of Christ" out of their immediate and redemptive-historical context. Subsequently, in the place of the principles and consistent application of God's objective revealed moral will found in both testaments, they have adopted Joseph Fletcher's situation ethics and fallaciously renamed it "the law of love."

The Queer Gay Theology assertions are a non-argument, they simply don't like what Scripture teaches and so for their own political agenda they seek to twist God's Word as their father did in the Garden of Eden. The fruit of the theology of these leaders is clearly seen in the MCC as a revival of the pagan Ancient Near Eastern religions that synthesizes Christian theological terminology and sacraments with cultic sex acts. This is a clear demonstration of the very thing Paul describes in Romans

1 which is a result of the suppression of the revelation of God that incurs His wrath and subsequently being turned over to the enslavement of their lusts and the depravity of their futile thinking.

Finally, we have seen that a person who experiences same-sex attractions are not a member of a third gender and that such inclinations are acquired, albeit often at a very early age. The solution then is not to capitulate to the desires of the flesh, but walk in the Spirit.

2. Final Word

There are many other important issues that have not been addressed this book. Namely, etiology of same sex attractions as well as the possibility of changing homosexual desires and the Biblical methodology for doing so. The purpose for this book has been to respond to the theological arguments of the Gay Theological movement. Consequently the personal and practical matters of applying the hope of the Gospel to the Christian who struggles with same-sex attractions has not been discussed. If the Lord wills, I will address these matters in a subsequent work in which I hope to provide Biblical counsel to the Christian who has SSA without depending on the worldview of secular psychology or a hybrid of Freudian-Christian psychobabble that offers conflicting theories and unbiblical solutions that dominates the marketplace of ideas.

Bibliography

<u>Pro-Gay Theology Books</u>:

John Boswell, *Christianity, Social Tolerance, and Homosexuality* (University Of Chicago Press; 8th Edition, 2005)

Rick Brentlinger, *Gay Christian 101 - Spiritual Self-Defense For Gay Christians* (2007)

Patrick M. Chapman, *"Thou Shalt Not Love": What Evangelicals Really Say to Gays* (New York, NY: Haiduk Press, 2008)

Candace Chellew-Hodge, *Bulletproof Faith: A Spiritual Survival Guide for Gay and Lesbian Christians* (San Francisco, CA: Jossey-Bass, 2008)

J. Michael Clark, *Defying the Darkness* (Cleveland, OH: The Pilgrim Progress, 1997)

Gary David Comstock, *Gay Theology Without Apology* (Cleveland, OH: Pilgrim Press, 1993)

Susannah Cornwall, *Sex and Uncertainty in the Body of Christ: Intersex Conditions and Christian Theology (Gender, Theology and Spirituality)* (Sheffield, England: Equinox Publishing, 2010)

L. William Countryman, *Biblical Authority or Biblical Tyranny* (Harrisburg, PA: Trinity Press, 1994)

L. William Countryman, *Dirt, Greed & Sex: Sexual Ethics in the New Testament and Their Implications for Today* (Minneapolis, MN: Fortress Press; Revised edition, 2007)

John F. Dwyer, *Those 7 References: A Study of 7 References to Homosexuality In The Bible* (John F. Dwyer, 2007)

Tanya Erzen, *Straight to Jesus: Sexual and Christian Conversions in the Ex-Gay Movement* (University of California Press; 1 edition, 2006)

Robert Goss, *Jesus Acted Up: A Gay and Lesbian Manifesto* (New York, NY: Harper Collins, 1993)

Robert E. Goss, *Queering Christ: Beyond Jesus Acted Up* (Resource Publications, 2007)

Daniel Helminak, *What the Bible Really Says About Homosexuality* (Estancia, NM: Alamo Square Press, 2000)

Tom Horner, *Jonathan Loved David: Homosexuality in Biblical Times* (Philadelphia, PA: Westminster Press, 1978)

Theodore W. Jennings Jr., *The Man Jesus Loved* (Cleveland, OH: The Pilgrim Press, 2003)

Samuel Kader, *Openly Gay, Openly Christian: How the Bible Really Is Gay Friendly* (San Francisco, CA: Leyland Publications, 1999)

Dale B. Martin, *Sex and the Single Savior: Gender and Sexuality in Biblical Interpretation* (Louisville, KY: Westminster John Knox Press, 2006)

John J. McNeill, *Taking a Chance on God* (Boston, MA: Beacon Press, 1988)

John J. McNeill, *The Church and the Homosexual* (Boston, MA: Beacon Press, 1988)

Jeff Miner; John Connoley, *The Children Are Free* (Indianapolis, IN: Jesus Metropolitan Church, 2002)

Martti Nissinen, *Homoeroticism in the Biblical World: A Historical Perspective* (Louisville, KY: Fortress Press, 2004)

Michael S. Piazza, *Gay By God* (Dallas, TX: Source of Hope Publishing, 1998)

Murray A. Rae and Graham Redding, *More Than a Single Issue* (Hindmarsh, SA; Australian Theological Forum, 2000)

Jallen Rix, *Ex-gay No Way: Survival And Recover From Religious Abuse* (Findhorn Press, 2010)

Jack Rogers, *Jesus, the Bible and Homosexuality* (Louisville, KY: Knox Press, 2006)

Robin Scroggs, *The New Testament and Homosexuality* (Philadelphia, PA: Fortress Press, 1983)

John Shelby Spong, *The Sins of Scripture* (New York, NY: Harper Collins, 2005)

Letha Scanzoni, Virginia Mollenkott, *Is The Homosexual My Neighbor?* (San Francisco, CA: Harper Collins, 1994)

David W. Shelton, *The Rainbow Kingdom: Christianity & the Homosexual Reconciled* (Lulu, 2006)

Andrew Sullivan, *Virtually Normal* (New York, NY: Vintage, 1996)

Nikki Sullivan, *A Critical Introduction to Queer Theory* (New York, NY: New York University Press, 2003)

R.D. Weekly, *Homosexianity* (Judah First Ministries, 2009)

R.D. Weekly, *The Rebuttal: A Biblical Response Exposing Deceptive Logic of Anti-Gay Theology* (Judah First Ministries, 2011)

Mel White, *Stranger At The Gate: To Be Gay and Christian in America* (New York, NY: Penguin Books, 1994)

Dan O. Via; Robert A.J. Gagnon, *Homosexuality and the Bible* (Minneapolis, MN: Fortress Press, 2003)

<u>Anti-Gay Theology Books</u>:

Greg Bahnsen, *Homosexuality: A Biblical View* (Grand Rapids, MI: Baker Book House, 1978)

Richard Davidson, *Flame of Yahweh: Sexuality in the Old Testament* (Peabody, MA: Hendriksen Publishing, 2007)

James B. De Young, *Homosexuality: Contemporary Claims Examined in the Light of the Bible and Other Ancient Literature and Law* (Grand Rapids, MI: Kregel, 2000)

Robert A. J. Gagnon, *The Bible And Homosexual Practice* (Nashville, TN: Abingdon Press, 2001)

Peter Jones, *One or Two: Seeing A World of Difference* (Escondido, CA; Main Entry Editions, 2010)

Peter Jones, *The God of Sex* (Eastbourne, England: David C. Cook, 2006)

Charles & Donna McIlhenny, *When the Wicked Seize A City* (New York, NY: Authors Choice Press, 2000)

Michael Saia, *Counseling The Homosexual* (Minneapolis, MN; Bethany House Publishers, 1988)

Thomas Schmidt, *Straight & Narrow?* (Downers Grove, IL: InterVarsity Press, 1995)

Ronald M. Springett, *Homosexuality In History and The Scriptures* (Washington DC: Biblical Research Institute, 1988)

William J. Webb, *Slave, Women & Homosexuals: Exploring the Hermeneutics of Cultural Analysis* (Downers Grove, IL: IVP Academic, 2001)

James R. White, Jeffrey Niell, *The Same Sex Controversy* (Minneapolis, MN: Bethany House Pub., 2002).

Other Works Cited

Jay Adams, *A Theology of Christian Counseling* (Grand Rapids, MI; Zondervan, 1979)

Jay Adams, *Marriage, Divorce, and Remarriage in the Bible* (Grand Rapids, MI; Zondervan, 1980)

Greg Bahnsen, *By This Standard* (Tyler, TX: Institute for Christian Economics, 1985)

Greg L. Bahnsen, *Pushing the Antithesis* (Powder Springs, GA: American Vision, 2007)

Geoffrey Barraclough, ed. *The Christian World: A Social and Cultural History* (New York: Harry N. Abrams Publishers, 1981)

S.M. Baugh, *A New Testament Greek Primer* (Philipsburg, NJ: P & R Publishing, 1995)

James Boice, *Foundations of the Christian Faith* (Downers Grove, IL: InterVarsity Press; 2 Sub edition, 1986)

Wilhelmus á Brakel, *The Christian's Reasonable Service* (Vol. 3) (Phillipsburg, NJ: Soli Deo Gloria Pub., 1984)

Andrew Bonar, *A Commentary on Leviticus* (Carlisle, PA: Banner of Truth, 1998)

F.F. Bruce, *Commentary on Galatians* (Grand Rapids, MI: Wm. B. Eerdmans Publishing Company, 1982)

F.F. Bruce, *Romans* (Grand Rapids, MI: Wm. B. Eerdmans Publishing Company, 1985)

John Calvin, *Institutes of the Christian Religion*, (Volume 1), (Louisville, KY: Westminster John Knox Press, 1960)

R. L. Dabney, *Systematic Theology*, (1871; reprint, Carlisle, PA: Banner of Truth, 1985)

Gary DeMar, *The Debate Over Reconstruction* (Powder Springs, GA: American Vision Press, 1988)

Jacques B. Doukhan, *Hebrew for Theologians* (University Press of America, 1993)

John Frame, *Doctrine of the Christian Life* (Philipsburg, NJ: P & R Publishing, 2008)

John Frame, *The Doctrine of the Knowledge of God*, (Phillipsburg, NJ: P&R. Publishing, 1987)

John Frame, *Worship in Spirit and Truth: A Refreshing Study of the Principles and Practice of Biblical Worship* (Phillipsburg, NJ: P&R Publishing, 1996)

Roy Gane, *Leviticus, Numbers* (NIVAC 3) (Grand Rapids, MI: Zondervan, 2004)

Norman Geisler, *Christian Ethics* (Grand Rapids, MI: Baker Book House, 1989)

Norman L. Geisler, Ronald Brooks, *When Skeptics Ask* (Wheaton, IL: Victor Books, 1990)

Norval Geldenhuys, "Revelation and the Bible" in *Authority and the Bible*, Carl F. Henry (ed.) (Grand Rapids, MI: Baker Book House, 1958),

John Gerstner, *Wrongly Dividing the Word of Truth: A Critique of Dispensationalism* (Brentwood, TN: Wolgemuth & Hyatt Publishers, Inc., 1991)

William Hendriksen, *New Testament Commentary: Galatians and Ephesians* (Grand Rapids, MI: Baker Book House, 1968)

Wesley Hill, *Washed and Waiting: Reflection on Christian Faithfulness and Homosexuality* (Grand Rapids, MI: Zondervan, 2010)

Zane Hodges, *The Gospel Under Siege* (Redencion Viva; 1st edition, 1981)

Zane Hodges, *Absolutely Free!* (Grand Rapids, MI: Zondervan Publishing House, 1989)

Michael Horton, *The Law of Perfect Freedom* (Moody Publishers, 2004)

Peter Jones, "Androgyny: The Pagan Sexual Ideal" *Journal of the Evangelical Theological Society* 43/3 (September 2000)

Peter Jones, *Spirit Wars: Pagan Revival in Christian America* (Escondido, CA; Main Entry Editions, 1996)

C.F. Keil, *Keil & Delitzsch, Commentary on the Old Testament: Volume 1 – The Pentateuch* (Peabody, MA: Hendrickson Publishers, 2001)

J.N.D. Kelly, *Early Christian Doctrines* (San Francisco, CA: Harper Collins, 1978)

George W. Knight III, *The Pastoral Epistles* (Grand Rapids, MI: Wm. B. Eerdmans Publishing Company, 1992)

Meredith G. Kline, *Kingdom Prologue: Genesis Foundations For A Covenantal Worldview* (Overland Parks, KS: Two Age Press, 2000)

Martin Luther, *The Large Catechism* Translated by F. Bente and W.H.T. Dau Published in: *Triglot Concordia: The Symbolical Books of the Ev. Lutheran Church* (St. Louis, MO: Concordia Publishing House, 1921)

Martin Luther, *Commentary on Galatians* (Grand Rapids, MI: Fleming R. Revell, 1988)

J. Robertson Mc Quilkin, *Understanding and Applying the Bible* (Moody Publishers; Rev Sub edition, 1992)

Douglas J. Moo, *The Epistle To The Romans* (Grand Rapids, MI: Wm. B. Eerdmans Publishing Company, 1996)

John Murray, *Principles of Conduct* (Grand Rapids, MI: Wm. B. Eerdmans Publishing Company, 1957)

Ronald H. Nash, *Worldviews In Conflict* (Grand Rapids, MI: Zondervan, 1992)

Gary North, "Hermeneutics and Leviticus 19:19" *Theonomy: An Informed Response* (Tyler, Texas: Institute For Christian Economics, 1991)

J.I. Packer, *New Dictionary of Theology* (Downers Grove, IL: InterVarsity Press, 1988)

W.C. G. Proctor, *Baker's Dictionary of Theology* Everett Harrison, ed., (Grand Rapids, MI: Baker Book House, 1987)

Herman Ridderbos, *Paul: An Outline of His Theology* (Grand Rapids, MI: Wm. B. Eerdmans Publishing Company, 1977)

Rousas John Rushdoony, *Exodus* (Vallecito, CA: Ross House Books, 2004)

Rousas John Rushdoony, *Leviticus* (Vallecito, CA: Ross House Books, 2005)

Rousas John Rushdoony, *Romans & Galatians* (Vallecito, CA: Ross House Books, 1997)

Charles Ryrie, *So Great A Salvation* (Moody Publishers, 1997)

Paul H. Seely, "The Firmament and the Water Above Part I: The Meaning of raqiaà in Gen 1:6-8" *Westminster Theological Journal* - Vol. 53, No. 2 (Fall 1991).

James W. Sire, *The Universe Next Door: A Basic Worldview Catalogue*, expanded ed. (Downers Grove, IL: InterVarsity, 1988)

R.C. Sproul, *Lifeviews: Make a Christian Impact on Culture and Society* (Grand Rapids, MI: Fleming H. Revell Publishing, 1986)

Peter M. J. Stravinskas, *The Catholic Response* (Our Sunday Visitor Publishing Division, 2001)

Wayne Strickland, "The Inauguration of the Law of Christ with The Gospel of Christ: A Dispensational View" *The Law, The Gospel, And the Modern Christian: Five Views* (Grand Rapids, MI, Zondervan Publishing House, 1993)

Ray Sutton, *That You May Prosper: Dominion By Covenant* (Tyler, Texas: Institute for Christian Economics, 1987)

Ernest Trice Thompson, *Presbyterians in the South*, Vol. 2, 1861-1890 (Richmond, VA: John Knox Press, 1973)

Jeffrey H. Tigay, *The JPS Torah Commentary: Deuteronomy* (Jewish Publication Society of America; 1st edition, 1996)

Cornelius Van Til, *The Defense of the Faith* (Phillipsburg, NJ: P&R, 1967)

Williston Walker, *A History of the Christian Church* (New York, NY: Scribner; 4th edition, 1985)

William J. Webb, *Slave, Women & Homosexuals: Exploring the Hermeneutics of Cultural Analysis* (Downers Grove, IL: IVP Academic, 2001)

Craig A. Williams, *Roman Homosexuality* (Oxford University Press, USA; 2 edition, 2010)

Douglas Wilson, *Fidelity* (Moscow, ID: Canon Press, 1999)

Michelle Wolkomir, *Be Not Deceived: The Sacred and Sexual Struggles of Gay and Ex-Gay Christian Men* (New Brunswick, NJ; Rutgers University Press, 2006)

Christopher Wright, *Deuteronomy* (Peabody, MA: Hendriksen Publishers, 1996)

N. T. Wright, *The Climax of the Covenant: Christ and the Law in Pauline Theology* (Minneapolis, MN: Fortress Press, 1991)

Index

www.ingramcontent.com/pod-product-compliance
Lightning Source LLC
Chambersburg PA
CBHW030409100426
42812CB00028B/2883/J